Opusculum de Sectis apud Sinenses et Tunkinenses (A Small Treatise on the Sects among the Chinese and Tonkinese): A Study of Religion in China and North Vietnam in the Eighteenth Century

Father Adriano di St. Thecla
Olga Dror, translator and annotator,
with collaboration of Mariya Berezovska in Latin translation,
with a Preface by Lionel M. Jensen

Opusculum de Sectis apud Sinenses et Tunkinenses (A Small Treatise on the Sects among the Chinese and Tonkinese): A Study of Religion in China and North Vietnam in the Eighteenth Century

SOUTHEAST ASIA PROGRAM PUBLICATIONS
Southeast Asia Program
Cornell University
Ithaca, New York
2002

Cornell Southeast Asia Program Publications
640 Stewart Avenue, Ithaca, NY 14850-3857

Studies on Southeast Asia No. 33

Printed in the United States of America

ISBN 978-0-87727-732-3

Cover: Cover design by Judith Burns, Publications Services, Cornell University

With all my love to my son Michael, who has endured it all.
In hope that he always will firmly follow his own faith,
but will get acquainted with other faiths and will respect them.

- Olga Dror

TABLE OF CONTENTS

Acknowledgments

You are about to read a very old and unique document, *Opusculum de sectis apud Sinenses et Tunkinenses* (A Small Treatise on the Sects among the Chinese and Tonkinese), relating the state of religion in Tonkin, and partly in China, through the eyes of a Discalced Augustinian missionary, Adriano di St. Thecla, who spent almost thirty years in Northern Vietnam in the eighteenth century. I found this in the Archives of the Foreign Missions in Paris while looking for materials on the cult of Princess Liễu Hạnh, a Vietnamese female deity, the primary focus of the project I was working on. In the *Opusculum* I indeed found a passage referring to Liễu Hạnh. This passage changed the whole course of my work on my dissertation project. Having read the passage, I could not help but continue to read the whole text, and, while doing so, I became more and more assured that this work should be made known to a broad circle of specialists interested in Vietnam, China, and missionary activity. And, as Adriano di St. Thecla interrupted writing his *Opusculum* to work on his other tractate, *The Chinese and Tonkinese Chronology*, so I interrupted my dissertation project on Liễu Hạnh to submerge myself in this document and to bring it to light after some two hundred fifty years of neglect.

Now, approaching the end of this endeavor, I can only echo Adriano di St. Thecla. He said that his work on the *Chronology* was a great advantage for the completion of the *Opusculum*. The same is absolutely true for me: my work on the *Opusculum* has enormously enriched my other project, the one on Liễu Hạnh, interrupted because of the *Opusculum*. Furthermore, not only has it expanded the horizons of my other project, but it also gave me a much broader prospective on history and religion in Vietnam and China. And, what may be most important, my work on the *Opusculum* put me in contact with and gave me a chance to work with many people who helped me complete this project and whose assistance I greatly appreciate.

Father Moussay, the director of the Archive of the Foreign Missions in Paris, was the first person to encourage me with this project. His assistant, Brigitte Appavou, was most helpful in giving me a hand not only during my work in the Archive but also later, sending to Ithaca upon my request some materials that I discovered were important to me.

At Cornell I was extremely lucky to find a co-translator of the manuscript from Latin, Mariya Berezovska. It has been a cooperation, which again demonstrates "globalization" of the world or the absence of boundaries for scholarship. Two former citizens of the former USSR, one from Ukraine, one from Israel, worked in the United States on a manuscript found in the French archive, written in Latin about Vietnam by an Italian missionary in consultation with a Spanish missionary. Together, Mariya and I struggled with all the difficulties of the Latin text. When we felt helpless in some especially hard cases, Professor Danuta Shanzer was there to draw us back to the firm ground of comprehension.

Father Pietro Scalia, the Director of the Archives of the Order of the Discalced Augustinians in Rome patiently and promptly replied to my numerous questions about the Order and about Adriano di St. Thecla. Eventually he even sent to me a number of the private publications of the Order, which have assisted my understanding of the *Opusculum*. Working on the *Opusculum*, I established contacts with various other archives in Italy and Spain, including the State Archive of Italy. Many people provided their support and assistance; to name just a few, Father Ramón Hernández, an archivist of the Archive of the Dominican Order in Rome; Father Donato González of the Convent of St. Tomas of the same order in Avila, Spain; Father Renzo de Luca, of the Jesuit Order, from the Museum of the Twenty-six Martyrs of Nagasaki, Japan.

At different stages of the project, several scholars read the drafts and suggested their valuable comments. I am greatly indebted to Professor Charles Peterson (Cornell University) for his comments on the chapter on Confucianism; to Professors Dan Boucher (Cornell University) and Professor Nguyen Tu Cuong (George Mason University) for their comments on the chapter on Buddhism; to Professor Robert McNeal (Cornell University) for his advice on the chapter on Daoism, and to Professor Vincent Pecora (University of California, Los Angeles) for his comments on my Introduction. I benefited from consulting many other faculty at Cornell University, among whom I particularly want to mention Professors Kim Haines-Eitzen, James John, and Gary Rendsburg.

Professor Jurgis Elisonas of Indiana University and Dr. Michael Cooper of the University of Hawai'i helped me to decipher Japanese names that are obscurely garbled in the manuscript.

I was overwhelmed by the willingness of the most distinguished of Vietnamese scholars to discuss my work with me. Their sincere interest was my great inspiration. I was privileged to work with Professors Phan Huy Lê, Trần Quốc Vượng, Ngô Đức Thịnh, Đồ Quang Hưng, Nguyễn Tài Thư, Phan Văn Các, Trần Nghĩa, Nguyễn Duy Hinh, Dr. Ngô Đức Thọ, Dr. Nguyễn Tá Nhí, and Mr. Đinh Văn Minh. I express my most sincere appreciation for this cooperation. The librarians of the Institute of Social Science Information in Hanoi were very considerate, helping me to get the materials in spite of the reorganization of their library at the time when I worked there. Chu Tuyết Lan made every effort to create for me the most favorable atmosphere to work in the Institute of Sino-Vietnamese studies in Hanoi and to aid me in locating and photocopying materials from there. My very special thanks and admiration go to Professor Hà Văn Tấn, who was helping me resolve some of the most difficult conundrums in the manuscript until his illness prevented him from leading his usual scholarly life. But even in his grave condition, Professor Hà Văn Tấn was a great encouragement to my project. Being almost completely paralyzed and unable to speak, he kept inquiring about my project, remembering all the details we worked on together. I wish him all the best, and he will always be for me, as to his numerous students and colleagues, an example of a great scholar and a person of dignity.

This project became possible with the support of the Social Science Research Council and the Ford Foundation, who sponsored my trips to France and Vietnam, and of the Gilmore and the Mellon fellowships given to me by the Department of History and the Graduate School of Cornell University. To all these funds and the people administrating them goes my deepest gratitude. I am very thankful to the Directors of Graduate Studies of the Department of History of Cornell University, Professors Vicki Caron and Victor Koschmann, who have been so considerate of my project, and to Professor Michael Steinberg, who, as Director of Graduate Studies, gave me a lot of support during my first years at Cornell.

The copyeditor of this book, John LeRoy, was most helpful in giving the manuscript the shape it has now. Deborah Homsher, the manager of the Southeast Asian Publications, provided her full support in editing and solving numerous technical problems that appeared during my work on the manuscript.

I express my deepest gratitude to my first teachers at St. Petersburg State University, Professors Valeriy Panfilov and Igor Bystrov, who laid the foundation of my interest in Vietnam and developed my abilities for scholarly work. Without them I would never be who I am. Even now, separated as we are by thousands miles, they have been following my research and have commented on the manuscript. I respectfully and admirably remember my other teacher, the late director of the Institute of Linguistics in Moscow, Corresponding Academician of the Russian Academy of Science Vadim Solntsev, whose PhD student I was for two years and who reinforced my ability for linguistic analysis. He was a great person and a great advisor, whom I will always dearly remember. I am extremely grateful to my professors at Hebrew University in Jerusalem, who were not afraid to accept me to the University several months after my arrival in Israel despite my complete incompetence in Hebrew and my ignorance of the Western system of education. I thank them for their trust. My supervisor, Professor Yitzhak Shichor, was the one to encourage me to proceed with my studies in the United States because of the lack of materials and specialists on Vietnam in Israel. If not for him, I would hardly have dared to apply to Cornell University.

The members of my dissertation committee, Professor David Wyatt and Professor Jane Marie Law, have always been there when I needed them and for almost five years already have encouraged me in my research. They were especially supportive in my work on the *Opusculum*.

Professor Lionel Jensen, of the University of Notre Dame, an expert on missionaries in China, whom I first approached with some small questions, eventually found himself closely involved in my project. He read the manuscript in parts and in whole and gave his valuable comments and insights. I was moved by his consideration and desire to help me, and was delighted to find in him a very strong supporter of my work. How many times his encouraging messages helped me to again believe that this project should be completed! To work with him was very important, instructive, and pleasant to me.

This project would have collapsed in quite an early stage if not for the constant support of my supervisor, Professor Keith Taylor. He read innumerable numbers of different drafts, devoted many hours to discuss them with me, and stewarded me throughout the entire project. I greatly appreciate his assistance, encouragement, and indulgence. Not being able to repay my debt to him, I hope to be to my future students as helpful as he has been to me.

My parents and grandmother, far away in St. Petersburg, as always, supported me in my endeavor. My debt to them can hardly ever be settled. I appreciate the help that was given me by Alex and his family. My son Michael's eagerness to see this book published has been my main stimulus to complete the project. Michael has been my perpetual source of strength and joy, without which nothing would be possible. I give him my love and gratefulness, and dedicate this book to him.

While I will gladly share any possible success of my project with all the aforementioned people, all mistakes are mine.

FOREWORD

When, in autumn 2000, Olga Dror showed me Adriano di St. Thecla's *Opusculum* and her translations of passages from it that were of particular relevance for her research, I knew that this rare manuscript was important. It contains direct observations, which exist nowhere else, from the mid-eighteenth century, of religious life in northern Vietnam, along with a survey of contemporary Sino-Vietnamese intellectual trends. I know of no comparable work anywhere, even in Vietnam. Yet, despite its importance, it seemed to be destined to a subterranean existence in footnotes and collegial conversations, because the set of skills necessary to make it available in translation with annotations and the time necessary to complete such a task are rare commodities indeed.

Then, in December 2000, Ms. Dror mentioned to me the idea of her undertaking this task. I immediately grasped the logic of her proposal, for I know of no other person in the world with the devotion to scholarship and the linguistic abilities necessary to do this. Nevertheless, as her academic advisor, a series of reservations passed rapidly through the back of my mind. After all, Ms. Dror was in the midst of her dissertation work, and this would in effect amount to a second dissertation project. Furthermore, the manuscript is extraordinarily complex, with multiple languages, erudite references to dozens of prior texts, names of people and places difficult to identify, obscurities each begging for dissertations of their own; the manuscript appeared to be a morass into which a graduate student could disappear forever. However, I suppressed these doubts, because my estimation of Ms. Dror's capacity for scholarship, formed during the preceding three and a half years, inspired me to have confidence that she could do it. Moreover, as I observed how quickly Ms. Dror plunged into the work and, ably assisted by Mariya Berezovska, began to make steady progress, the more certain I became that this was not a mistake. As the months passed, she sorted out one problem after another. Consulting with specialists and archivists in France, Italy, Russia, Spain, the United States, and Vietnam, she was soon at the center of a network of contacts that confirmed the importance of what she was doing. Within fifteen months of commencing the project, Ms. Dror has brought it to completion. It merits consideration as a dissertation.

But there is something else that began to grow in my mind as I read and reread drafts of this work. This is the ghostly voice of Adriano di St. Thecla himself, which came echoing from the "wooded ridge" of the manuscript's "language forest" because Ms. Dror succeeded as translator in finding "that single spot where the echo is able to give." As Walter Benjamin wrote in "The Task of the Translator": "The task of the translator consists in finding that intended effect upon the language into which he is translating which produces in it the echo of the original."[1] Beyond the vicissitudes of grammar, of syntax, and of the thick wash of necessary annotation, some excess of sensibility lingers, which, for the sake of convenience, is named Adriano di St. Thecla. I imagine that this man, writing two and a half centuries ago, has found in Ms. Dror a translator able to demonstrate the "translatability" and to present the "afterlife" of a manuscript attributed to him (using these terms as Benjamin does).[2]

Ms. Dror's Introduction and her annotations represent a huge achievement. In her Introduction, she has fulfilled the obligations of a translator to present a text in relation to authorship, provenance, contents, academic significance, theorization, and technical matters. Some notes grew until they were on the verge of becoming separate articles, and two of them were eventually absorbed into the Introduction. The translation itself is securely nested in Ms. Dror's scholarship.

As a member of the Editorial Board of Cornell Southeast Asia Program (SEAP) Publications, I am especially pleased that we are able to make this work available. It is a new kind of publication for SEAP, with unusual technical challenges posed by extensive annotations and Chinese characters. This book will be of interest far beyond the study of Southeast Asia, to readers interested in China and East Asia generally, in early European missionaries, in the larger contact between "East" and "West," and in early manifestations of "Asian Studies."

K. W. Taylor
March, 2002

---

[1] Walter Benjamin, *Illuminations* (New York: Schocken, 1985), p. 76.

[2] Ibid., pp. 70-71.

PREFACE

LIONEL M. JENSEN

Adriano di Santa Thecla (1667-1765) was an inspired and intrepid member of a fiercely proud, primitivist order, the Discalced ("Unshod") Augustinians, whose labors among the people we would call the Vietnamese, but who were known to him as "Tonkinese," yielded a treatise on popular religion and folk practice, accidentally discovered by Olga Dror, a historian of imperial Vietnam, while pursuing research on an indigenous cult in the archives of the Missions Étrangères. The text, *Opusculum de Sectis apud Sinenses et Tunkinenses* (A Small Treatise on the Sects among the Chinese and Tonkinese), for reasons I will discuss below, is exceptional. Of course, not all texts otherwise undiscovered are remarkable, for the vast bulk of the buried record of missionary material life is undisclosed, no longer extant, or lost. However, when one considers the textual productivity of the various orders of the Asia missions in the interval from 1580 to 1750 and the great number of works lost, misplaced, miscataloged, destroyed, the discovery alone of the *Opusculum* is just cause for scholarly elation.

Judging from the text of the treatise, Adriano took the heritage of his order's namesake, Augustine (354-430), quite seriously. As the reader will learn, he vividly captured the performative quality of popular rite in his ethnography of Chinese and Tonkinese practice. The missionary is a preacher, a rhetorician who implicitly measures the space of scripture and its oral performance. Augustine possessed a supreme sensitivity for language, life, and text, something also found throughout Adriano's *Opusculum*. It may be that for the missionary it is the greater promise of the art of preaching, preaching in a condition of jeopardy that draws him. If so, then every missionary is a preacher and potentially an ally, if not a legatee, of Augustine. Would this not be even more so for a Discalced Augustinian? I aver it would be and is. And like the preaching of his Patristic forbear, Adriano's work was as prescient as it was controversial.

My acquaintance with the work of Adriano di Santa Thecla was acquired only recently and conveyed through the generous scholarly industry of Ms. Dror, who translated this small but significant text in collaboration with Mariya Berezovska. This past year in the course of answering her occasional pointed queries about the language of Sino-Jesuit missionary texts, I was introduced to Padre Adriano and quickly learned of his priestly order, the Southeast Asian reach of the Catholic mission, and the religious sensitivity of the *Opusculum*. From just this abbreviated catalogue I was drawn to this obscure figure and his text. Ms. Dror accommodated my curiosity by kindly sending a copy of the Latin original and their draft translation. Study of the manuscript in comparison with earlier missionary treatises on Chinese religion convinced me that the *Opusculum de Sectis apud Sinenses et Tunkinenses* was both rare and remarkable. Now, owing to a careful, exacting translation, author and text will likely receive their due. With admiration for the original treatise and an enthusiasm for the translation and notes, I offer a few reflections on Adriano di Santa Thecla and the *Opusculum*, beginning with a sketch of the eighteenth-century intellectual context and its implications for the Tonkin mission founded by the Discalced Augustinians.

* * *

The eighteenth century was an especially fateful one for politics and peoples of faith, religious and revolutionary. At this juncture, the far points of the globe were mapped to such an extent that knowledge of China, the Chinese, their customs and habits was common among a broad front of Europe's educated classes. By mid-century, Chinese like Arcadio Huang (a cataloger and translator of Chinese books in France) and John Hu (the erstwhile assistant of Father Jean-François Foucquet) were living in Europe, while a great number of European missionaries inscribed a wide arc of indigenous residence across China, the Philippines, Japan, as well as Tonkin and Cochinchina, otherwise known as Vietnam. Global transit of this modest magnitude was underwritten by the spirit rather than by specie and yielded a discourse of cultural interchange made from the vocabularies of European and Asian peoples.

What made this burgeoning global imagining possible was an avalanche of texts, translations, commentaries, atlases, chronologies, proto-ethnographies, some published *in situ* in Asia and others that circulated widely in Europe. The most celebrated of these texts were produced in the first century following the establishment of the Catholic missions in China and Southeast Asia (1585-1687) and were grounded on a theological assumption of the complementarity of indigenous religion and Christianity. This assumption inspired enculturation by missionaries and came to be known as "accommodationism," a systematic apologist strategy originally conceived by the Jesuits that demanded rigorous grounding in the language and customs of native peoples. There were two foundational works of accommodationism: Matteo Ricci's *Storia dell'Introduzione del Cristianesimo in Cina* ("Storia," 1610) and Philippe Couplet et al., *Confucius Sinarum Philosophus sive Scientia Sinensis* (1687). Both were known to all posted to the missions of the East Indies, and both influenced for centuries religious and lay commentaries on China. The *Opusculum* bears a prominent imprint of these formative missiological works in the organization of its contents and in its delicate negotiation of Christian truth and local religion.

Nearly a century later and a sea away, Adriano's work built upon that of Ricci and Couplet, but was undertaken in an atmosphere of peril. Particularly noteworthy is the interpretive architecture of Adriano's presentation, specifically how he re-engaged and modified the accommodationist program of the Sino-Jesuit community of the seventeenth century, describing and analyzing the local contrariety of sects, spirits and cults, fortune-tellers and diviners, and Christianity among the Chinese and Tonkinese. His observations and his theological argument bear an uncanny resemblance to Ricci's *Storia* and to the *Confucius Sinarum Philosophus,* and this similarity is not accidental but significant. Indeed, one familiar with the writings of earlier missionaries cannot but recognize that the *Opusculum* is in dialogue with ethnographic and catechismic practices of the Sino-Jesuit community. Yet, upon a closer reading, especially one guided by an understanding of the ecclesiastical politics of the eighteenth century, these surface similarities are overcome by the author's originality and his willingness to report exactly what he observed.

Particularly intriguing for me, especially in light of the increasingly censorious gaze of church authorities, was the unblinkered quality of his observations about village cults, ritual practitioners, sacrifice, and ancestor worship. The following excerpt from Chapter 2 of the manuscript is illustrative of Adriano's insight and precision as an observer:

> . . . All sacrifices made to Confucius, tutelary genies, and other spirits, as well as to the deceased, are performed with substantially the same ceremonies and with the same credulity. Indeed, in each of them an altar and the four-legged sacrificial table called *hương án* are present; one principal attendant, several assistants, other servants, and two masters of ceremonies participate in it; meat of killed animals and other food is offered; wine or drippings from rice is poured over a handful of straw, and libations and prostrations are made, and a leaf of offertory is read; incense is burnt and pieces of gold and silver paper money are set on fire; and, finally, people partake of the offerings with pleasure.

This kind of detailed transcript of popular practice reveals a dimension of the *Opusculum*'s contemporary value, in fact one that is confirmed in the recent work of Edward Davis on religion in medieval China. In studied contrast with conventional Redfieldian segregation of religion into the "great" and "little" traditions, Davis demonstrates that the sound of Chinese religion was polyphonic, loud, and, often, antagonistic; it was therapeutic and exorcistic, reaching, without period or comma, from village to city and running like a current through all levels of society.[1] Adriano di Santa Thecla would concur, the chief interpretative benefit of his undeviating attention to the details of ritual practice being a conclusion found at the beginning of his chapter "On the Spirits and their Cult": "The cult of spirits among the Chinese dates back to the most ancient tradition, which was inherited by the Sect of the Literati. They taught the cult of spirits, although they were not the first to introduce it." In a single remark Adriano collapsed the conventional dichotomy—more a faulty typology than an accurate description—between "elite" and "popular" religious consciousness that has until very recently prevailed as fact in both the social and intellectual history of China. However, his greater contribution to the history of the encounter lies in his creative resolution of the competitive theological claims of native religion and Christianity.

* * *

One of the defining tensions of the missionary experiment in Asia in the sixteenth through the eighteenth centuries was that between the theological center and a proselytizing periphery. In practice it was a creative tension; however, it

---

[1] Edward L. Davis, *Society and the Supernatural in Song China* (Honolulu: University of Hawai'i Press, 2001).

became the source of strident protest and recrimination in the first decades of the eighteenth century with the culmination of a global debate over the proper Chinese terms for God and whether the indigenous ancestral rites of the Chinese could be accommodated within Christianity. The debate, properly known as the Rites and Terms Controversy, occurred over the course of a century. It was a vicious rejoinder to accommodationism that was bred from highly contentious private politics and achieved inviolable authority in a series of findings by the Holy See. The successive Papal bulls *Ex illa die* in 1715 and *Ex quo singulari* in 1742 significantly reduced the creative space between the Vatican and missionaries in the field and rendered a very successful missiological strategy heretical, in effect reversing the gains of a century.

Ecumenism was overcome by exclusivism. Even those at work in the remote points of the Mission of the Indies faced the threat of expulsion for noncompliance, and as early as 1711, Pope Clement XI signed a decree of the Inquisition prohibiting writing on the Rites controversy. One creative response to such dogmatic pressures was Figurism, an intellectual diversion from Chinese religious practice in favor of a hermetic study of the abstruse symbolism of sinographs and of hexagrams in China's earliest texts bearing evidence of divine inspiration. Still, few missionaries in China were willing after this fateful moment to maintain the complementarity of indigenous practices and Christianity and thereby risk recall and excommunication. But, there was someone in Tonkin who ran this risk.

The eighteenth-century story of the Catholic Church's loss of native faithful in the controversy over rites and terms is well attested, and in recent years has been the focus of fruitful but melancholy scholarly reflection.[2] However, it is a story that acquires an unexpected power and effectiveness when told in the voice of a non-partisan like Adriano living far from the frontlines of theological polemic joining Rome and Beijing. And it was in this tense, precious moment of profound ideological change that the *Opusculum* and its accompanying, but now lost, *Chinese and Tonkinese Chronology* were produced.

There was, as there is always, an advantage to being on the margins; in the case of Adriano, a Discalced Augustinian in Tonkin, the benefits were evident in the painstaking detail of his representation of native practice, particularly in the encyclopedic chapter, "De Spiritibus, corum que cultu" (On Spirits and their Cult) and his unapologetic preservation of the accommodationist presumption of *sensus communis*, a theological consensus enabling persusasion. Here he could ponder, albeit under some noticeable strain, the multiple manifestations of the religious among Vietnamese. Vietnamese religious experience reflected a pluralism and complexity at the heart of indigenous cultic practice, yet common as well to the emergent national religions of eighteenth-century Europe.

Just like his sympathetic Sino-Jesuit colleague Joseph de Prémare (1666-1736), Adriano found that even his liminal post in eastern Tonkin stood on the shore of a sea of discord; he felt at his feet the raging tides of tempest brought by the Church's renunciation of Chinese ancestral rites and the native terms for God. The eastern Tonkin mission of the Discalced Augustinians was at best a fledgling enterprise, consisting of twelve members of the order and eight Vietnamese converts. Moreover,

---

[2] D. E. Mungello, ed., *The Chinese Rites Controversy: Its History and Meaning* (Nettetal: Steyler Verlag, 1994).

from the 1730s until its closing in 1761 the mission was particularly vulnerable to a rural ecology of predation spawned from a cycle of insurrection and repression that consumed Tonkin from the 1730s through the 1760s. Perhaps more significant in its debilitating effects on the mission was an increasingly aggressive commitment of the fellow missionaries of a different order to see through, to its logical and painful implications, the official policy of the church against accommodation with indigenous rites and terms. Prosecutors of *Ex quo singulari,* the Spanish Dominicans, brought pressure on the Propaganda Fide in 1749 to recall the Discalced Augustinians, which led shortly to the placement of their Tonkin missions under the aegis of the Dominicans.

Laboring under the shadow of his order's recall in defense of its accommodationist mission, Adriano assembled his comparative chronology and recorded the ethnographic detail of popular rites in a manner befitting Christian apologetics, but which was expressly disallowed by the Vatican. Thus, the question for those knowing of this precarious context is how did he construct his account of popular religion without drawing the suspicions of the Church? *Ex quo singulari* made many missionaries more creative in their work among native peoples, but perhaps no one was as creative as Adriano. For him the exigency of official theological demand provoked an innovative reconception of Christian apologetics that resembled a comparative history of world religion. This he accomplished through ethnography rather than theology, describing a great expanse of piety and practice enveloping China, Southeast Asia, and in turn the world.

The rhetorical mechanism for this reconception is set out in the very first lines of Adriano's introduction, "In Sectas Sinarum et Annamitarum" (On the Sects of the Chinese and Annamites), where he erects the foundation of a conjectural history of religion derived from a close reading of the Vulgate and his astute observation of Vietnamese popular cults. He opens with an orchestral movement of human frailty: Non diu post hominem per Orbem terrarum dispersionem in mundo exorta est Idololatria . . . (Soon after people dispersed over the face of the earth, idolatry appeared in the world), that endows the descriptions of Chinese and Vietnamese rites with a grand narrative sense. Although one might take this as boilerplate, a requisite recollection of the history of human failing that creates the conditions for redemption, Adriano's Latin inscription of the fall restates the language of Shemot (Creation), the first book of the Torah, and stands as a universal declaration of human ignorance and of the twin forks of self-imposed heresy—"I think that approximately at the same time, when idolatry was introduced by Nimrod among the Chaldeans, it was also established in China by one of the first kings of the Ha [Xia] dynasty."

In this implied descent from the patriarchs of Judeo-Christian tradition, one may recognize the genius of Adriano, justifying tolerance of native practice by appeal to the *longue durée* of scripture according to which the ancient sacrifices of Mosaic-era tribes and the early Chinese were inevitably overcome in the reenacted metaphorical sacrifice of the Savior—Old Testament yields to New. Thus, a thorough and even appreciative exposition of the sects and cults of the Chinese and Tonkinese is not heretical, but magically documentary; they are all children of Abraham and the record of their primitive practices bear the seeds that in their efflorescence will confirm that these inspired Asian brethren have always known of the one God.

Of course, it was language, or rather conflict over how it could be used, that sealed the fate of the accommodationist project of Adrianus di Santa Thecla, although at the same time opening a passageway of theological reaction through which he advanced a historical sociology of world religion that justified all heresy and idolatry as necessary stages in the refinement of human understanding of God. Furthermore, how could indigenous religion be so aggressively dismissed as idolatry, when, as Cardinal John Henry Newman wrote, "we must confess, on the authority of the Bible itself, that all knowledge of religion is from Him . . . we are expressly told in the New Testament, that at no time He left himself without witness in the world . . . there is something true and divinely revealed, in every religion all over the earth, overloaded as it may be, and at times even stifled by the impieties which corrupt the will and understanding of man have incorporated with it."[3] Such sentiment was creed for Adriano and goes far in explaining his election to document the local manifestations of the sacred faith in a punitive climate of intolerance.

This choice is evident in the *Opusculum*; however, Adriano di Santa Thecla reconceived the problem by placing all of the diverse religious traditions of China and Tonkin within a broader interpretative context wherein the attentive reader would discern the outline of a developing arc of native practice that inscribed the history of Christianity itself. In his response to the inexorable pressure exerted by Dominicans and the Holy See, Adriano preserved but negated his accommodationism through a brilliant gesture of comparative religion, recalling in every detail the sacrifices to ancestors against the backdrop of Christianity's evolution from the sanguine sacrificial rites of the Israelites to the doxology of the early modern Church. Expanding the number of those summoned by and contained within Biblical stories, he complicated the normative determinants of heresy.

* * *

An odd consequence of Adriano's elaborate Sino-Vietnamese description of ritual choreography and artifact is that it is easy to become lost, ethno-geographically speaking. Many times in my reading I had to remind myself that he was describing the religious architecture of the Annamite kingdoms rather than the Chinese; Chinese and Tonkinese blend one into the other throughout. And the strangeness of this experience for the reader is only exaggerated by the author's vulgar Latin with punctuations of Latinized Chinese, Portuguese, Italian, and Vietnamese Latinized script all rendering the multiple languages and practices of indigenous peoples. To my mind this heteroglossia of sorts is more evidence of the contemporaneity of the *Opusculum* for it is an appropriate reflection of the linguistic and cultural diversity definitive of Asia and the modern West.

This quality of heteroglossia is found throughout the manuscript and prompts one to conclude that the author made no distinction, or rather very little, between Chinese and Vietnamese imperial traditions. Yet, this indecipherability of referent assumes a curious political significance in light of the exigencies of ideological circumstance. The referential ambiguity of Sino-Vietnamese offered advantages; it assisted Adriano in his efforts to account fully for the panoply of cultic practices constituting the religious life of Tonkin, Annam, and China. The detail of his

[3] John Henry Newman, *The Arians of the Fourth Century* (Notre Dame, IN: University of Notre Dame Press, 2001), pp. 79-80.

descriptions would have alarmed any ecclesiastical reader who would have seen in them ample evidence of idolatry and pagan rite completely out of keeping with Christianity. As in this instance where Adriano describes in painstaking detail the sanguine preliminary choreography of the "solmemni Confutii sacrificio" (the solemn sacrifice to Confucius):

> Another attendant lights sticks of incense on the altar of Confucius . . . and two other attendants carry to the altar two small goblets of wine, that is, of drippings from steamed rice, and place them on the small table with food, put there for Confucius. Another of the most distinguished [participants] genuflects to the left of the principal attendant, and, after declaring the names of all of the participants, brings to Confucius's attention that the sacrifice will be made in the morning. . . . With these words the spirit of Confucius is implicitly invited to be present at the sacrifice. . . . Finally, an animal to be killed is led to the door of the temple, and the principal attendant examines it to ascertain whether it is fit for the sacrifice. . . . After the animal is selected in this way, the preparatory ceremony . . . is over. Immediately after that, the selected and approved animal, either a pig or a bull, is killed, and if one animal is not enough they kill two, and they also kill several goats. They disembowel the animals, shave their hair, butcher them, and half burn them; some of the meat they put on the sacrificial tables with food in front of the vessels with incense; the head, indeed, [they place] on the altar of Confucius, and the rest of the parts in the center in front of the altar behind the *hương án* sacrificial table, and in the same place they put a vessel containing the blood and hair of the killed animal.

Information of this sort a century previous would have been repressed or bowdlerized, as in the deletions found in the first Jesuit letterbooks and in Ricci's description of regional sacrifices to Confucius in the *Storia*.[4] The text is replete with such gruesome ritual detail and one wonders how its representation was received. Perhaps poorly, for until Dror's accidental discovery the *Opusculum* was extant but largely unknown, enduring a form of repression by desuetude.

The lavishly annotated and cross-referenced translation that follows is, like all very good scholarship, a work of love—love of the word, of texts, and a passion for history and for that rare moment of the past that Walter Benjamin once wrote, "flashes up at the instant it can be recognized and is never seen again." Such unexpected flashes are startling in that they compel us to divert our eyes from the certainty of historical conviction, to hold less tightly to what we take for granted and thus provide unique opportunities for revision of the record. This shock of the old registered by the hand of Adriano di Santa Thecla will inspire revision of our inherited conventions of interpretation. And, in the end it is the unexpected concinnity of the *Opusculum*'s portrait of a non-hierarchical, religious pluralism with current scholarly consensus that makes the reflective reader sad. In this respect, to recognize the treatise's modernity, as it were, is to behold a snapshot of lost chances.

As the text is recovered here in the form of an English translation, we may redeem the loss by reengaging the readings of another era remote in chronology, but

---

[4] On this significant deletion and its contents in the first Latin edition of the *Storia* (*De Christiana expeditione apud sinas*), see Pasquale M. d'Elia, ed., *Fonti Ricciane*, Vol. 1 (Rome: Libreria della Stato, 1942), pp. 118-119.

in message and meaning near-at-hand. It is to Olga Dror's enormous credit that such a hermeneutic can be performed and a melancholy understanding of lost opportunity may be ours in the intoxication of our global present. She deserves more lavish praise than I can offer, being a PhD student with generosity sufficient to recognize the value of an obscure work tangential to her dissertation and willing, moreover, as a service to scholarship to devote years to its translation and annotation. In bringing the *Opusculum* back to light, Ms. Dror has made a gift of herself for which historians of religion and of the modern conjunction of West and East will be long in her debt. And Adriano di St. Thecla, resting in that posthumous spiritual abode intimately familiar to both Chinese and Tonkinese is, I suspect, no less grateful.

TRANSLATOR'S INTRODUCTION

OLGA DROR

The Author and His Time

Opusculum de Sectis apud Sinenses et Tunkinenses (A Small Treatise on the Sects among the Chinese and Tonkinese)[1] was written in Tonkin (northern Vietnam)[2] in 1750 by an Italian missionary, Adriano di St. Thecla. He belonged to the Order of the Discalced Augustinians, also called Barefooted Augustinians, or Augustinian Recollects. The Order of the Discalced Augustinians appeared at the end of the sixteenth century as a result of reforms in the Order of the Hermits of St. Augustine.[3] The movement began in Spain. In 1588 at Toledo, the Augustinians of Castile decided to set apart from the Order of Augustinians a new Order in which the religious would observe a "stricter form of life."[4] Discalced Augustinians promptly appeared in Italy with the same proposal of rigorous observance. On November 16, 1593, the Order of the Discalced Friars of the Order of the Hermits of St. Augustine was granted official recognition in the decree issued by Father Andrea Securani da

[1] Archive of the Foreign Mission in Paris, vol. 667.

[2] The term *Tonkin* is a Latinized version of the Vietnamese compound Đông Kinh (*Dongjing* in Chinese), meaning "the eastern capital." It signified the name of the city now known as Hanoi, the traditional capital of Vietnam, which was then called Đại Việt (Dayue in Chinese; Great Viet). In the sixteenth–eighteenth centuries Vietnam was formally one country under the sway of the Lê dynasty (1533-1789), but in reality it was divided into two parts: the northern part, where Hanoi is located, was governed by the Trịnh family, whilst the southern part was ruled by the Nguyễn family. Upon their arrival in Vietnam in the seventeenth century, the Europeans introduced the term Tonkin (also written as Tunking, Tumking, Tonking, Tongking) into the European vocabulary to distinguish the northern part of Vietnam from the southern part, called Cochinchina. The term already existed in the work of one of the first European missionaries in Vietnam, Alexandre de Rhodes (1591?-1660), *Histoire du royaume du Tonkin,* written in 1650 (Jean-Pierre Duteil, introd. and notes; Paris: Éditions Kimé, 1999). The term *Vietnam* (*Yuenan* in Chinese; Southern Viet) did not come into circulation until the nineteenth century and became firmly established as a name of the country and its people only in the 1920s.

[3] The Augustinian Order or the Hermits of St. Augustine is a mendicant order, which appeared as a result of the unification of several religious communities in 1256. They based their doctrine on the teaching of St. Augustine of Hippo (354-430), one of the main Church authorities, whose works Adriano di St. Thecla cites in his manuscript.

[4] Eugenio Cavallari, "Servire l'Altissimo in spirito di umiltà" (To Serve the Most High in the Spirit of Humility), in *Presenza Agostiniana. Agostiniani Scalzi,* no. 2-4 (1992): 16.

Fivizzano, Prior General of the Augustinian Order, and was separated from the main body of the Order.[5] According to David Gutierrez, a historian of the Augustinian Order,

> By law they were subject in every case to the prior general of the Augustinian Order, to whom they promised obedience on making their profession; but in fact they separated themselves gradually from the center of the Order, especially the French and Italians, who no longer wished to participate in the general chapters.[6]

The Discalced Augustinians have their own constitution apart from other Augustinians. They favor "not only the prohibition of human ambitions, but a *special internal attitude,* which favored poverty, mortification, and detachment from the world."[7] As for the "discalcedness," it has had a special significance for the followers of this religious house, as one of the highest authorities of the Order, Father Giovannii Nicolucci di S. Guglielmo (1552-1621), expressed it: "Enter unshod into this land for it is sacred. First bare your feet, that is, the affections of your soul, and remain naked and free."[8] According to the *Catholic Encyclopedia*'s description of the Discalced Augustinians,

> They never sing a high Mass. As an apparent survival of the hermit life, the Discalced Augustinians practice strict silence and have in every province a house of recollection situated in some retired place, to which monks striving after greater perfection can retire in order to practice severe penance, living on only water, bread, fruits, olive oil, and wine.[9]

From the beginning, the Hermits of St. Augustine, in general, and the Discalced Augustinians, in particular, have devoted themselves to missionary activity, "to follow which the order, though retaining its name Hermits, exchanged the contemplative life for the active."[10] According to its Constitution (article 12), the calling of the Order was defined as "special Grace, useful to the renovation and the major expansion of the Church."[11] In accordance with this, members of the Order were among the first European missionaries to arrive in Asia.[12] The first Discalced

---

[5] Benedetto Dotto, "Gli Agostiniani Scalzi: origini e sviluppo storico" (The Discalced Augustinians: Origins and Historical Development), in ibid., p. 84.

[6] David Gutierrez, *History of the Order of St. Augustine*, vol. 2, *The Augustinians from the Protestant Reformation to the Peace of Westphalia. 1518-1648* (Villanova, PA: Augustinian Historical Institute, Villanova University, 1979), 2:102.

[7] Cavallari, "Servire l'Altissimo in spirito di umiltà," p. 32.

[8] Cited in ibid., p. 32. In fact, the Discalced Augustinians are not strictly discalced as they wear sandals.

[9] Max Heimbucher, "Hermits of St. Augustine," in *Catholic Encyclopedia* (New York: Robert Appleton, 1910), 7: 284.

[10] Ibid., p. 286.

[11] Cavallari, "Servire l'Altissimo in spirito di umiltà," p. 27.

[12] There is a book written by one of the monks of the Order of the Discalced Augustinians, Ignazio Barbagallo, on the missionary activity of the Order, which describes its missions not only to China and Vietnam, but also to some other parts of the world, for example Tripoli and Tunisia. Ignazio Barbagallo, *Sono Venuto a Portare il Fuoco sulla Terra. Lineamenti di Spiritualità Missionaria degli Agostiniani Scalzi* (They Came to Bring Fire on Earth. Lineaments of the

Augustinians in Asia were Spaniards sent to the Philippines in 1604.[13] The Italian house of the order, to which Adriano di St. Thecla belonged, launched its missionary activity in 1696, primarily focusing on China and Tonkin. On July 29, 1697, the Congregation of the Propaganda of Faith decided to entrust to the Discalced Augustinians the establishment of their own mission.[14]

The first two Discalced Augustinians to depart to China were FF. Alfonso Romano della Madre di Dio (1657-1698) and Giovanni Mancini dei Sts. Agostino e Monica (1664-1711). They departed from Rome in March 1697.[15] On the way, Father Alfonso Romano died near Bombay. Father Giovanni Mancini continued his trip, and arrived in China on October 25, 1698.[16] Preaching first in Fujian province, he moved later to Canton. In May 1701, the local mandarins urged Father Mancini to return to Europe, but because of the absence of any ship departing in this direction, they temporarily closed their eyes to his presence. However, in July of the same year, he was officially and unequivocally ordered to leave the country.[17] In October, 1701, after three years of apostolic work, he left China and entered Tonkin, where he established the first mission of the Discalced Augustinians.[18] For their mission, the Discalced Augustinians were assigned two districts in eastern Tonkin, namely Kẻ

Missionary Spirituality of the Discalced Augustinians) (Rome: Segretaiato per la formazione e spiritualità dei PP. Agostiniani Scalzi, 1979?). On the missions to China and Tonkin specifically, see the same author, Ignazio Barbagallo, "Le missioni degli Agostiniani Scalzi nel Tonchino e nella Cina," in *Presenza Agostiniana*, no. 2 (1978): 28-41, or the same article in *Presenza Agostiniana*, no. 2-4 (1992): 131-150. There is also a book that incorporates this article along with some other materials on the Discalced Augustinians in China and Vietnam. See *Gli Agostiniani Scalzi nel Vietnam e nella Cina* (Rome: Edizioni Presenza Agostiniana, 1997), pp. 7-38. Hereafter when referring to this article of Father Barbagallo, I will cite the last mentioned book, *Gli Agostiniani Scalzi nel Vietnam e nella Cina*.

[13] Barbagallo, *Sono Venuto*, p. 54.

[14] Ibid., p. 111.

[15] Their departure took place prior to the decision of the Congregation of the Propaganda of Faith, but based on this decision Father Mancini was able to establish his own missions upon his arrival at his destination.

[16] There was a third missionary who joined FF. Mancini and Romano on their way to China. His name was Father Nicola Agostino Cima di St. Monica (1650-1711). At that time he did not belong to the Discalced Augustinians, but was from the Augustian Order. Arriving together with Father Mancini in China in 1698, he propagated Christianity there. Upon his return to Italy, he joined the Discalced Augustinians in 1711. Pietro Scalia, "Gli Agostiniani Scalzi in Oriente," in *Presenza Agostiniana*, no. 3-5 (1997): 33; Barbagallo, "Le missioni...," p. 13.

[17] Barbagallo, *Sono Venuto*, p. 122.

[18] Barbagallo, "Le missioni," p. 16. The Discalced Augustinians succeeded in establishing their mission in China only after almost half a century had passed. The founder of the mission is considered to be Father Sigismondo Meinardi di St. Nicola (1712-1767). He arrived in China together with another Discalced Augustinian, Father Serafino da S. Giovanni Battista, who in 1742 was appointed to be the head of the mission, but he died in the same year, and Sigismondo Meinardi di St. Nicola took over. Besides these two Discalced Agustinians, the Order sent three other missionaries to China. But the missionaries were expelled from there in 1811 due to the persecution against Christians unleashed under Emperor Qing Jiaqing (1796-1821). Two Discalced Augustinians, Father Anselmo di St. Margherita (1751-1816) and Father Adeodato di St. Agostino (1760-1821), present at that time in China, were expelled and fled to the Philippines, where they proceeded with their mission. The death of Adeodato di St. Agostino ended the apostolic work of the Discalced Augustinians in that part of the world.

Vân and Kẻ Sặt.[19] Father Mancini is credited with constructing eighty churches or chapels there in addition to a seminary of the Discalced Augustinians in Kẻ Vân.[20]

During the sixty years of the Discalced Augustinians's presence in Tonkin, fourteen other missionaries departed Europe to conduct apostolic work in this country. Two of them died on their way, while twelve successfully reached their destination and preached in Tonkin.[21] There were also eight Vietnamese converts who joined the Discalced Augustinian Order and assisted the Europeans in their apostolic work.[22] The activity of the Discalced Agustinians in Tonkin lasted until 1761, when their mission was closed by the Congregation of the Propaganda of Faith for reasons discussed below.

At least three of the members of the Order of the Discalced Augustinians working in Tonkin wrote works on religious practice in China and Vietnam.[23] Father Domenico di St. Martino (1703-1741), who arrived in Tonkin together with Adriano di St. Thecla, wrote a two-volume work, *Chinese Superstitions and Rites.* Father Ilario Costa di Gesù (1714-1754), considered one of the most acclaimed missionaries of the Order of the Discalced Augustinians, who arrived in Tonkin in 1723 and in 1737 was appointed Apostolic Vicar of Tonkin Oriental, wrote more than a dozen different works,[24] some of which are mentioned in the *Opusculum.* The third author is indeed Father Adriano di St. Thecla, who wrote three or four tractates: the first one being the *Chinese and Tonkinese Chronology*,[25] written shortly before the *Opusculum*, which was completed in 1750. While the works of the first two missionaries have yet to be located, Adriano di St. Thecla's *Opusculum* has survived and is available to contemporary scholars.

The activity of the order was carried out during the period of the so-called Rites Controversy, which is several times mentioned in the manuscript. This controversy

[19] Kẻ Sặt is located in Hải Dương province. As for Kẻ Vân, this toponym is no longer in usage. On the map presented in Barbagallo's article "Le missioni," p. 17, it appears that Kẻ Vân was located north-east of Kẻ Sặt.

[20] Scalia, "Gli Agostiniani," p. 33.

[21] Many of the missionaries designated to work in Vietnam reached the country by traveling through China.

[22] For the list of the missionaries and their short biographies, see Scalia, "Gli Agostiniani," pp. 33-37.

[23] Barbagallo, *Sono venuto*, p. 116; Scalia, "Gli Agostiniani," pp. 35-36.

[24] The list of his works is found in Adriano di St. Thecla's other work that survived, the *Compendium Vitae D. ni P. Hilarii a Jesu, Episcopi Coricensis* (A Brief Description of the Life of Ilario di Gesù, the Bishop of Corycus). This work was written by Adriano di St. Thecla in 1756 upon the death of Ilario di Gesù and is located in the General Archive of the Order of Predicators (file XIII-27532, fasc.1-2) in the convent of S. Sabina in Rome. It was published by the Order of the Discalced Augustinians in Latin and in translation into Italian in Pietro Scalia, ed., *Epistoliario*, vol. 3, *Lettere di P. Ilario Costa di Gesù* (Rome: Edizione "Presenza Agostiniana," 2000), pp. 307-338. The list is on pp. 334-337. Hereafter, I will cite this printed edition as "Compendium Vitae."

[25] It is not clear whether the *Chronology* is one work or two. While the sources of the order consider it to be one (Scalia, "Gli Agostiniani, " p. 36), one phrase in the Introduction to the *Opusculum* makes me think that there were two separate works, the *Chinese Chronology* and the *Tonkinese Chronology*. Adriano di St. Thecla says: "the study combined with [my work on] each chronology was a great advantage for its [*Opusculum's*] completion." At the same time, Adriano di St. Thecla calls the work the *Chinese and Tonkinese Chronology*, not *Chronologies*, as would be expected if there were two books. It is possible that there were two *Chronologies* bound as one volume. This work has not yet been located.

was about the degree to which missionaries could adapt their teachings to local culture without compromising their faith. The first missionaries who arrived in China in the late sixteenth century initially failed to establish themselves there and to propagate their religion due to their inability to comprehend and adapt to local realities. Gradually, they began to understand that their attempts to evangelize the indigenous population were doomed unless they studied local languages and customs. The most drastic change in the missionaries' approach to the propagation of Christianity was brought about by the Jesuit Matteo Ricci (1552-1610), who came to China at the end of the sixteenth century. He mastered the Chinese language, and he studied the culture, ideology, religious practice, and traditions of educated people.

The most difficult problem for the missionaries lay in the domain of rites and ceremonies practiced from time immemorial, that is, the worship of ancestors and the cult of the greatest philosopher of antiquity, Confucius. Ricci's policy was to avoid conflict about these rites because the rejection of these ancient traditions, in his opinion, would inevitably deter people from the Christian religion. He argued that the cults of the deceased and of Confucius were not religious in their character and thus did not contradict Christian tenets. Ricci wrote:

> The most solemn thing among the *literati* and in use from the king down to the very least being is the offering they annually make to the dead at certain times of the year of meat, fruits, perfumes, and pieces of silk cloth—paper among the poorest—and incense. And in this act they make the fulfilment of their duty to their relatives, namely, "to serve them in death as though they were alive." Nor do they think in this matter that the dead will come to eat the things mentioned or that they might need them; but they say they do it because they know of no other way to show their love and grateful spirit toward them [the dead].[26]

As for Confucius, Ricci considered his teaching as a way of life. "... we came to the conclusion that this [Confucianism] is not a formal rule [*legge formata*], but is really only an academy set up for the good governance of the republic."[27] Thus, Ricci thought that the cult of the ancestors and the cult of Confucius were viewed as being not of divine nature and hence should be treated with tolerance, at least until the Christian community had been established. His approach proved to be extremely successful, confirmed by the Holy Office, and applied by the missionaries during Ricci's lifetime and for several decades after his death. It was eventually challenged by the Spanish Dominicans and Franciscans, who were alarmed by the threat to Christian purity in using Ricci's approach. Their doubts sparked a heated controversy about rites and ceremonies, which marred relations between the missionaries and the local population, between the missionaries and the Holy Office, and among different orders.

At the time Adriano di St. Thecla wrote his manuscript, the Rites Controversy had been formally terminated by the bull "Ex quo singulari," issued on July 11, 1742, which condemned any concessions to local customs, including the cults of the ancestors and of Confucius, which were declared to be purely superstitious, and,

---

[26] In *Fonti Ricciane: Storia dell'Introduzione del Christianesimo in Cina Scrittsa da Matteo Ricci*, ed. Pasquale M. d'Elia, vol. 1, no. 177. Cited in George Minamiki, *The Chinese Rites Controversy from Its Beginning to Modern Times* (Chicago: Loyola University Press, 1985), pp. 17-18.

[27] *Fonti Ricciane*, vol. 1, no. 191. Cited in Minamiki, *The Chinese Rites Controversy*, p. 20.

hence, to be regarded as anathema to Christianity. What were Adriano di St. Thecla's views on the Rites Controversy? In his chapter on Spirits, he addresses the Rites Controversy, though in an oddly ambiguous manner.

In the eleventh article of chapter 2 he makes "important remarks on sacrifices" and implies the existence of an argument for exempting the veneration of Confucius and of ancestors from the charge of idolatry:

> Thus, the first observation is that all these sacrifices [i.e. to Confucius, tutelary genies, other spirits, and the deceased] are equally stained or infected with superstition and idolatry, and, because of this, sacrifices to Confucius cannot be considered free [of superstition and idolatry], nor can sacrifices to the deceased ancestors be [considered] as customary [i.e., innocent common usage]; they are similar to sacrifices, which, according to tradition, are made to Thần Nông [the god of agriculture], *Thành Hoàng* [tutelary deities], and to other spirits; all [of these sacrifices] should be considered as filled with superstition and idolatry. If sacrifices to Confucius and to the deceased were free from the idolatrous and superstitious [character of the] cult, sacrifices to other spirits would also obtain this immunity, because in all of them the same sense is contained. Therefore, the Holy Office many times deservedly pronounced offerings to Confucius and to the deceased as infected with superstition. (pp. 54-55 of the Latin manuscript)

His larger argument in this section of the manuscript involves a comparison of sacrificial practice in Vietnam with Biblical sacrifices, in which he observes that sacrificial practices in Vietnam are corrupted versions of Biblical sacrificial practice and are inspired by demons in imitation of Biblical sacrifices. Adriano di St. Thecla shows a strong interest in sacrificial ceremonies, giving several very detailed descriptions of such rites in his manuscript; he has a tendency in several places to interpret Tonkinese sacrificial rites as a shadow of Biblical sacrificial practice, as if they were capable of being redeemed for Christianity or of acting as a vehicle for inculcating knowledge of Christian worship.

It appears that an obligatory confession of adherence to the Papal Bull of July 1742 was inserted into this discussion of sacrifices, yet in such a way as to acknowledge the existence of a dissenting opinion, according to which offerings to Confucius and to ancestors were not classified as idolatrous. Given the very sensitive, even sympathetic, descriptions in the manuscript of the veneration of Confucius and of ancestors, we can reasonably conjecture that Adriano di St. Thecla was inclined toward the unorthodox position in the Rites Controversy.

The materials on the order and of the order are dispersed in different archives. Some of them are located in the collection of Discalced Augustinians (sect. XVI – XIX) in the State Archives of Italy, in the collection of East India in the Archive of the Propaganda of Faith, in the Archive of the Order of Predicatores in Rome, and, apparently, a very few are held in the Archive of the Vatican. The information on Adriano di St. Thecla himself is very sparse.

Adriano di St. Thecla was born to Casal Monferratto da Orazio and Caterina Rubaliara in 1667. His secular name was Giambattista. He was consecrated as a member of the Milanese Province of the Order in 1715,[28] and later, along with another Discalced Augustinian, the aforementioned Father Domenico di St. Martino,

---

[28] Scalia, "Gli Agostiniani, " p. 36.

departed on a French ship on December 18, 1736. On April 29, 1738, they arrived in Tonkin via Macao. They carried a reply from the Congregation of the Propaganda of Faith to a letter written earlier by Ilario di Gesù—who at that time was Vicar Apostolic of Eastern Tonkin—on the question of superstitions.[29] Father Lorenzo Maria della Concezione (1693-1773)[30] wrote: "On April 29 arrived healthy and safe in this kingdom of Tonkin two new Fathers, Adriano da Santa Tecle [Adriano di St. Thecla] and Domenico Maria da San Martino ... , the first of the two stayed with me in Kẻ Vân to study the language, the other stayed in Dun Xuen with the same purpose."[31]

It appears that Adriano di St. Thecla adjusted himself to the new milieu and mastered Vietnamese fairly soon after his arrival, because already on July 22, 1739 the same Father Lorenzo relates in his letter to Attanasio da St. Giacomo that, in addition to the existing seminary, the order planned to establish a new seminary for young people, and that this new school "will pass under the direction and instruction of our F. Adriano, whom I assigned to the parish of the Eastern Vicariate,[32] and in the interests of our mission, it is not possible to expect for him any other more useful position."[33] It is not clear whether Adriano di St. Thelca indeed started to work in this new seminary, or whether it was created at all. But whatever he did, Adriano di St. Thecla definitely proved himself to be a capable person, at least in the eyes of his superiors, for we read in another letter of Lorenzo Maria della Concezione: "[Father Adriano] is a religious of great merit dear to me for his virtue."[34]

Ignazio Barbagallo reports that in the 1740s, during a major rebellion, "the administrative zone of Father Adriano di St. Thecla, which was located near the sea, remained uninhabited, it turned into a steppe [sic] and the hiding place of the royal troops."[35] This is a reference, albeit obscure, to the rebellion of Nguyễn Hữu Cầu, which spread over the plain from Hanoi, eastward and southward, to the sea during the years 1743-51. This rebellion was simply one of several that were sustained in various parts of Tonkin beginning in the 1730s and continuing through the 1760s. At that time the Trịnh family ruled Tonkin, or northern Vietnam, which Europeans

---

[29] Adriano di St. Thecla, "Compendium Vitae," pp. 322-323.

[30] Father Lorenzo, a classmate of Ilario Costa di Gesù, arrived in Tonkin in 1729 and was appointed to the seminary in Kẻ Sặt, the head of which he later became. In 1754 he returned to Rome to deliver some documents of the Synod of Tonkin, and then could not go back. Father Lorenzo is the author of *History of the Missions of the Discalced Augustinians in Tonkin*, written and sent in 1745 to Rome (Scalia, "Gli Agostiniani," p. 35).

[31] The letter of Lorenzo Maria della Concezione from July 30, 1738, in Lorenzo Maria della Concezione, *Epistolario* (Roma: Edizione di "Vinculum" – Rivista interna dello Studentato di Gesù e Maria dei PP. Agostiniani Scalzi, 1966),1:100.

[32] The Eastern Vicariate was located east of the Red River.

[33] Ibid., p. 108.

[34] Letter to Attanasio da St. Giacomo from August 5, 1940, in Lorenzo Maria della Concezione, *Epistolario*, 1:117.

[35] Barbagallo, *Sono venuto*, p. 216. This is a reference to the rebellion of Nguyễn Hưũ Cầu in Hải Dương province, where in 1742 he succeeded in gathering a considerable following, built some small warships, and turned the seaside locality of Đồ Sơn into a stronghold. See I. A. Ognetov, "Obostrenie klassovoi bor'by v Dangngoae" (Aggravation of Class Struggle in Đàng Ngoài), in *Novaya Istoriya Vietnama* (New History of Vietnam), ed. S. A. Mhitarian (Moscow: Nauka, 1980), p. 85.

distinguished from Cochinchina, in the central and southern parts of modern Vietnam, which was ruled by the Nguyễn family. The Trịnh ruled in the name of the Lê dynasty, while holding the Lê kings as virtual prisoners. There was unrest and rebellion during the entire period of Adriano de St. Thecla's time in Tonkin. This was a time characterized by abandoned villages, bands of desperadoes, predatory soldiers, and occasional movements of massed peasant armies under the banners of rebel leaders.

In March of 1749 Adriano di St. Thecla was selected by Ilario di Gesù to be Vicar General of the northern province, in the place named Xu Lac, to assume direction of missionary activity there. In June of the next year, unable to propagate Christianity in Xu Lac due to the scarcity of believers and the fear of persecution caused by a royal decree against Christianity, Adriano di St. Thecla left Xu Lac and returned to his previous place of habitation, Kẻ Nam. However, according to Adriano di St. Thecla, no persecutions resulted from the decree.[36] In 1753 Adriano di St. Thecla was appointed Provicar of the Eastern Vicariate.[37]

Ilario di Gesù died in 1754, and thereafter the fortunes of the Discalced Augustinians in Tonkin declined rapidly. Adriano di St. Thecla turned out to be the last Discalced Augustian in Tonkin, and his final years of service were marred by conflict between him and Dominican missionaries, who arrived from Spain and claimed authority over the mission. Adriano di St. Thecla refused to concede his power.[38] According to the version of events kept by the Discalced Augustinians, Adriano di St. Thecla's own superiors—and consequently, the missionary himself—had not been informed of the decision of the Congregation of the Propaganda of Faith of June 30, 1757, to discontinue the work of the Discalced Augustinians and to transfer all their missions under the aegis of the Dominicans.[39]

The argument about the Discalced Augustinian missionary activity had started several decades prior to the final decision, when the Dominicans first tried to get Eastern Tonkin completely under their sway. In 1745, the Congregation of the Propaganda of Faith prepared the "Project for recalling the Discalced Augustinians in Tonkin," but it was postponed.[40] Perhaps Ilario di Gesù's reputation and merits averted the expulsion of the Discalced Augustinians from Eastern Tonkin, but after his death there was no one of his stature to represent the interests of the Discalced Augustinians against the pressure of the Dominicans.

In the light of conflict between the newly arrived Dominican missionaries and Adriano di St. Thecla, the Congregation acted to bring the mission of the Discalced Augustinians to an end. Adriano di St. Thecla, however, did not leave the country to

---

[36] Adriano di St. Thecla, "Compendium Vitae," pp. 326-327. However, this statement sounds strange since in 1750 there indeed were harsh persecutions. The *Journal of the Society of the Foreign Missions* of 1751 accounts for this differently, saying that the destructive incursions of the rebels in the northern province, where Adriano di St. Thecla worked at that time, caused him to shelter in an eastern province. The following year the Christians in the northern province could start to rebuild their homes and churches. Cited in André Marillier, *Nos pères dans la foi. Notes sur le clerge catholique du Tonkin de 1666 à 1765* (Our Fathers in the Faith. Notes on the Catholic Clergy of Tonkin from 1666 to 1765) (Paris: Eglises d'Asie, 1995), 2:126.

[37] Adriano di St. Thecla, "Compendium Vitae," pp. 330-331.

[38] A letter of L. Néez of February 26, 1759 (Archive of the Foreign Missions in Paris, file 689, p. 290), cited in Marillier, *Nos pères*, 2:126.

[39] Barbagallo, *Sono Venuto*, pp. 234-237.

[40] Ibid., p. 237.

which he devoted half of his life, and he died in Tonkin in September 1765. The Apostolic Vicar of Beijing, Giovanni Damasceno, wrote about Adriano di St. Thecla as follows: "Father Adriano suffered much, and he must not be condemned if he shows himself very reluctant to obey the Saint Congregation, because the injustice was elsewhere."[41]

We know that the Dominicans were vociferous denouncers of the unorthodox position in the Rites Controversy, which may explain why they were so determined to displace the Discalced Augustinians in Tonkin, of whom Adriano di St. Thecla was the last. If this supposition is correct, then we can see the Rites Controversy in the background of the events of 1757, when the Discalced Augustinians in Tonkin were dismissed in favor of the Dominicans and Adriano di St. Thecla was eased into involuntary retirement from his position of authority in the mission. That he chose to remain in Tonkin until his death eight years later, rather than returning to Europe, may indicate the degree to which he had adapted to local forms of religious practice.

Considering the controversial relations between the Orders of the Discalced Augustinians and the Dominicans, it is especially important to mention briefly a person who belonged to the Dominican Order and who, in a sense, was almost a co-author of the *Opusculum*, for, in the manuscript, Adriano di St. Thecla refers to him as the source for some of his information and acknowledges him as an "editor" of the first version of the *Opusculum*. This person's name was Francisco Gil de Federich. His activities in Vietnam deserve a thorough study, which, unfortunately, is beyond the scope of this work and is yet to be done. Unlike the sparse information on Adriano di St. Thecla, there is a considerable amount of material on Francisco Gil de Federich.[42] He was born in Tortosa, Spain, in 1702. He arrived in Tonkin in 1735 from Batavia. Two years later, in 1737, shortly before Adriano de St. Thecla's arrival in Tonkin, he was seized by Vietnamese opposed to his missionary activity. Gravely sick, he was thrown into prison and condemned to be decapitated, but he remained under arrest for several years until his execution in 1745. Strangely enough, Father de Federich was able to conduct his missionary activity even in his confinement. According to a church historian, "On the Saint Thursday in 1742 he even had an opportunity to celebrate the liturgy in the chambers of the sixth son of the *chua* [the leader of the ruling Trịnh family] and of the maternal grand-uncle of the sovereign, being invited to explain the fundamental points of the Christian religion."[43] Judging from Adriano

[41] Barbagallo, "Le missioni," pp. 44-45.

[42] The materials include a lot of archival documents, as well as some printed editions. For the archival documentation, see, for example, in the convent of S. Sabina in Rome, files X.1124-X.1127, X.1131-X.1138; and in the archives of the Ordre in Avila, Spain: vol. 1, doc. 8, pp. 160-192, "Report on the imprisonment of Fathers Fransisco Gil de Federich and Mateo de Leciniana"; vol. 2, doc. 3, "A letter written from the jail in Tonkin by Father Gil de Federich after five years in prison"; vol. 2., doc. 4, "A report on the martyrdom of Fathers and God's servants Francisco Gil de Federich and Mateo Leciniana that took place on January 22, 1745"; vol. 4, doc. 9, "A letter of Father Francisco Gil de Federich to the Provincial Vicar in 1739." There are at least two books devoted to Father Franscisco Gil de Federich. One is Lorenzo G. Sempere, *El Bienaventurado Francisco Gil de Federich, O.P.: Su Vida y Martirio* (Valencia, 1906), written on the occasion of his beatification; the second is Lorenzo Gales Mas, *Francisco Gil de Federich. Dominico, Academico, Misionero y Martir en el Vietnam* (Barcelona: Instituto de Espana, Real Academia de Buenas Letras de Barcelon, Provincia Dominicana de Aragon, 1988), which appeared in connection with his canonization. In addition, there is another work that contains a substantial amount of material on Father Federich: Marcos Gispert, *Historia de las Misiones Dominicanas en Tungkin* (Avila, 1928). Practically all these materials are in Spanish or Latin.

[43] Guy-Marie Oury, *Le Vietnam. Des martyrs et des saints* (Fayard, 1988), p. 67.

di St. Thecla's references to Father de Federich, Federich's imprisonment did not prevent him from meeting Vietnamese scholars and officials nor from carrying on an extensive correspondence with other missionaries, one of whom was Adriano himself.

The Provenance of the Manuscript

The *Opusculum* is written in vulgar Latin with numerous insertions of passages in Sino-Vietnamese (Hán; Sino-Vietnamese, i.e. classical Chinese with Vietnamese pronunciation), and some phrases in vernacular Vietnamese, written not with demotic characters (Nôm), as was usual in the eighteenth century, but in the Latinized script (quốc ngữ) invented by European missionaries in the seventeenth century and systematized in 1651 with publication in Rome of the first Vietnamese-Portuguese-Latin dictionary, compiled by Father Alexandre de Rhodes (1591-1661), a Jesuit missionary to Vietnam.[44] Some of the Chinese names and toponyms, and some terms written in this Vietnamese Latinized script, are, in addition, supplied with their Chinese equivalents in a Latinized transcription.

The manuscript is in pretty good shape but not without some places difficult to read. It was found in the Archive of the Foreign Missions in Paris, France. This is a copy, not the original written by Adriano di St. Thecla himself. Adriano di St. Thecla's handwriting differs from that in the copy of the *Opusculum* in the Archive of the Foreign Missions.[45] Furthermore, the Vietnamese Latinized script (*quốc ngữ*) used in the *Compendium*, written in Adriano de St. Thecla's hand, differs considerably from that found in the *Opusculum*. Adriano di St. Thecla's *quốc ngữ* is very similar to the spellings found in Alexandre de Rhodes dictionary, while the *quốc ngữ* in the *Opusculum* reveals changes that bring it closer to modern Vietnamese orthography.

For example, in the Introduction to the *Opusculum*, there are mentioned two works of Ilario di Gesù spelled as follows: *Dị doan chi giáo* (The Doctrine of Superstitions) and *Đại học chi Đạo* (The Doctrine of Great Learning). While in the *Compendium* the first title is spelled in the same way, the second one is there spelled as *Đại haọc chi đạo*, that is, the word *học* "learning, to study," is written as *haọc*, in the form recorded in Alexandre de Rhodes's dictionary.[46] Another discrepancy is seen in the word spelled by Adriano di St. Thecla as *trạõ*, standing for the modern *trọng*: "important, solemn, pure." In the seventeenth century, the ending "-ng" did not appear after the vowels "o," "ô," and "u."[47] Instead, the "-ng" words had above the vowel a diacritic to indicate its nasalization. Alexandre de Rhodes's dictionary recorded the words which now end with "-ong," "-ông,"or "-ung" as ending with "-

[44] The Latinized script (quốc ngữ) did not become widespread in Vietnam until the twentieth century. Until then, the Vietnamese kept their traditional system of character writing. Only with the establishment of firm French rule in Vietnam did quốc ngữ gain acceptance among the Vietnamese and now it has completely replaced character writing.

[45] The comparison of handwriting was made with samples of Adriano di St. Thecla's handwriting in the manuscript of the "Compendium Vitae" and in his letter found in the Archive of the Foreign Missions in Paris (file 689, p. 55), in which the handwriting is identical.

[46] Alexandre de Rhodes, *Từ Điển Annam-Lusitan-Latinh* (Annamite-Lusitanian [Portuguese]-Latin Dictionary), reprint with translation by Thanh Lãng, Hoàng Xuân Việt, and Đỗ Quang Chính (Hanoi: Nhà Xuất Bản Khoa Học Xã Hội, 1991), col. 315.

[47] The exception was if the aforementioned vowels were a part of a diphthong, as, for example, *cuồng*, "crazy," or *xuống*, "to descend." Ibid., cols. 144 and 899, respectively.

aõ," "-oũ," or "-ũ."[48] In the *Opusculum*, words with the "-ng" ending appear according to modern spelling without exception.

Having established the fact that the *Opusculum* in the Archive of the Foreign Missions is not the original from Adriano di St. Thecla's hand, we then encounter the question of how did this manuscript appear in the Archive? André Marillier ascribes its provenance to Father Louis Néez,[49] citing his letter to the directors of Foreign Missions in Paris of December 15, 1749:

> I had the Chronology of China and Tonkin with an abridged chronology of the history of religion, composed by Reverent Father Adrien de Sainte Thecle, an Italian Augustinian, missionary of the Propaganda in Tonkin, written [= copied] by our students.[50] It is a new book, at least concerning Tonkin, and perhaps even concerning China. Since this Father sent this work to Rome, I guessed that I would do you a favor by sending a copy for your library. I wish it had been written better and more precisely. I corrected there quite a number of mistakes. Maybe there are still many more others there. Please be so kind as to excuse an old man who is alone and overloaded with affairs.[51]

I assume, however, that this letter accompanied Father Néez's posting of the *Chinese and Tonkinese Chronology*, not the *Opusculum*, for it is clearly stated in the letter that he was sending the *Chronology*. The fact that along with the *Chronology* Father Néez sent "an abridged chronology of the history of religion" could suggest that he included an outline or first draft of the *Opusculum*. Adriano di St. Thecla

[48] Here are only several examples of a systematic rule: *cũ* for the modern *cùng*, "together"; *đoũ* for the modern *đông*, "east, winter"; *saõ* for the modern *song*, "pair, couple." Ibid., cols. 146, 235, and 679, respectively. The word written by Adriano di St. Thecla as *trạõ*, "important, solemn, pure, transparent," is also found in this form in de Rhodes's dictionary in col. 831, with its earlier variation spelled as *tlạõ*. Ibid., cols. 805-806.

[49] Father Néez (1680-1764) was a missionary of the Foreign Missions of Paris in Vietnam. He arrived in Vietnam in 1715 and spent all of his life there. Father Néez, like Adriano di St. Thecla, was suspended, in 1759, from his religious duties in Vietnam due to the Rites Controversy and the reorganization of mission work among different Orders in Vietnam, in particular, and in the Far East, in general. See Marillier, *Nos pères*, 2:81-82.

[50] The Society of the Foreign Missions was founded in Paris in 1664 for the propagation of Christianity in China and Vietnam. On its history, see A. Launay, *Histoire générale de la Société des Mission Etrangère depuis sa fondation jusqu'à nos jours* (Paris: Téqui, 1894). Father Néez is talking about the indigenous Vietnamese students who studied under the patronage of European missionaries in several small colleges in Northern Vietnam where, among other subjects, they studied Latin and the Latinized script for Vietnamese, *quốc ngữ*. As Father Néez advised the new Apostolic Vicar of Yunnan, Father de Martilliat, on the principles for establishing small colleges, "... apprehension of the Latin script is a necessity for those striving to ascend some day to the superior ranks.... Indeed it will be demanded from those aspiring to become priests not only to know how to decipher several Latin expressions, but also an attempt will be made that they would know the quốc ngữ to be able to communicate in writing or be able to understand and transcribe the writings of the missionaries, who, as for themselves, study at first the language in quốc ngữ." See the letter from October 24, 1739, Archive of the Foreign Missions in Paris, file 689, pp. 384-385, cited in Alain Forest. *Les missionnaires français au Tonkin et au Siam (XVIIe-XVIIIe siècles)*, vol. 3: *Organiser une église convertir les infideles* (Organizing a church to convert infidels) (Paris: L'Harmattan, 1998), p. 130. For a brief summary on these colleges see ibid, pp. 124-134; see also Marillier, *Nos pères*, 1:113-124.

[51] Marillier, *Nos pères*, 2:126.

mentions in the present version of the manuscript that he "wrote the following *Opusculum* in a sketchy form" before he wrote the *Chinese and Tonkinese Chronology*. The date on the letter, December 15, 1749, corroborates my supposition, since in the present version it is stated that the manuscript was completed in September, 1750. Thus, any version of the manuscript that could have been sent by Father Néez accompanied by the aforementioned letter would have to have been an early sketch of it.

If Father Néez and his students did not copy the manuscript, then who did copy it, and when? Unfortunately, both questions are still unresolved. I first tried to approach the question of dating the copy by comparing the Vietnamese Latinized script (quốc ngữ) found in the *Opusculum* with that typical for the middle of the eighteenth century. The results are not conclusive or persuasive.

First of all, the aforementioned example of the discrepancy between the words *haọc* and *học* cannot provide any decisive information. This is because de Rhodes's dictionary provides variant spellings for two words analogous to *học* (which de Rhodes spells only as *haọc*) that are identical to modern spellings, suggesting that a style of usage we associate with modern orthography was already being used in the seventeenth century. The two words are *đọc*, "to read," and *mọc*, "to grow," which de Rhodes records as *đaọc* and *maọc*[52]; however, de Rhodes also provides several compounds in which these words are spelled according to modern orthography, as *đọc* and *mọc*.[53] Other comparable words for which de Rhodes provides variant spellings are *nọc*, "the sting of scorpion, venom," for which de Rhodes indicates the possibility of its being spelling as *naọc*,[54] and *dọc*, "lengthwise," recorded as *daọc* with the variation *dọc*. [55] Furthermore, many comparable words did not have variations different from modern orthography. See, for example, *bọc*, "embryo or to enclose"; *cọc*, "stake, picket"; *lọc*, "filter"; *tọc*, "to pry and tell tales."[56] Thus, it seems that there was a definite tendency already in the seventeenth century to eradicate "a" from the ending "-aọc." Even if we assume that in the seventeenth century *haọc* was the only spelling for the modern word *học*, as de Rhodes's dictionary has it (and strangely this is the only such case among that class of words!), this word definitely succumbed to the general tendency as time went on, and it is very conceivable that in the eighteenth century both variants could co-exist, *haọc* as used by Adriano di St. Thecla in the *Compendium* and *học* as found in the *Opusculum*. Hence, these words do not contribute to a solution for the question of dating the copy of the *Opusculum*.

The second example discussed above—words ending with the nasalized final "-ng"—seems to fit our purpose a little better. In the *Opusculum* the spelling of the words ending with "-ông" invariably appear in their modern forms: *ông* ("sir, man"), *công* ("office, official post"), *đồng* ("field"), etc. But the "-ong" words follow a transitional form of spelling between the "-aõ" of de Rhodes's dictionary and modern "-ong"; the letter "a" is retained between the preceding consonant and the "o," possibly to reflect the "openess" of "o" in contrast to the more "closed" pronunciation of "ô," and the "-ng" is added to produce "-aong," for example *laòng* (instead of modern *lòng*, "heart") and *traọng* (instead of modern *trọng*, "important,

[52] Rhodes, *Từ Điển*, cols. 205 and 405, respectively.

[53] Ibid., cols. 226 and 477, respectively.

[54] Ibid., col. 565.

[55] Ibid., cols. 168 and 176, respectively.

[56] Ibid., cols. 51, 128, 420, and 821, respectively

solemn, pure, transparent"). By the end of the nineteenth century, the letter "a" disappeared from these endings, and they assumed their modern form, as the dictionary compiled by Huình Tịnh Paulus Của and published in 1895 clearly shows.[57]

Relying on the fact that extant examples of the Latinized Vietnamese script of the eighteenth century still follow the rule requiring placement of a diacritic above the second vowel for nazalization in words ending with "-ng,"[58] and that the *Opusculum* still uses some forms earlier than what is known at the end of the nineteenth century, I could suggest that the manuscript was copied some time at the end of the eighteenth or the beginning of the nineteenth centuries. However, it is not impossible that someone at the time of Adriano di St. Thecla was already using a spelling system that was closer to the modern spelling system than what was used by Adriano di St. Thecla or than what can be found in contemporary writing samples available for me to examine.

Language usage does not instantly change according to decrees or the preferences of a few individuals. Its development and the establishing of new rules can cover considerable periods of time. It might be that at the time of Adriano di St. Thecla there was already an alternative system used by a few but which eventually evolved to become generally accepted by everyone. In such a case, it would be interesting to know who copied the manuscript, as it appears that he may have played a not insignificant role in the development of the Vietnamese latinized script, or he may have been a transmitter of a system elaborated by colleagues or teachers.

The style of transliterating Chinese in the manuscript is tentatively dated by Professor Lionel Jensen as that of the seventeenth century. According to him, this type of transliteration is a rather unusual mixture of the French, Portuguese, and Italian style, and it is closer to the way of transliteration used in the seventeenth century than to that of the nineteenth century. Even though the Chinese transliteration in the manuscript is unusual, it is consistent throughout the entire manuscript, and thus forms a system. Even if the *Opusculum* was copied in the nineteenth century, as it is possible to surmise on the basis of the Vietnamese script, the use of the seventeenth-century style of transliterating Chinese still seems very plausible if we conjecture that the copyist was not acquainted with more modern ways for transliterating Chinese, so that, while fixing the Vietnamese, he left the Chinese transliteration in its original form.

Although it is obvious that some changes were made by the copyist of the manuscript, it is unclear how far his intervention spread, whether he fixed only the orthography or also the content of the *Opusculum*. Only Adriano di St. Thecla's original can supply a definitive resolution of this question. My attempt to find the original in the Order of the Discalced Augustinians in Rome or in the Archive of the Vatican, as well as in the State Archives of Italy, which according to information given me by the Order, confiscated a major part of the Order's materials, rendered no results. For the purpose of this translation, I consider Adriano di St. Thecla as the author of the *Opusculum* and as the source of information in it, unless there be a

[57] Huình Tịnh Paulus Của, *Đại Nam Quấc Âm Tự Vị* (A Dictionary of Characters with the National Pronunciation of Great South) (reprint, Ho Chi Minh: Nhà Xuất Bản Trẻ, 1998), see pp. 584, 585, 921, 1106-1107, respectively.

[58] See, for example, a letter of François Hậu to Jean Davoust, Archive of the Foreign Missions in Paris, file 690, pp. 207-208.

name mentioned in the manuscript ascribing some piece of information to someone else.

Adriano di St. Thecla based his manuscript not only on his own close acquaintance with Vietnamese life, but also on numerous other sources. First of all, a considerable amount of information was conveyed to him by the aforementioned Francisco Gil de Federich. In addition, as he states in his Introduction, he relied on the works of Ilario Costa di Gesù: *Dị doan chi giáo* (Doctrine of Superstitions) and *Index Historicum*. Adriano di St. Thecla also used many Chinese and Vietnamese sources from which he quotes extensively. Among them are the Vietnamese annals, Classical Chinese books of history and philosophy, and works of the Neo-Confucian scholars and historians. I remain puzzled by his references to the *Chinese History*. I have not been able to locate any work of "Chinese History" covering the span of time from antiquity to the fifteenth century, such as is indicated in the *Opusculum*. "*Chinese History*" might be a generic term referring to different dynastic histories, or perhaps it was a collection of historical writings produced in Vietnam, either by Vietnamese or by the missionaries themselves.

Some seventy-five years after it was written, the *Opusculum* was given notice in *Journal Asiatique*, 2 (1823): 163-175 and 6 (1825): 154-165 with an outline of the contents and some extracts. Aside from this, in the two and a half centuries since it was written, the *Opusculum* has not, to my knowledge, received any particular attention by scholars or others.

Contents of the Manuscript

The work covers all religious currents known to Adriano di St. Thecla. The manuscript includes six chapters: Introduction, Confucianism, Spirits, the Sect of Magicians (i.e., Daoism), Fortune-tellers, Buddhism, and Christianity. The last chapter, on Christianity, is not completed, and ends abruptly. The manuscript formally consists of 121 pages, eight pages of which are Introduction. It is also supplied with a two-page table of contents. However, twelve pages are left blank,[59] hence reducing the volume of actual text to 109 pages. The blank pages are found at the end of the chapters on Confucianism, Daoism, and Fortune-tellers, and after the second article of the chapter on Buddhism. In all these cases, except for the chapter on Fortune-tellers, the last sentence preceding the blank space starts with the word "Testimonia," that is, Testimony, followed by the topic of the chapter. This sentence is absent at the end of the chapter on Fortune-tellers and no blank pages were left after the chapter on the Spirits.

I suggest that these blank spaces were left for bibliographical references that were subsequently left unwritten or uncopied. I make this assumption taking into consideration the fact that quotations from texts, or "testimonies," are inserted into these chapters. These "testimonies" come from a considerable number of primary sources and are used to document the doctrines presented in the chapters. It appears that Adriano di St. Thecla intended to provide bibliographies for some chapters listing all the works quoted therein and possibly some other sources that were of help to him in constructing his presentation of Confucianism, Daoism, and Buddhism. If this were so, it would be logical to omit mention of testimony at the end of the chapter on Spirits, since there the author evidently used his own experience and oral sources rather than written works.

[59] Pages 20-23, 72, 77-82, and 88 are blank.

The chapter on Fortune-tellers tends to undermine this supposition, but it should be noted that this is the shortest chapter of the manuscript, containing only four pages. It is clear from the table of contents accompanying the manuscript that this chapter, as is the case of the chapter on Christianity, simply was not completed or copied up to the end, and the blank pages were to include some additional information. The absence of the word "Testimonia" at the end of this chapter corroborates this assumption, since the content of this chapter, as that of the chapter on the Spirits, is based (at least in its existing form) on oral sources.

Adriano di St. Thecla titled his work *Opusculum de Sectis apud Sinenses et Tunkinenses* (A Small Treatise on the Sects among the Chinese and Tonkinese), thus presumably preparing his readers to become acquainted with religious practice in both China and Vietnam. In fact, however, the manuscript definitely focuses on the religious situation in Vietnam. There is no evidence that Adriano di St. Thecla had any direct experience of China. Nevertheless, most of the works he used in the *Opusculum* are what today would be conventionally considered of Chinese origin. However, there is no indication that he observes any distinction between the religious, cultural, and intellectual realms of China and Vietnam. In his "Introduction," when discussing the roots of polytheism in the world, he mentions the legendary emperors of Chinese antiquity as if they referred equally to China and Vietnam, while taking no notice of legendary figures specific to the Vietnamese. He continues this approach when announcing his plan for presenting religious currents originating in China and claiming that Tonkin, "ever since it was a subject to Chinese authority, has followed the habits and rites of the Chinese." In the preamble to the chapter on the Spirits, he writes: "In this chapter we speak of the spirits who are worshipped not only by the literati but also by all the others according to the customs of the *Chinese* nation." (emphasis is mine).

With such examples so numerous throughout the manuscript, inevitably a question arises: if he is talking of China all the time, is there information to be found in the manuscript specific to Vietnam? The answer is a definite and strong "yes." Even though the Vietnamese, as Adriano di St. Thecla correctly mentioned, were for almost a millennium under the imperial rule of Chinese dynasties, from 111 B.C.E. to 939 C.E., according to the conventional scheme of dating in Vietnamese historiography, they succeeded in establishing their own language and culture.[60] That the Vietnamese actively participated in what came to be known as the Chinese philosophical system, as did the Japanese and the Koreans, does not negate or compromise the existence of their own cultural tradition. As P. V. Pozner observed: the famous philosophers, "being Chinese by their origin, were treated as outstanding philosophers and scholars of world import. We encounter analogous tendencies in other philosophical-religious teachings; for instance, in Christianity Thomas Aquinas and his teaching have never been treated as exclusively 'Italian.'"[61]

In the *Opusculum*, even when Adriano di St. Thecla labels something as Chinese, as he does in the chapter on the Spirits, in reality he presents specific Vietnamese features as the content of the object of investigation that he names "Chinese."

[60] See, for example, K. W. Taylor, *The Birth of Vietnam* (Berkeley: University of California Press, 1983).

[61] P. V. Pozner, "Nauka i Ideologia" (Scholarship and Ideology), in *Novaya Istoria Vietnama*, ed. S. A. Mhitarian, p. 610.

Adriano di St. Thecla's apparent "Sinicization" of Vietnamese culture is not unusual, and it does not mean that he regarded Vietnam simply as a part of China, a view that has governed numerous works of nineteenth- and twentieth-century scholars. Rather, it is likely that Adriano di St. Thecla's view was not much different from that commonly held by educated Vietnamese of his day, who regarded Chinese antiquity in a way similar to the way eighteenth-century Europeans regarded their own antiquity, as something more than the property of its originators, the Greeks, the Italians, or the Jews.

Textual references in the *Opusculum* are largely based on written sources of Chinese origin complemented with Vietnamese sources that reflect a local context of adapting different Chinese religious currents and enriching them with indigenous cults and practices. Adriano di St. Thecla gives detailed descriptions of various rites and ceremonies connected to these cults and practices. His mixture of philosophical doctrines with specific ceremonies creates a unique picture of Vietnamese religious practice.

At first glance, the structure of the *Opusculum* appears to be quite similar to works written about China in the seventeenth and eighteenth centuries by European missionaries. All of them describe three "sects": Confucianism, Daoism, and Buddhism. Usually, the order of their presentations is Confucianism first, Daoism or Buddhism second, and the remaining one third. Adriano di St. Thecla follows the order of Confucianism, Daoism, and Buddhism and announces in his "Introduction" that "we will talk mostly about these three sects." But, in fact, Adriano di St. Thecla's approach differs significantly from that of the other missionaries.

First of all, in his "Introduction" Adriano di St. Thecla explains his choice of order for the topics as being based on the order set by Zhou Wudi, an emperor ruling in northern China from 561 to 578, who, a foreigner himself, ranked Confucianism first, Daoism second, and Buddhism third. Adriano di St. Thecla's ostensible imitation of Zhou Wudi reveals that he was well acquainted with historical information about the relative statuses of the "sects" he wrote about; he approached his writing analytically and did not randomly order his chapters. Although he cites Zhou Wudi as his authority for ordering the three, I do not think that his reasons for following this sequence were the same as Zhou Wudi's. For Zhou Wudi, Confucianism was an imperial ideology that assisted in governing the country, Daoism was an indigenous doctrine, and Buddhism was a foreign doctrine not useful for supporting dynastic rule. On the other hand, Adriano di St. Thecla ordered his discussion of the religious currents according to an evaluation of the potential and practical impediments each would pose to the dissemination of Christianity, starting with the one most tolerable for the missionaries, Confucianism, and culminating with Buddhism, which the missionaries viewed as an archrival to Christianity.

The largest difference between Adriano di St. Thecla and other Christian writers, and the most characteristic feature of the *Opusculum,* is that Adriano di St. Thecla added, without announcing his intention to do so, a chapter on spirits. This chapter, put directly after Confucianism, is the longest chapter of the manuscript, consisting of thirty-six pages, a substantial portion in a manuscript that numbers 109 pages. In comparison, he gives nineteen pages to Confucianism, twelve pages to Daoism, and twenty-four pages to Buddhism. Adriano di St. Thecla's work seems to be the only one of this kind to present so substantial a picture of different spirits, of their legends, and of the rites and ceremonies connected to their cults. While his neglect of this chapter in the Introduction might be ascribed to his intention to follow the structure of the works of his predecessors, it is exactly this chapter that makes the *Opusculum* stand out from all other missionary writings. If we assume that the order in which Adriano di St. Thecla presented religious practices is not random and that the main criterion for his ranking was potential harm vis-à-vis Christianity, we can only surmise that, as much as they were condemned by the missionaries, the spirits were not considered by Adriano di St. Thecla as the main evil; this was most probably due to the uncoordinated character of the spirit cults and to the absence of any erudite doctrine supporting them. Furthermore, I believe that Adriano di St. Thecla was so interested in spirits because he perceived all the religious currents in Vietnam as being fundamentally the worship of spirits.

It is also possible to see Adriano di St. Thecla's chapter on Spirits, which immediately follows his chapter on Confucianism, as being modeled after Matteo Ricci's chapter on Confucianism in his work *De Christiana expeditione apud Sinas*, published in 1615, which included discussion of village tutelary deities, apparently categorizing these as an extension of the cult of Confucius into the village level.[62] On the other hand, Ricci ordered his chapter on Buddhism ahead of his chapter on Daoism, which apparently reflects his relatively positive view of Buddhism at the beginning of his missionary work in China when he adopted the garb of a Buddhist monk.

The other unannounced chapter in the *Opusculum* is chapter four, dealing with fortune-tellers. This chapter is also unique in comparison with other missionary tractates, where fortune-tellers are only briefly mentioned, if at all. In the *Opusculum*, however, fortune-telling is singled out for a separate chapter. In my opinion, Adriano di St. Thecla saw fortune-telling as a part of Daoism. Yet, because of the "outrageously superstitious" practice of the fortune-tellers, which he considered in excess of the practices he mentions under Daoism, he granted this topic a separate chapter to itself, following Daoism and preceding Buddhism. The practice of fortune-tellers was probably perceived by Adriano di St. Thecla as one of the most evil of practices, second only to Buddhism. He apparently viewed the cults presented in the chapters on Confucianism, Spirits, and Daoism as a form of spirituality that could potentially be replaced by Christian monotheism. This, however, was not the case with the fortune-tellers, who were deeply rooted in Vietnamese social practice, providing guidance for people's everyday life in almost every aspect regardless of social position and educational level. Fortune-tellers would give a person immediate and concrete replies to the most worldly of questions, whether about business, building a house, or marriage. Christianity did not have any way to compete with this.

Adriano di St. Thecla's Introduction

In his "Introduction," Adriano di St. Thecla creates the framework for the *Opusculum*, presenting the roots of idolatry in the world as they were perceived and reputed by different religious authorities of the ancient and medieval clergy. The

[62] Matteo Ricci, *De Christiana expeditione apud Sinas.* For the French translation published two years later, see Matthieu Ricci and Nicolas Trigault, *Histoire de l'expédition chrétienne au royaume de la Chine 1582-1610* (Collection Christus no. 45) (Paris: Bellarmin, Desclee de Brouwer, 1978), p. 164. Hereafter I will use the French translation for the references to Matteo Ricci's work.

extensive detail with which he develops his argument about idolatry shows how Christian proselytizers in eighteenth-century Vietnam conceptualized the difference between their own religious world and the religious world in which they worked. The great pains taken by the author to establish a historical argument about idolatry means that he understood the importance of the question. He did not simply dismiss idols as if the reasons for doing so were obvious. He took the existence of what he called idol-worship as an ingrained and long-standing aspect of human experience, which needed to be thoroughly investigated. At the same time, the author launches an argument, which he endeavors to pull through the entire manuscript, that idolatry was not an essential "in-born" feature of human society everywhere in the world, including China and Vietnam. He insists that initially all people knew only one god, and as Chaldeans slipped into idolatry in the third century after the Flood, so did the Chinese. Contrary to many other missionary accounts, he does not suggest that idolatry was "imported" to China from western Asia. Adriano di St. Thecla perceives the legendary Chinese emperors Yao, Shun, and Yu as bearers of "true religion," free from idolatry and superstitions, after whose time people's morals were corrupted and the knowledge of "true God" disappeared from their hearts and minds.

Confucianism

The chapter on Confucianism is remarkable for the author's extensive knowledge of the Confucian Classics as well as of the works of the so-called Neo-Confucians. Adriano di St. Thecla refers to numerous books and authors with a high degree of preciseness. The author covers not only the major Confucian works and authors, but also dwells on Confucian philosophical ideas and on the Confucian curriculum. Moreover, he dwells at length on the Confucian vision of the creation of the world initiated by the element Thái Cực (*taiji*)—the Primary Source. The first observation that inevitably arises when reading his description of Confucian books and doctrines is that they were all written and expounded by Chinese. The question then arises: did the Vietnamese have anything of their own to contribute to Confucianism? In fact, no indigenous Vietnamese works elaborating Confucianism have been discovered.

In the book *Nho Giáo* (Confucianism)[63] by Trần Trọng Kim, probably the most comprehensive work on Confucianism written by a Vietnamese, the chapter on Confucianism in Vietnam comprises twenty-one pages[64] or approximately 2 percent of a 1,128 page work. The message conveyed in this chapter basically comes to a negation of the existence of a specifically Vietnamese Confucianism. Trần Trọng Kim says: "Vietnam is a small country neighboring China, the territory is narrow, the population is sparse ... it is a civilized country. However, as for the way of learning and ideology, we have always only followed the transmitted path of studies in China." If indeed there exist undiscovered and unstudied Vietnamese Confucian tractates, as has been conjectured,[65] their influence does not seem to have been very significant if they were so easily neglected by Vietnamese in favor of highlighting works written by Chinese philosophers.

[63] Trần Trọng Kim, *Nho Giáo* (Confucianism) (Hanoi: Éditions Lê Thăng, 1942), 4 volumes. This was first published in 1929-30.

[64] Ibid., 4:262-283.

[65] Pozner "Nauka i Ideologia," p. 610.

This can be seen as supporting the widespread view of Vietnam as having been molded by China. But, in my opinion, the case here is quite the opposite. The "underdevelopment" of Confucianism in Vietnam indicated by the absence of Confucian works in the manuscript should be attributed to the differences between China and Vietnam and not to their similarities. Confucianism in Vietnam never gained the status it acquired in China but has largely remained an artificial "superstructure" amidst a Vietnamese reality permeated with Buddhist and other religious practices. There was hardly any period in Vietnam, except for the reign of King Lê Thánh Tông (1460-1497), which could be characterized as a time of Confucian dominance. Beginning in the thirteenth century, Confucianism was mainly used in Vietnam as a curriculum for the selection of officials through an examination process. However, examinations did not result in the creation of a bureaucratic structure of government, as, for example, occurred in China and Korea. Most Vietnamese Confucians served in relatively loosely structured entourages and accepted Buddhism and/or Daoism.[66]

In spite of the numerous references to Confucian works that appear in the manuscript, Confucianism in Vietnam was not a philosophical teaching or doctrine, but rather a religious practice based upon the personalities of Confucius, his disciples, and their followers. The attention given in the manuscript to the practice of worshiping Confucius is quite extensive. According to Professor Lionel Jensen and my research of works written by European missionaries in China, Adriano di St. Thecla's might be the most detailed description of this religious practice from his time, even for China. Although Adriano di St. Thecla treats Confucius and his teaching with evident respect, he cannot avoid putting the worship of Confucius into the same basket as idolatry, which he criticizes throughout his work. His disapproval of venerating Confucius was probably reinforced by the Papal Bull of July 11, 1742, condemning the worship of ancestors and of Confucius. He presents the veneration of Confucius as a vivid example of how far people deviated from the idea of worshiping the "one and only true God." Hence, Confucius is but one of the spirits, even if the most respectable, with whom Adriano di St. Thecla opens his description of the myriad spirits that comprised the rich palette of Vietnamese and Chinese religious practice.

Spirits

The second and longest chapter of the manuscript is devoted to "the Spirits and their Cult." In this chapter Adriano di St. Thecla describes the spirits of Heaven and Earth, the spirit-saints or legendary sage-kings of Chinese antiquity, the spirits of military heroes, of tutelary deities, and miscellaneous spirits who became objects of worship. The knowledge of popular religious practice revealed in this chapter is exceptionally extensive. It is clear that the author took a particular interest in the details of local cults, in stories about various spirits and the manner of showing devotion to them.

Aside from descriptions of spirits, their legends and ways of worshiping them, in this chapter there is valuable information on other subjects. For example, Adriano di St. Thecla describes in detail the ceremony of welcoming spring as it was performed in Hanoi, the main patron of which was a Chinese God of Spring named Câu Mang (Gou Mang). The ritual of inaugurating spring with reference to Câu Mang came

[66] Ibid., p. 608.

from China and was elaborated by the Vietnamese with local practices. This ceremony, now extinguished, was a complicated ritual in which a considerable number of soldiers from special units were enlisted. A central feature of the ceremony was the distribution by soldiers of 1,300 elaborately painted clay buffaloes. Three hundred are first taken to the Lê king, who then distributes them to the temples of spirits and to the soldiers. However, one thousand are taken to the Trịnh lord, who then distributes them to officials and to temples. From this we can see the ritual role of the army and the preeminence of the Trịnh lord over the king. Adriano di St. Thecla's testimony is a rare, possibly unique, description of this ceremony. It suggests that public affairs were to a large extent military affairs, and such a perception is reinforced by the three following items.

Adriano di St. Thecla writes a detailed description of the Vũ Miếu (Wumiao in Chinese, Military Temple) existing in Hanoi in the eighteenth century. As I explain in my annotations, there were several Military Temples in Hanoi during different epochs, but all of them were destroyed, and there remains very little concrete evidence of their existence, except for the last one from the Nguyễn period (1802-1945). With his almost photographic description of the interior of the temple, Adriano di St. Thecla enables us to imagine what the Military Temple of the Lê dynasty looked like.

As a complete surprise comes a description of the ceremony named Tế Kỳ Đạo (The Ceremony of the Leader's Banner). Not only has it never before been described, but also none of the Vietnamese specialists with whom I spoke knew about it. This ceremony, the major element of which was a big banner of the Trịnh warlord, was meant to scare the spirits of rebels from the kingdom. This is a brilliant illustration—which would have been lost to human memory save for Adriano di St. Thecla's testimony—of ritual power under a regime that sank into oblivion shortly thereafter.

Adriano di St. Thecla then leads us to witness a ceremony of taking the Oath of Loyalty. Reading its detailed description, in my opinion, one cannot help but feel with all the officials and soldiers the importance of taking this oath, sealed with a mixture of wine and blood. It is very significant that, according to Adriano di St. Thecla, the person to whom allegiance was pledged was not the emperor but rather the Trịnh lord. Adriano di St. Thecla goes on to describe how oath ceremonies were generalized throughout society to bind servants and retainers to their masters, to bind villagers to local authorities, and to administer justice in matters of dispute. Oath-taking, according to Adriano de St. Thecla's observations, was a central means of insuring public order, which suggests that it was used in lieu of any strictly bureaucratic system of government as a means of guaranteeing compliance with the authority of the regime. This generalized practice of oath-taking appears to be an extension of military values into civil government.

The three rituals of welcoming spring, of the leader's banner, and of the oath of loyalty do not appear to be religious in the sense of acknowledging the supremacy of divine powers. They rather appear as ceremonies in which divine powers are called into service by human rulers to serve or to guarantee the security and well-being of their realm.

Adriano di St. Thecla presents an extensive discussion of the institution of tutelary genies. He addresses the issue of tutelary genie (*thành hoàng; chenghuang* in Chinese) both in Tonkin and in China, and describes ceremonies performed in their honor.[67] Moreover, he describes a system for the probation and ranking of spirits, some aspects of which are hardly, if at all, known at the present time, i.e. a public test conducted to prove the prowess of a certain genie. All that has been known in modern times, apart from Adriano di St. Thecla's testimony, is the existence of a system in which villages submitted requests to provincial officials for their local tutelary genies to be promoted, and, if provincial officials found convincing proof that a genie had benefited a village, they would pass the request on to the capital for consideration by an office in the Ministry of Rites. Up to this time, however, we have known little else about the ritual process of evaluating a genie's capabilities. Now, as a result of this manuscript, we learn how these cases were ritually decided in the capital.

The author's descriptions of two spirits mentioned in this chapter offer opportunities for examining Adriano di St. Thecla's value as a source of information and for exploring unusual cases of spirit cults that pose special problems for modern scholarship. These spirits are the Han general Mã Viện (Ma Yuan) and the celestial princess Liễu Hạnh, whose cult apparently began in the sixteenth century.

Mã Viện

One of the most interesting points in the chapter on the spirits is Adriano di St. Thecla's equation of Mã Viện (Mạ Yuan) [68] and Vua Bạch Mã (King Baima, the White Horse). Mã Viện was one of the preeminent generals of the Han dynasty, who was sent to what is now northern Vietnam to subdue the rebellion of the Trưng (Zheng) sisters in 42-44, which in Vietnamese historiography is a glorious event in a long history of struggle against foreign aggression. Not only did Ma Yuan successfully suppress the rebellion, but he also established the foundations for direct Han rule.[69] Returning to China in 44 C.E., he enjoyed the status of an imperial hero. His campaign is depicted in various Chinese and Vietnamese annals, in particular in *Đại Việt Sử Ký Toàn Thư* (A Complete History of Great Viet), from which Adriano di St. Thecla borrowed his story for the manuscript.[70]

Vua Bạch Mã, mentioned by Adriano di St. Thecla in connection with Ma Yuan, is the spirit-protector of Hanoi. His legend is found in Lý Tế Xuyên's fourteenth-century compilation, *Việt Điện U Linh Tập* (Departed Spirits of the Viet Realm).[71] There he appears under the name Long Độ, and his legend is connected to Cao Vương (Gao Wang) or Cao Biền (Gao Pian), a Tang general who was active in northern Vietnam in the ninth century,[72] to whom the spirit appeared as an immortal

[67] In China the *chenghuang* was a god of walls and moats, otherwise known as a city or town god, while in Vietnam the *thành hoàng* was a village god.

[68] Hereafter I will use the Chinese name Ma Yuan for this person in his guise as a Han general and the Vietnamese name Mã Viện when referring to the spirit worshipped by Vietnamese.

[69] See more on Ma Yuan's legacy in Taylor, *Birth of Vietnam*, pp. 45-48.

[70] *Đại Việt Sử Ký Toàn Thư* (Hanoi: Nhà Xuất Bản Khoa Học Xã Hoi, 1993), ngoại kỷ, 3:2a–3a (1:156–157), under the years 40–43 C.E..

[71] Lê Hưũ Mục, *Việt Điện U Linh Tập* (Departed Spirits of the Viet Realm) (Saigon, 1960), p. 43.

[72] Appointed in 864 as military governor of Annam, Cao Biền (Gao Pian) reestablished Tang rule there lost in 862 due to invasion of peoples from the mountains. Cao Biền is well remembered in Vietnam. He is credited with rebuilding Hanoi and with introducing the study of geography and geomancy; he was also a famous sorcerer. His activities in Vietnam are also described in *Đại Việt Sử Ký Toàn Thư*, ngoại ký, 5:12b–16a (1:197–200, under the years 864–868

riding a dragon. Later, the spirit reportedly demonstrated its superiority to Cao Vương, who, seeing that he could not overcome the spirit with sorcery, decided to go back north to his homeland.

Later, this legend was elaborated and the spirit obtained a new name, Bạch Mã (Baima), "White Horse." The new story goes as follows: when King Lý Thái Tổ (1009–28) decided to transfer the capital from Hoa Lư to Thăng Long (modern Hanoi), then called Đại La, he had difficulty constructing the walls, which repeatedly collapsed. The king and his subjects prayed, and then they saw a white horse appear from a temple. They made a plan of the city walls following the steps of this horse, and the walls erected according to this plan stood firmly thereafter.[73] This legend undoubtedly was created under strong Indian influence, since the symbol of the white horse was important in India from ancient times in domains both religious (it was worshipped by Brahmans) and state (the ceremony of drawing the borders of a state following the steps of a white horse). The Indian influence could have been introduced into this region either by the Cham people (since a considerable number of them, coming from the territory of modern central Vietnam and bearing their Hinduized culture, were resettled in regions near Hanoi) or from China (as the name "White Horse" was renowned there; for example, the temple where emperor of the Later Han dynasty, Han Mingdi (58-76), kept the *Sutra in Forty-two Chapters*, brought from India, was named the Temple of the White Horse). The main temple of Vua Bạch Mã in Hanoi is located at 76 Hàng Buồm street.

At first glance, Adriano di St. Thecla's statement that "Vua Bạch Mã, a military prefect who was called by the proper name Mã Viện [Ma Yuan], had an excellent reputation" seems to be a blatant mistake by a person who did not know Vietnamese realities well and was confused because the word *mã* (*ma*, horse) appears in both names. However, such a conclusion would be too hasty. It should be noted that Adriano di St. Thecla was not the only one to consider Bạch Mã and Mã Viện to be one and the same.

A Chinese traveler, Zheng Junan (Trịnh Tuấn Am), who visited Tonkin in the first decade of the eighteenth century, wrote as follows in his account:

> In Hà Khẩu quarter [modern Hàng Buồm street belongs to this quarter] in the capital there is a temple of Bạch Mã, and it is said that there people commemorate the story of general Phục Ba [Fu Bo] of the Mã [Ma] family, personal name Viện [Yuan], a man from the time of the Han dynasty. I just arrived in the Southern country and did not know anything, so I also believed it to be true, and when I came to the temple to read the steles, I saw it written there that the spirit of Phục Ba, a person from the time of the Han dynasty, is worshipped to request happiness for the country and to protect the people. However, it is not clear since when his spirit has been worshipped there, how this was started and from what dynasty. Only the following can be seen recorded on the stele:

C.E.). Also see Taylor, *Birth of Vietnam*, pp. 246–254, also K. W. Taylor, "A Southern Remembrance of Cao Biền," in *Liber Amicorum: Mélanges offerts au professeur Phan Huy Lê*, ed. Philippe Papin and John Kleinen (Hanoi: Nhà Xuất Bản Thanh Niên, École Française d'Extrême-Orient, 1999), pp. 241–258.

[73] *Tuyển Tập Văn Bia Hà Nội* (Collection of the Stele Inscriptions of Hanoi) (Hanoi: Nhà Xuất Bản Khoa Học Xã Hội: 1978), 1:44.

> Written in the autumn of the year Dingmao [Đinh Mão] in the reign title Zhenghuo [Chính Hòa) [1687]; the temple was built a long time ago; rafters and columns were damaged; merchants from the North [China], such as Zhan Zhonglian [Chiêm Trọng Liên], gathered all the people, raised money, and hired restorers, so the temple is now again as beautiful as new.
>
> I venture to shed doubt on the fact that Phục Ba, last name Mã, is also called Bạch Mã. What could be a reason for that?

In the autumn of the year Jiawu (Giáp Ngọ) (1714), Zheng Junan launched an investigation of the subject, and in his search he encountered the book *Việt Điện U Linh Tập*. He was surprised to find there only the aforementioned legend on Bạch Mã without any connection to Mã Viện. Zheng Junan's interviews of elderly people did not produce any new information, so he surmised that Chinese immigrants, misunderstanding the temple, considered Bạch Mã to be the same as Mã Viện and worshiped him as such. Zheng Junan concluded that Mã Viện and Bạch Mã are two different personalities and expressed his apprehension that this error would persist forever.[74]

We can see that Zheng Junan's foresight was not entirely unfounded, for the statue of Mã Viện was present in this temple until recent times, as described by Vũ Đăng Minh and Nguyễn Phú Hợi in 1956. Apparently unaware of the long history of confusion between Bạch Mã and Mã Viện, they connected Mã Viện's presence in the temple to the fact that "in recent times the Chinese, ignorant of the legend of the White Horse, turned the temple into that of Mã Viện because they saw in the word Mã the family name of the Han general."[75] The fact that residents worshiped Mã Viện in Bạch Mã's temple might be attributed, as the aforementioned authors suggested, to miscomprehension and a lack of historical or mythological knowledge of the Vietnamese past by the Chinese community and/or to linguistic confusion. But I would endeavor to expand the range of explanation with two other possibilities.

First, according to a modern study, "beginning from the seventeenth century, Chinese immigrants were allowed to settle in Thăng Long, and they concentrated in a number of streets, among which was Hàng Buồm street."[76] This is a reference to the significant increase of trade between Tonkin and China in the seventeenth century, which brought many Chinese merchants to settle in Hanoi. But there was a Chinese community in Hanoi for many centuries before then. It is conceivable that the Chinese in Hanoi started to worship Mã Viện as a Chinese hero who brought Han civilization and authority into the country where they had immigrated. Since this quarter of the city became predominantly Chinese, it is reasonable to assume that the new settlers appropriated existing temples and introduced their own spirit, whom they venerated. However, always remaining a minority, they did not dare to expel

---

[74] Zheng Junan (Trịnh Tuấn Am), *An Nam Thần Từ Khảo Chính* (The Corrections on the Temples of Spirits in Annam), Institute of Sino-Vietnamese Studies, Hanoi, ms. A 2753, pp. 1a–2a.

[75] Vũ Đăng Minh and Nguyễn Phú Hợi, *Temples et pagodes de Hanoi* (Hanoi: École Française d'Extrême-Orient, 1956), p. 35.

[76] Nguyễn Vịnh Phúc and Trần Huy Ba, *Đường Phố Hà Nội* (The Streets of Hanoi) (Hanoi: Nhà Xuất Bản Hà Nội, 1979), p. 155.

the previously worshipped spirit of Bạch Mã from his temple, but rather merged the two.

My second hypothesis is that the first inhabitant of this temple was not Bạch Mã but Mã Viện. When the Viet kingdom developed in the eleventh century, the temple was rededicated to Bạch Mã. This hypothesis might be supported by the fact that Thăng Long already existed under the name of Đại La long before Lý Thái Tổ (r. 1009-1028) transferred his capital there in the eleventh century. Moreover, when the famous Tang general Gao Pian (Cao Biền) was sent to pacify the country in the ninth century, he located his capital at this place. It is very plausible to assume that he fortified the preexisting cult of his martial predecessor and compatriot Ma Yuan or even established it if it did not exist before. According to the *Việt điện u linh tập,* Ma Yuan appeared to Gao Pian in a dream when he was at Đại La. Mã Viện's cult could have spread as a result of being imposed by authority from above.

On the other hand, it could also have been developed by the local people themselves, since Ma Yuan brought some positive changes into Vietnam at the beginning of the first millennium C.E., when he reorganized society and established a measure of order, which was lacking at that time. According to Philippe Papin,

> Next to the high Chinese officials and settlers, he put local civil servants, whose power was enhanced in the shadow of Chinese tutelage. Some of them could reach higher positions, such as governor. During subsequent centuries, the Chinese and the Vietnamese drew together. Sharing the same interests, families mingled, which was to the advantage of the fusion of beliefs and of cultural knowledge. Thus, a Sino-Vietnamese elite was formed thanks to which a modest fortified space dominating the Red River became a prestigious imperial capital."[77]

Later, possibly, with the establishment of an independent Viet monarchy, Mã Viện could have lost his popularity, or perhaps veneration of this spirit was subdued, and thus the legend of Bạch Mã came into circulation to replace the position previously occupied by Mã Viện. To attach an even greater authority to Bạch Mã, the legend conflated this spirit with a spirit (Long Độ) that was supposed to have been more powerful than Gao Pian, who, like Ma Yuan, had been a northern general.

At the temple of Bạch Mã in Hanoi, Mã Viện retained his position at least until 1984, as is reflected in the plan of the temple made by the Office of Cultural Affairs of the Administration of Hanoi, where Mã Viện's altar is located in the far left corner of the temple.[78] This place in the temple is empty today. The keeper of the temple, who has been working at the temple for the last three years, informed me that, to the best of his knowledge, there was indeed a statue of Mã Viện quite a long time ago, but not in this century in any case; he did not elaborate on his version of the story.

I obtained a similar, if more astute, reaction, denying Mã Viện's presence in the temple, from Chinese people still inhabiting the area near the temple (even though their number has dramatically decreased since 1979, as a result of the Sino-

[77] Papin, *Histoire de Hanoi,* p. 37.

[78] "Di Tích. Đền Bạch Mã. Hồ Sơ Khảo Sát Năm 1984" (Cultural Vestiges. The Temple of Bạch Mã. A Dossier of Research in the Year 1984), Phòng Bảo Tồn Bảo Tàng, Sở Văn Hóa Hà Nội, p. 21, unpublished.

Vietnamese war in that year, and they have gradually relocated to other districts of the city). I interviewed several elderly Chinese living practically next to the temple, but all of them rejected my attempt to engage them in conversation about Mã Viện, saying that they had never heard about worshipping Ma Yuan at the temple of Bạch Mã and that it was altogether inconceivable that Ma Yuan should be worshipped anywhere in Vietnam because he was considered by the Vietnamese as a fierce enemy. Their reaction seems to be a result of the eradication of the cult of Mã Viện in socialist Vietnam after the war of 1979, when Mã Viện's cult would have been identified as the cult of an invader and local Chinese were in danger of being associated with this invader.

According to Adriano di St. Thecla, Mã Viện's cult was started by one of the Trưng sisters themselves, who "remembered his virtue and service to the state. She erected a temple to sacrifice to him in Phúc Lộc district of Thanh Hóa province. Later, from there he obtained a cult among the Annamites." It is not clear what source provided Adriano di St. Thecla with this information since, according to the annals, the Trưng sisters did not survive Mã Viện's campaign and, hence, were not able to launch his cult, even if they had had such an inclination. Phúc Lộc, a toponym used for the home locality of the Trưng sisters, was not in Thanh Hóa province,[79] so there appears to be some confusion here. There are now no temples for Mã Viện in either Phúc Lộc or in Thanh Hóa, although there are temples to the Trưng sisters in both places. But, we cannot be sure that such temples did not exist in Adriano di St. Thecla's time. It is now very difficult to find hard evidence of Mã Viện's temples anywhere in Vietnam due to the obliteration of his cult after the August Revolution (1945), when virtually all the temples of Mã Viện were destroyed.

Nevertheless, we can find indications that temples to Mã Viện did exist in Thanh Hóa province. For example, Nguyễn Thuật (b. 1842), governor of Thanh Hóa province in the time of the Nguyễn dynasty (he served in Thanh Hóa in the 1870s), mentioned a temple for Mã Viện in a poem entitled "Quốc Triều Danh Nhân Mặc Ngân" (Ink Traces of Renowned People of the National Dynasties).[80] The location of this temple cannot be identified, but it was apparently one of several temples to Mã Viện in Thanh Hóa province. So Adriano di St. Thecla hardly makes a serious mistake claiming the existence of temples to Mã Viện in Thanh Hóa. Moreover, it is not improbable that in the temples of the Trưng sisters people also worshipped Mã Viện. I found an example of this in the report submitted by Thanh Bình hamlet of Đa Tiện village (Liễu Lâm canton, Thuận Thành district, Bắc Ninh province) to the École Française d'Extrême-Orient in 1938. It is stated there that the people of this hamlet regarded the Trưng sisters as their main spirit protectors, but in addition they also worshipped the conqueror of the sisters, Mã Viện.[81] Another indication comes from Nguyễn Đức Lân, writing in the mid-nineteenth century, who described a temple for Mã Viện in the vicinity of Loa Lake. The location of this lake is now uncertain, but it may possibly have been in the vicinity of Cổ Loa, an ancient site several kilometers northeast of Hanoi near the place where, according to Chinese historical records, the

---

[79] Today located in northern central Vietnam.

[80] *Thanh Hóa Tổng Đốc Hà Đình Nguyễn Thuật Thi Sao*; this text is in Hanoi at the Institute of Sino-Vietnamese Studies, ms. VHv.48, see p. 3.

[81] Series *Thần Tích Thần Sắc* (The Treasury of Deity Legends and Royal Deification Decrees) in Hà Nội at the Viện Thông Tin Khoa Học Xã Hội (Institute of Social Science Information), file 2981, pp. 339–340.

decisive battle was fought between Ma Yuan and the Trưng sisters.[82] Thus, Adriano di St. Thecla's statement that Mã Viện "obtained a cult among the Annamites" definitely seems to be correct.

My attempt to locate an existing temple of Mã Viện, or at least its vestiges, led me to Hoàng Xá village, Thạch Đà district of Phúc Yên province, since this village reported to the École Française d'Extrème-Orient in 1938 that Mã Viện was one of its spirit protectors.[83] There, a keeper of Linh Tự temple, Mrs. Nguyễn Thị Đường, kindly agreed to talk with me about the spirit-protector of her village. Mrs. Nguyễn Thị Đường, who is in her late seventies, told me that indeed their village worshipped Mã Viện, but in 1946, shortly after the August Revolution, the temple was destroyed. Now there is a post office on its spot. According to Mrs. Nguyễn Thị Đường, at that time, as best she could remember, there were no Chinese residents in the area. She could not explain why the village worshipped a Chinese general who had suppressed national heroines fighting for the independence of the country. All she could say was that the worship of Mã Viện was a tradition that local people had transmitted from one generation to another, and that worshipping the general was what she had been taught in her youth. This suggests that Mã Viện was worshipped by Vietnamese as well as by Chinese as a spirit-protector.

Liễu Hạnh

Another point of special interest in the chapter on the spirits is Adriano di St. Thecla's description of the cult of one of the most famous Vietnamese female deities, Princess Liễu Hạnh, who is paired in northern Vietnam with the hero of the thirteenth-century Mongol wars, Trần Hưng Đạo, as the mother and the father of the people.[84] She is also one of the Vietnamese four immortals and the main deity in the pantheon of the Mothers. Adriano di St. Thecla's identification of the place where her cult ostensibly appeared in the sixteenth century is identical to that of Vietnamese tradition. However, Adriano di St. Thecla definitely introduces some new details of Liễu Hạnh's life which are absent in modern Vietnamese tradition. He writes of her as follows: "Since she had sung, as they say, disgracefully and shamelessly, people, being jealous, killed her and threw her into the river." Even though this statement does not directly address the issue of Liễu Hạnh's identity, or the identities and motives of her jealous murderers, we can assume with a high degree of probability that she was murdered for sexual reasons.

The Latin word *impudica*, translated into English as "shameless," has a definite sexual connotation in Latin, thus suggesting that Liễu Hạnh was a woman of easy virtue, a prostitute who entertained her clients with songs of a sexual character, and the people who drowned Liễu Hạnh were apparently her lovers. This information fully accords with that provided by another missionary, François-Louis Lebreton from the Foreign Mission of Paris, who in 1782 conversed with some Vietnamese on

---

[82] Nguyễn Đức Lân, *Loa Hồ Bách Vịnh* (A Hundred Poems in Tribute to Loa Lake), Institute of Sino-Vietnamese Studies, Hanoi, ms. A.1450 (1852), p. 22b.

[83] *Thần Tích Thần Sắc*, file 11841, pp. 555–556.

[84] According to a common saying that refers to festivals on the death anniversaries of Trần Hưng Đạo and Liễu Hạnh: "Tháng tám giỗ cha, tháng ba giỗ mẹ," "In the eighth month the death anniversary of the father; in the third month the death anniversary of the mother." See Ngô Đức Thịnh, "Kết Luận," (Conclusion), in *Đạo Mẫu ở Việt Nam* (The Way of the Mothers in Vietnam), ed. Ngô Đức Thịnh (Hanoi: Nhà Xuất Bản Văn Hóa Thông Tin, 1996), 1: 313

the subject of different spirits and was told that the Princess Liễu Hạnh was "a prostitute worshipped in numerous locations."[85]

Adriano di St. Thecla and Lebreton pose a question that we cannot ignore: was Liễu Hạnh indeed a prostitute? Not being able to analyze the reliability of Lebreton's information about other issues, the only thing I can say is that Adriano di St. Thecla's information is in most cases very trustworthy. Even in dubious instances, for example in the case of Mã Viện and Bạch Mã discussed above, Adriano de St. Thecla's testimony does not appear without corroboration. In my view, Adriano di St. Thecla's description of Liễu Hạnh, supported thirty years later by Lebreton, is not smoke without fire.

It is especially interesting to consider this information vis-à-vis the novel *Vân Cát Thần Nữ Truyện* (Story of the Van Cat Goddess), written by the famous Vietnamese author Đoàn Thị Điểm (1705-1748) about a decade prior to the time Adriano di St. Thecla created his manuscript. Đoàn Thị Điểm portrays Liễu Hạnh as a *femme émancipée*, a figure to be emulated, symbol of a protest against Confucian dogmas in Vietnamese society. According to her story, Liễu Hạnh was a daughter of the Jade Emperor, banished from Heaven to Earth for breaking a precious cup. She was born into the family of a righteous man in Vân Cát village where she grew up to be a beautiful and virtuous young woman, and, after marrying a Confucian scholar, she died of no apparent cause. In fact, she returned to Heaven, since the period of her punishment had expired. But later she repeatedly came down to Earth and wandered all over Vietnam. She allegedly met with Phùng Khắc Khoan (1528–1613), one of the most prominent scholar-officials of the late sixteenth and early seventeenth centuries, as well as with many other literati, all of whom were captivated by her literary talents. Liễu Hạnh became known for her benevolent as well as for her mischievous deeds. In the seventeenth century, she was deified and received several honorific titles from the Lê dynasty. This brings to mind Durkheim's obscure and undocumented comment published in his essay "Concerning the Definition of Religious Phenomena" in 1899: "In Tonkin, it is frequently the case that some vagabond or beggar succeeds in persuading the inhabitants of the village that he is their divine protector."[86]

In an article, I have argued that, rather than being Liễu Hạnh's hagiography or even the recording of a legend existing at that time, this was indeed a piece of fiction, and it should be seen as a creative production of Đoàn Thị Điểm. In it, Đoàn Thị Điểm incorporated elements of her own biography and projected her intellectual inclinations and aspirations upon the cult of Liễu Hạnh, which was seemingly widespread at that time.[87] A literary analysis of the *Vân Cát Thần Nữ Truyện* in light of what Adriano di St. Thecla and Lebreton have written is beyond the scope of this introduction. However, my reading of Đoàn Thị Điểm makes me certain that she was well aware of Liễu Hạnh's reputation for "easy virtue," or, at least, aware of the versions of Liễu Hạnh's story that displayed this aspect of the deity. Her Liễu Hạnh balances on the verge between the liberty of a woman ascertaining her position in a

[85] A letter from Lebreton to Hody from July 26, 1782, in the Archive of the Foreign Missions in Paris, 691 fol. 152, cited in Forest, *Les missionaires français au Tonkin et au Siam*, 3:253.

[86] W. S. F. Pickering, ed., *Durkheim on Religion. A Selection of Readings with Bibliographies* (London: Routledge & Kegan, 1975), p. 81.

[87] See Olga Dror, "Đoàn thị Điểm's 'Story of the Vân Cát Goddess' as a Story of Emancipation," *Journal of Southeast Asian Studies*, 33, 1 (2002): 63-76.

male-dominated society and that of a prostitute or, I would rather say, a geisha. I believe that with her story Đoàn Thị Điểm inspired new features in an existing cult and elevated it to make it known to educated people. I will discuss the issue of how a prostitute or a prostitute-in-question could have become such a powerful spirit in the Vietnamese pantheon on another occasion, but worshipping people notorious for their negative deeds was indeed not unheard of in Vietnam. Tutelary deities of villages were not always embodiments of morality, but could be thieves, murderers, or other outcast personalities.[88] People commonly believed that those with sufficient potency to enable them to break norms of conventional behavior were worthy of worship.

Daoism

The chapter on Daoism is entitled "On the Sect of Magicians." The term "magicians" in reference to the Daoists was, according to Nicolas Longobardi, an eighteenth-century French missionary in China, put into circulation by the Europeans.[89] The replacement of "Daoism" by "magic" was apparently inspired by practices called Daoism that were witnessed by the missionaries, that is, practices dealing with evil spirits or communication with the deceased. Indeed, when the Europeans appeared in China, for the bulk of the population, Daoism had long lost its philosophical basis as expressed in Daoist texts such as the *Daode jing*, and had crumbled into numerous popular spirit cults larded with magical ceremonies. As such, it was not very interesting to the missionaries, who immersed themselves in the imperial cult of Confucius, whose teaching seemed to dominate the higher stratum of the society and whose doctrine could be grasped by means of European logic. Hardly any missionary "went down" to study, grasp, and describe Daoism, in general, and popular Daoism, in particular.

The European works of this time always mentioned "the sect of magicians" and its founder Laozi, but did not proceed much further in discussing the topic.[90] Adriano di St. Thecla was not very different from other European writers of his time in ignoring the philosophical aspects of Daoism, although, unlike others I have consulted, he did endeavor to make reference to Daoist doctrine, such as "the definition of things" as found in the *Daode jing*: "The law produced one, one produced two, two produced three, three produced four, four produced innumerable things, or everything: the great law is at the same time nothingness and itself."[91] But, if the philosophical aspect of Daoism was typically underrepresented in the *Opusculum*, Adriano di St. Thecla, in contrast to other writers, developed a historical survey of early Daoist worthies.

Even more remarkable is his detailed presentation of popular Daoism as observed in the activities of sorcerers and mediums. After an extensive description of

---

[88] Hà Văn Tấn, *Đình Việt Nam (Community Halls in Vietnam)* (Ho Chi Minh City: Nhà xuất bản Thành Phố Hồ Chí Minh, 1998), pp. 116-120.

[89] Nicolas Longobardi, "Traité sur quelques points de la religion des Chinois," in *Opera omnia*, ed. G. G. Leibnitz, vol. 4, part 1, "Continet Philosophiam" (Geneva: Fratres de Tournes, 1768), p. 92.

[90] See, for example, Nicholas Longobardi, ibid.; Athanasius Kircher, *China Illustrata*, trans. Charles D. Van Tuyl (Oklahoma, 1987), p. 123; Matthieu Ricci and Nicolas Trigault, *Histoire de l'expédition chrétienne*, pp. 170-171.

[91] For this citation see the chapter on Daoism.

these "magicians," he turns to the worship of spirits. He begins his discussion of what he calls "the religion of this sect" by equating Daoism with Confucianism in that both "worship spirits according to very old tradition." From this and from the contents of his chapters on Confucianism, Daoism, and the Spirits, we can see that he viewed all of these religious currents as fundamentally the worship of spirits.

A peculiar feature of this chapter on Daoism is Adriano di St. Thecla's description of the worship of twelve spirits, each of whom governs one year in a cycle of twelve years. From this we see that there are not only spirits manifested in material objects and beings, but also spirits presiding over the passage of time. He ends this chapter with discussion of a miscellany of spirits, beginning with the Jade Emperor, who is portrayed as being in some way preeminent over all the other spirits. The spirits thereafter enumerated include some that he discusses in his chapter on the spirits, and there consequently seems to be no clear border between Daoism and what he considers to be the worship of spirits.

Part of Adriano di St. Thecla's portrayal of Daoism is virtually identical to Durkheim's description of "magic" in contrast to what he calls "religion." While, for Durkheim, religion produces churches or church-like collectivities that take the form of cults (private, domestic, or public), magic does not. In Durkheim's words, "There is no Church of magic." Magicians have clienteles, not churches, and contacts among people using magic is "accidental and transitory" and does not produce "a society, whose members are united because they imagine the sacred world and its relations with the profane world in the same way, and because they translate this common representation in identical practices."[92] However, Adriano di St. Thecla's descriptions of some cults attributed to Daoism—that of the Jade Emperor, for example— could possibly be seen to fall under Durkheim's definition of religion as long as they are "celebrated by a group, the family, or the corporation," which he considers to be a church, in the broad sense, as long as the rites and ceremonies connected to those cults occur periodically.

Fortune-tellers

The fourth chapter describes the practice of the fortune-tellers. The very fact that Adriano di St. Thecla decided to incorporate it into his work is unique. Fortune-tellers hardly ever earned any significant attention in the works of his predecessors and contemporaries, and surely never merited a whole chapter. The topic was probably dismissed as too insignificant and superstitious. While Adriano di St. Thecla does not differ from the other missionaries in his perception of the practices of divination as superstitious, he definitely acknowledges them as an inherent element of Vietnamese life, which should not be disregarded but, quite the contrary, studied. We should not be deluded by the small size of this chapter (the shortest in the manuscript, containing only four pages). It was supposed to be considerably longer, as pages 77 to 83 are blank and the last sentence on page 76 is not completed, while the table of contents indicates that there should have been two more articles describing other kinds of. fortune-tellers and diviners. However, the manuscript only presents the Thầy Bói, who, according to the author, hold "the first place among the fortune-tellers," leaving out the other groups that Adriano di St. Thecla apparently wanted to discuss.

[92] Emile Durkheim, *The Elementary Forms of Religious Life*, trans. Karen E. Fields (New York, London: The Free Press, 1995), pp. 41-42, 59-60.

Adriano di St. Thecla presents the fortune-tellers as mediators between people and divine power. The information he provides enables us to recognize that fortune-telling rituals were related to a network of Tonkinese traditions and beliefs, that they were not merely "superstitious" methods to be condemned. The fortune-tellers' methods mediated between different philosophies and doctrines and popular practices of divination. We see here the syncretic combination of the trigrams from the *Yijing* (The Book of Changes), the theory of *yin* and *yang*, the five elements that are common to both Confucianism and Daoism, and even the practice of calling on the students of Confucius to assist fortune-tellers in casting lots. In my opinion, this is a beautiful example of the mutual connection, if not identity, of literati and popular culture, especially taking into consideration that, as Adriano di St. Thecla points out, most of these Thầy Bói were illiterate and blind or had been blinded.

Buddhism

The fifth chapter of the manuscript considers Buddhism. Originating in India in the sixth century B.C.E., Buddhism appeared in China in the late first century and in Tonkin by the late second century C.E.. Buddhism thereafter occupied a prominent position in Vietnamese culture and society. It was the dominant religious and intellectual current among educated Vietnamese until the fifteenth century, when Confucianism began to be acknowledged by rulers as the intellectual basis of their authority. Buddhism in Vietnam has traditionally had a very syncretic character. Cuong Tu Nguyen explains this by arguing that, in the early stages of their penetration into the country, in the absence of Buddhist temples, Buddhist missionaries settled down at temples and shrines dedicated to local deities, and thus the indigenous deities came to be incorporated into Buddhist thought and practice.[93] The *Opusculum* presents a very vivid example of Vietnamese Buddhist syncretism.

Adriano di St. Thecla bases his presentation of Buddhism on two Vietnamese texts, the *Tâm Đăng* (Lamp of the Heart) and the *Bí Chi* (Secret Branch). While the latter has remained unidentified, the former has survived, and it provides very strong evidence, both for the credibility of Adriano di St. Thecla's account and for the syncretic character of the Buddhism he observed. I located several copies of the *Tâm Đăng*. The first one, catalogued as AC 417 and kept at the Institute of Sino-Vietnamese Studies in Hanoi (Viện Hán Nôm) was carved and printed in the year Ất Hợi (Yihai); the second one, catalogued as A 2481 and also kept at the Institute of Sino-Vietnamese Studies in Hanoi, was carved and printed in the year Canh Tí (Gengzi). These two manuscripts are identical except for the first introductory page. In Paris at the Société Asiatique there is one more copy of the text.[94] It is identical to that catalogued as A 2481 in Hanoi.

There is no reign title indicated in either of the texts, and there are no other indications in the texts pointing to an exact date aside from the years in the sixty-year cycle named Ất Hợi and Canh Tí. However, the character for *tân* is replaced by a taboo character,[95] indicating that the texts were published in the seventeenth or early eighteenth centuries. The regular character for *tân* was withdrawn from circulation

[93] Cuong Tu Nguyen, *Zen in Medieval Vietnam, A Study and Translation of the Thiền Uyển Tập Anh* (Honolulu: A Kuroda Institute Book, University of Hawai'i Press, 1997), p. 14.

[94] Catalogued as PD 2372.

[95] AC 417, 25a.

in the early seventeenth century because it constituted a part of the name of Emperor Lê Duy Tân (r. 1600-1619) and, thus, was forbidden. Consequently, for many years thereafter, another character was substituted for it, and this is the character that we see in the *Tâm Đăng*.[96] Thus, plausible years for the appearance of the texts (or, at least, for the carving of these copies) range from 1619, the year of the death of Emperor Lê Duy Tân, to the time of Adriano di St. Thecla's work, i.e. 1750. In this stretch of time, the years corresponding to the names of years cited in the texts are 1635 or 1695 for Ất Hợi and 1660 or 1720 for Canh Tí.

Both manuscripts were carved in northern Vietnam, in Đại Thiền temple in Vĩnh Phúc province and in Bảo Phúc temple in Lưu Xá district (now Hoài Đức district) in Hà Tây province, respectively. My trip to the second temple, although confirming its existence, did not yield any results helping to date the manuscript. The temple does not have in its possession the original; neither does anyone there know the history of the manuscript. The gap between the dates of the carvings of these texts (at least twenty-five years) and the fact that one was published north and one south of the Red River suggest that the ideas reflected in this book were not characteristic of one locality only but were known and, apparently, were popular in different places, including places familiar to Adriano di St. Thecla.

My attempts to find a prior source or analogue of the *Tâm Đăng*, in Vietnam or in China, have not yielded any result. Since the texts are practically identical, it is logical to assume that they were copied from one original, or, because of the high resemblance in the style of carving, that one of them served as an original for the other. I strongly suspect that the text was not copied from a Chinese source but is a local Vietnamese production. First of all, the text contains some characters from the vernacular Vietnamese language; secondly, and more important, is its typical Vietnamese style. For example, Buddha's name Thích Ca Mâu Ni, transliterated from the Chinese Shijiamouni, which in turn is a transliteration of the Sanskrit name Sakyamuni, is not perceived in the text as a mere transliteration, but each syllable is interpreted as a separate expression. Thích (shi) is Earth, which does not conceive; Ca (jia) is Water, which does not give birth; Mâu (mou) is Fire, which does not grow old; Ni (ni) is Wind, which does not transfer suffering. That is why, the text explains, these characters were chosen to represent the name of Buddha, who himself is imperishable Void.[97] Here we see a deep-rooted tradition of Vietnamese language usage to provide a concrete grounding for all words and not to leave anything abstract or unexplained or unidentified. This is quite different from Chinese language usage, which does not gravitate towards such scrupulous precision.

Whatever the original was, the existing texts of the *Tâm Đăng* very clearly reflect specific features of Buddhism prior to the second half of the eighteenth century, notably its syncretic character, which incorporated elements of Buddhism, popular Daoism, and Confucianism. The description of Buddhist doctrine presented by Adriano di St. Thecla is a rather precise translation of excerpts from this book, supplemented with information from some additional sources, the most important of

[96] This character is listed in the table of tabooed characters in Ngô Đức Thọ, *Nghiên Cứu Chữ Huý Việt Nam Qua Các Triều Đại* (A Research on the Tabooed Characters in Vietnam during the Dynasties), trans. E. Poisson (Hanoi: Nhà Xuất Bản Văn Hóa, Publication du Centre de l'École Française d'Extrême-Orient au Vietnam, 1997), p. 91.

[97] AC 417, 13b.

which was *Bí Chi*, for information of which I have searched in vain during my trips to local temples.

Relying on the *Tâm Đăng*, Adriano di St. Thecla presents the Buddhist doctrine following nine ages, aeons, or kalpas of the creation of the world originally produced from a dewdrop. These nine ages are densely populated with numerous figures and ideas, all of which are the active agents in the creation of the world. Among them we will see Chinese mythical personalities, as for example, Bàn Cổ (Bangu), Nữ Oa (Nü Gua), and Thần Nông (Shen Nong) intermingled with Buddha, Buddhist ideas of *prajna* and *tathagatha*, Daoist Nguyên Thủy (Yuanshi, the Primordial Beginning), the Jade Emperor, and Laozi himself; to them are added some unidentified figures such as Maha Địa (Maha Di, the Great Earth) and Đại Ngô Chân Trí (Dawu zhenzhi, the Great Awakening of the Genuine Mind). However, this tradition can hardly be called Buddhist. I would say that it was shaped under strong Daoist influence. Evidence of this is seen not only in the significant number of names and ideas pertaining to Daoism, and especially to popular Daoism, but also in the list of the Five Emperors presented in the seventh age in the *Tâm Đăng*, and cited by Adriano di St. Thecla. There Buddha is put as the last of the Five Emperors following both the Jade Emperor and Laozi in accordance with the Daoist claim that Buddha is the reincarnation of Laozi, and thus Buddhism owes its source to him. Moreover, the *Tâm Đăng* did not exclude Confucianism from its tenets. There is a chapter in the *Tâm Đăng* devoted to Confucius.[98]

The *Tâm Đăng* is a very special manuscript still awaiting its researcher. But already now it is possible to say that it shows a certain distinctive pattern of Vietnamese religious practice. Cuong Tu Nguyen observed that "through the outset of the Lý dynasty (1010-1225), Buddhism in Vietnam was of a composite nature. It was a mixture of some Buddhist elements from India and China and the beliefs and practices characteristic of the indigenous people's religious sensibilities and popular cults."[99] The *Tâm Đăng* demonstrates the continuation of the Buddhist syncretic tradition in the eighteenth century. But not only this. It presents a different kind of Buddhist adjustment in Vietnam, which goes beyond its merging with Vietnamese indigenous popular cults. The *Tâm Đăng* was created as an intellectual alloy of Chinese personalities from the Confucian tradition, Chinese Daoist ideas and figures, and philosophical Buddhist ideas processed into concrete entities all equally participating in the creation of the world. Taking into account that the *Tâm Đăng* was most plausibly created in Vietnam, we see that instead of drawing upon local historical or religious personalities or indigenous spirits, the Tonkinese produced a manuscript deeply rooted in the larger culture they shared with the Chinese.

It is important to note that Adriano di St. Thecla does not mention any Buddhist canonical sutras but limits himself to the *Tâm Đăng* and the *Bí Chi*. This does not appear to be the result of negligence or of any deliberate omission, for as a rule he makes thorough presentations of information to the best of his knowledge, as we can clearly see in the chapters on Confucianism and Daoism, which cite classical books along with later works. I surmise that the *Tâm Đăng* and the *Bí Chi* were the only works available to Adriano di St. Thecla in the place of his missionary activity, and they, in fact, represent the character of Buddhism there.

[98] AC 417, 24a.

[99] Cuong Tu Nguyen, *Zen in Medieval Vietnam*, p. 7.

Another possible explanation lies in Adriano di St. Thecla's approach to his study of Tonkinese religious practice. Let us note that what Adriano di St. Thecla presents as Buddhist doctrine pays very little attention to moral instruction, which is, in fact, a salient aspect of Buddhism. The "Buddhist doctrine" described by Adriano de St. Thecla focuses on the creation of the world, an issue that Buddhism hardly addresses, considering that the goal of Buddhism is to escape from the contingent world. If we consider this perception of "Buddhist doctrine," along with the author's aforementioned perception of "Daoist doctrine" (exemplified by the law of creation he cites—"one produced two, two produced three, ..."—which does not represent the central issue of the Daoist doctrine either), as well as his coverage of the Confucian approach to the creation of the world, we can see that Adriano di St. Thecla was defining these doctrines in terms of Christian theology. Taking the Bible as the core of Christian doctrine, he looked for an analogue of it in the other religious traditions. The Bible starts from the creation of the world and states that God was the one and only creator of it, which is the basis of all later teaching. Thus Adriano di St. Thecla tried to find a similar starting point in Confucianism, Daoism, and Buddhism. The *Tâm Đăng* is apparently one of a very few works related to Buddhism that dwells on the creation of the world, and Adriano di St. Thecla would have found it useful for that reason.

This chapter on Buddhism is the most aggressive of the manuscript. This aggressiveness found its embodiment first of all in the author's language. The most frequent word Adriano di St. Thecla uses in regard to the Buddhist deities is *idols.* In no other chapter of the manuscript does this word appear so often, if at all. Furthermore, he defines Buddhism as "falsehood" and Buddha's hagiography as "amazing fables." No such strong epithets were used in regard to other religious currents, and the hagiographies of different spirits were never characterized as utterly delirious. Adriano di St. Thecla also cites Gil de Federich's opinion on the Buddhist books: "I did not see any book, or material displayed in it, where madness was not present."[100]

Adriano de St. Thecla's disdain for Buddhism is apparently rooted in the missionary tradition, for numerous other accounts reflect an acute hostility of European missionaries towards Buddhism. To say that it was a pagan belief, and therefore deserving of attack, does not fully explain the Christian missionaries' special hostility to Buddhism, since they did not show equal hostility toward Daoism or the cults of tutelary genies, which are no less pagan. I would like to suggest here two approaches to this question, one having to do with intellectual life in Europe and one having to do with a missionary understanding of the history of Buddhism as a spurious intrusion into Christianity's rightful place.

First, a certain role in this irreconcilable hostility might lie, strangely enough, in the ancient Greek philosopher and mathematician Pythagoras (580–500 B.C.E.). Pythagoras wrote nothing, or, at least, nothing of his writings is known. His teaching has reached us in the writings of others who lived after him, so that we know about these teachings only from secondary sources. In the seventeenth century, Pythagoras was presented as the source of Buddhist doctrine since two of the principles that he allegedly taught—the transmigration of souls and vegetarianism—resembled aspects of Buddhism.

---

[100] Let us notice here that whatever Adriano di St. Thecla's expressions of derision are, they are much softer than those ascribed to Gil de Federich.

One of the sources who reported aspects of Pythagorean thought was the Roman poet Ovid (43 B.C.E.-17 C.E.), who in the fifteenth book of his *Metamorphoses* writes on the abstinence from eating meat:

> He [Pythagoras] was the first man to forbid the use
> Of any animal's flesh as human food,
> He was the first to speak with learnéd lips,
> Though not believed in this, exhorting them.—
> "No, mortals," he would say, "Do not permit
> Pollution of your bodies with such food,
> For there are grain and good fruits which bear down
> The branches by their weight, and ripened grapes
> Upon the vines, and herbs."[101]

And on the transmigration of souls:

> The moving soul
> May wander, coming from that spot to this,
> From this to that—in changed possession live
> In any limbs whatever. It may pass
> From beasts to human bodies, and again
> To those of beasts. The soul will never die,
> In the long lapse of time. As pliant wax
> Is moulded to new forms and does not stay
> As it has been nor keep the self-same form
> Yet is the selfsame wax, be well assured
> The soul is always the same spirit, though
> It passes into different forms.[102]

Reference to Pythagoras as the source of Buddhism is seen in Matteo Ricci's (1552-1610) and Nicolas Trigault's (1577-1628)[103] *History of the Christian Expedition to the Kingdom of China.* It reads: "The doctrine of the transmigration of souls was mostly borrowed from Pythagoras, and to this they have added *other fabrications* [my emphasis] to disguise falsehood."[104] Later this idea was reproduced by another Jesuit, Athanasius Kircher (1602-1680), in his book, *China Illustrata,* published in 1667. In addition to quoting the aforementioned statement of Ricci and Trigault,[105] Kircher repeatedly refers to Pythagoreanism as the root of Buddhism. In reference to Buddha, for example, he says: "The first creator and architect of the superstition was a very sinful brahmin imbued with Pythagoreanism."[106] The connection between

[101] Brookes More, trans., *Ovid's Metamorphoses,* vol. 2, *Books IX through XV* (Francestown, New Hampshire: Marshall Jones Company, 1978), p. 1104.

[102] Ibid., pp. 1108-1109.

[103] A Belgian Jesuit who arrived in China in 1610 and carried out his missionary activities there until 1613, when he returned to Europe, Trigault translated Ricci's work into Latin, and published it with great success in 1615. It was the first publication of Matteo Ricci's work, originally written in Italian.

[104] Matthieu Ricci and Nicolas Trigault, *Histoire de l'expédition chrétienne,* p. 166.

[105] Athanasius Kircher, *China Illustrata,* p. 122.

[106] Ibid., p. 141, also see pp. 135, 138, 141, 142.

Buddhism and Pythagoreanism is also evident in the works of Domingo Fernandez Navarete,[107] and other missionaries.

In the seventeenth century, Pythagoras was commonly cited as the source of Buddhism, which explains why, in 1693, Whitelocke Bulstrode published a treatise "to vindicate the Honour of Pythagoras, whom, though I would not, with the Heathen, Deifie for his eminent Works; yet I would defend him from the Calumny of the World, so unjustly cast upon him, as the Author of an erroneous Doctrine."[108] Bulstrode wrote in his treatise:

> This opinion of Transmigration of souls, which is father'd upon Pythagoras, is mistaken everywhere; but very grosly [sic] believed in Pegu, Magor, and other parts of Asia: For believing that the Soul doth pass into some other Creature, after its departure from the Humane Body, they abstain from no sort of respect to the most contemptible Creatures, and superstitiously avoid doing any hurt to that Animal, whose Body, they think, contains the Soul of their deceased Father. Now, how they could tell, or why they should think, that this, or that Beast is thus animated, rather than another, I confess is strange; and what is more so, it seems from the Belief of those in Bengall, and other Parts of East-Indies, (who imagine that the Souls of Good Men pass into Cows, and such useful Creatures; and the Souls of Bad Men into Crows and such hurtful Birds or Beasts) that these People think it of the Immortal Rational Soul, rather than the Sensitive. For the Faculties of the Rational Soul are exerted naturally in the kind Offices of Beneficence and Humanity; but those of the Sensitive, only in Growth and Sense. It looks as if Folly begot, and Superstitious Fancy propagated this Opinion: Though to do Right to Pythagoras, who was doubtless a great Man, the absurdity of this Opinion is as far remote from his Sentiments, as the Manichean Heresie is different from the Christian Religion.
>
> But Philosophy and Religion have both suffered alike by Ignorant Expositors .... Thus are the best Things corrupted.[109]

Here we can see that the idea of placing together the "heresies" of Pythagoras and of Buddhism was strong enough to elicit this relatively passionate defense of Pythagoras. The obvious question is what is the connection, if any, between the sharp attacks on Buddhism and on Pythagoras. Was disapproval of Pythagoras expressed by associating him with a pagan religious tradition or was disapproval of Buddhism expressed by associating it with Pythagoras? Perhaps there is no logical answer to this question, and the conflation of Pythagoras and Buddhism was a random coincidence. But, there is an apparent logic in the idea that Christian antipathy toward Buddhism in the seventeenth century was reinforced by the Pythagorean overlap of this antipathy with the antipathy of the church toward the Copernican system. This seems plausible considering that Adriano de St. Thecla proposed a very positive view of Pythagoras in comparing him with Confucius

---

[107] Domingo Fernandez Navarete, *Tratados historicos, politicos, ethicos, y religiosos de la Monarchia de China* (Madrid: Imprementa Real, 1676), pp. 87, 101.

[108] Whitelocke Bulstrode, "The Preface to the Reader," in *An Essay of Transmigration, in Defense of Pithagoras or, a Discourse of Natural Philosophy* (London: printed by E. H. for Tho Basset, 1693), pp. 1-2.

[109] Ibid., pp. 1-4.

rather than associating him with Buddhism, and he was writing in the eighteenth century when the heat of the Copernican controversy had faded from the church.

Pythagoras came under attack by the church because of the astronomical discoveries that were being made in the sixteenth and seventeenth centuries. The first page of these discoveries was opened by the Polish astronomer Nicolas Copernicus (1472-1543) with the publication of his work, *De Revolutionibus Orbium coelestium* (On the Revolution of the Celestial Spheres), arguing for the heliocentric system of the Universe, a concept strongly condemned by the Church, which clung to anthropocentrism. Copernicus avoided all possible bitter consequences of his scientific rebellion as he agreed to publish his work only on his deathbed. But his Italian successor Galileo Galilei (1564-1642) was to drain his cup of woe defending and developing Copernicus's system. Galilei started advocating Copernicus's system as early as 1610. Later, His *Dialogo sopra i due Massimi Sistemi del Mondo* (Dialogue Concerning the Two Chief World Systems) enraged the Jesuits. Galilei was tried by the Inquisition, condemned of heresy, and compelled to recant his views.

Copernicus's name was closely connected with Pythagoras or Pythagoreans, by whom he was considered to have been anticipated. The Holy Office related Copernicus's doctrine to that of Pythagoras or Pythagoreans, announcing that Copernicus's teaching was nothing more than the ancient Pythagorean doctrine, which had inspired Copernicus.[110] The Decree of the Congregation of the Index of March 1, 1616, proscribed a book published in Naples in 1615 by Paolo Antonio Foscarini (1565-1616) entitled *Lettera del R. Padre Maestro Antonio Foscarini Carmelitano sopra l'opinione de' Pittagorici e del Copernico della mobilità della terra et stabilità del sole, et del nuovo Pittagorico sistema del mondo* (Epistle of R. Father Antonio Foscarini of the Carmelite Order on the judgment on the Pythagorean and Copernican system of the motion of the earth and the immobility of the Sun, and of the new Pythagorean system of the world); this book, which puts together the ideas of Copernicus and Pythagoras, argues that the immobility of the sun in the center of the Universe and the mobility of the earth indeed conform with reality and do not contradict the holy scriptures.[111] Pythagoras, viewed by the church as a precursor of Copernicus, whose theory, in turn, was developed by Galilei, inevitably fell into disgrace in religious circles, and his teaching was placed under critical scrutiny.

As European missionaries discovered Buddhism to be a strong rival religion, Pythagoras became doubly heretical, both for his association with the Copernican system and for his ideas about the transmigration of souls. However, in the eighteenth century, as a result of further scientific developments confirming Galilei's theories, the Copernican system was no longer anathematized, and Pythagoras was also no longer associated with Buddhism. Adriano di St. Thecla compares Confucius and Pythagoras in a positive light and omits any reference to the Pythagorean theory of the transmigration of souls being the source of the despised Buddhist doctrine.

---

[110] Pierre-Noël Mayaud, *La Condamnation des livres Coperniciens et sa Révocation à la lumière de documents inédits des Congrégations de l'Index et de l'Inquisition* (Rome: Editrice Pontificia Università Gregoriana, 1997), p. 49.

[111] Ibid., pp. 41-42. Paolo Antonio Foscarini (1565-1616), a Carmelite theologian, together with the Dominican renegade Thommaso Campanella (1568-?), who in 1616 wrote the famous *Apologia pro Galileo, mathematico florentino,* were practically the only two defenders of the Pythagorean-Copernican system besides Galilei at this time. An English translation of Foscarini's treatise is found in Richard J. Blackwell, *Galileo, Bellarmine, and the Bible* (Notre Dame, IN: University of Notre Dame Press, 1991), pp. 217-251.

From this it appears that, while hostility toward Buddhism was unrelenting, hostility toward Pythagoras and his conflation with Buddhism came and went with the Copernican controversy. Although Adriano di St. Thecla's hostility toward Buddhism did not involve animosity toward Pythagoras, we can nevertheless conjecture that his attitude toward Buddhism was to some degree affected by the intellectual legacy of previous generations of missionaries.

A second reason that missionaries were hostile toward Buddhism is that Buddhism was perceived as a systematic teaching capable of withstanding the pressure of the Christian faith. The stalemate of the two systems is very evident in Adriano di St. Thecla's version of the arrival of Buddhism in China. He based his account on Christian books, which interpret the well-known traditional Chinese narration as follows. Emperor Ming of the Han dynasty saw in a dream a man with a golden body sixteen cubits tall who, when asked by the emperor who he was, replied that he was from the western region. The royal dream interpreters said that holy men had always been in the west, and they congratulated the emperor for catching sight of a holy man; they said the dream was auspicious and indicated that the emperor would prosper for a long time. Consequently, the emperor sent messengers to the west to search for the holy man. When messengers had traveled as far as India, according to the Christian sources cited by Adriano di St. Thecla,

> ... they still had not covered half of the way to the remote West, but, terrified by the incommodities and difficulties of [going] the rest of the longer way, they took an image of an idol and the books that were kept there [in India] and brought them to the emperor, pretending that they brought the image and the books of the holy man from the West. Deceived by their words, the emperor trustingly accepted Phật [Buddha] and ordered his subjects to construct everywhere temples for this idol.

This narrative displays the conviction of the Christian missionaries that the people were naturally inclined to grasp and worship the God to whom Christians prayed, and that they followed other religious traditions due more to the vicissitudes of human weakness and ensuing circumstances than to their natural desire. This version of the story portrays the Chinese as aspiring to grasp and worship the God of the Christians, but they were averted from it only by the faintheartedness of the messengers, who feared the long road where the true God could be found. Victims of the deceitful messengers, the Chinese accepted Buddhism instead of Christianity. One of the points in the narration of the "unfulfilled" mission of the messengers is that they did not arrive at their final destination, i.e. the West.

The word "West," used in the version cited by Adriano di St. Thecla, requires special attention, for it is not immediately clear what the authors of the book implied by it, from where they borrowed it, or in what context they originally found it. In the Chinese texts, the term "West" or "Western region," more often than not, implies India. In the Christian version of the story, the envoys' exact destination, and thus the story's conclusive lesson regarding the delivery of Buddhist, rather than Christian, teaching to China, may be based on consciously or unconsciously mistaken premises. This approach, which assumes that monotheism was the initial and natural inclination of people, but that this natural inclination was subdued by outside factors, can be seen in this manuscript (especially in its preface) as well as in the works of Christian missionaries and European travelers during this period. For example, a very similar, if not identical, narrative is found in the Eurasian merchant Samuel Baron's account of Tonkin, written in 1685-1686:

> One of the Chinese emperors coming to the knowledge of a famous law that was taught in the west, which was very efficacious for instructing and conducting mankind to wisdom and virtue, . . . he therefore dispatched several sages to find out this law, and bring it to China. These ambassadors, after they had travelled, or rather erred, to and fro the space of almost three years, arrived either in Indosthan or Mallabar; where finding this sect of Boots [Buddha] very rife, and of mighty veneration, and being deceived by the devil, and weary of travelling any further, they thought they had found what they sought for . . . [112]

But what is even more important to my analysis is the fact that the Europeans considered Buddhism as a kind of counterfeit Christianity. The envoys brought to China a *teaching*, the wrong one, but still a teaching, something that by mishap occupied the space that should have been allotted to the Christian teaching. It should be noted that hostility towards Buddhism was not always characteristic of the European missionaries. During the initial phases of the missionaries' activity in China, Buddhism served as a bridge between them and the local people. In 1584, according to Jensen,

> Ricci takes Buddhist costume to be indexical of Chineseness and appears excited by the prospect of having crossed over.... In assuming the identity of *osciani* [Buddhist monks] the fathers did not imitate the natives but "went native" and in a formal sense at least ceased to be priests, having exchanged their Catholic vestments for the homespun robes of Buddhist priests.[113]

But a decade later the Jesuits replaced their Buddhist garments with Confucian apparel, aligning themselves with Confucianism as "a conduit to power."[114] Buddhism for them was transformed from an initial vehicle for their accommodation to China into a threatening rival. The very outward similarity between Christianity and Buddhism (a notion of heaven and hell, the monastic life, the vows of celibacy and poverty) that helped the Jesuits to comprehend Chinese society and seemingly to find a place for themselves in it, quickly turned into a hindrance to their goals. The missionaries recognized in Buddhism an institutionalized doctrine, which, exactly because of superficial similarities with their own doctrine and practice, threatened to impede the propagation of the faith they were determined to inculcate among the indigenous people.

Assuming a Confucian appearance, the European missionaries also absorbed the Neo-Confucianism hostility toward Buddhism. Both Confucianists and Christians viewed Buddhism as their main rival. One of the pillars of Neo-Confucianism, Cheng Hao (1032-1085), wrote: "The words of the Buddha and Lao Tzu (Laozi) are

---

[112] See Samuel Baron, "A Description of the Kingdom of Tonqueen," in *A Collection of Voyages and Travels*, ed. Awnsham Churchill (London, 1732), 6:39.

[113] Lionel M. Jensen, *Manufacturing Confucianism; Chinese Traditions and Universal Civilization* (Durham and London: Duke University Press, 1997), p. 43.

[114] Ibid., p. 48.

somewhat reasonable. This is why they are very much more harmful."[115] Although mentioned here with Buddhism, Daoism, as it was practiced in Vietnam, and also in China, held no coherent doctrine and did not have an institutional structure, but rather it took the shape of scattered spirit cults. Without a strong doctrinal focus or a threatening organization, Daoism did not compete as did Buddhism and Christianity, each of which posited transcendent power and a future life.

Christianity

The last chapter of the manuscript considers Christianity. Unfortunately, the manuscript itself or its copy was not completed, and the piece we have now discusses only the penetration to China of Nestorianism in the seventh century and the first Christian missions to China in the sixteenth–eighteenth centuries. In addition to this narrative, the author described or intended to describe persecutions of the Christians in China and the penetration of Christianity into Tonkin and the persecutions the Christians suffered there. The chapter as it is hardly provides any new information or insight except that it shows Adriano di St. Thecla was well acquainted with the activity of his predecessors in China and that he evidently appreciated their efforts. It should be noted that Adriano di St. Thecla does not express his own dissatisfaction with or disapproval of the missionaries he describes in this chapter, even though among the missionaries were representatives of both sides in the Rites Controversy. Adriano di St. Thecla creates the impression that a unified Christian front opposed pagan belief, which seems to be one of the main goals of this chapter.

The Significance of the Manuscript for Studying Religious Belief and Practice in Eighteenth-Century Tonkin

The *Opusculum* of Adriano di St. Thecla is the first known systematic description of religious belief and practice in Tonkin, or, indeed, in Vietnam generally. It provides an alert survey through the eyes and thought of an educated eighteenth-century European. Even though Adriano di St. Thecla was not free of biases and was influenced by concepts ingrained in the works of his predecessors and contemporaries, he nevertheless went far beyond the conventional attitudes of his time. If we compare Adriano di St. Thecla's approach to studying Vietnamese realities to, for example, that of the Jesuits, we see how different they were. Micheline Lessard characterized the Jesuit approach in the following way:

> The Jesuit *cohérence* of Vietnam was European in nature. First, the Jesuits concerned themselves, as did most European intellectuals, only with the highest stratum of given societies. Jesuit letters and diaries did not provide insight into the possible difference or similarities between various social and ethnic groups. Furthermore, the Jesuits described the Vietnamese only with their own intellectual framework. While they did provide useful information as to Vietnamese agriculture, natural resources, and geography, when it came to the

[115] Cited in Wing-Tsit Chan, trans., *Reflections on Things at Hand, The Neo-Confucian Anthology compiled by Chu Hsi and Lü Tsu Ch'ien* (New York and London: Columbia University Press, 1967), p. 280.

Vietnamese "character" the Jesuits were mostly interested in virtues or vices or in practices they considered good or sinful.[116]

Adriano di St. Thecla's approach to Vietnamese religious belief and practice is far broader. Very often, working on this manuscript, I could not help but recollect Christopher Isherwood's self-definition in *Goodbye to Berlin*, observing Germany in the 1930s: "I am a camera with its shutter open ... Some day, all this will have to be developed, carefully printed, fixed."[117] However, contrary to Isherwood, who, as he expresses it, was "quite passive, recording, not thinking,"[118] Adriano di St. Thecla was determined to participate actively in changing the Vietnamese religious scene. He understood that to achieve this he had to comprehensively study and deeply penetrate Vietnamese religious thought and practice. In my opinion, judging from the *Opusculum*, he tried hard and succeeded in doing as much as was possible for a European of his background and goals.

Adriano di St. Thecla demonstrated an approach discussed and advocated a hundred and fifty years later by another missionary, perhaps the most famous of all missionary scholars in Vietnam, Léopold Cadière of the Foreign Missions of Paris. Cadière advised his fellow missionaries to study indigenous beliefs in order to convert the people who followed them, and, furthermore, to study both indigenous beliefs and their adherents with respect. He wrote:

> This respect for the beliefs of others, as I understand it, is greatly useful, even indispensable to a missionary, not only if he simply wants to study the religion of the pagans who surround him, but also to convert them. It is not through utter disdain of religious practices that he will win the hearts and arouse the support of volunteers. Even when he enters religious discussions ... the missionary should, I believe, present himself as respecting the manifestations of religious sentiments that he does not approve but, which, being sincere, are, by themselves, worthy of respect.[119]

In my view, Adriano di St. Thecla, to his credit, was a protagonist of this approach, as he incorporated respect for the "others," mastery of their language, and cultivation of the scholarly abilities of an anthropologist to observe and to elicit information. His sometimes sharply critical observations do not necessarily contradict this evaluation. It is evident from his Introduction, as well as from the contents of the *Opusculum*, that he wrote not for Vietnamese but for Europeans, and mainly for those who were already propagating Christianity in Vietnam or those who were to come there for that purpose. As it is, Adriano di St. Thecla provided an excellent tool for them and an invaluable source of information for modern scholars.

Adriano di St. Thecla viewed Confucianism, Daoism, and Buddhism as "sects" and not as "religions." I think that, while this designation might be interpreted as a rhetorical discounting of non-Christian religious beliefs, it also expresses a certain

---

[116] Micheline Lessard "Jesuit Perceptions of the Vietnamese," in *Essays into Vietnamese Pasts*, ed. K. W. Taylor and John K. Whitmore (Ithaca, NY: Southeast Asia Program, Cornell University, 1995), p. 156.

[117] Christopher Isherwood, *Goodbye to Berlin* (New York: Random House, 1938), p. 13.

[118] Ibid.

[119] Léopold Cadière, "Instructions pratiques pour les misssionaires qui font les observations religieuses," in *Annales de la Société des Missions-Étrangères*, 1913, no. 92 (March-April), p. 64.

analytical perspective on a scene of multiple religious practices. The expression "three religions" or "three teachings" (*tam giáo*) had already been used among speakers of Vietnamese for several generations before the arrival of Adriano di St. Thecla. In the seventeenth century, Alexandre de Rhodes, in his dictionary, defines *giáo* as "sect" and goes on to define *tam giáo* as "the three sects of China" and lists them as *đạo bụt* (Buddhism), *đạo nhu* (Confucianism), and *đạo đạo* (Daoism).[120] The use of the word "sect" and the resonance of its place in the local expression "the three sects" imply a syncretic system of religious belief and practice. We might be tempted to imagine that Adriano di St. Thecla and other missionaries viewed "the three sects of China" as a formal nomenclature to indicate three currents of religious thought that were in practice unified by the worship of spirits.

It is noteworthy that in his chapters on Confucianism and Daoism, Adriano di St. Thecla has sections entitled "On the religion of this sect." Here he apparently uses the word "religion" (Latin *religio*) to mean "the practice of worship." But when he writes about "the Christian religion" he is using the word to mean a systematic doctrine or teaching, as well as religious practice. It is inconceivable that he could have a section in his chapter on Christianity entitled "the religion of Christianity," because for him Christianity already was a religion, and it would be impossible to isolate a part of Christianity as the "religion" of it, as he does in the case of "the three sects." The relation between the two ways that Adriano di St. Thecla seemingly uses the word "religion" is similar to the difference between what in the next section I call sites of enunciation and sites of reference. In the one case, there is a unity of belief and practice expressed in a systematic teaching; in the other case, there is no unity of belief and practice and no systematic teaching, but rather forms of worship without obligatory contents.

For Adriano di St. Thecla, the Christian religion is a unified system of belief and practice that stands at the center of authority, while "the three sects of China" represent an accumulation of dispersed beliefs and practices, the "religion" of which consists only in specific acts of worship addressed to a multiplicity of spirits. I am convinced that Adriano de St. Thecla was a careful and scrupulous observer. Residing in rural areas, he was a witness of religious practice there. For matters that he did not directly observe, he went to books or inquired among his informants, which included people who resided in the capital city. His attention to detail gives us confidence that, in general, whatever was there to be seen was recorded. What he and his informants saw and what he could know from the written sources available to him reveal a place where a basic form of religious practice—namely the worship of spirits—infused all religious currents, whether practiced by common people or by the governing class.

The Redfieldian approach to the idea of "popular" or "folk" religion, found among peasants, as representative of true, pure tradition in contrast to "elite" religion, which is "littered" with numerous borrowings from other cultures, has been contested for several decades already.[121] Analyzing Taiwanese religion, Steven Sangren says: "Elements of both Confucian or 'high' culture and 'folk' belief inform

[120] Alexandre de Rhodes, *Từ Điển Annam-Lusitan-Latinh*, col. 281.

[121] See, for example Philip M. Hauser, "Observations on the Urban-Folk and Urban-Rural Dichotomies as Forms of Western Ethnocentrism," in *The Study of Urbanization*, ed. Philip M. Hauser and Leo F. Schnore (New York: Wiley, 1965), pp. 503-517.

all Chinese institutions and are not uniquely ascribable to social classes."[122] G. William Skinner showed the failure of the Redfieldian approach with regard to China by demonstrating the unity of urban centers and hinterlands. He asks: "How urban were the Chinese elite?"[123] His answer to this question is that the Chinese elite was as rural as it was urban: ". . . it is clear that China stands out among traditional societies in having an elite that was by no means predominantly urban."[124] And: "The basic cultural cleavages in China were those of class and occupation and of region, not those between cities and their hinterlands."[125] He is in agreement with F. W. Mote, who wrote: "Chinese values did not sustain a self-identifying and self-perpetuating urban elite as a component of the population."[126] And: "Chinese civilization may be unique in that its word for 'peasant' has not been a term of contempt . . ."; and he affirms "the disappearance of the urban-rural separateness."[127]

Vietnam was even more agrarian than China; the economic and the social structures were mainly based upon villages. In Vietnam, the number and significance of cities was even smaller than in China. This lack of an urban-rural hierarchy is also apparent with regard to religion. For example, the *thành hoàng* (Chinese *chenghuang*) is understood as a village tutelary genie in Vietnam, while the *chenghuang* was a city god in China. The term literally means "emperor or god of the walls." "Walls," in my opinion, symbolize the stability of a place defended by them. If such a place was considered to be a city in China, in Vietnam it was a village. We can hardly speak about popular religion per se in Vietnam since there is no elite religion to which it can be contrasted. In China, as G. William Skinner observes, *chenghuang* "was seldom worshiped by the rural populace, and his annual birthday festival was organized by and for residents of the capital."[128] On the other hand, in Vietnam many city gods were also worshiped in villages. For instance, the spirit-protector of Hanoi, King Bạch Mã, has also been widely worshiped in the countryside. At the same time, Princess Liễu Hạnh, whose cult originated in a village, became a popular deity in the capital. Moreover, as is seen in the chapter on fortune-tellers, the blind and mostly uneducated soothsayers incorporated into their casting of lots appeals not only to Confucius but also to many of his disciples. Another example is Mã Viện (Ma Yuan), the Han general, whose cult reached far beyond the city boundaries. These are only a few of the examples found in the manuscript, and there are many more that were not included in the *Opusculum*.

Paraphrasing Skinner's question: "how urban were the Chinese elite?," I would like to pose the question: "How rural were the Vietnamese 'folks'?" In Vietnam we definitely see a blurring of boundaries between urban and rural culture, urban and rural beliefs. I think this can be partly explained by almost perpetual warfare, either with invaders or among rival groups within the realm of Vietnamese speakers,

---

[122] P. Steven Sangren, *History and Magical Power in a Chinese Community* (Stanford, CA: Stanford University Press, 1987), p. 3.

[123] G. William Skinner, "Introduction: Urban and Rural in Chinese Society," in *The City in Late Imperial China*, ed. G. William Skinner (Stanford, CA: Stanford University Press, 1977), p. 265.

[124] Ibid., p. 267.

[125] Ibid., p. 269.

[126] F. W. Mote, "The Transformation of Nanking, 1350-1400," in *The City in Late Imperial China*, ed. G. William Skinner (Stanford, CA: Stanford University Press, 1977), p. 102.

[127] Ibid., p. 103.

[128] Skinner, "Introduction," p. 262.

which by the time of Adriano di St. Thecla had characterized the country for many generations. This prolonged internal strife squeezed parts of the urban population into the countryside and brought peasants into the cities. In this whirlwind it was impossible to sustain differences between a city and its rural hinterland, even if such an intention existed.

Possibly an even more important factor is that Vietnam was one of the most, if not the most, literate countries in Asia. It produced a great number of educated people relative to the population as a whole because the institutions that sustained Confucian education, such as schools, academies, and examinations, were operating in a relatively small country. The number of educated people far exceeded the number needed as government officials, and many of them settled in the villages, bringing with them their mental and cultural outfit. As a result of this, works were produced such as the *Tâm Đăng* (Lamp of the Heart), on which Adriano di St. Thecla based his description of Buddhism, which incorporated many elements borrowed from Chinese cultural and religious heritage as appropriated and processed by the Vietnamese. In this melange, we cannot even speak of institutionalized and non-institutionalized religion since all major village spirits were in some way "institutionalized" by obtaining appointments and promotions from the royal court.

But probably the most important factor for the lack of an urban-rural divide is that real urban areas did not develop in northern Vietnam. Even today, Vietnamese describe Hanoi as morphologically a large village. There was no commercial townspeople culture comparable to the ones that developed in China and Japan. The commercial sector of old Hanoi operated as a gathering of market outlets for products from surrounding villages and was oriented more toward the vantage of these various villages than toward any potential identification with an urban viewpoint looking outward from the city. These factors help explain why the topic of "popular religion" is very problematic when applied to Vietnam.

In Vietnam today, there are two terms for religious experience: *tôn giáo (zongjiao,* 宗 教), usually translated as "religion," and *tín ngưỡng (xinyang,* 信 仰), usually translated as "belief." A literal translation of the characters constituting the term *tôn giáo* is "ancestral teaching" or "to follow a doctrine" and of the term *tín ngưỡng* is "to believe in and to look up to." We see that the second compound does not indicate the presence of a unified doctrine or teaching, but merely denotes trust in and a subordinate position vis-à-vis a power that can influence a human being. Furthermore, let us note that an element in both characters of the compound *tín ngưỡng* is the character *nhân* (*ren,* human being); the other elements are *ngôn (yan,* speech, to talk) for *tín,* meaning "human speech" or "a speaking person," and *ngang (ang,* to lift up or the pronoun "I") for *ngưỡng,* meaning a person in the attitude of looking up or lifting something up, as if in worship or in offering something up. The sense of this expression is oriented toward concrete human actions rather than abstract doctrine.

Sometimes *tín ngưỡng tôn giáo* or *tôn giáo tín ngưỡng* are together used as a collective noun to cover all religious practices. However, in Vietnamese, the term *tín ngưỡng* is hardly ever applied to Confucianism, Buddhism, Daoism, Hinduism, Christianity, Judaism, or Islam as religions. It is the term *tôn giáo* that is used for them. In turn, *tôn giáo* is never employed to discuss a belief in spirits. Although Buddhism and Daoism, in Vietnam as well as in China, incorporated the worship of spirits or dispersed into various spirit cults, *tôn giáo* can, strictly speaking, refer only to their canonical teachings. This is also the case with Confucianism, the term for which, Nho giáo (*rujiao*), includes the word *giáo (jiao*, doctrine). While Confucianism is more than anything else a philosophical teaching, religious components were incorporated and developed as concomitant elements. In the term *Nho giáo*, as well as in *Phật giáo* (*fojiao*, Buddhism) and *Đạo giáo* (*daojiao*, Daoism), the word *tôn* (to venerate) is absent, thus producing Confucian doctrine, Buddhist doctrine, and Daoist doctrine.

The difference in usage between the terms *tín ngưỡng* and *tôn giáo* is clearly seen in the analysis of the cult of the Mothers (one of whom is Princess Liễu Hạnh), which is presented by one of the most eminent scholars of Vietnamese religion, Ngô Đức Thịnh, as an example of *tín ngưỡng*. Characterizing the state of the cult in modern times, he writes: "thờ Mẫu đang trong quá trình chuyển hóa từ *tín nguỡng* nguyên thủy thành một tôn giáo dân gian sơ khai"[129] (emphasis is mine), that is: "Mother worship is in a process of transformation from a primitive belief into an early stage of a popular religion." The cult of Mothers, according to Ngô Đức Thịnh, evolved from a primitive belief similar to animism in a matrilineal society, where the role of mothers was comparable to natural powers such as Heaven, Earth, and Water, believed to protect people from natural disasters and to provide the necessities of everyday life; with the advent of Daoism, the cult acquired a cosmology and developed a pantheon that incorporated many other spirits. The Mother occupied the highest position in the new pantheon, "similar to the position of Buddha in Buddhism, Jesus in Christianity, Allah in Islam."[130]

The existence of a pantheon in a cosmological context in conjunction with popularity among the people, a system of legends, hagiographies, liturgical literature, a network of temples, and festivals are the distinguishing features of the cult of the Mothers, according to Ngô Đức Thịnh. What deters this *tín ngưỡng* from transformation into a *tôn giáo* is its materialistic aspect. In other words, if, for example, Buddhism and Christianity can be described as religions of cosmic "salvation," belief in the Mothers differs from these insofar as it focuses on everyday vital issues such as health, money, career, etc.[131] Instead of basing itself on doctrinal premises relatively distant from everyday human concerns, as "religions" (*tôn giáo*) typically do, Mother worship attends directly to everyday concerns; it is an egocentric form of belief (*tín ngưỡng*) with which people seek the satisfaction of their immediate personal requests. From this, it appears that modern scholarship on religion in Vietnam observes a distinction between *tín ngưỡng* and *tôn giáo* based upon the presence or absence of a systematic doctrine or teaching. Nevertheless, most Vietnamese who identify themselves with Buddhism or Daoism are uninterested in doctrine and simply seek material benefits. Hence, while *tôn giáo* has a theoretical or doctrinal aspect, *tín ngưỡng* exists wholly in a practical domain.

In Vietnamese discussions of religion, the expression *tín ngưỡng* is often modified with the term *dân gian* (*minjian*, 民 間), literally translated "among the people," which is usually translated as "popular" or "folk." In addition to being a component of the compound *tín ngưỡng dân gian*, *dân gian* is also used with nouns such as "literature" (*văn học dân gian*), "art" (*nghệ thuật dân gian*), "music" (*âm nhạc*

---

[129] Ngô Đức Thịnh, "Kết Luận," (Conclusion), in *Đạo Mẫu ở Việt Nam*, ed. Ngô Đức Thịnh 1:312.

[130] Ibid., pp. 314-315.

[131] Ibid., pp. 315-316.

dân gian), "culture" (*văn hóa dân gian*), and "spirit" (*tính dân gian*). In each of these instances, the term designates the "mass character" of what is being modified.

The term *dân gian* has not had a stable meaning in Vietnamese scholarship. After the August Revolution of 1945 and before the Đổi Mới era of the late 1980s, the term *dân gian* was used in Vietnam to name the spontaneous, nondoctrinal, uninstitutionalized area of human activity at the local level beyond the direct supervision of the state. Beginning in the late 1980s, however, it has been increasingly used in a sense that brings to mind Walter Benjamin's "dream world of mass culture,"[132] except that instead of this being a dream of the masses, it is a dream of the state about the masses, and instead of the dream being about capitalist commodification, it is about commodification of the nation, about finding artifacts of authenticity at the local level and nationalizing them. For example, the form of music called *ca trù* was proscribed after the Revolution because it was considered to be a relic of the old feudal culture. In the 1990s, however, it has been revived as an authentic example of Vietnamese culture, as *âm nhạc dân gian*. Another example is the revival of festivals devoted to various deities, belief in whom is now defined as *tín ngưỡng dân gian*. The annual festival of Liễu Hạnh was prohibited in 1975 as "having a superstitious character,"[133] but at present it is one of the most famous and advertised festivals to be attended by Vietnamese and foreigners alike.

The term *tín ngưỡng dân gian*, "popular beliefs," refers to nature deities, to spirit cults, and to the "by-products" of religions such as ancestor worship, which is often considered as a part of Confucianism, and such as the cults of the Jade Emperor and other deities in Daoism, or spirit beliefs incorporated into Buddhism. It is not understood in the Redfieldian sense as the authenticity of rural culture in contradistinction to elite culture, because, as we have already noted, the Vietnamese do not make such a distinction, for cultural and religious practices have been and are being constantly exchanged between educated and uneducated people. Sangren suggests the term "local religion" in place of "popular religion" and his definition of this appears to be similar to how the term *tín ngưỡng dân gian* is used in Vietnam today when he writes of Taiwan: "Both elites and common people participated in local religion."[134]

In his discussion of Mother worship, cited above, Ngô Đức Thịnh uses the term *tôn giáo dân gian*, which is an apparent equivalent of Sangren's term "local religion." However, this term is very rare in Vietnamese scholarship and appears to be used with two aims in mind. One is to suggest a stage in a process by which local practices develop a structure of systematic beliefs comparable to a religion in the Durkheimian sense. Another is to bring discussion of religion in Vietnam into what is considered to be an international academic vocabulary. In general, we can say that contemporary Vietnamese scholarship on religion is still in a process of formation.

---

[132] See Walter Benjamin, *Illuminations* (New York: Schocken, 1985), p. 241; Susan Buck-Morss, *The Dialectics of Seeing* (Cambridge, MA: The MIT Press, 1997), chapter 8.

[133] Phạm Quỳnh Phương, "Thờ Mẫu Liễu ở Phủ Giầy" (Worship of Mother Liễu at Phủ Giầy), in *Đạo Mẫu ở Việt Nam*, ed. Ngô Đức Thịnh, 1:143.

[134] See T. Steven Sangren, *Chinese Sociologics* (London: Athlone, 2000), p. 251, n. 66.

Theorizing Voice, Place, and Thought in the *Opusculum*

The voice, place, and thought of the *Opusculum* text can be theorized as an unstable translating motion between a site of enunciation and a site of reference.[135] As a site of enunciation, the voice is first of all a performance in the Latin language with the authoritative linguistic point of access to the "other" being Hán, or Classical Chinese, many passages of which are transcribed into the text as a material form of authentication. Behind the formal façade of Latin and Hán, the text has multiple lines of implicit and explicit reference to a polyphony of classical and vernacular tongues, not only Chinese and Vietnamese, but also European. The first dictionary of the Vietnamese language produced by Europeans was a trilingual rather than a bilingual dictionary: Latin, Portuguese, and Vietnamese.

As a site of reference, the text distinguishes between the classical language of Hán and the vernacular or "vulgar tongue," what we today call Vietnamese. We can imagine the text to have arisen from a multilingual context of men from several European countries for whom Latin was a common tongue, learned in school and imbued with the authority of what was regarded as the highest civilization and the "true church." The *Opusculum* represents a translation into Latin of other texts and of talk in several tongues. It is the result of choices made among options available in the Latin vocabulary, which inevitably produced semantic slippage from the experiences and the non-Latin words being translated. This slippage is the perpetual motion between the site of reference and the site of enunciation.

This translation of the *Opusculum* into English has been produced by a similar motion between the multilingual vocabularies in the *Opusculum*, as well as the multilingual vocabularies of other materials consulted for the study of the text, and the vocabulary available in English. Choices were made on the basis of expediency rather than equivalency. Compared with the "full" voices of the materials and experiences upon which the text is based, the Latin text and its English translation are "empty" in the sense that, as approximations of what is being referenced, they represent choices that range from plausible to expedient, thus trailing off without clear boundary to randomness. This "emptiness," in fact, is a necessary feature of authority in a voice claiming categorical control over a field of experience or knowledge that can never be entirely absorbed by a single epistemological strategy or perfectly translated by a change of vocabulary. Instead of the excess of experience and knowledge beyond language, this is the excess of emptiness beyond experience and knowledge, which is nothing more than the authority asserted to control that experience and knowledge with words that, at best, approximate but can never represent. This empty place of slippage in translation produces the voice of authority. A similar place of slippage and authority can be theorized for mapping the text in space.

---

135 Here I am revising Michel Foucault's discussion of "the enunciative function" in *The Archaeology of Knowledge* (New York: Pantheon books, 1972), Part III, to theorize a text that moves between two enunciative sites, one of which I am calling a site of reference to distinguish between two discursive formations, both of which are found in the text. One discursive formation enables the site of enunciation, which is similar to what Naoki Sakai calls constituted, representable subjectivity (*shukan*), while the other is produced from what Sakai calls the unrepresentable "body of enunciation" or the hybrid excess of real life experience (*shutai*). See Naoki Sakai, *Translation and Subjectivity* (Minneapolis: University of Minnesota Press, 1997), chapter 4.

Whether we theorize the place of authority for the text to be Rome, Europe, or the West is unimportant, for they all work out to the same thing when we spatialize the sites of enunciation and of reference. As a convenience I will use the term Europe as the name for the text's site of enunciation. The text identifies the spatial "other" of Europe, the site of reference, as China. Tonkin is for the text a vernacular locality of China. Today, we do not even have a stable place in our modern vocabulary for Tonkin. We tend to treat it as if it is the same as Vietnam, but in fact this is a modern fiction. In the eighteenth century, Vietnam, as we know the country today, did not exist. For the Europeans, there was Tonkin and Cochinchina. Speakers of Vietnamese had their own terms to distinguish between the two countries. Even as beneath the text's vocabulary of equivalency between China and Tonkin lay the difference between what we today name China and Vietnam, so in our modern vocabulary of equivalency between Tonkin and Vietnam lies the difference between what was then named Tonkin and Cochinchina, and more recently named North Vietnam and South Vietnam. The slippage of terminology apparent in these examples is simply the empty space upon which the authority of Asian studies as a category of the modern academy has been built in the West. Beneath the empty European subjectivity of the text lies a multinational crew of Europeans posing as a Christian united front facing China—and all the heterogeneity masked by China—as a figure for Asia.

When we consider the thought of the text, at the site of enunciation we encounter the one Christian religion of Europe and the three sects of China as its false foil. However, the site of reference is full of Chinese and Tonkinese spirits, so prolific that they cannot even be contained in chapters dedicated to the three sects, but spill out to fill up another chapter, which becomes the largest in the manuscript, and then trail off in lists of spirits that seem to extend far beyond the last page. The plenitude of spirits that burgeons beyond the precincts of the three sects mirrors the sectarian multiplicity of the Europeans, not only between Protestants and Catholics, but also among the missionaries themselves with strife among Jesuits, Augustinians (discalced or not), Dominicans, and Franciscans, which is apparent in the Rites Controversy and in the vicissitudes of Adriano de St. Thecla's last years. The site of authority, where the text thinks, is the empty gesturing of a single truth toward a reality of multiple differences. This can also be seen in the text's conflation of China and Tonkin.

The degree of openness toward the spirit world is apparent when we consider how so-called Chinese spirits are fully accepted as legitimate spirits in Tonkin. The Tonkinese have no sense that spirits come with exclusive ethnic or political identities. Spirits are spirits, regardless of where they come from. Does this represent the effects of forced Sinicization, as some might conjecture? Or does it represent a degree of experience with China and a correlating confidence to participate as members of a larger cultural world? In certain formulations, these options may not be mutually exclusive, but I believe the *Opusculum* reflects the latter case more than the former, for there is not even a whisper of tension between China and Tonkin in this text.

Of course, the text reflects what is interesting to Europeans, and its epistemological mastery over China and Tonkin is gained by marking equivalency between them. At the same time, the text does enable us to perceive what was adapted from China in Tonkin or, at least, what Chinese elements were crucial to European perceptions of Tonkin. In general, these elements have to do with formal philosophical doctrine and whatever spirits could be gleaned from narratives associated with such doctrine, whether these spirits be Confucius and his disciples, sages and mythical beings of antiquity found in classical texts, Laozi and his followers, buddhas and boddhisatvas, or the Jade Emperor and his divine entourage. The Tonkinese appear uninterested in creating new doctrines or philosophies. If we were to imagine that this was in fact the case, as materials other than the *Opusculum* indeed suggest, then we might conjecture that the sense of participation in a larger civilized world felt by educated Vietnamese in the past precluded any necessity to create new intellectual systems.

Whether we look at the *Opusculum* as an exercise of language, as a formulation of space, or as a descriptive intellectualization of religious experience, we encounter sites of textual subjectivity that require a theorization of motion between enunciating authority with empty formal assertions and referencing an overflowing content that is constantly bustling off the page, off the map, off the altar. One of the delights of this text is that, despite its formal obeisance toward sites of enunciation, it surrenders to the pleasures of referencing the endless details that make such sites appear relatively unimportant.

Note on the Translation

The goal animating this translation was to stay as close as possible to a literal reading of the original, keeping the spirit and style of the *Opusculum* intact, and not trying to turn the translation into a modern English narrative. It has been a difficult task because the syntax of the sentence in Latin is very different from that in English. For example, extremely long sentences have been broken into two or even three shorter sentences in this translation. The subject of the Latin sentence is often replaced by a personal pronoun or is named only once at the beginning of a long sentence, a syntactical pattern that would render sentences incomprehensible if replicated in English. In such cases we inserted words in brackets to supplement the English structure of the sentence with the indispensable information. Also inserted in brackets is the pagination of the Latin manuscript to enable readers to easily find the corresponding page of the original. The words originally placed inside parentheses in the original text by Adriano di St. Thecla are set in braces in the translation. The words or phrases underlined in the original are italicized and underlined in the translation.

There are a significant number of Chinese names, book titles, terms, and toponyms in the *Opusculum* given in Vietnamese. For some of them, Adriano di St. Thecla provided their Chinese equivalents. I supplemented his Chinese equivalents with modern Chinese pinyin transliterations, which are placed in parentheses. His Chinese transliterations have diacritics to indicate tones, but these have not been reproduced in the translation; however, readers can consult the original text for these tonal marks. In the cases of Chinese names, book titles, terms, and toponyms for which Adriano di St. Thecla did not provide Chinese transliterations, I have inserted the appropriate Chinese words to assist readers unacquainted with the Vietnamese language who are accustomed to seeing these names in pinyin transliteration. In such cases, my Chinese transliteration is set in parentheses the first time it appears in a chapter, next to the Vietnamese names, book titles, and toponyms. In the footnotes, the titles and authors' names for Chinese books published using the Wade-Giles transcription are not rendered into pinyin.

When a Vietnamese term and its Chinese transliteration appear in the manuscript, I add an English translation unless additional explanation is required, in which case the translation along with the explanation is given in a footnote. When I discuss Chinese personalities, books, toponyms, and terms in the footnotes, I initially use terms as they are given in the text of the *Opusculum*—that is, first in Vietnamese followed by their Chinese equivalent—but I subsequently refer only to the Chinese and omit the Vietnamese term. In the case of a footnote that includes Chinese names, books, toponyms, or terms not found in the manuscript, or if they are not found in the sentence or passage to which the footnote relates, I do not provide the Vietnamese equivalent.

Some terms are in the vernacular Vietnamese language, that is, they were not borrowed from the Chinese language, so I did not insert any Chinese equivalent for them, and they are followed only by their English translation in parenthesis. Vietnamese names and toponyms are not transliterated into Chinese.

Adriano di St. Thecla quotes a significant number of Chinese and Vietnamese sources and also reproduces some expressions from Vietnamese oral tradition. I did my best to render into characters all phrases and sentences given in Sino-Vietnamese (Hán) to make them intelligible to scholars, for the Sino-Vietnamese language is hardly understandable in the absence of characters, since each pronunciation stands for a number of possible characters. The results of this endeavor are put into footnotes corresponding to the phrases and sentences in the *Opusculum*. In those cases when I was not sure about the plausibility of some character in a given sentence, this character is followed by a question mark in parentheses. When I was unable to suggest any character that would match the pronunciation found in the manuscript, I inserted a question mark in brackets. Due to the technical difficulties, the appearance of the sentences rendered into characters might be sometimes distorted. A passage in vernacular Vietnamese in the chapter on the spirits has not been rendered into characters due to technical difficulties in printing demotic Vietnamese characters (Nôm).

Adriano di St. Thecla provided his translation for most of the phrases and sentences in the *Opusculum*. For those few that he left untranslated, I provide my own translation in the footnotes corresponding to these sentences. In the footnotes, I also comment on his translations if my translations are different from his.

All spellings in Vietnamese are kept exactly as found in the original, including capitalization. Some of the words are misspelled or their orthography has changed since the time of the writing or copying of the manuscript. In both cases I point out the discrepancy when it is encountered in the text for the first time.

The translation is supplemented with three glossaries. First, there is a glossary for all Chinese names, terms, and toponyms that appear more than once in the manuscript according to Adriano di St. Thecla's transcription of Vietnamese pronunciation (and thus do not have pinyin equivalents in parentheses after the first appearance). Second, there is a glossary indicating differences between Adriano di St. Thecla's spelling of Vietnamese and modern *quốc ngữ* spelling. Third, there is a glossary indicating the differences between Adriano di St. Thecla's spelling of Chinese and modern pinyin spelling.

Opusculum de Sectis apud Sinenses et Tunkinenses

Father Adriano di St. Thecla

ON THE SECTS OF THE CHINESE AND ANNAMITES

Soon after people dispersed over the face of the earth, idolatry appeared in the world; since the corruption of moral habits grew from day to day, love for truth and honesty gradually disappeared, and absolute ignorance of things filled human minds. It happened, therefore, that almost all nations lost the true knowledge of God, and most of them descended miserably to idolatry. The first idolater was Nimrod,[1] who began to be a mighty one on the earth {Gen. 10},[2] as has been shown by Eusebius and St. Jerome, and by Saint Father Augustine in chapter 7 of the sixth book of *De Civitate Dei* (On the City of God).[3] "The beginning of his kingdom was

[1] This statement, by Adriano di St. Thecla, that Nimrod was the first idolater, should be specified as referring to after the Flood, for, according to the Old Testament, people first began to perform idolatry in the time of Enosh (the son of Seth and a grandson of Adam): "To Seth also a son was born; and he called his name Enosh. At that time men began to call upon the name of Jehovah" (Genesis 4:26, Standard Version; hereafter all biblical citations are according to the *New Oxford Annotated Bible with the Apocrypha,* ed. H. G. May and B. M. Metzger [New York: Oxford University Press, 1977]). Jewish commentators interpret this as the beginning of idol worship when people applied the name of the Creator to created things: "Then to call in the Name of Hashem became profaned." *The Chumash,* ed. Rabbi N. Scherman and Rabbi M. Zlotowitz (Brooklyn, NY: Mesorah Publications; The Artscroll Series/The Stone Edition, 2000), p. 23. According to the Book of Genesis, after the Deluge idolatry indeed reappeared, as the author states, in the time of Nimrod, a grandson of Noah's son Ham. Nimrod not only introduced idolatry but also claimed to be a god himself, forcing people to worship him instead of the true God, as it is said in Genesis 10:9: "He was a mighty hunter before Jehovah: wherefore it is said, 'Like Nimrod a mighty hunter before Jehovah.'" This phrase was interpreted by later commentators as describing Nimrod to be a hunter for people's souls, i.e., averting them from the true God. See, for example, the commentaries of Rashi (1040–1105), one of the leading Jewish commentators, in *Humash. Sefer be Reshit* (Pentateuch. The Book of Genesis), (Jerusalem: Or ha-Sefer), p. 44. St. Augustine, repeatedly cited by the author below, is also explicit with regard to Nimrod. He adduces a quotation from Genesis translated (or actually mistranslated) as follows: "Cush begat Nimrod; he began to be a giant on the earth. He was a giant hunter *against* the Lord God: wherefore they say, 'As Nimrod the giant hunter *against* the Lord'" (emphasis mine). See St. Augustine, *On the City of God* 16.3, in *Basic Writings of Saint Augustine*, ed. Whitney J. Oates (New York: Random House, 1948), 2:320. Except for later commentaries on the Genesis, which place the appearance of Nimrod in the third century after the Flood, there is no historical evidence for when Nimrod lived or even for his historicity.

[2] Gen. 10:8.

[3] Eusebius Pamphili (ca. 260–340), bishop of Caesarea in Palestine, wrote extensively on historical issues and church history. St. Jerome (ca. 340–420) was a famous translator and commentator of the Old Testament and other sacred Hebrew texts. St. Augustine (354–430),

Ba'bel" {ibid. 10}, and there he undoubtedly ruled, according to some narrators and chronologists, in the third century after the Flood, and in the second [century] after the scattering of people [over the world] according to the dating of the Vulgate.[4] And also during the same century, in Chaldea,[5] the capital of which was Babylon, we already have the flourishing cult of idols, revealed by the testimony of Joshua;[6] in chapter 24, he said to the sons of Israel: "Thus says the Lord, the God of Israel, 'Your fathers lived of old beyond the river {Euphrates}, Terah, the father of Abraham and Nahor {the father of Terah}, and they served other gods. . . . Now therefore {he says later} fear the Lord . . . put away the gods which your fathers served living in Mesopotamia, and in Egypt, and serve the Lord.'"[7] The Nahor mentioned there is not Nahor the brother of Abraham and son of Terah, but Nahor the father of Terah;[8] so when Joshua says: *your fathers lived beyond the river, and served* [p. II] *other gods*, this Nahor, mentioned together with Terah, must be the father of the sons of Israel, about whom Joshua says that there are many fathers, as mentioned earlier; if this Nahor really had been a brother of Abraham and a son of Terah, then not many fathers of the sons of Israel but only one would have been mentioned; and therefore it would have been said inconsistently [in Josh. 24]: *your fathers lived beyond the river, and served other gods*.[9] Nahor then gave birth

considered a philosophical and theological genius, is one of the Doctors of the Church. *De Civitate Dei* (On the City of God), one of two major books written in 413–26, contains Augustine's polemics against pagan ways of life and presents biblical history from Genesis to the Last Judgment. The author's citation of the book and the chapter is inaccurate: chapter 7 of book 6 is titled "Concerning the Likeness and Agreement of the Fabulous and Civil Theologies," and in this chapter St. Augustine does not deal with either idolatry or Nimrod. The reference here may be to book 16, which recounts history from Noah to Abraham; Nimrod is mentioned here. There is a similar citation to that adduced by Adriano di St. Thecla from Genesis, chapter 11: "Nimrod lived to the time in which Babylon was founded and the confusion of tongues occurred, and the consequent division of the earth" (Augustine, *On the City of God* [ed. Oates] 16.); or see the passage from 16.3 mentioned in note 1.

[4] The Vulgate, a Latin translation of the Old Testament made by St. Jerome between 390 and 405, suffered corruption, especially through copyists, and was revised several times during the next centuries. The modern version of the Vulgate dates Creation as happening in 4004 B.C.E. and the Flood in 2349 B.C.E., in correspondence with calculations made in the middle of the seventeenth century by Archbishop Ussher. The *Septuagint*—a Greek version of the Old Testament translated in the third century B.C.E., which was the main authority prior to St. Jerome's translation—designates these dates as 5200 and 2957 B.C.E., respectively.

[5] The name Chaldea was frequently applied to the land in southern Mesopotamia.

[6] The Book of Joshua is one of the historical books of the Old Testament that supplements the Pentateuch.

[7] Josh. 24:2, 24:14.

[8] In the Genesis there are two people called Nahor, a grandfather and a grandson. The first Nahor was a descendant of Noah's son Shem, and he begat Terah (Gen. 11:24). Terah in turn begat Abraham, Nahor, and Haran (Gen. 11:26).

[9] In fact, Joshua 24:2 is absolutely explicit (in the original Hebrew) that the reference is to Terah, the father of both Abraham and Nahor: This passage reads:

"בעבר הנהר ישבו אבותיכם מעולם תרח אבי אברהם ואבי נחור ויעבדו
אלהים אחרים."

"Your fathers always dwelt beyond the river—Terach [Terah] the father of Abraham and *the father of* Nahor—and they served gods of others." Emphasis is mine; cited from *The Book of Joshua*, trans. and comment. Reuven Drucker (NY: Mesorah Publications, 1998). As my emphasis in this quotation from the Vulgate indicates, the word *father* is repeated in front of the name *Nahor* with the possessive particle *of;* this eliminates the interpretation of Adriano di St. Thecla to Terah in the year 221 after the Flood, as it appears from the calculation of years of all generations after the Flood, according to the dating of the Vulgate: after he gave birth to Terah, Nahor lived 119 years {Gen. 11:26}. Thereupon he, together with his son Terah, could have worshipped gods during many years in the same third century, when Nimrod, the son of Cush,[10] established their cult. For that reason Abraham, by the order of God, came out from the land of the Chaldeans in order not to worship gods whom his fathers worshipped there.[11] Witness to this event is Achior, who in Judith, chapter 1, says to Holofernes:[12] "This people is

---

that the Nahor referred to here is the father of Terah. The sense of the passage is that indeed there was more than one father of the Israelites, and one of them was the father of both Abraham and Nahor, and he served idols. The argument launched by Adriano di St. Thecla is based on the Vulgate's potentially ambiguous translation of the passage "trans fluvim habitaverunt patres vestri ab initio Thare *pater Abraham et Nachor* servieruntque diis alienis" (your fathers lived of old beyond the river, Terah, *the father of Abraham and Nahor,* and they served other gods); *Biblia Sacra. Iuxta Vulgatam Versionem,* ed. B. Fischer et al. (Stuttgart: Deutsche Bibelgesellschaft, 1984), p. 320 (emphasis mine). The genitives here are not specified grammatically due to the lack of a possessive particle and to the identical form for the nominative and accusative case for the name of Nahor. By his analysis of the adduced phrase, Adriano di St. Thecla is either trying to solve a grammatical issue, which, in his opinion, would be an imprecision in the *Book of Joshua,* or developing a theological argument. Tracing idolatry among the Jews to the generation prior to Terah, as he wants to do, does not, in fact, contradict even Jewish commentaries. For example, Louis Ginzberg quotes *Baraita di Masseket Niddah* (a part of Mishna on women's purity) as follows: "In olden times children were brought up by their grandparents. When Abraham was four years old, his father Terah entrusted him to the care of Nahor, who tempted him to worship idols." L. Ginzberg, *The Legends of the Jews* (Philadelphia: The Jewish Publication Society of America, 1967-69), 5:216, n. 48. However, the Jewish commentaries emphasize the importance of the fact that, in this passage, Terah is the father of Abraham and of Nahor, and thus Nahor is the brother of Abraham, explaining that this is supposed to highlight that Abraham, chosen from among all the people to learn the true belief, was surrounded by pagans, not only from the previous generations (his father Terah), but also from his own generation (his brother Nahor). Furthermore, this relation between Terah, the father, and Abraham and Nahor, the sons, serves, according to the sixteenth century Rabbi Moshe Alshich, as an indication that idolatry was not inevitable among the Jews (as might be surmised from Adriano di St. Thecla's insistence, if not for the linguistic reasons, that the Nahor in question is Abraham's grandfather rather than his brother, potentially suggesting a genetic predilection towards idolatry): "The worship of idols, however, is not an inherited inclination. The proof of this is that Terach [Terah] was both the father of Abraham who recognized his Creator and of Nachor who was a pagan. Joshua did not mention Haran, although he too was a son of Terach [Terah], because he was neither a pagan nor a man committed to god." Cited in *The Book of Joshua,* Drucker, trans. and comment, p. 450.

[10] Cush was a grandson of Noah by his son Ham.

[11] Note that whereas the author perceives a passage from the Book of Joshua ("Your fathers lived of old beyond Euphrates, Terah, the father of Abraham and Nahor, and they served other gods . . .") as potentially inconsistent because of the presence of only one father (Terah), he does not seem to see any inconsistency in here ascribing to Abraham not one father but "fathers." His use of *fathers* in the plural here would be reasonable, if we bear in mind that the term denotes ancestors as a generic term, had he not previously argued at length against using the word *fathers* in a similar context with reference to the Book of Joshua: "Your fathers lived beyond the River, and served other gods."

[12] Achior was an Ammonite general who warned Holofernes against attacking the Jews; the Ammonites, he said, had engaged in sporadic armed conflicts with the Israelites and had found it difficult to gain an upper hand. Holofernes was a general of the Assyrian king Nebuchadrezzar II (630–561 B.C.E.) sent to subdue Palestine. A Jewish woman, Judith, attracted Holofernes with her beauty and with her prediction of his victory over Palestine and was invited to attend him

descended from the Chaldeans. At one time they lived in Mesopotamia, because they would not follow the gods of their fathers who were in Chaldea. For they had left the ways of their ancestors, and they worshipped the God of heaven."[13] From the aforementioned it becomes known that already during the lifetime of Noah idolatry reached people, and was contemporary with him [Noah] for many years, since Noah lived 350 years after the Flood {Gen. 9}.[14] Certainly, it is recognized that the descendants of Shem were involved in [idolatry], for Nahor and Terah were from the same posterity of Shem.[15]

Among the gods whom Chaldeans worshipped at that time was Fire, Ur in Hebrew, after which the city of the Chaldeans was named, the first [city] left by Abraham,[16] because the Chaldeans {as Tirinus[17] says [in his commentary on] Genesis, chapter 12} were worshipping Fire as a god, exactly as the neighboring Persians were doing in places, which for that reason were called Pyrea by Procopius[18] and others [who cited him]. We can rightly assume that the Sun, the Moon, and the Stars were also gods for the Chaldeans, since the Chaldeans greatly occupied themselves with astronomy and were distinguished in it above all other [people]; [but] with this observation and study of celestial bodies they [Chaldeans] could have easily fallen into error, considering [the stars], which they admired for their beauty, to be [p. III] gods, knowing nothing about their [the stars'] creator. So, the first people who considered creations of God to be gods happened to appear among the ancient Chaldeans, as we read in the thirteenth chapter of the *Sapientia* (Wisdom [of Solomon]):[19] "For all men who were ignorant of God were foolish by nature; and they were unable from the good things that are seen to know him who exists, nor did they recognize the craftsman while paying heed to his works; but they supposed that either fire or wind or swift air, or the circle of stars,

---

in his tent. When Holofernes, after a feast with her, fell into a drunken sleep, Judith cut off his head. The Assyrians, leaderless, lost their campaign.

[13] The reference is to the Book of Judith from the Apocrypha, excluded from the Hebrew and Protestant canon but included in the Roman canon and the Greek version of the Hebrew Bible. The indication of the chapter is inaccurate, this quotation is from Jth. 5:6–8. See the Vulgate, in *Biblia Sacra*, p. 695.

[14] Gen. 9:28.

[15] Nahor's father was Serug, a descendent of Shem, one of Noah's sons, in the sixth generation (Gen. 11:10–22).

[16] Ur, an important city of ancient southern Mesopotamia (Sumer), was situated some 140 miles from the site of Babylon, near modern Baghdad. The people of Ur worshipped Sin (the god of the moon) and the god of fire.

[17] Jacobus Tirinus (1580–1636), the principal of the Jesuit College in Antwerp from 1615 to 1625, wrote a number of commentaries on the Scriptures. I could not locate his works.

[18] Procopius, a Byzantine historian who lived in Palestine in the fifth century, was a member of the personal staff of Belisarius (527–65), a famous general of the Byzantine Empire who led a campaign against Persia and other countries. Procopius was a witness of these campaigns and described them in his earliest and most famous work, the eight-volume *De Bellis* (On the Wars). Pyrea is a possible Latin transliteration of a Greek word *πυρεῖα*, the plural of *πυρεῖον*. In the plural this word usually refers to two sticks used to start a fire. When discussing the Persian campaign of Belisarius in the first two volumes of *De Bellis*, Procopius uses it (in singular) to denote the "place of fire," or the temple of fire. Procopius, *History of the Wars*, ed. and trans. H. B. Dewing (London: William Heinemann; New York: Macmillan, 1914), 1:473.

[19] One of the apocryphal books of the Biblical canon, The Wisdom of Solomon was composed during the later part of the first century C.E.

or turbulent water, or the luminaries of heaven were the gods that rule the world. If through delight in the beauty of these things men assumed them to be gods, let them know how much better than these is their Lord, for the author of beauty created them."[20]

The cult of the deceased was also started among the Chaldeans. Terah, the father of Abraham, erected a statue in honor of his dead son Haran,[21] as Epiphanius in the first book of *De Hoeresibus* (On the Heretics) and Suidas in his entry on *Abraham* explains,[22] and for that he [Terah] was severely censured by Abraham. Contemporary to Terah was Ninus[23] {this [is affirmed by] Tirinus [in his commentary] on *Sapientia*, chapter 14}, the son of Nimrod or Belus,[24] who erected a

[20] Wisd. of Sol. 13:1–3. The citation is from the Vulgate, in *Biblia Sacra*, p. 1018. The only discrepancy is that in one place at the beginning of the citation Adriano di St. Thecla changed the word order: instead of "vani sunt autem omnes hominus" (for foolish are all men) he wrote "vani autem sunt omnes hominus," although this does not affect the meaning of the sentence. It is possible, however, that a different version of the Vulgate gives the translation exactly as Adriano di St. Thecla presents it.

[21] Gen. 11:28. "Haran died before his father Terah in the land of his birth, in Ur of the Chalde'ans." The Jewish tradition ascribes Haran's death to his vacillation between worshipping the true God and the idols of Nimrod. Haran's death is considered as especially important, showing the gravity of his sin, since it was the first time when a son died before his father.

[22] Epiphanius of Salamis (ca. 310–ca. 402) lived and preached in Egypt and Judea before becoming bishop of Constantia (Salamis) on Cyprus. He was known for his asceticism and his zeal for the monastic life. I assume that *De Hoeresibus* (On the Heretics) is a reference to Epiphanius's earliest work, *Anchoratus* (The Well-Anchored), also known as *Panarion* (Medicine Chest), written in 374. In this work, Epiphanius analyzes a list of eighty heretical sects from the earliest to those of his own time. *Anchoratus* or *Panarion* includes three books, the first of which dwells on the heresies prior to Jesus. In his summary to book 1, section 1, Epiphanius says: "they introduced the error of idolatry by means of statues as well, paying honor to their forefathers by fashioning likenesses of them and making images of those who died before them." See Ph. R. Amidon, trans. and ed., *The Panarion of St. Epiphanius* (New York: Oxford University Press, 1990), pp. 10, 28–29.

Suidas was a famous lexicographer who lived in about the tenth century in Constantinople (modern Istanbul) and was the author of one of the most important Greek lexicons or encyclopedias. His encyclopedia entry on Abraham is in *Suidae Lexicon ex recoginitione Immanuelis Bekkeri* (Berolini: Typis et impensis Georgii Reimeri, 1854), pp. 5–6. The English translation of *The Lexicon* exists only on the web; consult the Suda on Line website of the University of Kentucky (http://www.stoa.org/sol/). In this work, Terah indeed is reprimanded by his son Abraham—not exactly on the issue of the cult of the deceased, but rather for his worshipping of idols. The passage reads: "he admonished his father, saying 'Why do you lead the people astray for guilty profit and idols? There is no other God but the One in heaven and the Creator of the whole universe.'"

[23] Ninus, allegedly of the second half of the third millennium B.C.E., was a king of Assyria. According to the works cited below, he began to worship his deceased father, thus defiling the concept of the one God.

[24] Belus, also Bel or Belos in English, is a Hellenized form of the Hebrew word *baal* (lord, master, owner), the name of one of the highest gods of the Canaanites, the god of rain and, consequently, of fertility. Worship of Baal was later introduced into Mesopotamia as well, or at least identified with Marduk, the chief god of the Babylonians. According to some works cited below, Belus, the father of Ninus, was the first king of Assyria, and was deified by his son and his people. (See, for instance, Eusebius, Ambrose, Jerome.) Since Belus was the first man whom people worshipped, he is identified in the manuscript with Nimrod, who, as Adriano di St. Thecla writes, introduced idolatry. In my opinion, it is Ninus, not Belus, who should be identified with Nimrod and the cult of idolatry.

public statue, altars, and a temple to his deceased father—as say Eusebius in *Chronicon* (Chronicle),[25] St. Jerome in [his commentary on] *Osea* (Hosea), chapter 2,[26] St. Ambrose in chapter 1 of *Ad Romanos* (To Romans),[27] and St. Augustine in the sixteenth book [of] *De Civitate,* chapters 7 and 22,[28] and in *Contrà Faustum* (Against Faustus), chapter 17.[29] This is said in chapter 14 of *Sapientia* against the Chaldeans: "For a father, consumed with grief at an untimely bereavement, made an image of his child, who had been suddenly taken from him; and he honored as a god what was once a dead human being, and handed on to his dependents secret rites and initiations. Then the ungodly custom, grown strong with time, was kept as a law, and at the command of monarchs graven images were worshiped."[30] But the later chronologists say that Belus, the father of Ninus, reigned in Babylon many centuries after Nimrod, most possibly from the year 2628 after the creation of the world, and they also think that Belus the Babylonian, who was later considered

---

[25] *Chronicle* or *Chronological Canon* was written in 325 and describes a universal history. The first part of the book is devoted to the history of the Chaldeans and the Assyrians. In his introduction, Eusebius writes that the Assyrians deified Belus after his death. See Eusebius, *Chronicon* (Venice: E. Ratdolt, 1483), pp. b1–b2.

[26] Hosea (Salvation) is the name of one of the prophets active in the eighth century B.C.E. Accordingly, Hosea is one of the twelve books of prophets in the Old Testament. In 406 C.E., St. Jerome wrote a commentary on this book, to which the author refers.

Patrologiae Cursus Completus (Paris: J.-P. Migne Editorem, 1845), vol. 25, book 1, p. 838, point 24, says that in the struggle with the great king of Bactria, Ninus, the son of Belus and the first king to reign in Asia, acquired such a glory that he referred to his father Belus as God.

[27] St. Ambrose (ca. 340–97), bishop of Milan, was another illustrious Father of the Church. He commented widely on both the Old and the New Testaments. Many of his works have been lost, and quite a few works, on the contrary, are falsely attributed to him. *Ad Romanos* (To Romans), a work containing commentaries on the Epistles of St. Paul, is one of the works falsely attributed to St. Ambrose. Scholars have reached the consensus that the author, who was writing between 363 and 384, should rather be called Ambrosiaster (pseudo-Ambrose). Angelo di Berardino, ed., *Patrology,* in *The Golden Age of Latin Patristic Literature: From the Council of Nicea to the Council of Chalcedon* (Allen, Tex.: Christian Classics, 1986), 1:180–181. *Ad Romanos,* which includes commentaries on the letters of the Apostle St. Paul (ca. 10–ca. 66), traces the starting point of idolatry to the time when people began to worship animals, snakes, and birds as gods, and the first to do it were those who deified the image of Belus. Henricus Iosephus Vogels, ed., *Ad Romanos,* in *Corpus Scriptorum Ecclesiasticorum Latinorum* (Vindobonae: Hoelder-Pichler-Temsky, 1966), vol. 81, pt. 1, chap. 1, point 23, pp. 44–45.

[28] *On the City* is, of course, an abbreviation of *On the City of God* (De Civitate Dei). The reference seems to be imprecise, since chapter 7 of book 16 dwells on the animals preserved during the Flood and their dispersion over the earth, while chapter 22 deals with Abraham's struggle against Sodom. However, Belus and Ninus are indeed mentioned in chapter 17, but without any connection with the cult of the deceased (Oates, *Basic Writings of Saint Augustine,* 2:338).

[29] This title is also an abbreviation for one of St. Augustine's famous works, *Contra Faustum Manichaeum* (Against Faustus the Manichaeum), which was written ca. 400 and comprises thirty-three books. Here St. Augustine argues with some aspects of Manichaeism, a syncretic religion founded in Persia in the latter half of the third century that incorporated elements of Zoroastrism, Buddhism, Christianity, and Babylonian beliefs and was considered as a Christian heresy. I consulted *Contra Faustum Manichaeum* in *Patrologiae, Cursus Completus,* vol. 42 (Paris: J.-P. Migne Editorem, 1845), pp. 207–518. There might be an inaccurate reference in the manuscript here, for book 17 (pp. 339–344) broaches the issue of Christ's declaration that he came not to destroy the law but to fulfill it. I failed to identify a reference to Belus and Ninus in any of the other books that include at least seventeen chapters.

[30] Wisd. of Sol. 14:15–16.

by the Chaldeans to be a god and named Jove Belus,[31] was not Nimrod but Evachus,[32] who lived three centuries later than [Nimrod] and who started ruling in the year 2242 after the creation of the world; this can be found in the holy scholarly chronology of the College of Siam;[33] so much for the origin of idolatry among the Chaldeans.

I think that approximately at the same time, when idolatry was introduced by Nimrod among the Chaldeans, it was also established in China by one of the first kings of the Hạ [in Vietnamese], or [p. IV] Hia (Xia) [in Chinese] dynasty.[34] Since the Chaldeans fell into idolatry in the third century after the Flood, it is certainly possible to believe that the Chinese also slipped into it at the same time. Indeed, since the Chinese people were living, as they do now, in a part of the world far remote from the places which Noah and his sons inhabited, they, like the Chaldeans, could have heard nothing about the true doctrine and religion. I really think that Đế Nghiêu (Di Yao), Đế Thuấn (Di Shun), and Đại Vũ (Da Yu)[35] were

[31] Jove (Jupiter) was the chief god among the Romans. Belus was the counterpart of Jove in Chaldea. In its article on *Baal* (Belus), Paulus's encyclopedia, perhaps the most comprehensive source on the classics, considers Jove and Belus as parallel ideas of gods among different peoples. See Augustus Fredierichus von Paulus, *Real-Encyclopädie der Classichen Altertumswissenschaft* (Stuttgart: J. B. Metzlerscher Verlag, 1896), 2:2650–2651. Berossus, a third-century Babylonian priest, also mentions in his history that Bel "is to be translated (into Greek) as Zeus." Stanley M. Burstein, "The Babyloniaca of Berossus," in *Sources and Monographs: Sources from the Ancient Near East*, vol. 1, fascicle 5 (Malibu, Calif.: Undena Publications, 1978), p. 15. Zeus, in turn, is a Greek analogue of Jupiter. In Eusebius's *Chronicon* I found that Belus is identified as the first Assyrian king and was, after his death, called Saturn (Eusebius, *Chronicon*, p. b1). Saturn was the Roman god of agriculture.

[32] Evachus is not identified. The most similar name is found in Berossus's Babyloniaca. He mentions a Euechsios "who ruled after the flood over the land of the Chaldeans" (Burstein, "Babyloniaca of Berossus," p. 21).

[33] The College of Siam, organized in the last third of the seventeenth century by the European missionaries in Mahapram near the city of Ayutthaya (central Thailand) with the intention of instructing indigenous people in European sciences, became a major center for the preparation of indigenous clergy. The students included not only Siamese but also indigenous people from Tonkin, Cochinchina (southern Vietnam), the Philippines, and elsewhere. A number of brilliant European theologians taught there until the middle of the eighteenth century. The college played an important role in the evangelization of Southeast Asia. For the history of the College of Siam, see Alain Forest, *Missionaires français au Tonkin et au Siam (XVI–XVIII siècles)* (Paris: L'Harmattan, 1998), vol. 1, *Histoires du Siam*. I could not locate the chronology to which Adriano di St. Thecla refers. Most of the documents from this college have been lost.

[34] The dates traditionally assigned to this dynasty are 2207–1766 B.C.E. However, this dynasty's very existence is disputable. Traditional Chinese historiography did not question the historical reality of this dynasty and its predecessors. There are chapters on this dynasty in the *Shujing* (Book of History) and the *Shiji* (Historical Records), as well as in many other Chinese historiographical works. In the twentieth century, however, a number of Chinese and non-Chinese historians have questioned the historicity of the Hạ (Xia) dynasty. For a discussion of this, see Sarah Allan, "The Myth of the Xia Dynasty," *Journal of the Royal Asiatic Society*, no. 2 (1984): 242–256.

[35] According to tradition, Nghiêu (Yao, r. 2365–2356 B.C.E.) and Thuấn (Shun, r. 2255–2205 B.C.E.) were the last of five legendary Chinese emperors, considered as paragons of virtue, righteousness, and wisdom by Confucian scholars. Yao was praised for passing his throne not to his son but to a poor, ordinary man named Shun, who proved himself an obedient and dutiful son to his own parents, despite the fact that they treated him cruelly and even tried to kill him. After being chosen as a husband for Yao's two daughters, Shun demonstrated his ability to live in harmony with them, which confirmed to Yao the rightness of his choice. During Shun's reign, Vũ (Yu) was the most distinguished official of that time, successfully dealing with a devastating

still free from idolatry. We mention them as the first Chinese kings in our preface to the Chinese chronology, where we claim that only Đế Nghiêu, or in Chinese Ty Yao, could have been the founder of the Chinese nation. This first king had the knowledge of the true God, just as did all other sons and descendants of Noah when the Lord dispersed them over the earth at the beginning of the second century after the Flood, when there was only one nation and one language, when they started building a tower {Gen. 11},[36] and, accordingly, they had one religion, taught by Noah and his sons. We must believe that this king passed on this knowledge of God to his relatives [subjects] and kept it during his lifetime, since for his outstanding righteousness this king is distinguished by the Chinese to be among the Thánh Đế, or in Chinese the Xing Ty (Shengdi, Saintly or Sage Emperors). Among them is also honored Đế Thuấn, or Ty Xun (Di Shun), while his successor Đại Vũ is reckoned for his great virtue among the Thánh Vương, or in Chinese the Xing Vuong (Shengwang, saintly or sage king or prince), and they are strongly believed to have kept to the knowledge of God, which had already been given them by Đế Nghiêu. These two first kings were ruling in the second century after the Flood, and the third king, Đại Vũ, was ruling at the beginning of the third century, as we have shown in the aforementioned preface. This time antedates the rule over the Babylonians by Nimrod, who, according to several chronologists, started to reign after the first half of the third century after the Flood, and who was the first to introduce idolatry, as already said. Hence, according to the *Chinese History*,[37] these kings appear to have learned and worshipped the true God, [for] it is said there that Đế Thuấn sacrificed to Thượng Đế (Shangdi), that is, to the Supreme King.[38] And these kings happened to take this name to indicate God; but later

---

flood that was then affecting China. For his success he was called Tamer of the Flood. Shun passed on the throne to him, bypassing his own children. Yu reigned from 2205 to 2197 B.C.E., and, in addition to earning respect for his virtue and wisdom, became known as one who gained an upper hand over the Great Flood. Yu's death marks the beginning of hereditary rule in China. People rejected Yu's designated successor and instead proclaimed Yu's son the emperor, creating the first imperial dynasty in Chinese history, the above-mentioned Hạ (Xia).

[36] Gen. 11:1–4.

[37] It is not clear what *Chinese History* Adriano di St.Thecla refers to. I could find no Chinese history book covering a span of time from the legendary period to the sixteenth century that includes all the citations adduced by the author and ascribed by him to this book.

[38] Or Lord on High, Creator. The term "Thượng Đế" (Shangdi) initially designated the main spirit of the Shang dynasty (ca. 1750–1050 B.C.E.), "who ruled the other world just as the Shang king ruled the earthly one, and is analogous to Yu Huang Ta Ti [Yuhuang Dadi, the Jade Emperor] in modern folk religion. He 'ordered' *(ling)* the natural phenomenon—rain, thunder, clouds, and his 'messenger' *(shi)* the wind—and he 'sent down' *(chiang [jiang])* drought to either bring favor to or curse the world below." Sarah Allan, "Shang Foundations of Modern Chinese Folk Religion," in *Legend, Lore, and Religion in China: Essays in Honor of Wolfram Eberhard on His Seventieth Birthday*, ed. Sarah Allan and Alvin P. Cohen (San Francisco: Chinese Materials Center, 1979), p. 8. In the worldview of the people living during the Shang dynasty, Shangdi was not only the highest god but also their forefather and protector.

Adriano di St. Thecla consistently translates Thượng Đế (Shangdi) as "Supreme King," not "Supreme Emperor," as might be expected for the word *đế* (*di*, emperor). This translation might demonstrate his refusal to assign *đế* the highest dignity, despite the fact that he definitely understood the difference between *đế* (*di*, "emperor") and *vương* (*wang*, "king"). (See article 2 of the chapter on the spirits, where he notes that the former title expresses more dignity than the latter.) Possibly for the same reason, the author also calls Ngọc Hoàng (Yuhuang), the highest deity of popular Daoism, the "Jade King," not the "Jade Emperor," despite the fact that his title incorporates the word *hoàng* (*huang*, emperor). Apart from this, Adriano di St. Thecla's

Chinese, when the knowledge of the true God was forgotten, assigned this name to Heaven, or to its power. However, it is indeed mentioned in the *Chinese History*, that Đế Thuấn sacrificed not only to the Supreme King but also to the Sun, the Moon, [p. V] the stars, mountains, streams, and to others,[39] and also that Đại Vũ offered exquisite food to spirits, and even that he sacrificed to his deceased father, Cổn (Gun),[40] and to the king Đế Cốc, or in Chinese Ty Ko (Di Ku);[41] it is clear from what is said above that these kings practiced a cult of the creations [of God]. It must be noted that these [rituals] were wrongly ascribed to these kings by the Chinese, so that their mistakes [i.e., those of the Chinese] would certainly have been corroborated by the example of the first kings [who were] distinguished with so ancient a righteousness and authority. On that account, they [the Chinese] say in their *History* that Hoàng Đế (Huang Di),[42] who lived prior to the three kings mentioned above, built a temple to worship the Supreme King and all the spirits. This king must certainly be excluded from the real Chinese chronology, since he lived before the universal Flood.[43] [For information] on him see our preface to the *Chinese Chronology*. Therefore, the three aforementioned—Đế Nghiêu, Đế Thuấn, and Đại Vũ—must be believed to have known and worshipped the true God, and to have been free from any idolatry. Not long afterward their successors were gradually forgetting their legacy and their example, and they fell into idolatry together with the nation, approximately at the same time that Nimrod introduced

discrimination in applying the Latin *Rex* or *Imperator* to different historical Chinese emperors appears to be unsystematic.

[39] *The Shoo King;* James Legge, trans., *The Chinese Classics* (reprint, Taipei: SMC Publishing, 1991), 3:33–34. This information was later cited in chapter 28 of Sima Qian's book *Shiji* (Historical Records); see Burton Watson, trans., *Records of the Grand Historian of China* (New York: Columbia University Press, 1961), 2:14.

[40] Cổn (Gun) is mentioned in the *Shujing* (Book of History) in the sections titled "Documents of Tang" and "Documents of Yu." He preceded his son, Đại Vũ (Da Yu), in the position of minister of works, attempting to cope with the flood, but since his actions in this regard turned out to be a complete failure, Gun was banished from the court and held a prisoner until his death on Mount Yu. Legge, trans., *The Shoo King*, in *Chinese Classics*, 3:25, 39–40. Furthermore, we find a number of different legends on the birth of Da Yu that assign a very important role to his father, Gun. One of these legends, for example, says that Gun, while being in charge of controlling the flood, stole from heaven some magical object in hopes that it would help him in his task. The Supreme Celestial King was angered by this theft and punished Gun with death. Gun's body, however, was miraculously preserved, and after three years it was split open and Da Yu appeared from it.

[41] Đế Cốc (Di Gu) seems to be a mistake, and the intended reference is to the emperor Đế Khốc (Di Ku), a legendary predecessor of Yao, Shun, and Yu, who ostensibly ruled from 2435 to 2365 B.C.E. Adriano di St. Thecla consistently uses Cốc instead of Khốc throughout the manuscript.

[42] The Yellow Emperor—another legendary Chinese emperor and predecessor of emperors Nghiêu (Yao) and Thuấn (Shun)—allegedly ruled between 2697 and 2597 B.C.E. Upset by death among his people, the Yellow Emperor, along with his associates, was able, it was said, to obtain a recipe for prolonging the span of human life. He is, as well, credited for inaugurating Chinese civilization.

[43] Here Adriano di St. Thecla is clearly using the dating of the Flood according to the Vulgate (2349 B.C.E.). In accordance with the dating of the *Septuagint* (2957 B.C.E.), Hoàng Đế (Huang Di), as well as his two legendary predecessors Phục Hi (Fu Xi) and Thần Nông (Shen Nong), lived after the Flood. In accordance with the dating in the Jewish tradition (2104 B.C.E.), the time of reign of emperors Nghiêu (Yao), Thuấn (Shun), and even Đại Vũ (Da Yu), in the twenty-fourth to the twenty-third centuries B.C.E., would also fall into the period prior to the Flood, and the first emperor governing after it would be Shao Kang (r. 2079–2057 B.C.E.).

idolatry among the Chaldeans, as has been said. All these testimonies of the *Chinese History* about the earliest kings practicing the cult of Heaven, Earth, the Sun, the Moon, the stars, streams, and mountains, and also the cult of the deceased, prove only that this idolatrous cult is perhaps the oldest in China and that it was exercised by the first kings who followed the three aforementioned kings or emperors distinguished by their virtue; however, these [testimonies] cannot be applied toward these three [kings], as the arguments given above irrefutably prove.[44]

Thus, Chinese idolatry is very ancient, and it has continued to this day; however, it successively accepted new idols and new superstitions; for that reason numerous sects were brought into [China] and made known [there]. There are three main sects from which the rest originated: namely, the sect of Literati, the most powerful [one], which preserves the primary idolatry by worshipping Heaven and Earth, stars, mountains, streams, and other [objects], as well as the deceased; the sect of Magicians, which engages itself in magic mostly for the purpose of healing the weak; and the sect of worshippers of Phật, or in Chinese Phoe (Fo, Buddha), which is younger than the two others and is generally accepted among people. These three sects flourish also in the kingdom of the Annamites,[45] which, ever since it was subject [p. VI] to Chinese authority, has followed the habits and rites of the Chinese.[46] In this treatise we will talk mostly about these three sects, which are also mentioned in the Chinese books, in the order set for them by King Chu Cao Tổ (Zhou Gaozu), who ruled during the reign of the Trần (Chen) dynasty[47]; [it is said] of him [King Chu Cao Tổ] in the *History:* "Chu Cao Tổ định tam giáo tiên hậu, dĩ Nho vi tiên, Đạo vi thứ, Thích vi hậu,"[48] that is, "King Cao Tổ (Gaozu)

[44] This passage reflects Adriano di St. Thecla's aspiration to uncover in each nation a faith in one God, which initially existed but was later diluted by idolatry. I find his argument unpersuasive since he does not really present any data to support his analysis. Furthermore, there seem to be no reliable sources on the historicity of the three emperors he discusses, let alone their beliefs.

[45] The Annamites are the people inhabiting the territory of Annam. *An Nam* (Annan in Chinese) means "Pacified South." This title was originally applied to the territory of modern northern Vietnam and a part of central Vietnam when it became a frontier province of the Tang Empire (618–907) in the seventh century. Previously, this region was called Giao Châu (Giaozhou, Giao province). When the Europeans appeared in Vietnam in the seventeenth century, they used the term *Annamites* as a generic term for the inhabitants of Vietnam. After the French colonization of Vietnam in the second half of the nineteenth century the central part of Vietnam was called Annam.

[46] Vietnam was governed by Chinese imperial officials from 111 B.C.E. to 939 C.E., according to the conventional scheme of dating in Vietnamese historiography. During this period, Han and Tang culture spread into Vietnam, and many political, social, and religious institutions were established in Vietnam following the Chinese pattern.

[47] The Trần (Chen) is a Chinese dynasty (557–89 C.E.) that ruled in southern China during the period of the division of the country between the South and the North (420–589). In the North at that time one of the ruling dynasties was the Northern Chu (Zhou) dynasty (557–89).

[48] 周 高 祖 定 三 教 前 後 以 儒 為 前 道 為 次 釋 為 後 . This is reminiscent of a similar phrase found in *Beishi* (History of the Northern Dynasties). It is attributed to Emperor Chu Vũ Đế (Zhou Wudi, 561–78), whose complete title there is Zhou Gaozu Wu Huangdi. In the second year of Jiande reign period (572–78), i.e., in the year 573, he assembled scholars of different currents and established the above-mentioned order among Confucianism, Daoism, and Buddhism. See Li Yanshou, *Beishi* (Shanghai: Zhonghua shuju, 193–), vol. 3, chap. 10, p. 6b. The emperor, himself being of a foreign origin, tried to adopt Chinese customs and to enforce them. Thus, he ranked Confucianism (the national traditional

established the order for three sects, he put the sect *Nho* (Ru, Confucianism) first, the sect *Đạo* (Dao, Daoism) in the middle, and the sect Thích (Shi) {Thích Ca} (Shijia)[49] last." We will also talk about other sects that originate from them.

The possibility of writing this treatise was provided by the *Index Historicus* (Historical Index) of the Tonkinese Mission, which our Illustrious Father Ilario di Gesù, bishop of Corycus and vicar apostolic of Eastern Tonkin,[50] compiled for use by his brothers living in this Mission, in which he discussed these three sects following the information that previous missionaries passed on in books transcribed from Chinese and Annamite scripts. It seemed necessary to me to reexamine and to make a new investigation of the sects and to consult the Chinese books, literati, and experts. When it was done, I discovered many contradictions and followed the most trustworthy of the suggested versions, to which I added others. For this we are deeply indebted to the venerable martyr Father Francisco Gil de Federich,[51] whom I consulted when he was captured in the royal city Thái Hà;[52] I also sent him this treatise, which at that time was still sketchy, to examine and to correct; he diligently investigated many [matters], studied [them], and sent to me descriptions of them; he would have added much more had he not accepted a glorious death for Christ. Many other things still remain unexplored, but they are difficult to investigate because the royal ministers are extremely reluctant to be questioned about matters that concern the king; they are afraid that something bad might happen to them in the event of such openness. The aforementioned martyr wrote about this in a letter dated August 6, 1744: "For surely I did not neglect the task given to me; but they created a great difficulty in undertaking an enquiry on the issues concerning the king." To this is added another recent testimony of the Right Reverend Administrator Father Wenceslas Paleczek,[53] who in his reply to me on

ideology) first, followed by Daoism (also originating in China), and then by Buddhism, an alien religion brought from India but acquiring a significant influence in China by this time. The next year, 574, this emperor issued a decree proscribing both Buddhism and Daoism.

[49] This is an abbreviation of the name of Buddha Sakyamuni (Thích Ca Mâu Ni in Vietnamese, Shijiamouni in Chinese). Thus, the allusion is to Buddhism.

[50] Ilario Costa di Gesù (1696–1754) was an Italian Augustinian from the same Order of the Discalced Augustinians as Adriano di St. Thecla. He arrived in Tonkin in 1723. In 1735 he was appointed bishop of Corycus and coadjutor of the vicar apostolic of Eastern Tonkin by Father Tommaso Bottari, whom he succeeded in 1737. In 1737 Ilario di Gesù was appointed apostolic legate to Cochinchina. On March 31, 1754, he died in Tonkin. Pietro Scalia, "Gli Agostiniani Scalzi in Oriente," *Presenza Agostiniana* 126, 3-5 (1997): 35. See the translator's introduction.

As for Ilario di Gesù's title, bishop of Corycus, Adriano di St. Thecla gives it in a concise form. His full title was bishop of Corycus of Cilicia (ibid., p. 35). Corycus was a coastal town in Cilicia, an ancient district of Asia Minor, located in modern Turkey. In the first century C.E. it became a Roman province and was one of the strongholds of Christianity. The Catholic Church used to confer appointments to ancient defunct ecclesiastical jurisdictions on priests of high rank.

[51] Francisco Gil de Federich (1702–45) was a Spanish Dominican who arrived in Tonkin in 1735. Two years later he was imprisoned as a result of religious persecutions and was decapitated in 1745. See the translator's introduction.

[52] This Vietnamese name is difficult to read in the manuscript but appears to be Thái Hà, now a part of Hà Nội, but in the eighteenth century it was actually a place outside of the royal city in Hà Đông Province.

[53] Wenceslas Paleczek was a Jesuit from Bohemia. He came to Tonkin in 1738 and became chief of the Jesuit mission in 1746; he stayed in Tonkin until 1755. André Marillier, *Nos pères dans la foi. Notes sur le clergé catholique du Tonkin de 1666 à 1765* (Paris: Eglises d'Asie, 1995), 2:104.

the twentieth of May of this year, 1750, said the following about the *Tế Kỳ Đạo* (*Ji qidao*, sacrifice to the leader's banner) ceremony: "Having delivered the report on [p. VII] the *Tế Kỳ Đạo* {ceremony}, I came to a certain mandarin of the military service who censured it and who told military officials that it was not known to all, but only to those who were privy [to it], as he himself [was]. He shared [a description of the ceremony] with me, requesting to burn it after it is transcribed into European characters, because the promulgation [of this ceremony] was prohibited under the penalty of decapitation." I experienced another difficulty because of the civil war, which was disturbing the kingdom for more than ten years.[54] It was a wrong and inappropriate time to make such inquires among the ministers and among literati, who lost a lot of [their] books at that time.

I wrote the following *Opusculum* in a sketchy form before [I wrote] the *Chronologia Sinensis et Tunkinensis* (Chinese and Tonkinese Chronology), and this year I resumed, fixed, and completed [the writing], interrupted mostly because of [the chronologies]; the study combined with [my work on] each chronology[55] was a great advantage for its [*Opusculum*'s] completion. In the meantime the illustrious D. of Core,[56] mentioned above, wrote an admirable work on Annamites, *Dị đoan chi giáo (Yiduan zhijiao,* Doctrine of Superstitions),[57] against oblique and aberrant doctrines, in which especially the doctrine of the sect of Phật was explained and refuted; many [facts] from that [book] I incorporated into our *Opusculum*. Already long ago this same person, who is foremost among all the learned, wrote another very scholarly book in Annamite script, titling it *Đại học chi Đạo (Daxue zhidao)*,[58] that is, the Doctrine of Great Learning. In it, by using their books, he endeavored to move the literati toward the knowledge of God, which many who read this book grasped.

The Christian religion is added to the three above-mentioned sects, since it was preached in this kingdom of the Annamites, had an extensive development, and also suffered numerous persecutions. It is certainly reasonable and consistent for idolatry, which came from these three sects, to form an opposition to the true religion. In this work I also used the *Index Historicus* of our Illustrious D. of Core, the last part of which narrates the missionaries and their deeds in the Tonkinese mission. I reverently submit this *Opusculum* to my superiors and to my missionary friends staying in this mission; I think that it will be useful for them in the form it now has. I completed it in September of the year of Christ 1750, Canh Ngũ[59] in

---

[54] The author is referring to the major rebellions that paralyzed northern Vietnam in the early to mid-eighteenth century. It is interesting that he calls them a "civil war"; Vietnamese historians called them rebellions, but in fact they were very much like a civil war between the provinces of the Hồng River plain and the southern provinces of Thanh Hóa and Nghệ Tĩnh where the Trịnh recruited their soldiers.

[55] The *Chinese and Tonkinese Chronology* was apparently one item incorporating two separate works, a Chinese chronology and a Tonkinese chronology.

[56] The *D.* stands for "Dominus," an honorific preceding a prelate's name.

[57] The work has not been located.

[58] This work has not yet been found.

[59] Years in Chinese and Vietnamese tradition were designated not by numbers but by a combination of ten heavenly stems and twelve earthly branches. With the sixty possible variations, each name reappears once every sixty years, and these combinations of the heavenly stems and earthly branches served as practically the only form of dating, sometimes in conjunction with a reign title of a ruling emperor, as is the case in this manuscript, which

Annamite, in the eleventh year of [the reign title] Cảnh Hưng (Jingxing)[60] of King Lê.[61]

I am Father Adriano di Santa Thecla, discalced hermit of the Order of [p. VIII] our Holy Father Augustine, an apostolic missionary in the Tonkinese Kingdom.

---

considerably alleviates the difficulty of determining the exact date. Here the name of the year should be Canh Ngọ (gengwu) in modern Vietnamese orthography, denoting the year of a horse. *Ngọ (wu)*—the name of the seventh of the twelve earthly branches and the sign of a horse as a component for designating hours, days, and years—appears several times in the manuscript spelled *ngũ*, and only once (in the chapter on Buddhism) does it appear in its modern spelling, *ngọ*. At the present time, the Vietnamese use only *ngọ* and do not recognize this word if pronounced or spelled *ngũ*. However, the dictionary compiled by Huình Tịnh Paulus Của and published in 1895 records two variant pronunciations for the seventh earthly branch, *ngọ* and *ngũ*. See Huình Tịnh Paulus Của, *Đại Nam Quấc Âm Tự Vị* (A Dictionary of Characters with the National Pronunciation of Great Nam) (reprint, Ho Chi Minh City: Nhà Xuất Bản Trẻ, 1998), pp. 709, 721. On the other hand, Alexandre de Rhodes's dictionary, written in the seventeenth century, a hundred years before Adriano di St. Thecla's time, recorded only *ngọ*. See Alexandre de Rhodes, *Từ Điển Annam-Lusitan-Latinh* (Annamite-Lusitanian [Portuguese]-Latin Dictionary), trans. Thanh Lãng, Hoàng Xuân Việt, and Đỗ Quang Chính (reprint, Hanoi: Nhà Xuất Bản Khoa Học Xã Hội, 1991), col. 530. This might be either because de Rhodes's dictionary, although an invaluable source of information, is rather concise or because the variant pronunciation *ngũ* appeared some time during the 250 years between the publications of the two dictionaries, only to sink into oblivion in the twentieth century.

[60] Beginning from the second century B.C.E., the emperors of the Chinese Han dynasty (206 B.C.E.–220 C.E.) started the tradition of glorifying and identifying their reigns by giving them specific titles. For example, the title Cảnh Hưng (Jingxing) means "luminous and flourishing." A reign could have more than one title. Subsequently, this tradition was adopted among the Vietnamese. The first Vietnamese king to use a reign title was Lý Bôn (r. 544–47), who established his own court separate from that of China. His reign title, Thiên Đức (Tiande), is translated as "Heavenly Virtue." His separate court as well as his proclamation of an imperial reign title clearly affirmed his independence from the Chinese empire. After Lý Bôn was defeated in 547, the tradition of proclaiming reign titles appeared again at the end of the tenth century with the Vietnamese king Đinh Bộ Linh (r. 968–79). After him, and until the end of the monarchy in Vietnam in 1945, each king had a reign title. In both countries it became a custom to identify a certain point of time using the ordinal number of the year in a reign title of the ruling emperor. In this text I will not translate reign titles into English. The period of the Cảnh Hưng (Jingxing) reign title covered the years 1740–87.

[61] The reign of King Lê Hiển Tông lasted from 1740 to 1786.

CHAPTER ONE

ON THE SECT OF THE LITERATI

[p. 1]

Article 1: On Confucius, the Founder of This Sect

The Sect of Literati, called *Ju* or *Jo* (*Ru* or *Ro* in Chinese),[1] in Annamite *Nhu* or *Nho*,[2] plays the leading role in China. The founder of this sect is Confucius, who, however, was not the first to teach his doctrine called *đạo (dao)*,[3] for he received it from [his] forerunners and ancient sages, and brilliantly passed [it down to his disciples]. This man, the most famous teacher of China, was born in Lu kingdom[4] of Xang Tung (Shandong)[5] province, Lỗ San Đông in Annamite, in the twenty-first year of Emperor Cheu Ling Vuang (Zhou Lingwang),[6] Chu Linh Vương in Annamite, in the year 3454 of the world, [the year] 550 before Christ was born.[7] He

[1] "The definition of *ru [nho]* is a hotly contested issue. One of the earliest meanings was something like 'weaklings.' It did not seem like a very good title for the followers of the First Teacher. Whatever the term originally meant, it seems to have designated a whole class of ritual specialists." John H. Berthrong and Evelyn Nagai, *Confucianism. A Short Introduction* (Oxford: Oneworld, 2000), p. 48. Subsequently, this term came to indicate variously the doctrine of Confucius and a broadly educated person.

[2] *Nhu* and *nho* are variant pronunciations in Vietnamese.

[3] The word *đạo (dao)* came into circulation in China during the age of philosophers (the eighth to third centuries B.C.E.). "Originally meaning 'way' or 'road,' it began to be used everywhere by the philosophers to denote the way to do something, or the (right moral) 'Way' or (later) the 'Way' of all nature." David Nivison, "The Classical Philosophical Writings," in *The Cambridge History of Ancient China: From the Origins of Civilization to 221 B.C.*, ed. Michael Loewe and Edward L. Shaughnessy (Cambridge: Cambridge University Press, 1998), pp. 750–751. The Confucian *dao* should be distinguished from that of Daoism.

[4] A small feudal state known for its preservation of the musical and ritual traditions of the ruling Chu (Zhou) dynasty, the traditional dates of which are 1122–255 B.C.E. These dates, however, were contested by Edward L. Shaughnessy, who suggested 1099–771 B.C.E. See Edward L. Shaughnessy, *Sources of Western Zhou History: Inscribed Bronze Vessels* (Berkeley, CA: University of California Press, 1991), pp. 217–287. For the purpose of this translation I will use the traditional dates ascribed to this and other Chinese dynasties, since they correspond to the dates used by Adriano di St. Thecla.

[5] A province on the northern coast of China.

[6] R. 571–544 B.C.E.

[7] The exact date of Confucius's birth has not been established, although 552 or 551 B.C.E. have been mentioned as possible dates. In 1949, H. Dubs, analyzing different sources of Confucius's

lived seventy-three years and died in the forty-first year of Emperor Chu Kính Vương (Zhou Jingwang).[8] He was called by numerous names: first, and most often, he is named Kieu (Qiu) [in Chinese] or Kheo [in Vietnamese],[9] after the name of the mountain where his parents prayed for a son;[10] second, Chung Ny (Zhongni)[11] or Traọng Nơi [in Vietnamese],[12] the literary name given to him; third, Kung Zu (Kongzi)[13] and Khổng Tử [in Vietnamese] by the name of his family; fourth, Fu zu (Fuzi)[14] and Phu Tử [in Vietnamese], with which name [the title of] Master is designated and is descriptively given to Confucius; fifth, and finally, he is called with a conjectured double name Kung fu zu (Kong Fuzi) [in Chinese] and Khổng Phu Tử [in Vietnamese].[15] He is usually mentioned in books under all these names,

---

biography and applying to them his calculations based on the Chinese calendrical system, drew the conclusion that Confucius was born in 552 B.C.E. See Homer H. Dubs, "The Date of Confucius' Birth," *Asia Major*, n.s., 2 (1949): 139–146. However, in later historiography the date of his birth is commonly given as 551 B.C.E. The date mentioned in the manuscript (550) is a minor discrepancy.

[8] R. 519–475 B.C.E. If Adriano di St. Thecla used this dating for the reign of Chu Kính Vương (Zhou Jingwang), then Confucius would have died in 478 B.C.E. His dating must have been slightly different, however, for if Confucius were born 550 B.C.E., then, subtracting seventy-three years, he would have died in 477 or 476 B.C.E. The traditionally accepted date, on which there is no argument in modern scholarship, is 479 B.C.E. "That date is not only found in the *Historical Records*, but also in the very early continuation of the *Spring and Autumn*, a work which is said to have been written by the disciples of Confucius, in order to continue his history down to his death." Dubs, "Date of Confucius' Birth," pp. 139–140.

[9] *Kheo* is a vernacular pronunciation of the character 丘, which in Sino-Vietnamese is read as *Khâu*, meaning "a hillock or a mound"; *Khâu*, not *Kheo*, is normally used for the personal name of Confucius.

[10] The legend says that Confucius's mother did not have children and realized that her husband was growing old, so she decided to make a pilgrimage to the Mountain Niqiu. Upon her return from the pilgrimage, she became pregnant and delivered a son. "When Confucius was born, it was noticed that the top of his head was concave and that the circumference of the vertex formed an amphitheater, like the mountain Ni-k'ieou-chan [Niqiu san]." Henri Doré, *Recherches sur les superstitions en Chine*, vol. 13 (Shanghai: Imprimerie deT'ou-sè-wè, 1918), *Popularisation du Confucéisme, du Bouddhisme et du Taoïsme en Chine*, p. 10. This peculiarity, though without connection to Niqiu Mountain, was mentioned already in the *Shiji* (Historical Records) of Sima Qian, the first general history of China, written between the end of the second and beginning of the first century B.C.E., where it is also said that because of this resemblance the boy was given the name Qiu. Edouard Chavannes, trans. *Les memoires historiques de Se-Ma Ts'ien* (Leiden: E. J. Brill, 1967), 5:290. It is also mentioned in a number of other ancient texts, among which is *Kongzi jiayu* (Discourses of the Confucian School).

[11] The first word means "the second in order of birth," for Confucius was the second son to his father (the first was by a concubine); the second word designates a mountain, implying the mountain after which Confucius was named.

[12] "Traọng" is written *Trọng* in modern Vietnamese spelling (see more on the changes in the spelling of this word in the translator's introduction); "Nơi" is a vernacular pronunciation of the Sino-Vietnamese *Ni*.

[13] Khổng (Kong) is the family name of Confucius. Tử (Zi) has several meanings. One of them is "son"; another is "gentleman, master." Describing this name of Confucius as a family name, Adriano di St. Thecla seems here to use the first meaning, "son," as if it were a term of kinship; he leaves the other, more common meaning, "gentleman, master," for the next examples.

[14] The first word means "sage"; the second, "master," an honorific suffix added to the names of many philosophers. Together they produce a title of respect often applied to Confucius.

[15] Khổng Phu Tử (Kong Fuzi)—the Master or the Sage Kong. The "Fuzi" added to his surname is an honorific equivalent to saying "the Master Philosopher Kong." "This form, K'ung Fu-tzu

except for the first, which literati omit for the sake of honor, since the first name given him by his parents is considered shameful in Chinese.[16] He produced six books of admirable works [containing] his wisdom, called *Lo King* (*Liujing*, Six Books)[17] or *Lục Kinh* [in Vietnamese], which he composed when already an old man, drawing upon and editing the books of his literate forerunners. The titles of his books [p. 2] in Annamite are *Thư Kinh* (*Shujing*, Book of History), *Thi Kinh* (*Shijing*, Book of Odes), *Dịch Kinh* (*Yijing*, Book of Changes), *Lễ Kinh* (*Lijing*, Book of Rites), *Nhạc Kinh* (*Yuejing*, Book of Music), and *Xuân Thu Kinh* (*Chunqiu jing*, Spring and Autumn Annals).[18] The last of these he wrote when he was seventy. In

---

[Kong Fuzi], was Latinized by sixteenth- and seventeenth-century Europeans as Confucius." Frederick W. Mote, *Intellectual Foundations of China* (New York: Alfred A. Knopf, 1971), p. 36. However, according to L. Jensen, this term "Kong Fuzi" did not appear in the Chinese ancient classical texts and became popular only with the advent of the European missionaries to China in the sixteenth century, as "the Jesuits felt compelled to confer an incomparable respect upon Kongzi and, for this reason, granted him the superlative honorific 'Kong Fuzi.'" Lionel M. Jensen, *Manufacturing Confucianism; Chinese Traditions and Universal Civilization* (Durham, NC: Duke University Press, 1997), p. 86.

[16] The word translated as "shameful" is *indecorum* in Latin. The author's reference to the shamefulness or disgracefulness of Confucius's personal name Khâu (Qiu) might have several explanations. First, it might be that *indecorum* for Adriano di St. Thecla meant "impolite," since Qiu was the name given to Confucius by his parents, and the Chinese would consider it disrespectful for the Master to denote him with the name that only his closest relatives would use. A second explanation might lie in the possibility presented by L. Jensen on the basis of some Chinese texts, which have their roots in popular lore, that Confucius's mother was impregnated by a monk on the mountain where she came to pray for a son. For example, the text *Yan Kong tu* (Explanatory Kong Chart) reads: "Kongzi's mother Zheng Zai wandered onto the slope of a large mound and fell asleep. She dreamt of the Black Lord [one of the Five Celestial Emperors] whose envoy invited her to go to the marsh on the *yisi* day to copulate. He said to her: 'You will give birth in the center of a hollow mulberry.' After she awoke she felt pregnant and gave birth to the mound in the center of a hollow mulberry. For this reason he was called dark sage; when he was born the top of his head [looked like] *niqiu* a dirt mound, thus [he was given] the name." Cited in Lionel Jensen, "The Wise Man of the Wilds," *Early China* 20 (1995): 428. Even though here a celestial birth is ascribed to Confucius, it could be that the Chinese did not want to be reminded of the story about the sage's mother and her extramarital relation. Third, perhaps Adriano di St. Thecla implies here that the Chinese restrained themselves from using the name Qiu for Confucius because of the phonetic homonymy of that name with the word *qiu* "the male organ." See R. H. Mathews, *Chinese-English Dictionary* (reprint, Cambridge, MA: Harvard University Press, 2000), p.175 no. 1219. Even though these two words are currently pronounced with different tones (the first with the first tone and the second with the second tone), it is possible that in ancient times they were pronounced identically, since the first and the second tones might derive from the same tone. Another theory is that this word, associated with a mound, is also associated with the burial and worshipping of ancestors, and this could be a reason to avoid it. The last possibility is that Adriano di St. Thecla misunderstood the explanation he received from his informants.

[17] The present canon of Confucian classics is considered to include only five books, and that is why it is called *Wujing (Ngũ Kinh)*—the Five Classics. These Five Classics constitute the basis of a Confucian education. In 124 B.C.E., during the Han dynasty, they constituted the core curriculum for study at the state universities, and later a meticulous knowledge of the Five Classics and the ability to interpret them became a major requirement for passing the official examinations to obtain a government post in China and in Vietnam, as well as in Korea and Japan. The sixth book, *Nhạc Kinh* (*Yuejing*, Book of Music), perished.

[18] Most of the texts incorporated into the *Thư Kinh* (*Shujing*, Book of History) are usually considered to have been written around the fourth century B.C.E. or earlier. This book narrates the deeds of the most illustrious rulers of ancient China. Some scholars question Confucius's authorship of this book.

Thư Kinh the deeds of the Chinese kings are collected, beginning with Đế Nghiêu [in Vietnamese] or Ty Yao (Di Yao) [in Chinese]; and also the narration about the deeds of the kings in Lỗ kingdom;[19] in *Xuân Thu Kinh* and also in *Thi Kinh,* which is the *Book of Odes,* the Chinese kings are mentioned. In *Dịch Kinh,* figures of lines,

---

The *Book of Odes,* or, as it is also called, the *Book of Poetry,* is the first anthology of Chinese poetry. It was ascribed to Confucius, but scholars contest his part in it. "The *Historical Records* states that the *Book of Poetry* had previously consisted of 3,000 pieces, but that Confucius reduced them to 305, selecting the best. We must regard this statement with caution, for the *Historical Records* is not always reliable concerning Confucius. Scholars ancient and modern have questioned the statement that Confucius reduced the size of the *Book of Poetry,* pointing out that very few poems outside of this corpus are quoted in early literature. . . . Moreover, he [Confucius] quotes one poem that is not in our *Book of Poetry* and twice condemns (once calling them licentious) a whole group of verses that is included: this is strange if he edited the book. . . . This may mean that he made some sort of rearrangement of the pieces, but that is probably the most that he did to the *Poetry.*" H. G. Creel, *Confucius: The Man and the Myth* (London: Routledge and Kegan Paul, 1951), pp. 112–113.

The *Book of Changes* was originally used for divination; it presents sixty-four hexagrams, which will be discussed below. These hexagrams were used by the Chinese to explain and foretell the events of their daily life. Furthermore, the *Book of Changes* exerted a great influence on Chinese philosophical thought. The book became a source for interpreting the universe as having been created from constant cosmic changes, and it offered an example of harmony that people should emulate. But it caused numerous arguments among scholars, who held that the very idea of divination was alien to Confucius and that he could not have recognized it as part of his teaching. In the course of time, however, the arguments have faded away and the *Book of Changes* has gained a firm place among the Five Classics. Its authorship will be discussed below.

Lễ Kinh (Lijing) is the original title of the *Lễ Kí (Liji,* Record of Rites). It is believed to have been compiled by Confucius, whose authorship is ascertained in the *Shiji* (Historical Records). Later, in the first century C.E., it was apparently significantly changed by other scholars and, consequently, the word *ji* (record, collection) was substituted for the word *jing* (sacred book). This change might be explained by the intention of scholars to distance this re-edited work from other, less edited, books of Confucius, which incorporate in their titles the word *jing.* Consequently, the title of this book in the Five Classics is known as *Liji.* The *Record of Rites* is a manual regulating the rituals, sacrifices, education, and behavior of people. "There seems, however, to be no early evidence to justify the statement of the *Historical Records* that Confucius 'put in order' the *li,* if by this it is meant that he either wrote or edited a book on the subject." Creel, *Confucius,* p. 115. There is a theory that the *Liji* was compiled at the end of the last century B.C.E.; see Ch'u Chai and Winberg Chai, eds. and trans., *The Sacred Books of Confucius and Other Confucian Classics* (New Hyde Park, NY: University Books, 1965), p. 337. Adriano di St. Thecla calls the book *Lễ Kinh (Lijing)* in the manuscript. I will call it *Lễ Kí (Liji)—Record of Rites.*

The *Book of Music,* "with its harmonizing influence," as the great Taoist philosopher Zhuangzi (ca. 369–ca. 289 B.C.E.) characterized it in his book *Zhuangzi,* was once a part of the Confucian canon. Herbert A. Giles, trans., *Chuang Tzu: Taoist Philosopher and Chinese Mystic* (reprint, London: George Allen and Unwin, 1961), p. 314.

The *Spring and Autumn Annals* is the first Chinese chronological history, covering the reign of twelve rulers of Lỗ (Lu) kingdom (the native place of Confucius), from 722 B.C.E. to the last years of Confucius's life. It is usually called simply *Xuân Thu* (*Chungqiu,* Spring and Autumn), an abbreviation of the original title *Spring, Summer, Autumn, and Winter,* which was given because events used to be dated not only by the year they took place but also by the season. This work, ascribed to Confucius, has also not escaped questions about its authorship.

[19] The semicolon here is a mistake because it separates the subject "the narration about the deeds of the kings in Lỗ kingdom" from the source where it is depicted. The reference should be to the *Xuân Thu Kinh* (*Chungqiu jing,* the Spring and Autumn Annals), since this book focuses on the rulers of Lỗ (Lu) kingdom.

invented and designated by Emperor Phục Hi (Fu Xi),[20] are explained; there are eight main figures, which have multiplied [to the number] of sixty-four. In *Lễ Kinh*, examples of moral rules are displayed. Judging from the meaning of its title, *Nhạc Kinh*, which has perished, was about music. Confucius did not write other books, or at least knowledge of them has not been preserved. However, his disciples collected his numerous sayings, or replies to .questions, in their books, which are [*Khổng Tử*] *Gia Ngữ* ([*Kongzi*] *Jiayu*, Discourses of [the Confucian] School), *Luận Ngữ* (*Lunyu*, Analects), *Đại Học* (*Daxue*, Great Learning), and *Trung Daong* (*Zhongyong*, Doctrine of the Mean).[21] There were seventy-two of his disciples, and

---

[20] Phục Hi (Fu Xi), a legendary Chinese culture hero and one of the Chinese legendary emperors (traditional dates of reign are 2852–2737) is indeed credited, according to some sources, with the invention of these three-line symbols, on the basis of which the system of hexagrams was developed. No classical historical books confirm this. However, we find a similar statement in the *Yijing* (Book of Changes), where it is said: "When Fu Xi ruled the world in early antiquity, he looked up and contemplated the images [*xiang*] in Heaven, and looked downward to contemplate the patterns [*fa*] on Earth. He contemplated the markings of birds and beasts and their adaptations to the various areas. He proceeded directly from himself and indirectly from objects. Thus he invented the eight trigrams in order to enter into communication with the virtuous power of the spiritual intelligence [*shenming*] and to classify the conditions of all things." Richard J. Smith, *Fortune-Tellers and Philosophers: Divination in Traditional Chinese Society* (Boulder, CO: Westview Press, 1991), p. 13. "Other myths credit either Fu Xi, his successor Shen Nong [Thần Nông], or the fully historical King Wen [Văn] with developing a system of sixty-four hexagrams based on the eight trigrams." Ibid. Adriano di St. Thecla discusses this possibility in his chapter on the fortune-tellers, and there I will adduce a very similar account of some other European missionaries on the appearance of trigrams and hexagrams.

[21] The full name of *Gia Ngữ* (*Jiayu*) is *Khổng Tử Gia Ngữ* (*Kongzi jiayu*, Discourses of the Confucian School). The followers of Confucius compiled this book sometime between the third century B.C.E. and the third century C.E. The *Discourses* contains the biography of Confucius and sayings ascribed to him. However, this book can hardly be considered to be a reliable source, since no proven materials on Confucius's life exist, and their absence led to numerous attempts to reconstruct his life, most of which were based on imagination. The *Discourses* is, apparently, one of these attempts.

The *Analects*, the traditional English translation of *Luận Ngữ* (*Lunyu*), is an unsystematic collection of sayings, attributed to Confucius, which covers all the basic concepts of his doctrine. They were collected and written down by Confucius's disciples, especially by Zengzi or Zeng Shen (ca. 505–ca. 435 B.C.E.), mentioned by the author later in the manuscript.

The *Great Learning* is generally attributed to the aforementioned Zengzi. "Modern scholars, however, discredit his share in the book because of several passages which are definitely of a much later origin. But, whoever its author may be, the book represents the genuine interpretation of the Confucian political and ethical views." Chai and Chai, *Sacred Books of Confucius*, p. 293. At first, this text constituted a part of the *Record of Rites*, but in the twelfth century Zhu Xi published it as a separate book, constituting the *Four Classics*. The *Great Learning* concentrates on the concept of good governors and good government and on the measures that should be undertaken to achieve harmony between a ruler and his subjects. It emphasizes the necessity of personal development and the nurturing of virtues, which are the consequences of wisdom, gained by learning.

The *Doctrine of the Mean*, like the *Great Learning*, was a part of the *Record of Rites*. (In the spelling of Vietnamese used in this manuscript, *ao* is equivalent to *o* in the spelling of modern Vietnamese, so today this title appears as *Trung Dong*.) The authorship is attributed to Zi Si (483–402 B.C.E.), a grandson of Confucius. The book presents a Confucian doctrine of moderation, objectivity, honesty, and freedom from bias and prejudice—distinctive attributes of a perfect man—and avoidance of both great grief and great joy as extremes that lead a person away from a balanced life.

they are enumerated by name in the book *Gia Ngữ*,[22] which also contains an epitome of Confucius's life. It becomes clear from these books that Confucius was gifted with talent, a sharp genius, and a mighty mind, to which long experience of things was added, and that he was especially eminent in the knowledge of ethics and politics. But also from his books it appears very pitiable that he did not know the true God; following pagan superstition together with the delusion of his nation, he eloquently taught the cult of Heaven and Earth, stars, mountains, and other objects, as well as the cult of the dead; he also understood Heaven under the name of the Supreme King, whose cult he greatly promoted, as his testimonies, presented below, clearly show.

Confucius was a contemporary of Pythagoras—the founder of an Italian sect among the Greeks—who, originating from Samos,[23] taught philosophy to a large concourse of listeners in Croton,[24] near Tarentum, in about the year 3515 of the world, when Confucius was sixty.[25] They both had the same moderation of soul and the same modesty. Pythagoras wanted to be called not a *sophon*, that is, a sage, but a *philosophon*, that is, a lover of wisdom. From this the word "philosopher" appeared. Once, Confucius was asked {as they say, but nowhere in his books is it possible to find this} whether he was *thánh*, in Chinese *Xing (sheng)*,[26] that is, "wise"; he replied that he knew a lot, but would not dare to call himself wise.[27]

[22] Wang Su, *Kongzi jiayu* (Discourses of the Confucian School) (Shanghai: Zhonghua shuju, 193–?), vol. 2, chap. 9.

[23] A Greek island in the Aegean Sea.

[24] A port city in southern Italy. Pythagoras (580–500 B.C.E.), a great Greek philosopher and mathematician, left his native Samos, allegedly to escape the tyranny of the dictator Polykrates. He first traveled to Egypt and stayed there for quite a long time, but in the end he settled down in Croton, founded on the shores of the Gulf of Tarentum (Taranto) in the eighth century B.C.E. by Achean Greeks. There he established his school among the Greeks, and there he developed and taught his doctrine based on the significance of numbers in the real world, which, according to him, was mathematical in nature. He used his theory of numbers for analysis not only of worldly affairs, but music as well. His views became extremely influential. However, eventually Pythagoras and his followers were expelled from Croton, and he died in Metapontum, a Greek city in Italy. See Peter Gorman, *Pythagoras: A Life* (London: Routledge and Kegan Paul, 1979).

[25] This figure is slightly inaccurate. According to conventional reckoning, Confucius turned sixty years old in 490 B.C.E. and Pythagoras had already died around 500 B.C.E.; the school of Pythagoras flourished in Croton in the 530s B.C.E.

[26] The character pronounced *thánh (sheng)* means also "holy, sacred, reverend, divine"; but applied to Confucius or some other personalities known for their wisdom, it is understood and translated as "sage."

[27] We might even extend Adriano di St. Thecla's parallel between Confucius and Pythagoras. Both doctrines are based on strict rules and regulations. The Pythagorian doctrine has at its center mathematics, and Pythagoras applied his theory of numbers to worldly affairs and music. On the other hand, Confucius assigned a significant role to human relations, and music in his philosophy was an instrument of, or a pattern for, governing relationships among people. The doctrines of both Pythagoras and Confucius were not recognized in their native places, and both of them left their homeland and taught their doctrines elsewhere. Both created doctrines of their own, and in both cases their doctrines became known to us mostly through the writings of others. Pythagoras wrote nothing, or, at least, nothing of his writings is known. His doctrine became known to us thanks to the writing of another Greek philosopher, Aristotle (384–322 B.C.E.). Confucius's doctrine was mainly reflected in the *Lunyu* (Analects) and written down by his disciples. The doctrines of both philosophers have developed through propagation by disciples and followers, which has made it difficult to distinguish between original doctrines

[p. 3] Confucius's doctrine indeed did not grow strong immediately after his death, for a little bit later the doctrine of Dương Chu (Yang Zhu)[28] and Mạc Địch (Mo Di)[29] was made known and spread, and it became an obstacle to the doctrine of Confucius, so that the latter would not develop, as testified by Mạnh Tử (Mengzi)[30] in his book, tractate three, where he refutes both doctrines with the following words: Dương Mạc chi đạo bất tức, Khổng Tử chi Đạo bất trứ;[31] that is: If the doctrine of Dương Chu and Mạc Địch were not diminished, the doctrine of Confucius could not shine.[32] Mạnh Tử was writing in the third century after

---

and later developments. Contrary to Confucius, Pythagoras, while teaching, enjoyed official recognition and was influential in Croton, even if temporarily, whereas Confucius failed to see the impact of his doctrine on rulers, to whom he tried to preach it. On the other hand, several centuries after the death of its founder, Confucianism succeeded in gaining a stronghold, not only in China but far beyond its borders, and has remained influential till today. The philosophical school of Pythagoras came to an end by the fourth century, even though his influence was felt in the writings of Plato and Aristotle, as well as in medieval European thought, and today Pythagoras is better remembered as a brilliant mathematician than as a philosopher. Despite these outward parallels, however, the inner doctrines and philosophical teachings of these two masters are completely different. Nevertheless, the comparison drawn by Adriano di St. Thecla indicates a high level of erudition.

[28] Dương Chu (Yang Zhu, 440–360? B.C.E.) was an early Daoist philosopher in China. An adherent of individualism, who preached the importance of self in preference to the importance of others, he was accused by the Confucians of propagating extreme hedonism. In the Daoist book *Liezi* (fifth century B.C.E.?) there is a chapter devoted to the teaching of this scholar. See A. C. Graham, *The Book of Lieh-tzu: A Classic of the Tao* (New York: Columbia University Press, 1990).

[29] The name is pronounced *Mặc* in Vietnamese. Adriano di St. Thecla consistently uses *Mạc* intead of *Mặc* in the manuscript. Mặc Địch (Mo Di) is the original name of the Chinese philosopher Mặc Tử (Mozi, ca. 470–ca. 391 B.C.E.), who, contrary to Dương Chu (Yang Zhu), stood for collectivism. Being initially a follower of Confucianism, Mozi later distanced himself from it, regarding it as too formal and overloaded with rituals and regulations. He subsequently founded his own doctrine of universal love, which served as a basis for the movement of his followers known as Mohism. Mohism was quite influential for several centuries and challenged Confucianism.

[30] Mạnh Tử (Mengzi), like Kongzi (Confucius), was Latinized by the Europeans to become "Mencius" and remained in this form in Western historiography. Mencius (371–289? B.C.E.) is the second "sage" of the school of Confucian thought. Following the tenets of Confucianism, which he learned from a student of Confucius's grandson Zi Si, he elaborated Confucius's doctrine. His main idea is that human nature was inherently good and that is why, to establish order and govern a country, a ruler should appeal, first of all, to human nature, and not to law. According to Mencius, the ruler was to provide for the livelihood of ordinary people, their education, and their moral development. Like Confucius, Mencius traveled extensively, offering his services to different rulers. And, like Confucius, he did not succeed in admonishing the rulers to rely on human nature rather than on power. His book, the *Mengzi* (Mencius), which contains his sayings and accounts of his activities, reflects his thoughts on government; it shows the connection between the benevolence and righteousness of the ruler and the mandate of heaven to care for the people's welfare. Another important issue discussed in the book is filial piety; this issue was considered by Mencius as a cornerstone of society. His book became one of the *Sishu* (Four Classics).

[31] 楊墨之道不息孔子之道不著. *Mencius;* see James Legge, trans., *The Chinese Classics* (reprint, Taipei: SMC Publishing, 1991), 2:282–83.

[32] In fact, Adriano di St. Thecla adduces here only one part of the statement made in the *Mengzi* (Mencius), which in full reads as follows: "If the principles of Yang and Mo be not stopped, and the principles of Confucius not set forth, then those perverse speakings will delude the people, and stop up the path of benevolence and righteousness." Ibid., p. 283. Lyall, in whose translation the same statement is found in book 6, chapter 9, suggests a similar translation: "If

Confucius. Shortly after that, the doctrine of Confucius overcame another obstacle. Since Emperor Thần Thỉ Hoàng (Shen Shi Huang),[33] ignorant of literature, was hostile to literati, who were not faithful to him and who censured him, he ordered all the books of Confucius found in the entire kingdom to be burnt, and the literati or scholars studying his books to be buried alive.[34] Then a certain literatus intentionally hid the books of Confucius inside a wall, from where, after the persecution, at the beginning of the rule of the Han dynasty, they were extracted and scholars could copy them. There was no *Nhạc Kinh* among them, however, and it has been lost from that time. At the same time, a certain literatus named Phục Sinh (Fu Sheng), being already ninety, who had kept *Thư Kinh* in his memory, dictated

---

the ways of Yang and Mo are not stopped, if the way of Confucius is not seen, crooked words will bewitch the people, and choke love and right." Leonard A. Lyall, trans., *Mencius* (London: Longmans, Green, 1932), p. 97. The difference between the extract as interpreted by Adriano di St. Thecla and as rendered in the modern translations consists in the conditions stipulated by Adriano to guarantee the development of Confucianism: the doctrine of Confucius may shine only if the other two doctrines are stopped. The two other adduced translations stipulate that the flourishing of the doctrines of Yang Zhu and Mo Di, together with the neglect of Confucianism, would lead to moral decay—not that the mere existence of the first two schools would bar the development of the last. Reading the original, it becomes understandable why Adriano di St. Thecla could use the excerpt the way he did. Since in Chinese it is not necessary and not customary to use grammatical conjunctions, it was possible for him to link the two parts ("the ways of Yang and Mo are not stopped" and "the way of Confucius is not seen") through a conditional clause in which the second is stipulated by the first. But if one continues to read the following phrase of the text, it will be seen that, actually, these two parts are together a stipulation for the next part of the sentence, which begins with the word *thị* (*shi*, the verb "to be"), which usually introduces the main part of a sentence.

[33] Thần is a mistake for Tần (Qin), the name of the dynasty. Thus, the reference is to Tần Thỉ Hoàng Đế (Qin Shi Huangdi, r. 221–209 B.C.E.), "The First Emperor of Qin," the founder and in fact the only major ruler of the Qin dynasty, who in 221 unified the warring kingdoms of China and assumed the title of the "The First Universal Ruler." In modern Vietnamese, this name, Thỉ (Shi, the first, beginning) is pronounced *Thuỷ*. But *Thỉ* was a normative pronunciation in earlier centuries. In the nineteenth century, both pronunciations were acceptable, as revealed in Huình Tịnh Paulus Của's dictionary, which lists the character corresponding to modern *thuỷ* as *thỉ*; see Huình Tịnh Paulus Của, *Đại Nam Quấc Âm Tự Vị* (A Dictionary of Characters with the National Pronunciation of Great South) (reprint, Ho Chi Minh City: Nhà Xuất Bản Trẻ, 1998), p. 1005. In the manuscript, Adriano di St. Thecla consistently uses the pronunciation *thỉ* for the character 始, found as a noun (beginning) or a verb (to start), or included in a proper name as in the case of Tần Thỉ Hoàng Đế (Qin Shi Huangdi) or Nguyên Thỉ (Yuanshi, Primary or Primordial Source).

[34] The reference is to 213 B.C.E., when Confucian books were burned by Tần Thỉ Hoàng Đế (Qin Shi Huangdi)'s order. Destroying literature and persecuting scholars was a step in his plan to consolidate the empire, since reading books inevitably led to a critical perception of the present. Shi Huangdi's hatred of Confucianism was especially strong as a result of Confucian attempts to criticize the present, using examples from the past, and also because the Confucians advocated governing by using people's moral nature, and not by strict laws as proposed by legalism, the dominant thought during the Qin dynasty. However, according to Mark Lewis, the burning of the books "was not an attempt to destroy the scholarly traditions, since some copies were to be preserved in the imperial collection. Instead, it sought only to bring these scholars under state control and thereby create the identity of political and intellectual authority that was a shared postulate or ambition of most scholars in the third century." Mark E. Lewis, "Warring States Political History," in *Cambridge History of Ancient China*, ed. Loewe and Shaughnessy, p. 645. For a detailed analysis of Shi Huangdi's role in Chinese history, see Ulrich Neininger, "Burying the Scholars Alive: On the Origin of a Confucian Martyrs' Legend," in *East Asian Civilization: New Attempts at Understanding Traditions*, ed. W. Eberhard, K. Gawlikowski, and C.-A. Seyschab (Munich: Simon and Magiera, 1983), pp. 121–136.

it to another [literatus], for he had memorized it when he once studied it. This is mentioned in the preface to *Thư Kinh*.[35] In such a way the doctrine and the sect of Confucius could grow strong under the rule of the Han dynasty;[36] the first [emperor] of this dynasty, Cao Tổ (Gaozu),[37] saw Confucius's tomb when going through his native district, and made a sacrifice to him. The literatus Đạo Nguyên Lưu Thị (Dao Yuan Liu Shi),[38] who is mentioned below in article 4, counted a thousand years of worshipping Confucius, starting from the time of Cao Tổ.

Article 2: On the Studies, Books, and Doctrine of This Sect

The Chinese and Tonkinese literati dedicate themselves mostly to learning their characters, and the number of these characters is so large [and they are] so variable, and each of them is so hardly comprehensible, [p. 4] that even the course of a whole lifetime would scarcely be enough to grasp the knowledge of them. The literati indeed have their dictionaries, where all the characters are collected and each is explained according to all its meanings; from them our Europeans borrowed their dictionaries of Chinese characters, explaining them in Latin. While studying the characters, they also study the events that are depicted in the books, with the help of these characters; so they simultaneously learn the characters and events described by means of these characters. Furthermore, it must be noted that the Tonkinese, or Annamites, use the same characters as the Chinese do, but pronounce them in a different way, keeping the same meaning, so that if one Chinese literatus and one Tonkinese speak, they cannot understand each other, but if they write, they understand each other pretty well.

To become a literatus, they study the following books. First, *Ngũ Kinh (Wujing)*, that is, the Five Books of the aforementioned Confucius collected in one volume. Once there were six [books], but after *Kinh Nhạc*[39] was lost, only five remained. The main commentaries inserted in these books were [made] by extraordinary literati—Trình Tử (Chengzi), Chu Tử (Zhuzi or Zhouzi), and Thẩm Tử (Shenzi)[40]—who were disciples of Chu Văn Công (Zhou Wengong),[41] the author of

[35] See Legge, *Chinese Classics*, vol. 3, Prolegomena, pp. 16–17.

[36] Under the Han dynasty (206 B.C.E.–220 C.E.) Confucianism gained recognition as an official doctrine.

[37] R. 206–194 B.C.E.

[38] There is a mistake in the text. The name in Vietnamese should read Đạo Nguyên Lưu Thư (Dao Yuan Liu Shu). Đạo Nguyên (Dao Yuan) is a literary name of Liu Shu (Lưu Thư), a famous historian in the Song dynasty who lived from 1032 to 1078.

[39] While the original for the Book of Music in Chinese is *Yuejing* (*Nhạc Kinh* in Vietnamese), the author reverses the word order: *Kinh Nhạc*, which would be Jing Yue in Chinese. This is a plausible variation in Vietnamese, but impossible in Chinese. Adriano di St. Thecla's rendering suggests that the author heard about this book from a Vietnamese source.

[40] For Trình Tử (Chengzi), Chu Tử (Zhuzi or Zhouzi), and Thẩm Tử (Shenzi), Adriano di St. Thecla recorded only the family or clan names, replacing their personal names with the word *tử (zi)* denoting a respected person or a gentleman, which makes it difficult to identify these scholars. *Chengzi* most certainly refers to one or both of the Cheng brothers, Cheng Mingdao (1032–85) and Cheng Yichuan (1033–1107), also known as Chen Hao and Cheng Yi, respectively. Because their philosophies are often considered together, it might be that Adriano di St. Thecla perceived them as one person. Both brothers based their concepts on the principle of *li*, the universal law that determines all existence. But in fact their concepts were quite different. Whereas Cheng Hao, interested in Buddhism and Taoism in his youth, applied an idealist approach to his theory, emphasizing the importance of calm introspection and

meditation in order to grasp *li,* Cheng Yi confined himself to a rationalist current, advocating an active investigation of things in which *li* is present. Both are considered major contributors to the development of Neo-Confucianism. However, Cheng Yi's approach became more influential, especially when, after his death, his ideas were developed by his followers—mainly Zhu Xi (1130–1200), of whom we will talk below—into the rationalist school of thought, which remained influential till the beginning of the twentieth century. Taking into consideration the works and citations adduced by Adriano di St. Thecla in the manuscript, I suggest that under the name Chengzi he implied Cheng Yi.

Zhuzi or *Zhouzi:* Sino-Vietnamese *chu* can stand for two different characters for surnames pronounced in Chinese as *zhu* or as *zhou.* In this case, two people actually had surnames pronounced in Sino-Vietnamese *Chu.* One of them was Zhou Dunyi (1017–73), the most famous precursor of Neo-Confucianism. In his treatises he laid a basis for the revival and further development of Confucianism. The other person called by the name Chu Tử (Zhuzi) was the greatest Chinese philosopher of Neo-Confucianism, Chu Hi (Zhu Xi, 1130–1200). In spite of the fact that later in this same sentence Zhu Xi is unambiguously referred to as Chu Văn Công (Zhu Wengong), I am inclined to think that here the author implies Zhu Xi. My conclusion is based on the works ascribed by Adriano di St. Thecla to Chu Tử (Zhuzi) later in the manuscript. In my opinion, Adriano di St. Thecla simply did not realize that Zhuzi and Zhu Wengong refer to one and the same person, Zhu Xi, and thus this confusion arose. Zhu Xi is credited with restoring the dominant position of Confucianism, which had been lost in previous centuries to Buddhism and Taoism. He wrote almost one hundred works, among them *Tongjian gangmu* (Outline of the Comprehensive Mirror) and commentaries on the *Sishu* (Four Classics) and other Confucian books. Some of them are mentioned and cited in the manuscript. Zhu Xi died in political disgrace due to his uncompromising position of criticizing government policy and his general outspokenness; his name was rehabilitated only after his death in 1209. His commentaries became a part of the required curriculum for the civil service examinations for seven centuries, until 1905 when the exams were abolished. For an analysis of Zhu Xi's works and a description of his life, see, for example, Hoyt Cleveland Tillman, *Confucian Discourse and Chu Hsi's Ascendancy* (Honolulu: University of Hawaii Press, 1992); Wing-Tsit Chan, ed., *Chu Hsi and Neo-Confucianism* (Honolulu: University of Hawaii Press, 1986); Percy J. Bruce, *Chu Hsi and His Masters* (London: Probsthain, 1923).

Shenzi: None of the Song scholars with the surname *Thẩm (Shen)* can be referred to as being both a disciple of Zhu Xi and the author of the commentaries on the *Shujing* (Book of History), which Adriano di St. Thecla mentions later in the manuscript. Since my extensive search in dictionaries, encyclopedias, and the books on Song Neo-Confucianism have not yielded any result, I suggest that here Adriano di St. Thecla had in mind Zhu Xi's student, Cai Chen or Cai Shen (蔡 沈 , Sái Trầm in Vietnamese, 1167–1230). The character used for his personal name (沈) is usually read as *trầm (chen),* except for cases when it stands for a surname, in which case it should be pronounced *Thẩm (Shen).* Adriano di St. Thecla, seemingly, did not make this distinction and read the character as though it stood for the surname *Thẩm (Shen),* perhaps due to this character's frequent usage in this capacity. Cai Chen or Cai Shen, was one of the closest disciples and friends of Zhu Xi, and was tied to him with bonds of deep affection. He stayed with his master from the beginning of his illness until Zhu Xi's last day and was present during his death. Bruce, *Chu Hsi and His Masters,* p. 90. Cai Chen wrote two major works: *Shujing jizhuan* (Collected Commentaries on the Book of History) and *Hongfa huangji* (Grand Norm and Supreme Ultimate). Under the Yuan dynasty his commentaries on the *Shujing* (Book of History) became required reading for the civil service examination. As will be seen later in the manuscript, Adriano di St. Thecla cites a passage found in Cai Chen's work and attributes it to Thẩm Tử, which confirms this identification.

I think that Cheng Yi, Zhu Xi, and Cai Chen are the names implied by Adriano di St. Thecla. All three were famous Neo-Confucian scholars in the time span suggested by the author (1068–1225).

[41] Chu (Zhu) is a family or clan name; Văn Công (Wengong) is a posthumous name of Chu Hi (Zhu Xi), which is still widely used in Vietnam, and it is a tradition to use it especially in connection with his book *Gia Lễ* (*Jiali,* Family Rituals). See, for example, a modern Vietnamese edition: Bùi Tấn Niên, *Gia Lễ* (Ho Chi Minh City: Nhà Xuất Bản Thành Phố Hồ Chí Minh, 1992), p. 8.

the book *Gia Lễ* (*Jiali*, Family Rituals);[42] and they lived during the reign of Emperors Thần Tông (Shenzong), Hiếu Tông (Xiaozong), and Ninh Tông (Ningzong)[43] of the Tống (Song) dynasty.[44] Second, *Tứ Thư (Sishu),*[45] that is, Four Books united in one volume, their titles being *Luận Ngữ, Đại Học, Trung Daong,* and *Mạnh Tử;* these books contain different sayings of Confucius and his followers, collected unsystematically. Two disciples of Confucius, named Hữu Tử (Youzi) and Tăng Tử (Zengzi),[46] wrote the book *Luận Ngữ;* Tăng Tử alone wrote the book *Đại Học;* Tử Tư (Zi Si),[47] a disciple and descendant of Confucius, wrote the book *Trung Daong;* someone very famous called Mencius wrote the book *The Mencius* together with his disciple Vạn Chương (Wan Zhang),[48] who lived in the third century after Confucius at the time when the Chinese empire was divided into seven kingdoms.[49] In these books, the main comments belong to the aforementioned Chu

---

[42] *Family Rituals,* or *Family Etiquette,* a manual for carrying out the ceremonies of weddings, funerals, and sacrifices to the ancestors, is ascribed to Zhu Xi. It was written in 1169 and concentrates on adjusting previously used rituals, described in *Zhouli* (Rituals of Zhou), *Liji* (Record of Rites), and *Yili* (Etiquette and Ritual), which had been written more than a millennium and a half before, to the realities of his own time. "In the 1720s the French missionary Jean-François Foucquet (1665–1741) reported that the book was second in popularity only to the *Analects,* and that copies of it would be found in almost every home in China." John W. Witek, *Controversial Ideas in China and in Europe: A Biography of Jean-François Foucquet, S.J. (1665–1741)* (Rome: Institutum Historicum, 1982), pp. 285–286 n. 90, cited in *Chu Hsi's Family Rituals,* trans. Patricia Buckley Ebrey (Princeton, NJ: Princeton University Press, 1991), p. xiii. However, Wang Maohung (1668–1741), an authority on the study of Zhu Xi's scholarship, cast serious doubt on Zhu Xi's authorship of this book, which was a view not accepted by others. See Kao Ming, "Chu Hsi's Discipline of Propriety," in *Chu Hsi and Neo-Confucianism,* ed. Wing-Tsit Chan (Honolulu: University of Hawai'i Press, 1986), p. 317.

[43] R. 1068–86, 1163–90, and 1195–1225 respectively.

[44] During the Song dynasty (960–1279), China experienced a large cultural upheaval. Society was torn between those advocating reforms and those who favored the restoration of traditional Chinese values, language, and historical heritage. This period, often characterized as a Confucian revival, was in fact a successful attempt by a number of brilliant scholars to elaborate the doctrine created by Confucius fifteen hundred years before, and to adjust it to the contemporary conditions and needs of China. As a result, Confucianism regained its position in society and a new elite formed. Prior to the Song dynasty, the Chinese elite was a hereditary aristocracy. Under the Song, the civil service exams, based on the Confucian curriculum, were established on a regular basis, thereby opening the door to upward mobility not only for noblemen but potentially for any person capable of passing the exams. Beginning from the Song, this examination system became a characteristic feature of Chinese society; and it eventually spread over East Asia and to Vietnam.

[45] The *Sishu* (Four Classics) were four ancient Confucian texts, including the *Lunyu* (Analects), *Mencius, Daxue* (Great Learning), and *Zhongyong* (Doctrine of the Mean), published with commentaries of Zhu Xi in 1190. From 1313 to 1905 they, together with the *Wujing* (Five Classics), were used as official curricula for civil service examinations.

[46] Hữu Tử (Youzi) was a disciple of Confucius of whom it is said that he was so holy that Confucius's other pupils wanted to serve him as they served their master. Lyall, *Mencius,* p. 80. But Youzi thought that no one could be greater or equal to Confucius. I could not find any materials supporting Youzi's authorship of *Lunyu.* On Tăng Tử (Zengzi) see note 21 above.

[47] 483–402 B.C.E.

[48] In modern Vietnamese, the correct spelling is Vặn Chương. *Shiji* (Historical Records) says that when Mencius retired, he, "together with his disciple, Wan Chang [Wan Zhang], and others, . . . composed the *Mencius* in seven books." See Feng Yu-Lan, *A History of Chinese Philosophy,* trans. D. Bodde (Princeton, NJ: Princeton University Press, 1952-53), 1:107.

Tử. The book *Gia Ngữ* is added to these four; it was circulated separately, not combined with the other books at all; it contains the sayings of both Confucius and his disciples; another disciple of Confucius from the later generation, called Túc Tử Ung (Su Zi Yong),[50] wrote it. Third, books on the history of the Chinese kings, the three volumes of which have [p. 5] the following titles written on them: *Thông Giám* (*Tongjian,* Comprehensive Mirror) [written] by Ôn Công (Wengong)[51] during the reign of Emperor Tống Thần Thần Tông (Song Shen Shenzong)[52] [written] by the aforementioned author Chu Tử during the reign of Emperor Tống Hiếu Tông, and *Kang Giám* [written] by Liêou Phàm (Liaofan)[53] during the reign of Emperor Minh Thần Tông (Ming Shenzong);[54] on these see our *Chinese Chronology*. Scholars study these books to become literati, and they use all their persistence in this study, learning these books by heart to achieve the ranks of literati, to which they are led once triennially from previous examinations based on these books or on their contents.[55] There are three ranks, the lowest is called *Sinh Đồ (shengtu),*[56] the

[49] The reference is to the Warring States period (453–221 B.C.E.), when seven major kingdoms and a number of minor ones existed on the territory of modern China. The kingdoms were in a permanent state of war with one another, alternately making allies and enemies of their neighbors.

[50] Adriano di St. Thecla conflates two names of a third-century Confucian scholar, Vương Túc (Wang Su), also known as Tử Ung (Zi Yong). There are different opinions about Wang Su's connection with the *Jiayu* (*Gia Ngữ,* Discourses of [the Confucian] School). Some claim him as the author of the book, thus suggesting that the *Discourses* is not a genuine book from Confucius's time, but rather a forgery written by Wang Su; others ascribe to him the role of an editor of the *Discourses,* while still others think that the truth is somewhere in between—they believe that Wang Su inserted his own opinions into a genuine text. For discussion of this topic and Wang Su's biography, as well as a translation of ten chapters of the text, see R. P. Kramers, trans., *K'ung Tzu Chia Yu: The School Sayings of Confucius* (Leiden: E. J. Brill, 1950).

[51] Ôn Công (Wengong) is an honorific title, meaning "friendly and just," that was conferred upon the great Chinese historian Sima Guang (1009–86). *Thông Giám (Tongjian)* is an abbreviation of Sima Guang's major work, *Zizhi tongjian* (Comprehensive Mirror for Aid in Government). This work was written in 1084.

[52] Here is an apparent mistake in the manuscript. The phrase is corrupt. It mentions Emperor Song Shenzong, reduplicating the word Thần (Shen) and omitting the title of Chu Tử (Zhu Xi)'s work.

[53] This is the Chinese historian Yuan Liaofan (1533–1606), Nguyễn Liễu Phàm in modern Vietnamese spelling. *Kang Giám* (spelled as Cương Giám in modern Vietnamese) is an abbreviation of *Gangjian hebian* (Collated Annals of the Mirror of Law).

[54] Ming Shenzong, r. 1573–1620.

[55] The system of official examinations came to Vietnam from China. The first laureates obtained their ranks in 1277, and from then on the exams were organized with varying degrees of regularity. In Vietnam under the Trần dynasty (1225–1400), they were generally held once every seven years. Beginning with the Hồ dynasty (1400–1407), they were held on a regular basis once every three years, excluding some periods of warfare. After 1374 the system of three levels of examinations was established, and those who passed one level could be admitted to take the examination for the next level. Joseph Nguyen Huy Lai, *La Tradition religieuse spirituelle et sociale au Vietnam* (Paris: Beauchesne, 1981), pp. 129–130.

[56] Meaning "junior bachelor." The examination for this rank was held in the provinces.

middle is called *Hương Cống (xianggong)*,[57] and the highest is called *Tấn Sĩ (jinshi)*.[58]

These books tell mainly about the right way to live, and they incorporate history in order to make clear from the deeds of others what to follow and what to avoid. One sees there, however, no method to explain these virtuous ways and to learn a moral discipline, but one is told there what is appropriate about virtue in order to support the events described. All the virtues are brought down to five, the Annamites call them *Ngũ đức* (*wude*, five virtues, or five human relationships), and also they name them *Nhân (ren)*, *Nghĩa (yi)*, *Lễ (li)*, *Trí (zhi)*, [and] *Tín (xin)*; that is, humanity or compassion, justice, politeness, sagacity, and faith or faithfulness. They [the literati] teach these five virtues, together with moral honesty, according to five states of human [relationships], so that reciprocal order might be observed among them: first, [the relationship] between a king and his subjects; second, that between a father and his sons; third, that between a husband and his wife; fourth, that between elder and younger brothers; and fifth, that between allies or friends. These states or relationships of people the Annamites call *Ngũ luân* (*wulun*, five moral obligations), and they enumerate them as *quân thần (jun-chen)*, *phụ tử (fu-zi)*, *phu phụ (fu-fu)*, *huinh*[59] *đệ (xiong-di)*, and *bạng*[60] *hữu (peng-you)*.

Literati teach very little of natural philosophy, or natural science. At the beginning of their history they offer this system concerning the state of things: Thái cực sinh lưỡng nghi, lưỡng nghi sinh tứ tượng, tứ tượng biến hoá nhi thứ loại phiên hĩ;[61] in other words, The primary source, or the element *Thái cực (taiji*, first principle, primitive chaos, the Great Ultimate), produced Heaven and Earth, Heaven and Earth produced the four elements, or qualities;[62] that is, major and minor *âm (yin)* and major and minor *dương (yang)*, *âm* being imperfection or the materiality of a thing, and *dương* being perfection or [p. 6] the immateriality of a thing; and these four qualities constitute all kinds of things; or [in other words] from these four qualities, or elements, all things are made. To this they add that when initially Heaven and Earth were separated in the disorder of things,

---

[57] A title for those who passed inter-provincial examinations, organized at the capital.

[58] This title, now commonly called *tiến sĩ* in Vietnamese (*jinshi* in Chinese), denotes a third-degree graduate, an equivalent to the Western PhD. Those who wanted to obtain this rank took the examination in the capital at the Royal Palace.

[59] Spelled *huynh* in modern Vietnamese.

[60] *Bạng* is now pronounced and spelled *bằng (peng*, friend*)* in Vietnamese.

[61] 太 極 生 兩 儀 兩 儀 生 四 像 四 像 變 化 而 庶 類 繁 矣 . Yuan Liaofan, *Gangjian hebian* (Collated Annals of the Mirror of Law) (Shanghai: Shijie shuzhu, 1937), vol. 1, 1:1a. The next-to-last character, transcribed as *phiên* in the manuscript, is read as *phồn*, "many," in modern transcriptions of Sino-Vietnamese, but Anthony Trần Văn Kiếm lists *phiền* as its possible pronunciation. See Anthony Trần Văn Kiếm, *Giúp Đọc Nôm và Hán Việt* (An Aid for Reading Demotic Vietnamese and Sino-Vietnamese) (Hue: Nhà Xuất Bản Thuận Hóa, 1999), p. 718. Huình Tịnh Paulus Của has *phiền* as the only pronunciation for the character 繁 . See *Đại Nam Quấc Âm Tự Vị*, p. 812. The absence of the tone in the manuscript is a very easy mistake to make.

[62] Even though the compound *lưỡng nghi (liangyi)* has the meaning of "Heaven and Earth," it might have been better to use here another meaning for this compound, namely, "*yang* and *yin* principles," for it is generally considered that these principles evolved from *thái cực (taiji)*—the primordial source.

immediately after that the first man[63] appeared: Hỗn độn chi thế thiên địa thỉ phân, tức hữu Bàn Cổ thị xuất.[64] There is no active cause shown there [in the books] which created that first element *Thái cực*, and produced other things out of it, there is also no first woman introduced for reproduction, since mention was made only of the first man.

Moreover, they say in the book *Dịch Kinh* that Heaven and Earth are one source from which all things are created. Confucius, in the treatise *Hệ Từ (Xici)*[65] of this book, says the following: Thiên địa chi đại đức, viết: sinh;[66] that is: The great power of Heaven and Earth is called creative, or creativity.[67] Chu Tử elucidates these words of Confucius in the following way: Thiên địa dĩ sinh vật vi tâm;[68] that is: Heaven and Earth have a heart, or nature, to create things. He adds: Duy Thiên xác nhiên ư thượng, địa tắc đồi nhiên ư hạ, nhất vô sở, chỉ dĩ sinh vật vi sự;[69] that is: Since solid or firm Heaven remains above, round Earth indeed remains underneath, they both do nothing but only produce things.[70] He concludes: Cố Dịch viết: Thiên địa chi đại đức, viết: sinh;[71] that is: Therefore it said in the book *Dịch [Kinh]* that the great power of Heaven and Earth is called creative.[72] The glossator

---

[63] The "first man" in this phrase is Bàn Cổ (Pangu), a legendary being, first mentioned in a text attributed to the third century B.C.E., who allegedly evolved from chaos or a cosmic egg, grew for 18,000 years, and in his dying gave birth to the universe. "When he died, his eyes became the sun and moon; his blood, the rivers and oceans, his hair, the grasses and trees. Humans and animals derived from his body lice." Conrad Schirokauer, *A Brief History of Chinese Civilization* (New York: Harcourt Brace Gap College, 1991), p. 24. Pangu is "the Chinese version of Purusa, who breaks open the original egg and transforms himself into the world." Livia Kohn, *God of the Dao; Lord Lao in History and Myth* (Ann Arbor, MI: University of Michigan, Center for Chinese Studies, 1998), p. 191. An identical legend exists among some minority peoples in China and Vietnam. Pangu is mentioned by Adriano di St. Thecla in the chapter on Buddhism below.

[64] 混 沌 之 世 天 地 始 分 則 有 盤 古 是 出 . The text (Yuan Liaofan's *Gangjian hebian*, 1:1a) actually says: "According to tradition, there was born a ruler named Bàn Cổ (Pangu), also named Hỗn độn (Hundun)." The quotation in the manuscript is apparently corrupt. H. Giles defines *hundun* as follows: "This term is generally used to denote the condition of matter before separation and subdivision into the phenomena of the visible universe." Herbert A. Giles, trans. *Chuang Tzu*, p. 90. For a detailed analysis of Pangu and *hundun* and relations between them, see N. J. Girardot, *Myth and Meaning in Early Taoism: The Theme of Chaos (hun-tun)* (Berkeley: University of California Press, 1983).

[65] *Hệ Từ* (*Xici*) is an abbreviation of *Xici zhuan* (Commentary on the Appended Phrases) and consists mainly of interpretations and commentaries of Confucius on relations between Heaven and Earth and their creativity.

[66] 天 地 之 太 德 日 生 . These words of Confucius are quoted by Cheng Yi in *Xingli daquan shu* (Metaphysical Compendium) (Taipei: Taiwan shangwu yinshu guan, 1974), 7:35:1a.

[67] The translation into English of this version of the *Yijing* (Book of Changes) is in Richard John Lynn, *The Classic of Changes: A New Translation of the I Ching as Interpreted by Wang Bi* (New York: Columbia University Press, 1994). *Hệ Từ* (*Xici*) is on pages 47–101, and the particular quotation here is on page 77 (where it is translated as "the great virtue of Heaven and Earth is called generation").

[68] 天 地 以 生 物 為 心 . (*Xingli daquan shu*, 7:35:7b).

[69] 維 天 確 然 於 上 地 則 頹 然 於 下 一 無 所 只 以 生 物 為 事 .

[70] The word *đồi* (tui), translated by Adriano di St. Thecla as "round," in fact means "soft."

[71] 故 易 日 天 地 之 太 德 日 生 .

[72] I cannot locate the last two quotations ("He adds . . ." and "He concludes . . .") in the *Xingli*. The *Xingli* may have taken the first quotation from another text that contains all three quotations.

of the text *Tử Hạ* (Zi Xia) in the book *Gia Ngữ,*[73] in which Confucius was questioned, referred to this commentary of Chu Tử, saying: Chúa Thiên địa dĩ sinh vạn vật;[74] that is: The governor [named] Heaven and Earth produced innumerable things. In the same *Dịch Kinh,* they [the literati] ascribe to Heaven the leading role in making things and they explain there the first figure of eight [trigrams], *Càn Nguyên* (*qian-yuan,* heavenly origin or heaven), which had been invented and delineated by the first emperor Phục Hi. Confucius, amazed by [the figure], said: Đại tai Càn nguyên vạn vật tử[75] thỉ nải[76] thống thiên,[77] which the text of Trình Tử shows in this way: Đại tai thần tử, nguyên đại dã, Càn nguyên thiên đức chi địa chỉ Cố vạn vật chi sinh giai tư chi dĩ vi thỉ dã; that is: The characters *Đại tai (dazai)* are admirable, *Nguyên* (*yuan,* source, origin, cause or reason) is also mighty, and *Càn Nguyên* indicates the great source of Heaven's power; for that reason all the things created are based on this [p. 7] power, which they [the literati] consider to be the primary source.[78] Really, the power to create things,

---

[73] *Tử Hạ* (Zi Xia) is the title of a chapter in *Gia Ngữ (Jiayu),* after the name of one of Confucius's disciples, Zi Xia, which includes Zi Xia's conversations with the master, mostly on the issue of rituals and human relations. See Wang Su, *Kongzi jiayu* (Discourses of the Confucian School), chap. 10.

[74] 主天地以生萬物 .

[75] This is a mistake. In Vietnamese this word should be read as *tư (xu)* meaning "all, everybody."

[76] This word should be pronounced *nãi* (*nai,* "then," disjunctive particle). *Nảy* is a vernacular Vietnamese pronunciation of the same character with a different meaning. None of the dictionaries confirm Adriano di St. Thecla's version of this character's pronunciation, which persist throughout this chapter. I assume that it could have been a local dialectic pronunciation.

[77] 大哉乾元萬物資始乃統天 . "How great are *Càn (qian)* [and] *Nguyên (yuan),* [being] the origin of all creations and governors of Heaven." The phrase as it appears in the manuscript is a summarized version of the passage in Chao Cai's edition of *Zhouyi Cheng Zhu zhuanyi zhezhong* (The Weighing of Opinions and Teaching of Righteousness of Cheng and Zhu from the Zhouyi) (Shanghai: Shangwu yinshu guan, 1935), 1:18a. See also a translation into Vietnamese in Ngô Tất Tố, trans., *Kinh Dịch* (Book of Changes) (Ho Chi Minh City: Nhà Xuất Bản Thành Phố Hồ Chí Minh, 1995), p. 75.

[78] As it is, the passage is difficult to render in characters to produce an intelligible sentence. I could not locate the origin of the citation. Several words are problematic. The only guide available is Adriano di St. Thecla's translation. Relying on it, I endeavored to render it in characters. The fourth word in the phrase is written unclearly: it could be either *tử* or *sử,* and there are at least a dozen possible meanings based on characters with these pronunciations. None of them, however, makes any sense in this position in conjunction with the preceding word *thần,* which has also more than one possibility when written as a character. Moreover, this *thần tử* or *thần sử* is not reflected in Adriano di St. Thecla's translation itself. I assume that the word *thần* is a mistake here, and the correct word should have been *càn (qian). Càn* would fit better into the structure of the sentence for two reasons. First, the two words preceding the *thần* in question are *đại tai (dazai),* an expression which by itself means "great indeed" or "how admirable"; it does not, as Adriano di St. Thecla states, mean that the characters *đại tai (dazai)* themselves are admirable. It is not clear whether he misunderstood the term or merely chose a bad phrasing. If he misperceived the term, there should be a subject for this part of the sentence defined as "admirable," which is absent in the manuscript version. If we read the word *càn* instead of *thần,* not only would we get a plausible subject, but we would also see a more balanced grammatical structure, since the second part of the sentence is built on the subject of *nguyên (yuan)*—"Nguyên is also mighty"—and the third part of the sentence explains the conjunction *càn nguyên;* according to Adriano di St. Thecla's translation, *nguyên* appears in the second part of the sentence while *càn* does not appear until the third part. This possible solution for the third word in the phrase is of no help in solving the riddle of the fourth word. *Tử* or *sử* remains obscure, unless we arbitrarily substitute a final particle for it. The other

which is ascribed to Heaven, is different from the visible material sky, or from its image, which appears to the eye. And this distinction is clarified in the same book. Therefore, Trình Tử first explained the figure *Càn Nguyên* in this way: Càn Thiên dã, phù[79] Thiên chuyên ngôn chi tắc Đạo dã, phận nhi ngôn chi tắc dĩ hình thể vị chi Thiên; dĩ chúa tể, vị chi Đế, dĩ công dụng, vị chi Quỉ Thần; dĩ diệu dụng vị chi Thần; dĩ tính tình, vị chi Càn; Càn giã;[80] vạn vật chi thỉ; cố vi Thiên, vi Dương, vi Phụ, vi Quân;[81] that is: The character *Càn (qian)* means: heaven, oh heaven! When it is pronounced only in its absolute form, it means law or rationale. When it is pronounced differently: if it accepts the meaning of visible image, it is said in a special way to denote Heaven; if it accepts the meaning of governing, it denotes a king; if it accepts the meaning of action, it denotes an acting spirit, or active power; if it accepts the meaning of eminence, or power of doing [something], it denotes spirit;[82] if it accepts a natural condition, it is called *Càn;* this thing *Càn*

---

problematic place is with the thirteenth and fourteenth words, *địa chỉ (dizhi),* which, if read as the compound meaning "address," does not fit either Adriano di St. Thecla's translation or even a potentially plausible meaning of the phrase. I would suggest that the word *địa* (*di,* earth) is most certainly mistakenly written instead of the word *đại* (*da,* great). The following word *chỉ,* which can be written with a number of different characters, most probably was erroneously put into the text instead of the word *thỉ* or *thuỷ* (*shi,* source, beginning). With all these corrections, the phrase would look as follows: Đại tai Càn . . . , nguyên đại dã, Càn nguyên thiên đức chi đại thỉ Cố vạn vật chi sinh giai tư chi dĩ vi thỉ dã , 大哉乾 [?] 元大也乾元天德之大始故萬物之生皆資之以為始也 , the translation of which, with the exception of the first four words, is very similar to that of Adriano di St. Thecla.

[79] The word should be read as *phu* (fu), an initial particle 夫 . The tone is a mistake.

[80] Here *giã* is mistakenly written for *giả (zhe)*—the pronoun "this" or a particle to highlight the meaning of the previous word.

[81] 乾天也夫天專言之則道也分而言之則以形體謂之天以主宰謂之帝以功用謂之鬼神以妙用謂之神以性情謂之乾乾者萬物之始故為天為陽為父為君 . (*Zhouyi Cheng Zhu zhuanyi zhezhong,* 1:3b). The manuscript presents a slightly abbreviated version of the passage.

[82] The part of the sentence "dĩ công dụng, vị chi Quỉ Thần; dĩ diệu dụng vị chi Thần — 以功用謂之鬼神以妙用謂之神 — the author translated into Latin as "acceptâ operatione, dicitur spiritus operaus, seu virtus operativa; acceptâ excellentia, seu virtute operandi, dicitur spiritus." Thus, he distinguishes the words *quỉ thần (guishen)* and *thần (shen)* as "acting spirit" and "spirit." *Quỉ (gui)* are disembodied spirits of the dead. They were "popularly depicted as skeletons in all but the features, which are hideous and repulsive. They were not at first regarded as evil, though they came to be so regarded later on. . . . practically all are malicious demons, constantly seeking to deceive and harm. They have nothing to fear from man (though, as compared with man, they are regarded as only three-tenths brave), and are the authors of plague, famine, and pestilence. They enter into human bodies, causing sickness, insanity, and death. They are the instruments of the gods in governing the universe and punishing the evil doer." E. T. C. Werner, *A Dictionary of Chinese Mythology* (Shanghai: Kelly and Walls, 1932), p. 231, s.v. "kuei." *Thần (shen)* is "a term, dating from the Chou [Zhou] Period, in its original form meaning lightning. . . . The essence of the word is thus spirit, whether abstract or concrete, intelligence, mind, etc., and inscrutable, unfathomable, miracluous, etc., as though the work of spiritual beings" (ibid., p. 417, s.v. "shên"). In Neo-Confucianism *guishen* is also understood as "positive spiritual force and negative spiritual force." Chen Chun (1153–1217) said that *quishen* "should be discussed under four categories: that of the Confucian Classics, he meant the Classics as interpreted by the Neo-Confucians, according to whom *kuei-shen* [*guishen*] stood for the positive and negative forces behind events. Thus, expansion is *shen* while contraction is *kuei* [*gui*]. This materialistic and philosophical meaning should always be kept entirely distinct from the other meaning in the first three categories,

is the source of all things; so this *Càn* is self-sufficient, that is, it is Heaven, it is brightness,[83] it is the father, it is the king.[84] There you see that the power of Heaven, or the power ascribed to Heaven, is different from sky, or a visible image of Heaven.

Moreover, it is clear from this testimony that *Đế* (*di*, emperor), or the king who is called Thượng Đế (Shangdi), that is, Supreme King, is indeed different from the image of Heaven which is seen by eyes, nevertheless it makes a unity with this Heaven. Although [in the books] *Đế* is different from *Thần* (*shen*, spirit, god, divine, supernatural), that is, the king [is different] from the spirit, in any other place both are considered to be one and the same, especially in relation to Heaven, and they are mentioned as its two properties, or two duties. Thus, Kheo Thị,[85] being mentioned in history, says provocatively to Emperor Tống Huy Tông (Song Huizong):[86] Mặc tôn ư Thiên. Thiên thần chi tối tôn giả, Thượng Đế dã. Đế chúa tế chi xưng;[87] that is: There is nothing higher than Heaven, the highest spirit of Heaven is the Supreme King; this king is called the governor. Also they call this

---

namely, *kuei-shen* [*guishen*] as 'spiritual beings.' In ancient times *shen* usually refers to the spirits of deceased human beings. In latter-day sacrifices, the words *kuei-shen* [*guishen*] together refer to ancestors. In popular religion *shen* means gods (who are good) and demons (who are not always good). In Neo-Confucianism *kuei-shen* [*guishen*] may refer to all these three categories but more often than not the term refers to the activity of the material force *(ch'i [qi])*. Chang Tsai's [Zhang Zai, 1020–77] dictum, 'The negative spirit *(kuei [gui])* and positive spirit *(shen)* are the spontaneous activity of the two material forces *(yin* and *yang)*,' has become the generally accepted definition." See Wing-Tsit Chan, trans., *Reflections on Things at Hand, the Neo-Confucian Anthology Compiled by Chu Hsi and Lü Tsu-Ch'ien* (New York: Columbia University Press, 1967), pp. 366–367. Hence, Adriano di St. Thecla conveyed the sense of the compound *quỉ thần (guishen)* in accordance with its Neo-Confucian understanding.

[83] The word *dương*, which Adriano di St. Thecla translates as "brightness," is in fact the male principle of *yang*, the positive element in nature, of heavenly source and, consequently, light, brightness, as opposed to the dark, earthly, female element of *âm (yin)*.

[84] This phrase is based on the polysemy of the character *càn (qian)*, which is especially evident in different compounds. Ye Cai, a thirteenth-century Neo-Confucian scholar, defined *càn (qian)* as follows: "*Ch'ien [qian]* means heaven. Heaven is the physical body of *ch'ien [qian]*, whereas *ch'ien [qian]* is the nature and feelings of Heaven [nature]. *Ch'ien [qian]* means strength. What is strong and is unceasing in its activity is called *ch'ien [qian]*." Cited in Wing-Tsit Chan, trans., *Reflections on Things at Hand*, p. 9. It should be noted that the character here transcribed as *càn*—with the meaning of "heaven, male, father, sovereign," and the first of the trigrams—was pronounced by Vietnamese Confucians as *kiền*. This character also has a meaning of "dry, empty," and Confucians pronounced it *càn* with this meaning. Vietnamese Buddhists, however, used the pronunciation *càn* in place of *kiền*, and this became the more popularized form in Vietnamese usage. For a translation of the passage into Vietnamese see Ngô Tất Tố, *Dịch Kinh*, p. 66.

[85] The first word in the name is identical to that Adriano di St. Thecla used for the name of Confucius. Thus, the name would be Khâu Thị in Vietnamese or Qiu Shi in Chinese. The scholar, however, remains unidentified.

[86] R. 1101–26.

[87] 莫 尊 於 天 天 神 之 最 尊 者 上 帝 也 帝 主 宰 之 稱 . This is an abbreviated version of a quotation that appears in the chapter on Daoism, the source of which I have not been able to identify. It is apparent from comparing the two citations and from semantic analysis that the third-to-last word should be read *tể* (*zai*, ruler, to govern) and not *tế* (*ji*, to make a sacrifice) as it appears here.

Supreme King the master of heaven. Trình Tử in the book *Tính Lý (Xingli)*[88] says: Thiên chúa hà, Thượng Đế dã;[89] that is, Who is the master of Heaven? The Supreme King is. In the same book Tư Dương,[90] explaining the character *đế*, says: Đế giả, Thiên Chúa tế dã;[91] that is: This king is the governing master of Heaven. [p. 8] It clearly appears from this that, among the literati, Thượng Đế, or the Supreme King, was not different from Heaven, but was united with Heaven, and he himself was Heaven. It will be clarified below that Confucius understood and used [the name] of Thượng Đế in this sense.

In addition to the supreme spirit of the whole Heaven, called Thượng Đế, Chinese Xang Ty (Shangdi), they also recognize in Heaven certain other spirits, especially spirits of the Sun, the Moon, and the stars. Similarly, in addition to the general spirit of Earth, they also recognize other special spirits, especially of mountains and streams. They call the spirit of Heaven Thiên Thần (Tianshen); the spirit of Earth they indeed call Địa Kỳ (Diqi). Moreover, they recognize spirits of other things, namely of the winds, rain, cold, heat, and other numerous spirits, whose number is the same as the number of things in which there is an acting power far remote from ordinary understanding. All these spirits or powers of things are called Quỉ Thần, Chinese Kuei Xin (guishen), this name indicates an acting power inside things, which cannot be perceived by the sense of ordinary understanding. This power is also called with another name, *Linh* (*ling*, spirit, supernatural, efficacious). Besides, according to Confucius, the name *Thần (shen)* and the name *Linh* mean eminence, which is deep inside of things, and cannot be examined by people in its innermost [parts].[92] This is all about the doctrine of the Sect of Literati. The Chinese also have books on geometry, arithmetic, astronomy, and especially on medicine, although the foundations and the theory of their sciences hardly developed to the same perfection as in Europe. They expand these sciences in private study, and they do not teach them publicly in schools. Hence, in commentaries to the book *Kinh Thư (jing shu)*[93] and in the history *Kang Mục (Gangmu*, Outline),[94] which narrate the deeds of Đế Nghiêu, Chu Tử methodically

[88] *Xingli daquan shu* (Metaphysical Compendium), compiled in 1415, by Ming imperial command, as a text for academic examination studies, includes discourses of famous Confucians. Wing-Tsit Chan, *Chu Hsi: Life and Thought* (New York: St. Martin's Press, 1987), p. 46.

[89] 天 主 何 上 帝 也 .

[90] This name can be read in Chinese in different ways: the first syllable as Si or Xu or Zi, the second as Yang. I would suggest that this is a reference to Yang Shi, known also as Yang Guishan (1053–1135), a native of Fujian province, one of the outstanding disciples of the Cheng brothers, who transmitted their learning from northern to southern China.

[91] 帝 者 天 主 宰 也 . Here, as I have noted above, *tế (ji)* should be read as *tể (zai*, ruler).

[92] These two words *thần (shen)* and *linh (ling)* are often used as a compound, designating a collective idea of gods or supernatural powers.

[93] The title of the *Book of History* in Vietnamese is given in reverse order, reflecting a Vietnamese vernacular version of the classical title, which in Sino-Vietnamese should have been *Thư Kinh (Shujing)*.

[94] The author mixes languages in this title, using the classical, or Chinese, pronunciation for the first word and the Vietnamese pronunciation for the second. It should be read as *Cương Mục* in Vietnamese. The most plausible reference would be to *Tongjian gangmu* (Outline of the Comprehensive Mirror), in the creation of which Chu Tử (Zhu Xi) participated as a supervisor and author. This book is a remake of Sima Guang's history *Zizhi tongjian* (Comprehensive

talks about the movement of the Sun and the Moon regulated by the intercalary month. Scholars do not study this thing with great diligence; they skip it and turn to other things, which are narrated in the same books, on the deeds of the kings, [as their objects of] research.
[p. 9]

Article 3: On the Religion of This Sect

The literati worship Heaven and Earth, which they consider to be the primary source of all things, namely, the spirit of Heaven and the spirit of Earth, and also other spirits, both celestial and terrestrial, and they teach the cult of all [these spirits] in their books. In [the chapter] Lễ vận (Liyun, Changes in the Ceremonies)[95] of *Lễ Kinh*, Confucius says about this cult: Tiên Vương huận lễ chi bất đạt ư hạ dã, cố tế Đế ư giao, sở dĩ đinh Thiên vị dã, tự xã ư cuốc[96] sở dĩ liệt địa lợi dã;[97] that is: Primeval kings were very concerned about rites, so that their subjects would not neglect them, and for that reason they sacrificed to the king {supreme} in the territory of *giao* (*jiao*)[98] to establish the dignity of Heaven, and they sacrificed to Earth in the kingdom to ordain the usefulness of Earth.[99]

Mirror for Aid in Government). Zhu Xi's *Gangmu* does not go as far back as Yao and Shun; it starts after the time of Confucius in the Warring States period, so the reference here is obscure.

[95] Lễ vận (Liyun) is the title of chapter 7 of the *Lễ Kinh (Lijing)*.

[96] In modern Vietnamese this word is spelled *quốc* (*guo*, country, state). *Cuốc* was a normative spelling before the nineteenth century, as seen in the writings of other missionaries and also in Alexandre de Rhodes's dictionary, compiled in the seventeenth century. See Alexandre de Rhodes, *Từ Điển Annam-Lusitan-Latinh* (Annamite-Lusitanian [Portuguese]-Latin Dictionary), trans. Thanh Lãng, Hoàng Xuân Việt, and Đỗ Quang Chính (reprint, Hanoi: Nhà Xuất Bản Khoa Học Xã Hội, 1991), col. 142.

[97] 先王患禮之不達於下也故祭帝於郊所以定天位也祀社於國所以列地利也. This passage with the characters can be found in the French translation by S. Couvreur, *Li Ki*, 2nd ed. (Ho Kien Fou: Imprimerie de la Mission Catholique, 1913), 1:525–526. An English translation (without the characters) is found in James Legge's *Li Chi, Book of Rites* (New Hyde Park, NY: University Books, 1967), 1:385. I use Couvreur's translation to verify the characters, and that of Legge for comparison to Adriano di St. Thecla's translation.

[98] This term designates an open space beyond the cities, specially allotted for sacrifices to Heaven.

[99] Legge translates this passage as follows: ". . . it was that the ancient kings were troubled lest the ceremonial usages should not be generally understood by all below them. They therefore sacrificed to God in the suburb (of the capital), and thus the place of heaven was established. They sacrificed at the altar of the earth inside the capital, and thus they intimated the benefits derived from Earth." Legge, *Li Chi, Book of Rites*, 1:385. This translation is almost identical to Adriano di St. Thecla's. A potential discrepancy may be seen in the part of the phrase *sở dĩ đinh Thiên vị dã* (所以定天位也), which Legge translates as ". . . and thus the place of heaven was established," while Adriano di St. Thecla suggests establishing the dignity of Heaven. But "place" and "dignity" should be understand as synonyms in this case, as is evident in Couvreur's translation. He writes: ". . . to establish the place of heaven, that is to make the supreme dignity of heaven acknowledged." See Couvreur, *Li Ki*, 1:525. The only apparent difference between Legge's and Couvreur's translations and that of Adriano di St. Thecla seems to be in the translation of the word *quốc (guo), cuốc* in the manuscript, which the first two translate as "inside the capital" while the last has "in the kingdom." In fact this character may be used for both of these meanings, but in Legge's and Couvreur's translations we evidently see the distinction between the sacrifice to the Supreme Emperor outside the capital and that to the Earth in the capital itself. In Adriano di St. Thecla's translation this distinction disappears.

Confucius adds in the same [book]: Cố Lễ hành ư giao, nhi bất thần thụ chức yên, Lễ hành ư xã nhi bất hoá khả cực yên;[100] that is: The sacrifice is made in the territory of *giao*, and numerous spirits receive their offices; the sacrifice takes place in the territory of *xã* and many of the greatest things happen.[101] From this testimony of Confucius another testimony of his, in the book *Trung Daong*, becomes known, in which he says: Giao xã chi lễ, sở dĩ sự Thượng Đế dã;[102] that is: Ceremonies that take place in the territories of *giao* and *xã* are in honor of the Supreme King and the Queen of Earth;[103] the second [name] is understood from the character mentioned earlier, *xã (she)*, as Chu Tử interprets it there by saying: Giao Tế Thiên, xã tế Địa, bất ngôn Hậu Thổ gỉa tỉnh văn dã.[104]

Moreover, the first king who performed a sacrifice to Thượng Đế, or to the Supreme King, and to other spirits, is introduced in the *Chinese History* as Hoàng Đế (Huang Di) with the following words: Đế tắc[105] cung thất chi chế[106] toài[107] tắc[108]

---

[100] 故 禮 行 於 而 百 神 受 識 焉 禮 行 於 社 而 百 貨 可 極 焉 . Couvreur, *Li Ki*, 1:526–527. The word *bất* (found twice in the citation) should be read as *bách* (*bai*, one hundred, all).

[101] Legge's translation is as following: "By means of the ceremonies performed in the suburb, all the spirits receive their offices. By means of those performed at the altar of the earth, all the things yielded (by the earth) receive their fullest development." Legge, *Li Chi, Book of Rites*, 1:385. Some differencies are seen in the two translations. Adriano di St. Thecla in his translation accompanies both words *giao (jiao)* and *xã (she)* with the Latin *loco*—place or territory. He does not specify what he understood by *jiao* and *she*. The word *jiao* has been explained above; the word *she*, in turn, means "village or hamlet" and also "god or goddess of Earth" or "altar to this god." The translation of the end of the phrase *nhi bất hoá khả cực yên* (而 百 貨 可 極 焉) given by Adriano di St. Thecla significantly differs from that of both Legge and Couvreur. I cannot explain his translation.

[102] 郊 社 之 禮 所 以 事 上 帝 也 . *The Doctrine of the Mean*; Legge, *The Chinese Classics*, 1:404.

[103] Legge translates as follows: "By the ceremonies of the sacrifices to Heaven and Earth they served God." Ibid.

[104] 郊 祭 天 社 祭 地 不 言 后 土 者 省 聞 也 . "*Giao (jiao)* is the sacrifice to Heaven, *xã (she)* is the sacrifice to Earth, which is not an abbreviated expression for 'the God of the Earth.'" See Legge's note for an explanation of the controversy alluded to here. Ibid., n. 19.6.

[105] The only semantically plausible character for the word *tắc (ze)* is "thereupon, consequently," but it is syntactically impossible in this phrase, for then there would be no verb. Here, in my opinion, the word *tắc* should be read as *tác (zuo)* meaning "to do." The same confusion will be seen in several more phrases in the other chapters of the manuscript, where Adriano di St. Thecla writes *tắc* instead of *tác*.

[106] Adriano di St. Thecla omitted altogether the word *chế* (*zhi*, laws, regulations) in his translation.

[107] The word *toài* does not exist in Vietnamese. I believe it is an error for *toại* (*sui*, consequently, then).

[108] Here I surmise *tắc* should be read as *tạc*, (胙 , zuo) "to worship ancestors," as it appears in the abbreviated version of this quotation cited in the chapter on the Spirits. This *tạc* will work better semantically.

hợp cung tự[109] Thượng Đế, tiếp vạn linh,[110] that is: The king built a house for sacrificing to Thượng Đế and to innumerable spirits. According to Confucius in *Thư Kinh,* the first to perform [the sacrifice] was Đế Thuấn (Di Shun), of whom it is said: Tứ loại vu Thượng Đế, yên vu lục tông, vạn[111] vu sơn xuyên, biến vu quân thần;[112] that is: He indeed sacrificed to the Supreme King, to the Sun, the Moon, the stars, to the four seasons of the year, to cold and heat, to water and drought; they [all these spirits] were indicated by the name *lục tông (liuzong),*[113] or "six things" that must be venerated; he sacrificed [p. 10] to the mountains and streams, also to hills, to raised and flat places,[114] and in this way this text is clearly and distinctively interpreted by Thẩm Tử in [his commentary on] that book *[Thư Kinh].*[115] The way they worship Heaven and Earth will be discussed in chapter 2. The aforementioned testimonies of Confucius also show that by the name Thượng Đế he did not mean God of Heaven, or true God, but Heaven itself, or its power or omen. He also spoke there about the cult of Thượng Đế and the cult of Hậu Thổ (Houtu), or the Queen of Earth, and of other spirits; these cults of Earth and of other objects can hardly be combined with the cult of the Supreme King Thượng Đế, if by this name the true God is understood.

Besides this, the literati teach and practice the cult of the deceased. Confucius accepted and approved it, although he did not define any rites for this cult. His followers indeed invented and passed on to others many [additions]; because of them the cult of the deceased is performed with proper ceremonies. For that purpose they set out the *Ritual Gia Lễ,* called in China *Kia Ly* (*Jiali,* Family Rituals), in which numerous ceremonies exercised in this cult on the occasion of burial or commemoration are clearly described, and they are observed in common usage. The literatus Chu Văn Công brought to light this *Ritual* in the sixth year of

---

[109] There are two plausible possibilities for the character pronounced *tự*. The first is the character (自 , zi) , the preposition "from"; the other one is (祀 , si), "to make a sacrifice."

[110] 帝 作 宮 室 之 制 遂 胙 合 恭 祀 (自) 上 帝 接 萬 靈 . If the character for *tự* was 祀 , the translation is as follows: "The emperor established a law of [having an] official house, and thereupon worshipped [there] ancestors as well as made sacrifices to the Supreme Emperor and welcomed the ten thousand spirits." If *tự* stood for the character 自 the translation is: "The emperor thereupon established a law of [having an] official house, and thereupon worshipped [there] ancestors as well as made sacrifices starting from the Supreme Emperor and including the ten thousand spirits." I prefer the first version because the syntax is more idiomatic.

[111] Here *vạn* is an error for *vọng* (*wang*, the name of a sacrifice offered by the emperor to the mountains and streams).

[112] 肆 類 于 上 帝 禋 于 六 宗 望 于 山 川 徧 于 群 神 . *The Shoo King;* Legge, trans., *Chinese Classics*, 3:33–34.

[113] Legge says in his commentary: "Who the 'six Honoured ones' were, it is not possible to ascertain. . . . According to Gan-kwo, followed by Wang Suh [Wang Su] the six honoured ones are 'the seasons, cold and heat, the sun, the moon, the stars, and drought.'" Ibid., 3:34, n. 6.

[114] Legge suggests the following translation of this phrase: "Thereafter, he sacrificed specially but with the ordinary form, to God; sacrificed purely to the six Honoured *ones;* offered their appropriate sacrifices to the hills and rivers, and extended his worship to the host of spirits." Ibid., 3:33–34.

[115] Cai Shen, *Shujing jizhuan* (Collected Commentaries on the Book of History), 1:12b–13a, in *Wujing* (Five Classics) (Chengdu: Bashu shushe, 1989).

Emperor Tống Hiếu Tông, the year of Christ 1168.[116] Therefore, the literati teach the worship of, and they themselves worship, Heaven and Earth, that is, the power of Heaven and Earth as the highest deities, and also [they worship] the Sun, the Moon, the stars, mountains, streams, winds, rain, or their acting powers together with powers of other inanimate things, as well as the images of deceased people. The doctrine and the cult are idolatrous because the cult that must be exhibited to the true God they attribute, and want it to be attributed to, creations [of the true God]. They also condemn and deride idols in the sect of Phật, [or in] Chinese Foe (Fo, Buddhism), who is called by the old name Thích Ca, Chinese Xe Kia (Shijia, [Buddha] Sakya); and they attack the cult of idols with many [words] criticizing Emperor Hán Minh Đế (Han Mingdi),[117] who introduced this cult in China. Yet, because of the tradition of the kingdom and the action of habits, the idols of this sect became formed and are venerated openly, and all other superstitious things follow them, led and corrupted by love for wealth, rank, vainglory, and health.

[p. 11] There are many literati, mainly in China, who believe in no God, [who are] the atheists, of whom mention is made in the apostolic decrees issued on the problem of the Chinese rites. These [atheists] indeed openly withdraw and stay away from or avoid the doctrines of their Sect of Literati which worships Heaven and Earth and spirits of other things, as is evident in their books.

Article 4: On the Cult of the Famous Confucius

Since the literati honor their Teacher with a special cult, we undertake a special discussion about him here, and we will talk about the rest of the spirits, worshipped by everybody, in some later place. So all the literati and even the king himself, together with others, dedicated a cult to their great Confucius, both in the Chinese empire and in the kingdom of Annamites. Confucius became honored with this universal cult long ago; already in olden times the literatus Lưu Thị [Liu Shu], who lived during the reign of Emperor Tống Nhân Tông (Song Renzong),[118] declared [the cult], as can be read in the *History Thông Giám* (*Tongjian*, Comprehensive

[116] In the *Family Rituals* (or *Family Etiquette*), one of Chu Văn Công's (Zhu Xi's) students is quoted as saying that "in the 9th month of the 5th year of the Ch'ien-tao reign (1169) Chu Hsi [Zhu Xi] was in mourning for his mother and authored the *Family Etiquette.*" See Kao Ming, *Chu Hsi's Discipline of Propriety*, p. 333 n. 12. The phrase in Latin is "Illud autem Rituale in lucem dedit litteratus Chu Văn Công anno sexto Imperatoris Tống Hiếu Tông, christi 1168." Because of the word *autem*, it can be also understood that in 1168 Zhu Xi brought to light "another" ritual. In this case, the author apparently refers to the predecessors of Zhu Xi's *Jiali*. One of them, with the same title, was published in the late seventh or early eight century by a high official named Meng Xian; Ebrey, *Chu Hsi's Family Rituals*, p. xviii.

[117] R. 58–76. Adriano di St. Thecla twice attributes the title of emperor to this ruler—once in Latin *(imperator)* and once in Sino-Vietnamese (*đế* [*di*]); this redundancy is similar to his reference, for example, to "King Wen Wang" (Văn Vương, Wen Wang, "King Wen"), and some others, whose names already incorporate their titles. To avoid this redundancy, in the Western academic tradition this ruler is usually referred to either as King Wen or as Wen Wang (without a Western equivalent for his royal title). This redundancy is evident in many accounts of European missionaries and travelers. Adriano di St. Thecla's work differs from them in this regard by having relatively few such places in the manuscript.

[118] R. 1023–64.

Mirror),[119] written under the forty-first year of Emperor Chu Kính Vương: Tự Thiên Tử chí ư thứ nhân, mặc bất tông phượng[120] lịch xiên[121] dư niên, vị hữu như Khổng Tử chi thịnh gỉa, Khỉ[122] phi quân thần phụ tử, nhân nghĩa, lễ nhạc chi giáo;[123] that is: From the son of Heaven {namely the king} down to his subjects, there is nobody who does not venerate and worship perfect Confucius, to whom no one has appeared equal during more than one thousand years; he taught the theory of right relationships between a king and a subject, a father and a son.[124] Emperor Hán Cao Tổ, when he was passing through the land of Lỗ kingdom, saw the tomb of Confucius and was the first among all the emperors to sacrifice to him there in the twelfth year of his reign,[125] approximately two centuries before Christ was born. Numerous subsequent emperors indeed decorated Confucius with various honorific titles. First, Hán Hậu Đế (Han Houdi), four centuries after Cao Tổ, made Confucius a nobleman among the elite who accompany the king at the court, by saying: Truy thị[126] Khổng Tử vi Bao Thành Hầu tuyên noi[127] công;[128] that is: We confer this

---

[119] The reference here is to Liu Shu's *Tongjian waiji* (Outer Records of the Comprehensive Mirror), which covers the ancient times before Sima Guang begins his book *Zizhi tongjian* (Comprehensive Mirror for Aid in Government).

[120] This word, meaning to venerate, to offer up as a tribute or sacrifice, is now pronounced *phụng* in Vietnamese; however, *phượng* seems to be a correct pronunciation of this word in Adriano di St. Thecla's time. In Alexandre de Rhodes's dictionary we find this word in a form identical to that in the manuscript. Alexandre de Rhodes, *Từ Điển Annam-Lusitan-Latinh*, col. 611. Both pronunciations are listed with the same meaning in Huỳnh Tịnh Paulus Của's dictionary, *Đại Nam Quấc Âm Tự Vị*, pp. 825, 827.

[121] The correct pronunciation is *thiên* (*qian*, thousand). This pronunciation apparently reflects a local peculiarity of pronunciation from the place where Adriano di St. Thecla lived or from his Vietnamese tutors. Rhodes's dictionary lists this word in the form known at the present time. Ibid., col. 763, s.v. "thien."

[122] The standard pronunciation of this interrogative particle is *khởi (qi)*. It is not found in de Rhodes's dictionary. *Khởi* is found as a possible variation for *khỉ* in Anthony Trần Văn Kiếm's dictionary, *Giúp Đọc Nôm và Hán Việt*, p. 532, and as the standard pronunciation in Huỳnh Tịnh Paulus Của, *Đại Nam Quấc Âm Tự Vị*, p. 488. Throughout the manuscript Adriano di St. Thecla consistently uses the three words *phụng*, *thiên*, and *khởi* in the form seen in the citation.

[123] 自天子至於庶人莫不宗奉歷千餘年未有如孔子之盛者豈非君臣父子仁義禮樂之教. Liu Shu, *Tongjian waiji* (Outer Records of the Comprehensive Mirror) (Shanghai: Shangwu yinshu guan, 1936), 9:22a.

[124] I agree with Adriano di St. Thecla's translation of this passage except for the last part starting from *khỉ phi* (豈非). *Khỉ phi* is an interrogative compound, meaning "how can it be?"; this does not appear in his translation, and neither do the last four words of the sentence, *lễ nhạc chi giáo*, 禮樂之教.

This part of the sentence I would translate: "How could it be [otherwise since Confucius taught] the theory of right relationships between a king and a subject, a father and a son, [and] the theory of ceremonies and music."

[125] Yuan Liaofan, *Gangjian hebian*, p. 264.

[126] The word should be read *thụy (shi)*, meaning "to confer a posthumous title on the emperor or a high official." (In the form *thị* it will be found in the two following citations.)

[127] *Noi* is apparently a misspelling of a vernacular Vietnamese word *nơi* (the pronunciation of the Sino-Vietnamese word *ni*) as the name of the mountain after which Confucius was named. Apparently here, as at the beginning of the chapter, Adriano di St. Thecla used the vernacular pronunciation *nơi* for the character *ni*, but misspelled it.

[128] 追諡孔子為褒成侯宣尼公

dignity upon [p. 12] Confucius to be a noble courtier of the king.[129] Second, Đàng Huyền Tông (Tang Xuanzong)[130] in the twenty-seventh year of his reign, in the year of Christ 738,[131] declared Confucius *Vương* (*wang*, king, prince or ruler), saying: Truy thị Khổng Tử vi Văn Tuyên Vương,[132] that is, We confer the dignity upon Confucius to act as an official governor of scholarship.[133] Third, Tống Chân Tông (Song Zhenzong),[134] in the first year [of his reign], year 998 of Christ, promoted Confucius to the rank of *Thánh* (*sheng*, saint or sage), saying: Gia thị Khổng Tử vi huyền Thánh văn tuyên Vương;[135] that is: We additionally confer the dignity upon Confucius to appear as a person of complete virtue or a sage, the official governor of scholarship.[136] He made this announcement in the temple of Confucius in his native land,[137] where he also made a sacrifice to him. Moreover, he ordered

[129] I suggest the following translation of this phrase: "We confer upon Confucius the posthumous honorific title Meritorious and Perfect Marquis Universal Duke of Ni" (Ni is the mountain after which Confucius was named). Chinese honorific titles are very elaborate and difficult to translate. Adriano di St. Thecla usually describes them rather than translates.

As for the origins of the citation, they have remained obscure. Hán Hậu Đế (Han Houdi, r. 223–65) indeed reigned four centuries after Emperor Hán Cao Tổ (Han Gaozu). He was the second and last emperor of the Minor Han dynasty (221–65), established in Sichuan. I checked references to this emperor in Sima Guang's and Yuan Liaofan's works and in *Sanguo zhi* (Annals of the Three Kingdoms) (Chen Shou, *Sanguo zhi*, ed. Lu Bi [Beijing: Guji chuban she, 1957], 6:23: 893–903), but found nothing similar to this statement. It might be a reference to someone else. This emperor is generally referred to in the annals as Han Houzhu rather than Han Houdi. Furthermore, he was definitely not the first emperor to confer on Confucius an honorific title as there is almost an identical (except for two characters) phrase in *Hanshu* (History of the Han dynasty) under the second year of Han Bingdi (1–6 C.E.). It reads: Truy thụy Khổng Tử viết Bao Thành Tuyên Ni Công, 追 謚 孔 子 日 褒 成 宣 尼 公 . We confer upon Confucius the posthumous honorific title Meritorious and Perfect Universal Duke of Ni). Ban Gu, *Hanshu*, ed. Yan Shigu ([China]: Hanjiang Shuju, 1962), 1:351.

[130] R. 712–56. In modern Vietnamese the name of the Tang dynasty (618–907) is conventionally pronounced *Đường*. Adriano di St. Thecla consistently uses Đàng instead of Đường throughout the manuscript. However, there exists an identical character, but with a different meaning, in demotic Vietnamese pronounced *đàng* until modern times. It is possible that in Adriano di St. Thecla's time the Sino-Vietnamese character for the name of the Tang dynasty was also pronounced *Đàng*. This supposition is supported by Alexandre de Rhodes's dictionary, which, even though it does not have a word for the name of the Tang dynasty, lists the word for "road," pronounced *đường* (*tang* in Chinese) in modern Vietnamese, as *đàng*. Rhodes, *Từ Điển Annam-Lusitan-Latinh*, col. 200. He mentions *đường*, too, but does not say anything about this word, except to refer the reader back to *đàng*. Ibid., p. 244. In the nineteenth century, both pronunciations were acceptable, as Huình Tịnh Paulus Của shows it, even though he also gives this character under the pronunciation *đàng*, suggesting in the entry for *đường* to consult *đàng*. Huình Tịnh Paulus Của, *Đại Nam Quấc Âm Tự Vị*, p. 266, s.v. "đàng"; p. 335, s.v. "đường."

[131] 追 謚 孔 子 為 文 宣 王 The year should be 739.

[132] Yuan Liaofan, *Gangjian hebian*, p. 1153.

[133] My translation is "[We] confer upon Confucius the posthumous title Universal Ruler of Literati."

[134] R. 998–1023.

[135] 加 謚 孔 子 為 玄 聖 文 宣 王 .

[136] The compound *huyền Thánh* 玄 聖 , meaning "profoundly saintly," is also often used as a name for Confucius. I translate this phrase as follows: "We promote Confucius conferring upon him the posthumous honorific title Profoundly Saintly Universal Ruler of Literati."

[137] It is not clear whether the land in question is native to the king or to Confucius; the pronoun *suus* in the Latin text refers back to the king, but, if there is a scribal error, the reference may be to an imperial trip to Confucius's native land.

in the fourth year [of his reign] to build temples in honor of Confucius in cities in every region called *Chu (zhou)*:[138] Chiếu chu thành tắc[139] Khổng Tử miếu.[140] Fourth, finally Nguyên Vũ Tông (Yuan Wuzong),[141] as soon as he ascended to the throne in the year of Christ 1307, conferred the highest honor on Confucius, proclaiming him as the most virtuous or the wisest, with these words: Gia phung[142] Khổng Tử vi Đại thành chi[143] Thánh Văn Tuyên Vương;[144] that is: We confer the dignity upon Confucius to play the role of a great highly accomplished saint, or sage.[145]

So, according to the aforementioned edict of Emperor Tống Chân Tông, temples to Confucius were erected in each region, and you will also find these [temples], called *Miếu (miao)* and *Nhà thánh* (sacred house, place for prayers), everywhere in the kingdom of Annam, in any region, even in the minor [ones] called *Tổng* (*zong*, canton). Indeed, among the Annamites, in these temples no tablet of Confucius is kept, as is usually done in China, except for the temple in the royal city, where his [Confucius's] tablet, covered with gold and inscribed with silver characters, is kept on the altar. In general, there is also no image of Confucius, which nevertheless exists, although it is situated in another place. Once King Trần Thái Tông[146] in his twenty-seventh year [of reign], 1253 year of Christ, established a school, and painted in it images of Confucius, Chu Công (Zhou Gong),[147] and seventy-two disciples of Confucius to honor them, as it is said in the *History of Đại Việt* (Dayue)[148] with these words: Lập cuốc học viện tổ[149] Khổng Tử, Chu Công Á

---

[138] Another, and currently conventional, pronunciation in Vietnamese is *châu*, which signified an administrative division during the time from the Han to the Tang dynasties.

[139] As above, here *tắc* should be read as *tác* (zuo, to do, to make).

[140] 照 州 城 作 孔 子 廟 .

[141] R. 1308–12.

[142] Here *phung* should be read as *phong* (*feng*, to confer nobility) in modern Vietnamese. While more recent dictionaries do not provide Adriano di St. Thecla's pronunciation, Alexandre de Rhodes confirms that the pronunciation *phung* was the correct one, at least in the seventeenth century. Rhodes, *Từ Điển Annam-Lusitan-Latinh*, col. 609, s.v. "phung chức".

[143] The word is erroneously written *chi*. It should be *chí* (*zhi*, the extreme, best).

[144] 加 封 孔 子 為 大 成 至 聖 文 宣 王 . Yuan Liaofan, *Gangjian hebian*, p. 2025.

[145] My translation is "[We] raise Confucius to the rank of Great Perfection Holiest Universal Ruler of Literati."

[146] A Vietnamese emperor, reigned 1225–58.

[147] The Duke of Zhou, who lived in the twelfth century B.C.E., was a brother of Wu Wang, the first emperor of the Zhou dynasty. He solidified the power of the dynasty and is considered as a paragon of virtue and sagacity in Chinese history for his rejection of the throne after his brother's death and for his role as regent during the reign of Wu Wang's young son, when he provided wise guidance in governing the country.

[148] The reference is to *Đại Việt Sử Ký Toàn Thư* (Complete History of Great Việt). These court annals, compiled in various dynasties by several authors, are traditionally ascribed to the fifteenth-century historian Ngô Sĩ Liên, who completed an early edition of them in 1479. Later historians continued the work, and the annals were eventually published at the end of the seventeenth century, covering the period from the legendary Vietnamese kings up until 1675. Its title contains the name of Vietnam, Đại Việt (Dayue), "Great Viet," which was in circulation from the eleventh century until the nineteenth century when the dynasty (1802–1954) changed it to Đại Nam (Danan), "Great South."

[149] The word *tổ* should be spelled as *tố* (*xu*, to model in clay).

Thánh họa, thất thập Nhị Hiền tương[150] phượng sự.[151] But the first [p. 13] to draw the image of Confucius was Emperor Tống Thái Tổ (Sung Taizu),[152] who ascended to power in the year of Christ 960, as is read in the *History* ———.[153] Moreover, by the edict of Emperor ——— Confucius is called the most virtuous or wisest during sacrifices with these words from the offertory leaf: Đại Thành Chí Thánh Văn Tuyên Vương (Great Perfection Holiest Universal Ruler of Literati);[154] and the same words are written on the tablet of Confucius, if it is used there.

All the literati in every region come to the temple built for Confucius twice a year, as the law prescribes, namely, at the second and the eighth moons, approximately at the vernal and autumnal equinoxes, and there they make a solemn sacrifice; for that purpose all the village inhabitants in the region assemble. At the same second and eighth moons, schoolteachers together with their students also perform less solemn sacrifices to Confucius in their schools, where instead of the altar they put in the center one four-legged sacrificial table, on which there is neither a tablet of Confucius nor a scroll with any name written on it. Whoever has recently been granted one of the ranks of literati comes to the temple of Confucius built in his district, and in the presence of all the literati of this district offers food to his teacher, Confucius, and worships him with prostrations. With this ceremony he makes his newly attained rank known to everyone. In addition, literati in China make offerings twice a month, at the new and at the full moons. Apparently, this is not practiced among the Tonkinese, or Annamites.

[p. 14]

---

[150] Here *tương* should be read as *tượng* (*xiang*, statue).

[151] 立 國 學 院 塑 孔 子 周 公 亞 聖 畫 七 十 二 賢 像 奉 事 . The translation in the manuscript omits the name of Mencius, called in the original *Á Thánh* (Ya Sheng), and the manuscript's punctuation with a comma after *họa* is an error (the pause should be before this word). For the original, see *Đại Việt Sử Ký Toàn Thư* (Hanoi: Nhà Xuất Bản Khoa Học Xã Hội, 1993), bản kỷ, 5:19a.

[152] R. 960–76.

[153] A long dash indicates a blank space in the manuscript.

[154] 大 成 至 聖 文 宣 王

Descriptio Loci pro Sacrificio Confucii

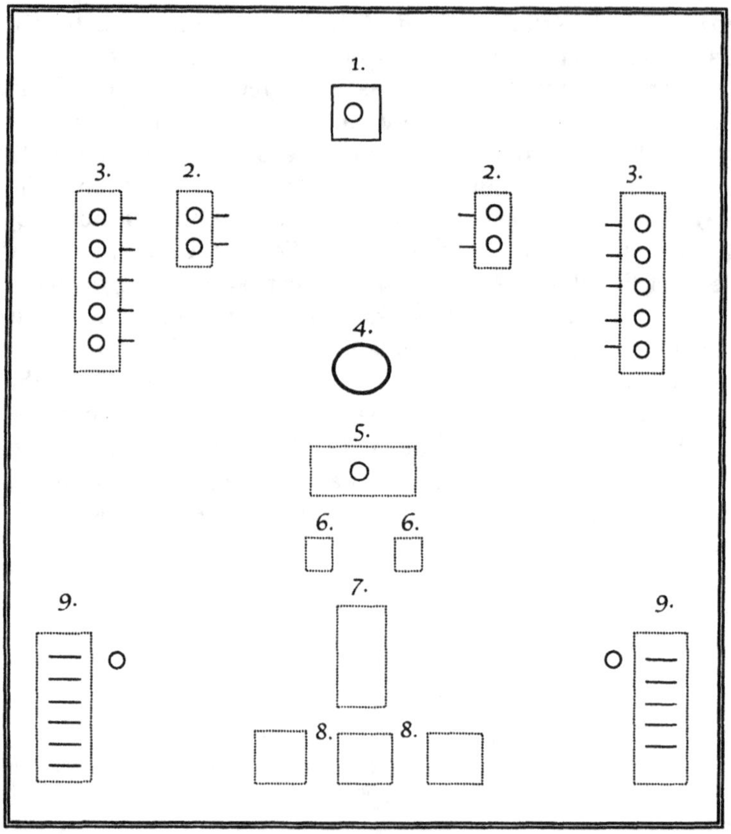

Description of the Place [Constructed] for the Sacrifice to Confucius

1. The altar of Confucius, on which a small vessel with incense and a sacrificial table with food are placed.
2. The altars of the four most distinguished disciples of Confucius.
3. The altars of ten distinguished disciples of Confucius.
4. The place where the half-burnt meat of animals and a small vessel with blood and hair are put.
5. The *hương án (xiang'an)* table, on which incense is burned and in front of which the rite of sacrifice is performed.
6. Two masters of ceremonies, who announce every [action], stand here.
7. The principal attendant, who sacrifices, stands here, and from that place he approaches the *hương án* table.
8. Three or more assistants, who help the principal attendant, stand here.
9. Two tables, on which several things that must be used for sacrifice [p. 15] are prepared, and near which two four-footed vessels for washing hands are placed.

Article 5: On the Solemn Sacrifice to Confucius

Paragraph 1: On Preparation for the Sacrifice

The sacrifice, which all the literati carry out twice a year in the temple of Confucius, is prepared with the help of the following actions and rites. In the center of the altar is placed a small vessel with incense. On both sides of the altar, and a little bit behind it, two four-legged sacrificial tables are positioned lengthwise, each of them holding two small vessels with incense representing the four most distinguished disciples of Confucius, called *Tứ Phối* (*sipei,* the Four Worthiest);[155] two other sacrificial tables are put on each side [behind these sacrificial tables, between them and the walls of the temple], and on each of them there are placed five small vessels with incense for ten other distinguished disciples of Confucius, called *Thập Triết* (*shizhe,* the Ten Sages).[156] For the sacrifice, they also put on these sacrificial tables or altars a lot of gold and silver paper money, several candles or lamps, and also one very small sacrificial table with food in front of each vessel with incense. Behind all the aforementioned sacrificial tables, in the middle [of the temple], is a place for offerings of the cooked meat of killed animals. Immediately behind, right in the center against the altar, stands a small, skillfully ornamented gilt table, the sacrificial table called *hương án,* which bears incense and two lamps or candles; this sacrificial table can be thought of either as an outer altar or as part of the inner altar. On both sides, a little bit behind, stand two other four-legged sacrificial tables, and [on them] are prepared various things intended to be used in sacrifice. In front of every sacrificial table, fixed on a four-legged support, is a vessel with water for washing hands. Between these lateral sacrificial tables in front of the sacrificial *hương án* table is a space for the principal attendant of the sacrifice and for his other assistants.

[p. 16] The day before the sacrifice, in the first part of the night, all the literati enter the temple, dressed in simple, rather long clothes of light violet color, their heads covered with a round beret of the same color. Two of them approach the sacrificial *hương án* table and stand on either side facing each other; they perform the duties of master of ceremonies through the entire ceremony of the sacrifice, announcing in raised voices every action they must do. They are called *Thầy Lễ* (masters of ceremony); numerous attendants called *Chấp sự* (*zhishi,* managers of the ceremony) stand in various places to help; numerous assistants, three at least, called *Bọi tế quan,*[157] stand in a line in the center, facing the sacrificial *hương án* table; and, finally, a senior, or the most distinguished [participant] among them, proceeds to the center in front of the same sacrificial

[155] The first of them is Zi Yuan or Yan Hui (514–483 B.C.E.), the favorite disciple and a kinsman of Confucius. "He surpassed all the pupils who gathered round the great Master in wisdom and quickness of perception. At the age of 29 his hair had grown white, and at 32 he died. He ranks first among the Four Assessors of the Sage." William Frederick Mayers, *The Chinese Reader's Manual* (Shanghai: American Presbyterian Mission Press, 1910), p. 295, no. 913. The three others have already been mentioned: Zeng Shen, Zi Si, and Mengzi.

[156] The ten are An Yuan, Minzi Qian, Ran Boniu, Zhong Gong, Zai Wo, Zi Ye, Ran You, Ji Lu, Zi You, and Zi Xia.

[157] *Bọi* is apparently a mistake for *bồi* (*pei,* assistant). The remaining two words *tế quan (jiguan)* mean "official [responsible for] sacrifice, or ceremonial official." Thus, the compound means "assistant to the ceremonial official."

table, where he stands before these assistants and performs the duties of the principal attendant; he is called the *tế quan* (*jiguan*, ceremonial official), and deservedly he can also be called a priest who performs the sacrifice. But, in fact, the clothes that he and his assistants wear are no different from those of the six others who are standing by.

After that, the principal attendant, when one master of ceremonies announces it, approaches the *hương án* sacrificial table, remains a short distance away for some time, and then genuflects in front of it. Another attendant lights sticks of incense on the altar of Confucius and other [altars],[158] and two other attendants carry to the altar two small goblets of wine, that is, of drippings from steamed rice, and place them on the small table with food, put there for Confucius. Another of the most distinguished [participants] genuflects to the left of the principal attendant, and, after declaring the names of all the participants, brings to Confucius's attention that the sacrifice will be made in the morning, saying: Kim vi ư lai nhật sự vu tiên thánh khẩn cáo;[159] that is: We reverently announce to the ancient saint or sage that we designate tomorrow morning for performing the ceremony. With these words the spirit of Confucius is implicitly invited to be present at the sacrifice. After these words are said, the principal attendant honors [Confucius] with a single prostration and returns to his place, where he bows deeply four times. Finally, an animal to be killed is led to the door of the temple, and the principal attendant examines it to ascertain whether it is fit for the sacrifice; it is not tested by pouring liquid into its ears, however, as happens among the Chinese. After the animal is selected in this way, the preparatory ceremony called *Lễ tức yết* (ceremony of reverent acknowledgement)[160] is over. Immediately after that, [p. 17], the selected and approved animal, either a pig or a bull, is killed and if one animal is not enough they kill two, and they also kill several goats. They disembowel the animals, shave their hair, butcher them, and half burn them; some of the meat they put on the sacrificial tables with food in front of the vessels with incense; the head, indeed, [they place] on the altar of Confucius, and the rest of the parts they place in the center in front of the altar behind the *hương án* sacrificial table, and in the same place they put a vessel containing the blood and hair of the killed animal.

Paragraph 2: On the Ceremony of Sacrifice

The next morning, starting at dawn, they conduct the sacrifice. Two masters of ceremonies, attendants, assistants, and the principal attendant stand, each in his place, as in the preparatory ceremony. When everyone is positioned in his place, the principal attendant proceeds with examining each sacrificial table and the altar, [to see] whether all the necessary [accessories] are arranged, and for this reason he also interrogates the attendants, who are standing in front of these sacrificial tables. After the inspection is completed, and when the master of

[158] The translation is quite approximate, since the syntax of the sentence in Latin is unclear.

[159] 今 為 於 來 日 事 于 先 聖 懇 誥 .

[160] Instead of the word *tức* there should have been *túc (su)*, "respectful, reverent," and the name of the ceremony would read in Chinese *li suye*. Even though all the words here are Sino-Vietnamese, the word order is vernacular Vietnamese.

ceremonies announces it, one attendant accepts the vessel with blood and hair and proceeds to bury it outside the temple without any preceding offering, which is usually performed in China, as testified by Episcope a Leonissa[161] in the *Exposita Sacrae Congregationi* (Replies to the Holy Congregation). With this ceremony they try to show that the meat offered is free of blood inside and of hair outside. Then the master of ceremonies announces the welcome of Confucius by saying: Nghinh Thánh Vương (ying shengwang), that is, Let us welcome the saint or wise king, or, better, the governor; and the first attendant, the assistants, and all the participants accept his arrival with four prostrations.

After that, whenever one master of ceremonies or another announces a subsequent action, the principal attendant proceeds to the chosen sacrificial table, washes his hands in the vessel placed on the four-legged [support], and wipes his hands with a towel offered by the appointed attendant; then he returns to the center, and, genuflecting in front of the *hương án* sacrificial table, offers or makes libations of one ladle[162] or a small goblet of wine—that is, of the drippings—raising it with both hands to his eyes, [and then] after offering [it], returns it to [p. 18] the attendant who had given it to him; this [attendant] carries it to the altar accompanied by three other attendants, who also carry to the altar three other goblets with drippings, and they place them on the sacrificial table with food [on the altar]. Another attendant brings a piece of cloth, or a white square of rolled silk, and puts it on [the altar]. Then the principal attendant honors [Confucius] with a single prostration, stands up, and then, after a little while, steps back to his place, where he genuflects. Immediately after that, one among the most distinguished [participants] approaches the *hương án* sacrificial table and, after genuflecting in front of it, recites an offertory from the leaf, called *văn tế* (*wenji*, sacrificial letters or writing, i.e., an oration), placed on a small table, showing it to himself, holding it in [his] hand; and after he reads it, he puts it on the altar and, simultaneously, the first attendant together with the assistants venerate [Confucius] with double prostrations.

In this offertory, all the literati who are present, preceded by the current year, month, and day, are enumerated, starting from the name of the principal attendant performing the sacrifice. Then, first, [the text of the offertory] offers the drippings, called *rượu* (wine), the food, and everything else that has been prepared; second, [it] praises Confucius for the books written by him and for the doctrine passed on to posterity; third, [it] asks that this doctrine be granted to them, so that they might follow it, as sages imitating wise ancestors, and [they] also [ask that Confucius] preserve this doctrine and give it to their posterity forever. Finally, they conclude [the offertory] with the following words: *Thượng hưởng* (*Shanxiang*, Mayest thou enjoy this offering), with which the spirit of Confucius is invited for the feast in a spiritual manner. Actually, Confucius is named with these honorific words: Đại thành chí Thánh Văn tuyên Vương, which we have already explained. Together with calling the name of Confucius, they also mention his four most distinguished disciples, [who] in common speech [are called] *tứ Phối*, and ten other distinguished

---

[161] Jean François Aleonissa, of the Order of Friars Minor, was a vicar apostolic in China. Being asked by Cardinal Casante to express his opinion on Chinese rites, he wrote his *Exposita*. Aleonissa's replies are kept in the Library of Port-Royal, according to Joseph Nguyen Huy Lai, *La Tradition religieuse*, p. 190.

[162] The word translated as "ladle" is *cyathus* in Latin. It refers to a ladle for filling the goblets with wine from the bowl.

disciples, [called] in common speech *thập Triết*. The four most distinguished disciples are: first, Nhan Tử (Yanzi, i.e., Yan Hui); second, Tàng Tử;[163] third, Tử Tư (Zi Si); fourth, Mạnh Tử. The title of *Thánh (sheng)*, that is, of saint or sage, is assigned to them by Emperor Nguyên Văn Tông (Yuan Wenzong), in his first year [of reign], [the year] of Christ 1307.[164]

After the offertory is read in this manner, the principal attendant offers four goblets of drippings to the four previously mentioned most distinguished disciples, to each of them one after another; [p. 19] after that, four attendants successively carry [the goblets] to the two tables [of the disciples], and place them in front of the four vessels with incense, keeping the same order we have just described; at the same place they also put for each of them a rolled piece of silk cloth, and after having placed each cloth, the principal attendant venerates [the disciples] with one prostration. Finally, ten small goblets of drippings are put for the ten other distinguished disciples of Confucius, but they are hardly offered and the silk clothes are not laid down either.[165] And all these [actions] are repeated for a second and third time, first for Confucius, then for his disciples in the order mentioned above. When everything is repeated for the third time, the principal attendant genuflects in front of the *hương án* sacrificial table and drinks from one goblet, turning his face aside from the altar; this goblet is taken from the sacrificial table of Confucius by the appointed attendant, and is carried to him [the principal attendant]; it is believed that with this drink he obtains happiness bestowed on him by Confucius and for that reason one master of ceremonies announces the drinking by saying: "Ẩm phúc (yinfu)," that is, *To drink happiness.* And when the goblet is empty, another master of ceremonies instructs the attendant to give thanks for such a gift; he immediately expresses his gratitude by venerating [Confucius] with double prostrations and returns to his place. After that the master of ceremonies instructs all the attending [literati] to thank the spirit of Confucius, saying: "Từ Thần (cishen),"[166] and the principal attendant, his assistants, and all the participants honor [Confucius] with four prostrations; with this ceremony they intend to see off the departing or "quasi"-departing spirit of Confucius by expressing [their] gratitude. Finally, outside the temple in the courtyard they burn the *văn tế* leaf, all the silk clothes, and also gold and silver papyri, which have been put on the altar; however, in the royal city this leaf and the offered silk clothes are not burnt, but they are put inside small bags and thrown in a pit in the courtyard; this occasionally is also observed in some other places. After the sacrifice is completed, they distribute meat and all the food offerings among the attendants, assistants, and other participants who are noble, and they eat some of it there, [and they] take some home for their relatives and friends.

---

[163] An apparent mistake for Tăng Tử (Zengzi), a disciple of Confucius menioned above.

[164] There is a mistake here. It should read "Emperor Nguyên Vũ Tông" (Yuan Wuzong, r. 1308–12). Adriano di St. Thecla introduces a minor discrepancy, which might have been caused by the different calendar systems of Europe and China.

[165] The grammar of the Latin sentence is corrupt, and the suggested translation is an attempt to guess what the author implied.

[166] Without the characters, the meaning of this compound is not monosemantic. If this pronunciation stands for the characters 辭 神, it might mean "bid farewell to a spirit," but if the original characters were 慈 神, the compound would mean "a merciful spirit." This compound is used in the manuscript several more times, and in each case, as is the case here, either meaning can be made to fit the context.

[p. 20] The names of Confucius, Books and Testimonies, about which [it has been said] in this chapter———

[This remainder of this page, as well as pp. 21–23 of the manuscript, are blank.]

CHAPTER TWO

ON THE SPIRITS AND THEIR CULT

[p. 24]

The cult of spirits among the Chinese dates back to the most ancient tradition, which was inherited by the Sect of Literati. They taught the cult of spirits, although they were not the first to introduce it. We have already talked in the preceding chapter about the doctrine of the literati pertaining to spirits. In this chapter we speak of the spirits who are worshipped not only by the literati but also by all the others according to the customs of the Chinese nation. However, I am not thinking of all the spirits or individual spirits who are honored in popular religion, but only of the most famous, to whom the greatest worship is exhibited.

Article 1: On the Spirits of Heaven and Earth

The literati as well as illiterates—the king and the people—together worship and venerate first of all Heaven and Earth, or the spirit of Heaven and the spirit of Earth. They call Heaven "King Hoàng Thiên" (Huangtian, High Heaven) and Earth "Queen Hậu Thổ" (Houtu, Empress of Earth), and they also call the spirit of Heaven "Thiên Thần" (Tianshen) and "Thượng Đế" (Shangdi, Supreme Emperor) and the spirit of Earth "Địa Kỳ" (Diqi);[1] and there is a certain temple called Thượng Đế inside the palace of the king, which in the vulgar [language] is called *Nhà Kính Thiên* (House for Veneration of Heaven). In no other place in the whole kingdom does there exist another temple dedicated to the cult of Heaven. There is no image inside the temple, not even a tablet, but only one four-legged gilt sacrificial table. In this temple the king makes a solemn sacrifice once a year, on the first or the second or the third day of the new year. He enters the temple with a few courtiers, leaving the rest of the train of nobles at the threshold outside the temple, since they consider themselves not deserving to enter this place, and

[1] This cosmic unity of heaven and earth in China is reflected in the expression from the Warring States period: "The way of Heaven is circular, that of Earth is square," which conveys the idea of a cohesive system whereby the circle of heaven encloses the square earth within its circumference. See Michael Loewe, "The Heritage Left to the Empires," in *The Cambridge History of Ancient China: From the Origins of Civilization to 221 B.C.*, ed. Michael Loewe and Edward L. Shaughnessy (Cambridge: Cambridge University Press, 1998), pp. 997–998.

nobody except the king is believed to be the appropriate person, who deserves to sacrifice to Heaven. So, it is by common consent that only the king is worthy to sacrifice to Heaven in its temple. There the king washes his hands, and while the tympani are sounding, together with other musical instruments, he burns incense over the sacrificial table, and then he honors Heaven, or Thượng Đế, with prostrations and a libation of wine; at the same time the *văn tế (wenji)* leaf, or the offertory, is read by one of the high priests, [p. 25] during which the king offers wine and food placed on the sacrificial table and asks Thượng Đế for help and protection for the entire kingdom. Also during the aforementioned three days the king offers sacrifices to Earth in her temple with three victims—a cow, a goat, and a pig. When the king comes to the temple dedicated to Heaven with the intention to make sacrifice, the following phrase is said: "Vua ra giao," which means: the king goes to the temple of Heaven, which is called Giao (Jiao), and in the same way the temple of Earth is named Xã (She). In addition, during these days, the king, with the help of his assistants or the nobles, sacrifices to mountains, streams, the four seasons of the year, cold and heat, winds and rain, or to their spirits in their separate temples, following the example of the ancient emperor Đế Thuấn (Di Shun), who sacrificed to all of them, as Confucius testifies in *Thư Kinh* (*Shujing*, Book of History).[2] In China there are five mountains which stand out among others, namely, Mount Tần (Qin) in the eastern part,[3] Mount Hoa (Hua) in the western part,[4] Mount Hành (Heng) in the southern part,[5] Mount Thương (Shang) in the northern part,[6] and Mount Tung (Song)[7] ——— in between these four parts. The emperors sacrifice to these five mountains. See chapter 1 on [everything] said above.

Not only the king but also his subjects honor Heaven, and they sacrifice to him in all the cities and villages once a year on some day of the first month. Whenever they wish, they sacrifice to the Supreme King, or Thượng Đế. The sacrifice to him, or the ceremony, is called *Kỳ yên*, which means supplication for tranquillity. They perform this sacrifice in any place: in the public building of the community, or in the marketplace, or in the road, or in a tent called *Nhà quán*. Nevertheless, they do not perform it in any temple, or *miếu* (*miao*, temple or shrine), since they do not have a temple dedicated to Thượng Đế, except the one described above inside the royal palace in the city. Also once a year, in the last month, all the prefects and soldiers inside and outside the country[8] pronounce a solemn oath, in which they promise to be faithful to the king on pain of death from Heaven and Earth and from

---

[2] *The Shoo King;* James Legge, trans., *The Chinese Classics* (reprint, Taipei: SMC Publishing, 1991), 3:33-34.

[3] The name of the mountain is Thái (Tai). Adriano di St. Thecla was apparently confused by the similarity of two characters , 秦 , tần (qin), and 泰 thái (tai). The mountain is located in Shandong province of China.

[4] In Shanxi province of China.

[5] In Hunan province.

[6] The name of this mountain is Hằng (Heng). Why Thương (Sheng) appears in Adriano di St. Thecla's manuscript has remained obscure. Heng mountain is located in Hebei province.

[7] In Henan province of China. In the manuscript a blank space follows.

[8] In Latin this part of the sentence reads "omnes Praefacti, et milites, tam in civitate quàm extrà," and we provided a verbatim translation of it: "all prefects and soldiers inside and outside the country," although the reference to those outside the country remains obscure.

all the spirits, to all of which they make a solemn sacrifice. We will describe this ceremony in the fifth article.

Moreover, there is a common belief that the king, on the day when he sacrifices to Heaven, after the sacrifice, goes out into the field, takes a plow and for a short time ploughs the field.[9] After a very diligent investigation in the city, questioning those who accompany the king each time he comes out of his palace to other places, it has been revealed that [p. 26] the king never takes the plow and ploughs the field. His companions, the Gentiles as well as the Christians, after being interrogated on this, answered that they had never seen the king taking the plow and plowing, neither the one currently ruling, nor his predecessors, his father, grandfather and great-grandfather. Venerable Father Francisco Gil de Federich, mentioned in the Preface, made me even more assured of this.

On the other hand, in the book *Lễ Kinh* (*Lijing*, Book of Rites), this ritual, performed by the king, is described with the following words: Thiên Tử nải dĩ nguyên nhật, kỳ cốc vu Thượng Đế, nải trạch nguyên thân,[10] Thiên Tử thân tái lỗi trĩ, suất tam Công cửu Khanh, chư hầu đại phu, cung canh đế tịch, Thiên Tử tam xôi, tam Công ngũ xôi, Khanh chư hầu cửu xôi.[11] This means: the son of Heaven, namely the king, receives on the first day?——— and disposes,[12] or takes hold of the plow, and orders the courtiers to open it for the king, or to split the ground. The son of Heaven ploughs going back and forth three times, the courtiers *tam Công* (*sangong*, first three highest-ranking mandarins at the court) go five times, the courtiers *Khanh* (*qing*, high ministers) and the *chư hầu* (*zhuhou*, great officers) nine times.[13] Henceforth, this ritual started falling into decay at the Annamite court, as well as at the Chinese court.[14]

---

[9] As it is said in the *Liji* (Record of Rites): "This was not because the son of Heaven and the princes had not men to plough for them . . . ; it was to give the exhibition of their personal sincerity. Such sincerity was what is called doing their utmost, was what is called reverence." James Legge, *Li Chi, Book of Rites* (New Hyde Park, NY: University Books, 1967), 2:239.

[10] This word should be read as *thần* (*chen*, a favorable day) instead of *thân*.

[11] 天子乃以元日祈穀于上帝乃擇元辰天子親載耒耜帥三公九卿諸侯大夫躬耕帝籍天子三推三公五推卿諸侯九推. Adriano di St. Thecla omits, however, a part of the original passage. The original reads, 天子乃以元日祈穀于上帝乃擇元辰天子親載耒耜帥措之于參保介之御閒三公九卿諸侯大夫躬耕帝籍天子三推三公五推卿諸侯九推. S. Couvreur, trans., *Li Ki ou mémoires sur les bienséances et les cérémonies* (Ho Kien Fu: Imprimerie de la Mission Catholique, 1913), 1:334–335. Legge translates the omitted passage: (措之于參保介之御閒) as "placed between the man-at-arms who is its third occupant and the driver." Legge, *Li Chi,* 1:254.

[12] This part of the sentence is corrupted.

[13] James Legge gives the translation of this phrase as the following: "The son of Heaven on the first (*hsin* [*xin*]) day prays to God for a good year; and afterwards, the day of the first conjunction of the sun and moon having been chosen, with the handle and share of the plough in the carriage, placed between the man-at-arms who is its third occupant and the driver, he conducts his three ducal ministers, his nine high ministers, the feudal princes and his Great officers, all with their own hands to plough the field of God. The Son of Heaven turns up three furrows, each of the ducal ministers five, and the other ministers and feudal princes nine." Legge, *Li Chi,* 1:254–255 (or ibid., 1:254–255).

[14] Legge (1815–97) states that this ceremony was still performed in his time, that is, in the nineteenth century, "in substance, by the emperors of China and their representatives

Article 2: On the Kings Called Thánh, and Especially on Those to Whom Sacrifices Are Made Four Times a Year

There are nine kings, whom the Sect of Literati, as well as all the others, treat and honor as the <u>*Saints,*</u> or as [ones] endowed with exceptional virtue, whom the Annamites call Thánh, and the Chinese call Xing (sheng). They are divided into two categories: the elder [kings] are called Thánh Đế (Shengdi); more recent are called Thánh Vương (Shengwang). These two titles *Đế* (*di*, emperor) and *Vương* (*wang*, king) are considered to be different in the following way: the name *Đế* expresses more dignity, the name *Vương*, less. There are five kings, who are called Thánh Đế, and for that reason [they are called] Ngũ Đế (Wudi), namely, Thái Hảo Phục Hi (Tai Hao Fu Xi),[15] Viêm Đế Thần Nông (Yandi Shennong),[16] Hoàng Đế (Huang Di), Đế Nghiêu (Di Yao), and Đế Thuấn (Di Shun).[17] There are four kings called Thánh Vương: Đại Vũ (Da Yu) is, of course, the first, from the Hạ (Xia) dynasty; Thành Thang (Cheng Tang)[18] is the first from the Thương (Shang) dynasty;[19] Văn Vương (Wen Wang) and his son Vũ Vương (Wu Wang)[20] are the

---

throughout the provinces. . . . The grain produced by it was employed in the sacrifices or religious services of which God (Shang Tî [Shangdi]) was the object, and hence arose the denomination" (Legge, *Li Chi,* 1:255 n. 1). In Vietnam, it is recorded that the emperor performed the plowing ceremony at least as early as the tenth century. See, for example, *Đại Việt Sử Ký Toàn Thư* (Complete History of Great Việt) (Hanoi: Nhà Xuất Bản Khoa Học Xã Hội, 1993), bản ký, 1:18a (1:224) under the year 987, and bản ký, 2:25b (1:259) under the year 1038. In the second case, even the argument between King Lý Thái Tông (1028–54) and his courtiers was recorded. The courtiers tried to persuade Lý Thái Tông that plowing is not an occupation for kings, but Lý Thái Tông replied: "If We [the king] do not personally plough, then what will We use for rice offerings, and what will We use as an example for others to follow?"

[15] Thái Hảo (Tai Hao) is Fu Xi's dynastic title, translated by Legge as "the Grandly Bright." See Legge, *Li Chi,* 1:250 n. 1.

[16] The god of agriculture, or the "Divine Farmer" (in the traditional Chinese chronology his years of rule are 2737–2697 B.C.E); Viêm Đế (Yandi) is his dynastic title, meaning "Flaming (Brilliant) Emperor." Thần Nông (Shen Nong) appeared relatively late in Chinese literature. Mencius spoke of a school of agriculture that traced its origin back to Shen Nong. He is also mentioned in the *Zhuangzi.* "Both reports show that Shen-nung [Shen Nong] must have been a quite well-known figure already in the fourth century B.C.E., but probably not in the whole area of the high-Chinese culture." Wolfram Eberhard, *The Local Cultures of South and East China,* trans. Alide Eberhard (Leiden: E. J. Brill, 1968), p. 219.

[17] The composition of the group of the Five Emperors varies in different sources. This list and order of the Five Emperors, which Adriano di St. Thecla cites, appeared in commentaries in various sources as early as the Han dynasty, but for some time thereafter it was not clearly set. See a discussion on the Five Emperors by Luo Genze in Gu Jiegang, Luo Genze, and Lü Simian, *Gushi bian* (Discrimination of Ancient History) (Beijing: Pushe minguo, 1926–41), 5:621–636.

[18] Thành Thang (Cheng Tang, traditional dates of reign are 1766–1753 B.C.E.) is credited with overthrowing the wicked ruler of the declining Hạ (Xia) dynasty and founding a new Thương (Shang) dynasty. For his ability to bring back virtuous rule, Cheng Tang is considered one of the righteous or saintly kings in traditional Chinese historiography, and described as such in both *Shujing* (Book of History) and *Shiji* (Historical Records).

[19] There are different versions of the time of reign of the Thương (Shang) dynasty. The traditional dates are 1766–1122 B.C.E. While these dates have been contested, as with the dating of the Zhou dynasty, I will use here the traditional dates, as did the author of the manuscript.

first from the Chu (Zhou) dynasty. All these kings are treated under one name of Thánh Vương in the illustrious encomium in the Preface [p. 27] to the classical book *Đại Học* (*Daxue*, Great Learning) with the following words: Tích giả Thánh Vương kế thiên lập cực dĩ đạo trị Thiên hạ, tự Phục Hi, Thần Nông, Hoàng Đế, Nghiêu, Thuấn, Vũ Thang, Văn Vũ tương truyền thụ.[21] This means: at that time, when the Saintly Kings or the kings of exceptional virtue were writing a law, they accepted a rigid doctrine of ruling the people, which the aforementioned kings, starting from Phục Hi (Fu Xi) successively passed on.[22] They make sacrifice to the first five emperors on the same day when they sacrifice to Heaven and to Earth.

Four times a year the king, with the help of the nobles of the court, sacrifices to the ancient emperors, as it is prescribed in *Lễ Kinh*.[23] At the end of winter he sacrifices to the East of Giao region, to Emperor Phục Hi, and to the spirit Câu Mang (Goumang),[24] who was his officer, to inaugurate spring, *lập xuân (lichun)*.[25] At the end of spring he sacrifices to the South of Giao region to Emperor Thần Nông and to the spirit Chúc Daong[26] (Zhurong),[27] bringing in summer, *lập hạ (lixia)*;[28] at

---

[20] King Văn (Wen) was a ruler of the state of Chu (Zhou), one of the many ancient principalities in the territory of modern China. He, together with his son Vũ (Wu), started a military campaign against the Thương (Shang) dynasty. King Wen did not complete the campaign, as he was killed in the fight. His son (Wu) succeeded him, won the war, and beheaded the last ruler of the Shang dynasty, Trụ Tân (Zhou Xin), whom Adriano di St. Thecla will mention below. Kings Wen and Wu are considered as founders of the Zhou dynasty; they received special respect from the Confucian scholars since the Zhou was a cradle of Confucianism.

[21] 昔 者 聖 王 繼 天 立 極 以 道 治 天 下 自 伏 義 神 農 黃 帝 堯 舜 禹 湯 文 武 相 傳 收 受 . This is not the exact citation from the preface written by Chu Hi (Zhu Xi), but a very close paraphrase of one of its passages. *Daxue zhangju* (Great Learning: Chapters and Paragraphs [with commentaries of Zhu Xi]) (Kyoto: Santo Shorin, 1900?), p. 1b. I suspect that Adriano di St. Thecla used some other Chinese or Vietnamese source commenting on Zhu Xi's preface, and took it as the original, because I could not find an exact match to the adduced phrase in several other editions of *Daxue* (Great Learning) I have consulted.

[22] Adriano di St. Thecla's explanation of the phrase quite precisely conveys its sense. The translation of this sentence is: "In olden times the Sage (or Saint) Kings following [the way] of Heaven established the law to govern the world, [and] starting from Phục Hi (Fu Xi), Thần Nông (Shen Nong), Hoàng Đế (Huang Di), Nghiêu (Yao), Thuấn (Shun), Vũ (Yu), Thang (Cheng), Văn (Wen) [and] Vũ (Wu) successively passed it down." However, it has remained unclear whether he treated emperors Vũ (Yu) and Thang (Cheng) as one person, since they are not separated by a comma, as were Nghiêu (Yao) and Thuấn (Shun). The same absence of a comma is also seen in the next pair, Văn (Wen) and Vũ (Wu). I wonder whether Adriano di St. Thecla failed to recognize that there are actually four names here, not two. If so, that might explain why he did not provide the list of the emperors, as he definitely could not find emperors named Vũ Thang (Yu Cheng) and Văn Vũ (Wen Wu). On the other hand, he may have left out the names in the translation because he considered the entire list unimportant for his readers. In the original the names of Vũ (Yu), Thang (Cheng), Văn (Wen), and Vũ (Wu) are absent.

[23] Legge, *Li Chi*, 1:224–225.

[24] The God of Spring, who "had the body of a bird and wore plain-color clothes in three tiers." See Eberhard, *Local Cultures*, p. 187. He allegedly was a son of another legendary emperor Thiếu Hạo (Shao Hao). See Legge, *Li Chi*, 1:250.

[25] Legge, *Li Chi*, 1:249–257.

[26] Chúc Dong or Dung in the modern style of writing. Neither Huình Tịnh Paulus Của nor Alexandre de Rhodes incorporates the second character used for this emperor's name or its pronunciation. Huình Tịnh Paulus Của, *Đại Nam Quấc Âm Tự Vị* (A Dictionary of Characters with the National Pronunciation of Great Nam) (reprint, Ho Chi Minh City: Nhà Xuất Bản Trẻ, 1998); Alexandre de Rhodes, *Từ Điển Annam-Lusitan-Latinh* (Annamite-Lusitanian

the end of summer he sacrifices to the West of Giao region to Emperor Thiếu Hiệu (Shao Hao)[29] and to the spirit Nhục Thu (Rushou),[30] designating the beginning of autumn, *lập thu (liqiu);*[31] at the end of autumn he sacrifices to the North of Giao region, to Emperor Xuyên Húc[32] (Zhuan Xu)[33] and to the spirit Huyền Minh (Xuanming),[34] starting winter, *lập đông (lidong).*[35] Three days before, an astrologer decides on the time of introducing each period and informs the king about the day determined. The king, in the process of preparation for the ritual, fasts by abstinence from meat. These emperors receive sacrifice due to their services to the state; definitely, sacrifice is performed to Phục Hi and Câu Mang, since being obedient to or complying with Heaven they introduced the law, or the rigid doctrine, as Chu Tử (Zhuzi) says in the commentaries to the above mentioned *Lễ Kinh:* Thánh Thần kế thiên lập cực sinh hữu[36] công đức ư dân, cố hậu ư xuân tự chi.[37] They also sacrifice to Thần Nông and Chúc Daong, since they taught agriculture to their subjects, as is mentioned in the *Chinese History:* Trác mộc vi tử, như mộc vi lỗi, thỉ giáo dân nghệ ngũ cốc.[38]

They observe a special ritual in welcoming spring, or in establishing *lập xuân.* It can be easily described with the same words used by venerable F. Francisco Gil de Federich, in order to picture it accurately. "Around *lập xuân* [day]," he says,

---

[Portuguese]-Latin Dictionary), trans. Thanh Lãng, Hoàng Xuân Việt, and Đỗ Quang Chính (reprint, Ho Chi Minh City: Nhà Xuất Bản Khoa Học Xã Hội, 1991). However, it is known that the combination *ao* was replaced by *o* or *u* in modern Vietnamese.

27 God of Fire, whose connection with fire is indicated by his name "the melter." His life is reported with great variations. For a discussion of accounts in different sources, see Eberhard, *Local Cultures,* p. 68. Apparently, it is not a coincidence that he is coupled here with Thần Nông (Shen Nong), whose dynastic title was "Flaming Emperor."

28 Legge, *Li Chi,* 1:268–272.

29 R. 2597–2513 B.C.E. He allegedly was the eldest son of Hoàng Đế (Huang Di).

30 The spirit of autumn, and according to Legge one of the sons of Emperor Thiếu Hiệu (Shao Hao). Legge, *Li Chi,* 1:283.

31 Ibid., pp. 283–286.

32 Chuyên Húc in modern Vietnamese spelling. It is difficult to say whether *xuyên* is a mistake for *chuyên* or is an outdated variation of pronunciation.

33 R. 2513–2435 B.C.E. All four emperors belong to the legendary period of Chinese history.

34 "The Dark and Mysterious." He is identified with Yushi, a god of rain, and held as one who personifies the aqueous influences of the atmosphere. See N. B. Dennys, *The Folk-lore of China and its Affinities with that of the Aryan and Semitic Races* (London: Trubner; Hong Kong: "China Mail" Office, 1876), p. 124.

35 Legge, *Li Chi,* 1:296–301. In fact, the description of these seasonal rites is in the book *Yueling* (Monthly Commands) of the *Record of Rites,* and, according to this book, the rituals to the respective spirits are to take place not once a season, as it is said in the manuscript, but thrice, though in reality these rites were not celebrated so frequently.

36 This word is garbled in the manuscript. *Hữu* (*you,* to have) is the best version I could come up with, even though I do not think that it is the perfect syntactical solution for this phrase.

37 聖 神 繼 天 立 極 生 有 (?) 功 德 於 民 故 後 於 春 祀 之 . "Sages and spiritual men, following [the way of] Heaven, established the rule of life, showed merit and virtue toward the people; consequently, later [people started] to make sacrifices to them in the spring."

38 斫 木 為 籽 如 木 為 耒 始 教 民 藝 五 穀 . "[They taught] to hew trees to produce seeds of grain, as [to use] wood to make a plough and started to teach people the skill of [growing] the five kinds of grains [i.e., agriculture]."

The day before, the soldiers *Đội lí hình* (*dui lixing*)[39] go to the house of *Nhà Môn Ngưu* (Office of Buffaloes or the Office of Slaughtering Buffaloes) and [p. 28] take 1,300 small buffaloes there. In the gate Hàng Chiếu[40] a house is erected open to the four winds. A big clay buffalo is put inside the house, and on every buffalo a statue of Câu Mang is put—for a small buffalo, a small one, for a big, a big one—as if it guards the buffalo itself. After they take 1,300 buffaloes they bring them to the eastern prison, and put them down at the court of the prison. The clay buffalo stays in the house erected in Ngõ Hàng Chiếu (Hàng Chiếu lane) during the entire day and until midnight, and after that [through the] *phố phường (pufang)*[41] it is led to the courtyard, or the temple, of Vua Bạch Mã (King Baima, King White Horse),[42] where they put it outside; and only Thần Câu Mang (Shen Goumang, spirit Goumang) is lifted up in the center of the courtyard, where Quan Phủ Doản (guan fuyin)[43] sacrifices to Thần Câu Mang. After the sacrifice, Nhà Môn (people from the office [of buffaloes]) cover Thần Câu Mang with a mat and carry it out for burial; the soldiers of this prison bring down the buffalo to this prison, take a part of his head, one foot, and a part of the tail, and carry them away to offer to king Vua,[44] who is waiting together with other chiefs on both sides of the courtyard; to this place they also bring 300 out of the aforementioned small buffaloes. The soldiers take 55 of them and distribute them evenly among the sacrificial tables, called *mâm* (tray) in vulgar speech; 5 buffaloes per each of the eleven tables. They cover them with saffron *lụa* (silk) and leave them there. Later the king sends them to all the *đền thờ* {the temples of spirits} together with the buffaloes remaining from 300. After that, the king orders to divide [the rest] between all the soldiers, who always assist him *ex officio;* they bring the thousand small buffaloes out of the prison to Phủ Đang[45] and proclaim this to king *Chúa* (*zhu*).[46] Then all the *Nhà Môn Sáu Hiệu* {six cohorts} approach and take the

[39] The meaning of this compound is not clear in modern Vietnamese, but it seems to designate a certain kind of police unit.

[40] The place is in Hanoi near the eastern gate of the citadel.

[41] As a compound *phố phường* means "streets." Thus, a translation of this part of the sentence is "after that it is led through the streets to the courtyard."

[42] The temple to Bạch Mã (Baima), for centuries worshipped as the protector deity of the capital, is located in the old quarter of Hanoi. See more on him below.

[43] The final word in the compound should read *Doãn* (*yin*, official position), not *Doản*, which does not, and apparently did not exist. There is a redundancy in this title, as *quan (guan)* means "official," and *phủ doãn (fuyin)* is already a self-sufficient compound, meaning "the governor of a prefecture." This compound often refers to the governor of the province where the capital is located. In this case the mayor of Thăng Long (modern Hanoi) is meant.

[44] The reference is to the figurehead Emperor Lê.

[45] According to Professor Trần Quốc Vượng, there was a temple erected in the seventeenth century by the Trịnh lords outside of Hanoi to commemorate their female ancestors from the Đang clan. This temple no longer exists.

[46] *Chúa (zhu)* originally designated a generalissimo of the army and refers to the actual rulers from the Trịnh family, who in the seventeenth century became an analogue to the Japanese *shogun.* See Philippe Papin, *Histoire de Hanoi* (Paris: Fayard, 2001), p. 147. In this passage the author uses the term "king" (*regius or rex* in Latin) for both the Vua Lê (the de jure king of Vietnam) and the Chúa Trịnh (the de facto ruler), thus demonstrating that the position of the warlords was at least as high as that of the kings.

buffaloes to all the mandarins who belong to this *Hiệu* (xiao, cohort), for distribution. The buffaloes are put on the altars, which are dedicated to an idol, or a *thần* (*shen*, spirit or deity), or to the ancestors. They make clay buffaloes, which are 5 or 6 fingers high {as he [i.e., F. Fransisco Gil de Federich] says in another, earlier, writing}, and they paint them differently, the head, the body, and the tail with different colors according to the rule. For painting they use five principles of Chinese philosophy, namely *hỏa* (*huo*, fire), *thổ* (*tu*, earth), *kim* (*jin*, metal), *thủy* (*shui*, water), and *mộc* (*mu*, wood), which are also assigned to days and years and the five colors corresponding to these principles. If the first day of spring corresponds to the fire or *hỏa*, they cover the head of the buffalo with the corresponding color, they also make next to the buffalo a clay image of a boy-guardian, whom they call Thần Câu Mang, and whom they also cover with a different [color of] paint in accordance with a different time of the year.

[p. 29] The *Chinese History* tells that Xuyên Húc performed the *lập xuân* ceremony in the first month and on the first day early in the morning. Nothing there mentions that any of his predecessors performed this ritual before him. In the year Mậu Thìn (wuchen), the ninth [year] of King Lê's [title of reign] Cảnh Hưng (Jingxing), this ceremony was performed on the eighteenth day of the last month before the new year; in China it was made in the same year on the sixteenth day of its last month. According to our calendar, it was February 1749. They have a special custom of welcoming summer; namely, after making a sacrifice to Emperor Thần Nông in his temple, the prefect called *phủ Doản*, in the garden or in the adjacent field, takes a plow and ploughs, turning three times back and forth, and plants a small amount of rice or turnips called *củ khoai* (edible tuber). This ritual seems to be used as a substitute for the ritual that in *Lễ Kinh* is prescribed to be performed by the king in the first month.[47] We described this ritual earlier.

Moreover, in some villages the sacrifice to Emperor Thần Nông happens twice a year, during the sixth or the seventh lunar months, when the transplanting of rice starts, which is called *hạ điền (xiadian)*, in the vulgar [language] *xuống đồng*, or "descending to the fields," and when this transplantation ends, it is called *thượng điền (shangdian)*, in the vulgar [language] *lên đồng*, or "ascending from the fields." The sacrifice for the descending to the fields is skipped in many regions, and only the simple offering of food takes place. No image or tablet of Thần Nông is used in the sacrifice. In the offertory, which they read from the leaf, they first praise him with many words, calling [him] Thánh Đế, wise, unearthly, the noblest, the most excellent, and the co-helper of the Supreme King Thượng Đế in feeding and caring for his subjects, in teaching them agriculture, and in handing down this kind of useful privilege from his time to eternal posterity. Second, they ask him to grant them complete happiness, namely fertility of the fields, abundant harvests, also wealth, peace, and the proper mixture for bronze, since the saint king himself helps and gives strength. This is said in the offertory, or the formula of sacrifice. However, the aforementioned emperors, to whom they sacrifice four times a year, cannot be treated as real Chinese kings. It appears, indeed, that they lived before the universal flood. This is discussed by us in our Preface to *The Chinese Chronology*, where we said that Thần Nông [p. 30] was nobody else but Noah,

[47] Legge, *Li Chi*, 1:253–257.

about whom it is said in Gen. 9 that after the flood "[Noah] *was the first tiller of the soil*."[48]

Article 3: On the Spirits Whom the Military Worship

The military worship many people who are famous for their courage in battle. Most of all, they venerate Thái Công (Tai Gong), earlier called by his family name Lã (Lü) and by his personal name Vaọng[49] (Wang), as the highest master and protector. He lived during the reign of Emperor Chu Vũ Vương (Zhou Wu Wang) more than a thousand years before Christ was born; he fought on his [the emperor's] side against Emperor Trụ (Zhou), the last [ruler] of the Thương (Shang) dynasty.[50] He surrounded the emperor with a siege so intense that he [Emperor Trụ of Thương], having no place to flee, threw himself and his retinue into the fire. In such a way Vũ Vương (Wu Wang) acquired power over the entire state, which his father Văn Vương (Wen Wang) had for the most part already subdued to himself,[51] and having gained power, he made him [Thái Công] the master of military service, or the highest [supreme] prefect.

They grant the second honor upon an extremely famous man named Trương Lương (Zhang Liang), who, during the rule of the Tần (Qin) dynasty,[52] was a prefect of the first rank in the kingdom of Hàn[53] during the reign of King Thành (Cheng).[54] After he [the king] was killed by Emperor Tần Nhị Thế (Qin Ershi),[55] he [prefect Trương Lương] with the army joined King Hán Lưu Bang (Han Liu Bang), to whom he subsequently handed down the entire power over the state; and he [Hán

---

[48] Gen. 9:20. With this statement Adriano di St. Thecla contradicts what he wrote in the preface, where he says that Hoàng Đế (Huang Di) "must certainly be excluded from the real Chinese chronology, since he lived before the universal flood." Thần Nông (Shen Nong) was one of Huang Di's predecessors according to the traditional Chinese chronology. Thus, he could not be Noah, who lived before and after the flood.

[49] Vọng in modern Vietnamese style.

[50] Thương Trụ Tân (Shang Zhou Xin, r. 1154–1122 B.C.E.), known as Zhou the Cruel.

[51] The information on the struggle between the Thương (Shang) and the Chu (Zhou) is mainly available from the sources of Confucian tradition, which elevates the prestige of the Zhou dynasty that defeated the Shang dynasty. The *Shujing* (Book of History) in the Zhou Annals says the following: "Show [Zhou Xin], the king of Shang, does not reverence Heaven above, and inflicts calamities on the people below. He has been abandoned to drunkenness, and reckless in lust. He has dared to exercise cruel oppression. Along with criminals he has punished all their relatives. He has put men into office on the hereditary principle. He has made it his pursuit to have palaces, towers, pavilions, embankments, ponds, and all other extravagances, to the most painful injury of you, the myriad people. He has burned and roasted the loyal and good. He has ripped up pregnant women. Great Heaven was moved with indignation, and charged my deceased father Wan [Wen] reverently to display its majesty; but *he died* before the work was completed." *The Shoo King;* Legge, trans., *Chinese Classics*, 3:284-285.

[52] 255–206 B.C.E.

[53] One of the kingdoms of the Warring States period in China.

[54] *Sử Ký Tư Mã Thiên* (Historical Records of Sima Qian), trans. Nhử Thành (Hanoi: Nhà xuất bản Văn Học, 1988), p. 284

[55] Tần Nhị Thế Hoàng Đế (Qin Ershi Huangdi, r. 209–206), the emperor who succeeded Tần Thuỷ Hoàng Đế (Qin Shi Huangdi).

Lưu Bang] got the name Cao Tổ (Gaozu).[56] Then, since he [Trương Lương] was afraid that the emperor might kill him, suspecting him of an intent to seize power over the kingdom, he asked for permission to leave and to lead a solitary life with spirits; he left the court, where he had served the emperor for six years, and hid himself for thirteen years until the sixth year of the reign of Huệ Đế (Huidi),[57] when he passed away from life, nine centuries after the aforementioned Thái Công Vaọng (Tai Gong Wang).[58]

In a public decree, Emperor Đàng Huyền Tông (Tang Xuanzong)[59] gave instructions about the cult of Thái Công and Trương Lương in the nineteenth year of his reign, in the year 730 after Christ was born, with these words: Trí Thái Công miếu, dĩ Trương Lương phối hưởng, tuyển cổ danh tướng dĩ bị thập, Triết, Tĩ [60] nhị bát nguyệt thượng mạu . . .[61] trí tế như Khổng Tử lễ.[62] [This says:] He ordered to build the temple for prefect Thái Công, to accept Trương Lương [into the temple], and to make him almost equal to Thái Công, to select generals with ancient names, and to appoint ten [p. 31] who were wise, or of high morality [from the generals], to adopt the second and the eighth moon [for the ceremony], and to sacrifice on the day prior to *mạu*, just as the sacrifice to Confucius was made. From this it is clear that Thái Công received from the military the same honor and cult as that which the literati devoted to Confucius; a little bit later Emperor Đàng

---

[56] The reference here is to Liu Bang who founded the Han dynasty and was posthumously honored as Hán Cao Tổ (Han Gaozu).

[57] R. 194–187 B.C.E.

[58] Thus, according to the author, Trương Lương (Zhang Liang) died in 188 B.C.E., which is in accordance with other sources. Adriano di Santa Thecla writes more of him in the chapter on Taoism.

[59] R. 713–56.

[60] The word *tĩ* does not appear in modern Sino-Vietnamese dictionaries. I surmise that the word implied here is either the character 俾 —"so that, to accord, to cause" or the character 比 —"to follow, when, by the time," now pronounced *tỉ*. The latter character is recorded as *tĩ* in Huình Tịnh Paulus Của's dictionary, as well as some other characters presently pronounced *tỉ*: 徙 — "to move," 姊 — "an elder sister." Huình Tịnh Paulus Của, *Đại Nam Quấc Âm Tự Vị*, p. 1047. The character 俾 is not listed among them, but then it is not listed in the dictionary at all (at least, under any similar pronunciation, and phonetic principle is the only key to working with this dictionary), which still leaves a chance that this character was pronounced the way Adriano di St. Thecla has it in his manuscript.

[61] The word *mạu* is not identified. It does not exist in Sino-Vietnamese or demotic Vietnamese dictionaries. I suggest two possibilities. One is to read this word as *mão (mao),* meaning the first ten days of a lunar month. The other is to consider *mạu* as indicating a compound current in seventeenth-century vernacular language as *mạu thìn (maochen),* which, according to Alexandre de Rhodes, is the same as *thìn (chen);* see Alexandre de Rhodes, *Từ Điển Annam-Lusitan-Latinh,* col. 460, s.v. "mạu thìn." While *thìn* is one of the twelve "earthly branches" to designate time (7–9 A.M.), it is also used in compounds like *ngày thìn* (the day of *thìn*); ibid., col. 766, s.v. "thìn." According to Anthony Trần Văn Kiệm, *thìn* also means "a memorable or commemorating event." See Anthony Trần Văn Kiệm, *Giúp Đọc Nôm và Hán Việt* (An Aid for Reading Demotic Vietnamese and Sino-Vietnamese) (Hue: Nhà Xuất Bản Thuận Hóa, 1999), pp. 829–830. Despite referring to an identical day for the sacrifices to Confucius in the chapter on Confucianism, Adriano di St. Thecla does not use this term, so it is impossible to establish a correspondence with the date used in that chapter. Between the words *mạu* and *trí* there is some unreadable two-letter word, which looks like a failed attempt to write *trí*.

[62] 置 太 公 廟 以 張 良 西 饗 選 古 名 將 以 備 十 哲 俾 (比) 二 八 月 上 [?] 置 祭 如 孔 子 禮

Túc Tông (Tang Suzong),[63] a direct successor of Huyền Tông (Xuanzong), granted him the title Vũ Thánh Vương (Wu Shengwang, Holy King of Military [Service]). Everything mentioned above on Thái Công and Trương Lương is borrowed from the *Chinese History*.

In the royal city of the Annamite kingdom a temple stands, named Vũ Miếu (Wumiao, Temple of Military Men),[64] where fifteen brave generals have a cult, and talented Thái Công Vaọng is their leader. There are two rooms in this temple; one is usually open, another is always closed. In the open room, there are twelve generals, or their images, six on each side. In the closed room, Thái Công stays with another twelve generals, one of whom is Trương Lương, and another one with the same grade of *phối* (*pei*, worthy); and ten others with the name Triết (zhe, wise or sage). It seems to me that, according to the emperor's decree quoted above, there is also another *miếu* in this country, established in the *bải* region,[65] called Nhà Chải[66]

---

[63] R. 756–63.

[64] The temple was more widely known as Võ Miếu, a variation for pronouncing the same name. The first known Võ Miếu was apparently built in Hanoi during the Trần dynasty (1126–1400). A stele corroborates this fact; see Hà Văn Tấn, "Bài Bia của Trương Hán Siêu và Vấn Đề Phong Thành Hoàng" (A Stele of Trương Hán Siêu and the Question of Tutelary Genies), *Nghiên Cứu Lịch Sử* (Historical Studies) 1 (1999): 42–50. This temple did not survive, and under the Lê dynasty a new Võ Miếu was erected in the year 1683, during the reign of Lê Hy Tông (1675–1705), as is affirmed in a manuscript containing notes on the vestiges of the capital Thăng Long. This is apparently the temple to which Adriano di St. Thecla refers. According to the manuscript, this Võ Miếu was located in the southern part of the then-existing Thăng Long, and there ten Worthy Sages were venerated along with some famous generals of previous dynasties. See *Thăng Long Cổ Tích Khảo Tịnh Hội Đồ* (Notes on and Plan of Ancient Thăng Long), compiled in 1956 by École Française d'Extrême-Orient, (kept in the Library of the Institute of Sino-Vietnamese Studies, archive no. VHv. 2471, p. 55). This manuscript was translated into modern Vietnamese by Phạm Thị Thoa in 1997 (unpublished). The Võ Miếu described by Adriano di St. Thecla shared the fate of its predecessor and perished during the Tây Sơn wars at the end of the eighteenth century. In the nineteenth century a new Võ Miếu was established in Hanoi by the Nguyễn dynasty (1802–1945), and it stood through the first part of the twentieth century until it was destroyed during the French War (1945–54). The Võ Miếu in Hanoi has not yet been restored.

[65] In modern Vietnamese this word is read *bãi*, and it denotes a shore or a ground with no buildings. The word *bải* in the form given by Adriano di St. Thecla is found in Rhodes's dictionary with the meaning "a coastal region." Rhodes, *Từ Điển Annam-Lusitan-Latinh*, col. 19.

[66] The temple does not exist anymore. The etymology of its name is obscure. However, it is known that there were in Vietnam a number of Võ Miếu temples devoted to military men; some were big constructions, some were only small shrines. In 1916, Mr. Delamarre, Resident of France in Sơn Tây, noted the following about maintaining ritual buildings: "The Võ Miếu exist only in major ancient provinces. In this temple is kept the memory of Thái Công (a military officer of the Chu [Zhou] dynasty) and that of Quan Công [Guan Gong] or Vân Chương [Wen Zhang], a military officer who was in the service of Lưu Bị [Liu Bei], a famous king of the Thục [Shu], about which the facts are recorded in the history of Tam Quốc [Sanguo, the Three Kingdoms] (the epoch of the Han). Twice a year, in the spring and in the autumn, on the next day after the ceremony in Văn Miếu [Wenmiao, the Temple of Literature], the military officers accompanied by the civil officials perform a ritual ceremony in honor of these heroes of Chinese antiquity to pay a tribute to military virtues." See note of Delamarre no. 126 from 15.03.1916, Vietnamese National Archive, Hanoi, fond of the Supreme Resident of Tonkin (RST) 72194, F90, p. 6. These temples apparently had a special significance in Vietnamese culture, judging from Mr. Delamarre's note: "At the time when we demand the indigenous population to participate on our side in the war against Germany, it seems that it would be correct to preserve the existing Võ Miếu. It would be, perhaps, even an opportunity to divert later in favor of the Protectorate sentiments the venerable existence of which are attested by Võ Miếu." Ibid., p. 6. I suspect that

in the vernacular language. Here a famous general named Quan Đế (Guandi) or Quan Vũ (Guan Yu)[67] is worshipped, whom soldiers treat with devotion greater than that which they show toward the aforementioned Thái Công. He lived during the reign of Emperor Hậu Hán Hậu Đế,[68] and he had an associate, another general called Trương Phi (Zhang Fei), and together with him he once fought for that emperor against the king of Ngô (Wu),[69] and they both were killed in the same battle in the twenty-fifth year of the emperor's reign, approximately in the middle of the third century after Christ was born. I received the first mention of these two *miếu* from the venerable martyr Father Francisco Gil de Federich, when he wrote me a letter in reply [to my query] dated August 6, 1744.

At the time when they start a war, they sacrifice first to the inventor of military service in front of the standard on which his image is depicted, and then the general, sitting on a horse, offers sacrifice. Later he [Father Gil de Federich] amended [his comments] in the following way: "the one who is given the title Vũ Thánh Vương (Wu Shengwang) [is] in the middle, to his left [is] Tôn Vũ Tử (Sun Wuzi),[70] to the right is Trương Lương under the name of Trương Tiên Vương (Zhang Xianwang)."[71]
[p. 32]

Article 4: On the Ceremony of Tế Kỳ Đạo

Every year during the second lunar month, on the day designated by the chief astrologist known as Quan Tư Thiên (guan sitian, official accomplished in Heavens),[72] a great ceremony called *Tế Kỳ Đạo* (*ji qidao*, sacrifice to the leader's banner) takes place at the court and in all the provinces. In a sand pit near the city a very large enclosure is made of reeds, inside of which thirty-six altars are erected. The first altar, in honor of Heaven and Earth, is in the left part of the

---

Adriano di St. Thecla here mentions a Võ Miếu located outside of Hanoi that did not survive into modern times.

[67] Quan Vũ (Guan Yu), an associate of Liu Bei, the founder of the Shu Han dynasty, was canonized in popular religion as Quan Đế (Guandi), "Emperor Guan," the God of War.

[68] It is not immediately clear whom the author intends to identify as Hậu Hán Hậu Đế (Hou Han Houdi). Hậu Hán (Hou Han) is the Later Han dynasty (25–221). However, an emperor with the name Hậu (Hou), called Hậu Chủ (Houzhu), r. 223–65, not Houdi, existed under the Minor Han dynasty (221–65), a successor to the Han dynasty. In my opinion, there is some confusion here as Adriano di St. Thecla definitely refers to Liu Bei, a general and descendant of the Han imperial family, who gained power when the Later Han dynasty collapsed and the state disintegrated into several kingdoms, each one founding its own dynasty. In 211, at the dawn of the period, known as the Three Kingdoms period, Liu Bei established himself in Sichuan (western China), and Guan Yu and Zhang Fei joined him in the wars of the Three Kingdoms, which led to the founding of the Shu Han kingdom in 221 under the aegis of Liu Bei, who assumed the title of emperor.

[69] The Ngô (Wu) dynasty arose in southern China during the Three Kingdoms period, after the downfall of the Han dynasty.

[70] Sunzi is the name of an eminent general of the Warring States period (he lived in the fourth century B.C.E.), who served the Wu kingdom. Sun Wu is his personal name. He was the author of the famous treatise "The Art of War." Sunzi is considered to be a Chinese Clausewitz.

[71] Zhang the Ancient Ruler or Zhang the Immortal Ruler, depending on what character stood for the pronunciation *tiên*, 先 or 仙 .

[72] This is Vietnamese word order; in Chinese it is *sitian guan*.

enclosure, and the rest of the altars, consequently, are positioned in many lines to the right of the first altar. In the first line stand the numerous altars in honor of ancestors and of the kings and governors of the kingdom who served the state well; among the altars of the kings are two dedicated to the two most ancient kings, namely, Kinh Dương[73] and Lạc Laong Quân,[74] who are the first in the *Annamite Chronology*. In the second line are five altars in honor of the five highest generals or military leaders who served under the five ancient kings called Ngũ Đế (Wudi). At the head of this line is placed a big flag, called *Kỳ Đạo*, which is the personal flag of the highest prefect of the whole army, from which the name of the ceremony *Tế Kỳ Đạo* was taken. Furthermore, many altars are arranged in two lines in honor of the spirits of the highest grade, Thượng đẳng Thần (shangdeng shen), and on each altar is placed a tablet inscribed with the name of its spirit; indeed, among them there are altars for Tản Viên Sơn,[75] Đông Thiên Vương or vulgar Vua Giaóng,[76] Lý Ông Traọng[77] or vulgar Vua Trèm;[78] we will speak about them in detail in article 8. The governor of the kingdom, or *Chúa*, comes down with his entourage to the house of convalescence called a *nhà lầu*,[79] which stands at a distance from the place of sacrifice and from which he observes the ceremony. The royal army stands in order in the sand pit with the horses and elephants, whose bodies are covered with black bitumen. The appointed prefects go inside the enclosure and sacrifice there to the aforementioned spirits on the prepared altars; they express gratitude for the tranquillity which came over the kingdom, and in addition they ask for their [the spirits'] protection for maintaining and increasing this tranquillity by drawing away the spirits of rebels so that they would not disturb the peace.

After the sacrifices are completed, the one who is in charge of the military equipment, being three times alerted by the triple [p. 33] appearance of an equestrian messenger, three times fires a siege-engine named *ống lậnh*[80] (a pipe-cannon), which looks like a large mortar.

---

[73] According to Vietnamese tradition, King Kinh Dương was a descendant in the third generation of Thần Nông (Shen Nong), the legendary king of Chinese antiquity venerated as the god of agriculture. Kinh Dương, in his turn, ostensibly was the father of Lạc Long Quân, discussed in the next note. Kinh Dương is the first Vietnamese person mentioned in *Đại Việt Sử Ký Toàn Thư* (Complete History of Great Viet), and with him these annals start from the year Nhâm Tuất (renxu), which, according to the calculations of Ngô Đức Thọ, is the year 2879 B.C.E. *Đại Việt Sử Ký Toàn Thư*, ngoại ký, 1:1b (1:131–132 and 1:131 n. 7).

[74] Lạc Laong Quân, spelled in modern Vietnamese as Lạc Long Quân (Dragon King Lạc), is the original culture hero in Vietnamese mythology. He came from the sea, subdued demons, civilized the people, and protected them from intruders. From the children born of the union between him and Âu Cơ, a mountain fairy, came the earliest kings in Vietnamese mythology; ibid., 1:2a (1:132–133). Lạc Long Quân and Âu Cơ are considered mythical progenitors of the Vietnamese.

[75] The mountain spirit; in article 8 of this chapter, he is described under the name Sơn Tinh.

[76] Variously Vua Gióng or Vua Dóng in modern Vietnamese orthography; he is discussed in article 8 below.

[77] Lý Ông Trọng in modern Vietnamese orthography; he is also discussed in article 8 below.

[78] This spirit is discussed at length in article 8.

[79] *Nhà lầu*, meaning a multistory building in modern Vietnamese, used to denote a royal recreational house. See Rhodes, *Từ Điển Annam-Lusitan-Latinh*, col. 404.

[80] This should be *lệnh* in the standard Vietnamese orthography.

Later a large standard at the door of the aforementioned house is raised, together with other small flags; immediately afterward a larger cannon called a *báo laong* (a big mortar)[81] located at the same place is fired, and subsequently other cannons are fired thrice, and also each soldier shoots his catapult, uncovers a sword, and lifts up a spear. With these actions they intend to scare the spirits of rebels, to drive them far away from the kingdom, so that they will not become hostile and disturb the common tranquillity. At the end, the *ống lệnh* is again fired once, and this indicates that the firing of the cannons is over. Then all the soldiers assemble and take positions with horses and elephants around the house of the *Chúa;* and some [of them] wrestle in front of the *Chúa* and the [rest of the] army, and other pleasure contests are also held. After that the assembly is dismissed and they all go back, each to his appropriate place.

Among the provincial rulers called Quan Trấn (guan zhen, mandarins of regional jurisdictions)[82] the ceremony *Tế Kỳ Đạo* was held with only one altar erected and one *hương án (xiangan)* sacrificial table in the year Canh Ngũ, the eleventh year of the reign [title] Cảnh Hưng, in the year 1750 of Christ. This ceremony took place on the tenth day of the second month, corresponding to the seventeenth day of the month of March.

Descriptio loci ad Juramentum

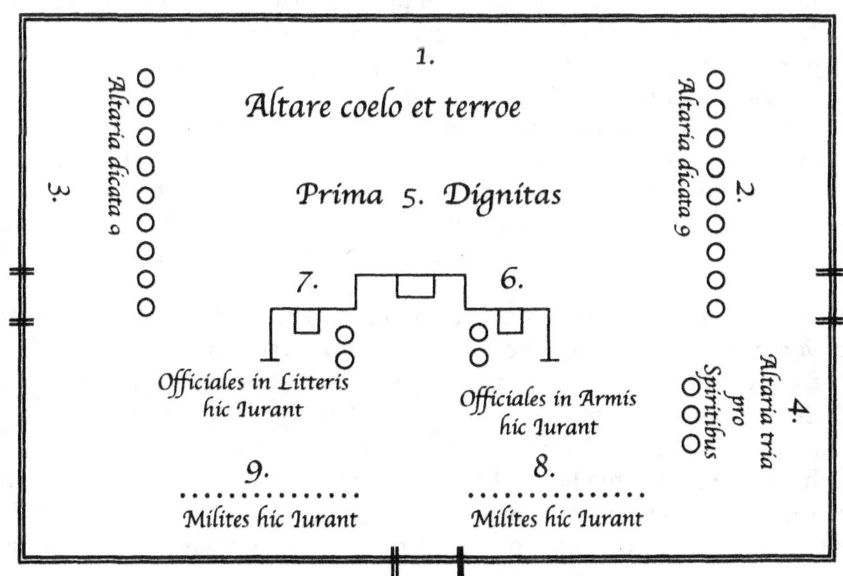

Plan of the Place where the Oaths are Taken:
1, altar dedicated to Heaven and Earth; *2, 3*, nine dedicated altars; *4*, three altars dedicated to the spirits; *5*, the highest officials take the oath here; *6*, military officials take the oath here; *7*, scholarly officials take the oath here; *8, 9*, soldiers take the oath here.

[81] *Báo long* in modern Vietnamese orthography.

[82] This is the Vietnamese word order; *zhenguan* in Chinese.

[p. 34]

Article 5: On the Ceremony Hội Minh, or on Taking the Oath of Loyalty

The *hội minh* (*huimeng*) ceremony[83] is one during which all the nobles and prefects, or people of any position or rank whether civil or military, pronounce the solemn oath of faithful service to the king; so it is called *hội minh,* that is, an assembly for taking the oath. The ceremony is held in the royal city as well as in other provinces by their rulers once a year during the last month, and it is celebrated in the city with the following ceremonies. A very spacious square enclosure is constructed of reeds, which can be entered from both the sides and from the front. In the front part of the enclosure an altar dedicated to Heaven and to Earth is erected, to the left of this altar are nine altars dedicated to the nine kings, *Vua*, from the most recent one down to the ancestors. On the right side there are also nine altars dedicated to the governors of the kingdom, *Chúa*, from the most recent one down to the ancestors; and immediately to the left, after the altars of the kings, three altars follow, dedicated, the first, to all the spirits of the highest grade, or *thượng đẳng thần* (*shangdeng shen*); the second, to the spirits of waters; the third, to the spirits of earth. Each altar is shaded with two parasols, and over each altar is placed a small half-burnt bull, some steamed rice, called *xôi* in the vulgar [language], and wine for the sacrifice. In the center of the enclosure are three small, four-legged *hương án* sacrificial tables; sticks of incense are burnt on them; underneath them on the sides are small vessels filled with wine mixed with the blood of hens, and on the central sacrificial table is placed the golden sword of the *Chúa*. In front of the central table, the highest prefect or highest official takes the oath; in front of the table on the left, all the military officials do the same; and in front of the sacrificial table on the right, all the civil officials. In the rear part of this enclosure, on both sides, are fourteen sacrificial tables, in front of which soldiers swear, and near them are small vessels filled with wine and the blood of bulls. From each sacrificial table hangs a scroll bearing the formula of the oath, which those who swear read while genuflecting. In order for everything to be clear, [p. 35] we showed the plan of the enclosure on the preceding page 33 [of the manuscript].

Thus, early in the morning, from the *Phủ* (*fu*, official residence),[84] or the palace of the governor of the kingdom, the *Chúa*, to the above-mentioned place of taking the oath are brought an amphora of good wine, a hen, and the golden sword of the *Chúa*; there, a prefect accepts the sword, raises it to the sky, and then draws with it three circles on the ground; three officials enter the circles. One holds a hen or a rooster; the second holds the head of the hen with pincers; and the third, standing between these two, cuts off the head of the hen with the golden sword. The amphora with wine is put there for the blood to flow into, and over it one leaf of

[83] This ceremony first appears in the Vietnamese annals during the reign of Lý Thái Tông (1028–53); see *Đại Việt Sử Ký Toàn Thư*, bản ký, 2:14b–15a (1:251), under the year 1028.

[84] Apparently, there was more than one governor's residence. There is no consensus among scholars where a residence or residences were located, even for a given time. See, on the discussion of this question, Nguyễn Thừa Hỷ, *Thăng Long—Hà Nội: Thế Kỷ XVII-XVIII-XIX* (Thăng Long—Hanoi: The Seventeenth-Eighteenth-Nineteenth Centuries) (Hanoi: Hội Sử Học Việt Nam, 1993), pp. 35–40.

the oath to be pronounced is burnt, so that the ashes fall into the amphora. The wine is stirred six times and then the amphora is emptied into six small vessels standing in pairs at the three *hương án* sacrificial tables, in front of which all the prefects take the oath. Numerous vessels of wine are prepared for the soldiers, which contain the blood of a bull, instead of that of a hen, mixed with *sơn*, or cinnabar. After that, sacrifices are made to Heaven and Earth, to the nine kings, and to the nine governors of the kingdom, as well as to the spirits, with the sons of the *Chúa* or with the highest prefects performing the sacrificial duties. At first, a *văn tế*, or offertory, is recited in front of the altar dedicated to Heaven and Earth. When the word *duy (wei)*[85] is pronounced, all the offertories are read aloud at the same time at each altar. After the sacrifices are completed, everyone takes the oath in successive order, each one according to his rank, in front of the sacrificial table corresponding to his rank; after the oath is pronounced, everybody takes a small swallow of wine mixed with blood and ashes.

The formula of this oath is: (A) Tôi lạy hiệu Thiên Thượng Đế,[86] Hoàng Địa Kỳ, or[87] Hoàng Thiên Hậu Thổ, or Blời Đất,[88] cập chư linh Thần đẳng. (B) Tôi ở mỗ phủ, mỗ huyện, mỗ xã, tên tôi là mỗ, tôi niên sinh tôi là mỗ tuổi. (C) Tôi làm tôi Vua mỗ tôi; tôi làm tôi Chúa mỗ tôi cho hết laòng[89] (D) Ví bằng tôi ở chẳng hết

---

[85] The word signifying the end of the ceremony.

[86] I surmise that, despite the absence of a capital letter in the word *hiệu* (*hao,* name, to invoke), it most probably should be considered as a part of the title "Hiệu Thiên Thượng Đế." This compound designates the title ascribed to Heaven, pronounced in modern Vietnamese "Hạo Thiên Thượng Đế" (Haotian Shangdi), which Mathews translates as "Sovereign on high in the vast heavens." See R. H. Mathews, *Mathews' Chinese-English Dictionary* (Cambridge: Harvard University Press, 2000), p. 308, no. 2072:2. The first character was indeed pronounced *hiệu* earlier, at least a hundred years ago, when Huình Tịnh Paulus Của incorporated it into his dictionary with this pronunciation. See Huình Tịnh Paulus Của, *Đại Nam Quấc Âm Tự Vị* (A Dictionary of Characters with the National Pronunciation of Great South) (reprint, Ho Chi Minh: Nhà Xuất Bản Trẻ, 1998), p. 421. I assume that the sentence is much better idiomatically if *hiệu* joins *Thiên Thượng Đế* than if it is joined with *lạy* (reverently pray) because the two words preceeding *hiệu, tôi* (I) and *lạy* (reverently pray) are in vernacular Vietnamese, while the three following it, *Thiên Thượng Đế (Tian Shangdi),* are in Sino-Vietnamese. The structure of the sentence, in my opinion, vividly displays social stratification. It contrasts vernacular Vietnamese, as an embodiment of human agency to venerate, with Sino-Vietnamese, as the denominator of the heavenly object of this veneration. It is very obvious that the sentence was purposely constructed using different language levels. The lower status of the vernacular Vietnamese *tôi lạy* (I humbly pray) is especially evident when the honorific title of Heaven and Earth in Sino-Vietnamese, to be spoken by high officers, is replaced by its vernacular equivalent *blời [trời] đất* when, according to Adriano di St. Thecla, the formula was to be pronounced by soldiers. This does not concern the superior position of the gods and spirits addressed in vernacular Vietnamese vis-à-vis their worshipers but rather expresses an established stratification of the worshippers, which can be interpreted in at least two ways. On the one hand, it might be said that a low-ranking person should not desecrate a deity by addressing him or her in the language to which he does not belong. On the other hand, it might be said that an aura of intimacy between the worshipper and the deity is reflected in the way that each group uses the language with which it is most comfortable.

[87] The author uses the Latin word *vel* ("or") inside the Vietnamese phrase to distinguish versions of the oath taken by different stratums of people.

[88] *Blời* (heaven, sky) was a standard pronunciation of the word *trời* through the eighteenth century. One can see the use of the phoneme *bl* instead of *tr* in Rhodes's dictionary, *Từ Điển Annam-Lusitan-Latinh*, col. 45.

[89] *Lòng* (heart) in modern Vietnamese spelling.

ngay, thì tôi uống chén son máu này. (E) Nguyện hiệu Thiên Thượng Đế, Hoàng Địa Kỳ, or Hoàng Thiên Hậu Thổ, or Blời Đất, cập chư linh Thần đẳng đánh chết tôi.

The sense of this formula is: (A) I worship the Supreme King of great Heaven, and the spirit of the queen of Earth, or the king of Heaven and the queen of Earth, or Heaven and [p. 36] Earth, and all the spirits; (B) I am from such and such a district, from such and such a region, from such and such a city, I am called by such and such a name, and I am of such and such an age. (C) I am wholeheartedly a subject of King N and the governor of the Kingdom N. (D) If I do not stay faithful, after I drink from this vessel of wine and blood, (E) I pray reverently the Supreme King of Great Heaven, and the spirit of the Queen of Earth, or the king of Heaven and the queen of Earth, or Heaven and Earth, and all the spirits, to strike and kill me.

All who swear use this one formula for the oath, using differently the name of Heaven and Earth; certainly, prefects of the highest rank, or the nobles, say: "hiệu Thiên Thượng Đế" (Haotian Shangdi, Sovereign on high in the vast heavens), "Hoàng Địa Kỳ" (Huang Diqi, Emperor or Empress of Earth); prefects of the lower rank say: "Hoàng Thiên Hậu Thổ" (Huangtian Houtu, Emperor of Heaven [or High Heaven] and Empress of Earth); soldiers say: "Blời Đất." On the same day, in the palace of the *Vua* and in the palace of the *Chúa* all *Đức Bà* (*depo*, reverend ladies), or queens, and "quasi"-queens, all *quan thị (guanshi)* or *Thụy (rui)*,[90] that is, eunuchs, the guards of the queens, and all the members of the *Vua*'s and *Chúa*'s families take the oath of loyalty. After that, in every house of *Bà Chúa* (*pozhu*, lady or mistress) and *Đức Ông* (*deweng*, lord or master), all who belong to their family take the same oath; also all the military *chầu* (attendants) who serve the mother or grandmother of the governor of the kingdom *Chúa*, in addition to the oath already taken concerning keeping loyalty to *Vua* and *Chúa*, take another oath in the house of their mistresses, concerning their faithful service to them.

Besides, in many villages, once a year, mostly in the first month, they take a common oath of serving their village or the region in concord and unity. And they take the same oath every time that all the inhabitants of a village or a district engage in a common affair, and so they are called *ăn thề* (swearing loyalty or brotherhood). Then they swear in a communal house in front of the tutelary genie, or in his temple, called *miếu*, or even under the open sky, using the potion of hen's blood mixed with wine; and after taking the oath they make a food offering. Moreover, the elders of the village use this kind of oath, taken in a public place, to bring together two arguing sides [in a dispute] in order to resolve the discord that separates them.

It is useful to note, concerning the oath of loyalty to the king taken with drinking a blood potion, that ancient tradition [p. 37] introduced this kind of oath taking. It started by chance, as the *Chinese History* narrates, when Emperor Hán Cảo Tổ requested an oath of loyalty from his servants, using a potion with the

---

[90] Professor Ngô Đức Thọ explained to me the difference between *quan thị (guan shi)* and *quan thụy (guan rui)* as follows: *quan thị*, literally meaning "an administrator or governor of women," had a bad connotation, and eunuchs did not like to be called by this name. Thus, the second word *thị (shi)* was replaced by the similarly sounding word *thụy (rui)*, since the phonemes *i* and *uy* were interchangeable at this time in Vietnam. In this case, *thụy* does not bear any semantic load, but serves as a euphemistic substitution.

blood of a horse. Trình Tử (Chengzi) presents this tradition as unworthy and rejects it in the commentaries to Confucius's book *Xuân Thu (Chunqiu*, Spring and Autumn Annals), in which Confucius himself had criticized the habit of taking from subjects a simple oath of loyalty. Everything that has been said on the aforementioned *Hội minh* ceremony, celebrated in the royal city, we owe to the educated venerable Father Francisco Gil de Federich, from the order of Brother Preachers, who studied and found this with his outstanding diligence, and he sent it to me in a description with the plan of the enclosure of the place for taking the oath, which we exhibited earlier.

Article 6: On the Tutelary Genies Called Thành Hoàng

The literati and all the others traditionally honor the spirit of the fortress, or the protector of the village, and [who is] the ruler, [called] *Thành Hoàng* in common speech, or *Ching hoang (chenghuang)*[91] among Chinese. In most cases he is some ordinary man raised to this honor due to his services to the state, and he is considered to be and is worshipped as a spirit protecting the place, or as a tutelary genie—although it happens not seldom that some person famous for his impiety, or a certain animal or inanimate thing, is, because of some event, proclaimed by the inhabitants to be a tutelary genie of the place, which in a normal sense is quite ridiculous and even lamentable. There are some villages around that worship the spirit of a tiger; moreover, many days before the day of sacrifice, [the villagers] secretly capture a poor man, and then on the appointed day they kill him in order to offer his meat to the spirit; because of that, tigers kill, dismember, and devour people. There are others who honor the spirit of a dog; and, because dogs eat human excrement, they take a small vessel and place inside it the first excrement that someone produces in the morning after fasting the previous day, and then offer it to the spirit with other food. You might find many other spirits of this kind, in whom anyone who does not live in these regions can hardly believe.

All the tutelary genies to whom any grade is ascribed, which are discussed later, have a special sacred place called *miếu*. Some of them who are not ranked and have only [p. 38] the name *Thành Hoàng* usually do not have a special sacred place, but they enjoy a place assigned [to them] in the public house of the community, which in most cases is decorated with engravings. In any place, the spirits, both ranked and unranked, have a tablet covered with gold, on which the name of the spirit is written in silver characters with these two characters 大 王 , that is, *Đại Vương* (*Dawang*), with which the <u>*Great Governor*</u> is

[91] In China this name was used to designate a god of walls or of the ramparts, that is, a god of the city. When it was introduced from China to Vietnam, however, this term came to be applied to the genies of the villages. Scholars differ in their opinions about when the idea of Thành Hoàng (Chenghuang) was borrowed by the Vietnamese. For example, Nguyễn Duy Hinh suggests the period of the Tang dynasty (618–907); Nguyễn Duy Hinh, *Tín Ngưỡng Thành Hoàng Việt Nam* (Belief in the Tutelary Genies of Vietnam) (Hanoi: Nhà Xuất Bản Khoa Học Xã Hội, 1996), p. 60. Meanwhile, Nguyễn Hồng Kiễn talks about the end of the thirteenth and beginning of the fourteenth centuries, the time when Confucianism started to develop, as the time when it came into usage; Nguyễn Hồng Kiễn, *Đình Làng Việt Nam* (The Communal Houses of Vietnamese Villages) (Hanoi: Nhà Xuất Bản Văn Hóa, 1993), p. 13. According to Nguyễn Duy Hinh, a tutelary genie in Vietnam is to be defined as a main deity of the village, who was given recognition by the feudal state; Nguyễn Duy Hinh, *Tín Ngưỡng*, p. 92.

designated.[92] On both sides of the tablet there is something stretching out as [though they were] arms, and on the top there is a certain unfinished figure of a face, in the center of which there is a very small mirror; in some places they also put a piece of cloth around it.

The origin of these tutelary genies is traced to the following event, which happened at the beginning of the reign of the Tấn (Jin) dynasty that started ruling approximately in the year 270 after Christ was born;[93] the emperor ordered that a temple be built in the kingdom in honor of the celestial spirit, the protector of the kingdom, and that a tablet be put inside it with the following inscription: *Thành hoàng thần vị (chenghuang shenwei)*, which means "throne of the spirit who rules the city." These things are mentioned in the Christian book *Văn Lâm Quảng (Wen lin guang)*[94] with these words: Đại Minh Trung cuốc ư nhất thiên tứ bách niên tiền vận đang[95] Tấn kỉ linh cuốc trung tắc nhất từ dĩ tự thủ cuốc Thiên Thần dĩ tứ thự đề vu bản viết Thành Hoàng Thần vị.[96] I am most uncertain about this thing, since the *Chinese History* does not have it, and since by the name of Thiên Thần (Tianshen, heavenly spirit) the Chinese understand not an angel, or a spirit, but only the power of Heaven inside Heaven itself, and also the powers of the Sun, the Moon, and the stars inside themselves as well, as it appears from what has been said in article 2 of chapter 1. We must consider it to be true that the tutelary genies of the regions, [in the way they] are worshipped by the Chinese and Annamites, are brought in by the Demon with the intention to put them in opposition to the guardian angels of the regions and to the saint protectors of the regions, whom the Saintly Church venerates.

At least three times a year a sacrifice is offered by the community to these spirits ruling over the regions and to protectors, mainly on the first day of the first month, and it is called in the vernacular language *Kỳ yên*, supplication for tranquillity, which is made to the Supreme King but not to the tutelary genie, see article 1 on this; [it also happens] in the tenth month, and [p. 39] is called in the vulgar [language] *cống vua* (to pay tribute to a king or to make offerings to a king); [there is] an offering of the first fruit, and [it takes place] in the eleventh month and is called *Kỳ phúc (qifu)*, supplication for happiness. A simple food offering is

---

[92] Strictly speaking, *vương* means a king or a prince. Here it reflects the high status assigned to tutelary genies.

[93] The Jin dynasty (265–420).

[94] The absence of the characters does not allow an exact translation of the title. The book has not been identified.

[95] In modern Vietnamese this word is pronounced *đương* (*dang*, a temporal particle, "at this time"), but *đang* was a normative pronunciation for this word earlier. Alexandre de Rhodes lists this word with the same meaning as *đang* (Rhodes, *Từ Điển Annam-Lusitan-Latinh*, col. 199) Later, in the nineteenth century both pronunciations were acceptable (Huình Tịnh Paulus Của, *Đại Nam Quấc Âm Tự Vị*, pp. 265, 335), but in the twentieth century, *đương* became standard.

[96] 大明中國於一千四百年前運當晉紀令國中則一祠以祀守國天神以賜書題于板曰城隍神立. "In the Great Ming Central Kingdom, one thousand four hundred years ago, at the time of the Jin dynasty, it was ordered that a temple be erected in the capital of the country to worship a celestial spirit-protector of the country, honoring it by writing the following inscription on the tablet: throne of the spirit who rules the city." "Great Ming," a reference to the Ming dynasty (1368–1644), appears in some Vietnamese texts of the fifteenth century and later as a general reference to "China." The style and syntax of this passage, as well as the mode of dating the events, suggest that it was not written by a Chinese or a Vietnamese.

also added, which happens at the end of the last month in some places to express gratitude for the favors of that year. Finally, when a village is affected by some disease or another evil, the community makes a sacrifice to the tutelary genie, which is called *Tống ách (songe)*, drawing misfortune away. They also sacrifice to him when they need rain for agriculture and harvest, and it is called *Đảo vũ (daoyu)*, supplication for rain. There are also other sacrifices, performed in more wealthy villages, to please the senior rulers of the village or community, who, perhaps being fond of food and jokes, command the performance of more sacrifices at the expense of the community, mainly for their own belly rather than obeying the tutelary genie.

Moreover, almost every year, unless poverty occurs, in the first month, or in the third, or in the ninth, or in the eleventh month they organize a song celebration that continues for many days, sometimes up to a month, and takes place in the communal house. During these days a sacrifice to the spirit is made once a day, in the morning or in the evening, and only one sacrificial table with food is offered; after completing the sacrifice, songs are sung, continuing throughout the whole night or day. Singers sing praise in honor of the spirit, although, in the manner of performers, between the songs they insert the most filthy, humorous, ridiculous, and vile satires, with which they please the ears of those standing around and receive much money given to them willingly as a reward. Meanwhile, tympani and other musical instruments sound, and all the people who are present there feast from the sacrificial tables with food, which is hardly offered during the sacrifice and is prepared with the contributions of all the inhabitants of the village. This song celebration is prohibited for a triennial period of mourning following the death of the king.

Besides, at that same time they organize many games in honor of the tutelary genie; mainly they wrestle, and the name of this game is *Đánh vật;* they fight with sticks, and this game is called *Đánh thó;* two lines meet at the board of the game-table of Italian chess, and this game is called *Đánh cờ;* they strike from both sides a wooden ball, so that it runs to the opposite part, and this game [p. 40] is called *Đánh cầu.* Whoever gains victory gets the promised reward and praise.

On the Sacrifice to the Tutelary Genie

Sacrifice to a tutelary genie is held with the following rites. A tablet, on which a name of the spirit is written with his honorific title Đại Vương, that is, the Great Governor, is put on the altar; if the spirit has a special temple this tablet is solemnly transported from there to the communal house in the appropriate skillfully ornamented tabernacle. In front of the tablet they put a small vessel with sticks of incense, and one sacrificial table with steamed rice called *xôi,* one whole head of a cow, pig, or bull, and a lot of square gold and silver paper money; in addition, they put on the ground near the altar a lot of sacrificial tables with food, arranged in many lines; and they place in the center, in front of the altar, meat of an animal killed and dismembered, which is killed earlier without any offering or ceremony. In front of all these objects stands one four-legged sacrificial table, a *hương án,* on which incense, two candles, or a lamp are burned. After the preparation is finished, the elders of the village, dressed in court clothes, come into the [public] house or into its yard; two masters of ceremonies stand close on either side of the *hương án* sacrificial table. In the center, in front of the same sacrificial table, stands the principal attendant, and behind him several assistants; these events are described more precisely in the first chapter, where we were talking about the sacrifice to Confucius.

After everyone takes his place, one of the masters of ceremonies pronounces with a clear voice: "Nghinh Đại Vương" (ying dawang), [which means] let us meet the great governor; and the principal attendant and the assistants with the rest [of the participants] prostrate themselves four times, reverently greeting the arriving spirit, who, they believe, shows his presence in his tablet. Then the principal attendant proceeds with washing his hands in the basin prepared in advance, and, after having dried them, he returns to the center close to the *hương án* sacrificial table, where, genuflecting, he makes a libation of wine, raising the small goblet up to [p. 41] eye level, offering it, and then returning it to the attendant, who carries it to the altar and puts it on the sacrificial table with the food already placed there. After that, one of the dignitaries comes to the *hương án* sacrificial table and, genuflecting beside the principal attendant, who is also kneeling, reads the offertory, the *văn tế* leaf. After it is read, the principal attendant bows once, and after that prostrates twice. According to this offertory leaf, all the elders of the village or community first praise the spirit for the excellence of his nature and his knowledge, power, and protection; second, they offer him food and other things placed there, asking him to consider them worthy to be accepted; and third, they ask him to protect them by keeping away all the misfortunes and by granting tranquillity and all good things so that they might [be enabled to] spend their days in joy. And it is extraordinary that between the praises with which they extol the spirit, they say that he has reverence and is obedient to the king with these words: Thượng hưởng khâm phượng Đế đình;[97] all the spirits are certainly considered to be the subjects of the king, because the king raises them to their rank and allows them to be honored in his kingdom, as we will mention later.

After the offertory is recited in this manner, the principal attendant again makes libations of wine a second and third time, in the same way as he did the first time, and then another attendant carries the goblets of wine to the altar and places them on the sacrificial table with food. Later a master of ceremonies reminds them to thank the spirit and see him off, saying, "Từ thần" (cishen, farewell, spirit; or a merciful spirit); immediately after that the attendant together with the assistants and other participants prostrate four times, attending the departing spirit with grateful souls. Later they feast at the common banquet composed of the offerings, which have been prepared at the common expense of the whole village or city.

[97] 上 饗 欽 奉 帝 廷 . My translation of the phrase is: "Mayest thou enjoy the offering and [be] respectfully received by the imperial court."

Article 7: On the Ceremony Tạo Khoa bạt Thần (zao keba shen, establishing the ranks and promotions of the spirits), That Is, on the Probation and Ranking of Spirits

Among protective spirits of these places there are many who are given rank by a royal certificate. There are three ranks: supreme, [p. 42] middle, and the lowest, according to which they are called *Thượng đẳng (shangdeng),*[98] *Trung đẳng (zhongdeng),*[99] or *Hạ đẳng Thần (xiadeng shen).*[100] The spirits are ascribed to their ranks by means of a public test, this test is held with these ceremonies. An altar for all *Thần* under examination is erected inside a certain enclosure at the designated place in the city, and on this altar names of all *Thần* are inscribed. After this, bulls are led close to the enclosure, in the same number as the number of spirits on probation, and on each bull the name of a *Thần* is written, to which the bull belongs. The highest prefect, sent here by the king, commands a *Thần* by calling his proper name; if the spirit wants to increase his rank, he kills the bull, and for that reason the bull is led inside the enclosure; and if this *Thần,* after being named, kills it, he is promoted by a royal certificate in which his services are praised, and his name is put into the register where other ranked spirits are listed. Later, after much preparation on the appointed day, the whole village whose protective spirit has been promoted comes out to welcome this certificate; they honor it with many prostrations, and they bring it to the communal house, where they sacrifice to the promoted spirit, after which they feast and rejoice in different ways. At the present time, nobody has seen this ceremony of promoting spirits, which is described as having taken place long before. All spirits that are mentioned in the royal register and are given one of the three ranks mentioned above have a special temple called *miếu* where, once a year, the officials of the district in which the temple stands—namely, *ông Phủ* (*wengfu,* prefectural officials), *ông Giáo* (*wengjiao,* educational officers), *ông huyện* (*wengxian,* district officials)—sacrifice to them. These three [officials] make their sacrifices at the same time, each in a temple of the ranked spirit in his own district and within the limits of his jurisdiction. One of the royal officials, sent by the king, sacrifices to the spirits that have been promoted to the highest rank. He is allowed to carry a parasol and to raise a battle flag; every year he also receives from the hands of the king a clay [yellow] bull for the ceremony of *lập xuân,* which has been described earlier. Whoever passes in front of the temples of the spirits belonging to the highest rank, *Thượng* [p. 43] *đẳng Thần,* wears a cap on his head and takes off his shoes; and he descends from the palanquin, in which nobles and other people of rank are usually carried; if they ignore these signs of honor, they are punished. What I have written above about the ceremony of promoting spirits is almost in the same words that the venerable

[98] Genies of the supreme rank. "These are the genies of famous mountains, big rivers, and also the celestial genies. . . . All the genies, whose history and actions are famous, whose names are clearly known, received from successive dynasties the rank of 'Thượng đẳng thần'"; Phan Kế Bính, *Viet-Nam Phong-Tuc (Moeurs et coutumes du Vietnam),* trans. Nicole Louis-Hénard (Paris: École Française d'Extrême-Orient, 1975), 2:79.

[99] Genies of middle rank. These have been worshipped in the villages for a long time, but their deeds are not widely known. They are also quite powerful, and they demonstrate it by obeying the orders of the king to produce rain or good weather. Ibid., pp. 79–80.

[100] Genies of the lower class. Their histories are unknown; they are venerated mostly in groups. The court grants them official titles upon the request of the villagers. Ibid., p. 80.

martyr Father Francisco Gil de Federich wrote to me, when I consulted him during his captivity in the city. In short, in this probation of spirits and in the promoting of them, the highest craft of the demon is transparent. If indeed he [the demon] has introduced this rite of the spirits' probation, of promoting them to a rank, and of writing their name in the register, he [the demon] did it in order to deceive the sacred church, which after examination pronounces men saints, famous for their chastity and virtue, and mentions them in the register of the Blessed or the Saints.

Article 8: On Vua Daóng and Vua Trèm and Several Others

Among the spirits of the highest rank, *thượng đẳng*, there are two with great reputations, mentioned above, in this kingdom, whom even the followers of the Sect of Magicians fervently worship. The first, Vua Daóng or Siaóng,[101] was born in Phù Đổng village of Vũ Ninh district in the northern province.[102] It happened in the eighth [year] of the rule of Hùng Vương (Hùng King), who belonged to the sixth generation among the ancient kings.[103] After he was attacked, the king issued an order to find out who could fight against his enemies. During the search, a small boy with the name Daóng, who was only three years old and who had never before spoken a word, suddenly asked his mother to call the royal minister. The boy said to him: Nguyện đắc nhất kiếm, nhất mã, quân vô ưu dã,[104] which means: I ask for a sword and a horse; the king should not be worried. He went to fight as a leader, and he destroyed the enemy in the bloody battle near Vũ Ninh mountain,[105] so that the greater part of the hostile army was demolished and the rest quickly surrendered; they prostrated before him and worshipped him, calling him celestial general hô Thiên Tướng (hu Tianjiang).[106] The boy, still riding his horse,

[101] King Daóng, in modern spelling Ông Dóng or Ông Gióng, is one of the Vietnamese immortals. For a detailed discussion of the roots of his name, as well as of his cult, see Trần Quốc Vượng, "The Legend of Ông Dóng," in *Essays into Vietnamese Pasts*, ed. K. W. Taylor and John K. Whitmore (Ithaca, NY: Cornell University, Southeast Asia Program, 1995), pp. 13–41. *Daóng* or *Siaóng* are the author's versions of the modern Vietnamese variations *Dóng* or *Gióng*, which shows that in the eighteenth century people also had varying perceptions of his name. Even though both of these words are from the vernacular Vietnamese vocabulary, the story of Vua Dóng first appeared in texts with a Sino-Vietnamese version of the name: *Đổng* (*Dong* in Chinese), which means "storm."

[102] In modern Bắc Ninh province, about fifteen kilometers northwest of Hanoi. Here is located the main temple of this spirit, which is still worshipped in many locations in Vietnam, especially in the North.

[103] There were eighteen generations of Hùng Vương (Hùng King[s]) comprising a legendary dynasty dated 2809–258 B.C.E. by Vietnamese historians in the fifteenth century. There is no way to fix the time of reign of the sixth king of this dynasty. On this dynasty, see *Đại Việt Sử Ký Toàn Thư*, ngoại ký, 1:3a–5b (1:133–135).

[104] 願得一劍一馬君無憂也. Ibid., 1:3b (1:134).

[105] In Bắc Ninh province.

[106] In fact, according to *Đại Việt Sử Ký Toàn Thư* (see for the characters ngoại ký, 1:3b), he was called Thiên Tướng (tianjiang), meaning Heavenly General. The character *hô (hu,* 呼 *)* incorporated by the author at the beginning of the title, means "to name, to call out." Adriano di St. Thecla's incorporation of this word into the title might be a result of his direct citation from *Đại Việt Sử Ký Toàn Thư*—namely, that the people "called [Ông Dóng] Heavenly General"—and somehow in the manuscript it was joined to the title "Heavenly General" itself. Another possibility is that Adriano di St. Thecla misread the character standing for *hô*, confusing it with the character *hoà (huo,* 和 to be in harmony), in which case the author could imply the

was elevated into the air and went away, [p. 44] or disappeared. Later the king ordered that a temple [dedicated] to this boy be built in the garden where he used to live, and sacrifices be made to him at proper times. When many centuries had passed, King Lí Thái Tổ,[107] who was ruling more than seven hundred years after that, in his edict proclaimed [the boy a] king, or the spiritual governor over Heaven: Phung Vi Trùng[108] Thiên Thần Vương.[109] All the events, described above, are narrated at the very beginning of this *History of Đại Việt kingdom.*[110]

The spirit Sơn Tinh (Mountain spirit) was also one of great fame. In the *History of Đại Việt* in [the section on] King Hùng Vương in the last generation or *thế (shi)* [of this dynasty], the following story is told about him.[111] The spirit Sơn Tinh and another spirit Thủy Tinh (Water Spirit) came to King Hùng Vương and asked to marry his daughter. The king was surprised that both spirits asked for it together, and told them that he had only one daughter, and that he could not give her to both of them. The king also said that the first one who brought gifts on the following day would obtain his daughter. The next day the spirit Sơn Tinh was the first to bring numerous gifts, and he obtained the king's daughter. When he was carrying her to the mountain for the wedding, the other spirit, the water spirit Thủy Tinh, raised a tempest and tried to hinder their way with rain and wind. Thereafter, every year competitions were held between these two spirits, and the mountain spirit Sơn Tinh accomplished many miracles. King Lí Anh Tông,[112] in the sixth year of [the reign title] Chính Laong (Zhenglong),[113] or in 1170 the year of Christ, built a temple to him on that mountain, which is called Tản Viên[114] and is situated in the western province, and the name of this spirit is Tản Viên Sơn Thần.[115]

Vua Trèm,[116] earlier called Lí Ông Traọng, was born in Từ Liêm district of the western province;[117] he lived during the time of King An Dương,[118] who ruled

meaning "General in Harmony with Heaven"; but then it is strange that he still read it as *hô*. Another possibility is that it was a pure mistake.

[107] R. 1010–28.

[108] At present this word is customarily pronounced xung (chong). However, its normative pronunciation is indeed trùng (chong, to soar). See Thiều Chửu, Hán-Việt Tự Điển (Sino-Vietnamese Dictionary) (Ho Chi Minh City: Nhà Xuất Bản Thành Phố Hồ Chí Minh, 1997), p. 333, s.v. "trùng."

[109] 封 為 沖 天 神 王 . Ibid., 1:4a. The phrase can be translated as "Conferred [upon him the title] Soaring to Heaven Divine King."

[110] *Đại Việt Sử Ký Toàn Thư*, ngoại ký, 1:3b–4a (1:133–134).

[111] Ibid., 1:4a–5b (1:134–135).

[112] R. 1138–75.

[113] An abbreviation of the reign title Chính Long Bảo Ứng (Zhenglong Baoying), 1163–74.

[114] A mountain in Sơn Tây province, northwest of Hanoi; its name derives from the mountain's resemblance to a parasol.

[115] Spirit of Tản Viên mountain. The story of this spirit is also found in sources preceding the *Đại Việt Sử Ký Toàn Thư*, e.g., *Việt Điện U Linh Tập* (Invisible Powers of the Việt Realm) of Lý Tế Xuyến (early fourteenth century) (Lê Hữu Mục, trans., Saigon: Nhà Sách Khai Trí, 1961), pp. 109–111, and *Lĩnh Nam Chích Quái* (Mysteries Gathered from South of the Passes), edited in the late fifteenth century by Vũ Quỳnh and Kiều Phú (Hanoi: Nhà Xuat Bản Văn Hóa, 1960), pp. 72–75.

[116] King Trèm or Chèm is another name for Lý Ông Trọng, a legendary Vietnamese hero. Trèm/Chèm is the vernacular name of the locality in the northwestern suburbs of modern

when Tần Thỉ Hoàng (Qin Shi Huang) was the emperor, and he [Lý Ông Trọng] is said to have been twenty-three cubits tall. When he was young, a certain prefect struck him for performing his official duties in an inappropriate way; then he came to the aforementioned emperor and served him as a prefect titled Tư Lệ Hiệu Úy (sili xiaowei, commander-in-chief). He [Lý Ông Trọng] was sent by the emperor to protect the Lâm Đào (Lintao)[119] region from enemies of the kingdom, the Hung Nô (Xiongnu),[120] who were extremely afraid of him. After he accomplished his service, [and being] already an old man, he returned to his homeland, where he finished his life. Later, [p. 45] when the same enemies were repeatedly raiding the adjacent region, the emperor erected a bronze statue of Lí Ông Traọng of miraculous magnitude. In its belly thirty men were hidden, and the statue itself was put in the gates of the imperial city. When these enemies looked at the statue, they saw it moving, because thirty men were shaking it from inside. The enemies thought it was Lí Ông Traọng in the statue and, seized with terror, did not dare to invade and plunder that region any more. After many centuries [years] passed, during the reign of Emperor Đàng Đức Tông (Tang Dezong) at the beginning of the ninth century after Christ was born,[121] prefect Triệu Xương (Zhao Chang) built the temple to Lí Ông Traọng in order to sacrifice there to him.[122] Sixty years later, during the reign of emperor Đàng —— Tông (Tang zong),[123] prefect Cao Biền (Gao Pian), also called Cao Vương (Gaowang),[124] restored the temple, and put inside it a wooden statue, because it helped him in the battle against the rebel Nam Chiếu

Hanoi where this hero originated. This toponym, rendered into Hán characters, has become Từ Liêm, as it is officially known today. Lí Ông Traọng is written Lý Ông Trọng in modern Vietnamese.

117 Hà Đông province.

118 A quasi-legendary and quasi-historical king who ruled over Vietnam (then called Âu Lạc), according to *Đại Việt Sử Ký Toàn Thư*, between 257 and 208 B.C.E. *Đại Việt Sử Ký Toàn Thư*, ngoại ký, 1:5b–11b (135–140).

119 A region in northwestern China on the border with Mongolia.

120 A Turkish-speaking people who lived in the territory of modern Mongolia at that time.

121 R. 780–805.

122 On the Tang officer, Triệu Xương (Zhao Chang), and the cult of Lý Ông Trọng, see Lý Tế Xuyên, *Việt Điện U Linh Tập*, p. 68; Keith Taylor, *The Birth of Vietnam* (Berkeley: University of California Press, 1983), p. 222.

123 The reference is to Emperor Đường Ý Tông (Tang Yizong), r. 860–74.

124 A general of the Đường (Tang) dynasty in China, who in 864–65 led an army against the forces of the kingdom of Nam Chiếu (Nanzhao) (based in modern Yunnan province of southwest China) and reestablished Tang authority in northern Vietnam, which had been lost in 862 when Nanzhao forces had invaded it. His deeds are also described in *Đại Việt Sử Ký Toàn Thư*, ngoại ký, 5:12b–16a (1:197–200, under the years 864–68). Cao Biền (Gao Pian) is well remembered in Vietnam and is recorded in Vietnamese texts as a king, i.e., *vương (wang)*. He is credited with rebuilding Hanoi and with introducing the study of geography and geomancy; he was also a famous sorcerer. On Cao Biền see Taylor, *The Birth of Vietnam*, pp. 246–254, and "A Southern Remembrance of Cao Biền," in *Liber Amicorum: Mélanges offerts au professeur Phan Huy Lê*, ed. Philippe Papin and John Kleinen (Hanoi: Nhà Xuất Bản Thanh Niên, École Française d'Extrême-Orient, 1999), pp. 241–258.

(Nanzhao), whom he overcame. This temple stands in the small town of Thụy Hương[125] of Từ Liêm district. One can read about it in the *History of Đại Việt,*[126] whose authors could have seen what credence can be given to the height of twenty-three cubits for Lí Ông Traọng, equal in height to six men, and also to his statue, whose belly could hold thirty men. Others, nevertheless, tell the story or the fable about Vua Trèm differently. They say that when Emperor [Tần] Thỉ Hoàng was waging war against the inhabitants of Hung Nô kingdom he requested King An Dương to send him Lí Ông Traọng, who was known from his ambassadorship, which he undertook to pay tribute. King An Dương clearly replied that the man was dead. When the emperor ordered that the bones of the deceased be given him, King An Dương ordered that the man be killed and his bones sent to the emperor, because he was afraid of punishment by death for his lie. This is told in the book *Thuật Thiên Vĩnh Sử (Shutian yongshi).*[127] In the books of the *History of Đại Việt,* however, these events are hardly mentioned.[128]

Vua Bạch Mã, a military prefect who was called by the proper name Mã Viện (Ma Yuan), had an excellent reputation.[129] He was fighting on the side of Emperor Hán Quảng Vũ (Han Guangwu),[130] who sent him with troops into that kingdom or ———, in Giao Chu (Jiaozhou) province.[131] There he captured a woman called Trưng,[132] who, after she had by force of arms expelled the imperial governor, [p.

---

[125] The temple is called Trèm or Chèm, in Từ Liêm district, Hanoi.

[126] *Đại Việt Sử Ký Toàn Thư,* ngoại ký, 1:8a (1:137–138, under the year 221).

[127] The lack of characters suggest several possible translations of its title: *The Book Accounting for Heavenly Eternity* or *The Book Accounting for Ten Thousand Eternal [Things]* or *The Book Accounting for Eternity.* The book is not identified.

[128] This version is indeed not mentioned in *Đại Việt Sử Ký Toàn Thư,* but a similar version of it is in *Lĩnh Nam Chích Quái,* pp. 50–52. The only discrepancy between the author's version and that of *Lĩnh Nam Chích Quái* is that, in the latter, Lý Ông Trọng was not killed by imperial order but committed suicide to spare his king and the country from trouble (p. 50).

[129] On the issue of correspondence between Vua Bạch Mã (King Bai Ma) and Mã Viện (Ma Yuan), see the translator's introduction.

[130] The Vietnamese name of the emperor should be Hán Quang Vũ, r. 25–58.

[131] This name is usually pronounced in Vietnamese as Giao Châu. The character 州 standing for *Châu* might be read also as *Chu,* but Giao Châu is a more conventional pronunciation at the present time. The Han administrative jurisdiction comprising northern Vietnam and southern China was given the name Giao Châu in 203; prior to this it was called Giao Chỉ (Jiaozhi). It included seven prefectures, three of which were in northern Vietnam. In the decade 220–30, the Wu dynasty divided this jurisdiction and thereafter "Giao Châu" was applied only to northern Vietnam. This name was in circulation up to the seventh century when the Tang dynasty changed it to Annam. See Taylor, *Birth of Vietnam,* pp. 72, 87, 89. The *Đại Việt Sử Ký Toàn Thư* and other later texts anachronistically applied this name to earlier times.

[132] In fact, there were two Trưng sisters: Trưng Trắc and Trưng Nhị (this fact is also recorded in *Đại Việt Sử Ký Toàn Thư*), who rose in rebellion against the Han governor; *Đại Việt Sử Ký Toàn Thư,* ngoại kỷ, 3:2a–3a (1:156–157), from the year 40 through 43. Adriano di St. Thecla ignores the younger one, Nhị. The sisters are identified in texts as daughters of the leading figure in the local aristocracy of that time. According to Han dynastic records, the husband of the elder sister, Thi Sách, was imprisoned by the Han governor; Vietnamese legends say that he was killed by the governor and that he was the husband of both sisters. The sisters decided to take revenge and rose in rebellion in the year 40. Initially succeeding, they were subdued by Mã Viện (Ma Yuan) in 43. In modern Vietnamese historiography, this uprising is a golden moment in the national struggle for independence.

46] claimed to be the ruler, and for that reason she received the name Trưng Vương,[133] which we mentioned in the preface to the *Annamite Chronology*. In honor of this victory the general erected a large bronze column and wrote the following characters on it: Đồng trụ chiết Giao Chu duyệt. [134] They mean: when the bronze column is broken, the province of Giao Chu will be free, or the emperor will let it be free.[135] These events happened in the nineteenth year of the reign of the aforementioned emperor, or ten years after the death of Christ,[136] and they are described in the *History of Đại Việt*, where a story about Thục Đông Hán (Shu Dong Han) [dynasty] is found.[137] After that he came back to the emperor and died. That woman, whom he conquered, remembered his virtue and service to the state. She erected a temple to sacrifice to him in Phúc Lộc district of Thanh Hóa province.[138] Later, from there he obtained a cult among the Annamites.[139] Now there is also another temple in the royal city, built not long ago in his honor, in the

---

[133] King or Prince Trưng. According to Vietnamese texts, the sisters proclaimed themselves kings, the title given usually to male representatives of the imperial line or to great heroes deified under this title. Here the title has no gender context but is used as an indication of sovereignty. The sisters are still frequently referred to in Vietnam as Trưng Vương, "the Trưng kings."

[134] In *Đại Việt Sử Ký Toàn Thư*, ngoại kỷ, 3:3b, this phrase appears as "Đồng trụ chiết Giao Châu diệt" 銅 柱 折 文 州 滅 ; the manuscript reads the last word here as *duyệt*, which has no plausible meaning in this sentence, and is apparently a mistake or an alternative pronunciation of *diệt*. Both Alexandre de Rhodes and Huình Tịnh Paulus Của have it close or identical to the modern form. (Huình Tịnh Paulus Của, *Đại Nam Quấc Âm Tự Vị*, p. 234, s.v. "diệt"; Rhodes, *Từ Điển Annam-Lusitan-Latinh*, col. 172, s.v. "diẹt").

[135] The translation suggested by the author differs from the meaning of the phrase as it appears in *Đại Việt Sử Ký Toàn Thư*: "When the bronze column crumbles down, Giao Châu will perish" (1:157, under the year 43). On the one hand, this phrase equates the difficulty of destroying a column made of bronze with the difficulty of overthrowing Giao Châu and suggests the stability of this province. On the other hand, the translation suggested by Adriano di St. Thecla is that the province's prospects for freedom are as meager as the prospects for breaking a bronze column. Both of these thoughts might well mean the same thing, however. Mã Viện (Ma Yuan) was sent to Giao Châu to reestablish Han rule, and after he succeeded he installed bronze columns marking the southern border of the Chinese empire, and on one of these columns the adduced citation was carved. If we understand it in the sense that only when the bronze column crumbles down will Giao Châu perish as one of the provinces of the Chinese empire, then Adriano di St. Thecla's interpretation would perfectly fit the framework of the phrase as it appears in the Vietnamese annals.

[136] The year 43.

[137] See *Đại Việt Sử Ký Toàn Thư*, ngoại kỷ, 3:2a–7b (1:157–160).

[138] This is an apparent mistake in the text as there is no evidence of a Phúc Lộc in Thanh Hóa province; see ibid. Apparently Adriano di St. Thecla meant Phúc Thọ district of Hà Tây province (previously Sơn Tây province). On the historiographical confusion about localizing the jurisdiction of Phúc Lộc, see Taylor, *Birth of Vietnam*, app. 1, pp. 327–329.

[139] The two last phrases on the veneration of Mã Viện (Ma Yuan) by Princess Trưng might be a result of a misunderstanding by the author of the actual text in *Đại Việt Sử Ký Toàn Thư*, ngoại kỷ, 3:3b (1:157), where it is said that "the local people loved the Princess/es Trưng, and built a temple to venerate [her/them]." So the temple was built in honor of Princess Trưng and not of Ma Yuan. And indeed, this famous temple, dedicated to the Trưng sisters, is still in the place mentioned by the author. Furthermore, Adriano di St. Thecla makes an erroneous (or at least, unproved) supposition that the princess was still alive after Ma Yuan returned to China, since according to his interpretation, she erected a temple to venerate Ma Yuan. Han dynastic record say that Ma Yuan beheaded the sisters and sent their heads to the Han capital; see Taylor, *Birth of Vietnam*, p. 40.

marketplace.[140] It is called in the vulgar language Chợ Vua Bạch Mã (Market of King Bạch Mã),[141] and people attend it mainly on the first and fifteenth day of each month.

A very famous woman named Bà Chúa Liễu Hạnh (Princess Liễu Hạnh)[142] is added to them [i.e., to the most prominent spirits]. She was born in Thiên Bản district of the southern province.[143] Since she had sung, as they say, disgracefully and impudently, people, being jealous, killed her and threw her into the river. The Devil took her shape and name and introduced, developed, and secured her cult in many provinces.[144] She is worshipped mainly in Quình Lưu district in Cửa Tuần village[145] of Nghệ An province.[146] Her temple, or *miếu*, is built there, where two girls attend on her. When one of them leaves, another is put in her place. The girls are selected from all the girls of that district by Bà Chúa Liễu Hạnh herself or by a demon with her name. The one selected is assigned to serve as one of the two attendants, or zealous servants. She is [expected] to speak when possessed by her [Bà Chúa Liễu Hạnh] or by the demon. The girl, upon leaving the temple, is paid a considerable amount of money, according to the way of life she chooses.[147]

Furthermore, the tutelary genie of Kẻ Sặt city in the eastern province[148] [p. 47] was once a daughter of a certain military prefect.[149] Before rushing into battle, he promised to sacrifice her to the idol if he was victorious. He gained the victory, but when his boat was passing by the sacred place in front of the idol he did not want to keep the oath and sacrifice his daughter. The demon, with its power, made his boat stand still, and it could not move forward until he threw his daughter into the waters to honor the idol. The inhabitants of Kẻ Sặt city adopted and worshipped her as their tutelary spirit. The demon caused many supernatural acts to happen

140 The reference is to Bạch Mã temple located now at 76 Hàng Buồm Street in Hanoi. In earlier times there was a marketplace here, also named Bạch Mã, built, or rebuilt, according to legend, in the eleventh century. The temple has undergone numerous reconstructions. It was expanded during the years 1680–1705 and refurbished in 1740, during the time Adriano di St. Thecla was in Vietnam. See Nguyên Văn Uẩn, *Hà Nội: Nửa Đầu Thế Kỷ XX* (Hanoi: The First Half of the Twentieth Century) (Hanoi: Nhà Xuất Bản Hà Nội, 1995), 2:136–137. I think that it was this temple that led Adriano di St. Thecla to merge Bạch Mã and Mã Viện (Ma Yuan) into one personality since in this Bạch Mã temple there was a statue of and an altar for Mã Viện. This temple is discussed in the translator's introduction.

141 In the first quarter of the twentieth century the market was moved from there and became Chợ Đồng Xuân (market Đồng Xuân). The temple remains in the same place.

142 Princess Liễu Hạnh, known as a female spirit of Vân Cát village.

143 Modern Vụ Bản district, Nam Định province.

144 See more on Princess Liễu Hạnh in the translator's introduction.

145 This village seems not to exist anymore, or at least my search in the region proved unsuccessful. According to a missionary map of 1889, missionaries resided in a place called Cam Tuang. Cam could be a misspelling of Cửa, Tuang that of Tuần. This place does not appear on the modern maps, but it was located east of the town of Quỳnh Lưu. Map "Tong-King Méridional," in Adrien Launay, *Atlas des Missions de la Société des Missions-Étrangères* (Lille: Société de Saint-Augustin Desclée de Brouwer, 1890).

146 A province in north-central Vietnam.

147 The author refers here to a major feature of Liễu Hạnh's cult, i.e., spirit possession. She is one of the most popular of deities to be invoked and is widely reckoned as one of the most helpful.

148 Now Bình Giang district in Hải Dương province.

149 It is not clear to which prefect the author refers.

there; because of that she, being a small girl, or her spirit, was attended with the greatest cult by the Gentiles, until the Christians devastated the temple of that spirit. This matter was subsequently a cause of great discord between the Christians and the Gentiles, and a great amount of money was lost because of it.[150] There are also many other tutelary genies in different regions, Vua Mê Hê,[151] Chúa Trì,[152] and Chúa Quế.[153]

Among these [spirits] Vua Bạch Mã is the most prominent tutelary genie of the royal city, or Kẻ Chợ.[154] There they have his temple next to quite a large

[150] I could find no trace of this legend in any texts or scholarly works. It is also unknown to the scholars with whom I discussed it. My trip to Kẻ Sặt did not reveal any significant new information either; in none of the temples of Kẻ Sặt did anyone know this story. This fact by itself cannot definitively refute the information provided by Adriano di St. Thecla, but only suggests that for some time the people of Kẻ Sặt have not worshipped this spirit anymore. Kẻ Sặt is located on the bank of Sặt river. Kẻ Sặt was one of the most "christianized" places in Vietnam at the time of Adriano di St. Thecla. One of the leaders of the Christian community of Kẻ Sặt, Nguyễn Tới Đích, told me that he remembered the old people telling the story about a temple or a shrine to some spirit, which was destroyed during the turmoil between the Christians and non-Christians, but no one could identify this spirit by name.

[151] This spirit is not identified. Dr. Nguyễn Tá Nhí suggested that it is a plausible variation of pronunciation for the name of Mỵ Ê. I found a possible corroboration for this suggestion in one of the descriptions of the tutelary genie submitted by Đông Trữ village, Lý Nhân district, Hà Nam province, to the L'École Française d'Extrême-Orient in 1938, in which her name is written as Mỵ Hê; See Series *Thần Tích Thần Sắc* (The Treasury of Deity Legends and Royal Deification Decrees) in Hanoi at the Viện Thông Tin Khoa Học Xã Hội (Institute of Social Science Information), file 5505, p. 93. Thus, there is a good possibility that the first syllable, pronounced *my* in modern Vietnamese, was in the eighteenth century pronounced *mê*. That a woman was called by the male title Vua (King) might be explained by the fact that sometimes female deities were called by the title Đại Vương: for example, the words *đại vương* are incorporated into the honorific title of Princess Liễu Hạnh in the account on the tutelary genie of Đông Duyên village, Tín An district, Há Đông province (ibid., file 1456, p. 283), as well as in a number of others. The vernacular analogue of the Sino-Vietnamese word *vương* is *vua*, and it is possible to assume that the people adopted this title for the female deity, Mỵ Ê. Mỵ Ê was the wife of the Cham king Sạ Đẩu, who was defeated by King Lý Thái Tông (1028–54) in 1044. She was captured during the war and on the way back to Vietnam was summoned to Lý Thái Tông's vessel. Preferring to stay faithful to her husband, Mỵ Ê committed suicide by jumping into the river. Moved by her faithfulness, Lý Thái Tông conferred upon her an honorific title, recognizing her as a powerful spirit. This story is found in *Đại Việt Sử Ký Toàn Thư*, bản ký, 2:35a (1:266–267, under the year 1044). Her story is also in *Đại Việt U Linh Tập*, pp. 61–62, and in *Lĩnh Nam Chích Quái*, pp. 113–114.

[152] Prince or Princess Trì was a spirit of ponds or other watery places. According to information given to me by Professor Trần Quốc Vượng, her cult still exists in Thanh Trì district, which now belongs to the city of Hanoi. I could not find a legend for this deity in Vietnam, but it exists in Chinese folklore.

[153] Princess Quế was a deity assigned by the Jade Emperor to accompany Princess Liễu Hạnh, mentioned above, on her second journey to Earth. She is widely worshipped in northern Vietnam together with Princess Liễu Hạnh.

[154] Literally meaning "market area," this vernacular Vietnamese compound eventually came to designate an urban area. From the fifteenth to the eighteenth century it was the name used by the common people for the capital, of which the official name at that time was Thăng Long. See Đinh Xuân Vịnh, *Sổ Tay Địa Danh Việt Nam* (A Notebook of the Places Names of Vietnam) (Hanoi: Nhà Xuất Bản Lao Động, 1996), p. 273. "The Western merchants and missionaries talked only about Ca-Cho, Cha Cho, Kacho, or else Cachao. A capital of the kingdom, shrunk and politically contested, the city of Soaring Dragon from now on seemed to reduce its functions to commerce." Papin, *Histoire de Hanoi*, p. 161.

marketplace, and people attend it mainly on the first and fifteenth day of each month.

Article 9: On Tiên Sư, Thổ Công, Vua Bếp, and Others, Who Have a Cult among Ordinary People

All craftsmen and merchants worship the first master of their craft or of their trade, or the inventor, whom they call Tiên Sư (Xianshi, originator or founder).[155] At home they assign his altar to a certain place; here they have his image, in which he appears as an old man, painted on papyrus; they refresh it at the beginning of every year, and during the first three days [they] make food offerings and burn incense in front of it. They often venerate it and invoke it with a food offering, especially when they start some business, [or] in any place where they find themselves at the moment, in order to succeed in their undertakings. They also make the same offering every time they are going to participate in a feast. Indeed, craftsmen and merchants, who constitute one community, once a year assemble in a public place and make a solemn offering to their first teacher. I consider that the origin of Tiên Sư's cult definitely comes from nothing else but from the [cult], [in] which the [p. 48] Chinese worship not only parents and dead ancestors but also the ancient teachers. For this reason the literati honor their Confucius as the first, or most distinguished, who passed on his doctrine to them; and the Magicians worship their Lão Tử (Laozi), as the first and most distinguished, who taught them magic. For the same reason all the craftsmen and merchants honor their first teacher [or chief master], who supports [them] and gave them the profession that they practice.

Ordinary people especially honor the spirit Thổ Công (Tugong), that is, the protector of the Earth, or of the place where they live. He has acquired this cult from the following [events]. Once, in China, an extremely ferocious tigress was killing many travelers, and nobody dared to approach and kill it. Because of this, the emperor in a public edict promised an award to any person who would kill it. Five brothers from the Lê (Li) family came and murdered it. For that reason, the emperor, in addition to other awards, made them officials and proclaimed them protectors of the five parts of his kingdom. In such a way ordinary people started to worship and invoke them under the name of Thổ Công.[156]

Ordinary people also venerate another spirit, called Thổ Chủ (Tuzhu), the lord of the place where they live. Its origin, as it is said, is as follows. During the rule of the Tấn dynasty, which came to power in the year 265 after Christ, was born someone called Vương Chất (Wangzhi),[157] a poor and humble man who occupied himself with gathering wood. When he encountered some demons enjoying

[155] Craft guilds still worship their founders in Vietnam.

[156] To the best of my knowledge, this legend is not known in Vietnam now—not, at least, with any connection to the spirit in question. The cult of Thổ Công (Tugong) as one of the spirits belonging to the house is, nevertheless, still popular.

[157] The name means "lord of a wooden block."

abacus,[158] out of curiosity he took himself to look at the game. Meanwhile, it happened that the demon with his craft made him [the man] believe that his iron-firm scaffolding[159] was gnawed away by moths, and he [the man] escaped with his appearance changed because of his thinness. When he returned back home, he was not recognized by his relatives, and his wife did not want to admit him although he proclaimed himself the lord of the village and the house. He barely managed to get [permission] from her to build his own rough and modest hut in a quiet corner of the garden,[160] where he lived and later died. Then he was indeed recognized as the lord of that village, and so his cult was established among ordinary people, who repeatedly lauded[161] him as prefect Thái Giám (Taijian, eunuch).[162]

Women also greatly worship Vua bếp,[163] the spirit called the King of the Kitchen, about whose origin it is narrated as follows. Someone named Traọng Cao[164] had a fight with his wife, named Thị Nhi, on account of wealth, each of them claiming it. The husband struck the wife, who, indignant, [p. 49] left all the goods to the spouse, tore her hair, and left to live above a bridge in the place where the three rivers meet; then a man called Phạm Lang, who was passing by this place, married her, and [he] acquired great wealth from then on. But the first husband, who became extremely poor because of misfortune and intrigues, accidentally came to them while begging for food; although he did not recognize his wife, she recognized him; she talked with him about his various experiences while her husband was out hunting. Having compassion for him, she gave him food and drink in abundance, so that he, well satiated and drunk, lay down and fell asleep. Since the wife was afraid that he might be discovered by her husband when he returned, she ordered the slaves to carry the sleeping man down to a heap of straw, and to cover him entirely with it until he woke up and went away. When Phạm Lang returned from his hunt bearing a deer, he set the heap of straw on fire to roast the deer. There, Traọng Cao, enveloped in flames, finished his life. Seized with compassion for him, Thị Nhi threw herself into the flames and perished. When her husband Phạm Lang saw that, being upset about his wife, he jumped into the fire and died. Uneducated common people started to worship these three taken by fire

---

[158] The manuscript says that the demons were playing "abacus." While in English this word denotes a calculating instrument, Latin *abacus* means "a square board" and by extension "a gaming board divided into compartments."

[159] In the text the Latin word *fala* is used, which literally means a wooden tower from which missiles were thrown into a besieged city. Taking into consideration that the posthumous name of this person, as will be seen below, is Eunuch, it might be that under the word *fala* Adriano di St. Thecla masked "phallus."

[160] In the text the word that we translated as "modest" is *mediam*, which literally means "the middle, everyday life."

[161] In the manuscript it is actually written *dularatus*, a word that does not exist in Latin. The translators took the freedom to consider *dularatus* as a mistake for *laudatus*.

[162] This cult is not particularly observed in Vietnam at the present time. According to Professor Trần Quốc Vượng, this spirit is worshipped in Tiên Du district of Bắc Ninh province. There are several spirits of the eunuchs famous for their service to different dynasties, whose cults indeed were observed until recent times or can still be observed. None of the people I asked knew the legend recounted by Adriano di St. Thecla concerning Thái Giám.

[163] This is a vernacular Vietnamese expression. In Chinese, the corresponding deity is called Zaojun.

[164] Trọng Cao in the modern Vietnamese writing style.

under the name of the King of the Kitchen: Vua bếp hai ông một bà (King of the Kitchen, two men and one woman). They say that three bricks, which they put under the pan for cooking food, indicate those three [persons]; they consider that the fourth brick, which is put over the fire covered with ashes, indicates a woman-maid of that couple, named *con đòi*. So every year, on the first day, they hang in the kitchen the image of these four painted on a leaf of papyrus, which is bought in advance. During the first three days they also make for them an offering of one sacrificial table with food, and they burn incense, and ask them for help in cooking and preparing food well for the family that year, and all such similar [things]. There is a special tradition: when a new wife enters the house of a husband, she honors Vua bếp, and asks to be assisted in her duties around the kitchen.[165]

Besides those spirits, women also worship spirits in different regions, where a small mount rises from the ground, or where some tall tree, a *cây đa* (banyan tree), stands. Women passing by usually invoke *ông đổng*,[166] that is, the master of the mount or the spirit who rules there, and promise him that if they acquire wealth due to successful trade they will, on their way back, throw a lump of soil so that the heap will grow. Or [they will leave] some gold and silver paper money [p. 50] or wreaths of flowers, or they will put there sticks of incense. They make offerings to them on the way back from the marketplace to become free from their vow; because of this a lot of lumps are seen accumulated there. They also often construct on those mounts a certain small hut, and they put inside a small statuette in honor of the spirit who rules [lives] there. They also usually invoke Bà Nàng (Lady) when passing a tree of the aforementioned kind, inside of which they consider a spirit to stay, and they think it is a woman. For the sake of their business and their health, and in her honor, they hang flower wreaths on the branches of the tree and small bunches of golden and silver paper money, and they throw at its bottom small vessels made of gypsum and sticks of incense.

Article 10: On the Spirits of the Deceased

They exercise the cult of the spirits of the deceased with many ceremonies; there is no space [to discuss all the ceremonies] here, since this would demand a longer treatise; but it seems useful to talk about the offerings and sacrifices with which this cult of the deceased is mostly performed. They make many simple offerings to their deceased and also numerous offerings with sacrifice. They make simple offerings every day from the day of death until the body—which is usually kept inside the house—is buried enclosed in a coffin; [they do so] during many months, and [they also make simple offerings] every year on the first three days,

---

165 This cult is still very popular in Vietnam as well as in China, and Adriano di St. Thecla's version of the legend is in full accordance with what people still practice nowadays.

166 The compound is not identifiable in the form given in the text. It might be a mistake. Relying on the translation or explanation suggested by Adriano di St. Thecla, I conjecture that the implied word could be the vernacular Vietnamese word *đống*, meaning "a heap or a low hill." If, disregarding Adriano di St. Thecla's explanation of the compound, and assuming that this word is indeed correctly reproduced, then it is the Sino-Vietnamese *đổng* (*dong*, to lead people in the right way, to correct); and *ông đổng (wen dong)* would be translated as "master-in-control." It seems that this cult has not survived in Vietnam, since no one whom I questioned could recognize this term.

and four times a year; at these times they offer food with a single invitation to the soul, without a libation of wine or a dripping [from the rice] and without a recitation of the offertory leaf [text]. They make offerings with a sacrifice on the day of burial, followed by two more days—the fiftieth and hundredth day after the death—and on the anniversary day every year; especially in the triennial mourning period, [they make offerings] twice on the seventh moon of the first three years after death.[167] For these offerings, if a corpse is still kept in the house, they use a certain white band of silk, fitted to the appropriate form with the help of a wooden stick, which they call *hồn bạch*, Chinese *hoen pe* (*hunbai*, white [band] of the soul). If the corpse has already been buried, they use a wooden tablet made in a certain determined form, called *chủ*, Chinese *chu (zhu)*. They consider that the soul shows its presence [p. 51] at the offering in either of them [i.e., the *hồn bạch* or the *chủ*]. This band is stretched over two sticks in the form of a one-cubit-high cross to represent to some extent the image of the deceased. For that purpose the part on the top is raised in place of the head, the two parts on the sides are in place of the arms, and two parts, or extremities, descend all the way down, in place of legs and feet. This is the way of decorating the band, outlined in the *Ritual Gia Lễ* (*Jiali*, Family Rituals), to designate a human figure, so that the soul will stay there; for that reason it is called *hồn bạch*, that is, the white band of the soul.[168] In order to portray this image with greater clarity, they dress *hồn bạch* in casual clothes, and put over it a felt cap. A tablet, approximately one palm high, [has] its upper part, which is shaped as a semicircle, projecting out, while the rest of it goes inside, and in the middle it is made hollow lengthwise.[169] [The tablet] is inscribed with many characters, and two [words], *Thần vị (shenwei)* or *Thần phủ (shenfu)*, by which a *Throne of the Spirit* is indicated, are at the end of the line in the center [of the tablet]. The use of a tablet of this kind and of a band is believed to have been started by Chu Văn Công (Zhu Wengong) since no mention is found of the tablet and of the band of the soul before the time of this author;[170] he created the *Gia Lễ*, Chinese *Kia Ly (Jiali)*, on the ceremonies in honor of the deceased in the sixth year of Emperor Tống Hiếu Tông (Song Xiaozong),[171] which coincides with the year 1168 of Christ. Indeed, worshipping the deceased by means of offerings is recognized to be the oldest cult in China. It is undoubtedly reported in the *Chinese History* that Emperor Hạ Đại Vũ (Xia Da Yu) sacrificed to his father Cổn (Gun), and to Đế Cốc (Di Ku), and the words of the text "Đế Cốc giao Cổn" (Emperor Ku joined Emperor Gun) are added. [The aforesaid] helps to describe the offering with the sacrifice that people make—when they return home from the burial of the corpse—in front

[167] The redundancy in the translation of this phrase ("triennial period"—"three years after death") corresponds to the original.

[168] Patricia Buckley Ebrey, *Chu Hsi's Family Rituals: A Twelfth-Century Chinese Manual for the Performance of Cappings, Weddings, Funerals, and Ancestral Rites* (Princeton, NJ: Princeton University Press, 1991), pp. 77–78 and nn. 34–37.

[169] For a more detailed description with pictures of this type of tablet, see Gustave Dumoutier, *Le Rituel funéraire des Annamites, étude d'ethnographie religieuse* (Hanoi: Imprimerie Typo-Lithographique F. H. Schneider, 1904), pp. 140–141.

[170] The reference is to Chu Hi (Zhu Xi), the author of the *Gia Lễ* (*Jiali*, Family Rituals). In fact, a tablet is mentioned in the *Liji* (Record of Rites) several times. For instance, book 18, section 1, part 2. "The spirit tablet (which had been set up over the coffin) was buried after the sacrifice of Repose" (Legge, *Li Chi*, 2:142). As for the band, I did not find it mentioned in the *Liji*.

[171] A Chinese emperor, r. 1163–90.

of the tablet, which is sacred, [the same] as it is described in the *Ritual Gia Lễ*. So, after coming back home, they put the tablet on the bed, and they put in front of it a sacrificial table supplied with the most tender food, and they place many other sacrificial tables with food on both sides of the bed, and also on the bed, as well as on mats on the ground close to the bed with the tablet. A little bit below, in the center, a small *hương án* (*xiang'an*) table is placed in front of the tablet. Nearby, on both sides of this small table, stand two masters of ceremonies to guide the action. All the sons and descendants, dressed in funeral clothes and holding incense, proceed to the center in front of this table, where they sit down on the ground on the unrolled mats, women on the right, men on the left; the first-born son stands alone in the center in front of all the others, and there [p. 52] they mourn and lament together. Thereafter, the first-born son, or the principal attendant, who plays the leading part in the sacrifice, called in the ritual *Chúa Nhân (zhuren),*[172] and in the vulgar speech *Trưởng Nam (zhangnan),*[173] goes to the appointed place; there he washes his hands in the vase on the prepared four-legged [table], again steps back to the center and burns incense on the same small table where two candles are also burning, and he venerates the tablet with a single prostration. Two noble men, after washing their hands in a similar way in the same place, carry a small flask of wine, that is, a vessel of drippings from the rice, to the principal attendant; then, genuflecting together with him and on either side, in front of the small *hương án* table, they help him [in this manner]: the man who is on the right side stretches out the flask with drippings, the one who is on the left holds a flask in his hand, and the principal attendant fills it with the drippings. When he takes the flask, he pours out the liquid entirely, remaining kneeling, onto a handful of straw heaped on the ground. This [ceremony] is called *sa mao* (to drop into capillaries). After having performed the libation [of the wine], he venerates [the tablet] by bending his head to the ground, after that he rises and steps back, and there, together with his brothers, sisters, and other relatives, he worships [the tablet] with a double prostration. With this libation of wine they intend, according to the *Ritual Gia Lễ,* to attract the spirit of the deceased back, or to indicate his descent. For this reason the master of ceremonies says, "Giáng thần," or kiang xin (jiangshen) in Chinese, that is, "descend the spirit," [sic][174] or, in accordance with the rules of the Latin language, he asks, "make the spirit descend." After the libation, the first-born and other sons with the rest of the relatives make two prostrations, reverently accepting the spirit of the deceased descending to the

[172] A lord, a master, a host, thus, the chief of the ceremony.

[173] It is not clear why the author denotes this expression as vernacular, as it is also a Sino-Vietnamese compound with practically an identical meaning, that is "senior master."

[174] Adriano di St. Thecla tried to provide a verbatim translation of the phrase *Giáng thần (jiangshen),* which invites a spirit to descend. While, according to the rules of the Vietnamese and Chinese languages, the grammar of this compound is very viable, Adriano di St. Thecla's suggestion in Latin, "descende spiritum," is syntactically corrupt as the verb is in the imperative and the noun is in the accusative. That is why Adriano di St. Thecla suggested a different version of translation, "in accordance with the rules of the Latin language." This example gives us another wonderful piece of evidence for how it is impossible to apply mechanically the rules of one language to another language. The fact that Adriano di St. Thecla gave us two translations, stipulating that only one of them complies with the rules of the Latin language, shows his interest in linguistics, his fair knowledge and sense of both languages, and his abilities as an interpreter or translator.

tablet, which for that purpose is inscribed as a seat or a throne of the spirit. After accomplishing the libation, one of the attendants takes a bowl filled with steamed rice and puts it on the sacrificial table with food, placed in front of the tablet. Thereupon the principal attendant again pours wine or drippings over the handful of straw, except for a few drops from the flask, which the appointed attendant carries back to the sacrificial table with food, and he [the principal attendant] alone, after the libation, venerates [the spirit] with a double prostration.

After the second libation of drippings is over, one of the nobles, among those present, approaches the small *hương án* table, and, kneeling, reads with humble and somewhat tearful voice the offertory from the leaf, [p. 53] which another kneeling [person] is showing to him. He reads aloud from the leaf, mentioning first the current year, month, and day, the names of the first-born and of other sons, and the descendants, and in their name he praises the merits of the deceased parent, enumerates all his gracious acts, produces various feelings of compassion and love, and offers food, asking him to taste it, pronouncing the words "Thượng hưởng" (shangxiang, Mayest thou enjoy this offering); their meaning is explained in the next article. After the leaf is recited, all the sons and descendants prostrate themselves three times, and lament together. Then the principal attendant approaches the *hương án* and, kneeling together with two other attendants, once again pours a little bit of drippings onto the handful of straw left there, and honors [the deceased] with a double prostration. Then he [the principal attendant] steps back, again approaches the table, and makes the fourth libation in the way described earlier. Meanwhile musical instruments of different kinds sound in mournful harmony.

Then they wrap the tablet and the sacrificial table placed in front of it with a long cover, and one of the attendants, with hands raised and crossed in front of his face, twice invites the deceased in a raised voice to eat of the offered food; at this time all the sons and descendants do not look at the place of the tablet, and turn their faces to another side, as if they do not dare to look at the place where the deceased father, or ancestor, is eating. After some time they raise the cover and carry it away from the tablet and from the sacrificial table, as if the deceased has already eaten, or tried, the food; and an attendant places one bowl of the potion *chè* (tea) on that sacrificial table.

Thereafter, one of the two masters of ceremonies, who advise on every action that must take place, announces the ceremony finished and complete by saying, "Lị thành (licheng)"; and the other reminds them to praise the spirit of the deceased by saying, "Từ thần." Then the first-born, or the principal attendant, and other sons, descendants, and relatives, lamenting, make a double prostration; in this ceremony, according to the *Ritual*, they thank the spirit for showing his presence in the sacrifice, and they let him go and lead him away with grateful hearts. Immediately afterward, the *văn tế* leaf, or offertory, is burnt; the tablet is covered and closed up inside its depository, with the sacrificial table of food left in front of it; [p. 54] all non-relatives who are present, or neighbors who came for the funeral, honor the deceased with four prostrations; the first-born son greets each of them with four, two, or only one prostration, or with a single bow, depending on the merit and rank of the person. Later they all joyfully feast at the common banquet from the prepared sacrificial tables, with one special sacrificial table placed in front of the tablet for the deceased.

Article 11: Important Remarks on Sacrifices

It is evident from what was narrated in this second chapter, and from the preceding one, that all sacrifices made to Confucius, tutelary genies, and other spirits, as well as to the deceased, are performed with substantially the same ceremonies and with the same credulity. Indeed, in each of them an altar and the four-legged sacrificial table called *hương án* are present; one principal attendant, several assistants, other servants, and two masters of ceremonies participate in it; meat of killed animals and other food is offered; wine or drippings from rice is poured over a handful of straw, and libations and prostrations are made, and a leaf of offertory is read; incense is burnt and pieces of gold and silver paper money are set on fire; and, finally, people partake of the offerings with pleasure. They believe, first, that the spirits exhibit their presence during the sacrifices in the tablets that they commonly use for that purpose, and which they call a seat of the spirit, *Thần vị (shenwei),* and they welcome arriving spirits and see them off with special ceremonies; second, the spirits receive offerings and enjoy them, and for that reason at the end of the *văn tế*—the leaf of sacrifice [read] at the conclusion of the offertory—[the participants] pronounce the following words: Thượng hưởng; third, the spirits have the ability to bestow blessings on their worshippers and because of that [the participants] thank them for received favors and ask for new [blessings while reading] from the aforementioned leaf. Thus, the first observation is that all these sacrifices are equally stained or infected with superstition and idolatry, and, because of this, sacrifices to Confucius cannot be considered free [of superstition and idolatry], nor can sacrifices to the deceased ancestors be [considered] as customary [i.e., innocent common usage]; they are similar to sacrifices, which, [p. 55] according to tradition, are made to Thần Nông, *Thành Hoàng,* and to other spirits; all [of these sacrifices] should be considered as filled with superstition and idolatry. If sacrifices to Confucius and to the deceased were free from the idolatrous and superstitious [character of the] cult, sacrifices to other spirits would also obtain this immunity, because in all of them the same sense is contained. Therefore, the Holy Office many times deservedly pronounced offerings to Confucius and to the deceased as infected with superstition.

Observation two: A sacrificial table, or a *hương án* table [for incense], must be decorated and should stand at some distance from the altar, on which is put the [other] sacrificial table with food to the spirit, which must be considered to constitute unity with the altar itself; since wine or drippings [from rice] are poured, or libations of wine or of drippings are performed in front of it, and prostrations are made, and a leaf of sacrifice is read, it [the sacrificial table] seems to be used in place of an altar, and the attendant, assistants, and servants must stand at a distance from it in front of the sacrificial tables with food, which are placed around. Since on that *hương án* sacrificial table incense is burnt, and no food or drink offerings are arranged, it seems to be introduced by a demon to represent the altar of incense, which in the tabernacle and in the temple of the Lord existed beyond the altar of burnt offerings, about which the Lord instructed in Exod. 30: "You shall make an altar to burn incense upon; of acacia wood shall you make it. . . . You shall offer no unholy incense thereon, not burnt offering, nor cereal offering, and you shall pour no libation thereon."[175]

---

[175] Exod. 30:1, 9.

Observation three: The animals, which are killed so that their meat may be offered in the sacrifice, represent victims, which formerly were killed in sacrifices to the Lord. But yet the offering of them has been far different from the offering of victims. Indeed, the animals for sacrifices to Confucius, to the deceased, and to other spirits are not killed in an actual sacrifice, they are killed before the sacrifice without any ceremony or offering; after they are killed, they are usually cut into pieces and offered in this way. Animals in sacrifice to the Lord are killed during an actual sacrifice, and are not offered dead, as it appears from the first chapters of the book of Leviticus, which instructs that when a man offers an animal victim to the Lord, he should lay his hand over the head of the victim, kill it in front of the Lord, or at the side of the altar, or at the entrance of the tabernacle, or in its vestibule, and the priests should pour the blood [p. 56] around the altar, or onto the base of the altar, and the same priests should burn the pieces into which the animal had been cut, all of them or some of them, on the altar according to the type of sacrifice. The sense of a sacrifice is certainly in killing a victim, and the victim to God is killed in a solemn praise of the highest Lord, because the same God stays with us in life and in death as the theologians teach according to St. Thomas 2.2 q 85;[176] there is no sense in the killing of animals in the sacrifices to Confucius, to the deceased, and to other spirits; in a proper sense they cannot be called sacrifices, but only solemn offerings, and are usually called with this name in decrees of the Holy Office.

[People] started to offer animals to God early at the beginning of the world, in this way Abel[177] offered {Gen. 4} of the first-born of his herd and of their fat; "Then Noah built {Gen. 8} an altar to the Lord [after the flood], and he took of every clean animal and of every clean bird, and offered burnt offerings on the altar."[178] The first to offer animals in sacrifice to Thượng Đế, or to the Supreme King, according to the *Chinese History*, was Hoàng Đế, about whom it is said there that he built a house for making sacrifice to Thượng Đế, and for worshipping all the spirits: Đế toài tạc hợp cung tự Thượng Đế tiếp vạn linh,[179] and literatus

[176] The reference is to St. Thomas Aquinas (1224?–75), an Italian Dominican, one of the most famous theologians, who wrote two major philosophical works: *Summa Contra Gentiles* (ca. 1258–64) and *Summa Theologiae* (ca. 1265–73), numerous biblical commentaries, and liturgical hymns. Adriano di St. Thecla cites here his *Summa Theologiae* 2.2, question 85; see S. Thomae Aquinatis, *Summa Theologiae* (n.p.: Marietti, 1952), 2:406–407.

[177] Abel, the second son of Adam and Eve, was a shepherd. He was slain by his brother Cain, a tiller of the ground, who was jealous of God's preference for Abel's sacrifice, the firstlings of his flocks, to Cain's sacrifice of fruits. See Gen. 4:1–16.

[178] Gen. 8:20.

[179] 帝 遂 胙 合 恭 祀 上 帝 接 萬 靈 . Adriano di St. Thecla cites a slightly expanded version of this phrase in the chapter on Confucianism. As noted in that chapter, to make this phrase intelligible, the word *toài* here should be read as *toại* (*sui*, consequently). The phrase in the chapter on Confucianism has the word *tắc* (*ze*, thereupon, a pattern) instead of the word *tạc* (*zuo*, to worship ancestors), which is hardly plausible in either chapter; to the best of my knowledge, it is not used in conjunction with the word *toại* (*sui*, consequently). Certainly the word *tạc* (*zuo*, to worship ancestors) works better in the phrase. In spite of the fact that Adriano di St. Thecla adduces here an abbreviated citation compared to that in the chapter on Confucianism, he keeps here the same translation. In the form given here this phrase should be translated: "The emperor thereupon worshiped ancestors as well as made sacrifices to the Supreme Emperor and welcomed the ten thousand spirits."

Thiên Thai[180] added to this, saying: Tạc Thần y nhân nhi huyết thực, nhân hưởng Thần nhi hữu sở; that is: Hence, spirits feed on blood {i.e., animals} because people venerate them, and people have the place {mentioned above} because they make offerings to the spirits.[181] Usually the Chinese and the Annamites in their sacrifices and offerings offer to spirits meat of the animals of six species: namely *mã (ma)*, horse; *ngưu (niu)*, buffalo; *dương (yang)*, goat; *thỉ (shi)*, pig; *kê (ji)*, rooster; and *khuyển (quan)*, dog. These six species are called *lục súc* by the Annamites, and *lo cho* (*liuchu*, the six domestic animals) by the Chinese. Among them there are three that coincide with those that were once sacrificed to the true God, namely the buffalo, the goat, and the rooster. The buffalo and the goat belong to the cattle and the rooster to the birds. Noah offered burnt offerings of both kinds [of animals], and in Levit. 1 the rites about the sacrifices of both kinds, cattle and birds, are mentioned, where, in explanation, bulls and sheep are understood under the name of cattle with these words: "When any man of you brings an offering to the Lord, you shall bring your offering of cattle from the herd or from the flock."[182]

[p. 57] Observation four: The literati feel differently concerning the presence of the spirits at sacrifices; some say that this presence is real, others that it is imagined, and imitative. And the latter support their theory with the testimony of their teacher Confucius, who in the book *Luận Ngữ (Lunyu*, Analects) says: Tế như tại, tế Thần như Thần tại;[183] this means: *Sacrifice is made to the spirits as if they were present*; where the word *như (ru)*—that is, *as if*, or *just as*—represents the imitation of presence, but not the presence itself. Chu Thị (i.e. Zhu Xi) in

---

[180] This person has not been identified. Due to the lack of the characters, there are several possibilities for reading the first syllable of his name in Chinese: Tian or Qian or Shan or Pian, and the second one is read in Chinese as Tai.

[181] I am not sure how to render this phrase into characters. It seems that something is missing in front of the first word of the sentence because, as it is, the beginning of the sentence means "to offer a sacrifice to the spirits," and it does not fit the structure of the rest of the sentence. I think that before the word *tạc* (*zuo*, to make a sacrifice) there was an agent who makes the sacrifice or a signifier of the passive voice. The best version I could think of is: 胙 神 依 人 而 血 食 因 饗 神 而 有 所 . This phrase can be translated as: "To [obtain] a sacrifice, spirits rely on people to partake of sacrificial offerings; in order to make the sacrifice to the spirits, there should be a place [for it]." If we rely on Adriano di St. Thecla's translation of the second part of the sentence ("because people venerate them, and people have the place {mentioned above} because they make offerings to the spirits"), then the second character with the pronunciation *nhân* (*yin*, because, in consequence of) should be replaced with the character *nhân* (*ren*, person). This is also a plausible version, but then the word *nhi* (*er*, and, still) is in a slightly grammatically worse position than it is in the construction *nhân (yin)* . . . *nhi* (*er*, because of). In any case, this could produce the following translation: "To [obtain] a sacrifice, spirits rely on people to partake of sacrificial offerings; people make sacrifices to the spirits, and there should be a place [for it]." Adriano di St. Thecla's notion of the spirits "eating blood" is apparently caused by literally translating the words *huyết* (*xue*, blood) and *thực* (*shi*, food or to eat). If the meaning were really "to eat blood," then the word order in the compound would be reversed: *thực huyết (shixue)*, and not *huyết thực (xueshi)*, as it is. The compound *huyết thực* has the meaning "to partake of a sacrificial offering—of the gods." See R. H. Mathews, *Mathews' Chinese-English Dictionary*, 19th ed. (Cambridge: Harvard University Press, 2000), no. 2901:62, p. 434.

[182] Lev. 1:2.

[183] 祭 如 在 固 神 如 神 在 . The object of the sacrifice in the first part of the sentence is absent. Legge suggests it is "the dead." He translates this passage as "He sacrificed *to the dead*, as if they were present. He sacrificed to the spirits, as if the spirits were present." *Analects*; Legge, *Chinese Classics*, 1:159 and n. 12.

[commentaries to] the book *Thi Kinh* (*Shijing*, Book of Odes) rejects representation of the real presence with the following words: Nhược phụ mẫu chi kí một, daong[184] mạo chi bất khả dĩ phục kiến, âm hưởng chi bất khả dĩ phục văn, tuy hữu cam chi[185] khinh noản,[186] vô sở phương chi dã.[187] This means: If father and mother are sent away {that is, died}, their faces are no longer seen, their voices are no longer heard; in spite of this, delicious food is offered and single-layer and double-layer clothes are offered without them {aforementioned father and mother} [being present]. It is a common belief that spirits reveal their presence to them [the worshippers] at the sacrifices. Moreover, some literati may admit the presence of Confucius at the sacrifices to him [rather than there being only] an image of him. Since the literati hold their sacrifices in the morning of one and the same day during the second and eighth lunar month, in all his temples built in any place, then the spirit of Confucius is believed to be present at sacrifices in many places at the same time if his presence is considered to be real and not imagined.

Observation five: The meaning of the words *Thượng hưởng*, in Chinese *Xang hiang (shangxiang)*, which are read at the end of each *văn tế*, or the leaf of the sacrifice, is: *the spirit, whom we venerate, is pleased*, or *is delighted by the offerings*. The phrase *Thượng hưởng* indicates veneration of the spirits who are addressed by the person who makes the offering throughout the entire offertory. He reads [the words] from the leaf, and they [the words] do not show any doubt in [the fact that the spirit will] enjoy [the offering], as if the sense were: *perhaps he* [the spirit] *may enjoy the offerings*, as some literati translated it for me, and they commonly believe that in reality the spirits are delighted by the offerings. If they [the spirits] really are [delighted], those who understand the word *Thượng* as *perhaps*[188] would express doubt whether spirits are pleased with the offerings, [p. 58] [yet] with their doubt they show that they believe that spirits are able to take pleasure from the offering; if they did not have this belief, they would not be able to say that the spirit perhaps would enjoy the offerings, *Thượng hưởng*. The ritual of pronouncing at the end of the leaf of sacrifice these two words *Thượng hưởng*, with which the spirit is asked whether he likes the offerings, seems to have been introduced by a demon with the intention to liken the offerings made to the spirits even to the sacrifices offered to God, in which God accepted the offerings, and clearly [the demon tries to liken them] to the sacrifice that Noah offered to God

---

[184] This word is spelled *dong* or *dung* (*rong*, appearance) in the modern orthography. As is the case with other words in the manuscript ending with *-aong*, this combination lost the *a* in the course of time. *Daong* started to be spelled as *dong*.

[185] This word is an apparent mistake for *chỉ* (*zhi*, good, excellent, delicious). The compound *cam chỉ (ganzhi)* means "delicacies—for aged parents." Mathews, *Chinese-English Dictionary*, no. 3223:13, p. 484.

[186] This is a mistake for the word *noãn* (*nuan*, warm). The compound *khinh noãn* (qingnuan) means "light and warm." In this context it might imply light and warm clothes, even though the word "clothes" is absent. Adriano di St. Thecla translated it as "single-layer and double-layer clothes."

[187] 若 父 母 之 既 歿 谷 貌 之 不 可 以 復 見 音 響 之 不 可 以 復 聞 雖 有 甘 旨 輕 煖 無 所 挙 之 也 .

[188] This argument is caused by the different possibilities for characters read as *thượng*: 尚 , which usually means "to honor, to ascend," or 倘 , meaning "if, supposing."

after he came out of the ark, as it is said in Gen. 8, "God smelled the pleasing fragrance."[189]

Finally, in the feast, which they have after the sacrifice, they imitate the Hebrews who in the desert offered burnt offerings and peace victims in front of a golden calf {Exod. 32:6}, and the people would sit to eat and drink, and would stand up to play. They appear completely similar to them [the Hebrews], since they not only feast after the offering but also play different games, as it has been said in the appropriate place about the spirit *Thành Hoàng* or the tutelary [genie]. Among the Hebrews a habit also existed after the sacrifice to God to feast from the offerings, and the first to feast in this way were Jacob[190] and his brothers: when Jacob made a covenant with Laban {Gen. 31}, "he swore by the fear of his father Isaac; and Jacob offered a sacrifice on the mountain and called his kinsmen to eat bread; and they ate bread and tarried all night on the mountain."[191] When Jethro, a relative of Moses,[192] came to him in the desert {Exod. 18:12}, "he offered a burnt offering and sacrificed to God; and Aaron came with all the elders of Israel to eat bread with Moses' father-in-law before God." And Moses taught them: {Deut. 12} "and thither you shall bring your burnt offerings and your sacrifices, your tithes and the offerings that you present, your votive offerings, and the firstlings of your herd and of your flock; and there you shall eat before the Lord your God."[193]
[p. 59]

Article 12: On Sacrifice to Living Vua and Chúa

Among the sacrifices that are made, it is necessary to discuss those that are performed, according to tradition, to the living *Vua* and to the living *Chúa*. So, they sacrifice before the king or living *Vua* several times a year with all the ceremonies that are observed in other sacrifices. Since the sacrifice must take place twice a month, namely, at the new moon and full moon, during these days all the officials or the prefects come to fulfill their duties at the court. In reality the king often orders that the sacrifice be skipped, sure that it will happen sometime [later]; usually it is celebrated annually on the king's birthday.

---

[189] Gen. 8:21

[190] Jacob, a Hebrew patriarch, was one of Abraham's grandsons, the son of Isaac and Rebekah. He is traditionally considered the ancestor of the Israelis. On Jacob, see Gen., starting from 25:19.

[191] Gen. 31:54. Laban was Rebecca's brother, whose daughters, Leah and Rachel, Jacob married after he had fled from his homeland due to conflict over the birthright with his twin first-born brother, Esau. Jacob stayed with Laban more than twenty years before he could return home with his wives and children. On his way back, Jacob and his household were chased by Laban, who was searching for the statues of gods that had disappeared from his house after Jacob's departure. Not having found his gods, Laban made a covenant with Jacob, which is referred to in the manuscript. On Laban, see Gen. 29:5–31:55, and on the covenant 31:43–55.

[192] Jethro, a priest of Midian, gave refuge to Moses after Moses had murdered an Egyptian who had smitten a Hebrew. Moses married one of Jethro's seven daughters, Zipporah (Gen. 3:1). After the Exodus of the Hebrews from Egypt, Jethro heard about all the assistance God was giving to the Hebrews, and he joined Moses at Mount Sinai, bringing along Zipporah and Moses' two sons. Adriano di St. Thecla refers here to the episode when Jethro recognized the God of the Hebrews as the greatest of all gods and made a burnt-offering sacrifice to God (Gen. 18).

[193] Deut. 12:6–7.

Undoubtedly, this honor is exceptional, since it might make the king, who is staying among humans, equal to all the spirits whom the Annamites venerate with sacrifices; furthermore, it reveals human arrogance, because of which kings accept such a high honor. They would have acted sensibly if they had never admitted such sacrifices and prohibited them from taking place, shouting out the words of Paul and Barnabas,[194] who restrained the citizens of Iconium[195] from the sacrifice that [the citizens] arranged for them: "Men, why are you doing this? {Acts 14} We also are men, of like nature with you."[196]

Also it is mentioned that because of excessive honor the king is descriptively called Son of Heaven, Thiên Tử (Tianzi), and one can see [this] in books of the literati or Đạo Nho (dao ru),[197] and in the *Chinese History* they usually write this name on the back side of their epistles, according to their tradition. For this reason, they say that the king has Heaven as father, and Earth as mother, just as it is written in the *History:* Phụ Thiên, Mẫu Địa nhị vị Thiên Tử.[198]

Similarly, a sacrifice is made to the governor of the kingdom, or to the living *Chúa* in the second and in the eighth month, twice a year, in front of his statue, preserving all the ceremonies of the sacrifice. The sacrifice happens, as I was told, in Bố Chính district of Thuận Hóa province,[199] and I also believe it happens in the fatherland of the *Chúa* in Thiên Thiên district[200] of Thanh Hóa province.[201] They also reveal with this honor that governors of the kingdom, who are called *Chúa*, claim to be equal in everything to the kings [p. 60] or *Vua*, whose power they have already usurped.

---

[194] The Apostles St. Paul and St. Barnabas lived in the first century. They were among the first Jews converted to Christianity after Christ's crucifixion. Fervent Christians, they became the first missionaries. St. Paul and St. Barnabas went together on mission to a number of remote places in Asia Minor, and as a result of their work some Christian communities were founded in Cyprus, Jerusalem, and elsewhere. Later, due to conflicts between them, St. Paul and St. Barnabas dissolved their companionship and preached separately (Acts 14:20, 16:2).

[195] Modern Konya, a city in central Turkey. In the time of St. Paul and St. Barnabas it was a colony of the Roman Empire, and they preached there sometime after 40 C.E. while on their missionary journey.

[196] Acts 14:15.

[197] Here again a Vietnamese word order. The compound implies Confucianism.

[198] 父 天 母 地 二 為 天 子 . "The Father being Heaven and the Mother being Earth, the two make the Son of Heaven."

[199] In modern Quảng Bình province, central Vietnam. At the time Adriano di St. Thecla was writing the manuscript, the border with the Nguyễn warlords was in Bố Chính, and they (the Trịnh lords, or *chúa*, in Hanoi) erected there a temple dedicated to their family. See Đinh Xuân Vịnh, *Sổ Tay Địa Danh Việt Nam*, pp. 521–522.

[200] Four villages are considered to be native places of the Trịnh family (Kẻ Nưa, Thủy Chú, Sóc Sơn, and Hổ Bái).

[201] A province in north-central Vietnam.

CHAPTER THREE

ON THE SECT OF MAGICIANS

Article 1: On Lão Tử, the Founder of This Sect

This sect is descriptively called *Đạo* (*Dao*),[1] and its doctrine is *called Đạo Đạo* (*Dao Dao*).[2] Its principal is someone known by his vulgar name, Lão Tử, Lao zu (Laozi) in Chinese,[3] who is also called by other names: Lão Tiên (Lao Xian), Lão Đam (Lao Dan), Lão Nhiễm (Lao Ran), Lão Quân (Laojun);[4] in European speech he was called Lautius by the first missionaries.[5] He was born in China in Hu Kuang (Huguang) province, Hồ Quảng in Annamite,[6] to the father ——— Trụ (Zhu or Zhou)[7] and mother Huyền Diệu (Xuanmiao)[8] in the seventh year of the

[1] A great principle; the primary source of all being; the governor, law, and way of all life; relationships in nature and among humans.

[2] Doctrine of the Dao.

[3] Lão Tử (Laozi) might be understood as "an old child" (according to the legends, when Laozi was born, he had white hair, which is why the boy was called "old child"), "venerable elder," or "Master Lão." Laozi is a mythical rather than a historical figure. All the information about his life relies on later accounts. The information on him first appears as early as third century B.C.E. in numerous places in the *Zhuangzi* (Writing of Master Zhuang). For a detailed analysis of Laozi's hagiography and role in Daoism, see Livia Kohn, *God of the Dao: Lord Lao in History and Myth* (Ann Arbor, MI: Center for Chinese Studies, University of Michigan, 1998).

[4] These are various honorifics for Lão Tử (Laozi).

[5] Contrary to the Latinized forms of the names of Confucius and Mencius, the Latinized name of Laozi—Lautius—did not strike roots in Western tradition.

[6] In modern Hunan province, in central China. In Laozi's time the Chu (Zhou) kingdom was located in this territory.

[7] None of the sources mentions Lão Tử (Laozi)'s father, but only his mother. Laozi's family tree starts with his appearance, and genealogies were developed only for his descendants. (Such is the case, for example, when Laozi is identified as an ancestor in the genealogy of the Tang emperors.) None of the texts traces Laozi's own ancestors. This seemingly indicates his mythical personality and divine appearance into this world.

I think that Adriano di St. Thecla gathered the information given in the text from a Vietnamese source. It is a characteristic feature of Vietnamese tradition not to leave anything unexplained or incomplete, and it is plausible that Vietnamese sources or Vietnamese lore complemented the story by introducing an absent father for Laozi.

[8] An abbreviation of Huyền Diệu Ngọc Nữ (Xuanmiao yunü) which means Jade Maiden of Mystery and Wonder. She appeared as a result of the combination of three energies: the mysterious, the primordial, and the creative. According to legend, Xuanmiao became

reign of Chu Linh Vương (Zhou Lingwang),[9] year 565 before Christ; and he died in [his] eighty-first year,[10] in the thirty-fifth year of Emperor Chu Kính Vương (Zhou Jingwang),[11] in the mountains called Cửa ải Hàm Cốc (Hangu Pass) of Huề Lí (Xieli) district,[12] where he had fled when those who set up the younger brother [of Chu Kính Vương] as an emperor were getting the upper hand in war over Kính Vương (Jingwang).[13] He was a master of ceremonies or of instruction at the court of Cảnh Vương (Jingwang),[14] and later at the court of his son Kính Vương. He wrote several small books, and [united them] under the title *Đạo Đức Kinh (Daode jing)*, which contains various instructions on ethical doctrine.[15] He had many disciples, and Confucius himself received some education from him, as can be seen from the book *[Khổng Tử] Gia Ngữ* (*[Kongzi] Jiayu*, Discourses of [the Confucian] School) in the epitome of his life, where it is mentioned that, at the age of thirty-four years, Confucius *Thích Chu vấn lễ Lão Đam*;[16] this means:

---

pregnant from swallowing a pill consisting of these three energies. She was prompted to swallow this pill when Lord Lao decided to appear in human form on earth and needed a human mother. The eleventh-century text *Youlong zhuan* (Like unto a Dragon) describes it in the following way: "She carried him for eighty-one years, after which he splits open her left armpit and steps out, already able to walk. Blessed by the gods of the sun, moon, and stars, and bathed by nine dragons who spring up from the earth, he next takes nine steps. With each step a lotus blossom sprouts forth, announcing his superior stature in heaven and on earth." Cited in Kohn, *God of the Dao*, p. 235.

[9] R. 571–544 B.C.E.

[10] Year 484 B.C.E.

[11] R. 519–475 B.C.E..

[12] In modern Shanxi province in China.

[13] It is not clear what source served as a basis for Adriano di St. Thecla's statement on the struggle between two brothers. The traditional version says that Laozi left his homeland when he felt that the dynasty was in decline.

[14] R. 544–519 B.C.E.

[15] The Book of the Dao and of Virtue, the greatest Daoist classic. *Đạo Đức Kinh (Daode jing)* displays many of the fundamental Daoist ideas: the prevalence of the state of nonbeing over that of being, of nonaction over action, and of the negative over the positive. This highly suggestive work became one of the most commented upon of all Chinese texts. During the past two thousand years, there have been numerous unresolved debates about the date and authorship of this book. Proposed dates range from the sixth century B.C.E. to the third century B.C.E. It might be a product of a certain philosopher or of a collective authorship. For a bibliography of this discussion, see Ellen M. Chen, *The Tao Te Ching: A New Translation with Commentary* (New York: Paragon House, 1989), pp. 4–6; and Kohn, *God of the Dao*, p. 1. The *Shiji* (Historical Records) has the following information: "After living in Chou [Zhou] for a long time, he [Laozi] saw Chou's [Zhou's] decline and left. When he reached the pass, the Prefect of the Pass, Yin Hsi [Yin Xi], said, 'Since you are going to retire from the world, I beg you to endeavor to write a book for us.' Lao Tzu [Laozi] thus wrote a book in two sections which spoke of the meaning of the Way and its virtue in five thousand and some characters and then departed. No one knows where he finally ended." See William H. Nienhauser, Jr., ed., *The Grand Scribe's Record: The Memoirs of Pre-Han China by Ssu-ma Ch'ien* (Bloomington: Indiana University Press, 1994), 7:22.

[16] 適 周 問 禮 老 聃 *Kongzi jiayu* (Discourses of the Confucian School) (Taiwan: Zhonghua shuju, 1968) published in *Kongzi jiayu suizi suoyin* (A Concordance to the *Kongzi jiayu*) (Hong Kong: Xianggang zhongwen daxue zhongguo wenhua, Shangwu yin shuguan, 1992), p. 20. The phrase there is slightly different from that in the manuscript. In the original it reads: (至 周 問 禮 於 老 聃). Adriano di St. Thecla uses the word *thích* (*shi*, to go) instead of the original character *chí* (*zhi*, to arrive). Also in the manuscript the word *ư* (*yu*, in this case, a preposition "from") is absent. Its presence in the original is

[Confucius] came to the court of the emperor of the Chu (Zhou) dynasty to question Lão Đam on rituals.[17]

Magicians consider him the principal of their sect, who used magic for medicine and gave them instructions on this subject, and who also taught them that there were five elements or principles in a human body, namely: *hỏa (huo), thổ (tu), kim (jin), thủy (shui),* and *mộc (mu);* that is, fire, earth, metal, water, and wood.[18] Furthermore, they tell delusive miracles about him, namely, that he was in the womb of his mother for eighty-one years, and he was born [p. 61] in an unusual way. Standing in the womb, he bit the left side of his mother, and emerged from there, and his mother died because of that; when he died, a green bull appeared to him, and seated on the bull he ascended to Heaven.

Also, many literati think that Lão Đam did not pass on his magic to anyone, nor did he practice it [himself], but [rather] those who lived after him taught it in a significantly changed form using the book of Lão Nhiễm, so that with the name of such a great man they obtained authority for their doctrine. Their opinion may be supported by the consideration that Confucius did not write or say anything against *Đạo* Lão Đam (Dao Lao Dan), or Lão Nhiễm, which he would certainly have done if, at the time he lived, his [Lão Đam's] doctrine had already been full[19] of magic, since Confucius died six years after Lão Đam, in the forty-first year [of the reign of] Chu Kính Vương.[20] Moreover, Chu Tử (Zhuzi, i.e. Zhu Xi), in the book *Lao Ngữ (Laoyu,* Discourses of Lao*)*,[21] assumes that the doctrine of Lão Tử was the same as the doctrine of Dương Chu (Yang Zhu), and affirms that Mạnh Tử (Mengzi) by attacking Dương Chu at the same time attacked Lão Tử; he says: Lão tiện thị Dương thị Mạnh Tử tích[22] Dương tiện thị thích Lão.[23] And in the preface to the book *Đại Học* (*Daxue,*

grammatically better. There exist several versions of the *Discourses*. It is not clear whether Adriano di St. Thecla used some version that I could not trace, relied on a corrupted secondary source, decided himself to "fix" some characters, or simply paraphrased it. The main point is that his citation is almost identical with that of the original.

[17] The earliest surviving mention of this meeting of the two great masters is probably in *Liji* (Record of Rites). James Legge, trans., *Li Chi, Book of Rites* (New Hyde Park, NY: University Books, 1967), 1:325. There are also several references to their having met in the *Zhuangzi* and the *Shiji* (Historical Records). For a detailed analysis of the meetings of Lão Tử (Laozi) with Confucius, see A. C. Graham, "The Origins of the Legend of Lao Tan," in *Studies in Chinese Philosophy and Philosophical Literature*, ed. A. C. Graham (Albany, NY: State University of New York Press, 1990), pp. 111–124.

[18] This concept of the five primary elements also exists in the Confucian philosophical system. Chu Hi (Zhu Xi), commenting on Cheng Yi's statement "that which receives the Five Agents in their highest excellence becomes man," said in the *Zhuzi yulei* (Classified Conversations of Master Zhu): "Only the Five Agents, and not yin and yang, are mentioned because man requires the Five Agents to be produced. Yin and Yang are inherent in the Five Agents." Zhu Xi, *Zhuzi yulei*, ed. Li Jingde (Taipei: Zhengzhong shuju, 1962), 2:1303.

[19] The word is hard to read; it looks like *scatuisset* (to be abundant).

[20] That is, the year 478; Lao Tử (Laozi) died in 484, according to the author.

[21] I could not locate the book. It might be that *Lao Ngữ (Laoyu)* is not a book but a chapter in one of the numerous books by Chu Hi (Zhu Xi). However, in the book *Zhuzi yulei* (Classified Conversations of Master Zhu) Zhu Xi indeed affirms that the doctrine of Yang Zhu is identical to that of Laozi. Ibid., 4:2158–2519.

[22] There seems to be no character pronounced in Vietnamese as *tích* that is suitable in this context (the best possible one would be 析 , meaning "to separate, to divide, to analyze"), but, in my opinion, it would stand out of the phrase. Taking into consideration the

Great Learning), the same Chu Tử calls the sect of Lão Tử Dị đoan hư vô thí[24] giáo;[25] this means: sect of nothing, contradictory, and oblique.[26]

They also teach in this sect about the following source for the origin and the definition of things: Đạo sinh nhất, nhất sinh nhị, nhị sinh tam, tam sinh vạn vật, hư vô tự nhiên chi đại đạo;[27] that is: The law produced one, one produced two, two produced three, three produced innumerable things, or everything: the great law is nothingness, which appeared out of itself. Furthermore, they teach that there are five immortals: heaven, earth, water, spirit, and the human soul.

Article 2: On the Growth of This Sect

The Sect of Magicians grew significantly during the period of the Hán (Han) dynasty; at that time, indeed, there lived some of the Trương (Zhang) family, who were distinguished in this sect; namely Trương Nghi (Zhang Yi),[28] Trương Đạo Lang[29] (Zhang Daoling), and Trương Giác (Zhang Jue).[30] [p. 62] Some mention as their predecessor a certain Trương Lương (Zhang Liang), a very famous man who at first served as a prefect under King Thang[31] in the Hàn kingdom; later, under Emperor Hán Cao Tổ (Han Gaozu) and afterward, he

translation of Adriano di St. Thecla, which precedes the Vietnamese phrase, the grammatical and semantic structure of the sentence, and the absence of a plausible option for the character 刺 pronounced in Vietnamese as *tích*, I propose that *tích* is an error for *thích* (*ci*, to lampoon, to criticize), which is used again in this citation in front of the name of Lao to say that Mencius criticized Laozi.

23 老 便 足 楊 氏 孟 子 刺 （ 析 ） 楊 便 足 刺 老 .

24 This is a mistake. This word stands for the character 之, a possessive pronoun, pronounced *chi* in Vietnamese.

25 異 端 虛 無 之 教. *Daxue zhangju* (Great Learning: Chapters and Sentences [with commentaries of Zhu Xi]) (Kyoto: Santo Shorin, 1900?), p. 3b. The exact original definition of the doctrine is found in the preface by Chu Hi (Zhu Xi), from which Adriano di St. Thecla quotes partially. The original reads: 異 端 虛 無 寂 滅 之 教.

26 Adriano di St. Thecla's translation conveys the sense of the passage. A more precise translation is "useless, false, empty, inert, and destructive doctrine."

27 道 生 一 一 生 貳 貳 生 三 三 生 萬 物 虛 無 自 然 之 大 道 The citation is from the *Daode jing*. Zhang Songru, *Laozi shuojie* (Laozi Explains) (Jinan, China: Jilu shushe, 1987), p. 279.

28 The identity of this person has remained obscure. I could not find any mention of him in the annals, legends, or secondary sources I have consulted.

29 It should be Trương Đạo Lăng in modern Vietnamese.

30 Trương Giác (Zhang Jue), who lived in the second century C.E., was known for his vast knowledge of the Daoist occult arts and his ability to heal. He was reckoned a patriarch of the Daoist sect Taiping dao (the Way of Great Peace). This sect was a messianic current that incorporated some features of Chinese cosmology and philosophical Daoism along with numerous popular beliefs. Its main deity was Huang Lao, a combination of the Yellow Emperor, Huangdi, and Laozi. According to the doctrine of this sect, disease was a result of human sin. Thus, the members of the sect often organized various religious activities to purify themselves through public confession and collective trances, called assemblies *(hui)* and "fasts of purification" *(chai)*.

31 A mistake in the text. The king's name was Thành (Cheng). He is mentioned in the chapter on spirits.

Chinese History under the ninth year of Emperor Hán Linh Đế. As you can see, the aforementioned prefect Trương Lương, killed in battle, was different from the preceding Trương Lương (Zhang Liang, 張 良) who served as a general under Emperor Hán Cao Tổ, and his name Lương (Liang 梁) is written in a way different from the name of the former.

Article 3: On the Magic of This Sect

Those who teach [the doctrine] of this sect are called *Thầy Phù thủy* (masters of sorcery); they exercise magic with their whole heart, and apply it mostly for treatment of the sick. On that account, they say that the spirits and the deceased are malignant toward humans and that they bring in illnesses and weaknesses and that there are twenty-four spirits of this kind, of which five spirits, called *Thần hung* (*shen xiong*, ferocious or malevolent spirits),[45] are especially pernicious to [people's] life; and, furthermore, they [the magicians] boast that they have power from [p. 64] Lão Tiên and Ngọc Hoàng (Yuhuang, Jade Emperor)[46] to expel them [the spirits], and to force them not to hurt the sick anymore. Moreover, they perform many superstitions to treat the weak, namely, they [the magicians] offer food to the spirits and to the deceased, they burn gold and silver paper money in their honor, and they beg them to stop hurting the sick. They fill their prayers with much shouting in the house of the sick, or at the bank of a river, or in any other place; they terrify them [the spirits] with shouting and clattering, invoking black *hắc hổ (heihu)* tigresses to [make them] go away terrified, and at such times they also strike a small bell and hold a staff. They often decorate a cymbal of paper with oars of reed and a sail and send it away into a stream or a fish-pond so that in it the harmful spirits, whom they compel to enter the cymbal, are driven away. They also enclose in a glass flask a firefly, that is, a shining insect with wings, and say that a soul that is harassing a sick person is contained in it, and with much swearing and with loud clapping they attempt to expel it; after that they open the flask, the firefly flies away, and they say that the soul fled from the sick person and will no longer torment him. They also order to carry the sick to another house, so that the souls of the deceased and the spirits of their own house will not find them and afflict [them] with a worse disaster. Sometimes they order the bones of the deceased to be exhumed and transferred to another tomb, so that, pleased with a new place, they will stop being malicious to living people; and they even advise that some of the bones be left unburied and exposed to the violence of the air, so that they will lose their ability to cause damage. They also often pretend that the souls of deceased parents are tormenting their children and descendants with illnesses, since they are burning

---

dynastic authority, according to them, was to be eliminated. Zhang Jue, together with his two brothers, one mentioned here as Zhang Liang and the other Zhang Bao, were at the head of the uprising. Even though the rebellion was suppressed, the Han dynasty was irreparably weakened and soon came to its end.

[45] The word order in the compound *thần hung* is Vietnamese. In Sino-Vietnamese it should have been *hung thần (xiongshen)*.

[46] One of the highest Daoist deities. See article 5 below.

in Hades and they want to be liberated from there with their [children's] help; for that reason they make a ceremony [called] Phá ngục (poyu, destruction of prison), of which we will talk in an article in Chapter Five; they borrowed this ritual from the sect of the worshippers of Phật (Fo, Buddha). They make somebody sit in the center and, with words, gestures, and fumigations, make it so that he [the person in the center] leaves [his body] having no power over it, and he becomes possessed by some demon or a spirit of the higher rank; then the possessed person takes a branch and strikes or breaks something in which he thinks the spirit hurting the sick one is hiding, and expels him [the spirit]; or he hits numerous times [p. 65] a small piece of paper on which is written the name of the deceased who is hostile to the sick one; magicians compel his soul, present in this piece of paper, quickly to stop hurting the sick person; after those actions he [the possessed] returns to his mind. Magicians also distribute small pieces of paper, inscribed with different superstitious characters, chiefly at the beginning of a new year; many people buy them and put them in their houses, or attach them to their necks, to free themselves from misfortunes. Cards of this kind are called *bùa phép* (magic amulets), that is, magic endowed with preserving power.

Among those characters there are two, Thần [and] Đồ, Chinese Xin tu (Shentu),[47] which denote the name of the spirit who is the chief among the malevolent spirits, and who restrains them from causing damage. There are so many [amulets] to exercise salutary magic that even the governor of the kingdom, Chúa (zhu), orders the attendants of elephants and horses to get these cards from the master magicians *Thầy Phù thủy* at the beginning of every year or even two or three times a year; and [they] attach them over the thresholds of stables, and if they do not do this and accidentally some elephant or horse gets sick or dies, the attendants are punished with a heavy penalty.

Magicians also perform evil deeds; they make spirits and demons appear to them and order them to inflict damage upon others, and for that they often use certain small figurines, or statuettes, made of straw, representing people in the form of the Roman numeral ten [X] called *mô đền*,[48] which are moved and instructed by the Devil; they [magicians] distribute these "quasi alive" [figurines] in the houses and on the tops of the roofs,[49] and they set them on fire

---

[47] This is the elder of two brothers (the younger one is Yulei) – the Door-spirits. Their fame came as a result of their power over evil spirits. Chinese legends relate their appearance to a huge peach tree growing on one of the mountains whose branches covered an extremely large area. "The longest branches, which inclined toward the north-east, formed the Door of the Devils (*kuei* [*gui*]), through which millions of them passed in and out. Two spirits, named Shên T'u [Shentu] (or T'u Yü [Tuyu]) and Yü Lei [Yulei] had been instructed to guard this passage. Those who had done wrong to mankind were immediately bound by them and given over to be devoured by tigers. When Huang Ti [Huang Di] heard of this he had the portraits of the two spirits painted on peach-wood tablets and hung above the doors to keep off evil spirits. This led to the suspension of the small figures or plaques on the doors of the people generally. Gradually they were supplanted by paintings on paper pasted on the doors, showing the two spirits armed with bows, arrows, spears, etc." See E. T. C. Werner, *A Dictionary of Chinese Mythology* (Shanghai: Kelly and Walsh, Ltd., 1932), p. 420, s.v. Shên T'u.

[48] The meaning of this expression is unclear. It could mean something like "model [figure to obtain] recompense."

[49] It is not clear whether the manuscript has *tectis* or *lectis*. In the former case it is on the top of the roofs, in the latter, on the beds.

in many places and burn them entirely, and they also openly throw clods of soil into houses. They take food out of jars or cauldrons and put excrement inside instead [of food], dig out cavities [searching] for money, move the house equipment from here to there, and harass inhabitants with other ill-treatments, so that they [the inhabitants] are compelled to return to the same magicians for liberation from such incommodities or misfortunes; and they [the magicians] themselves destroy the previous evil deeds with a different magic. It is true that while this art has been prohibited by the king under punishment by death, they exercise it secretly; whenever, on the other hand, [another] king has ordered that those who make magic to offset such misfortunes be captured and questioned, to determine whether they have performed prior evil deeds, such [practice of magic] happens but seldom, because they [the magicians] gain no profit and expose [themselves] to great danger, so they do it [magic] only out of hatred. Similarly they do love magic, by which means they attract women whom they meet [p. 66] in narrow paths and use them for their pleasure; in certain circumstances they rob these disoriented women and then clear these events from their [victims'] minds, and after that they release them and retreat somewhere before the women return to themselves in several hours, when the power of evil fades. To other people they sell philters to make spouses love each other or hate and reject each other; and they inflict much damage on people who are not careful enough.

There are other magicians called *Thầy Thiếp tính*,[50] who search for and reveal information on the status of the deceased; for that purpose they put a man or a woman in the center,[51] then with fumigations and different gestures they make [it happen] that one's senses are abducted, and one seems to be lifeless or dead; after some time miraculously one returns to one's senses and revives and narrates what one has seen—with the help of the demon in the tomb, or in Hades, or in heaven—about the status of some deceased; one affirms that one's soul, which indeed left the body, came to these places, and on the way it [the soul] used the pieces of gold and silver, into which the paper money was turned that it [the soul] was holding with the hand of the corpse. After one returns back to one's senses, one feels exhausted and also deprived of strength because of the power of the abduction, or of taking away the soul [out of the body]. You see, furthermore, in these [examples] a description of the [spirit] abductions, which [are similar to what] the male and female servants of God suffer through the working of grace.[52] Moreover, in order to find food, the

[50] This compound is not used or known in the form found in the manuscript, at least not in the present time. Its usual form is *thầy thiếp*. The role of the last word, *tính* (most plausibly Chinese *xing*, meaning "nature, disposition, or people"), remains unclear.

[51] The text says that a man or a woman is put *in medio*, that is, "in the center," but does not specify in the center of what. Having seen some séances, I assume that Adriano di St. Thecla implied the center of a circle or a group of people in the séance. Usually the séances take place next to the altar, which, in turn, is located in the center of a temple, if it happens in the temple. Briefly, I think that whatever this center is, it is the center of attention for everybody.

[52] It is astonishing that Adriano di St. Thecla compares the experience during the séances with that of the Christian idea of "working of grace." Here he is definitely referring to the God that he believed in, since he uses the word *Dei*, which he does not apply to indigenous deities anywhere in the manuscript. His comparison is quite out of keeping with the perception of séances by missionaries, including himself, who invariably attributed them to

aforementioned magicians do many other [things] that belong not to this sect but to another; they perform for that purpose the ceremonies and rituals of the sect of the worshippers of Phật, and they also exercise the art of fortune-telling, about which [we speak] later.

In addition, this Sect of Magicians has women prophetesses, called *Bà Cốt,*[53] female mediums, who also do many magical things. To treat the sick they make offerings of food to the spirits and to the deceased, to whom they invoke, honor, and sing superstitious prayers, without any sense and order and mixed together with shouting. They also set up a branch of a tree on a sacrificial table, asking a benevolent spirit to come down to it, and holding in their hands the well-tied branch,[54] they carry it to sick people, so that their weak bodies will revive with its help. They make different images appear in a mirror, and they call them the souls of the deceased, with whom they pretend to speak secretly and thus have many things revealed to them. Also, very often, a prophetess asks these souls questions when they enter [p. 67] her body, and, with various movements of her body, she pretends that she is moved by those who are inside of her now; and meanwhile she orders children and grandchildren to venerate the souls of their parents, which are now staying within her, with different prostrations made toward her; later she pretends as if they want this thing or that thing, to eat and to drink, and she herself eats and drinks what is offered. She announces useless things about the miserable or happy condition in which she imagines the deceased to be in the other world, and also predicts good or bad things that their children or descendants want to know. Some men called *Cốt đực*[55] engage themselves in the art of these women, and they wear women's clothes and completely pull out their beards. They want to be called *Bà (po),*

---

the work of the devil, but perhaps he saw a similarity here with the raptures of Christian mystics.

[53] The first word in the compound, *bà* (*po*), means "a lady." The second word, vernacular Vietnamese *cốt* (骨) does not have any meaning that could explain its incorporation into the compound designating "a female medium." The Chinese equivalent for a female medium is 巫 . Maurice Durand, *Technique et panthéon des médiums vietnamiens* (Paris: École Française d'Extrême-Orient, 1959), 45:10.

The institution of mediums has a long history and is deeply integrated into Vietnamese society. It includes a whole pantheon of spirits whom mediums contact and solicit assistance from. One of the main spirits of this pantheon is discussed in chapter 2: Princess Liễu Hạnh, who, in my opinion, gained through it a great deal of her popularity. For a detailed analysis of Vietnamese mediums see Durand, *Technique et panthéon,* and P. J. Simon and I. Simon-Baurouch, *Hầu Đồng, un culte vietnamien de possession transplanté en France* (Getting into Trance: A Vietnamese Cult transplanted into France) (Paris: Mouton-LaHaye, 1973).

[54] The text says that they are holding "bene collegatium" (well-tied) branches, which I surmise should be understood as tightly entangled.

[55] A male medium. The first word in this compound is the same as in the compound for a "female medium." The second one is also a vernacular Vietnamese word used to determine "maleness." However, it is curious to note that this word is mainly used for naming male animals, as in, for example, *dê đực* (he-goat). A usual name for male mediums is *ông đồng,* meaning "Sir Medium" (a Chinese equivalent of which is 覡). The name for a male medium adduced by Adriano di St. Thecla in the manuscript might have some derogative connotation, reflecting a pejorative attitude toward male mediums among the Vietnamese (at least, among those with whom Adriano di St. Thecla communicated). My reason for thinking so is that, instead of the term of respect "Sir," the compound substitutes a word that more narrowly refers to male gender.

that is, <u>*mistress*</u>, and they get very angry if they are addressed with the masculine name *ông (weng)*, or <u>*master*</u>. They make use of similar images and nonsense, in which often the demon intervenes. Magicians, both men and women, get the money of others, since incautious ordinary people have faith in them, being possessed with superstitions, and are greatly confused, never using the light of the mind for examining and discerning such open lies.

Article 4: On the Religion of This Sect

The followers of this sect worship spirits according to very old tradition, just as the followers of the Sect of Literati do; most of all they exhibit reverence to Lão Tử, whom they treat as the principal and the instructor, and they address him with the following names: Đức Thánh (Desheng, Virtuous Sage), Đức Tiên (Dexian, Virtuous Forerunner), and Đức Tổ (Dezu, Virtuous Ancestor), that is, King Famous for Virtue, Ancient King, and Young King;[56] and, moreover, they say, that he is the master of all the things in Heaven, the master of kings on land, and the greatest king among the stars, with these words: Lão quân tại thiên vi vạn vật chi Chúa, giáng thế vi bách vương chi sư, tại tinh viết Hoàng Thái Đế.[57] Emperor Tống Chân Tông (Song Zhenzong)[58] significantly promoted the cult of Lão Tử when, in a public edict in the seventh year of his rule on the first moon in 1034 after Christ was born, he gave him the rank of the greatest Supreme King: Đế yết Lão Tử [p. 68] gia hiệu viết: Thái Thượng Lão Quân;[59] you can see this edict in the *Chinese History*. Others add that the emperor in this edict also declared that Lão Tử was the creator of Heaven and Earth, idols and spirits: sinh thiên, sinh địa, sinh Bụt, sinh thiêng; although in the *History* it is hardly mentioned.[60] Once a year, on a predetermined month and day and in an appropriate house where an altar is erected without a tablet or an image, all *thầy phù thủy* make to Lão Tử either a solemn sacrifice—strictly according to the ritual by which a sacrifice is made to the tutelary genie Thành Hoàng (chenghuang), which we discussed in article 6 of the second chapter—or a solemn recitation of prayers lasting through the entire night and day with a

---

[56] Even though the translation in the manuscript of the term Đức Tổ (dezu) corresponds to "Young King," I am inclined to attribute this imprecision to a mistake in Latin rather than to a mistake in the translation, for although the manuscript has the word *primaevus* (young), it apparently should have *primarius* (distinguished) or *primoris* (most illustrious) instead.

[57] 老 君 在 天 為 萬 物 之 主 降 世 為 百 王 之 師 在 星 曰 皇 太 帝 . The exact translation of the text is: "In Heaven Laozi is a lord of ten thousand things [that is, everything], down on the Earth he is a master of hundreds of kings, among the stars he is called the Highest Emperor."

[58] R. 1023–64.

[59] 帝 揭 老 子 加 號 曰 太 上 老 君

[60] And rightly so. This phrase could not be expected in the *Chinese History* and was certainly read in a Vietnamese source or heard by the author from Vietnamese Daoists, for it includes the vernacular Vietnamese words *Bụt* (Buddha) and *thiêng* (awe-inspiring [spirit]), and the very structure of the sentence is Vietnamese. The phrase can be translated as follows: "Laozi produced Heaven, produced Earth, produced Buddha, produced awe-inspiring [spirits]." Adriano di St. Thecla's translation of *Buddha* as "idols" reflects, first of all, his treatment of Buddhism as pure idolatry and, secondly, the source from which he got his information, since it indicates the Daoist aspiration to present Buddhism as having derived from Daoism, and to present Laozi as the founder of Buddhism.

simple offering and the same ceremonies with which the worshippers of Phật celebrate this ceremony of the recitation of prayers, called *đọc canh đọc kệ*,[61] in honor of their idols. In the offertory, or *văn tế (wanji)*, which they read during the sacrifice, they first praise Lão Tử because he has wisdom and foresight in spiritual affairs, possesses the entire world and governs it, and has power over the spirits and commands them; second, they offer the food and everything else arranged [on the table]; third, they say that they reverently care for him who is able to destroy like the wind and work like the rain;[62] fourth, they ask him to guard them from misfortunes and all evil things, and also to grant happiness, wealth, and good reputation.

They especially worship twelve spirits, who govern the same number of years in a cycle, and follow each other one after the other in governing and in the ability to harm, for that reason they are called Hành Khiển Vương (xingqian wang), that is, governors bringing evil. They are distributed in this order: in the first year, *Tí* (*zi*, mouse), Chu Vương (Zhouwang) rules; in the second, *Sửu* (*chou*, buffalo), Triệu Vương (Zhaowang) rules; in the third, *Dần* (*yin*, tiger), Ngụy Vương (Weiwang) rules; in the fourth, *Mão* (*mao*, cat), Trinh Vương (Zhengwang) rules; in the fifth, *Thìn* (*chen*, dragon), Sở Vương (Chuwang) rules; in the sixth, *Tị* (*si*, snake), Ngô Vương (Wuwang) rules; in the seventh, *Ngũ* (*wu*, horse), Tần Vương (Qinwang) rules; in the eighth, *Vì*,[63] Tống Vương (Songwang) rules; in the ninth, *Thân* (*shen*, monkey), Tế Vương (Qiwang) rules; in the tenth, *Dậu* (*you*, rooster), Lỗ Vương (Luwang) rules; in the eleventh, *Tuất* (*xu*, dog), Việt Vương (Yuewang) rules; in the twelfth, *Hơi* (*hai*, pig), Lưu Vương (Liuwang) rules. They [members of the sect] make offerings to these spirit-rulers, to each of them in his year, namely, at the beginning and at the end of the year. At the beginning they do it to accept reverently his arrival, and at the end, indeed, to see him off with thanksgiving, and to make their farewells. It is customary among the magicians that the name of the spirit [p. 69] governing the current year, written on a papyrus together with the words "Đang niên hành khiển,"[64] is given to sick [people] to drink with medicine, so that they will get well from the sickness

---

[61] This is a vernacular Vietnamese phrase corresponding to the Sino-Vietnamese *độc kinh độc kệ (dujing duji)*, meaning "to read sutras." Alexandre de Rhodes gives this phrase exactly in the same form as it is found in the manuscript, *đọc canh đọc kệ*, that is, reading the second word of the compound not as *kinh* but as *canh*. He explains the phrase as "reading prayers to idols." Rhodes, *Từ Điển Annam-Lusitan-Latinh* (Annamite-Portuguese-Latin Dictionary), trans. Thanh Lãng, Hoàng Xuân Việt, and Đỗ Quang Chính (reprint, Ho Chi Minh City: Nhà Xuất Bản Khoa Học Xã Hội, 1991), col. 86.

[62] The manuscript here has *operaturum ut pluviam*, the translation of which is "to work like the rain."

[63] The regular pronunciation of this character in Vietnamese, meaning the sign of goat (未) is *mùi (wei)*. It is also listed as such in Alexandre de Rhodes's dictionary (Rhodes, *Từ Điển Annam-Lusitan-Latinh*, col. 489). However, Thiều Chửu put this character with the pronunciation *vị* in his dictionary, mentioning that "we got accustomed to read it as *mùi*." Thiều Chửu, *Hán Việt Tự Điển* (Sino-Vietnamese Dictionary) (Ho Chi Minh City: Nhà Xuất Bản Thành Phố Hồ Chí Minh, 1997), p. 280. It seems that in the manuscript this pronunciation is used with an erroneously changed tone. Adriano di St. Thecla will use the same pronunciation *vì* for this sign in the chapter on the fortune-tellers.

[64] 當 年 行 譴 . The phrase means "[The one who] inflicts punishments during this year."

with his [the spirit's] protection and power. They believe that Mạnh Tông (Mengzong) is the author of the aforementioned distribution of the twelve spirits who govern the corresponding number of years;[65] he was very famous for [his] magic, and he is believed to have lived in the period of rule of the Tống (Song) dynasty. They also venerate the spirits or the powers of nine constellations, and they make an offering to them as well. They assign the spirits and constellations in successive order among the nine months; when they make a full cycle, they go back to the first constellation and complete the cycle by repetition. They have a special book on the twelve spirits whom we discussed earlier, distributed in twelve years, and on the nine other spirits whom we discussed just now, assigned to the same number of [nine] months.[66] Moreover, they have another book divided into fourteen chapters about curing illnesses, and averting and driving away other evils.

Article 5: On Ngọc Hoàng and Others, Who Are Worshipped

Magicians greatly worship a Ngọc Hoàng (Yuhuang), that is, the Jade King,[67] who is Trương Nghi,[68] about whom [we talked] above in the second article; however, now he is called by the family name Trương Đại Đế (Zhang Dadi), that is, the great King Trương (Zhang). The author of the book *Văn Lâm Quảng (Wen lin guang)* and the author of the book *Giảng Đạo (Jiangdao,* Preaching the Way*)*[69] wrote on that account that Trương Nghi was pronounced Ngọc Hoàng Thượng Đế (Yuhuang Shangdi, the Jade Monarch-Supreme Emperor) by Emperor Tống Huy Tông (Song Huizong).[70] However, it is evident from the *Chinese History* that this emperor attributed these names to Heaven, and not to any human being. Thereupon, the literatus Kheo Thị (Qiu Shi) in the same *History* [in the section under] the sixth year of [the reign title] Chính Hòa

---

[65] The nature of this calendar and the identity of its author have remained unclear. The most obvious correspondence would be "The Twelve Lords" from Sima Qian's *Historical Records* (Edouard Chavannes, trans., *Les Memoires Historiques de Se-Ma Ts'ien* [Leiden: E. J. Brill, 1967], 3:15–21), but the twelve lords there do not exactly correspond to those in the manuscript. The creator of the calendar has also remained unidentified.

[66] This is an obvious mistake. There are *ten* signs, called "heavenly signs," which, in conjunction with the twelve previously mentioned earthly signs, comprise a combination of characters to designate each year in a sixty-year cycle used in China and other countries of East Asia. Moreover, Adriano di St. Thecla has not discussed above and will not discuss below these ten heavenly signs.

[67] Adriano di St. Thecla translates Ngọc Hoàng (Yuhuang) as *gemmeus Rex.* In the English language, there is no adjective form of the noun *gem,* so, complying with the traditional translation of this name into Western languages, translators use the word *jade* to translate *gemmeus.*

[68] The Jade Emperor is usually identified with Trương Đạo Lăng (Zhang Daoling), not with Trương Nghi (Zhang Yi). See, for example, de Groot, *Fêtes,* 1:79.

[69] The book has not been found.

[70] R. 1101–26. De Groot adduces the year 1116 as the date of imperial canonization of the Jade Emperor. He writes: "In 1116, God of Heaven, who already was completely identified with Tchang Tao Ling [Zhang Daoling] received from emperor Hwoui Tsoung [Song Huizong] a new title, that of Giok-Hong Sion-Te [Yuhuang Shangdi] or the Jade Monarch, the Supreme Emperor." See de Groot, *Fêtes,* 1:79.

(Zhenghe)[71] argues with the aforementioned emperor—for he [the emperor] wanted to designate Heaven, which did not want to be called with human titles, with the aforementioned words [i.e., human titles by which Heaven did not want to be called]; because of this he suffered misfortune: Mạc tôn ư Thiên, Thiên Thần chi tối tôn giả Thượng Đế dã, vị chi hiệu Thiên Thượng Đế,[72] Đế giả Chúa Tể chi xưng dĩ Đế, xưng chi Thiên chi đại bất khả danh Đế chi tôn, vô dĩ đối Tống Huy Tông thượng Ngọc Hoàng huy hiệu ư Chính Hòa ư thị hồ, hưu Hoàng laong[73] chi họa, ô hô khả úy dã tai.[74] But Emperor Huy Tông (Huizong) [p. 70] was so influenced by the Sect of Magicians that in the seventh year of the same reign title Chính Hòa, in the year 1117 of Christ, he proclaimed himself a king of this sect in a public edict: Sách Đế vi giáo Chúa Đạo quân Hoàng Đế.[75]

A literatus, who was also a magician and bore the name Phạm Nhan (Fan Yan), has his cult among the magicians; since he was involved with the empress, whom he was treating, he was killed by order of the emperor, cut into three parts, and thrown into the sea. However, his corpse happened to be brought by the waves into a river, and then it accidentally fell into the net of a certain fisherman; after the fisherman dragged his net out [of the water] and found the corpse in the net, he drew it down to the riverbank and asked it—if it was a corpse of some spirit or *thần (shen)*—to help him in his fishing, and later he caught plenty of fish; for that reason he built a small hut to the spirit and started worshipping him in each of his three parts, which ignorant ordinary

---

[71] The reign title Chính Hòa (Zhenghe) of Emperor Tống Huy Tông (Song Huizong) was 1111–18; thus, it was the year 1117.

[72] I believe that here "hiệu Thiên Thượng Đế," as it was in the chapter on the Spirits, should be read Hạo Thiên Thượng Đế" (Haotian Shangdi, Sovereign on high in the vast heavens).

[73] *Long (long)* in modern Vietnamese spelling, meaning dragon.

[74] 莫 尊 於 天 天 神 之 最 尊 者 上 帝 也 謂 之 昊 天 上 帝 帝 者 主 宰 之 稱 以 帝 稱 之 天 之 大 不 可 名 帝 之 尊 無 以 對 宋 徽 宗 尚 玉 皇 徽 號 於 正 和 於 是 乎 有 (?) 皇 龍 之 禍 嗚 呼 可 畏 也 哉 . As the author of the citation has remained unidentified, so did its source. Adriano di St. Thecla provides only a partial explanation of this citation. Its first part was translated by him in the chapter on Confucianism, where it appears in an abbreviated version. I could not find a suitable character for the word pronounced *hưu* in Vietnamese. The only plausible one is 咻 "to shout out," but even this one hardly fits the phrase. It is possible that instead of *hưu* there should have been the word *hữu* (*you*, to have, there is, there are). If we accept this as plausible, the phrase can be translated as follows: "There is nothing more revered than Heaven; among heavenly spirits the most revered is the Supreme Emperor, called the Sovereign on high in the vast heavens. As for the [word] *đế* (*di*), it is a way of calling the [earthly] rulers by [the word] 'emperor'; the appellation of the greatness of Heaven is beyond the reverence [contained] in the term *đế* (*di*); unable to be in accord with this, Tống Huy Tông (Song Huizong) honored [God] with the honorific title 'Jade Emperor' in [the period of the reign title] Chính Hòa (Zhenghe), and thereupon there were [?] disasters for the Imperial Dragon [i.e., of the Chinese empire]. Alas! How dreadful!" This argument is caused by the polysemy of the word *đế* (*di*), which, along with its meaning "emperor, ruler," came to designate the Supreme Ruler of Heaven or a god. On different appellations of Heaven see Howard J. Wechsler, *Offerings of Jade and Silk: Ritual and Symbol in the Legitimation of the T'ang Dynaty* (New Haven: Yale University Press, 1985).

[75] 冊 帝 為 教 主 道 君 皇 帝

people also venerate under the name of three masters: his head is named the first master; the loins, the second master; and the feet, the third master.[76]

Magicians also honor criminals, Tư Dương[77] among them; he was born in China during the rule of the Hán dynasty and was killed by order of the emperor for his crimes. Since he terrified others with his impiety, he is venerated in order to restrain him from doing harm. Also, three brothers, being rebellious against the emperor, were beaten to death with sticks; the Devil appeared in their form and predicted the future, and for that reason they received a cult and were called Thiên Phủ (Tianfu, Governor of Heaven), Địa Phủ (Difu, Governor of Earth), Thủy Phủ (Shuifu, Governor of Water).[78] There are other spirits, whom [magicians] call *tướng (jiang)*, that is, leaders or generals who are distinguished among others; magicians send them to expel other hostile spirits bringing misfortune. They are the following Tướng: Thổ Địa,[79] Mạnh Tông (Mengzong),[80] Đục Cước,[81] Thiên Lôi,[82] Tam Danh Sưng Sỏ Sắt,[83] Chúa Quế, and Chúa Liễu—the last two are the spirits of two women.

---

[76] This legend is very well known in Vietnam in several variations.

[77] This spirit is not identified.

[78] This is a Daoist idea, in which "Heaven bestows happiness, Earth pardons sins, and Water protects from evils. Each of these powers received the honorary title of Great Ruler (Dadi). This concept goes back to the reign of Emperor *Han linh ti* [Han Lingdi], the first year of his reign title *H'i p'ing* [Xibing, 172 B.C.E.]." See Henri Doré, *Recherches sur les superstitions en Chine*, vol. 6, *Le panthéon Chinois* (Shanghai: Imprimerie deT'ou-sè-wè, 1914), p. 16. However, it appears that Adriano di St. Thecla refers here to the three Zhang brothers, leaders of the Daoist sect of the Great Peace in the second half of the second century in the lower plain of the Yellow River in China, who were at the head of the Yellow Turban rebellion. But they were called "Lords General of Heaven, Earth, and Men." Jacques Gernet, *A History of Chinese Civilization*, trans. J. R. Foster and Charles Hartman (Cambridge: Cambridge University Press, 1999), p. 155.

[79] Thổ Địa ("land and earth") refers to earth spirits in general. One of the possibilities is that Adriano di St. Thecla talks about Hậu Thổ Phu Nhân (Empress Earth Lady). An account of this spirit is in *Việt Điện U Linh Tập*, trans. Lê Hữu Mục (Saigon: Nhà Sách Khai Trí, 1960), pp. 97–98, according to which King Lý Thánh Tông (r. 1053–72) encountered this spirit as a woman dwelling in a tree during his expedition against Champa; she assisted him in gaining success on the battlefield, and he established a temple to worship her at the capital upon his return. The name of this spirit is taken from a popular goddess worshipped during the Tang dynasty in China. The main temple of this spirit is in Hanoi. However, there exist a significant number of other spirits identified with the earth.

[80] This spirit is not identified. This name is identical to one mentioned above. See note 65.

[81] In modern Vietnamese this name reads Độc Cước, meaning "one-legged genie." This is a genie-warrior brought from China, according to G. Dumoutier, by some unknown Daoists. His cult is closely associated with mediums and sorcerers. Độc Cước's power is implemented through amulets and magic words of a special character in a book of magic spells. The description of the rites devoted to this genie and the magic spells comprise two books, which are held by the guardians of his cult. G. Dumoutier, "Essai sur les Tonkinois," *Revue Indo-Chinoise*, 1 (1908): 22–24. Độc Cước is worshipped in many localities in Vietnam; one of his main temples is in Sầm Sơn, Quảng Xương district, Thanh Hóa province. For a description of the temple, as well as Độc Cước's hagiography, see Lê Kim Lữ, *Đền Độc Cước* (Temple of Độc Cước) (Thanh Hóa: Nhà Xuất Bản Thanh Hóa, 1998).

[82] A Thunder genie, his cult is not widespread in Vietnam anymore.

[83] The author divides this name by inserting a comma: "Tam Danh, Sưng Sỏ Sắt"; it is in fact a single entity. Tam Danh means "three names," and it embraces the names of the three brothers Sưng, Sỗ, and Sắt. Tam Danh is also the name of the temple in Vũ Bản district of

They offer food to all these spirits twice a month on the new moon and on the full moon as if to *cô hồn (guhun)*, or abandoned souls, of which [we will talk] later in article 4 of chapter 5; they [the spirits] want offerings to be made to them, and if any offering is omitted, they, offended, ruin the house of the magician who skipped [the offering] and kill pigs, dogs, bulls, [p. 71] and hens there, since they [the spirits] are deprived of their usual food. To prevent suffering from such a disaster, the followers [of the sect of] magicians are sagacious in offering food to spirits twice a month on the occasion of curing somebody or burying some deceased person; if neither occasion arises [the magicians conduct the offerings] at the expense of their own households.

Moreover, the magicians also usually invoke with their magic the aforementioned spirits together with the following ones: Vua Giaóng,[84] Vua Càn,[85] Vua Bạch Mã,[86] Vua Bạch Hạc,[87] Vua Đinh,[88] Vua Sử Hi,[89] Tam Đầu,[90]

Nam Định province, dedicated to these three brothers, who allegedly originated during the time of the legendary Hùng kings. The brothers are worshipped as mighty spirits who repeatedly helped the people and the country. Their legend and the temple dedicated to them are considered to be one of six wonders in Vũ Bản district. See a detailed discussion of this legend in Bùi Văn Tam, *Thiên Bản Lục Kỳ Huyền Thoại, Đất Sơn Nam* (Manuscript of Legends on Six Wonders, Sơn Nam Region) (Hanoi: Nhà Xuất Bản Văn Hóa Dân Tộc, 2000), pp. 17–30.

[84] This spirit is discussed in chapter 2.

[85] It is not immediately clear what spirit Adriano di St. Thecla is referring to, since in the present time this name hardly exists in this form. I can suggest two possibilities. The first is a historical king, Lý Càn Đức, known under his posthumous name Lý Nhân Tông (r. 1072–1127). Nhân Đồng village of Huệ Lai district in Hưng Yên province lists him under his tabooed name Càn Đức as its tutelary genie. See *Thần Tích Thần Sắc* (Treasury of Deity Legends and Royal Deification Decrees; hereafter TTTS) at the Institute of Social Science Information (Viện Thông Tin Khoa Học Xã Hội) in Hanoi, file 11981, pp. 79–81. Another possibility is that it is an abbreviation of the name of the tutelary genie Càn Hải after the place Càn Hải (Nghệ An province in north-central Vietnam), where the wife and daughters of Emperor Song Dihe (1278–79) fled when the Song dynasty in China fell under the Mongols in 1279. When Vietnamese emperor Lê Anh Tông (r. 1293–1314) went to fight with the adjacent kingdom of Champa, he passed through Càn Hải and asked the assistance of these four women to abate the horrible weather that was impeding his advance. After the emperor received the requested help, he conferred upon them an honorific title and later they were recognized as Mothers. See Pham Minh Thảo, Trần Thị An, and Bùi Xuân Mỹ, *Thành Hoàng Việt Nam* (Tutelary Genies of Vietnam) (Hanoi: Nhà Xuất Bản Văn Hóa-Thông Tin, 1997), pp. 443–445. While their main temple is in Nghệ An province, they are also worshipped in a number of other places in northern Vietnam. The story has been known for generations. One of their main temples is called Đền Cờn. The pronunciation of *Cờn* and *Càn* is interchangeable and, in the eighteenth century, the latter could have been a normative pronunciation for these spirits united under one roof.

[86] This spirit is discussed in chapter 2.

[87] King White Crane. His story is included in *Việt Điện U Linh Tập*, trans. Lê Hữu Mục, pp. 114–115, according to which a Tang governor, Lý Thường Minh, built a temple in the Bạch Hạc region and invited all powerful local spirits to come into the temple to be worshipped. Two spirits appeared to him in a dream and competed for precedence. The one who prevailed was then worshipped as the spirit of this region.

[88] This is the name of the Vietnamese King Đinh Bộ Lĩnh (r. 968–79), the first and practically the only king of the short-lived Đinh dynasty (968–80), who is known and appreciated in Vietnam for having unified the country, bringing to a close the period of the so-called Twelve Warlords in the tenth century. He is credited as well with establishing the Vietnamese imperial tradition. See O. W. Wolters, "Historians and Emperors in Vietnam and China: Comments Arising out of Le Van Huu's History, presented to the Tran court in

Tam vị Tản Viên,[91] Cửu Vĩ,[92] Chúa Trì, Thủy Tề,[93] and Thủy Tục[94]—the last two being the spirits of two large fish and of some big or extraordinary thing, which is seen in the water.

1272," in *Perceptions of the Past in Southeast Asia,* ed. Anthony Reid and David Marr (Singapore: Heineman Educational Books, 1979), pp. 69–89; also K. W. Taylor, "The Twelve Lords in Tenth Century Vietnam," *Journal of Southeast Asian Studies* 14, 1 (1983): 46–62. His main temple is located in Hoa Lư (in modern Ninh Bình province), the capital established by Đinh Bộ Lĩnh.

[89] This spirit is not identified.

[90] Three Heads. There is no spirit under this name worshipped in Vietnam at the present time. Initially, I was inclined to consider it as a possible variation of the name Tam Đảo, being the spirit of the mountain of the same name, located in Sơn Đình village, Tam Dương district, Vĩnh Phúc province. This spirit is the mother of the mountain spirit Tản Viên, mentioned next in the text. However, relying on the title of the spirit discussed in the final footnote of this chapter, it is possible to assume that it was a water spirit. It seems that worship of Tam Đầu as a separate spirit has come to an end.

[91] "Three Honorables of Tản Viên" is an alternative name of the spirit Sơn Tinh or Tản Viên, the mountain spirit described in chapter 2. It refers to the shape of Tản Viên mountain, which has three peaks.

[92] Nine Tails. This spirit seems to have lost his popularity in modern Vietnam. I could not locate any places of worship for him. However, this spirit, under the name Cửu Vĩ Hồ Tinh, is described by Nguyễn Đồng Chi. Cửu Vĩ was a malicious monster dwelling in the region of modern Hanoi. He inflicted immeasurable harm on the people living in the area, destroying their houses and fields. He was harmful to such an extent that people moved away and lived elsewhere, but Cửu Vĩ reached them there, too. He used to transform himself sometimes into a young man, sometimes into a beautiful woman who seduced, raped, and killed men. Lạc Long Quân, the dragon-ancestor of the Vietnamese, heard about this monster and decided to pacify him. In a ferocious fight, Lạc Long Quân gained the upper hand and killed Cửu Vĩ. At this moment the monster transformed into his "true self," a huge nine-tailed fox. Lạc Long Quân carried its corpse into the mountains, into Cửu Vĩ's den, where the women captured by the monster were held. Delivering them, Lạc Long Quân set out to destroy the den, and he brought Cái river to pour its water for days into this place. As a result of this a lake appeared, which is now called Hồ Tây, or West Lake, in Hanoi. See Nguyễn Đồng Chi, *Lược Khảo về Thần Thoại Việt Nam* (A Sketch of Vietnamese Mythology) (Hanoi: Nhà Xuất Bản Văn Sử Địa, 1956), pp. 146–148.

[93] One of the main spirits of the water world, his name is pronounced in two ways. Sometimes it is Thủy Tề, as for example in the account of the tutelary genie of Yen Thị village, Lạng Phong canton, Nho quan district, Ninh Bình province, where it is usually called Mr. Dragon (TTTS, file 16143). In other cases, this name is spelled as Thủy Tế. See, for instance, the account of An Đạo village, Cát Xuyên canton, Xuân Trường district, Nam Định province (TTTS, file 6994, pp. 45–46). There is apparently no unified way to spell the name of this spirit among modern scholars either. The *Dictionary of Cultural Vestiges of Vietnam* lists it as Thủy Tế, describing his temple in Mộ Đạo commune, Vũ Tiên canton, Vũ Thư district, Thái Bình province (Ngô Đức Thọ, ed., *Từ Điển Di Tích Văn Hóa Việt Nam* [A Dictionary of the Vietnamese Cultural Vestiges] [Nhà Xuất Bản Khoa Học Xã Hội, Nhà Xuất Bản Mũi Cà Mau, 1993], pp. 649–650), while Ngô Đức Thịnh spells it as Thủy Tề (Ngô Đức Thịnh, "Thờ Thành Hoàng" [Worshipping Tutelary Genies], in *Góp Phần Nâng Cao Chất Lượng Sưu Tầm Nghiên Cứu Văn Hóa Văn Nghệ Dân Gian* [Contribution in the Improving of Quality in Studying Popular Culture and Art] [Hanoi: Nhà Xuất Bản Văn Hóa Dân Tộc, 2000], p. 272). He is believed to be a guardian of the underwater palace. There are several versions of the legend about Thủy Tế. One of them goes as follows: Once a couple went into the sea to cast a fishnet and suddenly from the water appeared a huge serpent. That same night the husband had a dream that one of the water spirits requested to be reincarnated into earthly life to help the Lý king save the country. Sure enough, the wife became pregnant and then gave birth to a sac. Growing up, this sac developed into an usually strong and tall man, called Chàng Hai, who helped the king to fight with Champa.

Indeed it must be mentioned that many spirits have a cult both in the Đạo sect and in the Phật sect, or are worshipped by the followers of [both] these sects, as it appears mainly in the account on Ngọc Hoàng. The aforementioned spirits with the title *Vua* (king) are the tutelary genies of various regions, or villages, who are worshipped by the inhabitants in this kingdom.

Testimonies Concerning Lão Tử and His Sect Đạo

[This chapter of the manuscript ends here. Page 72 is blank.]

When the time came for Chàng Hai to separate from his earthly life, the sky became dark and waves appeared in the river. A water serpent appeared and swallowed him. See Ngô Đức Thọ, *Từ Điển Di Tích*, pp. 649–651; see also the report of Tứ Kỳ village, Thanh Liệt canton of Thanh Trì district in Hà Đông province, where Thủy Tế was the tutelary genie (TTTS, file 1218, p. 653).

[94] The modern spelling is Thủy Tộc, meaning aquatic clan. It is a water spirit worshipped in a number of localities. One of the versions of his legend, as it appears in the account of Kiều Mộc village, Kiều Mộc canton, Quang Oai district, Sơn Tây province, claims that he was one of a hundred sons of Âu Cơ and Lạc Long quân; when they decided to separate, Thủy Tộc, together with forty-nine of his brothers followed their father into the sea, and he was the first one to enter the water (TTTS, file 1959, p. 51). Sometimes there is a conflation of several of these spirits. For instance, the tutelary genie in Ngọc Chấn village (Ngọc Chấn canton, Nghĩa Hưng district, Nam Định province) is called Thủy Tế Tam Đầu Cửu Vỹ Bát Hải Thủy Tộc, thus combining, into a single entity, five different spirits, seemingly all or most of them connected to water: Thủy Tế (Shuiqi), Tam Đầu (Santou), Cửu Vỹ (Jiuwei), Bát Hải (Bahai), and Thủy Tộc (Shuisu) (TTTS, file 6564, p. 427).

CHAPTER FOUR

ON FORTUNE-TELLERS AND DIVINERS

[p. 73]

We are going to talk here about fortune-tellers and diviners, since they also form a class of magicians and they often use the examples of the literati for divinations.

Article 1: On the Fortune-Tellers Thầy Bói and Thầy Khoa [1]

The first place among the fortune-tellers is held by so-called *Thầy Bói*, who prophesy using the figures invented by the oldest king of China, Phục Hi (Fu Xi). As is said in the *Chinese History*, when this king saw in the waters of a river some image of a horse or of a dragon, [with some markings] on its back, he took this occasion to introduce eight figures of lines according to these signs [which he saw in the river] for dividing and marking the parts of the world, which are called by the Annamites with the following names: *càn (qian), khảm (kan), cấn (gen), chấn (zhan), tốn (xun), ly (li), khôn (kun),* and *đoài (dui)*;[2] and, by their general name, they are called *quái*, in Chinese *kua (gua,* trigram [of the Book of Changes]*)*, in the common [Vietnamese] speech *quẻ*. Later, the same Phục Hi made sixty-four {64} other figures from these eight figures, called with the same name *quái*, for distinguishing and recognizing different things. Each figure consists of six small lines, continuous or

[1] While the term *thầy bói* is widely used in Vietnam, the term *thầy khoa* is hardly known to anyone, and it does not appear in de Rhodes's dictionary. The other known name for fortune-tellers is *thầy cúng*. The difference lies in the way the fortune-teller makes predictions: a *thầy bói* does so on the basis of how he or she senses or perceives a person. For a *thầy cúng*, on the contrary, magic and sorcery are instrumental.

[2] *Càn (qian)*, the first of the trigrams, called Creator, represents heaven. *Khảm (kan)*, the fourth trigram, called Impenetrability, represents water. *Cấn (gen)*, the fifth trigram, called Immobilization or Immobility, represents mountain. *Chấn (zhan)*, the third trigram, called Awakening, represents thunder. *Tốn (xun)*, the sixth trigram, called Mildness or Smoothness, represents wind. *Ly (li)*, the seventh trigram, called Adherence, represents fire. *Khôn (kun)*, the second trigram, called Receptor or Recipient, represents earth. *Đoài (dui)*, the eighth trigram, called Joy, represents lake. Joseph Nguyen Huy Lai, *La Tradition religieuse spirituelle et sociale au Vietnam* (Paris: Beauchesne, 1981), p. 211.

interrupted, and they contain two of the eight main figures mentioned above combined in different ways; and in total there are 384 of these lines, which are called *hào*, or *yao* in Chinese. The aforementioned sixty-four figures are included, explained, and illustrated in the book called *Dịch Kinh (Yijing*, Book of Changes), which is written solely about them. There, in the first part, you have all sixty-four figures called *quái;* in the second part is their interpretation made by Chu Văn Vương (Zhou Wen Wang); then, there are explanations of every line or *hào* contained in the sixty-four figures by Chu Công (Zhou Gong, i.e., the Duke of Zhou), a son of Văn Vương; and, finally, [there is] an inserted explanation by Confucius about the figures,[3] to which the commentaries of other literati are added, [p. 74] especially [the commentary] of Trình Tử (Chengzi), who wrote the preface to this book, and also [that] of Chu Tử (Zhuzi), who had a great reputation among the literati.

Thus, those who occupy themselves with fortune-telling, *Thầy Bói*, use the aforementioned figures for prophesying future and secret things, by inquiring and exploring which figure comes up for a person who requests a divination. After the figure is explored and confirmed, they announce their sentences with special and general words, skillfully hiding their lies. If they do not know what to prophesy, they say that the figure for this person is the figure *bất thuần (bushun*, unfavorable), which does not have any explanation in the book: "quẻ này là quẻ bất thuần" (this lot is unclear or impure). Some literati prophesy by using these figures. However, fortune-tellers, those called *Thầy Bói*, are mostly illiterate, and not only do they have no idea about the aforementioned figures but, moreover, they are blind, or have been blinded; they usually sit in marketplaces, where there are crowds of people, prepared to sell their divinations, and they invite passers-by in a vexing manner, and attract [their attention] to [ask for a] divination. People usually consult them about the future outcome [in matters] of life or death, health or sickness, wealth or poverty, or whether there will or will not be a promotion in

---

[3] There is a seventeenth-century account of the origins of *Yijing* by a Jesuit missionary in China, which is almost identical with that offered by Adriano di St. Thecla and which reconciles all the myths: "The third Volume [of the Five Classical Books] is called *Ye Kim* [*Yijing*, Book of Changes]. In this volume, which is the Ancientest, if it may be called a Volume, nothing but Obscurity and Darkness is observed. *Fohi* [Fu Xi] had no sooner founded his Empire, than he gave Instructions to the *Chineses;* but the use of Characters and Writing being unknown, the Prince, who could not teach them all with his Voice, and who was moreover imploy'd in the Advancement of his growing Monarchy, after a long and serious Consideration, thought at last upon making a Table, composed of some little lines which it is not necessary to describe. The *Chineses* being as yet dull and rustick, 'tis probable that his prince laboured in vain; and if it is true, that he accomplished his Design, by the clear and easie Explications, which he himself gave for the understanding of these Lines, it happen'd, at least insensibly, that this Table became useless. For it is certain that after his Death nothing could make use thereof. Two thousand Years from the Foundation of the Monarchy were near elaps'd, no one being able any way to decypher this Mysterious Table, when at last an *Oedepis* was seen to appear: 'T was a Prince named *Venvam* [Wen Wang]. This Prince endeavoured to penetrate the sense of these Lines by a great number of others, which he did disposed after different ways; they were new Enigmas. His Son, viz. *Cheucum* [Zhou Gong], attempted the same thing; But had not the good fortune better to succeed. In brief, five hundred Years after appeared *Confucius*, who endeavoured to untie this *Gordin*'s Knot. He explain'd, according to his Understanding, the little Lines of the Founder, with the Interpretations that had been made before him, and refers all to the Nature of Beings and Elements." Cited from Philippe Couplet et al., *The Morals of Confucius, the Chinese Philosopher* (London: For Randal Taylor, 1691), pp. 12–13. This is an English translation of *Confucius Sinarum Philosophus sive Scientia Sinensis.*

rank. Moreover, if someone loses something in a theft, he asks a fortune-teller where the thief fled, whether he returned to the east, west, south, or north, and then he makes up his mind about the person whom he suspects: whether someone among those whose houses stand in the direction indicated by the fortune-teller really stole what belonged to him.

These fortune-tellers also draw upon many superstitions [for their prophesies]. Before the divination, they throw two coins, and if the coins fall on the same side, heads or tails, they say that they have *âm (yin)*, which they consider bad for the divination. If they fall differently, one heads and another tails, they say they have *dương (yang)*, and this is good for divination; and only then do they proceed with it; for that reason, they throw coins until they come out different and render *dương*, so that they [the fortune-tellers] can continue with the prophecy. Also, they often issue orders to the five senses of the body of the person who is demanding a divination to grant [the divination], by saying: "let khẩu bốc, nhĩ bốc (koubu, erbu)," that is, let the mouth make a divination, let the ears make a divination; and in such a way [they mention] each [part of the body]. They also use the names of five elements: *kim (jin)*, metal; *mộc (mu)*, wood; *thủy (shui)*, water; [p. 75] *hỏa (huo)*, fire; and *thổ (tu)*, earth; [and] the names of twelve animals, with which they name and count the years, months, days, and hours:[4] *tí (zi)*, [the name of the] mouse; *sửu (chou)*, ox; *dần (yin)*, tiger; *mão (mao)*, cat; *thìn (chen)*, dragon; *tị (si)*, snake; *ngũ (wu)*, horse; *vì (wei)*, goat; *thân (shen)*, monkey; *dậu (you)*, rooster; *tuất·(xu)*, dog; and *hợi (hai)*, pig. So they judge in accordance with these names of elements and animals, and declare [their decisions] about the agreement or disagreement among things and people. They are to a great extent responsible for keeping or breaking a marriage, for they look at what day a man and a woman, already married or going to be married, were born, and if they see that the man was born on the day of the cat, and the woman on the day of the mouse, they say that they should not join each other, but be separated, because a cat captures a mouse and eats it; however, if they see that a man was born on the day of the bull and a woman on the day of the goat, they say that they can join each other and stay together, because a bull and a goat fit together and [can] coexist. The same [thing] happens concerning the elements: if a man was born on the day of fire and a woman on the day of water, the fortune-tellers declare that they should not get married, or if they are married, that they should separate, because water kills fire; certainly, if [a man] was born on the day of earth and a woman on the day of wood, they are allowed to get married, or to stay together if they are already married, since wood springs from earth and flourishes in it. Years, months, and days are indicated in the common calendar or the lunar calendar called *lịch (li)* with the same names of the five elements and of twelve animals; this calendar is published every year for the use of the community,[5] so that decisions can be made about marriages and undertaking

[4] The day is divided into twelve parts, each two hours long, and each two-hour period is associated with one of the twelve aforementioned animals. It was customary to designate the time of the day not by the European idea of hours and minutes but with the sign of the animal "reigning" over its two-hour period. To each of the animal signs is ascribed the *yin* (female) principle or the *yang* (male) principle, which are considered among the main factors for judging the compatibility of the signs.

[5] The Vietnamese lunar calendar was borrowed from China in the early period of the Han dynasty, not later than the beginning of the Common Era, when Chinese culture spread among the people inhabiting the territory of modern northern Vietnam. P. V. Pozner, *Drevniy Vietnam:*

other things. Predictions of this kind, according to those names [mentioned above] are even displayed in the lunar calendar for daily use.

In addition, fortune-tellers, or *Thầy Bói,* often perform this prayer for divination: (A) Tiên sư, tiên thành, tiên hiền, chiếu lâm giáng hạ, thính văn[6] Thượng Đế; (B) Phục Hi, Đại Vũ, Văn Vương, Chu Công, Khổng Tử, cập Quỉ Thần giáng quyết minh bạch; (C) Khổng môn Nho Đạo thất thập nhị hiền, liêm lạc quân môn trần mục, lí thiệu viên thiên hạ phàm, lí thuần phung, thiệu Khang tiết, liệt vị đại Thánh đại hiền đồng lai trở[7] quái;[8] (D) Tuế thử mỗ niên, mỗ ngoạt,[9] mỗ

Problema Letopisaniya (Ancient Vietnam: Problem of Compiling Annals) (Moscow: Nauka, 1980), pp. 76–77.

[6] Relying on Adriano di St. Thecla's translation, I surmise that *thính văn* (聽 聞 *tingwen,* to hear) is a mistake for *thỉnh vấn* (請 問 *qingwen,* to request, to ask for).

[7] *Trở* (*zu,* to hinder, to obstruct) seems to be erroneously written instead of *trợ* (*zhu,* to assist).

[8] The part of this sentence starting from *liêm lạc* can hardly be properly translated or understood in the absence of characters. Adriano di St. Thecla's translation of phrase (C) implies that some Confucian scholars were enumerated here. His translation is also supported by the fact that if these words, or some of them, are not names, it is impossible to find a set of characters corresponding to the given pronunciations that would render a plausible meaning for the phrase. I see these two considerations as a hint for understanding the phrase, in spite of the fact that these words are not capitalized (as would be expected in the case of personal names). In this case *liêm (lian)* most plausibly refers to a student of Confucius named Liêm Khiết (Lian Qie), also called Tư Dung (Zi Yong). *Lạc (le)* then refers to another student of Confucius named Lạc Khái (Le Ke) or Lạc Hân (Le Xin), also known as Zi Sheng. *Lí thuần phung* (li chun feng) most obviously designates Lí Thuần Phong (Li Chunfeng, 602–70), an author of numerous works during the Tang dynasty, one of whose books, *Zhouyi xuanyi* (Dark Meanings of the Zhou Changes), was a commentary on the legendary *Zhouyi* (Zhou Changes), a kind of manual for divination. As for *thiệu Khang tiết,* this refers to another famous scholar, Thiệu Khang Tiết (Shao Kangjie, 1011–77), also known under the name Shao Yong. Originally a Daoist, Shao Yong later became a Confucian and exerted a considerable influence on the development of the idealist current of Neo-Confucianism. He was extremely interested in divination and the *Yijing* (Book of Changes), on the premises of which he developed a theory of numbers, which he considered to be the basis of all existence. The words between Liêm Lạc and Lí Thuần Phung, "quân môn trần mục, lí thiệu viên thiên hạ phàm," are apparently also some names, which, when rendered into Chinese pronunciation from the Vietnamese syllables, might be read as follows: the first group "quân môn trần mục" corresponds to the Chinese syllables *jun* or *yun, men, chen,* and *mu* respectively, and the second group "lí thiệu viên thiên hạ phàm" corresponds to *li, shao, yuan, qian* or *tian, xia* or *he,* and *fan,* respectively. In this group Viên Thiên (Yuan Tian) might be the name, albeit in a strangely abrupt form, of an associate of the aforementioned Li Chunfeng, Yuan Tiangang (d. 627), with whom he co-authored a famous book of political prophecy *Tuibei tu* (Chart of Extrapolation from the Back). But neither these two nor any other syllables in this group have been identified with certainty. Transferring the syllables of both groups into all the possible Chinese characters corresponding to the given pronunciation would give too wide a variety of different options, and thus is hardly possible or relevant here. Each syllable can be a representation of an entire name, as it was with the syllables *liêm* and *lạc,* or two or three of them can be composites of a name given in full. But if we assume that these syllables, or at least some of them, are not personal names but regular words, the most plausible sense of the part "liêm lạc quân môn trần mục, lí thiệu viên thiên hạ phàm" is 廉 樂 均 門 陳 目 理 萃 圓 天 下 凡 "All the incorrupt and joyful disciples cast [your] glance; aptly arrange [the lot], explain the order of Heaven, come down to the world of mortals." Then, the whole phrase (C) would be translated as "[Ask] the seventy-two benevolent disciples of Confucius, all the incorrupt and joyful disciples to cast [their] glance; to aptly arrange [the lot], to explain the order of Heaven, [and] to come down to the world of mortals, [ask] Lí Thuần Phong (Li Chunfeng), Thiệu Khang Tiết (Shao Kangjie), great wise gentlemen, great benevolent people, to come down together to assist [in casting] lots." However, this phrase is as unwieldy in Chinese as it is in English. This inclined me to Adriano di St.

nhật, mỗ thà,[10] mỗ tuyết,[11] hoạc thượng hạ tuần hốt ngộ hoạc nam nữ nhân bốc vấn cầu sự; (E) Các các kì sự cát tắc cát thần triệu, hung tắc [p. 76] hung thần triệu, chư vị thánh hiền đồng lai giáng hạ.[12]

The sense of this prayer is as follows: (A) Great masters, great prefects, great virtuous ones, illuminate the world, beseech the Supreme King with a prayer;[13] (B) the kings Phục Hi, Đại Vũ (Da Yu), and Văn Vương, Chu Công, Khổng Tử (Kongzi), or Confucius, and all the spirits descend to reveal [the truth] clearly and distinctly; (C) the seventy-two good disciples of Confucius {other literati or sages are enumerated one by one up to Khang Tiết (Kang Jie)}, all [people] praiseworthy for [their] dignity, great prefects, great virtuous [people], all together, assist [in casting] lots; (D) [let] a man or a woman requesting a divination ask for something

---

Thecla's translation and a consideration of all the problematic syllables, or at least some of them, as personal names. Assuming this to be the case, the translation will be as follows: "[Ask] the seventy-two benevolent disciples of Confucius, Liêm [Khiết] (Lian Qie), Lạc [Khái] (Le Ke), [several unidentified names here], [ask] Lí Thuần Phong (Li Chunfeng), Thiệu Khang Tiết (Shao Kangjie), great wise gentlemen, great benevolent people, to come down together to assist [in casting] lots."

[9] The word *ngoạt* is used here instead of the conventional *nguyệt* for the word "month" since *nguyệt* belonged to the category of tabooed *(húy)* characters, being a part of the name of a deceased principal wife of the Emperor Trần Nhân Tông (r. 1278–93). It was taken out of circulation by a decree of 1299. See Ngô Đức Thọ, *Nghiên Cứu Chữ Huý Việt Nam Qua Các Triều Đại* (A Study of Vietnamese Tabooed Characters through the Great Dynasties), trans. E. Poisson (Hanoi: Publications du Centre de l'École Française d'Extrême-Orient au Vietnam, Nhà Xuất Bản Văn Hóa, 1997), pp. 38, 47–49, 53–54. The substitution of *ngoạt* for *nguyệt* in this phrase leads me to assume that this formula appeared in the fourteenth century, since the taboo against using this character was lifted in 1395 (ibid., p. 48).

[10] *Thời (shi)* in modern Vietnamese. This word denotes "period of time." The author translated it as "hour."

[11] It is plausible to expect that this also means a certain period of time less than a year—a month, a day, or an unspecified period of time. But Vietnamese dictionaries do not suggest any such meaning for *tuyết*. In Alexandre de Rhodes's dictionary one finds the word *tüết*, an equivalent for *chó* (dog), used also as a denominator of a certain hour, day, month, or year corresponding to the celestial sign of dog. See Alexandre de Rhodes, *Từ Điển Annam-Lusitan-Latinh* (Annamite-Lusitanian [Portuguese]-Latin Dictionary), Thanh Lãng, Hoàng Xuân Việt, and Đỗ Quang Chính, trans. (reprint; Hanoi: Nhà Xuất Bản Khoa Học Xã Hội, 1991), col. 843. Adriano di St. Thecla apparently understood *tuyết* as "moment."

[12] **(A)** 先師先聖先賢照臨降下（請問）聽閗上帝
(B) 伏羲大禹文王周公孔子及鬼神降決明白
(C) 孔門儒道七十二賢廉樂均（？）門（？）陳（？）目（？）理（？）斉（？）圓（？）天（？_）下（？）凡（？）李淳風邵康節列位大聖大賢同來助卦
(D) 歲此某年某月某日某時某【？】或上中下旬忽遇或男女人卜門求事望事
(E) 各各奇事吉則吉兆凶則凶神兆諸位聖賢同來降下

[13] The more accurate translation of this phrase is "The ancient masters, the ancient sages, the ancient worthies throw light upon [casting the lots], come down to earth, beseech the Supreme Emperor." The translation of the parts (B) and (D) does not require any commentaries.

and hope for something in the year N, month N, on the day N, in the hour N, moment N, in the new, full, or old moon; (E) all and every ——[14]

[The chapter breaks off here. Pages 77–82 of the manuscript are blank.]

[14] The translation of the last phrase is incomplete; the Vietnamese appears to mean something like "Each and every strange event, if [it is] auspicious, then [it gives] an auspicious spirit omen; if inauspicious, then an inauspicious spirit omen; [may] all saints and benevolent [people] come down [from heaven]."

CHAPTER FIVE

ON THE SECT OF WORSHIPPERS OF [BUDDHA][1]

[p. 83]

Article 1: On Thích Ca, the Founder of This Sect among Indians

The founder of the sect of the worshippers of Phật (Fo)[2] was a very famous man, called Thích Ca[3] by the Annamites, who was born in India—[then] called Thiên Trúc (Tianzhu)—in Ấn Độ (Yindu) kingdom,[4] when Chu Chiêu Vương (Zhou Zhaowang)[5] was ruling China in his twenty-fourth year, on the eighth day of the first moon in the year 1029 before the birth of Christ; and he died, at ninety years old, after eight years of the reign of Emperor Chu Cung Vương (Zhou Gongwang).[6]

[1] The chapter title in the manuscript has two blank spaces: "On the Sect of Worshippers of ——— or ———."

[2] Fo (Phật) means Buddha. There are many definitions and explanations for the meaning of the word Fo. I will adduce here only one found in the book *Lihuo lun* (On the Settling of Doubts), written by Mouzi (Mâu Tử) or Mou Bo (Mâu Bác), who lived in what is now northern Vietnam in the late second and early third century C.E. When asked about the meaning of the word *Buddha,* Mouzi replied: "The word Buddha is a posthumous title, like calling the three sovereigns 'divine' or the five emperors 'sage.' Buddha is the original ancestor of the power of the Way, our ancestral link to spiritual understanding. The word *buddha* means awakened." John P. Keenan, *How Master Mou Removes Our Doubts* (Albany: State University of New York Press, 1994), p. 64. For the translation into Vietnamese published together with the characters see Mâu Tử, "Lý Hoặc Luận," in Trần Nghĩa, *Sưu Tầm và Khảo Luận Tác Phẩm Chữ Hán của Người Việt Nam trước Thế Kỷ X* (Search for and Examination of Works by Vietnamese in the Sino-Vietnamese Language before the Tenth Century) (Hanoi: Nhà Xuất Bản Thế Giới, 2000), pp. 389–390.

[3] *Sakya* in Sanskrit, "one from the Sakya clan," an abbreviation from Thích Ca Mâu Ni Phật (Shijiamouni fo)—Buddha Sakyamuni, whose name at birth was Siddhartha Gautama.

[4] Both terms, Thiên Trúc (Tianzhu) and Ấn Độ (Yindu), designate India, the first one is a descriptive term meaning Heavenly Bamboo, while the second one is a phonetic approximation.

[5] R. 1052–1001 B.C.E.

[6] R. 946–934 B.C.E. The name in modern Vietnamese is read Chu Cộng Vương. There are several versions about dating the appearance of Sakyamuni. See, for example, Trần Văn Giáp, *Việt Nam Phật Giáo Sử Lược* (Historical Survey of Vietnamese Buddhism) (An Hanh: Phật Học Viện Trung Phan, 1942), p. 27, where he adduces as one of the possible dates of Siddhartha Gautama's birthday the year 1027 B.C.E. One of the reasons why such early dates have been used may have

His father was King Tịnh Phạn (Jing Fan),[7] his mother was Mada,[8] his wife was Da Thị (Ye Shi),[9] his concubine was Như La (Ru Luo);[10] Thích Ca himself was earlier called Nhẫn Nhục (Renru).[11] When his father skipped for three years the payment of the yearly tribute he owed King Lí Hổ (Li Hu),[12] the indignant king threatened to punish him. The petty king Tịnh Phạn [Thích Ca's father], to avert from himself the impending menace, ordered that the tribute owed King Lí Hổ be sent to him. Since all the ministers refused, because of fear, to go as ambassadors, his son Nhẫn Nhục volunteered to take upon himself this service. He was sent by his father with many gifts, and he conducted the affair with King Lí Hổ so skillfully that he not only restored the king's good feelings toward his father but also gained the king's favor [for himself], and he [became] so dear to the king that the king gave him his daughter Wadu as a wife. When he returned to his father, he was received with the deepest gratitude and exultation of all [the people of the kingdom], and his father bestowed upon him a special honor by giving him an oriental palace to live in.[13] But, indeed, he, to cover his name with even more

---

been competition among Buddhists and Taoists with Confucians on the issue of the primogeniture of their sects and, accordingly, the antiquity of their founders, which led to the appearance of several hagiographies according to which Laozi and Buddha were born long before the sixth century B.C.E. The established academic version, based on materials found in Sri Lanka, says that Sakyamuni was born ca. 563 B.C.E. and died in 483. However, there is still quite an active debate on the dates of Buddha's appearance. See Heinz Buhert, "The Problem of the Determination of the Date of the Historical Buddha," *Wiener Zeitschrift für die Kunde Südasiens und Archiv für Indische Philosophie* 33 (1989): 93–170.

[7] Suddhodhana (in Sanskrit), the father of Sakyamuni, was the king of a small kingdom on the periphery of the greater Indian monarchies. Its capital was Kapilavastu. This territory is now in Nepal.

[8] An abbreviation of Maha Mada or Maha Maya, the mother of Sakyamuni. Some legends present her as his immaculate mother, an accomplished person, who "searched so intensely for a spiritual absolute that she denied the pleasures of the body. . . . King Suddhodhana desired his wife passionately, but he loved her so deeply that he refused to insist on his rights and respected the wishes of this companion who was so avid for perfect purity." Maurice Percheron, *The Marvelous Life of the Buddha*, trans. Adrienne Foulke (New York: St. Martin's Press, 1960), p. 48. Queen Maya, according to legend, died a week after she gave birth to Siddhartha Gautama, and he was lovingly raised by Maya's sister, Mahapajapati, who was also Suddhodhana's wife.

[9] Da Thị (Ye Shi), "woman of the Da (Ye) clan," is apparently a reference to Da Du Đa La (Yeshuduoluo, Yasodhara). She gave birth to Buddha's son, Rahula, and after that she retreated to a monastery, becoming enlightened herself. Siddhartha had two other wives: Gopika and Urganika. Đoàn Trung Còn, *Phật Học Từ Điển* (Dictionary of Buddhism) (Ho Chi Minh City: Nhà Xuất Bản Thành Phố Hồ Chí Minh, 1997), 2:211.

[10] Siddhartha is said to have had more than one hundred beauties to entertain him. My search for one by the name of Như La (Ru Luo), in numerous dictionaries and in the different primary and secondary sources and in consultations with specialists, has not produced results. Even Noël Peri's article "Les femmes de Sakya-muni," *Bulletin de l'École Française d'Extrême-Orient* 18, 2 (1918): 1–35, which concentrates on the female circle around Siddhartha Gautama, does not mention Như La.

[11] *Kshanti* in Sanskrit, meaning "patience" and "forbearance."

[12] Suddhodana, Siddhartha's father, was a vassal of the king of Kosala, but the reference here seems to be to some other unidentified king.

[13] I could not locate the source of this story of Buddha's mission to King Lý Hổ (Li Hu) and his marriage to Wadu, whose identity remains uncertain. The orthodox version runs as follows: Having been raised in luxury, Siddhartha hardly knew suffering. But on his trips he had four encounters that changed his life: Siddhartha saw an old man, a sick man, a corpse, and a

glory, left the court secretly, keeping his father ignorant,[14] and retreated to the mountains.[15] There he met two demons on the road, called A la la (Aluoluo) and Hắc la la (Heiluoluo),[16] and for many days they taught him a doctrine, which later he passed on to the members of his sect, who called him with a new name, Thích Ca Mâu Ni Phật (Shijiamouni, Buddha Sakyamuni);[17] having at the same time accepted [this] new name from those who called themselves Di Đà (Mituo) and Di Lặc (Milei).[18] He was sitting between [p. 84] the two devils, who, from the left and from the right, were giving him instructions as [his] assistants; he listened to [the instructions] and wrote them down in forty-two treatises,[19] according to the testimony collected in the next article, and not four thousand, as some [people] wrote in the books of Christians. We will present astonishing fables about Thích Ca in the third and fourth articles.

---

religious mendicant. These experiences were traumatic, and all the pleasures of palace life and even of his recently born son lost their appeal for him. So, at the age of twenty-nine, he left his family and set off on a long journey, searching for a means to deliver people from suffering. Through his studies with different people, but mainly through introspection, he became the Buddha, "the Enlightened or Awakened One," that is, he found the way to achieve Nirvana, the state in which there is no more suffering, the state that interrupts the chain of reincarnation. His teaching was based on the Four Noble Truths: life is suffering; the cause of this suffering is craving; to stop suffering, desire must be stopped; and it is possible to achieve this through right living. His teaching spread far beyond the borders of his native land and became one of the major world religions.

[14] "Numerous texts mention that Siddhartha himself requested permission to become a hermit and that his father refused." Henri Doré, *Recherches sur les superstitions en Chine,* vol. 15, *Vie illustrée du Bouddha Cakyamouni* (Shanghai: Imprimerie deT'ou-sè-wè, 1929), p. 73, n. 2.

[15] Adriano di St. Thecla apparently rejects here the traditional motivation that allegedly prompted Siddhartha to leave the palace and search for the way to avoid suffering, and instead ascribes to him a purely vainglorious motivation.

[16] A la la (Aluoluo) is Alara Kalama in Sanskrit. I could not identify Hắc la la, but it may be a corruption of Uất-Đa-La (Yuduoluo): Udraka Ramaputra. According to tradition, Siddhartha Gautama had two teachers whom he met upon his departure from the royal palace in search of his own way of life. One of them was Alara Kalama and the other was Udraka Ramaputra. They both were acclaimed teachers of Brahmanic scriptures and practiced meditation and Yogic asceticism. However, their teaching did not satisfy Siddhartha Gautama, and he continued his quest. Marie Gallaud, *La Vie du Bouddha et les doctrines bouddhiques* (Paris: Maisonneuve, 1931), p. 16. In Alexandre de Rhodes's dictionary the name of Udraka is listed as Calala, which is close to what appears in the text, Hắc La La. Alexandre de Rhodes, *Từ Điển Annam-Lusitan-Latinh* (Annamite-[Lusitanian] Portuguese-Latin Dictionary), trans. Thanh Lãng, Hoàng Xuân Việt, Đỗ Quang Chính (reprint, Ho Chi Minh City: Nhà Xuất Bản Khoa Học Xã Hội, 1991), col. 761, s.v. "Thic ca."

[17] *Muni* means virtue, perfection, or asceticism. Thus, Buddha's name became "The Virtuous or Perfect or Ascetic One from the Sakya clan." It seems that Adriano di St. Thecla borrowed Buddha's hagiography from local texts in Vietnam, such as the one that he draws on in his presentation of Buddhist doctrine.

[18] Di Đà (Mituo) is an abbreviation from the epithet A di đà Phật (Amituo fo): Buddha Amitabha, "Immeasurable Radiance," who presides over the Western Pure Land. Di Lặc (Milei) is Maitreya, the Buddha who is to come to succeed Sakyamuni.

[19] The reference here is to the *Sutra in Forty-two Sections,* which, according to the legend recounted below, was brought back to Han China by an imperial envoy sent to India to find out about Buddhism. The sutra, however, seems to be a later production compiled in the fourth or fifth centuries. See Kenneth K. S. Ch'en, *Buddhism in China: A Historical Survey* (Princeton: Princeton University Press, 1964), pp. 34–36. The text of the *Sutra in Forty-two Sections* has been translated into English; see Donald S. Lopez Jr., ed., *Religions of China in Practice* (Princeton, NJ: Princeton University Press, 1996), pp. 360–371.

The aforementioned name, Phật, with which Thích Ca was called, means *celestial person*. This character [亻天] is composed of two characters, namely *nhân (ren,* 亻*)*, which is "human being," and *thiên [tian,* 天], which is *Heaven*. This character *phật* is also written in a different way [佛], and it is composed of the characters *phật* [弗],[20] or *not*, and *nhân* [*ren,* 亻], or *human being*, as if it *meant not human*, since he undoubtedly became an idol, which is higher than a human being; and the same name *phật* has another secret meaning in the inner doctrine of this sect: the point [of this secret meaning] is that the previously mentioned character, *phật* [亻天], consists of a double character *nhân* [人 and 亻] or *human being*, and a character *nhị* [*er,* 二] or *two*, which means a man and a woman, or a mother and a father bringing a child to life.

Article 2: On the Spread of This Sect in China

During the rule of the Hán (Han) dynasty the Phật sect was brought into China from India by order of Emperor Minh Đế (Mingdi)[21] in the eighth year of his reign, approximately in the seventieth year after Christ was born.[22] These events are narrated in the Christian books, and first of all in the book *Văn Lâm Quảng (Wen Lin Guang)*, in the following way: they say that Hán Minh Đế (Han Mingdi) saw in a dream a man with a golden body sixteen cubits tall. Being asked by the emperor who he was, he responded that he was a man from the western region. When this dream was presented to the royal dream interpreters to get them to provide its interpretation, they said that holy men had always been in the West, and they congratulated the emperor for catching sight of a holy man; they also interpreted that dream [to predict] that the emperor would be prospering for a long time. Because of this the emperor himself wanted to go to the West to inquire there and to bring back the image and the law of that holy man. [p. 85] Since the dream interpreters were against the trip of the emperor because in his absence the state might be thrown into turmoil, he sent two ambassadors, named Thái Am (Cai An) and Tần Cảnh (Qin Jing), to look for [the image and the book] and bring them to him.[23] When they came to India, or Thiên Trúc, they still had not covered half of the way to the remote West, but, terrified by the incommodities and difficulties of

[20] This character is, in fact, read as *phất* in Vietnamese.

[21] R. 58–76.

[22] Usually the date is reckoned to be 65 C.E. On the discussion of other possible dates see Eric Zürcher, *The Buddhist Conquest of China: The Spread and Adaptation of Buddhism in Early Medieval China* (Leiden: Brill, 1972), pp. 18–22. In fact, Adriano di St. Thecla would also arrive at this date if he counted from the year 58, the first year of the reign of Emperor Hán Minh Đế (Han Mingdi). It seems to be just a mistake in writing since on the next page of the manuscript he adduces a phrase unambiguously pointing to the year 65.

[23] The book *Văn Lâm Quảng (Wen lin guang)*, to which Adriano di St. Thecla refers, was apparently compiled from several sources. One of them could be the book *Lihuo lun*. The name of one of the two envoys mentioned above, Tần Cảnh (Qin Jing), a palace guard, is, according to this text, among the envoys dispatched by Hán Minh Đế (Han Mingdi) to India. See Keenan, *How Master Mou Removes Our Doubts*, p. 123. The name of the second envoy, Thái Am (Cai An), is not directly mentioned in *Lihuo lun*. Cai An is, however, mentioned along with Qin Jing in the version of this story found in the book *Gaoseng zhuan*, written during the Liang dynasty (502–57) by the monk Hui Jiao. *Gaoseng zhuan* (Lives of Eminent Monks) (Beijing: Zhonghua shuju: Xinhua shudian, 1992), chap. 1, p. 1.

[going] the rest of the way, they took an image of an idol and the books that were kept there [in India] and brought them to the emperor, pretending that they brought the image and the books of the holy man from the West.[24] Deceived by their words, the emperor trustingly accepted the cult of Phật and ordered his subjects to construct everywhere temples for this idol, and forbade under penalty of death that anyone should kill an animal in the future, according to the doctrine of this sect. This fact became known from the Christian books.[25]

Indeed, this fact is interpreted in a different way in the books of *Chinese History*, which we must take into account when talking with literati. There it is put in this way: Ất Sửu bát niên sơ, Đế văn Tây vực hữu Thần, kì danh viết Phật nhân khiển sứ chi Thiên Trúc cầu kì đạo, đác[26] kì thư, cập sa môn dĩ lai, ư thị Trung Cuốc thỉ đắc kì thuật, đồ kì hình tượng;[27] that is: In the eighth year [of his reign], the emperor {Minh Đế} heard the rumor that in the Western region there was a spirit called Phật, and he ordered ambassadors to go to Thiên Trúc {India} to ask about his [the spirit's] doctrine and to get his book; then his falsehood appeared in this kingdom and his image was created.[28] The literatus Phan Thị

---

[24] The question of envoys being sent to the West to investigate is very arguable. There exist several versions of reports that tell of dispatching envoys, but their names and number vary as well as the dates of their departure and return. See Zürcher, *Buddhist Conquest of China*, pp. 19–21.

[25] See more on this episode in the translator's introduction.

[26] *Đác* is presently spelled as *đắc* (*de*, to obtain, to receive). But I suppose this was not always the case. Alexandre de Rhodes's dictionary does not include this word, but neither does it contain any entries at all with a combination of *đ* and *ă*. Moreover, other words with different tones that are spelled with *ă* in modern Vietnamese are recorded there with *a* as, for example, the word *đạc* (solid, thick), spelled *đặc* in modern Vietnamese orthography. See Alexandre de Rhodes, *Từ Điển Annam-Lusitan-Latinh*, col. 191–192. By extension we can surmise that the same is true with regard to *đác* and *đắc*. It should be noted that the absence of *ă* following a consonant is seen only in the case of the consonant *đ*, as there are numerous examples in de Rhodes's dictionary of combinations of all the other consonants with *ă*, as well as examples of the combinations *ăc*, *ắc*, and *ặc* in final position as they exist in modern Vietnamese. Apparently, there was some distinctive phonetic quality of *đ* that made it incompatible with *ă*, but later this feature disappeared, as is seen in Huình Tịnh Paulus Của, *Đại Nam Quấc Âm Tự Vị* (A Dictionary of Characters with the National Pronunciation of Great South) (reprint, Ho Chi Minh City: Nhà Xuất Bản Trẻ, 1998), pp. 257–258, where we find the word for "solid or thick" written *đặc*. In the phrase we are discussing, the word with the same meaning "to receive, to obtain" appears twice, once here as *đác* and then as *đắc* (the seventh word from the end). This might be a scribal error, in the first instance, or a reflection of the phonetic and spelling processes taking place in the eighteenth century.

[27] 乙 丑 八 年 初 帝 聞 西 域 有 神 其 名 曰 佛 因 遣 使 之 天 竺 求 其 道 得 其 書 及 沙 門 以 來 於 是 中 國 始 得 其 術 塗 其 形 像 .

[28] This account is very similar to that in the first part of the previous passage and also can be found in *Linhuo lun*. See Keenan, *How Master Mou*, pp. 123–124, or in Mâu Tử, "Lý Hoặc Luận," pp. 447–449. Adriano di St. Thecla rather precisely conveys the sense of the passage. However, we should restore his omission of the word *sơ* (*chu*, at the beginning) and remedy his neglect of the phrase *cập sa môn dĩ lai* (及 沙 門 以 來), which means "along with Buddhist monks to come." Thus, the translation of the phrase is: "At the beginning of [his] eighth year [of reign under the sign] Ất Sửu (yichou) [i.e., the year 65], the emperor heard that in the western region (India) there was a saint, whose name was Buddha; [he] dispatched envoys to India to ask about his doctrine and to get his books and also [to invite] the Buddhist monks to come, and, thereafter, in China his mystery was accepted and his images were painted." Another point deserving our attention is Adriano di St. Thecla's translation of the word *thuật* (*shu*) as

Vinh (Pan Shirong or Pan Shiyong), in the book *Tổng Luận* (*Zonglun*, General Discussion), which was written before the historical books *Thông Giám* (*Tongjian*, Comprehensive Mirror),[29] adds something to it by saying: Minh Đế khiển sứ chi Thiên Trúc, đắc Phật kinh tứ thập nhị chương, giam chi Lan đài thạch thất, dĩ Phật tượng hội chi, Thanh Lương đài hiển thiết[30] lăng;[31] that is: Minh Đế ordered ambassadors to go to Thiên Trúc and to get the book of Phật [which consisted] of forty-two treatises, and to place it into the palace called Lan (Lan),[32] in its stone compartment, and to accept the image of Phật and paint it in the palace called Thanh Lương (Shengliang) on the mound or the heap of earth called Hiển Tiết (Xianjie).[33] From this it has been discovered that the aforementioned emperor sent [ambassadors] to India with the intention to bring to China the book and the image of Thích Ca called Phật, [p. 86] but [the emperor did not send them to the remotest

"falsehood," which I translate as "mystery." This word can be translated as "trick" (i.e., the author's "falsehood"), "mystery," "art," "magic," or "technique." Adriano di St. Thecla's choice here suggests that he either translated relying on the overall anti-Buddhist context of the document or that he chose the meaning that reflected his own disdain of Buddhism.

[29] This work, as well as its author Phan Thị Vinh (pronounced *Pan Shirong* or *Pan Shiyong* in Chinese), has remained unidentified. At the the end of this chapter Adriano di St. Thecla mentions that Phan Thị Vinh lived during the Minh (Ming) dynasty (1368–1644). If so, it is not clear to what work, following Phan Thị Vinh's *Tổng Luận* (*Zonglun*, General Discussion) and titled *Thông Giám (Tongjian)*, Adriano di St. Thecla refers. All the works incorporating the words *tongjian* mentioned in the manuscript—namely, Sima Guang's *Zizhi tongjian* (Comprehensive Mirror for Aid in Government), written in 1084; *Tongjian waiji* (Outer Records of the Comprehensive Mirror), written by Lưu Thư (Liu Shu), also in the second half of the eleventh century; and the twelfth-century *Tongjian gangmu* (General Outline of the Comprehensive Mirror) of Chu Tử (Zhu Xi)—were created long before fourteenth century. The words of the title *Tổng Luận* (*Zonglun*, General Discussion), seem to be the last words of a longer title, which, in the absence of the initial words and the unclear name of the author, is yet to be revealed.

[30] This name should be read *Hiển Tiết*, as it appears below in the text, and also should have been capitalized.

[31] 明帝遣使之天竺得佛經四十二章監之蘭臺石室以佛像繪之清涼臺顯節陵.

[32] The palace was located in Luoyang, an ancient city in modern Honan province in China.

[33] This is an exact translation of the passage except for two places. Lan đài (Lantai) was, according to *Lihuo lun*, the place where the Sutra in Forty-two Sections was brought and kept. *Đài (tai)* could be read as "tower or palace," making the reference here to a stone compartment in a tower or palace named "Lan," as the author has it; but Adriano di St. Thecla failed to recognize that in historiography Lan Đài is known as a proper name. In addition, there are two possible translations of the phrase *Lan đài thạch thất (Lantai shishi)*. John P. Keenan's translation is similar to that of Adriano di St. Thecla: "the cubicle of the Stone Chamber at Lan-t'ai [Lantai]" (Keenan, *How Master Mou*, p. 123), while Trần Nghĩa translates it as "the compartment of stone-built Lantai" (Mâu Tử, "Lý Hoặc Luận," pp. 447–449). Grammatically both possibilities of "stone chamber of Lantai" and "stone-built Lantai" seem plausible. As for the place called Thanh Lương (Shengliang) in the text, it was not itself a palace but a tower located in the palace called Nam Cung (Nangong, Southern Palace) (Mâu Tử, "Lý Hoặc Luận," pp. 447–449). Keenan gives the name of the tower as Qinjing (Keenan, *How Master Mou Removes our Doubts*, p. 123). The second imprecision is that the author refers to Hiển Tiết lăng (Xianjie ling) as a mound or heap of earth. The word *lăng (ling)* indeed has the adduced translation as one of its meanings, but here another meaning, "mausoleum," would serve better. *Lihuo lun* states that, while still alive, Emperor Minh (Ming) built in advance a mausoleum for himself, which was called Hiển Tiết. See Xianjie, "The Illustrious Integrity of Purity." "On its peak he placed a likeness of Buddha." Ibid., p. 124; Mâu Tử, "Lý Hoặc Luận," pp. 447–449.

West or Europe or even to Palestine to bring from there the image as well as the doctrine of the saintly people who lived there. It is not difficult to figure out from where it would have become known to this emperor that in India there was a spirit named Phật, for long ago Emperor Hán Vũ Đế (Han Wudi)[34] extended Chinese authority as far as India, which he overcame with arms more than one hundred seventy years before Minh Đế; in the *History*, under the twenty-seventh year of this emperor, it is mentioned that the emperor sent messengers or ministers to Đại Hạ (Daxia) kingdom[35] and other adjacent kingdoms, that is, to the Indian kingdoms; and so a passage from China to India, or communication between the two, was opened.[36] From then on, the Chinese learned about the Indian Phật, who was honored by the Indians; and since his fame was preserved in China, Emperor Minh Đế accepted him [his doctrine], according to legendary tradition. Thereafter they knew Phật also under the name of Thiên Chúa (Tianzhu), or Lord of Heaven; it is also narrated in the same *Chinese History*, under the first year of the aforementioned emperor, that he [the emperor] highly esteemed Bạng Trừ kingdom,[37] which was adjacent to the kingdoms of the Indians, and they [the inhabitants of the kingdom] made there a golden statue of a man dedicated to the Lord of Heaven: Đế dĩ Bạng Trừ tắc kim nhân vi tế Thiên Chúa.[38] This Thiên Chúa (Tianzhu),[39] or the Lord of Heaven, is none other than Thích Ca, who is considered and honored by Indians and other neighboring nations as the Lord of Heaven, or even as the founder of Heaven

Later many other emperors promoted the cult of Phật; the first [among them] was Hán Linh Đế (Han Lingdi), who ruled a century after Minh Đế,[40] and who first built inside his palace a temple for the idol Phật, as testified the aforementioned Phan Thị Vinh: Thỉ lập tư[41] vũ cung trung dĩ phượng chi.[42] Emperor Lương Vũ (Liang Wu), [43] who ruled in the fourth century after Minh Đế, constructed a large tower in a temple of idols, where he later retreated and devoted himself to their

---

[34] R. 140–86 B.C.E. He was known for his very active expansionist policy. During his time, Han successfully struggled against its enemy on the northern and western borders, the Xiongnu (Hung Nô), whose constant raids restrained the development of the country. With at least partial pacification of the Xiongnu, Han was able to increase its trade with Central Asia and other regions.

[35] Bactria, an ancient country located near the mountains of the Hindu Kush in the territory of some parts of modern Afghanistan, Tajikistan, and Uzbekistan.

[36] One of the envoys was Trương Khiên (Zhang Qian). He was sent to Bactria and India to conduct negotiations with the Yuezhi people concerning a possible alliance against the Hung Nô (Xiongnu) in 138 B.C.E., returning in 125 B.C.E. In some legends he is considered to be the first to bring knowledge of the scriptures of Buddhism. He is also mentioned in *Lihuo lun*. See Keenan, *How Master Mou Removes Our Doubts*, p. 123; Mâu Tử, "Lý Hoặc Luận," pp. 447–448.

[37] I failed to identify this kingdom exactly; hence its Chinese pronunciation remains obscure. It might be either Bangchi or Bangchu.

[38] 帝 以 [?] [?] 作 金 人 為 祭 天 主 . "[The inhabitants of the kingdom of] Bạng Trừ made a golden statue for the emperor to worship the Lord of Heaven."

[39] This term was also used as an apellation of the Christian God.

[40] R. 168–90 C.E.

[41] This word, relying on Adriano di St. Thecla's translation, is an error for the word *tự* (*si*, temple).

[42] 始 立 寺 宇 宮 中 以 奉 之 .

[43] R. 502–49 C.E.

cult, and there he was captured by the rebel Hầu Cảnh (Hou Jing).[44] Also, in the ninth century after Minh Đế, after a certain idol of a great name had been accepted into the temple called Phượng Dương (Fengyang or Fangyang), it was accessible there [every] thirtieth year, and in that same [thirtieth] year the idol granted an abundance of fruit [to the people] and tranquillity in the state;[45] Emperor Đàng Hiến Tông (Tang Xianzong)[46] sent an ambassador to India to bring the idol's bones to him. At the beginning of the [p. 87] fourteenth year of this emperor['s reign],[47] the ambassador brought to the court the hand bones of the idol, and on the second moon carried them around to all the temples: Chính ngoạt trung sứ nghinh Phật cốt chí kinh sứ;[48] nhị ngoạt nảy lịch tống chư sư.[49] The [number of] worshippers of Phật grew so much in the sixth century after the introduction of this sect [to China] that the number of men and women staying in temples and engaging in the cult of Phật ran to one hundred thousand during the rule of Emperor Đàng Cao Tổ (Tang Gaozu),[50] as the literatus Phó Dịch (Fu Yi) testifies in a letter of petition to this emperor,[51] saying: Kim Thiên hạ Tang[52] ni số duanh[53] thập vạn.[54] This all is [written] in the *Chinese History.*

---

[44] Emperor Lương Vũ (Liang Wu) was an outstanding patron and generous supporter of Buddhism, which he made the official religion, and he even banished wine and meat from the imperial table. He wrote a number of commentaries on Buddhist scriptures, built many temples, and sometimes resided in Buddhist monasteries. Hầu Cảnh (Hou Jing) was one of the regional leaders of a Turkish tribal federation of Toba. He rose to power sometime after 545 C.E., invaded China, and captured its capital in 549. Emperor Wu was killed.

[45] On this, see: Ch'en, *Buddhism in China,* pp. 279–282.

[46] R. 806–21.

[47] That is, the year 820.

[48] *Sứ* is erroneously written instead of *sư* (*shi*, capital city), a component of the compound *kinh sư (jingshi)* with the same meaning.

[49] 正 月 中 使 迎 佛 骨 至 京 師 二 月 乃 歷 送 諸 師 :"In the first month, the envoy respectfully received Buddha's bone and arrived at the capital; then in the second month [he] carried it [or it was carried] around the entire capital."

[50] R. 618–27. During the Tang dynasty (618–907) and its predecessor the Sui ddynasty (589–618), Buddhism in China reached its apogee. These two cosmopolitan dynasties allowed significant freedom in the development of intellectual and religious life. Although it did not replace Daoism, which was also strongly favored by the rulers, Buddhism became widespread and adjusted itself to the Chinese environment; it developed different schools and became much more closely identified with Chinese culture and government. The Buddhist clergy grew numerous and powerful and enjoyed support from many influential families. Disaster struck in 845, when Emperor Đường Vũ Tông (Tang Wuzong, 841–47) unleashed a very severe persecution. Buddhism recovered and has since played an important role in China, but it never regained the strong hold it had earlier. For a detailed analysis of Buddhism during this period see Stanley Weinstein, *Buddhism under the T'ang* (Cambridge: Cambridge University Press, 1987).

[51] Fu Yi (Phó Dịch) was a Daoist scholar who lived from 554 to 639. In 621 he presented a memorial to the emperor in which he attacked Buddhism. To support his point, he gave intellectual, economic, and nationalistic reasons. Emperor Gaozu (Cao Tổ) did not want to confront Buddhism and alienate its many supporters, but as a response to Fu Yi's memorial he issued a decree aiming to limit both Buddhist and Daoist activity in China. The decree was never carried out, however, for Emperor Gaozu was compelled to abdicate just several weeks after issuing it. See Arthur Wright's chapter on Fu Yi's memorial in *Studies in Chinese Buddhism* (New Haven: Yale University Press, 1990), pp. 112–123.

[52] *Tang* here is a mistake for *tăng* (*seng*, Buddhist priest). For some reason, when this word appears in quoted passages or phrases in the manuscript, it is erroneously written as *tang*,

Testimonies on Phật from the Chinese Books

[The rest of this page and p. 88 are blank.]

[p. 89]

Article 3: On the Doctrine of This Sect

The doctrine which Thích Ca received as a student of the two demons, his teachers, and which he as a teacher passed on to his disciples, is twofold: one [part of it] is external, another is internal; the former deals with the cult of idols, the latter with atheism. The internal doctrine explains the external one; it clarifies the origin of the human [race], and also the shameful parts of the human body, of a man as well as of a woman, which in the external doctrine are masked under different signs and names of idols. If, in the external doctrine, many [things] appear interwoven in stories and fables, in the internal doctrine they have their real appearance. Thích Ca passed along the external doctrine and made it known to everybody; the internal doctrine, however, he shared only with one, or in any case with a few well-tested and faithful students, and strictly ordered them to keep it in secret, often saying: Bí chi,[55] Bí chi, xiên kim bất kha[56] truyền chi;[57] that is: This doctrine should be secret, one must not pass it on and reveal it [even] for a thousand measures of gold. For that reason even now it is usually shared only with the highest and the most well-tested priests who perform sacrifices, being concealed from others. Thích Ca gave the book of this sect, titled *Bí Chi* (*Mizhi*, Secret Branch),[58] to one of the followers among his disciples, who in turn gave it to another, and others handed it down successively to yet others. Their names are enumerated in the preface to this same *Bí Chi* in the order it [the book] was used; the last of the disciples is named Huyền Quang (Xuan Guang).[59] It is amazing that the tenth [disciple] after Thích Ca is someone from the Tống (Song) dynasty,[60] since

while when mentioned in the course of the author's exposition, separate from a citation, it is correctly recorded as *tăng*.

[53] The modern spelling of this word is *doanh* (*ying*, surplus, to overflow, to exceed). This word appears neither in Alexandre de Rhodes's nor in Huình Tịnh Paulus Của's dictionaries. But it is known that sometimes the combination *oa* was written as *ua* in the earlier centuries.

[54] 今 天 下 僧 尼 數 盈 十 萬 . "Now in the empire the number of Buddhist monks and nuns has exceeded a hundred thousand."

[55] The pronunciation of the compound *bí chi* can stand for a number of different characters, none of which are perfectly suitable idiomatically. The variation closest to Adriano di St. Thecla's translation of *bí chi* as "secret doctrine" is 秘支 , meaning "secret branch."

[56] *Kha* should be *khả* (*ke*, to be able, may) to give the sense of the phrase.

[57] 秘 支 秘 支 千 金 不 可 傳 之 .

[58] I could not locate this book.

[59] I could find no Chinese person with this name. There was a Vietnamese monk, the third patriarch of the Buddhist Trúc Lâm (Bamboo Grove) school with this name, but he lived a bit later, 1254–1334, than is indicated below in the text, and his school virtually ended with his death. See Cuong Tu Nguyen, *Zen in Medieval Vietnam: A Study and Translation of the Thiền Uyển Tập Anh* (Honolulu: University of Hawai'i Press, 1997), p. 342 n. 49. For more on Huyền Quang, see Nguyễn Lang, *Việt Nam Phật Giáo Sử Luận* (A Historical Essay on Vietnamese Buddhism) (Saigon: Nhà Xuất Bản Lá Bối, 1973), pp. 355–378.

[60] 960–1279.

almost two thousand years had passed from [the time of] Thích Ca to the Tống dynasty; and a thousand years [from Thích Ca] to the earlier dynasty of Tống, or Bắc Triều (Beichao);[61] and either period of time demands much more than ten [generations of disciples] who accepted the book handed down in succession.

The doctrines of this sect are mainly described in his [Sakyamuni's] books according to nine *kiếp* (*jie*, kalpa),[62] that is, ages or aeons, especially in the aforementioned book *Bí Chi* and in the book *Tâm Đăng* (*Xindeng,* Lamp of the Heart).[63] In the first age, they say, before all things, a drop of dew first appeared from nothing,[64] out of itself, and this is the nature of Phật, or of the idol; this [p. 90] drop produced three drops out of itself: one green, which created Heaven; another yellow, which is Earth; and the third white, which produced a human being;[65] and soon after that, the name Nguyên Thỉ[66] (Yuanshi), or Primary Source, was given [to them]. Then these three drops merged into one and produced something looking like a stone egg, which broke into four pieces, and of one piece Heaven was made; of another, Earth; of the third, father; of the fourth, mother; and Tổ Nguyên Thỉ (Zu Yuanshi),[67] or Original Primary Source, appeared out of itself, and it produced four parts: East, West, South, and North, which were like four brothers, and those four brothers, together with Nguyên Thỉ, made Heaven and Earth.[68] At that time Nguyên Thỉ was in the world, and it was called Tì Lô (Pilu),[69] since both together

---

[61] The Liu Song dynasty, 420–78.

[62] A kalpa is a period during which a physical universe is formed and destroyed, which lasts for hundreds of millions of years, and is marked by its stability. "A thousand Buddhas appear in the course of it. Our present period is a Bhadrakalpa and four Buddhas have already appeared. It is to last 236 million years, but over 151 million years have already elapsed." Ernest J. Eitel, *Hand-book of Chinese Buddhism* (Hong Kong: Lane, Crawford, 1888), p. 29.

[63] The title of the book is a Buddhist term reflecting the state of non-passivity. See Kim Cương Tử, ed., *Từ Điển Phật Học Hán Việt* (A Sino-Vietnamese Dictionary of Buddhism) (Hanoi: Nhà Xuất Bản Khoa Học Xã Hộ, 1998), p. 1158. In the Institute of Sino-Vietnamese Studies (Hán-Nôm) in Hanoi there are two copies of this book, catalogued as AC 417 and A 2481. At the Société Asiatique in Paris there is one more copy of the text (PD 2372), identical with A 2481 in Hanoi. Due to the high degree of similarity (except for the preface) between these texts of the *Tâm Đăng* with which I have worked, hereafter, I refer to only one, AC 417 (the pagination of A 2481 and PD 2372 is identical to that of AC 417), which I suspect was written earlier. See the translator's introduction for more information on the *Tâm Đăng*.

[64] This entire passage is a slightly garbled summary of the passage in the *Tâm Đăng*. See AC 417, pp. 1a–b. In fact the primordial drop is not described there as a drop of dew, a Hindu idea of the primary source, but it is said to be a "drop pregnant with emptiness, 一 滴 孕 空 ." Ibid., p. 1a.

[65] The *Tâm Đăng* does not have "Heaven," "Earth," and "a human being" (although Adriano di St. Thecla may have consulted a text that does). The texts I have consulted have, first, "nature, sex, disposition" 性 ; second, an unidentified character ; and third, "body" 身 .

[66] He was discussed in the chapter on Daoism.

[67] This is a vernacular Vietnamese word order. In Chinese it would be Yuanshi zu, "Proto" Primary Source.

[68] In the *Tâm Đăng* there is no direct connection between Nguyên Thủy (Yuanshi) and the four brothers in the creation of Heaven and Earth, as Adriano di St. Thecla states. It says: [These four directions], pretending to be brothers, created Heaven and Earth, [and there] appeared in the center of the world two ancestors: the first named Nguyên Thủy (Yuanshi), the other one, *kalpa.*" (AC 417, p. 1b).

[69] These two characters can correspond to Vairo (an abbreviated form of Vairocana, Tì Lô Giá Na, Piluzhena), the Buddha Supreme and Eternal, who is present only in the Northern (Mahayana) Buddhist school and is a product of Buddhist mysticism and meditation; he plays a

[Nguyên Thỉ and Tì Lô] are the same idol, Phật, that appeared before Heaven and Earth. After Heaven and Earth were made in the first place, Nguyên Thỉ made Mục Mũi,[70] who is remarkable and unearthly by his nature, but at that time he was still indistinct; neither was the sky structured, nor was the earth condensed. In such a way only vapor, or a drop of water, which appeared from nothing, created the idol of Phật, Heaven and Earth, human beings, and all things. In the internal doctrine, Nguyên Thỉ is the primary state of human generation.

In the second age, they say, there was a couple, a man with the name Tu La Thiên (Xiuluo Tian)[71] and a woman with the name Maha Địa (Maha Di);[72] who dedicated their bodies to serve Heaven and Earth, and they produced day and night, water and fire, Heaven, Earth and man, the four elements or qualities, the Sun and the Moon, and also the eight figures of the lot:[73] Dụng thân tư trợ Thiên Địa tạo vi Càn, Khôn,[74] Tí ngọ,[75] Thủy hỏa, Tam tài,[76] tứ tượng,[77] nhật nguyệt, bát quái chi nhân[78] dã.[79]

---

special role in Tantrism. According to this school, in the state of Nirvana, Buddha became invisible, immaterial, and immortal; in this state he is called Vairocana Buddha. He is worshipped as an eternal being, the source and originator of all things. Buddhism shared its idea of Vairocana with Taoism, and many Taoist temples have statues of him. Another possibility is that Tì Lô (Pilu) means, as Alexandre de Rhodes puts it, "The second period of the human life when a fetus takes shape in the mother's womb. This period is called by the people worshiping idol images a second stage of a person, or *kiếp* (*jie*, kalpa) as they usually say it." According to Alexandre de Rhodes, Tì Lô corresponds to the next name mentioned in the text, Mục Mũi. Rhodes, *Từ Điển Annam-Lusitan-Latinh*, col. 417, s.v. "lô."

[70] The *Tâm Đăng* does not patently equate Nguyên Thủy (Yuanshi) to Tì Lô (Pilu) and to Buddha. It indeed does equates the two latter, saying "Tì Lô, one and the same with Buddha, first created Heaven and Earth, and then Nguyên Thủy reappeared as Mục Mũi." (AC 417, p. 1b). The characters corresponding to Mục Mũi 目 每 in the text are nowadays read as *mục mỗi (mumei)*. Mục Mỗi is apparently not widely known in Buddhist literature since I have not encountered this name either in the Buddhist texts I consulted nor in the secondary sources. Nor was it familiar to the specialists I consulted. However, Alexander de Rhodes in his dictionary gives an entry for *mộc mỗi* (the phonemes *ộ* and *ụ* were interchangeable in the seventeenth and eighteenth centuries): "*Mộc mỗi* is the body created when first endowed with a rational soul. This is an expression [used] by the idolatry sect." See Alexandre de Rhodes, *Từ Điển Annam-Lusitan-Latinh*, col. 477, s. v. "mộc mỗi." Moreover, another missionary, Manu de Rivas, mentions a certain *Muc-Mni* (possibly a mistake for to Mục Mũi) as being worshipped in the pagodas of Tonkin. Manuel de Rivas, *Idea de Imeperio de Annam, de los Reinos Unidos de Tunquin y Cochinchina* (Manila: Imprenta de los Amigos del Paris, 1858), p. 140. Adriano di St. Thecla's phrase "Nguyên Thủy made Mục Mỗi" apparently comes from his literal translation of the word *vi* (*wei*, to do, to make, to be). I think that the construction 元 始 再 現 後 為 一 祖 名 曰 目 每 from the original should be translated as "then Nguyên Thỉ reappeared as Mục Mũi."

[71] Tu La (Xiuluo) seems to be an abbreviated form of A Tu La (Axiuluo), signifying Asura, the mightiest of all demons, who rules over the kingdom of spirits in Heaven. Thiên (Tian, Heaven) might here denote benevolent spirits, devas, composing together with Asura and his kind a class of celestial titans.

[72] Maha Địa (Maha Di) means "Great Earth." This name or image is rarely, if at all, used in Buddhism. In the text, I think Tu La Thiên (Xiuluo Tian) and Maha Địa (Maha Di) are used as two juxtaposed and at the same time united entities, Heaven and Earth, the male and female sources.

[73] The sense of "lot" here is as in "to cast lots" and is a reference to the use of the eight basic trigrams of the *Yijing* (Book of Changes).

[74] *Thiên Địa (tian-di)* and *Càn Khôn (qian-kun)* are Sino-Vietnamese terms (unlike their vernacular equivalent, *Trời Đất*), and each has a similar meaning of Heaven and Earth, male and

female, superior and inferior. However, their usage differs. *Qian-kun* has been used mostly in the scholarly domain, in doctrines of different religious and philosophical currents, and consequently by the literati discussing these issues. *Qian-kun* signifies the combination of the male principle *dương (yang)* and the female principle *âm (yin)*, the two primordial symbols of existence and the two basic trigrams in the book *Yijing* (Book of Changes) from which the other trigrams have evolved. As the thirteenth-century Neo-Confucian scholar Ye Cai put it, *qian* emphasized strength and activity; *kun*, harmony and tranquillity (cited in Wing-Tsit Chan, trans., *Reflections on Things at Hand: The Neo Confucian Anthology Compiled by Chu Hsi and Lü Tsu-Ch'ien* [New York: Columbia University Press, 1967], p. 59). The term *tian-di* does not have the same mystico-philosophical aura as does *qian-kun* and is thus used more often by people in oral and written speech, while it is retained in the vocabularies of educated people, who use it in the formation of numerous philosophical and religious ideas. It seems that Adriano di St. Thecla may have translated the pair *tian-di* in this sentence as "Heaven and Earth," while *qian-kun*, which has among its meanings "sun and moon," he translated as "day and night." It is more likely however, that he translated *qian-kun* as equivalent to *tian-di* ("Heaven, Earth") because there are no other plausible words to be translated this way in the sentence, and also because he cites these two words using a comma between them: *càn, khôn* (in this case "day and night" would be an exuberance of his translation). Here, Adriano di St. Thecla uses the same punctuation as is found in the passage, not a copulative conjunction as appears with other pairs in the sentence. Adriano di St. Thecla's translation may be explained by the difficulty of conveying in translation the difference between these two pairs. I surmise that the text of the *Tâm Đăng* (*Xindeng*, Lamp of the Heart) implies that a more grounded *tian-di* produced a more mystical *qian-kun*.

75 *Tí ngọ* (*zi-wu*, the signs of the elephant and the horse) are omitted in Adriano di St. Thecla's translation. These are two of the twelve earthly branches used for indicating the names of years. Thus, it seems plausible to suggest that the author(s) of the *Tâm Đăng* inserted them to communicate an idea of the creation of this system of the twelve earthly branches. But the choice of *tí ngọ* for denoting the twelve branches is unsystematic because they are the first and the seventh signs respectively, and there is no apparent logic for their choice. Alternatively, the expression "elephant and horse" might have served as a generic term for animals, but then it stands out in the order of enumeration of the created things, following immediately male and female source, or Heaven and Earth, and preceding fire, water, the sun and the moon. It might be conjectured that the elephant was perceived as male and the horse as female in some erudite subculture, a phenomenon of which I am not aware. However, here is the only place in the manuscript where Adriano di St. Thecla spelled the sign of the horse as *ngọ*, not *ngũ*. The reasons for this exception are unclear because, even if we assume that the pronunciation *ngũ* was customary in the names of the years while in other cases it was *ngọ*, Adriano di St. Thecla's usage of *ngũ* for the sign of the horse in the chapters on Daoism and fortune-tellers would eliminate this assumption.

76 *Tam tài* (*sancai*, the Three Powers) has also been left untranslated in the manuscript. This term encompasses the Power of Heaven, the Power of Earth, and the Power of Men.

77 *Tứ tượng* (*sixiang*), translated in the text as "the four elements or qualities," might rather mean the four secondary forms evolved from the first figures for Heaven and Earth, *càn khôn (qian-kun)*.

78 As for *chi nhân (zhi ren)*, the *Tâm Đăng* has the character *nhị (er)*, meaning "two," instead of the character *chi (zhi)* (AC 417, p. 2a). This is the only discrepancy between the citation in the manuscript and its textual source. If we follow the *Tâm Đăng*, this compound should be translated as "two people," which does not contradict the author's translation since he mentions the creation of human beings.

79 用身資助天地造為乾坤子午水火三才四象月日八卦二(之)人也 (AC 417, pp. 1b–2a). I suggest the following translation for this passage: "[They] used their bodies to serve Heaven and Earth and created the male and female source of everything, earthly branches [or animals], fire and water, the three powers [of Heaven, Earth and Man], the four secondary trigrams, the Sun and the Moon, the eight figures of the lot [i.e., for casting lots] and two people."

In the third age, they say, there were five brothers called *Tướng* (*xiang*, ministers),[80] that is, leaders of others, each being called by his own name. The first, Thái Dịch (Taiyi, Invisible), was 150 cubits tall; the second, Thái Sơ (Taichu, Beginning of All Things), 130 cubits tall; the third, Thái Thỉ (Taishi, First Principle or Primitive Chaos), 120; the fourth, Thái Tố (Taizuo, Primary Source or Ultimate Reason), 110; and the fifth, Thái Cực (Taiji, Supreme Ultimate),[81] was 100 cubits tall. They [the brothers] were transformed into five colors; the first into the green color, the second into red, the third into white, the fourth into black, the fifth into yellow. And they are also said to have established Heaven and Earth: Ngũ Tướng biến vi ngũ sắc đồng tạo Thiên Địa dã.[82] Besides, they add that Heaven produced thirty-six copies [of itself], [p.91] or thirty-six Heavens, one above the other, and, similarly, Earth reproduced itself with the same number of layers.[83]

In the fourth age, they say, there was Bàn Cổ (Pangu), who had the head of a dragon, and the rest of his body was human, and who was fifty cubits tall. When everything was disordered, he separated Heaven from Earth and created all things: every time he opened his eyes, he made day, every time he closed his eyes he made night, and later his left eye was turned into the Sun and his right eye was turned into the Moon; when [during the] day Heaven was rising up and Earth was being pressed down, his height grew taller, and he lived one thousand years. This is [described] in the book *Bí Chi*. In the book *Tâm Đăng*, they also add that Bàn Cổ[84] made heat by opening his mouth and cold by closing it, wind by exhaling, thunder by speaking, and rain by spitting. When he died, his body was transformed into all [existing] things: his hair produced herbs and trees, his bones produced mountains, his teeth produced rocks, his blood produced water, his excrement produced fish, his legs and arms produced birds, animals, and serpents.[85] Long ago the followers and worshippers of Phật took this man Bàn Cổ from the *Chinese History*, where he is exhibited as the first among all that exists, and, since he was described there [in the book] as faultless, they attributed to him this amazing appearance.

---

[80] In the text *Tâm Đăng*, it is not mentioned that they were brothers, neither is there the elaborate description of their heights and colors as is presented by the author.

[81] All these five names are in fact cosmological terms used in Daoism. Thái Cực (taiji), the primary cosmological notion, became one of the main ideas in Zhu Xi's Neo-Confucian metaphysics. But it was also "almost an out-and-out takeover from the Taoists." Allen Wittenborn, trans. and commentary, *Further Reflections on Things at Hand: A Reader Chu Hsi* (Lanham, MD: University Press of America, 1991), p. 189.

[82] 五 相 變 為 五 色 同 造 天 地 也 (AC 417, p. 2a). "The five ministers, transforming five colors, together created Heaven and Earth." The word *sắc (se)*, justly translated by Adriano di St. Thecla as "color," has a specific meaning in a Buddhist context as "being, appearance," as opposed to the idea of nonexistence. This might change the translation into "The five ministers transforming [their] five appearances [i.e., using their own bodies] together created Heaven and Earth." Since in the *Tâm Đăng*, contrary to the manuscript, there is no mention of colors, we can only guess whether this idea of colors emerged because Adriano di St. Thecla interpreted the 色 as "color," in which case we should translate the phrase in the *Tâm Đăng* as "being, appearance," or whether this concept of colors was contained in the other book, the *Bí Chi*, and the Adriano di St. Thecla interpolated it into his understanding of the *Tâm Đăng*.

[83] Ibid.

[84] See chapter 3.

[85] AC 417, p. 2:a–b.

In the fifth age, they say, there were Tam Hoàng (Sanhuang), or the Three Kings,[86] called by these names: Thiên Hoàng (Tianhuang, Emperor of Heaven), Địa Hoàng (Dihuang, Emperor of Earth), Nhân Hoàng (Renhuang, Emperor of Men).[87] The first was three hundred cubits tall, and in their books they describe him saying that he had one large prominent head of a man, six other smaller heads descending on one side, and five others on the other [side], and these [heads] are said to have been twelve brothers[88] who had been reigning together under the one name Thiên Hoàng for 18,000 years.[89] Địa Hoàng was one hundred fifty cubits tall, and about his appearance they mention that he had one large prominent head of a man and five other smaller heads on each of both sides, and for that reason they are considered to have been eleven brothers, who ruled together under the name Địa Hoàng, also for 18,000[90] {must be corrected to 15,000} years. Nhân Hoàng was one hundred cubits tall, and they describe his appearance as having one large prominent head of a man with four minor heads on each of both sides, and these are said to have been nine brothers, who all together ruled under the one name Nhân Hoàng for 45,600 [years] {must be corrected to 12,600 years}.[91] This number of years, 45,600, is the sum of all the years [p. 92] of all the three Hoàng, as it appears from the testimony of a certain literatus mentioned in the *Chinese History*, who said that these three Hoàng ruled one hundred fifty *thế* (*shi*, generation),[92] and each of these [generations] stands for thirty years.[93] So, the three Hoàng mentioned above were borrowed from the *Chinese History*, in which they directly follow the first man

[86] The manuscript has the Latin *reges* (kings), while *hoàng* (*huang*) is usually translated as "emperor."

[87] AC 417, p. 2:b. The description of these three that follows is completely absent from the *Tâm Đăng*. However, it is indeed found in the *Shiji* (Historical Records) of Sima Qian, in the chapter "Principal Annals of the Three Sovereigns," written by Sima Qian's father Sima. See Eduard Chavannes, trans. and ed., *Les memoires historiques de Se-Ma Ts'ien* (Leiden: E. J. Brill, 1967), 1:17–19.

[88] Chavannes warns against a literal understanding of the word *head*, which might lead one to imagine the emperor as a monster. He suggests reading *head* as a classifier, signifying a number of rulers. Ibid., p. 19 n. 1.

[89] The *Shiji* (Historical Records) does not provide this description, but states: "From the time Heaven and Earth were established for the first time, there were sovereigns of Heaven comprising twelve representatives. They were twelve brothers, each of whom reigned for 18,000 years." Ibid., p. 18.

[90] Ibid. However, there is a discrepancy between the manuscript and the *Shiji* (Historical Records). According to the latter, the brothers ruled successively, and the period of their reign lasted 198,000 years rather than 18,000 years as stated in the manuscript.

[91] The *Shiji* reads that these nine sovereigns reigned for 45,600 years. Ibid., p. 19.

[92] In the *Shiji*, the 150 generations are ascribed to the Emperor(s) of Men, and not to all the three emperors or clan reign periods. Ibid.

[93] I could not find the source to which the author refers, but this explains the corrections he made in the account of the Emperor of Earth (correcting 18,000 to 15,000 years) and the Emperor of Men (correcting 45,600 to 12,600 years). By adding these corrections to the 18,000 years attributed to the Emperor of Heaven, he indeed would come up with the sum of 45,600. I suspect that Adriano di St. Thecla misunderstood the explanation he received from the literati or that the literati upon whose advice he relied were not very knowledgeable about this issue.

Bàn Cổ;[94] however, many Chinese literati rightly consider them fabulous, and also Thiên Hoàng there includes in himself thirteen, not twelve, brothers.[95]

In the book *Bí Chi* they say that in the sixth age there was a woman called Oa (Gua).[96] When Heaven was still not fully joined and continuous, but rather looked as if perforated, she put above her head a stone of five colors, inserted it into weak Heaven, and made it [Heaven] imperishable. However, in the book *Tâm Đăng,* they say that at that age there were the Five Kings or Ngũ Đế (Wudi). The first, undoubtedly, was Nguyên Thỉ Thiên Tôn (Yuanshi tianzun), that is, Primary Source of High Heaven, or Highness of Heaven; the second was Hư Hoàng Đại Đạo (Xuhuang taidao), that is, King of Nothing, the Great Law; the third was Ngọc Hoàng Thượng Đế (Yuhuang Shangdi), that is, Jade King, Supreme Emperor; the fourth was Thái[97] Thượng Lão Quân (Taishang Laojun), that is, the highest and greatest king Lão Tử (Laozi); the fifth Cù Vân Thiên Sư (Quyun tianshi), that is, the clear, bright cloud and the celestial master.[98] These aforementioned Ngũ Đế

[94] These three emperors as well as Bàn Cổ (Pangu) occupied an important place in the pantheon of popular Daoism.

[95] According to Chavannes, this correction was made in the *Tongjian gangmu* (Outline of the Comprehensive Mirror) of Zhu Xi (Chu Hi). There it is indeed suggested that there were thirteen, not twelve, sovereigns of Heaven, each ruling for 18,000 years. Thus, the period of time of their rule would amount to 234,000. If one adds the 198,000 years' reign of the sovereigns of Earth, one comes up with 432,000. "This number is exactly the same as that which represents the duration of ten Babylonian dynasties after the Flood, according to Berose; it is also one that reflects the length of the period of Kali-yuga in India." See Chavannes, *Les memoires historiques de Se-Ma Ts'ien,* 1:18 n. 1. Chavannes suggests the possibility that after the Chinese expanded their contacts with India and the West they decided to adjust their history to correspond with the events in Genesis and with the Hindu Puranic theory of the creation of the world. Ibid., p. 18 n. 1.

[96] Oa (Gua) is the mythical sister or wife and successor of Phục Hi (Fu Xi), who allegedly existed in the period 2953–2838 B.C.E. She appears for the first time in the *Book of Liezi* (fifth century B.C.E.?). "Fu-hsi [Fu Xi], Nü-Kua [Nü Gua, Nữ Oa, 'Lady Gua'], Shen-nung [Shen Nong, Thần Nông], and the Emperors of the Hsia [Xia, Hạ] dynasty had snakes' bodies, human faces, heads of oxen and tigers' snouts. They did not look like men, but they had the virtue of great sages." A. C. Graham, *The Book of Lieh-tzu: A Classic of the Tao* (New York: Columbia University Press, 1990), p. 54. She is also found in the *Shiji*. See Chavannes, *Les memoires historiques de Se-Ma Ts'ien,* 1:9–12.

[97] In both versions of the *Tâm Đăng* that I consulted, instead of the character *thái* (*tai,* highest) there is the character *đại* (*da,* the great). The two characters are very similar and easily conflated; but this substitution does not affect the sense of the title.

[98] AC 417, p. 2b. "The clear, bright cloud and the celestial master," as we will see below, designates Buddha. It is not clear how Adriano di St. Thecla arrived at this translation, since the first syllable *cù (qu)* means "timid look of a bird" and not "clear, bright." However, this syllable is used for transcribing the original family name of Buddha, "Gautama," in which case the second syllable should be not *vân (yun),* or "cloud," but *đàm (tan),* or "dark cloud." And, in fact, this is indeed how it appears in the *Tâm Đăng*. The name should read Cù Đàm Thiên Sư (Qutan tianshi), or Gautama Celestial Master. It might be that the resemblance of the two characters *vân* (雲) and *đàm* (曇) led the author to pick the former for the manuscript and translation. Alternatively, a more plausible hypothesis is that Adriano di St. Thecla was not aware that the compound *cù đàm (qutan)* is a transliteration of *Gautama,* one of Buddha's names, and that the characters were used purely for their phonetic values and not for semantic ones. He might have reckoned that it would be implausible to assume that Buddha's followers ascribed such a "dark" name to their headmaster, so he accordingly amended the original text. I exclude the possibility of a mere error in writing because the pronunciation suggested by the author is in full accord with his translation.

were introduced in a way similar to [the way that] Ngũ Đế [were introduced] in the *Chinese History*. You should note that Lão Quân (Laojun) is wrongly put after Ngọc Hoàng, since the latter lived approximately three hundred years after the former, as is clear from the words about each of them whenever they are mentioned in other texts, and also both of them lived much later after Thích Ca, who is shown [in the book *Tâm Đăng*] as living after them in the next age.[99] Even more, at the time of the aforementioned Ngũ Đế, there also were, as they say, Maha (Great), Đại Ngộ Chân Trí (Dawu Zhenzhi, Great Awakening of the Genuine Mind),[100] and Ban Nhược (Banruo),[101] who made the Sun of five hundred pounds of gold and the same amount of bronze, and similarly they made the Moon of five hundred pounds of gems and the same amount of silver.[102]

In the seventh age, as the *Tâm Đăng* narrates, Thích Ca was born,[103] who in the book *Bí Chi* is wrongly said to have been born in the eighth age. His birth is described in the following way; they say that, first, he descended from Heaven under the name of Như Lai (Rulai),[104] and having met in the southern region [p. 93] Diêm Vương (Yanwang), a king of Hades,[105] immediately was [put] into the womb of a woman called Ma Da phu nhân (Maya furen),[106] and so he was conceived by her; second, later, the mother gave birth to him being surrounded by nine dragons who exhaled water on him, and then from Heaven to Earth a *tràng sinh* (*changsheng*, immortality)[107] plant sprang forth, and its leaves were thereafter

[99] The ordering of these names in the *Tâm Đăng*, which Adriano di St. Thecla perceived as mistaken, might well be explained by the characteristics of the Buddhism presented in this book. Daoism not only intermixed with Buddhism but also seems to have significantly diluted it, which may explain why Buddha is placed after Laozi and the Jade Emperor as if he were their product or follower, which increases the prestige of Daoism over Buddhism. On the other hand, we should not disregard here a potential attempt to appease Buddhists by placing Buddha last, that is, as the "crown" of the creation of the world. As for the Jade Emperor and Laozi, the placement of the former signifies his evidently higher position in the Daoist folk pantheon compared to Laozi, who, even though revered, is hardly considered a deity able to punish, defend, and reward as the Jade Emperor is able to do.

[100] In the *Tâm Đăng* the structure of the sentence is different; it reads: Maha Đại Ngộ (Maha Dawu), i.e., "the Great Awakening," and Chân Trí Phật (Zhenzhi fo), i.e., "the Buddha of the Genuine Mind," presenting them as two different figures. AC 417, p. 2b.

[101] This is an incorrect version of the pronunciation of the term 般 若, which reads *bát nhã (bore)*, or *prajna* in Sanskrit, denoting wisdom. The fact that the author reads this compound as *ban nhược*, the way it is usually read in non-Buddhist contexts, and not as *bát nhã*, as was used only for *prajna*, might indicate his better acquaintance with the spoken language than with Buddhist textual terminology. It is also possible, however, that he reproduces the way *prajna* was pronounced in the eighteenth century. In the *Tâm Đăng*, in any case, this name is absent from the sixth age; it is found in the eight and ninth ages below.

[102] AC 417, p. 2b.

[103] Ibid., p. 3a. The rest of the description, however, is not found in the *Tâm Đăng* and thus seems to be based completely on the *Bí Chi*.

[104] *Tathagata* in Sanskrit, meaning "the one who had gone the path to full awakening," an epithet the Buddha applied to himself and other buddhas. Later this term came to denote the essence of the buddha-nature found in everyone.

[105] Yama, god of the dead, appropriated by the Buddhist pantheon from Brahmanism.

[106] "Lady Mada" (Maya), the mother of Buddha Sakyamuni.

[107] The common modern pronunciation is *trường sinh (changsheng)*. Adriano di St. Thecla's spelling of the first word in this compound is in accordance with the spelling in the previous centuries in Vietnam (as it has been seen in the previous examples in the text).

used with water for the washing of mother and baby; third, when he came out of the womb of his mother, he took seven steps to the south, and the same number of steps to the north, east, and west, and beautiful flowers called *sen* (lotus) sprouted in his footprints; fourth, finally, when he was walking in such a manner, his left hand was raised up toward Heaven and his right hand hung down toward earth.[108]

In the eighth age, as narrated in the book *Tâm Đăng,* Thích Ca, imitating the three aforementioned men who made the Sun and the Moon, again made the Sun of five hundred pounds of gems and the same amounts of gold, silver, tin, and bronze; and in the same way he made the Moon of gems, silver, tin, and bronze using the same weight of five hundred pounds.[109] Nothing is mentioned about this event in the book *Bí Chi,* neither [in the section on] the eighth age nor in any other age. The birth of Thích Ca, ascribed in this book to this age, must be ascribed to the seventh age, and what is said there about the fish captured and offered to Thích Ca must be put under the [chapter on] the eighth age, although in the book *Tâm Đăng* these events refer to the ninth [age], as [can be seen in what] follows.

In the ninth age, they say in the book *Bí Chi,* a man and a woman, or a father and a mother, met each other, or discovered each other. The man looked down at the woman, and the woman looked up at the man, and so vacuum from above moved below, and was called Tì Lô, and its name was Ban Nhược, and a certain percussive musical instrument came into being. This [episode] is completely absent from the book *Tâm Đăng.* It is narrated there that the following events happened in the ninth age. Thích Ca, as they say [in the book], had compassion on people who were without means to sustain a long life. Because of this, his three servants were turned into three kinds of fish, three rivers, and five species of fruit, birds, and animals. The two above-mentioned Đại Ngộ Chân Trí[110] and Ban Nhược, who led solitary lives near the stream called Bàn Cổ, saw three fish, *cá chép* (carp) in the vulgar language, who were eating crops and shaking down grain, and Chân Trí took them [p. 94] and brought them to Thích Ca, who by chance was present there. Thích Ca ordered King Thần Nông (Shennong) to cultivate the fields, to plant rice, to feed these fish, and also to gather crops and winnow grain to feed people, and to pass on to subsequent generations the art of cultivating fields, gathering harvests, and winnowing grain for their sustenance.[111] In the book *Tâm Đăng,* you can see how unbelievable it is that Thích Ca ordered King Thần Nông to teach people agriculture, since Thần Nông lived two thousand years earlier than Thích Ca, for Thích Ca was born during the rule of emperor Chu Chiêu Vương in China. The discrepancy between the stories in the book *Bí Chi* and those in the book *Tâm Đăng,* in their accounts of these nine *kiếp* (*jie,* kalpa), shows how worthless are the events narrated in these [sections on] the nine ages or *cửu kiếp (jiujie);* this [discrepancy] is

[108] On the symbolism of this legend as well as on other versions of the legends of Buddha's birth, see Patricia E. Karetzky, *The Life of Buddha: Ancient Scriptural and Pictorial Traditions* (Lanham, Md.: University Press of America, 1992, pp. 9–31). This legend is very similar to the legend of the birth of Lão Tử (Laozi). For a comparison of the birth legends for Laozi and Buddha see Kohn, *God of the Dao,* pp. 239–242.

[109] AC 417, p. 3a.

[110] Đại Ngộ (Dawu, Great Awakening) is not mentioned in this age in the *Tâm Đăng;* only Chân Trí (Zhenzhi, Genuine Mind) is there. Apparently, Đại Ngộ was added in the manuscript as a result of the conflation of these two as one person as they appeared above.

[111] AC 417, p. 3b.

especially evident in the sixth, eighth, and ninth *kiếp*, [for which the two books] contain events absolutely different from each other.

Moreover, they also say in their books that, first, in the Sun there is a golden bird with three legs, which they call Chim Hạc (crane),[112] and in the Moon there is a white hare called Con Thỏ,[113] and in the same place [in the Moon] the queen called mother Chúa Tiên (zhuxian, chief fairy) has her palace;[114] second, in Heaven there is a certain messenger of Heaven called Trướng Sứ (Zhangshi), or Thiên Lôi (Tianlei),[115] that is, the lightning of Heaven, whom they portray in a human shape with wings of a hawk; and when he is talking, being angry, he makes thunder, lightning, and thunderbolts,[116] and sends fire onto the earth, spreading it among the parts of the world, and he also kills people and animals for pleasure, and he shakes, strikes, and destroys from afar; third, in Heaven, similarly, there is a dragon who from time to time descends to fill the sea, streams, and ponds with water, and who also tears out trees and snatches people, animals, and other things away up high [above ground]. These things often become visible in a whirlwind, which people truly consider to be this dragon and call it so.

They teach the following about a human being: in any human being, indeed, there are three souls with seven vital spirits in a man and nine [vital spirits] in a woman, which they call in the vulgar language: Đàn ông ba hồn bảy vía, Đàn bà ba hồn chín vía. These three souls are not present inside the body of a man or a woman immediately from the moment of birth or conception, but [they appear] only from the fifteenth year of life. Also, nine species of worms are present in the human body, and they produce illnesses inside it.[117] There is Paradise and Hades as a reward or a penalty for the souls [p. 95] in another age; Paradise is located in the western part of Heaven, and the highest king of it is Thích Ca; Hades is situated, indeed, inside of the Earth, it consists of eighteen levels or divisions,[118] ten of

---

[112] A crane is a symbol of longevity and is also considered as a means of transportation "of Taoist [Daoist] Immortals who fly from place to place seated on the backs of cranes." E. T. C. Werner, *A Dictionary of Chinese Mythology* (Shanghai: Kelly and Walsh, 1932), p. 372.

[113] The moon is symbolized by a hare, who, on its hind legs, pounds rice in a mortar. E. T. C. Werner, *Myths and Legends of China* (London: George G. Harrap, 1934), p. 176.

[114] This is a famous Chinese legend, which also became very popular in Vietnam. The legend narrates a story of a woman who stole from her husband the pills of immortality granted him as a reward for his help to divine beings. Having taken the pills, she flew from her house to the realm of heaven and dwelt there on the moon, of which she became the queen.

[115] It is Leigong, the spirit of thunder, "an ugly, black, bat-winged demon, with clawed feet, monkey's head, and eagle's beak, who holds in one hand a steel chisel and in the other a spiritual hammer, with which he beats numerous drums strung about him, thus producing the terrific noise of thunder. According to Chinese reasoning it is the sound of these drums, and not the lightning, which causes death." Werner, *Myths and Legends of China*, pp. 199–200.

[116] The manuscript reads *flumina*, "streams," although it seems to be a scribal error for *fulmina*, "thunderbolts," which better fits the text.

[117] This is also seen in Daoism.

[118] These are "The Eighteen Places of Torment" (*naraka* in Sanskrit). Eitel explains the idea of Naraka in the following way: "There are different torments in different hells; the length of life also differs in each class of hells. . . . It is not necessary that each individual should pass through all the above hells. The decision lies with Yama, who, assisted by eighteen judges and a host of demons, prescribes in each case what hells and tortures are appropriate. His sister performs the same duties with regard to female criminals." See Eitel, *Hand-book of Chinese Buddhism*, pp. 105–106. See for a detailed analysis Stephen F. Teiser, *The Scripture on the Ten Kings and the Making of Purgatory in Medieval Chinese Buddhism* (Honolulu: University of

which are governed by Diêm Vương (Yanwang, Yama), the other eight are ruled by eight families, who are Tao Ma Vu Tịch Xương Tiên Hậu Vi.[119] Souls can be released from Hades by praying and making offerings to the king and rulers, who remit sins and free [souls] from penalty. The priests who make sacrifices to idols boast that they are able to execute this liberation, and they often make a solemn procession, which we will describe in the proper place. Moreover, they teach the transmigration of souls, which they call Luân Hồi (lunhui),[120] saying that souls, having left the body, would—if they were good and especially if they were devoted to the cult of Phật—later move into the bodies of the sons of kings, nobles, literati, and rich men. If they were bad, they would reappear as the children of poor, ugly, and uneducated [men], merchants, or they would also move into lions, tigers, pigs, and dogs, et cetera. They claim that, of the three souls [after death], one migrates, another stays at the tomb, and the third one, indeed, after fifteen years, joins with others [i.e., other bodies]; others say, indeed, that one soul goes down to Hades and, released from the penalties, ascends to Heaven, another stays in the tomb or in any other place, and the third one moves into other bodies.

Moreover, in the internal doctrine, the three souls represent [or are] a father, a mother, and a son; seven *phách (po)* or *vía*[121] are not really seven vital spirits but seven internal organs of a human body,[122] and an equal number of *vía* is ascribed both to a man and to a woman, so there are seven of them for each of the two [i.e., seven each for a man and a woman]. Similarly, in the interior doctrine, *tam tài (sancai)*, that is, Heaven, Earth, and human beings, which [were discussed] in the second age or *kiếp*, means three parts of a human body, namely, the upper part, from the chest up to the head, is Heaven; the lower part, from the navel down to the feet, is Earth; and the part in the middle is a human being; similarly, five generals or kings, Ngũ Tướng Ngũ Đế (wuxiang wudi), of whom [we talked] in the third *kiếp*, are five human internal organs called *ngũ tạng (wuzang)*, namely the heart, the

Hawaii Press, 1994).

119 The Eight Grand Places of Torment (Bát Đại Địa Ngục, Ba da diyu) or Eight Hot Places of Torment (Bát Nhiệt Địa Ngục, Ba re diyu). See Đoàn Trung Còn, *Phật Học Từ Điển*, 1:227, 239. Even though I suspect that the words in Vietnamese represent the names of these Eight Places of Torment or that of the families governing them, I could not identify them or find Chinese equivalents for them. We might imagine that these surnames should be listed with commas, but the manuscript provides no punctuation. The phrase does not make sense if the words are not names.

120 Samsara, the endless migration of souls until one achieves Nirvana, when transmigration ceases.

121 *Phách (po)*, a classical Hán word, and *vía*, its vernacular Vietnamese equivalent, refer to inferior souls that go down into the earth after a person's death, contrary to *hồn (hui)*, the spiritual souls, which ascend to Heaven.

122 Mathews characterizes them as "the seven inferior souls of Taoism." See R. H. Mathews, *Chinese-English Dictionary* (reprint, Cambridge: Harvard University Press, 2000), p. 77, no. 579:32.

liver, the lungs, which, along with the kidneys, are very important, and the stomach.[123] All these things are narrated in the aforementioned book *Bí Chi*.

It seems proper to add here that venerable Father Francisco Gil de Federich, with due erudition, made a remark on the aforementioned in the last letter, written to me three days before his [p. 96] suffering of January 19, 1745. From these words it seems to me that the ages {*kiếp*} that they describe and all these kings are a transformation of an idol into them [into epochs and kings], since they talk about one idol {Phật}, and the effort is to explain the origin of Thích Ca; then the things that happen in reality in the development of the body during different months they explain with the help of these nine *kiếp;* so Thích Ca in the first *kiếp* and similarly in the second was what they describe there. When they explain this, they believe in the transmigration of the souls of Ngũ Đế [and] Bàn Cổ into [the] one [soul of] Thích Ca, and in such a way they convince [others] of this. But we must not stall here, since there would be no end of explaining all their insanities; I did not see any book or material displayed there where madness would not be present, this educated Father [said].

Article 4: On the Main Idols Worshipped in This Sect

Most of all, they worship Thích Ca, whose full name is Thích Ca Mâu Ni Phật (Buddha Sakyamuni), and who established his own sect in India, as we explained in the first article. His followers created amazing fables about him and made them known in their books; in addition to what we have said about his origin, in the third article under the seventh age, or *kiếp*, they add the following: mainly, that thirty-six Heavens were made of his head, that his tongue is a column of Heaven made of gold and gems, that his two arms and two feet are four kings of Heaven, that twenty ribs from both of his sides were turned into twenty idols, and the rest of the bones [were turned] into three hundred sixty {360} [idols], two knees [were turned] into eighty-four thousand {84,000} idols, five internal parts of the body [were turned] into five idols, and in addition major viscera were turned into large rivers, minor [viscera were turned] into small streams; they even worship and have as idols the father, mother, grandfather, and grandmother of the same Thích Ca. They also worship many other idols, which are older than Thích Ca, his parents, and his ancestors. The first among all of them is Uỷ Âm (Weiyin),[124] who is said to

[123] These five viscera are also enumerated as important elements in Daoism and Confucianism. First found in the *Hanshu* (Han Dynastic History), they traditionally were said to have been the sources of the "five characteristics" or traits: irritation, serenity, determination, aggression, and wisdom (Wittenborn, *Further Reflections on Things at Hand*, p. 191).

[124] Uỷ Âm (Weiyin) is apparently a mistake for Uy Âm or Oai Âm (*uy* and *oai* are variants of reading of the same character 威). The full name is Oai Âm Vương Phật (Weiyin wangfo), or Bhismagarjitasvara-raja Buddha. He is the Buddha of the previous kalpa. He "has appeared in the world since the beginning of time, in the age of chaos, and he was the founder of the Zen school." Cuong Tu Nguyen, *Zen in Medieval Vietnam*, p. 103.

have already existed before Heaven and Earth were separated in the first disorder of things: Thiên Địa vị phân, thỉ Uỷ Âm Phật;[125] that is, Heaven and Earth had not yet been separated and then, first, there was the idol Uỷ Âm. After him, five primary ages are counted, the first is [p. 97] Tì Lô, the second Di Đà, the third Di Lạc, the fourth Đại Bi (Dabei),[126] and the fifth Nhiên Đăng (Randeng).[127] Seven idols follow them,[128] namely, the first [is] Di Nha,[129] the second Di Thức,[130] the third Tuy Khí (Suiqi),[131] the fourth Ca Lưu (Jialiu),[132] the fifth Ca Na (Jiana),[133] the sixth Ca Diếp (Jiaye),[134] the seventh Thích Ca Mâu Ni Phật. You see now that Thích Ca existed in the form of many idols, to which in later times you should also add the idols that we have counted in the nine aforementioned ages or *kiếp*.

Besides [these], they venerate Thiên Phủ (Tianfu, Governor of Heaven), Địa Phủ (Difu, Governor of Earth), and Thủy Phủ (Shifu, Governor of Water),[135] [and they] honor Thái Nguyên Chân Quân (Taiyuan zhenjun, Venerable True Source Lord),[136] who is the first among all those who are called *tướng*, and they portray [him] in a shape of three men on one seat. They worship numerous idols, which they call *Bồ tát (pusa)*,[137] that is, those who have ability to release others from

---

[125] 天 地 末 分 始 威 音 佛 .

[126] An abbreviation of Đại Bi Bồ Tát (Dabei pusa), the bodhisattva Avalokitesvara, goddess of Mercy, who attends the Buddha Amitabha. Avalokitesvara is the most popular deity in China and in Vietnam. Originally Avalokitesvara was a male deity in India; in China and in Vietnam, Amitabha acquired female features.

[127] Buddha Dipanikara, the "Light-maker," one of the predecessors of Buddha Sakyamuni, who foretold his advent.

[128] This is the list of the Seven Ancient Buddhas, the last of whom is Buddha Sakyamuni himself. Adriano di St. Thecla took it from the book *Tâm Đăng*; AC 417, p. 18b–20a. In this manuscript the first three Buddhas from this list in the *Tâm Đăng* are given alternative names along with their usual ones.

[129] *Tâm Đăng*, AC 417, p. 18b has Duy Nha (Weiya), an alternative name for Buddha Tì Bà Thi (Piposhi), or Vipasyin. A short story of his transformation into Buddha under the latter name is found in ibid., p. 17b.

[130] His alternative name reads, in the *Tâm Đăng*, 18b, as Duy Sấm (Weichen), while the name under which he is widely known is Buddha Thi Khí (Shiqi), Sikhin. Elsewhere this Buddha has another name, Thức Khí (Zhiqi), the first element of which is incorporated into his alias in the *Tâm Đăng* and subsequently into the manuscript. The story of his enlightenment is found in the *Tâm Đăng*, AC 417, p. 17b.

[131] This follows *Tâm Đăng*, AC 417, p. 18a, being an alternative name for Buddha Tì Xá Bà (Pishepo), Visvabhu. A narrative of his enlightenment is in *Tâm Đăng*, AC 417, p. 18.

[132] An abbreviated form of Ca Lưu Đà Di (Jialiutuoyi), Kalodayin in Sanskrit, a disciple of Sakyamuni who is said to have been reborn later as a Buddha.

[133] An abbreviated form of Ca Na Già Mâu Ni (Jianajiamouni), Buddha Kanakamuni, a Brahman who converted many people and became one of the mythical Buddhas and predecessors of Sakyamuni.

[134] This is Buddha Kasyapa, also a Brahman, who converted a large number of people.

[135] A Daoist division of worldly powers.

[136] The author implies that this may be another name for Thái Dịch, "the Invisible," who was the first among the five Tướng (jiang) recited above in the "third age."

[137] *Bồ tát (pusa)* is "bodhisattva," one who is able to achieve the state of Nirvana but chooses not to complete the circle of his transmigration in order to stay with people and help them to achieve Nirvana.

misfortune. Among them is Quan Âm (Guanyin, Avalokitesvara), whose father is the idol with the name Di Đà, who is said to be the author of the philter, being endowed with the power to free people from marriage and to separate them with divorce. They also worship numerous women, especially Mọc Liên[138] and Màu Tiền.[139] They say that Mọc Liên was a daughter of Emperor Đàng Văn Tống (Tang Wenzong),[140] who secretly left her husband and came to a certain temple of Phật, and there she engaged herself in his cult. Màu Tiền, they say, indeed was a daughter of King Màu Trang Vương (Mou Zhuangwang);[141] since she was suffering because her father and mother did not love her, she left them and also devoted herself to the idol. Many scholars consider her to be the same [person] as the aforementioned Quan Âm.[142] They especially worship the following idols, which, they believe, release them from penalties in Hades, and on the assigned days of each month they fast in honor [of these idols] and invoke their names a thousand times. To each idol a day is assigned, in the book *Tâm Đăng*, in this order: the first day [is assigned] to Định Quang Vương Phật (Dingguang wangfo),[143] the eighth day to Dược Sư Lưu Li Quang Phật (Yaoshiliuli guangfo),[144] the fourteenth day to Hiền Kiếp Thiên Phật (Xianjie Qianfo),[145] the fifteenth day to Ami Đà Phật (Amituofo, Amitabha), the eighteenth day to Địa Tạng Vương Bồ Tát

[138] Today there is no Hán character pronounced *mọc*, but *mọc* is sometimes a variant pronunciation for *mục*. If it is so, then the name in the text may be an abbreviation of the name Mục Kiện Liên (Mu Jianlian in Chinese or Maudgalyayana in Sanscrit), usually called Mulian. However, Mulian is known to be a male, and his hagiography differs from that in the manuscript.

[139] The name of the person referred to here is commonly transcribed in Vietnamese as Miễu Tiên (Miaoshan).

[140] R. 827–41.

[141] The name is known as Miễu Trang Vương (Miao Zhuangwang), a ruler of Xinglin kingdom. "The kingdom of Hsing Lin [Xinglin] was, so says the Chinese writer, situated between India on the west, the kingdom of Tian Zheng on the south, and the kingdom of Siam on the north, and was 300 li in length." See Werner, *Myths and Legends of China*, p. 253.

[142] According to the legend, Miaoshan's father, Miao Zhuangwang, strove to have a male heir, but he did not have any children. He prayed to the gods, and the Jade Emperor was persuaded to meet Miao Zhuangwang's request and grant him children. However, it was decided that for the harm caused by the wars Miao Zhuangwang had waged, he would get female offspring; they would be reincarnations of three evildoers, who in their new lives would be able to perform good deeds. Thus, it happened that in the course of three years Miao Zhuangwang's wife delivered three daughters, the youngest of whom was Miaoshan. She started to observe the Buddhist law from her childhood, and, unlike her sisters, she refused to get married and retreated instead to a monastery. Outraged by her disobedience, Miao Zhuangwang decided to kill his daughter. The Jade Emperor, seeing Miaoshan's virtue, pronounced his decision to deliver Miaoshan, when she died, to Xiangshan (an abode of Buddha), where she could reach Nirvana. A thorough analysis along with different versions of the legend is found in Glen Dudbridge, *The Legend of Miao-shan.* (London: Ithaca Press London for the Board of the Faculty of Oriental Studies, Oxford University, 1978).

[143] Another name for Buddha Nhiên Đăng (Randeng), or Dipanikara. See Kim Cương Tử, *Từ Điển Phật Học Hán Việt*, p. 415.

[144] Buddha Bhaisajyaguru, the Healing Buddha. He is said to receive his healing power from Siddhartha Gautama. He usually dispels misfortunes and averts disasters.

[145] I could not identify this Buddha. Hiền Kiếp (Xianjie) denotes the modern kalpa, Bhadrakalpa. Thiên Phật (Qianfo) means a thousand Buddhas. It appears that the term Hiền Kiếp Thiên Phật (Xianjie qianfo) refers to the thousand Buddhas of the modern kalpa.

(Dizhangwang pusa),[146] the twenty-third day to Đại Thế Chí Bồ Tát (Dashizhi pusa),[147] the twenty-fourth day to Quán Thế Âm Bồ Tát (Guanshiyin pusa),[148] the twenty-eighth day to Lồ Xá Na Phật (Lushena fo),[149] the twenty-ninth day to Dược Vương, Dược Thượng, nhị Bồ Tát (Yaowang, Yaoshang, er pusa),[150] and the thirtieth day to Thích Ca Mâu Ni Phật. So they invoke their names, for example, [on day] thirty Nam Mô Thích Ca Mâu Ni Phật (Namo Buddha Shijiamouni, Homage to Buddha Sakyamuni) [and on] day fifteen Nam Mô Arida Phật (Namo Buddha Amitabha, Homage to Buddha Amitabha).[151] Many [worshippers] use for counting [the number of] these invocations a little crown[152] consisting of a hundred small balls, which they run through [their fingers] until [they count] a thousand [invocations].

Finally, they honor many other idols, for enumeration of which there is very little space [here], but you might look [for information on them] in the book *Tâm Đăng*. Their [i.e. the idols'] calendar is divided into months [p. 98] and days, where the first month contains twelve idols; the second month, fourteen; the third month, eleven; the fourth month, also eleven; the fifth month, ten; the sixth month, twelve; the seventh month, eleven; the eighth month, twelve; the ninth month, eleven; the tenth month, fourteen; the eleventh, thirteen; the twelfth contains twelve idols.[153] It is worth mentioning that the idols in this calendar are placed in triple order, and they are enumerated according to it; the idols of the first rank are given the name Phật (Buddha), [idols] of the second rank are called Bồ Tát (Bodhisattva), Pusa in Chinese, that is, [the name] of a liberator or guardian, those of the third rank are not assigned any similar name and are called each with [its] proper name. All [the idols] are known under the common name *Thánh*, Chinese *Xing* (*sheng*, saint), and this title is ascribed to each month: Chư Thánh dẫn nhật (Zhusheng yinri) or sinh nhật (shengri); that is, birthday of all saints or of men famous for [their] virtue.[154] Some [people] said that this calendar of idols was made by an apostate neophyte similar to the calendar of saints, which the Church has [in use].

---

[146] Bodhisattva Ksitigarbha, the Lord of the Underworld. He is mentioned later in the manuscript.

[147] Bodhisattva Mahasthamaprapta, a prince, who left his secular life and, in monastic seclusion, grasped Buddhism. He belongs to the retinue of Buddha Amitabha.

[148] Another name of Bodhisattva Avalokitesvara. See Kim Cương Tử, *Từ Điển Phật Học Hán Việt*, p. 1039.

[149] Buddha Lochana, Body of Absolute Completeness, is worshipped especially by Buddhist monks. He is a representation of Buddha's essence. Along with Vairocana (Tì Lố, Pilu) he is one of the states in Tantric Buddhism: the state of the ideal reflection of Buddha.

[150] Two bodhisattvas, Bhaichadyaradja and Bhaichadjyaradjasamudgata. They were brothers and royal sons, but instead of choosing a life of luxury they preferred to devote themselves to the doctrine of Buddha.

[151] While the manuscript appears to have "Arida," the vernacular should be A Di Đà.

[152] A *mala* (Sanskrit), or rosary.

[153] The calendar is indeed found in *Tâm Đăng*, AC 417, pp. 25a–34a, but it differs significantly from that suggested by Adriano di St. Thecla.

[154] In the *Tâm Đăng*, AC 417, this calendar is found on pages 23b–24a, where it is called slightly differently: Chư Phật sinh nhật ký (諸 佛 生 日 記), "Register of the Birthdays of All the Buddhas."

In addition to idols they also worship *cô hồn (guhun)*, or abandoned souls deserted by everyone; they say that they [the souls] are so weak that they cannot descend into the Earth, and they stay over the plants and gardens, and therefore on the first and fifteenth day of each month people cook broth from rice and throw it upward over the leaves of the plants to feed [the souls]; people make this broth very thin, because they say that the souls have throats too narrow to swallow. They also believe that these *cô hồn* are the messengers of the king of Heaven, and that they have a register of years of life, which fate had determined for each human being; according to that register, they kill those who have completed their number of years, and there is a fable about this. They say that once there was a woman called Nàng Hành Mãn (Damsel Xing Man), to whom thirty years of life were allotted; when she was sitting on the bridge selling food and drinks to passers-by, she saw three *cô hồn* approaching to kill her; she courteously welcomed them and provided them with food and beer in abundance; they [the souls], satiated, prolonged her life in return for such a favor by changing the years [written in the register] from the sign for ten to the sign for one thousand; since the sign for ten in the Chinese characters is written in the form [p. 99] of a cross [十], they put a small stroke over it, and with this addition the sign ten became one thousand [千], and, instead of thirty years assigned in the register, three thousand years appeared. So this woman lived an exceptionally long life.[155]

Article 5: On the Temples and People Devoted to the Cult of Phật

Temples or sacred places dedicated to Phật exist everywhere; each village has its own [temple], and larger villages have several, which in the vulgar [language] are called *Chùa*. They are situated outside the villages, although close [to them], in a place densely covered with many trees; for that reason it reminds one of groves that pagans in Europe consider dedicated to idols. They have a house for idols, and a house for their worshippers to live in, also a very wide atrium, and a wall going around the place. Major temples have numerous houses put in order one after another, in which the idols are placed; among these houses there is one larger than others, in the middle of which there is a big altar, and two altars stand on both sides lengthwise. On these altars there are wooden or clay images of the idols painted in different colors or covered with gold and silver. On the major altar, one or two or three images with terrible visages are placed together with one small bronze image approximately one cubit high, which is the image of Thích Ca. All other images, located on the side altars, are approximately of the same height. In the center of the house there is a table, on which numerous rods of incense fixed in a small vessel are burnt together with many wax candles. Also, in each temple, there is a bell, hanging high up, which is struck from the exterior on only one side with hammer blows by the hand of a specially appointed man. It is usually done on the new moon and also on the full moon and whenever any solemn offering takes place.

There are men and women devoted to the cult of Phật. They live in the temples of idols and perform ceremonies in honor of those [idols]. Men are called *Sãi* (temple

155 This legend reflects a tendency to ascribe a decisive role to written signs or characters in making vital decisions. As seen here, the character became instrumental as a mediator between a divine will and its implementation on Earth.

wardens), women are called *Vãi* (women helping in the temples); the literary [i.e., Sino-Vietnamese] name for the former is *Tăng* (*seng*, Buddhist priest, bonze), for the latter it is [p. 100] *Ni* (*ni*, Buddhist nun).[156] Some of the men have wives, others are not married; those who lead their lives with wives are called *Sãi Chùa* (temple wardens); those who live without wives are called *Thầy Tu* (bonze). Sãi Chùa are mostly uneducated, do not rigidly observe the rules of their sect, and are assigned to their temples by the elders of the villages; *Thầy Tu* are educated, adhere to the doctrine of their sect more rigidly, and are assigned to more famous temples by a special order of the king; they nourish and teach numerous disciples, conduct their ceremonies with great splendor, and are greatly respected by all. There are, indeed, many women devoted to idols, and they live unmarried, staying in special temples. The clothes of these men and women are dark or black; they have their heads shaved; they eat only rice and fruits of the earth; they always abstain from [eating] meat, fish, and fowl, since in their sect it is forbidden to kill living creatures. This abstinence, or fasting, is called *Trai (zhai)*,[157] or *Chay* [in vernacular Vietnamese].[158] Every day, in houses of idols, they recite many prayers, for which they use the book *Hoàng Đồ Vĩnh (Huang tu yong)*[159] and the book *Tâm Đăng*. There are five rules for them to observe: first, not to kill any living creature; second, not to steal; third, not to engage themselves in depravity; fourth, not to lie; and fifth, not to drink wine.

Finally, there are some persons among the aforementioned *Tăng* who endeavor to grasp Phật and, being eager to reach this highest honor, they burn themselves, since they believe that in combustion they will certainly enter Phật. And if someone offers himself to flames for this purpose, the ceremony is celebrated with a large gathering of worshippers of Phật in the atrium of the temple. Three years ago this ceremony was held in a certain temple of idols in Vĩnh Lại district of the eastern province,[160] close to my residence; but only the corpse was given to fire, since the priest performing the sacrifice was overtaken by death and could not burn in flames

---

[156] Strictly speaking, the vernacular *sãi* is not a complete synonym of the Sino-Vietnamese *tăng (seng)*, just as the vernacular *vãi* does not always coincide with the Sino-Vietnamese *ni (ni)*. The first meaning of the vernacular words in the pair, *sãi* and *vãi*, relates to people who live in temples and carry out auxiliary functions but do not rigidly adhere to the tenets of Buddhism, while the Sino-Vietnamese *tăng (seng)* and *ni (ni)* designate members of the clergy, people who devote their lives to observing the doctrine. Sometimes the secondary meaning of *sãi* and *vãi* as "middle-ranking bonzes/monks/nuns" overlaps with that of *tăng* and *ni*. But, several lines below, Adriano di St. Thecla definitely refers to the primary meaning of *sãi* when he refers to the people called *sãi* as uneducated and uncommitted to strict observance of the doctrine. A synonym of *tăng*, found below, is the compound *thầy tu* (bonze).

[157] This word designates fasting, in the sense of a restricted vegetarian diet. It has also come to denote Buddhist and Taoist sacrifices, and a period when the monks were not supposed to eat after the noonday hour.

[158] It can also mean libation to the dead or a thanksgiving service to images.

[159] I could not locate this book. There might be a mistake in the title. The words *Hoàng Đồ Vĩnh* are actually found on the title page of the book *Tâm Đăng*. They are the first three words of an invocation, "Hoàng Đồ Vĩnh Cố 皇 圖 永 固), which means something like "Let the fortune of the emperor be eternal and firm." Adriano di St. Thecla appears to have cut the phrase short. According to Professor Ngô Đức Thọ, this phrase is very often found on the title pages of texts written during the time of the Lê dynasty, and possibly Adriano di St. Thecla perceived them as a title of the book.

[160] Now it is Ninh Giang district in Hải Dương province.

alive as he intended. This ceremony is called *Thiêu Thân (shaoshen)*, that is, to burn a body. The number of the aforementioned *Tăng Ni* (*sengni*, bonzes and nuns) was indeed so great during the reign of Đàng Cao Tổ (Tang Gaozu),[161] in the sixth century after establishing the sect of Phật in China, that at that time their number was counted as a hundred thousand, as testified by the literatus Phó Dịch, who for that reason encouraged this emperor in the ninth year of his rule to throw them out of the temples and to oblige them to marry, so that later he [the emperor] would be able to summon many soldiers: Kim Thiên hạ Tang Ni số duanh thập vạn, thỉnh linh[162] thất phối, sản dục nam nữ thập niên trương[163] dưỡng nhất kỉ giáo huấn khả dĩ túc binh.[164] [p. 101] You see, however, in these *Tăng Ni* a representation of our native religious and sacred [personalities], whom the demon wanted to liken completely to his servants.

On the Famous Temples of This Kingdom[165]

Kings of the Lí dynasty[166] built numerous temples for idols and expanded their cult to a great extent.[167] King Thái Tổ,[168] in [his] first year, at the beginning of the

---

[161] R. 618-27.

[162] In modern Vietnamese this word is spelled *lệnh* or *lịnh* (*ling*, to give an order). It is not clear whether in the manuscript the sign of the tone under the letter *i* was skipped or the author for some reason indeed read the character 令 as *linh*, which is also possible, according to Thiều Chửu and Trần Văn Chánh, but with a different meaning. See Thiều Chửu, *Hán-Việt Tự Điển* (Sino-Vietnamese Dictionary) (Ho Chi Minh City: Nhà Xuất Bản Thành Phố Hồ Chí Minh, 1997), p. 17; Trần Văn Chánh, *Từ Điển Hán Việt. Hán Ngữ Cổ Đại và Hiện Đại* (Sino-Vietnamese Dictionary. Ancient and Modern Chinese Characters) (Ho Chi Minh City: Nhà Xuất Bản Trẻ, 1999), p. 127.

[163] This word should be read as *trưởng* (*zhang*, to grow up).

[164] 今 天 下 僧 尼 數 盈 十 萬 請 令 匹 配 產 育 男 女 十 年 長 養 一 紀 教 訓 可 以 足 兵 . This is a summarized version of the passage from the memorial sent by Phó Dịch (Fu Yi) to Đường Cao Tổ (Tang Gaozu) in 624, which has not survived but was cited in annals written in the tenth century. It appears in Liu Xu, *Jiu Tangshu* (Old Tang History) (Beijing: Zhonghua shuju qu, 1975), 8:2716. The translation of the phrase in the manuscript is: "Now in the empire the number of Buddhist monks and nuns exceeds a hundred thousand, please order [them] to get married, [then they will] produce men and women; [after] ten years of bringing them up and twelve years of instructing them, [the country will] have enough soldiers."

[165] All the dynasties, kings, and places in this article are Vietnamese unless otherwise indicated, and therefore I do not provide Chinese transcriptions. For a historical survey of Buddhist temples in Vietnam see Hà Văn Tấn, *Chùa Việt Nam* (Buddhist Temples in Vietnam) (Hanoi: Nhà Xuất Bản Khoa Học Xã Hội, 1998).

[166] 1009–1226.

[167] Cuong Tu Nguyen suggests the following explanation of the construction of numerous temples during the Lý dynasty: "During the early centuries when Buddhist missionary monks came to Vietnam (then Jiaozhou), Buddhist temples were still few and far between, so the monks often took up residence in temples or shrines dedicated to local deities. (This explains why the early Lý kings had so many emples built during their reigns.)" Cuong Tu Nguyen, *Zen in Medieval Vietnam*, p. 14. Adriano di St. Thecla concentrates in this manuscript on the temples built by the Lý dynasty, apparently, not only because the Lý dynasty was strongly Buddhist but also, and maybe mainly, because the construction of the temples by this dynasty was carefully reflected in the Vietnamese historical annals. As will be seen below, the data provided by Adriano di St. Thecla very precisely correspond to that of *Đại Việt Sử Ký Toàn Thư* (A Complete History of Great Việt) (Hanoi: Nhà Xuất Bản Khoa Học Xã Hội, 1993), which apparently served as the author's main source on Buddhist temples.

eleventh century of Christ, established two temples for idols, one inside the royal city, called Thiên Ngự, another outside of the city, called Thắng Nghiêm,[169] and he molded a bell of 168 pounds of silver.[170] Already in the seventh year [of this king's reign], more than a thousand worshippers of Phật were living there.

King Thánh Tông,[171] in his third year, established the temple called Báo Thiên,[172] and molded a large bell of twelve thousand pounds of bronze.[173] And, in the fourth year,[174] he built for it a tower three hundred cubits high, divided into twelve floors,[175] and also two other temples, where he placed two golden statues of Thích Ca and of his [Thích Ca's] father, Tịnh Phạn Vương (Jing Fanwang).[176]

King Nhân Tông[177] in the second year [of the reign title] Quảng Hựu,[178] or the year 1086 of Christ, established the Đại Lãm San temple[179] and two years later he built a tower there.[180]

Later, King Huệ Tông[181] abdicated the kingdom to his daughter[182] and went to the temple of idols called Giáo Thuyên,[183] in the year of Christ 1225, and devoted

---

[168] R. 1009–28. Thái Tổ, founder of the Lý dynasty, enjoyed very strong support from the Buddhist temples, enabling him to ascend the throne.

[169] This information is recorded under the year 1010 in *Đại Việt Sử Ký Toàn Thư*, bản kỷ, 2:3b (1:241). In this source the first of the temples mentioned by Adriano di St. Thecla, Thiên Ngự, is identified as Hưng Thiên Ngự Tự, meaning Hưng Thiên Royal Temple. The author misread this phrase, omitting the first character and taking *ngự* (*yu*, royal) as the second syllable of the temple name, which undoubtedly arose from the plausible habit of taking the two characters immediately preceding *tự* (*si*, temple) as the name of the temple.

[170] Ibid., bản kỷ, 2:4b (1:242). *Đại Việt Sử Ký Toàn Thư* records that the bell was made of 1,680 *lạng (ling)* of silver. One *lạng* is equal to an ounce, while Adriano di St. Thecla uses the Latin word *libra*, an equivalent to the Roman pound of twelve ounces.

[171] R. 1054–72.

[172] In *Toàn Thư*, this information is dated in the year 1056 and the full name of the temple is given as Sùng Khánh Báo Thiên, bản kỷ, 3:1b (1:271, under the year 1056). It was built on the site of the present-day Hanoi cathedral. Hà Văn Tấn, *Chùa Việt Nam*, pp. 101–102.

[173] *Đại Việt Sử Ký Toàn Thư*, bản kỷ, 3:1b (1:271, under the year 1056). *Đại Việt Sử Ký Toàn Thư* uses 12,000 *cân (jin)* as the unit of weight. One *cân* equals sixteen ounces, but Adriano di St. Thecla still translates *cân* as *libra*.

[174] The year 1057.

[175] Đại Thắng Tự Thiên tower, also called Báo Thiên. *Đại Việt Sử Ký Toàn Thư* records that the tower was twelve stories high and measured several tens of *trượng (zhang)*, a measure of ten Chinese feet, which does not have an exact equivalent to modern measures since it varied significantly, but it nonetheless suggests that the height was several hundred feet. *Đại Việt Sử Ký Toàn Thư*, bản kỷ, 3:2a (1:272, under the year 1057). *Đại Việt Sử Lược* (Short History of Great Viêt) records that the tower was thirty stories high (see Chen Chingho, ed., *Đại Việt Sử Lược* [Tokyo, 1987], p. 58), which suggests that Adriano di St. Thecla used *Đại Việt Sử Ký Toàn Thư* and not *Đại Việt Sử Lược* as his source.

[176] The construction of the two temples, Thiên Phúc (Kiều Thụy district, Hải Phòng) and Thiên Thọ, is recorded in *Đại Việt Sử Ký Toàn Thư*, bản kỷ, 3:2a (1:272, under the year 1057).

[177] R. 1072–1127.

[178] 1085–92.

[179] The tower was situated on Mount Lãm Sơn, Nam Sơn commune, Quế Võ district, Hà Bắc province. Its construction was completed in 1094 (*Đại Việt Sử Ký Toàn Thư*, bản kỷ, 3:11b, 12b (1:281, 283, under the years 1085, 1094). The remnants of it can still be seen there. Ibid., p. 281 n. 1.

[180] Ibid., 3:12a (1:282, under the year 1088).

[181] R. 1210–24.

himself to their cult. There, a little bit later, he was slain when, amid great clamor, he was required to pass the kingdom on to the Trần dynasty[184] from his daughter Chiêu Hoàng, who married a man from that dynasty called Cự.[185] This king experienced the same [thing] for which literati criticize [the Chinese] Emperor Lương Vũ [Đế] (Liang Wudi), namely, that Lương Vũ was not delivered by Phật, to which he was devoted, but even perished from hunger after being captured by his enemies in the temple. Similarly, Lí Huệ Tông was not delivered by Phật, to which he was devoted, but was killed there [in the temple]. You have these temples enumerated in the *Annamite History Đại Việt*.

The main temples of Phật, which now exist in different places, are the following: Chùa Đàng, very wealthy, situated in the upper part of the southern province;[186] [p. 102] Thày Chùa in the western province,[187] Chùa Quình Lâm in the eastern province in its lower part in Hiệp San district;[188] finally, Chùa Sùng Phủ Lai in the same eastern province. In these temples stay a lot of women from the nobility; these women, devoted to idols, live there unmarried; doubtless they are the daughters of nobles, even of a king, or often concubines; among these is the mother of the governor of the kingdom, called in the vulgar language Chúa (Zhu), who devoted herself to the aforementioned Quình Lâm temple and not long ago finished her life there.[189] Mọc Liên, the daughter of Emperor Đàng Văn Tông, and

---

[182] The Lý dynasty was declining, and the strong Trần clan sought to replace the Lý. King Lý Huệ Tông did not have a male heir, and thus he abdicated in favor of his daughter Chiêu Hoàng, who was married to one of the Trần clan members. According to *Đại Việt Sử Ký Toàn Thư*, she ascended the throne in 1224 (bản kỷ, 4:31b; 1:338). Later she abdicated the throne to her husband, Trần Cảnh, known under his posthumous name Trần Thái Tông, who became the first king of the new dynasty and reigned from 1226 until 1258. This gradual transfer of power was implemented to prevent an impression the the Lý throne had been usurped by the Trần, and to present the transfer as an internal family transition.

[183] According to *Đại Việt Sử Ký Toàn Thư*, Lý Huệ Tông retreated to Chân Giáo temple in the royal palace (bản kỷ, 4:31b–32a; 1:338). This temple was built in 1024 "so that the king could come and watch the chanting of prayers." Hà Văn Tấn, *Chùa Việt Nam*, p. 101.

[184] 1226–1400.

[185] The personal name recorded in the annals is Cảnh. *Đại Việt Sử Ký Toàn Thư*, bản kỷ, 5:1a (2:7). According to Professor Trần Quốc Vượng (personal communication), Cụ is an old local name for a kind of fish and the early Trần princes all had personal names from kinds of fish, which were changed into Sino-Vietnamese literary names when written down in texts.

[186] Chùa Đàng, Đàng Temple, is unidentified. Đàng is a vernacular, rather than a Sino-Vietnamese, word, which can mean highway, or dike, or edifice (as in *thánh đàng*, "saintly house" or "temple"), or a royal court of justice; see Rhodes, *Từ Điển Annam-Lusitan-Latinh*, col. 200–201.

[187] Another pronunciation of this temple's name is Thầy Chùa. It is located at the foot of Sài Sơn Mountain, in Sài Sơn commune, Quốc Oai district, Hà Tây province. For more, see Hà Văn Tấn, *Chùa Việt Nam*, pp. 188–193.

[188] The modern way of writing the name of the temple is Quỳnh Lâm, now in An Sinh commune, Đông Triều district, Quảng Ninh province. This temple, built during the Lý dynasty, was repeatedly rebuilt and repaired. For a description, see Trần Mạnh Thường, *Đình Chùa, Lăng Tẩm Nổi Tiếng Việt Nam* (Famous Communal Houses, Temples and Mausoleums in Vietnam) (Hanoi: Nhà Xuất Bản Văn Hóa-Thông Tin, 1998), pp. 526–527.

[189] I have not been able to identify this person. Inquiries at Quỳnh Lâm Temple, which was utterly destroyed during the French War of 1945–54 and is only now being rebuilt, have yielded no result.

Màu Tiên, the daughter of king Màu Trang, about whom we spoke earlier, were examples for these [women].

Article 6: On the Ceremonies in Honor of Phật

Every new and full moon they make offerings to the idols of Phật in their temples, [where] they offer balls of steamed rice, which they call *Vấn* and *Oản*,[190] and different fruits, especially small yellow figs, which for that reason are called in the vulgar language *Chuối Bụt*.[191] Indeed, they do not offer meat, because it is required in this sect not to kill animals. When the priest carries these [offerings] to the altar, he proceeds with a band on his mouth tied around his head, so that he will not exhale on the offered objects. In front of the statues on the altar they burn many black sticks of incense and several wax candles. Under the sacrificial table of the altar, on one step, they put much silver and gold paper money, and later they burn it in the atrium, when food has already been put on the altar. They strike tympans and other [musical] instruments, and they believe that the spirits of the idols descend, enter their statues, and are present at the ceremony. The priests repeatedly recite various prayers from a book, sitting close to the door outside the building in which the idols are placed, intermingling [their prayers] with different noises; they call this recitation *đọc kanh, đọc kệ* (to read sutras),[192] and they believe that during this recitation idols eat, or try to eat, the offerings. In addition they make different prostrations and prayers, but the prostrations are not done with genuflection, that is, they do not bend their knees as others usually do in sacrifices to the spirits and to the [p. 103] deceased. Also, in private houses, the worshippers of the idols, in the same new and full moon, make their offerings, putting the aforementioned rice on a small table, which they have in the house instead of an altar.

On the first day of every year they erect in front of the door of the house a high pole in honor of Phật to free themselves from demons;[193] the origin of this [tradition] is as follows. There is a story that, once upon a time, the idol Phật had a dispute[194] with a demon because the demon was leading everyone to stray toward his domain;

---

[190] *Vấn*, which does not exist in modern Vietnamese, is listed in Rhodes's dictionary as a synonym or maybe a variant pronunciation of the modern modern *oản*—pronounced then as *uấn* (Rhodes, *Từ Điển Annam-Lusitan-Latinh*, col. 858)—a cone-shaped cake made of roasted glutinous rice used for offerings.

[191] "Buddha's banana"—a kind of very small banana, especially widespread in Northern Vietnam. They are used for common consumption as well as for various ceremonies. There is no classical Latin word for banana, thus Adriano di St. Thecla calls them figs. The Italian Jesuit Christopher Borri, one of the first missionaries to Cochinchina, describes this definitely exotic fruit for Europeans at that time (1624) in the following way: "There is a sort of fruit which the Portuguese call *bananes*, and others Indian figs; though, in my judgement, the name of a fig is neither proper to those in India, nor in Cochin-China, because neither the tree nor fruit has any resemblance with our figs." Cristopher Borri, *Cochin-China* (London: Robert Raworth, for Richard Clutterbuck, 1633), chap. 3, p. 2.

[192] This expression was used also in the chapter of Daoism. There it was written as *đọc canh, đọc kệ*.

[193] The pole is usually erected on the eve of the New Year and stays for a week.

[194] The manuscript is unclear. *Rixam* is a probable reading, since the meaning of "dispute" is appropriate here.

and after many quarrels an agreement was arranged between them that the demon would not enter—and would yield to the idol—any house at the door of which a pole had been erected; other houses, indeed, would be in the possession of the demon. When they both accepted this agreement, the idol or Phật secretly, deceitfully, and immediately [sent] messengers, who warned inhabitants to put a pole in front of their houses in such a way as to become free from the devil. So this ritual has been instituted, and at the beginning of a new year they erect a pole in front of the doors of the houses on which they hang many bunches of silver and gold paper money so that the houses will be free of the demon, where he does not dare to enter, and he passes by as if [the houses] belong to Phật. This pole is called a *nêu*.[195]

Every year, on the eighth day of the fourth month, they celebrate in temples the birthday of Phật, that is, Thích Ca Mâu Ni Phật, whose bronze statue, which is kept over the altar, they wash by pouring over it perfumed warm water, just as newborn babies are washed and cleaned.

Whenever they want, they perform two solemn ceremonies in honor of the idols for the benefit of the deceased; the first ceremony is called *Tiếu (jiao,* ceremony of sacrifice and pouring libations to the death) and the second is called *Chay*.[196] The *Tiếu* ceremony is made in the temples of idols and continues throughout a whole day or night, and it is usually held for the benefit of all the deceased of one family, or one village. The other ceremony, *Chay*, is performed outside the temples in some spacious place, where for this ceremony they make a wide tabernacle called *rạp*. In the vulgar [language], this ceremony is called *Nhà chay* (house for the ceremony of a deceased person's soul), and it lasts for many days according to the desire [of the worshippers]; it is usually held for the benefit of one or more deceased during the triennial mourning period. In each of the two ceremonies, they sacrifice first to the three idols Thiên Phủ, Địa Phủ, and Thủy Phủ, and then to the other idols, and they recite many prayers; and they make sacrifices and prayers of this kind mostly in daytime. [p. 104] They also read the leaf of offering, on which the names of the persons who make offerings are enumerated, and the prayer is made for the deceased in order to obtain release from penalties in Hades; later, a large ceremony for the destruction of Hades takes place, called *Phá ngục* (*poyu*, destruction of prison), to release the soul of the deceased from Hades. It is said in the book *Tâm Đăng* that the author of the *Chay* or *trai (zhai)* ceremony was Emperor Lương Vũ: Lương Vũ lập vi trai hội;[197] this emperor began to rule at the beginning of the sixth century after Christ was born. Emperor Tống Huy Tông (Song Huizong)[198] was the first to establish and practice the *tiếu* ceremony, as Phan Thị Vinh testifies in the

[195] Trần Quốc Vượng explains the symbolism of the *nêu* in the following way: "*Nêu* is a kind of 'cosmic tree' (arbre cosmique), a concept of which exists in every nation. . . . *nêu* is a symbol of *dương* [yang, the male, positive source] fighting with demons, which in the East are considered as *âm* [yin, female, negative source]." See Trần Quốc Vượng and Vũ Tuấn Sán, *Hà Nội Nghìn Xưa* (Hanoi of Times Immemorial) (Hanoi: Sở Văn Hóa Thông Tin, 1975), p. 263.

[196] *Chay* is a vernacular analogue to both *trai (zhai)*, mentioned above and *tiếu (jiao)*. Anthony Trần Văn Kiệm, *Giúp Đọc Nôm và Hán Việt* (An Aid to Read Demotic Vietnamese and Sino-Vietnamese Characters) (Hue: Nhà Xuất Bản Thuận Hóa, 1999), pp. 330, 860, 874.

[197] 梁 武 立 為 齊 會 . AC 417, p. 5a. The exact citation would be Lương Vương lập vi trai hội: 梁 王 立 為 齊 會 that is, King Lương established assemblies for fasting. The translation in the manuscript replaced this royal title *vương* (*wang*, king) with the emperor's personal appellation Vũ (Wu).

[198] R. 1101-1126.

book *Tổng Luận*: Phượng đạo chi cần, thiết tiếu chi hậu hữu hà dĩ gia ư đạo quân;[199] that is: He respected the law eagerly, and established the *tiếu* ceremony, spending much on it; is there anyone greater than Emperor Huy Tông (Huizong) in this regard? {He is descriptively called Đạo quân (Daojun), or the king of the Đạo sect}. Huy Tông became emperor in the twelfth century after Christ was born. Both of these ceremonies are openly condemned and derided in the *Ritual, Gia Lễ* (*Jiali*, Family rituals), which deals with the question of *hồn bạch*, Chinese *hoen pe* (*hunbai*, soul on the white [band]),[200] in the sense that whoever performs ceremonies of this kind for the father and the mother does not respect them because he considers them sinners who need absolution and release from Hades. However, my opinion, not to say conviction, is that the *Phá ngục* rite, which will be described shortly, was brought in with the skill of a demon to set it in opposition to the sacred rituals, which by order of the Church the priest performs around the tomb of the deceased, and to prepare to the demon, in this ritual, a cult equal to [worship] rendered to God. Besides the aforementioned solemn ceremonies[201] in honor of idols for the benefit of the deceased, they also make another [ceremony], not a solemn one, called *xám hối* (repentance), which continues no more than an hour or two, in which they make only one offering with one recitation of prayers without a [special] ceremony.

The Phá Ngục (Poyu) Rite

Destruction of Hades, called *Phá ngục*, is performed with the following ceremonies: in the center, they construct a square hut of several reeds each separately inserted [into the ground], and they stretch around them, instead of walls, several bunches of woven material, or silk, or papyrus, to the height of one cubit. They also mark five doors in it, four [p. 105] on the four sides and one in the center, which correspond to the four parts of the world and its center. Each of these has its own guardian idol: the eastern door has Thanh Đế (Qingdi), the Green King; the western [door] has Bạch Đế (Baidi), the White King; the southern has Xích Đế (Chidi), the Red King; the northern has Hắc Đế (Heidi), the Black King;[202] and the central has Hoàng Đế (Huangdi), the Yellow King. The priest, with his assistants, approaches this structure, dressed in a capote resembling our rain cloak, his head covered with a very beautiful felt cap of a different color, and he holds a staff in his hand; sometimes three priests, not only one, are dressed this way. They make the sacrifice by offering food and burning sticks of incense, first, simultaneously to ten idols, who together reign in Hades, and are called *thập Điện*

---

[199] 奉 道 之 勤 設 醮 之 厚 有 何 以 嘉 於 道 君 .

[200] Mentioned in the chapter on Confucianism.

[201] There is a mistake in the text here. The manuscript reads *solemnem functiones*. Since later in the text these two ceremonies are opposed as solemn and non-solemn, one can assume that *solemnem* (acc. sing.) should really be *solemnes* (acc. pl.) as the attribute to *functiones*.

[202] The worship of these four emperors corresponding to the four directions traces back to antiquity. The first two were worshipped at least as early as the eight century B.C.E., while the last two were worshipped no later than the beginning of the Han dynasty (201 B.C.E.–221 C.E.). See Michael Loewe, "The Heritage Left to the Empires," in *The Cambridge History of Ancient China, from the Origins of Civilization to 221 B.C.*, ed. Michael Loewe and Edward L. Shaughnessy (Cambridge: Cambridge University Press, 1999), pp. 980–981.

Minh Vương (*shi dianmingwang*, Underworld Kings of Ten Palaces).[203] Second, they sacrifice to the idol Địa Tạng (Dizang, Kshitigarbha), who accompanies [people] to Hades and shows in what place a soul, which they ask to release, is held. Third, they sacrifice at each door to every guardian, so that they [the guardians] will open the door and let the soul out. Before every sacrifice they go around the hut three times, and, after the sacrifice is accomplished, they throw two coins, and if they fall different sides up, one face up and the other face down, idols are considered to have heard the prayers favorably. If the coins fall together face up or face down, spirits are considered unlikely to have heard the prayers; for that reason, they repeat sacrifices and prayers as many times [as it takes], until the thrown coins lie differently. After having obtained a sign that their prayers have been heard, the priest strikes and breaks with a staff, or throws down, some bowls placed on the door; after that they consider the door to Hades to be open; after all the sacrifices and prayers are over, and all the doors are unlocked in such a way, the *ngục* (*yu*, prison) hut is destroyed [in the following way]: many [participants] eagerly detach the woven material, silk or papyrus, placed around [the reed stakes]; in this way they believe the soul is liberated from Hades. Furthermore, for the purpose of clarity, it might be useful to show a drawing of the aforementioned *ngục* hut, as it is described in the book titled *Hoàng Đồ Vĩnh*, which the priests of the idols use for their prayers and ceremonies.

[p. 106]

---

[203] This expression reflects the division of Hades, traditionally located in the center of the earth, into ten parts, each of which is governed by a certain genie or Buddha. The ruler of the underworld is the god of the dead, Yama. All the gods of Hades and their assistants are subjects of the Jade Emperor, the supreme god of the Daoist pantheon. Henri Doré, *Recherches sur les superstitions en Chine, Le panthéon chinois* (Shanghai: Imprimerie deT'ou-sè-wè, 1914), 6:168. This is further evidence of conflation of Buddhism and Daoism into one popular tradition. For a detailed analysis of the Underworld Kings of the Ten Palaces, see Teiser, *Scripture on the Ten Kings*.

Figura ngục

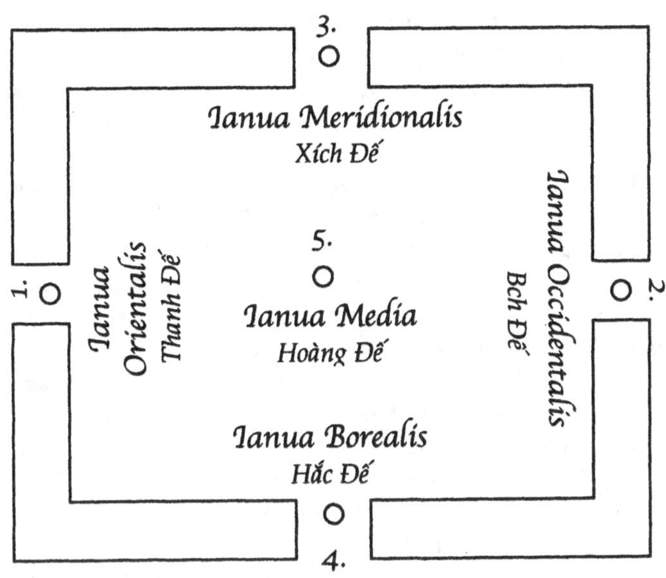

Picture of the *Ngục* (*yu*, prison): *1*, eastern door—Thanh Đế (Qingdi, the Green Emperor); *2*, western door—Bạch Đế (Baidi, the White Emperor); *3*, southern door—Xích Đế (Chidi, the Red Emperor); *4*, northern door—Hắc Đế (Heidi, the Black Emperor); *5*, central door—Hoàng Đế (Huangdi, the Yellow Emperor).

Besides [this ceremony], from time to time they make a solemn procession in honor of the idols, which is descriptively called *hội* (*hui*, to assemble or to hold a festival), or *kéo hội* (to assemble to parade images), and it is celebrated with a great concourse [of people] during many days. From all the villages of the *tổng* (*zong*, canton) or *huyện* (*xian*, district) come people who have been invited in advance by the village celebrating the festival. The day before the procession is made by the arriving villagers, the priest, with others, leaves the temple to which the guests will come in procession, and goes to another temple of another village in order to bring the idol of Phật from that place to his own temple. This action of leading the idol away does not happen by taking and carrying away his statue, but only by as if leading his spirit; from that place an empty tabernacle is carried without any statue or image, which several women, devoted to idols, follow, carrying over their heads a white band stretched out, which they say is a bridge, over which the spirit of the idol proceeds and comes into the temple. This [action] of leading the idol away, which in the vulgar language is called *rước Bụt* (to stage a procession for the Buddha), is also performed on other occasions. During the next several days, processions of the guest villages take place, each of them making its own procession, one by one at different times. They go in processions of this kind dressed in special clothing with the different sounds of [musical] instruments; they approach the temple [p. 107] and go around it, enter its atrium, and when passing the house of idols they venerate them [the idols] with prostrations. Several girls called *tướng* (*xiang*, ministers or assistants) go before them, dressed in ornamented clothing, with painted faces, and they proceed keeping their eyes fixed on an inscribed scroll, or on pincers, or on a knife which they hold with both hands, and they do not dare to look to either side, since, if they serve unsatisfactorily, they are despised and deprived of their reward. When they come to the atrium of the temple, they give the inscribed scroll or the leaf to the seniors of the village, who are standing and sitting there; on this [leaf is written] the name of the village which came to [participate] in the procession, and the amount of money that was offered is then marked. After the procession is over, they rejoice, play comedies, and, finally, they feast; and the banquet is prepared by the seniors of the village having the *hội*. So much for the ceremonies of idols.

To make this [narration] complete it is useful to add that literati criticized the sect and the cult of Phật in their numerous books; the most zealous among them are: the literatus Phó Dịch, who presented to Emperor Đàng Cao Tổ, in the ninth year of his rule, in 626 after Christ was born, a petition to plead for the expulsion of the law and the cult of Phật [from China]; the literatus Hàn Dù (Han Yu),[204] who also presented a letter against the sect of Phật to Emperor Đàng Hiến Tông[205] in the fourteenth year of his reign in 819 after Christ; also the literatus Phan Thị Vinh, who lived during the time of the first emperor of the Minh (Ming) dynasty,[206] in the book *Tổng Luận* on Chinese history mentioned above, [warned][207] the emperors strongly against worshippers of Phật.

Literati really have a triple reason to despise, reject, and criticize the sect of Phật. First, because Phật is an outsider and a foreigner, since Thích Ca lived in the mountains of India and there accepted from demons the idea of his sect. Second, because Phật is unaware of the proper obedience of subjects toward the king and of children toward their parents and, because of this, those who are especially addicted to the idol Phật do venerate kings or [their] father and mother not with prostrations, according to the tradition of that kingdom, but only with bows. Third, because Phật scarcely releases from evils, but his cult is rather a cause of evils, [because] kings [who were] followers of Phật endured much suffering and the state was much afflicted from the time they started worshipping Phật. They [the literati] declare and say this repeatedly in their books.

---

[204] Hàn Dù (Han Yu, 768–824) was the greatest Chinese prose writer after the historian Sima Qian. Han Yu was a notorious anti-Buddhist. This is a reference to his diatribe against the position and influence of Buddhism in China. It was written in response to moving a relic of Buddha into the imperial palace accompanied by fervent Buddhist adherents.

[205] R. 806–21.

[206] 1368–1644.

[207] This word is unreadable.

CHAPTER SIX

ON THE CHRISTIAN RELIGION AMONG THE CHINESE AND ANNAMITES

[p. 108]

After we have spoken on the sects of the Annamites and the Chinese, it is certainly fair to speak about the Christian religion, which has long been preached and widely propagated among both [peoples].

Article 1: On the Christian Religion in China

Faith in Christ was twice introduced to the Chinese.

First: At the end of the sixth century and the beginning of the seventh century after Christ was born. When Mahumetes[1] gained victory in war and subdued the Greek Empire,[2] at the end of the sixth century, he started a harsh persecution in

[1] The reference here is, apparently, to the prophet Muhammad or his followers. The end of the sixth century or the beginning of the seventh seems to be a premature dating of the events described here. Muhammad preached first in Mecca, and later, in 622, fled to Medina, where he and his teachings were recognized and where he established a Muslim community. Upon his death in 632, his successors launched military campaigns that within a century brought huge territories, from Spain across Central Asia to India, under the Arabs' sway.

[2] The Greek empire did not exist at that time, since it came to its end with the death of Alexander the Great in 323 B.C.E. The empire to which the author is referring is the Byzantine empire, heir to Hellenistic civilization; it lasted from 300 to 1453 C.E. and comprised the eastern part of the Roman empire, which survived for a thousand years after the western part disintegrated into various kingdoms. The Byzantine army was completely defeated by the Muslims at the battle of the Yarmuk River in 636, and in 642 Alexandria capitulated, opening Palestine and Syria to Arab Muslim control. From then the Arabs began their victorious march to Northern Africa, Persia (Iran), and India. It is also possible that Adriano di St. Thecla referred here not to the Arab conquest but to the incessant conflict in the Arabian Peninsula, in which Persia and Rome, during a nearly one-hundred-year-long war (540–629), tried to eliminate each other. The persecution mentioned in the manuscript might also be related to the hardships of Nestorianism in Zoroastrian Persia, although this was concerned not with the Arabs but rather with the Persians; there is no historical data, but only some speculation, about the penetration of Nestorianism into China before 635. "As early as 455, a Persian embassy had reached the Wei dynasty capital in north China just outside the Great Wall at Ta'tung, and Persian Nestorians might therefore conceivably have been in China before the end of the fifth century. But that is

Asia of those who were faithful to Christ. For that reason many Christians fled to foreign lands to escape persecution. At that time, a certain Palestinian presbyter with the name Isbuzaddes went first to India and then a little later came to China, where he arrived in Kuei Cheu (Guizhou) province[3] and turned many [inhabitants] to faith in Christ with his sermons;[4] [this happened] during the reign of the Sui

---

speculation." Samuel Hugh Mofett, *A History of Christianity in Asia* (Maryknoll, NY: Orbis Books, 1998), 1:290. See also Kenneth Scott Latourette, *A History of Christian Missions in China* (Taipei: Ch'eng-wen Publishing, 1966), pp. 48–51. As for the advent of Christianity into China—which, according to Adriano di St. Thecla, was caused by Arab persecutions—a more probable explanation is the Arab tolerance of Christianity and their willingness to include Christian missionaries in their foreign embassies. In short, in the seventh through eighth centuries Christianity, apparently, arrived in China not through force but through goodwill.

[3] Guizhou, a province in southwestern China, situated on a plateau and very difficult of access. Guizhou was not a province during the Sui or Tang dynasties but became one only later under the Ming dynasty (1368–1644).

[4] During the Tang dynasty, Christianity indeed arrived in China, but it was a Christianity of a special kind: Nestorianism, which originated in Asia Minor and Syria and spread widely over Sassanid Persia in the fifth and sixth centuries. Its founder, Nestorius, was born in Syria Euphoratensis (date unknown) and died in the Thebaid, Egypt, ca. 451. This branch of Christianity stressed the independence of the divine and human natures of Christ and, in effect, suggested that they were two persons loosely united. In Persia it proclaimed its full independence of Christian churches elsewhere, thereby freeing itself of suspicions about foreign links. In Chang'an, the capital of the Tang dynasty, there were a number of Nestorian churches, whose congregations, however, were mainly of foreign origin. Nestorian Christianity enjoyed state protection until it was forbidden along with other foreign religions in China in 842–45, and thereafter Nestorianism never reappeared in China. In the numerous sources that I have consulted, I could find no person with a name similar to Isbuzaddes whose biography fits this description. But someone with a clearly similar name is Izd-buzid (other versions of his name include Sazd-bozed, Yazd-bozed or I-ssu), a Nestorian priest and a native of the city of Balkh (in the territory of modern Afghanistan). In 781 he erected a stele, near Chang'an, known as the Nestorian monument, commemorating the mission (635–49) of another Nestorian, a Persian, named Alopen, mentioned below. See, for example, Paul Pelliot, "Chrétiens d'Asie Centrale et d'Extrême-Orient," *T'oung Pao* 15 (1914): 625. It is possible that "Isbuzaddes" is not Izd-buzid but someone else, but such a coincidence is unlikely. Mentioning Izdbuzzade, Adriano di St. Thecla relied on sources contemporary to him, among which two are mentioned below in the manuscript: *Mapamundum Historicum* (Historical Atlas of the World) by Antoni Foresti, and *China Illlustrata*, by Athanasius Kircher. While I could not consult the first source, the second makes explicit mention of Isbuzzade, whose name there is transcribed as Jyzbuzad. It is said of him, however, that he was the one who erected the stele at the end of the eighth century to commemorate the mission of Alopen, of whom the author writes below. The apparent reason that led to Adriano di St. Thecla's confusion is that Kircher's book mentions this person immediately following a description of persecutions of Christians in Syria, Egypt, and Ethiopia, as a result of which they fled first to Persia and later to Asia. Kircher then says: "It is likely that about 600 A.D. in the reign of the [Roman] emperor Heraclius [r. 610–41], when treacherous, perfidious Mohammed was gaining power, new colonies of Christians were planted in these eastern regions. Certainly the Babylonian and Syrian priests retreated before the fury of the infidels, and did not stop propagating the Christian faith with the passage of time. The above mentioned Syrian inscription [the Nestorian monument commemorating missionary activity of Alopen in the seventh century] amply shows this, where Jyzbuzad the priest and chorepiscopus of Cumdan [Chang'an] is said to be 'the son of Noe, a priest who came from a city of Turchestan called Belech.'" Athanasius Kircher, *China Illustrata*, trans. Charles D. Van Tuyl (Oklahoma, 1987), p. 47. It is possible that while reading this passage and skipping the translation and description of the stele, Adriano di St. Thecla jumped to the conclusion that Jyzbuzad appeared in China immediately with the rise of the Arabs. But since he provides in his manuscript a detailed description of the stele similar to that in Kircher's book, I would attribute this inaccuracy to the aberration of his memory, which is perfectly

dynasty, Tùy in Annamite,[5] which directly preceded the Tang, or Đàng, dynasty. Several Syrian priests closely followed him, and, inspired by his example, came to China from Syria during the reign of Emperor Tang Tai Zung (Tang Taizong), or Đàng Thái Tông,[6] who had been ruling for twenty-three years from the year of Christ 627. The most remarkable among them was the priest Olopuen (Alopen), who deservedly is called the Apostle of China, since he brought the Christian faith in Hu Kuang (Huguang),[7] Kiang Si (Jiangxi),[8] and Fo Kien (Fujian)[9] provinces.[10] A famous monument of this event was discovered in the year of Christ 1625 in the capital city Si Gan (Chang'an)[11] of Xen Si (Shanxi) province.[12] [It was] a stone board slab of pyramidal shape, which had a cross on top [p. 109] and many Syriac[13] and Chinese characters written on the bottom, indicating that the preaching of the Christian faith grew greatly in China from the year of Christ 636 due to priest Olopuen, mentioned above. This stele is located in the most frequented temple of idols in this country, where it is visible to everyone in the atrium or in the garden of the temple.[14] Father Athanasius Kircher from the Society of Jesus provides a picture of this stele in his *China Illustrata*,[15] which I saw in Milan in

---

understandable taking into account that he read the book in Milan and cited from it in Vietnam. On the whole, one can only admire Adriano di St. Thecla's memory.

[5] 581–618.

[6] R. 627–50.

[7] Huguang province existed in central China up to the seventeenth century, when it was divided into two provinces, Hunan and Hubei.

[8] Jiangxi is a rich agricultural province in south-central China, which, due to the construction of the Grand Canal, lay on the main route between northern and southern China during the Tang dynasty.

[9] A province located on the southeast coast of China, northwest of Taiwan.

[10] According to the Nestorian monument, Alopen was warmly received by Emperor Tang Taizong, who initiated the study of the new religion and ordered that books brought by Alopen be copied for the imperial library and disseminated. "Alopen was promoted to be Great Spiritual Lord, Protector of the Empire; the religion spread over the ten provinces; monasteries occupied every city." P. M. d'Elia, *The Catholic Missions in China* (Shanghai: The Commercial Press, 1934), p. 7 .

[11] Chang'an was a magnificent cosmopolitan capital of the Sui (581–618) and the Tang dynasties (618–907) and a place of attraction for numerous foreign traders, clergy, and immigrants. It was renowned for its beauty, wealth, and tolerance of new influences. Abandoned by later dynasties, the city ceased to play any significant role in Chinese history from the end of the ninth century.

[12] Shanxi, a province located northeast of Honan province, in its heyday was the site of the imperial capital during the Sui and Tang dynasties. It shared the fate of its capital, Chang'an, and fell into decay under later dynasties, and it has turned into one of the least developed and poorest provinces in China.

[13] Syriac was an ecclesiastical language.

[14] There are several works devoted to the discovery of this stele in a Nestorian church in Chang'an. See, for example, Pelliot, "Chrétiens"; also, J. Legge, *The Nestorian monument of Hsî-An fu in Shen-hsî, China: Relating to the diffusion of Christianity in China in the Seventh and Eighth Centuries* (London: Trubner, 1888); P. Y. Saeki, *The Nestorian Monument in China* (London: Society for Promoting Christian Knowledge, 1916). It is also cited in most of the works on the Tang dynasty and on early Christianity in China.

[15] The Society of Jesus (Company of Jesus, or Jesuits) is a religious order founded in the 1530s by Saint Ignatius Loyola (1491–1556) together with his followers, among whom was St. Francis Xavier, mentioned in the text below. The society is a mendicant order whose goal is

our library of the Convent of St. Cosma and St. Damian. For the description of these events, see the seventh volume of *Mappamundum Historicum* (Historical Atlas of the World) by Father Antonio Foresti,[16] in the description of the life of the second emperor of the Tamgu dynasty, that is, Tang dynasty, and in the description of the life of the fifteenth emperor of the Mina[17] dynasty, that is, Ming.[18]

Second: The Christian religion was preached to the Chinese six centuries later during the rule of Emperor Sung Ly Zung (Song Lizong), Tống Lý Tông in Annamite, who started ruling from the year of Christ 1229.[19] In his time, when the western Tartars[20] were subduing the Chinese empire to their power, two illustrious Venetian men arrived in China, the first among all Europeans, namely, Niccolo and Marco Polo, a father and son, who fought vigorously in China on the side of the Tartars against the aforementioned emperor, and who conquered numerous cities.[21] Also at this time two preachers of the Gospel from the order of Friars Minor came

---

apostolic work. It sent its first mission to China in 1552. In 1773 the Society of Jesus was disbanded.

Father Athanasius Kircher (1601–80), a Jesuit, was extremely broadly educated in the classics as well as in natural sciences. He was a professor of mathematics and philosophy at different universities in Germany, France, and Italy. He never voyaged to China; in fact, he never traveled outside of Europe beyond Malta. His syncretic *China Illustrata* (ca. 1666), based on the oral and written accounts of the European missionaries, examines numerous aspects of Chinese history, culture, and language. Translated into several European languages, it became very influential in the European perception of China. For its modern translation into English see Kircher, *China Illustrata*, trans. Van Tuyl. For an analysis see D. E. Mungello, *Curious Land: Jesuit Accommodation and the Origins of Sinology* (Honolulu: University of Hawaii Press, 1989). Mungello considers Athanasius Kircher a "proto-sinologist." Ibid., p. 340. The description of the stele borrowed by Adriano di St. Thecla is found in Kircher, *China Illustrata*, pp. 20–42.

[16] Father Antonio Foresti (?–1692) was an Italian Jesuit, a professor and the rector of a number of Italian colleges. He is the author of several works on the penetration of Christianity into different parts of the world. The four-volume *Mappamundum Historicum*, his last work, was published in Parma and Venice in 1690–94. See *Enciclopedia Universal Ilustrada Europeo-Americana* (Barcelona: Hijos de J. Esposa, 1924), 24:395. Since Adriano di St. Thecla refers in the manuscript to the seventh volume, I assume that he either used a different edition from the one mentioned in *Enciclopedia* or did not remember the exact volume number.

[17] Here the author apparently reproduces the spelling used in *Mappamundum Historicum*. In *China Illustrata* the Tang dynasty is designated as *Tam*, not *Tamgu*.

[18] Tang Taizong (627–50) and Minh Guangzong (1620–21) respectively.

[19] R. 1225–65.

[20] The reference here is to the Mongols, who took over the Chinese throne in 1280 and proclaimed the Yuan dynasty, which lasted till 1368.

[21] Niccolo Polo, together with his brother Matteo, made his first trip to China from 1254 to 1269. In 1271 they set off again, this time accompanied by Niccolo's son, Marco. They arrived in China at the time when the Sung dynasty was suffering defeat by the Mongols. Khubilai (who adopted the Chinese dynastic name Shizu, 1260–94) actually occupied the throne of China from 1280. He preferred to employ foreigners rather than Chinese officials to avoid dependence on the latter. Marco Polo (1254–1324), rather than conquering cities, as claimed in the manuscript, collaborated with the ascending dynasty as a mathematician, administrator, and diplomat; he was entrusted with governing the big commercial city of Yangzhou and other missions. Marco Polo left China in 1292 and returned home through Vietnam, Java, Malaya, Ceylon, the Malabar Coast, Mekran, and the southeast coast of Iran. He returned to Venice in 1295.

to China,[22] namely Father Nicholas Vicenza and Father Guillermo de Tripoli,[23] who not long before were sent to Tartary by Pope Gregory X;[24] to that place they were led by the aforementioned Niccolo of Venice (Niccolo Polo), who had requested [their appointment] from the highest pontiff;[25] due to their deeds, the Christian faith became known in China for the second [time]. It spread even wider, flourished for a long time, and had numerous worshippers and followers, for as long as the western Tartars held the Chinese empire. The aforementioned Marco Polo, when he returned back to Italy, was the first to bring information about the Chinese nation and make it known there.[26] You will have this in the seventh volume of *Mappamundum Historicum*.

Later, the Christian faith, three centuries after it had been introduced by the earlier sermonizing, was preached again in China by European preachers. First of all, Father Martin de Herrada tried this work; [he was] a Spaniard from our order of Brothers Hermits of St. F. Augustine.[27] In the year of Christ 1575—the third

[22] The Friars Minor (or Lesser Brothers) is one of the first orders of the Franciscans, founded by St. Francis of Assisi (1182–1226) in the thirteenth century. Because of their clothes, a gray tunic with a white cord at the waist, their English name is the Grey Friars. The first Franciscan with a special mission to China was Antonio de Santa Maria (?–1669), who was sent to China in May, 1633, and took an active part in their discussion over the Rites. In four years the Franciscans were expelled from China, due to the same Rites controversy, and resumed their activity later. The first Franciscan missionary to China was Father Pedro d'Alfaro; the first permanent mission was established in the 1660s.

[23] This is a mistake. Fathers Nicholas Vicenza and Guillermo de Tripoli belonged not to the Order of Friars Minor (the Franciscan Order), but to the Order of the Friars Preachers (the Dominican Order) in Paris. Jacobus Quétif et al., *Scriptores ordinis Praedicatorum recensiti: Notisque historicis et criticis illustrati* (Enumerated Authors of the Order of Preachers Famous among Known Historians and Critics) (Lutetiae Parisiorum: J. B. Christophorum Ballard, 1719–21), 1:264–265. The Order of the Friars Preachers was founded in 1215 in Spain and quickly spread over Europe. The members of the order combined the contemplative life with active community and missionary work. Thomas Aquinas, one of the most prominent of the church philosophers, belonged to this order.

[24] Gregory X (1210–76) was chosen to be the highest pontiff in 1271.

[25] Latourette writes of them: "Armed with papal letters to Khubilai and accompanied by two Dominicans, Nicholas of Vicenza and William [Guillermo] of Tripoli, and Marco, the son of Nicolo, the Polos made their second start in November, 1271. Before the party had proceeded far, a war so frightened the Dominicans that they turned back and left the Polos to go alone. The latter continued their journey, and in due course of time reached Cathay." Latourette, *History of Christian Missions*, p. 68.

[26] He wrote a well-known book of memoirs, *Il Milone*, which is usually translated into English as *Description of the World*.

[27] This name is used in Latourette, *History of Christian Missions*, p. 90, and in Pacifique-Marie Chardin, *Les Missiones Franciscaines en Chine* (Paris: Auguste Picard, 1915), p. 21, whereas Antonio Sisto Rosso in his *Apostolic Legations to China of the Eighteenth Century* (South Passadena, Calif.: P. D. and Ione Perkins, 1948), p. 48, and some other sources, use the name Martin de Rada. Other possible names include Arrada, Errada, and Rrada. See Isacio Rodriguez Rodriguez and Jesus Alvarez Fernandez, *Diccionario Biografico Agustiniano, Provincia de Filipinas* (Valladolid: Estudio Agustiniano, 1992), 1:93. Born in Navarra in 1533, educated in Paris and Salamanca, Father de Rada arrived in the Philippines in 1565. Ten years later he departed for China, becoming the first Spanish missionary to enter China. Expelled from China shortly after his arrival, he returned to Manila. He died in Borneo while accompanying the governor of the Philippines on his trip there in 1578. Manuel P. Merino, *Agustinos Evangelizadores de Filipinas (1565–1965)* (Madrid: Ediciones Archivo Agustiniano, 1965), p. 258. His detailed biography is found in Teofilo Aparicio López, *Misioneros y*

year of Emperor Ming Xin Zung (Ming Shenzong),[28] or Minh Thần Tông in Annamite—he came to the Chinese empire to preach the Christian faith. In June he came to Che Kiang (Zhejiang) province[29] from the Philippine islands with his companion Jeronimo Marin of Mexico;[30] but he could not stay in China for long, [p. 110] since by the order of the viceroy of this province he was made to return to Manila.[31] In a short time these two servants of the Gospel introduced the Faith into the islands called Luzon, to which, when these islands were first discovered, they came on the famous ship *Victoria* in the year of Christ 1569; these islands are located at a distance of one hundred forty gallic miles from the Chinese mainland, and they are called the Philippines by the Spaniards in honor of their king Phillip the Second, the largest [island] among them is called Manila. [There] the Spaniards established their principal commune in the year of Christ 1571. Later the Brothers Hermits of St. F. Augustine, Friars Minor of Saint Francis, also Spaniards, attempted to preach the Christian faith in China. First, on the twelfth of June in the year 1578,[32] Father Pedro de Alfaro[33] and four other associates[34] from the Philippines came to the capital city[35] of Kuang Tung (Guangdong) province;[36] but, accused by the prefects of being spies of the king of the Spaniards, they were forced to return to the Philippines. Again, in the year 1582, at the end of June, Father Martin Ignatius from [the order of] Saint Francis[37] and six other companions, also Spaniards, came to the same Kuang Tung province from the

Colonizadores, Agustinos en Filipinas (Valladolid: Imprenta Agustiniana, 1965), pp. 79–99, and in Rodriguez and Fernandez, *Diccionario,* 1:93–117.

[28] R. 1573–1620.

[29] Located on the central coast of China.

[30] Father Marin (?–1606), born in Mexico, became a Spanish missionary in the Philippines in 1571. His biography is found in López, *Misioneros y Colonizadores,* pp. 137–154.

[31] Father Martin de Rada (Herrada) and Father Jeronimo Marin were sent to China by the governor of the Philippines, Guido de Lavezaris, not only to reestablish the Catholic Church in China but also to make an alliance between China and the Philippines against the corsairs. Their mission lasted from June 12 to October 28, 1575. Rosso, *Apostolic Legations,* p. 48.

[32] In fact, he arrived in China in 1579.

[33] A Franciscan missionary. He was the first Custos of the Philippines' Custody of St. Gregory the Great. "It had never been the intention of the Pope to restrict their [Franciscans'] activities to the Philippines, but that their foundation in Manila was meant in the first place as a base whence they were to attempt the conversion of China." Achiles Meersman, *The Franciscans in the Indonesian Archipelago (1300–1775)* (Louvain: Nauwelaerts, 1967), pp. 23–24.

[34] Giovanni Battista Lucarelli, Sebastian of Baeza, Augustin de Tordesillas, and Estevan Ortiz; the last possessed some knowledge of Chinese. They arrived in Guangzhou (capital of Guangdong) on June 21, 1579. Fr. Ortiz later realized the difficulties of their enterprise and returned home. The mission of the four other people thus became more difficult, since none of them knew any Chinese, and they had to rely on their interpreters. Their mission failed, and, one after another, they were expelled from China under the pretext of being suspected of spying for the Spanish king. Rosso, *Apostolic Legations,* pp. 53–54.

[35] Guangzhou (Canton) was the first Chinese port regularly visited by Europeans.

[36] The southernmost part of mainland China.

[37] Father Martin Ignacio de Loyola, a Spanish Franciscan of the Discalced Order of the Friars Minor, came to the Philippines in 1582. In 1584 he approached the Holy See with his project of missionary activity in China. On his mission see Lorenzo Perez, *Origen de las Misiones Franciscanas en el Extremo Oriente* (Madrid: Imprenta de G. López del Honrno, 1916), pp. 64–91.

Philippines. There they at first were captured as spies. Later released, they started to preach the Christian faith; but they were captured again and thrown into jail because of the envy of the priests of the idols. They were freed with the help of a certain Lusitanian[38] general, and returned with him to Macao,[39] and from there to Europe. Moreover, other Friars Minor, Lusitanians, had already preached the Gospel prior to their brothers the Spaniards in the [countries] adjacent to China, namely on the island of Macao, where the Lusitanians built their commune after they obtained permission from the aforementioned Chinese emperor in the fifth year of his rule, in the year of Christ 1577. Finally, at the end of the twenty-seventh year of the same emperor at the beginning of the year 1600 of Christ, Father Matteo Ricci from the Italian [city] of Marcerata, from the Society of Jesus, first brought Faith into the court of Pe King (Beijing) through the scientific knowledge [astrology and mathematics] in which he was proficient.[40] And from that [time] the Christian religion has been marvelously spread in China. Earlier he came to the main city of Kuang Tung province in 1583. But he was forbidden by the governor to stay there and returned to Goa,[41] and he arrived there two years before Father Michele de Ruggieri,[42] of the same Society, [arrived] from Naples. All these [notices], as well as everything that follows, are taken from the aforementioned *Mappamundum.*

---

[38] Lusitania was a territory including modern Portugal and parts of the Spanish provinces of Estremadura and Toledo. Consequently, the name Lusitanians was applied to Portuguese.

[39] Macao is a small territory on China's southern coast. It consists of a peninsula rather than an island, as it is said below in the text, projecting out of Canton province. In the sixteenth century it fell under Portuguese domination, and missionaries carried over on Portuguese ships transformed Macao into an East Asian center of Christianity.

[40] Matteo Ricci (1552–1610) was a founder of the Catholic missions of China. He was born in the city of Marcerata, in central Italy. In 1571 he entered the Society of Jesus at the Roman College, where he studied theology, mathematics, astronomy, and cosmology. He arrived in China in 1583. "Dressed until 1595 in a Buddhist monk's robe, as was the custom with the missionaries in Japan and the Philippines, Ricci realized that to win over the most highly educated Chinese he would have to adopt their dress and manners and serve a long and difficult apprenticeship in the classical culture of China. He thus gradually succeeded in defining a method of evangelization which consisted in emphasizing the—at any rate apparent—analogies between Buddhism, Daoism, and popular beliefs, and in flattering the taste of the literati for the science, technology, and arts of Europe." Jacques Gernet, *A History of Chinese Civilization,* trans. J. R. Foster and Ch. Hartman (Cambridge: Cambridge University Press, 1999), p. 450. Being an extraordinary personality, Matteo Ricci left a long-lasting legacy in Chinese Christianity in particular, and in the relations between China and the West in general. Matteo Ricci left an account of his mission to China; see Matthieu Ricci and Nicolas Trigault, *Histoire de l'expedition chretienne au royaume de la Chine, 1582–1610* (reprint, Paris: Desclée de Brouwer, 1978). One of the best books on Matteo Ricci is Jonathan D. Spence, *The Memory Palace of Matteo Ricci* (New York: Viking Penguin, 1984).

[41] Goa, situated on the west coast of India, south of Bombay, was the capital of the Portuguese Indies in the sixteenth to eighteenth centuries.

[42] Father Michele de Ruggieri (1543–1607) came to India from Italy in 1578 and was summoned by Matteo Ricci to his mission in China. He came to Macao in 1579 and started there diligently to study Chinese. His labor was not wasted, for he turned out to be much more successful than any of his predecessors during two sojourns at Canton (1580–81). In 1583 he took up his residence with Father Matteo Ricci in Canton, where they established the first Christian mission of the modern period. In 1607 Father Ruggieri died in Europe, where he had been sent in 1588 to interest the Holy See more particularly in the missions.

When all these [events] were happening in China, the emperor called Faociba[43] started the first persecution of Christians in Japan in the year of Christ 1596,[44] after forty-eight years [p. 111] [had passed] since the Faith had been brought in for the first time by St. Francis Xavier.[45]

During this persecution, three Saint Martyrs of the Society of Jesus were crucified and stabbed with a spear; also six other martyrs from the order of Friars Minor all suffered martyrdom in one day on the fifth of February 1597. When this emperor died, the Christian religion became strong there, and spread far and wide under his two successor sons Samnua[46] and Ongozi.[47] When the son of the emperor

---

[43] The reference here is not to an emperor but to a warlord, Toyotomi Hideyoshi (1536–98), who could be described as the virtual military ruler of most of Japan from about 1582 until his death. He, as many other nobles, changed his name several times throughout his career. His original name, Hiyoshi, was changed to Hideyoshi in 1562. In 1575 he assumed the name Hashiba. "He affected the surname Kinoshita during his early career as a soldier and later, around 1573, assumed the surname Hashiba." Mary Elizabeth Berry, "Hideyoshi," *Harvard East Asian Monographs* 146 (Cambridge, MA: Council of East Asian Studies, Harvard University, 1982), p. 244 n. 5. Though he is usually referred to by his surname, Toyotomi (received in 1586), or by his given name, Hideyoshi, several early European accounts refer to him as Hashiba. The syllable *fao* in *Faociba* is a garbled version of the syllable *fa*, which would be used in a system of romanization devised in the sixteenth century on the basis of Portuguese orthography; in other words, it represents the same phoneme that would be transcribed *ha* in the current Hepburn system. In fact, neither *f* nor *h* accurately reproduces the Japanese sound, which actually is somewhere in between the two. The syllable *ci* was apparently written *xi* in the original source, used by Adriano di St. Thecla. It is, again, a transliteration of Japanese on the basis of Portuguese orthography—and the error was introduced by a scribe. *Xi* is the same phoneme that would be written *shi* in the Hepburn system. As regards another European source referring to Hashiba: in 1581 Visitor Valignano ordered a Jesuit Brother "vizitar a hum capitao de Nobunaga, por nome Faxiba Chicugendono [Chikuzen Dono]." Luis Frois, *Historia de Japam*, ed. Jose Wicki (Lisbon: Biblioteca Nacional, 1982), 3:269. Hidyeoshi issued an expulsion decree against the Christian missionaries in 1587 and in 1596 ordered the execution of twenty-six Christians in Nagasaki, a city with a considerable concentration of Christians, which took place in February 1597.

[44] The chain of events that unleashed this persecution began in 1593 with the arrival of a Franciscan mission to Japan under the patronage of Spain. Prior to this, evangelization was the monopoly of the Jesuit order, which was sponsored by Portugal. The rivalry between Portugal and Spain aggravated the antagonism between the two religious orders, planting suspicion in the minds of the Japanese rulers. The wreck of the Spanish galleon *San Felipe* off the Japanese coast in October 1596 was the turning point in Toyotomi Hideyoshi's policy toward the Christians, after which he considered all Christians as spies. On December 29, 1596, he issued a decree: "I will that there be no more preaching of this law hereafter." Cited in Jurgis Elisonas, "Christianity and the Daimyo," in *The Cambridge History of Japan*, vol. 4, *Early Modern Japan*, ed. John Whitney Hall et al. (Cambridge: Cambridge University Press, 1991), p. 364.

[45] St. Francis Xavier (1506–52), a founder and member of the Jesuit Order, came to Japan in 1549 after spending seven years on missions in Goa and Malacca. Upon his arrival in Japan, he devoted his first year to studying Japanese and translating some small treatises to be employed in preaching and catechizing. Xavier began preaching and made some converts, but these aroused the ill will of the bonzes, who had him banished from the city. Leaving Kagoshima about August 1550, he penetrated to the center of Japan and preached the Gospel in some of the cities of southern Japan. After working about two and a half years in Japan he left this mission in charge of Father Cosme de Torres and Brother Juan Fernandez and departed for Goa. His intentions were to go to China to evangelize people there, and he even got an appointment as ambassador from the Viceroy of India to go to China, but on his way there, he fell ill and passed away. He was canonized by Pope Gregory XV in 1622.

[46] The name in the manuscript is obscurely written. It can be read as Sanuma, Samnua or Sanmua. However, whoever these two, Sanuma and Ongozi, may have been, they were not sons

Samnua, called Zong gu Samnua, succeeded to the throne,[48] a new and most harsh persecution was unleashed in the year of Christ 1621.[49] In its course numerous Christians of all statuses, as well as missionaries, suffered cruel martyrdom through multiple kinds of penalties. And, among the missionaries, Father Luis Flores[50] from the order of the Friars Preachers,[51] Father Carol Spinola from the

---

of Hideyoshi, who was succeeded not by his own progeny, who never ruled, but by the Tokugawa family, who seized the realm by force in 1600. Hideyoshi's successor was Tokugawa Ieyasu, who came to power in 1600 and obtained the official title of shogun (a Japanese term for a military governor ruling in the name of the Emperor) in 1603, establishing the dynastic regime of Tokugawa, which lasted till 1868. Ieyasu resigned in 1605 to keep the post in his family. Adriano di St. Thecla calls the shogun "emperor"; although the shogun possessed real power in Japan, he did not enjoy the status of emperor. The shogun is almost universally called "emperor" in all European sources of the Tokugawa period. The "true" imperial sovereign (i.e., mikado) reigned but did not rule. The name "Samnua," "Sanmua," or "Sanuma" is presumably a garbled transcription of the Japanese word *Sama,* which simply means "Lord." These variants as well as "Samme" and "Samma" can be frequently found in the sixteenth- and seventeenth-century European sources.

[47] "Ongozi" most likely represents *Ogosho,* a Japanese word that literally means "Great Honorable Palace" and is a common honorific applied to rulers or retired rulers in general and Tokugawa Ieyasu in particular. Ieyasu (the first Tokugawa shogun) was known as *Ogosho-san* after his retirement in 1605. Although Ieyasu retired early, he remained mostly in charge until his death in 1616. He was known by this name after his nominal retirement in 1605. So, it appears that "Samnua" and "Ongozi" are references to one and the same person. This conjecture is corroborated by the following passage found in a letter dated January 1, 1617, to Sir Thomas Wilson in London, written by a British captain visiting Japan: "Since w'ch tyme Ogosho Samme, the ould Emperour, is dead and hath left the Empier in quiet pocession to his sonne Shongo Samme, now rayning, whoe is held to be the politikest prince that ever rayned in Japon." Anthony Farrington, "The English Factory in Japan, 1613–1623" (London: The British Library, 1991), 1:551. Indeed, under Ieyasu "the Christian mission was to enjoy a decade of calm weather and clear sailing. . . . Ieyasu at first took a conciliatory stance toward them, partially at least in consideration of the efforts of Christian daimyo who played important roles in the alliance that brought the Tokugawa to power in the great military conflict in 1600." Jurgis Elisonas, "Christianity and the Daimyo," in *Cambridge History of Japan,* 4:365.

[48] "Zong gu Samnua" most likely represents *shogun-sama,* the Lord Shogun. As seen in the previous footnote, the son and successor of Tokugawa Ieyasu—the second shogun of the Tokugawa family, Tokugawa Hidetada, who ruled as shogun from 1605 to 1623—was referred to as "Shongo Samme" by a Englishman in the early seventeenth century. Another Englishman, Richard Wickham, also uses a similar title for Hidetada. In January 1617 he wrote from Hirado to John Jourdain at Bantam: "It hath pleased God, the ould Emp' dep'ting this life the 17 of Ap' last, 1616, that his sonne Shongo Sama succeding him hath cut us of from most of our cheefe privelidges." Farrington, "English Factory," p. 585.

[49] The apogee of these persecutions was the Great Martyrdom of Nagasaki on September 10, 1622 (not in 1621 as Adriano di St. Thecla suggests), in which fifty-five Christians were executed. For a list and concise biography of the martyrs, see Juan Ruiz-de-Medina, *El Martirologio del Japon, 1558–1873* (Rome: Institutum Historicum, 1999), pp. 443–468. Smaller persecutions occurred in many other places throughout the country.

[50] Father Flores (ca. 1563–1622) was born in Belgium, educated in Spain, and later was sent to preach in Mexico. From there he went to the Philippines. In 1620 he volunteered to go to Japan, and set off for this mission together with Father Pedro Zuniga, mentioned below. Father Flores was beatified in 1867. Hilario Ocio and Eladio Neira, *Misioneros Dominicos en el Extremo Oriente, 1587–1835* (1895; reprint, Manila: Filipinas, 2000), pp. 75–76.

[51] In the 1580s the Dominicans began to preach in Japan.

Society of Jesus,[52] and Father Pedro Zuniga from the order of Brothers Hermits[53] were all burned in fire and were made famous for their miraculous firmness.

Article 2: On the Persecutions of the Christian Faith in China

The Christian Faith, within a century and a half, had already blossomed in the flourishing Chinese empire; it had spread through all its provinces and was honored due to the diligence and toil of the laborers of each order and position. Certainly, it suffered persecutions in different times. The first two [persecutions] were launched in Nan King (Nanjing) province.[54] The first one [occurred] in the year of Christ 1615, the thirty-ninth year of Emperor Ming Xin, another [occurred] in the year of Christ 1622, the forty-sixth year of the same emperor. Neither of the two persecutions lasted long, nor were they extensive. Of more weight was the third persecution, which was ignited by four nobles of the court, at the beginning of the reign of Zing Khang Hi (Qing Kangxi),[55] when the emperor was very young, with an edict published in the fourth year of this emperor, the year of Christ 1665, by which the promulgation of the Christian Faith and the arrival of its preachers into [the extent] of the sovereignty of China were prohibited; Christian books were set on fire in large numbers. Four years later, the missionaries were allowed to return to their churches and to exercise their ceremonies, although the restriction

[52] Carol Spinola (1565–1622) was an offspring of a noble family from Genoa. He received an excellent education at the Roman College, where he was a pupil (as was Father Matteo Ricci earlier) of a famous Jesuit mathematician and astronomer, Christofer Clavius (1538–1612), who is credited as well for promoting the Gregorian calendar. Joining the Society of Jesus in 1584 in Napole, the city of which his uncle, Cardinal Spinola, was a bishop, Carol Spinola aspired to go on mission to Japan. His dream came true in 1602. Laboring through all the hardships of his mission, Father Carol Spinola managed to establish good contacts with the indigenous people. During the persecution of 1622 he was sentenced to be burnt alive and accepted his fate with firmness and dignity during the Great Martyrdom of Nagasaki on September 10, 1622.

[53] Pedro Zuniga (ca. 1579–1622) was an Augustinian Hermit. Born in Seville, Spain, he went to the Philippines in 1610 and later shifted his missionary activity to Japan. In 1618, however, he came back to Manila because of the persecutions in Japan. In 1620 he decided to resume his mission in Japan. See Merino, *Agustinos Evangelizadores*, p. 356; Ruiz-de-Medina, *El Martirologio del Japon*, p. 400. Pedro Zuniga and Luis Flores tried to enter Japan in 1620 "disguised as Spanish merchants, but carrying letters from the ecclesiastical authorities at Manila which conclusively proved that they were missionaries bound for Japan." C. R. Boxer, *The Christian Century in Japan, 1549–1650* (London: Cambridge University Press; Berkeley: University of California Press, 1951), p. 346. Fathers Zuniga and Luis were captured by the English and handed over to the Dutch, who in turn delivered them to the Japanese authorities. The two men were burned alive with the captain of the ship on which they had come. Richard Henry Drummond, *A History of Christianity in Japan* (Grand Rapids, MI: William B. Eerdmans Publishing Company, 1971), p. 102. Contrary to Adriano di St. Thecla's grouping of them, these three missionaries were martyred at different times. The execution of Fathers Zuniga and Flores took place on August 19, 1622, and turned out to be a prelude to the Grand Martyrdom of Nagasaki three weeks later, in which Father Spinola perished. In 1867 Fathers Zuniga and Flores were beatified.

[54] Strictly speaking Nanjing, meaning "the southern capital," is a city, not a province. It is the capital of Jiangsu province in east-central China.

[55] His official years of reign are 1662–1723, but he actually ruled from 1668, being a minor before this time.

of preaching the Faith remained intact. [p. 112] A new persecution was started in Che Kiang (Zhejiang) province by its viceroy, who issued an edict in the thirtieth year of the aforementioned emperor, in the year of Christ 1693. He expelled Christians from the city and destroyed all the churches that they had built in this province. This persecution was stopped by a decree of the Ministry of Rites, published in favor of the Faith, according to the order of the emperor in the same year, on the twentieth day of March; it stated that Europeans were free to exercise their religion inasmuch as it conformed with common sense, and their churches had to be restored, and anyone was allowed to enter them whenever he wanted, and to exhibit reverence in them. This decree was ratified by the emperor himself, and made known in all the provinces. Up to this point, I follow the aforementioned *Mappamundum Historicum.*

When Emperor Kang Hi (Kangxi) was alive, the Christian religion developed peacefully;[56] however, disputes, which appeared earlier between the missionaries concerning the Chinese rites, broke out [and continued] for a long time during the rule of this emperor. Many apostolic decrees were issued to stop them [that is, stop traditional Chinese rites practiced among Christians] and for their enforcement two Holy Patriarchs [and] Apostolic Visitors were sent by Pope Clement XI,[57] namely, D. Carlo Tommaso Maillard de Tournon, patriarch of Antioch,[58] later a cardinal, who arrived in China in 1705, and D. Carlo Ambrose Mezzabarba, Patriarch of Alexandria,[59] who came to China in 1720.

After the death of Emperor Kang Hi, who ruled for sixty-one years, his son Yung Ching (Yongcheng), Ung Chính in Annamite,[60] succeeded him. At that time, the highest prefect of Fo Kien province published an edict against the Christian religion and obtained its ratification from the emperor, who at first tested and

---

[56] This might be explained by the fact that, assuming full power in 1669, Kangxi broke off with his advisors, dismissed them, and decided to conduct policies different from those of his regents. As an result, he changed the treatment of missionaries and of Christianity in the empire.

[57] 1649–1721. He was enthroned in the Vatican in 1700.

[58] Carlo Tommaso Maillard de Tournon (1668–1710), an Italian from Tourin, was consecrated by Pope Clement XI (1700–1721) in 1701. He left Europe in February 1703 as Apostolic Visitor with the faculty of Legate, stayed for some time in India and Macao, and reached Peking on December 4, 1705. He was received with great honor at the court, but later Chinese treatment of him drastically changed when the Chinese realized that his main goal was to abolish the traditional Chinese rites among the Christians. Patriarch de Tournon was ordered to go to Macao and was forbidden to leave from there before the return of the envoys sent by the emperor to Rome with an explanation of the emperor's objections to the interdiction of the rites. Patriarch de Tournon died in Macao in 1710. An account on his mission is found in Rosso, *Apostolic Legations.*

[59] The personal name of Patriarch Mezzabarba (ca. 1685–1741) differs, depending on the source. He is called Jean Ambrose Mezzabarba (Latourette, *History of Christian Missions*, p. 147) and also Carlo Ambrogio Mezzabarba (Rosso, *Apostolic Legations*, pp. 202–203). After the failure of the first legate, Clement XI tried to find a remedy for the situation and sent Patriarch Mezzabarba, of Alexandria, to China. He left Lisbon in March 1720 and in November, not without difficulty, was admitted to the emperor. The pope had authorized him to alleviate some of the Holy Office's requirements, but this measure did not produce the desired unity among the missionaries. Furthermore, the proposals brought by Patriarch Mezzabarba to China from the pope were condemned and annulled in 1742 by a papal bull which reimposed the need for a relentless struggle against superstitions, that is, rites not considered Christian.

[60] The imperial reign title from 1723 to 1736. For the emperors of the Qing dynasty (1644–1908) their title of reign serves as their imperial name.

approved it in the Ministry of Rites and later ratified it at the end of the first year of his reign under the Chinese title Kuei Mao (Guimao);[61] according to the Christian [chronology], [this was at] the beginning of 1724, on the twentieth day of January. It was demanded in this edict and decree that the servants of the Gospel, who were dispersed around the provinces, should arrive at the court of Pe King or leave and go to Macao;[62] and, their churches should be transformed into temples of ancestors or into the courts of literati. This was happening in the presence of Emperor Kan Lung (Qianlong), Càn Laong in Annamite.[63] In his second year another decree appeared from the Ministry of Rites against the holy religion, and afterward another one was issued by the emperor himself in his eleventh year, in the sixth month, that is, in the year of Christ 1746, on the [p. 113] twelfth of August. From this moment the persecution that had already been started in Fo Kien province immediately flared up in other provinces as well. In this completely new persecution, numerous missionaries together with many Christians were captured, and penalties were imposed on them. The most remarkable among the missionaries was the venerable Peter Sans[64] from the order of Brothers Preachers[65]—a Spaniard, bishop of Maurocastro, and Vicar Apostolic in Fo Kien province—who, together with [his] companions,[66] was captured on the thirtieth of June 1746 and repeatedly interrogated on account of his faith in front of the judges, and even in front of the viceroy, being tortured with heavy punches and further numerous whippings; finally, on the twenty-sixth of May 1747, he gladly accepted decapitation[67] in front of the people in the large city Fo Cheu (Fuzhou),[68] the capital of the province. His four companions, Spaniards as well, were tormented to death on the twenty-eighth of October of the next year, 1748. Also in the same

[61] The reference is to the name of the year corresponding to 1723–24.

[62] The missionaries skilled in astronomy, the knowledge of which was considered very precious and useful in China, were summoned to Beijing; the rest were supposed to leave the country immediately. Henri Cordier, "Documents pour servir à l'histoire ecclésiastique de l'Extrême-Orient," *Revue de l'Extrême Orient* 2 (1884): 54–55.

[63] R. 1736–96.

[64] Another way of writing his last name is Sanz (1680–1747). Ordained in 1704, he arrived in 1712 in Manila, and in 1715 came to Fujian province in China. For his biography, see Marie J. Savignol, *Les martyrs Dominicains de la Chine au XVIIIe siècle* (Soreze [?]: Imprimerie Abeilhou, 1893), pp. 23–40.

[65] The first Dominican missionary, Gaspar da Cruz (?–1570), arrived in China in 1555. The first Dominican mission was established in China in 1630. The Dominicans took a very active part in the controversy of the Rites. The main headquarters and the greatest field of activity for the Dominican Order was the Philippines. There, in Manila, starting from 1866, they began to publish *El Correo Sino-Annamita,* which included the letters from their missionaries in China and Tonking.

[66] Fathers Jean Alcober (1694–1748), Joachim Royo (1691–1748), Francois Diaz (1713–48), and Bishop Francisco Serrano (1695–1748). Their biographies are in Savignol, *Les martyrs Dominicains,* pp. 61–86, 51–60, 87–100, and 41–50, respectively.

[67] "It was known already that Fathers Serrano and Royo were in the same prison with Father Pierre Sanz. When the venerable bishop was given a letter addressed to him, he expressed a lot of joy towards Father Francisco Serrano and told him with a spark of happiness in his eyes: 'Know, my Father, that soon I will be decapitated.'" Ibid., p. 190.

[68] Fuzhou is a prosperous port city on the east-central coast of Fujian province. It played an especially important role in the history of China beginning in the sixteenth century when contacts with Europeans began to develop.

year, on the seventeenth of September, two French Fathers from the Society of Jesus in Nan King province experienced the same kind of death. But the first among all the martyrs in China before [them] was the venerable Father Francisco de Capillas of the same order of Fathers Preachers, who was decapitated for [his Faith in] Christ[69] during the time of Emperor Xun Chy (Shunzhi),[70] the first to rule in [this] dynasty in the year of Christ 1645.[71] This event was testified by the venerable Father Francisco Serrano[72] in his report on the martyrdom of the aforementioned bishop [Peter Sans]; he [Father Serrano] was captured together with him, and later he shared his fame.[73]

The following divine revenge fell upon the persecutors. The viceroy of Fo Kien province was deprived of his rank, and his property was assigned to the state treasury because of his poor governing. The viceroy of Nan King province was captured, indeed, on the suspicion of rebellion.

[The manuscript ends here.]

---

[69] Francisco Fernandes de Capillas (1607–48) began his mission in the Philippines in 1632. In 1642 he was transferred to China. A brilliant orator, Father Capillas traveled from village to village preaching his faith. He was arrested and executed on January 15, 1648. Pope Bendict XIV proclaimed him a protomartyr of China on September 16, 1748. He was beatified in 1909. Ocio and Neira, *Misioneros Dominicos,* p. 152.

[70] R. 1644–62.

[71] The first year of this first emperor of the Ming dynasty is conventionally dated 1644.

[72] An elected bishop of Tipasa (a city on the territory of modern Algeria).

[73] In 1893 all five martyrs (Fathers Sanz, Serrano, Alcobar, Royo, and Diaz) were beatified. The description of their martyrdom and beatification is found in Savignol, *Les martyrs Dominicains,* pp. 101–277.

GLOSSARY 1

This glossary lists Vietnamese words used more than once in any chapter. These words appear unaccompanied in the text by their Chinese equivalents or explanatory notes[1]

Vietnamese	Pinyin	Definition
Bạch Mã	Baima	"White Horse," spirit-protector of Hanoi
Bàn Cổ	Pangu	a legendary being, from whose body the world supposedly derived
Ban Nhược, known in modern Vietnamese as:		
Bát nhã	bore	prajna, "wisdom"
Bí Chi	*Mizhi*	*Secret Branch,* title of the book on which Adriano di St. Thecla based his description of Buddhism
Bồ Tát	pusa	bodhisattva
Càn	qian	polysemantic word, one of the numerous meanings of which is heaven.
Càn Nguyên	qian-yuan	heaven and source, heavenly origin,
Canh Ngũ, in modern Vietnamese orthography:		
Canh Ngọ	gengwu	name of a year; in the manuscript it corresponds to 1750
Cảnh Hưng	jingxing	reign title of Lê Hiển Tông: 1740-1786
Cao Tổ (Hán), see Hán Cao Tổ		
Câu Mang	Goumang	god of spring, worshipped at the ceremony to inaugurate spring
Chai	————	ceremony of libations to the dead
Chân Trí	Zhenzhi	Genuine Mind
Chu Chiêu Vương	Zhou Zhaowang	Chinese emperor whose reign according to Chinese tradition (and per the manuscript) dated 1052 -1001 B.C.E.
Chu Công	Zhou Gong	Duke of Zhou (twelfth century B.C.E.),

[1] A long dash indicates the lack of a Chinese equivalent because the word is vernacular Vietnamese.

		considered a paragon of virtue
Chu Kính Vương	Zhou Jingwang	Chinese emperor whose reign is traditionally (and per the manuscript) dated 519 to 475 B.C.E.
Chu Văn Vương	Zhou Wen Wang	ruler of the state of Zhou in ancient China and father of the first emperor of the Zhou dynasty
Chu Tử	Zhuzi	reference to Zhu Xi (1130-1200), the great scholar
Chu Văn Công	Zhu Wengong	see Chu Tử
chùa	————	temple
Chúa	zhu	ruler; reference to the Trịnh family governing Tonkin
Chúc Daong, in modern Vietnamese orthography:		
Chúc Dong or Chúc Dung	Zhurong	god of Fire, worshipped at ceremony to inaugurate summer
cô hồn	guhun	abandoned or lonely soul
Cổn	Gun	father of Đại Vũ (Da Yu)
Di Đà	Mituo	abbreviation of A di đà (Amituo; Buddha Amitabha)
Di Lạc	Milei	Buddha Maitreya
Dịch Kinh	*Yijing*	*The Book of Changes*
Điêm Vương	Yanwang	Yama, king of Hades, god of the dead
Dương Chu	Yang Zhu	philosopher, 440-360 B.C.E.?
Đại Học	*Daxue*	*The Great Learning*
Đại Ngộ Chân Trí	Dawu zhenzhi	Great Awakening of the Genuine Mind
Đại Vũ	Da Yu	legendary emperor, traditional reign dates 2205-2197 B.C.E.
Đại Vương	Dawang	Great King or Great Ruler
Đàng Cao Tổ	Tang Gaozu	Chinese emperor ruled 618-627
Đàng Đức Tông	Tang Dezong	Chinese emperor ruled 780-805
Đàng Huyền Tông	Tang Xuanzong	Chinese emperor ruled 713-756
Đàng Văn Tông	Tang Wenzong	Chinese emperor ruled 827-841
Đế	di	emperor
Đế Nghiêu	Di Yao	Chinese legendary emperor, traditional reign date 2365-2356 B.C.E.
Đế Thuấn	Di Shun	Chinese legendary emperor, traditional reign dates 2255-2205 B.C.E.
Địa Hoàng	Dihuang	Emperor of Earth
Địa Phủ	difu	Governor of Earth
đọc canh đọc kệ or đọc kanh đọc kệ, in modern Vietnamese orthography:		
đọc kinh đọc kệ	————	to read sutras
Gia Lễ	*Jiali*	*The Family Rituals*

Gia Ngữ	*Jiayu*	abbreviation of *Khổng Tử Gia Ngữ* (*Kongzi jiayu, The Discourses of the Confucian School*)
Giao Chu, in modern Vietnamese pronunciation:		
Giao Châu	Jaiozhou	the Han administrative jurisdiction in northern Vietnam and southern China
giao	jiao	an open space beyond the cities allotted for sacrifices to Heaven
Hán Cao Tổ	Han Gaozu	Chinese emperor ruled 206-194
Hán Linh Đế	Han Lingdi	Chinese emperor ruled 168-189
Hán Minh Đế	Han Mingdi	Chinese emperor ruled 58-76
Hào	yao	line of the trigrams from the *Book of Changes*
Hiệu Thien Thượng Đế, in modern Vietnamese pronunciation:		
Hạo Thiên Thượng Đế	Haotian Shangdi	"Sovereign on high in the vast heavens"
Hiếu Tông (Tống), see Tống Hiếu Tông		
Hoàng	huang	emperor
Hoàng Đế	Huang Di	Yellow Emperor, allegedly ruled 2607-2597 B.C.E.
Hoàng Thiên Hậu Thổ	Huangtian Houtu	High Heaven and Empress of Earth
Hội	hui	to assemble or to hold a festival
hội minh	huimeng	ceremony of taking the oath
hồn bạch	hunbai	white [band] of soul
Huy Tông, see Tống Huy Tông:		
hương án	xiang'an	sacrificial table
Kheo Thị	Qiu Shi	unidentified author cited in the manuscript
kiếp	jie	kalpa, a period during which a physical universe is formed and destroyed
Kính Vương, see Chu Kính Vương		
Kỳ Đạo, see Tế Kỳ Đạo		
Lão Đam	Lao Dan	one of the names referring to Laozi
Lão Nhiễm	Lao Ran	one of the names referring to Laozi
Lão Tiên	Lao Xian	one of the names referring to Laozi
Lão Tử	Laozi	an ancient philosopher, whose historicity is strongly doubted, called the founder of Daoism
lập xuân	lichun	ceremony to inaugurate spring
Lễ Kinh	*Lijin*	*The Book of Rites*
Lí Hổ	Li Hu	a king, of whom Buddha's father was a vassal
Linh Đế, see Hán Linh Đế		
Lỗ	Lu	native kingdom of Confucius
Luận Ngữ	*Lunyu*	*The Analects*
Lương Vũ [Đế]	Liang Wu[di]	Chinese emperor, ruling 502-549

Mạc Địch, a mistake for:		
Mặc Địch	Mo Di	philosopher, ca. 470-391 B.C.E.
Mạnh Tử	Mengzi	Mencius, a famous Chinese philosopher (371-289? B.C.E.); a book containing his sayings bears the same title
Màu Tiền, a name known in Vietnamese as:		
Miễu Tiên	Miaoshan	personality worshipped in Buddhism sometimes identified wih Guanyin
Màu Trang, a name known in Vietnamese as:		
Miễu Trang Vương	Miao Zhuangwang	ruler of Xinglin kingdom, father of Miaoshan
miếu	miao	temple or shrine
Mộc Liên, in modern Vietnamese orthography:		
Mục Liên	Mulian	personality worshipped in Buddhism, but the traditional hagiography of this person differs from that in the manuscript
Ngọc Hoàng	Yuhuang	Jade Emperor, the chief deity in the pantheon of popular Daoism
Ngũ Đế	Wudi	Five [ancient] emperors
Nhạc Kinh	*Yuejin*	*The Book of Music*
nhân	ren	person, human being
Nhân Hoàng	Renhuang	Emperor of Men
Nhẫn Nhục	Renfu Kshanti	"patience," "forbearance"; in the manuscript it is used as Buddha's name
Nho	Ru or Ro	reference to Confucianism
Nguyên Thỉ, in modern Vietnamese orthography:		
Nguyên Thủy	Yuanshi	Primary Source, an abbreviation of:
Nguyên Thủy Thiên Vương	Yuanshi Tianwang	Heavenly King of Primordial Beginning
ống lạnh	————	pipe-canon
phá ngục	poyu	a ceremony, destruction of prison or "Hades"
Phan Thị Vinh	Pan Shirong or Pan Shiyong	unidentified author of the Ming dynasty (1368-1644)
Phó Dịch	Fu Yi	scholar, 554-639, strong opponent of Buddhism
Phục Hi	Fu Xi	Chinese legendary emperor, traditional reign dates 2852-2737 B.C.E.
quái	gua	trigram of the Book of Changes
Quan Âm	Guanyin	Bodhisattva Avalokitesvara
Sơn Tinh	Sanjing	Mountain Spirit
tăng	seng	Buddhist priest, bonze
tăng ni	sengni	bonzes and nuns
Tâm Đăng	*Xindeng*	*The Lamp of Heart*, title of the book on which Adriano di St. Thecla largely

		based his description of Buddhism
Tần Thỉ Hoàng [Đế]	Qin Shi Huang[di]	the first emperor of the Qin dynasty, r. 221-209 B.C.E.
Tấn	Jin	Chinese dynasty, 265-317
Tế Kỳ Đạo	ji qidao	ceremony of the leader's banner
Thái Công	Tai Gong	general of the Zhou dynasty; spirit worshipped by soldiers
Thái Công Vaọng, see Thái Công		
Thái Cực	taiji	primordial source in philosophy
Thành Hoàng	chenghuang	tutelary genie
Thánh vương	shengwang	saint or wise prince or king
Thẩm Tử	Shenzi	apparently, a mistake for Sái Trầm (Cai Chen) Song philosopher, 1167-1230
thần	shen	spirit, divine
Thần Câu Mang, see Câu Mang		
Thần Nông	Shen Nong	legendary emperor, traditional reign dates 2737-2697 B.C..E; considered as god of agriculture
thập triết	shizhe	the Ten Sages (disciples of Confucius)
thầy bói	————	fortune-teller
thầy phủ thủy	————	master of sorcery
thầy tu	————	bonze
Thi Kinh	*Shijing*	*The Book of Odes*
Thích Ca	Shijia	Sakya
Thích Ca Mâu Ni	Shijiamouni	Sakyamuni
Thiên Hoàng	Tianhuang	Emperor of Heaven
Thiên Phủ	Tianfu	Governor of Heaven
Thiên Trúc	Tianzhu	India
Thổ Công	Tugong	spirit-protector of earth
Thủy Phủ	Shuifu	Governor of Water
Thủy Tinh	Shuijing	Water Spirit
Thư Kinh	*Shujing*	*The Book of History*
Thương	Shang	ancient Chinese dynasty, traditional dates of rule 1766-1122 B.C.E.
thượng đẳng	shangdeng	highest rank
thượng đẳng thần	shangdeng shen	spirit of the highest rank
Thượng Đế	Shangdi	Supreme Emperor, Lord-on-High
thượng hưởng	Shanxiang	Mayest thou enjoy this offering
Tì Lô	Pilu	Vairo, possibly an abbreviation of:
Ti Lô Giá Na	Piluzhena	Vairocana, Buddha Supreme and Eternal
Tiên Sư	Xianshi	originator or founder; spirit worshipped by professional guilds
tiếu	jiao	ceremony of sacrifice and pouring libations to the dead
Tịnh Phạn	Jing Fan	name of Buddha's father
Tống	Song	Chinese dynasty, 960-1279

Tống Chân Tông	Song Zhenzong	Chinese emperor, 998-1023
Tống Hiếu Tông	Song Xiaozong	Chinese emperor, 1163-1190
Tống Huy Tông	Song Huizong	Chinese emperor, 1101-1126
Trình Tử	Chengzi	reference to the Song philosopher Cheng Yi, 1033-1107
Trung Daong, in modern Vietnamese orthography:		
Trung Dong or *Trung Dung*	Zhongyong	*The Doctrine of the Mean*
Trương Đạo Lang, in modern Vietnamese orthography:		
Trương Đạo Lăng	Zhang Daoling	one of the eight Daoist immortals
Trương Giác	Zhang Yue	one of the patriarchs of the Daoist Taiping dao (second century C.E.)
Trương Lương	1. Zhang Liang	one of the founders of Daoist mysticism; died ca. 189 B.C.E.
	2. Zhang Liang	a prominent Daoist, one of the leaders the Yellow Turbans' rebellion;
	died ca. 184 C.E.	
Trương Nghi	Zhang Yi	the identity of this person has not been established; in the manuscript he was given the title of Jade Emperor
tứ phối	sipei	the Four Worthiest [disciples of Confucius]
từ thần	cishen	"bid farewell to spirit" or "merciful spirit"
tướng	jiang	general, minister
Uỷ Âm, mistake for:		
Uy Âm or Oai Âm	Weiyin	Bhismagarjitasvara-raja Buddha
Văn Lâm Quảng	*Wen lin guang*	title of an unidentified book, apparently written by Christian missionaries
văn tế	wenji	sacrificial letters or writing; oration
Văn Vương, see Chu Văn Vương		
vua	————	king
Vương	wang	king, prince, or ruler
xã	she	altar of the earth
Xuân Thu Kinh	*Chunqiu jin*	*The Spring and Autumn Annals*
Xuyên Húc, in modern Vietnamese orthography:		
Chuyên Húc	(Zhuan Xu)	legendary Chinese emperor, traditional reign dates 2513-2435 B.C.E.

GLOSSARY 2

This glossary notes discrepancies between spelling in the manuscript and in the modern Vietnamese orthography[1]

bải	bãi	a shore, a piece vacant ground
Ban Nhược	Bát Nhã	prajna
bất	bách	one hundred
Canh Ngũ	Canh Ngọ	the name of the year
chu	châu	an administrative division
Chúc Daong	Chúc Dong or Chúc Dung	
cuốc	quốc	country, state
daong	dong or dung	appearance
doản	doãn	an official position
duanh	doanh	surplus, to overflow, to exceed
đác	đắc	to obtain, to receive
đang	đương	a temporal particle, "at this time"
Đàng	Đường	Tang dynasty
Đế Cốc	Đế Khốc	
đọc canh đọc kệ or đọc kanh đọc kệ	đọc kinh đọc kệ	to read sutras
Đục Cước	Độc Cước	"one-legged genie"
Giao Chu	Giao Châu	
Hiệu Thiên Thượng Đế	Hạo Thiên Thượng Đế	"sovereign on high in the vast heavens"
Kang Mục	Cương Mục	
Kheo	Khâu	
khỉ	khởi	interrogative particle
Lạc Laong Quân	Lạc Long Quân	
laong	long	dragon
laòng	lòng	heart
Lí Ông Traọng	Lý Ông Trọng	

[1] This glossary shows in Vietnamese alphabetical order all words for which the spelling in the manuscript differs from that in modern Vietnamese orthography and which are found in this form more than once in the manuscript (and therefore cannot be dismissed as scribal errors) or are found in this form in other writings of the seventeenth through nineteenth centuries. I provide translations for words that are not names or that cannot be unambiguously identified to enable a reader to recognize them more easily.

Mạc Địch	Mặc Địch	
Màu Tiền	Miễu Tiên	
nải	nãi	then, a disjunctive particle
ngoạt	nguyệt	month
ống lạnh	ống lệnh	a pipe-canon
phiên	phồn	many
phung	phong	to confer a title of nobility upon someone
phượng	phụng	to venerate, to offer up as tribute or sacrifice
tắc	tác	to do, to make
tĩ	tỉ	to follow, when, by the time
Thái Công Vaọng	Thái Công Vọng	
thỉ	thủy	a source, beginning
thị	thụy	to confer a posthumous title
toài	toại	consequently, then
tràng sinh	trường sinh	immortality
Traọng Cao	Trọng Cao	
Trạong Nơi	Trọng Ni	
Trung Daong	Trung Dong	
trùng	xung	to soar to
Trương Đạo Lang	Trương Đạo Lăng	
Uỷ Âm	Uy Âm or Oai Âm	Bhismagarjitasvara-raja Buddha
vạn	vọng	the name of a sacrifice offered by the emperor to the mountains and streams
vì	mùi	sign of goat in the system of the twelve signs of earthly branches
Vua Giáong or Vua Gióng or Vua Siaóng	Vua Dóng	
xiên	thiên	a thousand
Xuyên Húc	Chuyên Húc	

GLOSSARY 3

Adriano di St. Thecla's transliteration of Chinese words.

Che Kiang	Zhejiang	province in China
Cheu Ling Vuang	Zhou Lingwang	emperor, for whose reign the manuscript uses the dating scheme of 571 to 544 B.C.E.
Chung Ny	Zhongni	one of the names by which Confucius was called
Fo Cheu	Fuzhou	province in China
Fo Kien	Fujian	province in China
Fu Zu	Fuzi	a title of respect for Confucius
Foe	Fo	Buddha
Hia	Xia	legendary dynasty; traditional dates: 2205-1766
hoen pe	hunbai	white [band] of soul
Hu Kuang	Huguang	province in China
Ju or Jo	Ru or Ro	reference to Confucianism
Kan Long	Qianlong	emperor of the Qing dynasty ruling from 1736 to 1796
Kia Ly	Jiali	the book *Family Rituals*
kiang xin	jiangshen	expression used during the ceremony of worshiping the deceased, means: "let the spirit descend"
Kieu	Qiu	the name of the mountain after which Confucius was called
Kuan Tung	Guandong	province in China
Kuei Cheu	Guizhou	province in China
Kiang Si	Jiangxi	province in China
kua	gua	trigram of the *Book of Changes*
Kuei Mao	Guimao	the name of a year corresponding (in the manuscript) to 1623-24 of the European calendar
Kuei Xin	guishen	spiritual powers of good and evil
Kung Fu zu	Kong Fuzi	the Master Sage Kong
Kung Zu	Kongzi	Confucius
Lao Zu	Laozi	

lo cho	liuchu	six domestic animal
Lo King	Liujing	the Six Classical Books of Confucianism
Lu	Lu	kingdom where Confucius was born
Ming	Ming	dynasty ruling from 1368 to 1644
Ming Xin Zung	Ming Shenzong	emperor ruling from 1573 to 1620
Nan King	Nanjing	capital of Jiangsu province in China
Pe King	Beijing	capital of China
Pusa	pusa	bodhisattva
Si Gan	Chang'an	capital during the Sui and the Tang dynasties
Sui	Sui	dynasty ruling from 581 to 618
Sung Ly Zung	Song Lizong	emperor ruling from 1225 to 1265.
Tang	Tang	dynasty ruling from 618 to 907
Tang Tai Zung	Tang Taizong	emperor ruling from 627 to 650
Ty Ko	Di Ku	legendary emperor, traditional dates of reign 2435-2365 B.C.E
Ty Xun	Di Shun	legendary emperor, traditional dates of reign 2255-2205 B.C.E.
Ty Yao	Di Yao	legendary Emperor, traditional dates of reign 2365-2356 B.C.E.
xang hiang	shangxiang	concluding expression in sacrificial oration: "Mayest thou enjoy this offering"
Xang Tung	Shandong	native province of Confucius
Xang Ty	Shangdi	Supreme Emperor, Lord-on-high
Xe Kia	Shijia	Sakya, abbreviation from Shijiamouni, name of Buddha Sakyamuni
Xen Si	Shanxi	province in China
Xin tu	Shentu	door-spirit
Xing	sheng	wise or saint
Xing Ty	Shengdi	saintly or sage emperor
Xing Vuong	shengwang	saintly or sage prince or king
Xun Chy	Shunzhi	Qing emperor ruling from 1644 to 1662
yao	yao	line of the trigrams of the *Book of Changes*
Yung Ching	Yongcheng	emperor ruling from 1723 to 1736
Zing Khang Hi	Qing Kangxi	emperor ruling from 1662 to 1723

Facsimile

Opusculum de Sectis apud Sinenses et Tunkinenses

Father Adriano di St. Thecla

Opusculum
de Sectis
apud Sinenses et Tunkinenses

Præfatio
In Sectas Sinarum et Annamitarum

Non diu post hominum per Orbem terrarum dispersionem in mundo exorta est Idololatria; si quidem crescente in dies in dies morum corruptione, decrevit paulatim veritatis et honestatis amor, ac profunda rerum ignorantia mentes hominum offudit: quo factum est, ut veram Dei notitiam omnes propemodum Nationes amiserint, atque in Idololatriam miserrime defluxerint. Primum autem Idololatriæ auctorem fuisse Nemrod, qui cœpit (Gen. C. 10) esse potens in terra, tradiderunt Eusebius, Hieronymus, et S. P. Augustinus lib. 6 de Civitate Dei. C. 7. Fuit autem (ibid. 10) principium regni ejus Babylon; ubi nimirum regnavit, juxta aliquos Expositores et Chronologos, sæculo tertio post diluvium, et secundo post hominum divisionem, ad veram Vulgata. Ac eo quidem sæculo in Chaldæa, cujus caput Babylon, Idolorum cultum viguisse compertum habemus ex testimonio Josue cap. 24, qui Filios Israel sic allocutus est — hæc dicit Dominus Deus Israel: trans fluvium (Euphratem) habitaverunt Patres vestri ab initio, Thare pater Abraham, et Nachor (pater Thare), servierunt que diis alienis. Nunc ergo (ait infra) timete Dominum ..... et auferte deos, quibus servierunt patres vestri in Mesopotamia, et in Ægypto, ac servite Domino. — Nachor ibi nominatus, non est Nachor frater Abrahæ, et filius Thare, sed est Nachor pater ipsius Thare; quippe cum Josue dicat: *Trans fluvium habitaverunt patres vestri*, *servierunt que*

Diis alienis; necesse est, ut Nachor internominatus cum Thare sit pater filiorum Israël, quos Josue alloquebatur, ut habeantur plures patres prius expresse: quod si Nachor ille fuisset frater Abraham, filius Thare, non utique plures patres filiorum Israel, sed unus nominaretur; sicque incongrue dictum esset: Trans fluvium habitaverunt patres vestri, servierunt que diis alienis. Nachor autem genuit Thare anno 221 post diluvium, ut patet ex calculo annorum omnium generationum post diluvium, ad veram Vulgatam: vixit que Nachor (Gen. 11.26) postquam genuit Thare 119 annis. Hinc potuit ille, et filius ejus Thare pluribus annis deos colere eo seculo tertio; quo Nemrod filius Chus cultum eorum induxit. Idcirco Abraham, Deo jubente, egressus est de terra Chaldaeorum, ne deos coleret, quos patres ejus ibi coluerunt. Cujus rei testem habemus Achior, qui Judith C. 5. ait ad Holofernem — populus iste ex progenie Chaldaeorum est; hic primum in Mesopotamia habitavit; quoniam noluerunt sequi deos patrum suorum, qui erant in terra Chaldaeorum. Deserentes itaque caeremonias patrum suorum, quae in multitudine deorum erant, unum Deum caeli coluerunt. — Illud insuper ex his innotescit, quod adhuc vivente Noë Idololatria homines pervasit, atque annis multis ei coaeva fuit; quando quidem vixit Noë post diluvium (Gen. C. 9) trecentis quinquaginta annis. Qua [illegible] vel nepotes Sem implicitos fuisse dignoscitur; Nachor enim et Thare erant ex progenie Sem.

Inter deos autem, quos eo tempore coluerunt Chaldaei, Ignis unus erat, hebraice dictus Ur, quo nomine civitas illa Chaldaeorum unde primum exivit Abraham, nominabatur: quia Chaldaei (inquit Tirinus in Gen. C. 12) Ignem ibi pro Deo colebant, sicuti et vicini illis Persae colebant in locis, quae inde Pyrea dicta vult Procopius, et alii. Sed et Solem, Lunam, et Sydera Chaldaeis deos fuisse non immerito possumus opinari, cum Chaldaei Astronomiae potissimum vacarent, et in ea super caeteros excellerunt: qua corporum caelestium inspectione, et cognitione abripi facile potuerunt in errorem eo, quae speciosa mirabantur,

mirabantur, Deos existimandi, eorum artificem ignorantes. Quapropter in priscos Chaldaeos primò cadunt, quae Sapientiae Cap. 13. legimus de illis, qui opera Dei deos putaverunt. — Vani autem sunt omnes homines, in quibus non subest scientia Dei, et de his quae videntur bona, non potuerunt intelligere eum, qui est, neque operibus attendentes agnoverunt, quis esset artifex: sed aut ignem, aut spiritum, aut citatum aerem, aut gyrum stellarum, aut nimiam aquam, aut solem, aut lunam rectores orbis putaverunt. Quorum si specie delectati deos putaverunt, sciant quanto his dominator eorum speciosior sit; speciei enim Generator haec omnia constituit.

Cultus quoque defunctorum apud Chaldaeos incepit. Nam Thare patrem Abrahae filio suo Aran defuncto statuam posuisse docent Epiphanius lib. 1. de haeresibus, et Suidas voce Abraham: ideo quod ab Abrahamo gravissime reprehensum fuisse. Apud eosdem coaevus Thare, Ninus, (hoc Ticinus in Sapientiae C. 14) filius Nemrod seu Beli defuncto parenti publicam statuam, aras, et templum posuit, ut tradunt Eusebius in chronico, Hieronymus in Osée C. 2 Ambrosius in C. 1 ad Romanos. Augustinus lib. 16. de civitate C. 7. et 22 contra Faustum C. 17. huc in Chaldaeos rursus cadit illud Sapientiae C. 14. — Acerbo luctu dolens pater cito sibi rapti filii fecit imaginem: et illum, qui tunc quasi homo mortuus fuerat, nunc tanquam Deum colere coepit, et constituit inter servos suos sacra et sacrificia. Deinde interveniente tempore, convalescente iniqua consuetudine, hic error tanquam lex custoditus est, et tyrannorum imperio colebantur figmenta. — Caeterum recentiores Chronologi tradunt Belum Nini patrem regnasse in Babylonia multis seculis post Nemrod, nimirum ab anno mundi 2628. et putant Belum Babylonium a Chaldaeis Deum postea habitum, dictum Jovem Belum, non fuisse Nemrod, sed Evechum, tribus seculis eo posteriorem, qui imperare coepit anno mundi 2262. de quibus in erudita chronologia sacra collegii Sinensis, haec de origine Idololatriae apud Chaldaeos.

Circa idem tempus, quo apud Chaldaeos inducta fuit a Nemrod Idololatria, et apud Sinas ab aliquo ex primis eorum regibus familiae Hia, seu bia illam censeo introductam fuisse. Si enim tertio seculo à diluvio Chaldæi in Idololatriam inciderunt, multo magis Sinenses in eam prolapsos eo tempore fuisse credendum est. Sinenses etenim populi versaban-tur, sicuti et versantur in plaga mundi quam distita à regionibus, quas Noë, ejusque filii incolebant, à quibus nihil audire poterant, sicut Chaldæi, de verâ doctrinâ et Religione. At verò Idololatriæ immunes fuisse puto Đế Nghiêu Đế Thuấn et Đại Vũ, quos primos Sinarum Reges statuimus in nostrâ præfatione de Sinensi chronologiâ, in quâ et ostendimus solum Đế Nghiêu Sinis Tý yáo esse potuisse Sinicæ gentis conditorem. Primus namque hic rex veri Dei notitiam habebat, quemadmodum et alii omnes filii et nepotes Noë, quando divisit eos Dominus in universas terras, evoluto uno seculo à diluvio, cum unus esset populus (Gen. C. 11) et unum labium, quando turrim extruere ceperunt, ac proinde una esset religio, instructoribus Noë, ejusque filiis. Eamque Dei notitiam Rex ille suis tradidisse, ac retinuisse, quoad vixit, credendus est, cum eximiæ probitatis Rex à Sinensibus habea-tur inter Thánh Đế, Sinis Xing Tý recensitos. Quos inter cum et Đế Thuấn seu Tý xun celebretur, nec non illius successor Đại Vũ ob magnam ejus virtutem inter Thánh Vương, Sinensibus Xing vuáng annumeretur, eâdem Dei notitiâ jam traditâ à Đế Nghiêu inhæsisse credendi sunt. Hi duo priores reges seculo secundo regnarunt post diluvium, et tertius Rex Đại Vũ initio tertii seculi regnavit, ut ostendimus in præfatâ præfatione: quod tempus prævenit tempus regni Nemrod apud Babylonios, qui reg-nare cœpit juxta chronologos non nullos post medium seculi tertii à diluvio, et primus Idololatriam invexit, ut dictum est. Porrò illos reges verum Deum cognovisse, et coluisse colligitur ex historiâ Sinensi, in quâ tradi-tur, quod Đế Thuấn sacrificavit Thượng Đế, id est, Supremo Regi. Quod nomen et illi Reges fortè usurparunt ad Deum exprimendum; sed in posterum Sinenses, amissâ veri Dei notitiâ, nomen illud cœlo, vel ejus virtuti attribuerunt. Quamvis verò in historiâ Sinensi referatur, quod Đế Thuấn sacrificavit nedum Regi Supremo, verum etiam Soli, lunæ,

Stellis, montibus, fluminibus, et aliis, nec non quod Đại Vũ spiritibus offerret edulia exquisita, ac rursus patri suo defuncto nomine Cỗn, et Regi Đế Cốc, Sinis Ty Kŏ sacrificaverit; quibus ostenditur illos Reges cultum creaturis impendisse; ex illis regibus à Sinensibus affictum esse dicendum est; ut nempe errores suos tam antiquâ priscorum Regum probitate excellentium exemplo, et auctoritate corroborarent. Quam in rem etiam tradunt in sua historiâ, quod Hoàng Đế, tribus regibus praefatis antiquior, templum construxerit ad colendum regem supremum, et omnes spiritus. Ipse rex profecto excludendus est à verâ Sinensi chronologiâ, eo quod diluvium illud universale antecessit: de quo vide nostram praefationem Sinensis chronologiae. Tres ergo praefati Đế Nghiêu, Đế Thuấn, et Đại Vũ Deum verum cognovisse, et coluisse credendi sunt, et ab omni idololatria immunes fuisse. Non multò autem post; eorum successores illorum documentum, et exempla paulatim obliviscentes, in idololatriam cum populo prolapsi sunt, circa illud tempus, quo Nemrod idololatriam induxit apud Chaldaeos, ut dictum est. Haec omnia testimonia Sinensis historiae de cultu exhibito à priscis regibus caelo, et terrae, soli, lunae et syderibus, fluminibus et montibus, nec non hominibus defunctis, id unum persuadent, quod cultus ille idololatricus vetustissimus sit apud Sinas, et exercitus fuerit à priscis regibus, qui praefatos tres reges seu imperatores virtute eximios subsecuti sunt, non tamen de illis tribus, pro quibus prolata sunt, admitti possunt, ut evincunt praedicta argumenta.

Sinensis itaque idololatria quàm vetusta sit, et suo in statu ad haec tempora permansit; nova tamen idola, et novas superstitiones deinceps admisit; quamobrem plures Sectae inductae sunt, et evulgatae. Tres autem sunt praecipuae ad quas reliquae reducuntur: nimirùm Secta litteratorum, quae potissima est, et primaevam retinet idololatriam, colendo caelum et terram, sydera, montes, flumina, et alia, atque defunctos; Secta Veneficorum, quae versatur circa veneficia maxime ad curationem infirmorum; Secta cultorum Thích, Sinis Foë, quae aliis duobus recentior est, et populo communis. Quae tres Sectae vigent etiam in hoc regno Annamitarum, quod cum subjectum sit-

ditioni Annami, Sinarum mores sequitur et ritus. De illis tribus Sectis potissimum agemus in hoc tractatu, de quibus quoque in libris Sinicis fit mentio, et eo quidem ordine, quem eis dedit Rex Chu Cao Tổ, qui regnavit, imperante familia Trần, de quo in historia: Chu Cao Tổ định tam giáo tiên hậu, dĩ nho vi tiên, Đạo vi thứ, Thích vi hậu, id est, rex Chu Cao Tổ statuit ordinem trium Sectarum, Sectam Nho fecit esse priorem, Sectam Đạo esse mediam, Sectam Thích esse posteriorem. De reliquis quoque Sectis, quae ad illas rediguntur verba faciemus.

Huic autem opusculo conscribendo occasionem dedit index historicus Missionis Tunquinensis, quem noster Illustrissimus Pater Hilarius a Jesu, Episcopus Coricensis, et Vicarius Apostolicus Tunkini Orientalis compilavit ad usum suorum confratrum in hac Missione existentium, ubi de illis quoque tribus Sectis sermonem habet, ea secutus, quae priores Missionarii tradiderunt in libris nonnullis Sinico et Annamitico charactere descriptis. At mihi visum est ea ad examen revocare, novamque de iis inquisitionem facere Sinicos libros, litteratos, et peritos consulendo: quo factum est, ut plura esse diversa deprehenderim, et veriora sim assecutus, quae illis subrogarentur; quibus et alia superaddidi. In his vero plurimum debemus Venerabili Martyri P. Francisco Gil de Federich, quem in urbe regia pro fide captivum consului, misso etiam ad illum hoc opusculo, tunc valde informi, ad examen et emendationem: qui multa diligentia plura exquisivit, et invenit, et descripta ad me transmisit; atque alia deinceps adjecisset, nisi necem pro Christo gloriose subiisset. Alia multa remanent inquirenda; sed eorum inquisitio magnam affert difficultatem; quando quidem Regii ministri aegre nimis opus suscipiunt talia inquirendi, quae ad Regem pertinent, metuentes, ne quid mali sibi obveniat ejusmodi propalando. Quam in rem laudatus Martyr in Epistola data die 6 Augusti 1744 haec scribit — Nec certe fuit negotii mihi mandati oblivio, sed maxima, quam isti opponunt difficultatem in inquirendo de rebus ad Regem pertinentibus. — Cui accedit aliud recens testimonium R. R. adm. P. Venceslai Paleczek, qui in responso ad me dato die 20 Maii hujus anni 1750, sic loquitur de functionibus Nam Giao — habita relatione

(functionis)

(functiones de [illegible]), conveni quemdam mandarinum officii militaris, qui hanc reprobavit, et dixit militum officialibus, non esse omnibus notam; sed solum qui intimi sunt, ut ipse; hinc mihi eamdem communicavit, rogavit ut illud combureretur, quando litteris europaeis describebatur, cum sub poena amissionis capitis promulgatio haec inhibita sit. — Aliam quoque passus sum difficultatem a bello civili, quo regnum hoc plusquam decennio exagitatur: quo tempore nec vacat, nec expedit de similibus inquirere apud ministros, et apud litteratos, qui plurimos libros hoc tempore amiserunt.

Opusculum porro illud scripsi jam informe ante chronologiam Sinensem, et Tunquinensem, et propter illas praecipue intermissum hoc anno reassumpsi, efformavi, et perfeci: cui profecto non leve emolumentum provenit ex studio intermixto utriusque chronologiae. Quo etiam tempore intermedio, cum Illmus D. Coricensis praelaudatus egregium opus annamiticum edidisset Di đoan chi gião inscriptum contra doctrinas obliquas et aberrantes, in quo praesertim explicatur, et refellitur doctrina secta Thật; plura ex eo ad opusculum nostrum derivarunt. Alium vero librum valde eruditum annamitico charactere jampridem edidit idem Praesul pro litteratis, eo titulo donatum Đại học chi Đạo, idest, magni addiscentis doctrina; in quo conatur litteratis, ex eorum libris, Dei notitiam persuadere; quam et multi illum legentes perceperunt.

Tribus insuper sectis praefatis accedit et Religio christiana, quae in hoc regno annamitarum praedicata est, et magnum processum habuit, pluresque persecutiones passa est. Aequum quippe est, et consentaneum idololatriae, quae ex tribus illis sectis descendit veram opponere Religionem, tamque in rem adhibui, et praedictum indicem historicum Illmi Di nostri Coricensis, cujus pars ultima agit de Missionariis, eorumque gestis in hac missione Tunkinensi. Hoc itaque opusculum reverenter exhibeo dominis meis, et amicis Missionariis hac in missione versantibus; quod, qualecumque sit, arbitror fore illis profuturum. Quod complebam mense Septembri anno christi 1750, Annamitis Canh ngọ Regis Lê Cảnh Hưng undecimo.

Ego Frater Adrianus a Sancta Thecla, Eremita discalceatus Ordinis.

VIII

Sancti Patris Nostri Augustini, Missionarius Apostolicus in Regno Tunquini.

Caput Primum

Opusculum de Sectis apud Sinenses et Tunkinenses

Caput Primum De Sectâ Litteratorum

Articulus Primus. De Confucio, hujus Sectæ Principe

Primas partes in Sinis habet Secta Litteratorum, quæ appellatur Sŭ vel Jô, Annamitis Nhu, vel nho. Cujus sectæ Princeps est Confucius, qui tamen doctrinam ejus nho dictam primus non docuit, sed à præcedentibus, et priscis Sapientibus acceptam egregiè tradidit. Celeberrimus ergò ille Sinarum Magister natus est in Regno Lŭ provinciæ Xang tung, Annamitis Lô San anno vigesimo primo Imperatoris Cheu Ling vuâng, Annamitis chu linh Vuong, Mundi 3454. ante christum natum ad Æram vulgarem annis 550. Annos vixit septuaginta tres, mortuus anno quadragesimo primo Imperatoris Cheu Kinh vuong. Pluribus autem nominibus appellatus est, et appellatur nimirum 1° Kiŭ, seu Khu à monte ubi ejus parentes filium petierunt. 2° Chung Ny, seu Trọng Ni à nomine litterario ei impertito. 3° Kung Zu et Khŏng Tư à nomine suæ familiæ; 4° Fu Zu et Phu Tư quo nomine significatur Magister, et antonomasticè illud appropriatur Confucio. 5° demum duplici nomine simul conjuncto dicitur Kung fu zu, et Không Phu Tư. Sed ex omnibus nominibus in libris promiscuè citari solet, pro-nomine excepto, à quo honoris gratiâ abstinent litterati, cum primum nomen à parentibus impositum à Sinensibus habeatur indecorum. Pro-tanta sapientia sua opera, quæ edidit, sunt sex libri Lŏ King et Luc Kinh appellati, quos ille jam tunc composuit, libris olim præcedentium litteratorum, eos que Reformans. Tituli eorum [illegible] sunt Thư Kinh, Thi Kinh, Dịch Kinh, Lễ Kinh, Nhạc Kinh, Xuân Thu Kinh, quorum ultimum ipse scripsit jam septuagenarius. In Thư Kinh gesta Regum [illegible] continentur, exordio facto à Đế Nghiêu, seu Ỷ Jao, de quo ut Regum gestis regiminis [illegible] similiter est sermo; in [illegible] Thi Kinh, necnon in Thi Kinh quondam Regis [illegible], qui est liber carminum. In Dịch Kinh figurae lineares ab Imperatore Phục Hi inventae et designatae explicantur, quae radicitus sunt octo, et in seipsas multiplicatae sunt sexaginta quatuor. In Lễ Kinh traduntur documenta de moribus. Nhạc Kinh, quae periit, juxta sui nominis significationem, agebatur de Musica. Alios libros non scripsit Confucius, aut saltem notitia eorum non habetur. Plurima tamen ejus dicta seu responsa ad interrogata allegarunt ejus discipuli auditores in libris suis, qui sunt Gia Ngữ, Luận Ngữ, Đại Học, Trung Dung. Illius autem discipuli numero septuaginta duo nominatim recensentur in libro Gia Ngữ, in quo et habetur historia vitae Confucii. Ut autem ex libris noscitur, Confucium egregia indole, acri ingenio, ac magna vi mentis cum longo rerum usu conjuncta praeditum fuisse, ac politissimum politica et morali scientia excelluisse: sed et illud summopere miserandum ex ejus libris apparet, quod ille Deum Verum ignoravit, cum errore gentis suae Ethnicam superstitionem secutus, cultum caeli et terrae, syderum, montium, aliarumque rerum, nec non et defunctorum, diserte docuerit, nec nisi caelum Regis superni nomine, cujus cultum maxime promovit, intellexerit, ut ejus testimonia mox producenda ostendunt luculenter.

Porro Confucius coaevus fuit Pythagorae, apud Graecos Italicae sectae principi, qui ex insula Samo oriundus, Crotone prope Tarentum magno auditorum concursu, Philosophiam professus est, circa annum mundi 3535, quo Confucius erat Sexagenarius. Utrique fuit eadem animi moderatio et modestia; Pythagoras quippe non se Sophon, id est Sapientem, sed Philosophon, hoc est Sapientiae amatorem voluit appellari. Unde Philosophi nomen promanavit. Confucius vero interrogatus, ut fertur (nullibi enim in ejus libris potuit inveniri) an ipse esset thánh, sive [illegible] King, id est, Sapiens, respondit se quidem multa scire, non tamen audere sapientem se nominare.

Ut

At vero Confutii doctrina non statim prævaluit ab ejus obitu. Namque exorta est doctrina Dương-chu et Mặc-Địch evulgataque est et prævaluit, atque obstante [illegible] doctrina Confutii [illegible] [illegible] Mạnh Tử in suo libro tract. 3° [illegible] doctrinam utriusque repellit in verbis: Dương Mặc chi đạo bất tức, Khổng Tử chi đạo bất trứ — ; hoc est, si doctrina Dương chu et Mặc Địch non extinguatur, doctrina Confutii effulgere non potest. [illegible] [illegible] [illegible] non [illegible] [illegible] [illegible] quoque persecutionem tandem passa est doctrina Confutii. Imperator quidem Tần Thỉ Hoàng litterarum ignarus, litteratos, qui sibi non adhærebant, sic obloquebantur, infensus, comburi jussit quotquot libri Confutii inveniebantur in toto Regno, atque litteratos seu scholasticos libros ejus addiscentes vivos sepeliri. Tunc quidam litteratus libros Confutii de industria intra parietem occultavit, unde post persecutionem [illegible] Imperii familiæ Hán extractos scholastici reperire potuerunt. Inter eos tamen non fuit Nhạc Kinh, et ideo deperditus est. Eodem tempore quidam litteratus jam nonagenarius nomine Phục Sinh memor Thư Kinh, quam olim addiscens memoriæ commendaverat, alteri scribendi dictavit, ut habetur in Præfatione libri Thư Kinh. Itaque Confutii doctrina, et Secta non nisi imperante familia Hán potuit invalescere; ex quo namque primus illius familiæ Imperator Cao Tổ pertransiens territorium patrium Confutii, sepulchrum illius invisit, eique sacrificavit. Hinc a toto tempore Cao Tổ [illegible] mille annos venerationis Confutii numeravit litteratus Đào [illegible] [illegible] Thị, infra citandus articulo 4°.

Articulus Secundus.

De Studio, Libris, et Doctrina hujus Sectæ.

Litterati Sinenses et Tunkinenses plurimum studium impendunt in suis characteribus addiscendis, quorum tanta est multitudo, et varietas, cum multiplex etiam uniuscujusque significatio;

nificatione et totius vitae cursus vix sufficiat ad eorum notitiam comparandam. Habent vero sua dictionaria, in quibus collecti habentur omnes characteres et singillatim explicantur juxta omnes eorum significationes, à quibus nostri Europaei sua characterum Sinensium dictionaria desumpserunt, illos explicantes locutione latinâ. Characteribus autem dum student, student et rebus, quae in libris traduntur per characteres; quare simul addiscunt characteres et res characteribus significatas. Illud porro observandum, quod Tunkinenses seu Annamitae, eisdem quidem characteribus utuntur ac Sinenses, eos tamen pronunciant diversâ loquelâ ab illis, eâdem retentâ significatione; ita ut si quis litteratus Sinensis, et alter Tunkinensis colloquantur, se nequeant intelligere; si vero scribant, se bene intelligant.

Libri autem, quibus student, ut evadant litterati, sunt 1° Ngũ Kinh, quinque libri Confucii praelaudati in unum corpus collecti, qui olim sex erant; sed uno deperdito Kinh Nhạc, remanserunt quinque. Praecipua commentaria in iis libris intersecta sunt illustrium litteratorum Trình Tử, Chu Tử et Thâm Tử discipuli Chu Văn Công authoris libri Gia Lễ, qui floruerunt sub Imperatoribus Thần Tông, Hiếu Tông, et Ninh Tông familiae Tống. 2° Tứ Thư, id est quatuor libri in unum corpus conjuncti quibus tituli sunt, Luận Ngữ, Đại Học, Trung Dung, Mạnh Tử; in quibus Confucii, aliorumque ejus sectatorum varia dicta in confuso collecta continentur. Librum Luận Ngữ duo discipuli scripserunt auditores Confucii nomine Nhan Tử et Tăng Tử; librum Đại Học unus scripsit idem Tăng Tử; librum Trung Dung scripsit Tử Tư Confucii nepos et auditor; librum Mạnh Tử scripsit quidam ex nomine vocatus Mạnh Tử, valde clarus, una cum Vạn Chương ejus discipulo, qui floruit tertio saeculo à Confucio, quo tempore Sinense imperium in septem regna dividebatur. In quibus libris commentaria praecipua sunt praefati Chu Tử. Quatuor illis libris accedit liber Gia Ngữ, qui solus circumfertur, aliis libris minime similis, et continet pariter Confucii dicta, ejusque discipulorum; eum scripsit alius Confucii discipulus aevi posterioris nomine Thúc Tử Lương. 3° Libri de historia Regum Sinensium, quorum tria corpora habentur, id titulis inscripta Shàng thuân, authore Đu Cống, sub Imperatore Tống Thần Thần Tông authore praefato Chu Sĩ, sub Imperatore Tống Hiếu Tông; et Hang yên authore Liêu Khâm, sub imperatore Minh Thần Tông: de quibus nostram vide Sinensem Chronologiam. Illis itaque libris studiunt Scholastici, ut fiant litterati, totis que viribus in ejusmodi studium intendunt, eos libros vel memoriter ediscendo, ut gradus litterarios consequantur, ad quos praevio examina circa eos libros, seu in iis contenta, semel in triennio provehuntur. Gradus autem illi sunt tres, minimum infimus dictus sinh Đồ, medius Cống, supremus Tấn Sĩ.

Agitur autem potissimum in illis libris de recte vivendi ratione, et ad illam historia adhibetur, ut ex aliorum actibus quid prosequendum, quid evitandum innotescat. Nulla tamen methodus ibi observatur ad morum honestatem explicandam, et addiscendam moralem disciplinam, ac solum pro opportunitate rerum enarratarum de virtutibus sermo habetur. Omnes virtutes ad quinque reducunt, quas Annamitae dicunt Ngũ thường, easque sic nominant Nhân, Nghĩa, Lễ, Trí, Tín, id est, charitas vel misericordia, justitia, urbanitas, prudentia, fides aut fidelitas. Easque virtutes et Moralem honestatem docent pro quinque hominum statibus, et reciprocus ordo observetur in illis; nimirum 1°. Inter Regem et subditos: 2°. inter Patrem et filios: 3°. Inter Maritum et uxorem: 4°. inter fratres majores et minores: 5°. Inter Socios seu amicos; qui ordines seu respectus personarum dicuntur ab Annamitis Ngũ luân, et ita recensentur, Quân thần, Phụ tử, phu phụ, huinh đệ, bằng hữu.

Pauca vero docent litterati de Philosophia naturali, seu de Physica. Illud proferunt systhema in exordio suae historiae, quoad rerum constitutionem: Thái cực sinh lưỡng nghi, lưỡng nghi sinh tứ tượng, tứ tượng biến hóa [illegible] [illegible]; hoc est primum principium, seu elementum Thái cực produxit coelum et terram. coelum et terra produxit quatuor elementa, seu qualitates, id est majus et minus âm, ac majus et minus dương. è quibus âm, est res imperfecta seu materialitas, et dương est res perfecta, seu

seu immaterialitas; atque quatuor illæ qualitates constituerunt omnes rerum species; seu ex illis quatuor qualitatibus, seu elementis factæ omnes sunt res. His addunt quod quando cælum et terra in rerum confusione primum sunt discreta, illico prodiit primus homo; Bàn đầu chi khi thiên địa chi phân, tắc hữu Bàn Cổ thị xuất. Nulla vero causa efficiens, quæ primum illud elementum Thái cực creaverit, et ex eo alia produxerit, ibi exhibetur; nec illa prima mulier ibidem inducitur ad propagationem; solius primi viri facta mentione.

Præterea dicant in libro Dịch Kinh .. cælum et terram unum esse principium a quo res omnes producantur. Confutius eo in libro, tractatu Hệ từ, hæc pronunciat: Thiên địa chi đại đức viết: sinh, hoc est, cæli et terræ magna virtus dicitur productiva, seu productio. Quæ Confutii verba Chu Tử sic elucidat: Thiên địa dĩ sinh vật vi tâm, id est, cælum et terra habet cor, seu naturam, ad producendas res. Subdit ille: Ngày thiên xác nhiên tại thượng, địa tắc đồi nhiên tại hạ, nhất vô sở [illegible], chỉ dĩ sinh vật vi sự: hoc est, idcirco cælum solidum seu firmum manet suprà, terra verò rotunda manet infra; utrumque nihil aliud agit, nisi res producere. Concludit ille: Cố Dịch viết: Thiên địa chi đại đức, viết: sinh; scilicet, propterea dicitur in libro Dịch .., cæli et terræ magna virtus dicitur productiva. Et ad illud commentarium Chu Tử respexit glossator tractus Tả [illegible] in libro Gia ngữ Confutium interrogantis dicens: [illegible] Thiên địa dĩ sinh vạn vật hoc est, gubernator cælum et terra producit innumerabiles res. Primas autem partes tribuunt cælo ad producendas res in eodem Dịch Kinh, ubi explicant primam figuram ex octo, quas invenit et designavit Primus Imperator Phục Hi, quæ est Càn nguyên, tam admiratus Confutius ait: Đại tai Càn nguyên, vạn vật tư thỉ [illegible] textum Chu Tử exponit: Đại tai Càn nguyên [illegible] Càn nguyên thiên [illegible] hoc est, litteræ Đại tai sunt admirantis. Nguyên est idem ac magnum, et principium Càn nguyên significat magnum principium virtutis cæli: quapropter omnes res productæ illi virtute nituntur, quam respiciunt ut primum principium. Ex quibus comperimus, quod Confutii mens, ejusque Sectatorum est, quod res omnes producantur à caelo tanquam à primo principio. Virtutem verò naturae productivam caelo inditam distinguunt ab ipso caelo materiali visibili, seu ab ejus figura, quae oculis videtur. Quae distinctio est ibidem manifesta. Siquidem Trình tử eamdem figuram Càn nguyên primò ita exponit: Càn thiên dã, phù thiên chuyên ngôn chi tắc đạo dã, phân nhi ngôn chi tắc dĩ hình thể vị chi thiên, dĩ chúa tể vị chi Đế, dĩ công dụng vị chi quỉ thần, dĩ diệu dụng vị chi thần, dĩ tính tình vị chi càn, càn giả vạn vật chi thủy, cố vi thiên, vi dương, vi phụ, vi quân. hoc est littera Càn significat caelum, oh, caelum! absolute solum loquendo de illo est lex, seu ratio; distinctim loquendo de illo, acceptâ figurâ visibili dicitur specialiter caelum; acceptâ gubernatione, dicitur Rex; acceptâ operatione, dicitur Spiritus operans, seu virtus operativa; acceptâ excellentiâ, seu virtute operandi, dicitur Spiritus; acceptâ naturali conditione, dicitur Càn; haec res Càn est rerum omnium principium; itaque illud Càn se habet, seu, est caelum, est clarum, est Pater, est Rex. Ubi vides, quod virtus caeli, licet caelo indita, distinguitur à caelo, seu à visibili caeli figurâ.

Manifestum est insuper ex eo testimonio, quod Đế seu Rex, qui et dicitur Thượng Đế, idest, Supremus Rex, distinguitur quidem à caeli figurâ, quae oculis videtur, unum tamen facit cum ipso caelo. Quamvis verò ibi Đế distinguatur à thần, hoc est Rex à Spiritu; alibi tamen uterque pro eodem accipitur, nimirum relatè ad caelum, de quo praedicantur tanquam duae illius proprietates, vel duo officia. Sic Khảo thị in historia relatus Imperatori Tống huy tông succensens ait: Mạc tôn ư thiên, thiên chi thần chí tôn giả, Thượng Đế dã, Đế giả chúa tể, id est, non est aliquid altius caelo, caeli spiritus ille altissimus, est supremus Rex; Rex ille gubernator praedicatur. Illum quoque supremum Regem dicunt dominum caeli. Trình tử ~~in libro [illegible]~~, ait: Thiên chi chúa tể, Thượng Đế dã. hoc est, caeli Dominus quis? est Supremus Rex. Thái Chinh in eodem libro explicans litteram Đế, dicit: Đế giả, thiên chi chúa tể, hoc est, Rex ille est caeli Dominus gubernans. Constat ex his luculenter quod apud litteratos Thượng Đế, seu Supremus Rex non est diversus à coelo, sed unum est cum ipso coelo, et ipsum est coelum. Ac eo sensu Confucium quoque Thượng Đế intellexisse, et usurpasse infrà patebit.

Praeter Supremum illum Spiritum totius coeli, qui dicitur Thượng Đế sive Xáng Dỷ, agnoscunt in coelo et alios spiritus particulares, Solis nimirum lunae, et Stellarum: Sic et praeter generalem terrae Spiritum, agnoscunt et alios spiritus speciales, praesertim montium et fluminum. Ac coeli spiritus vocant Thiên Thần, spiritus verò terrae dicunt Địa Kỳ. agnoscunt insuper spiritus aliarum rerum, nempè ventorum, pluviae, frigoris, et aestus, aliosque spiritus innumeros, sicut innumerae sunt res, quibus omnibus inest virtus operativa à sensibus remota. Omnesque illi spiritus seu rerum virtutes dicuntur Quỉ Thần, sive Kuỉ Xần, quo nomine significatur virtus operativa rebus indita, quae per sensus non percipitur. Quae virtus alio nomine dicitur etiam Linh. Nomen autem Thần, et nomen Linh ex Confutio significat excellentiam, quae rebus inest, et ab hominibus intimè scrutari non potest. haec de doctrina secta litteratorum. Caeterum Sinenses libros habent de Geometria, de Arithmethica, de Astronomia, et et maximè de Medicina, quamvis earum Scientiarum principia, et rationem ad tantam perfectionem minimè perduxerint, ac in Europa. Quibus scientiis privatim studium impendunt, nec publicè in gymnasiis eas addiscunt. hinc quamvis in commentariis libri Kinh thư, et in historia Kang mục, ubi sermo est de gestis Đế Nghiêu disertè agat Chu Tử de cursu solis et lunae aequando per mensem intercalarem; Scholastici tantam studium illi rei non adjiciunt; ea quae omissa, ad alia addiscenda intendunt, quae in iisdem libris de gestis Regum enarrantur.)

Articulus Tertius.

Articulus Tertius
De Religione hujus Sectae.

Caelum et terram, quae unum putant esse principium primum omnium rerum, colunt litterati, minimum Spiritum coeli, et Spiritum terrae, nec non alios Spiritus, tam coelestes, quam terrestres; atque cultum eorum omnium docent in suis libris. Confutius de eo cultu haec habet in Lễ Kinh Lễ vận: Tiên vương hoạn lễ chi bất đạt ư hạ dã, cố tế Đế ư giao, sở dĩ định Thiên vị dã, tế xã ư quốc sở dĩ liệt địa lợi dã, hoc est primaevi Reges fuerunt solliciti de ritibus ne ignorarentur à Subditis, ideo Sacrificarunt Regi (Superno) in loco Giao ad constituendam coeli dignitatem, et Sacrificarunt terrae in regno ad ordinandam terrae utilitatem.

Subdit ibidem Confutius: Cố lễ hành ư giao, nhi bách thần thụ chức yên, lễ hành ư xã nhi bách hoá khả cực yên, nempe Sacrificium fit in loco giao, et plurimi Spiritus recipiunt sua officia; sacrificium fit in loco xã et plurimae res producuntur optimae. Ex eo Confutii testimonio, et aliud ejusdem innotescit quod habetur in libro Trung Dung, ubi ait: Giao xã chi lễ, sở dĩ sự Thượng Đế dã: id est, caeremoniae quae fiunt in locis Giao, et xã, sunt in cultum Superni Regis, et Reginae terrae, quod secundum sub intelligitur ob litteram xã prius expressam, et Chu Tử ibi interpretatur dicens: Giao tế Thiên, xã tế Địa; bất ngôn Hậu Thổ giả tỉnh văn dã.

Primus autem Rex, qui sacrificium exhibuit Thượng Đế seu Regi Superno et aliis Spiritibus in historia Sinensi inducitur Hoàng Đế iis verbis: Đế tác cung thất chi chế, toại tác hợp cung tế Thượng Đế, tiếp vạn linh: hoc est, Rex construxit aedem cung ad sacrificandum Thượng Đế, et innumeris Spiritibus. Et apud Confutium in Thư Kinh primus occurrit Đế Thuấn de quo refert: Tứ loại ư Thượng Đế, yên ư lục tông, vọng ư sơn xuyên, biến ư quần thần; nempe sacrificabat Regi Superno, Sacrificabat Soli, lunae, stellis, quatuor anni temporibus, frigori et calori, aquae et siccitati, quae significantur nomine lục tông, seu sex rerum, quae debent venerari; sacrificabat montibus et fluminibus, nec non collibus, locis elevatis et locis planis. Eum que textum seu Shāin Tiī in eo libro expresse, et distincte interpretatur. Quonam vero modo colant coelum et terram conspectum fiet cap. 2. Illud autem ostendunt praecitata testimonia Confucii, quod nomine Shang ti Dē ipse non intellexerit Deum coeli, seu Deum verum, sed ipsum coelum, seu ejus virtutem aut praerogativam. Ibi enim locutus est de cultu Shang ti Dē, ac de cultu Hœu Thū seu Reginae terrae, et aliorum spirituum; qui cultus terrae, et aliarum rerum male conjungeretur cum cultu Regis Superni Shang ti Dē, si eo nomine verus Deus intelligeretur.

Cultum insuper Defunctorum docent et exercent litterati. Illum que admisit, et approbavit Confucius, qui tamen nullos ritus ad illum cultum praescripsit. Verum plura ejus sectatores adinvenerunt et tradiderunt, quibus cultus ergo Defunctos rite valeat exerceri. Quamobrem speciale ediderunt Rituale Kia li appellatum Sinis Kia ly, in quo plurimae caeremoniae ad eum cultum exercendum in funeribus, et commemorationibus distincte praescriptae sunt, et usu communi observantur. Illud autem Rituale in lucem edidit litteratus Chu Vän Cōng, anno sexto Imperatoris Sōng Hiāo Tōng, Christi 1168. Colendos ergo docent, et colunt litterati Coelum et Terram, id est, coeli et terrae virtutem, tanquam Suprema numina, atque Solem, lunam, stellas, montes, flumina, ventos, pluviam, seu virtutes operativas eorum, aliarum que rerum inanimatarum, nec non hominum Defunctorum manes. At ejusmodi doctrina et cultus sunt idololatria, cum cultum, qui vero Deo debetur, tribuunt, et tribui velint creaturis. Caeterum idola, quae in secta Thăc Sinis Fŏe, quae prisco nomine Shich Kia Sinis Xě Kiā appellatur, coluntur, contemnunt, et derident, cultum que eorum impugnant, multis traducentes Imperatorem Hán Ming Dē, qui cultum illum in Sinas evocavit. Attamen regni consuetudini, et moribus externe se conformantes idola illius sectae venerantur externe, et omnia alia superstitiosa exequuntur, amore ducti et correpti divitiarum, dignitatum, famae gloriae, et sanitatis.

Sunt

Sunt et multi litterati in Sinis politissimi, qui nullum Deum credunt, Atheistae, de quibus Sermo est in Decretis Apostolicis editis in causa rituum Sinensium. Verum illi à Doctrina Secta sua litteraria, de colendis coeli et terrae, aliarumque rerum Spiritibus, quae in libris eorum quam praecipua est, manifeste recedunt, deviant et apostatantur.

Articulus Quartus.
De Cultu celebris Confutii.

Quoniam litterati Speciali cultu Magistrum suum prosequuntur, specialem de eo Sermonem hic instituimus, de reliquis Spiritibus, qui ab omnibus coluntur, suo loco peracturi. Colunt itaque omnes litterati magnum suum Confutium, quin imò Rex ipse, et alii omnes cultum ei impendunt, tam in imperio Sinarum, quam in hoc regno Annamitarum. Quem cultum universalem jam diu Confutius consecutus est; Siquidem jam pridem litteratus Liu Shi, qui floruit, Imperante Tống Nhân Tông, ea pronunciavit, ut legitur in historia Thông Giám, ad annum 41. Imperatoris Chu Kinh Vương: Tự Thiên Tử chí ư thứ nhân, mạc bất tông phụng lịch xuân dư niên, vị hữu nhất Khổng Tử chi thịnh giả. Nhĩ phi quân thần phụ tử nhân nghĩa, lễ nhạc chi giáo ; hoc est, a coeli filio (nempe Rege) usque ad Subditos, non est, qui non reveratur et colat Confutium perfectum, cui à plusquam mille annis similis non fuit, eo quia Regis et Subditi, patris et filii rectam docuerit disciplinam. Imperator Hán Cao Tổ pertransiens terram regni Lỗ, Confutii Sepulchrum invisit, et primus Imperatorum ibidem ei sacrificavit, anno Regni sui duodecimo ante Christum natum fere duobus Saeculis. Plures verò Imperatores Subsequentes variis honoris titulis Confutium decorarunt. Primò Hán Bình Đế quatuor saeculis à Cao Tổ Confutium constituit Magnatum ex praecipuis, qui Regis obsequuntur in aula dicens: Truy thị Khổng Tử vi Bao Thành Tuyên Ni công, hoc est, confirmamus dignitatem

Confucio, ut sit magnus Regi aulicans. Secundo Đàng huyền tông anno Regni sui 27° christi 738. Confucium pronunciavit Vương, inquiens: Truy thì Khổng Tử vi Văn tuyên Vương; hoc est, conferimus dignitatem Confucio, ut se gerat litterarum publicum gubernatorem. 3° Tống Chân Tông, anno primo, Christi 998. Confucium evexit ad gradum Thánh dicens: Gia thì Khổng Tử vi Huyền Thánh văn tuyên Vương; id est, addimus dignitatem Confucio, ut se gerat profunde sanctum, vel sapientem litterarum publicum gubernatorem. Quam declarationem fecit in templo ipsius ~~Confucii [illegible]~~ nativitatis, ubi et ei sacrificium exhibuit. Mandavit insuper anno quarto erigi templa in honorem Confucii in urbibus cujusque Toparchiae Chu appellatae; Châu chu thành tạo Khổng Tử miếu. Quarto demum Nguyên Vũ tông regnum sibi consecutus, anno christi 1307, decrevit Confucio supremum honorem, declarans illum sanctissimum, vel sapientissimum, in haec verba; Gia phong Khổng Tử vi Đại thành chí Thánh văn tuyên Vương; scilicet conferimus dignitatem Confucio, ut se gerat magnum effectum summe sanctum, vel sapientem.

Itaque praefatum propter edictum Imperatoris Tống Chân Tông templa Confucio in unaquaque toparchia extructa sunt, et modo passim, ea invenies in hoc regno Annam, in quolibet territorio etiam minori dicto Tổng, quae Miếu et Nhà thánh nuncupantur. Illis vero in templis nulla apud communitas tabella Confucii asservatur, prout apud Sinas communiter habetur, praeterquam in templo Regiae civitatis, in quo tabella ejus super altare retinetur, auro obliniti, et argenteis characteribus inscripta. Nec ullum Confucii simulachrum, ut plurimum ibi habetur, quod tamen alicubi existit collocatum. Olim Rex Trần Thái Tông, anno ejus 27 christi 1253 scholam condidit, et pinxit in ea imagines Confucii, Chu Công, et septuaginta duorum discipulorum Confucii ad eos colendos, ut in historia Đại Việt iis verbis refertur: Lập quốc học viện tô Khổng Tử, Chu Công, Á thánh họa thất thập nhị hiền tượng phụng sự. Primus autem Confucii

Imaginem deposuit Imperator Tông thái Tổ imperium adeptus anno Christi 910, quod legitur in historia. Bội tước autem Imperatoris Confucius in sacrificiis sanctissimus ac sapientissimus modo nominatur ex schedula offerendi iis verbis: Đại thành chí thánh văn tuyên vương; ac eadem verba scribuntur in ejusdem Confucii tabella, ubi adhibetur.

Omnes litterati cujuscumque territorii, ad templum Confucii in eo constitutum conveniunt ex legis praescripto bis in anno, nimirum luna secunda et octava circa aequinoctium veris, et autumni, ibique peragunt solemne sacrificium: ad quod pluribus in locis omnes pagi incolae conveniunt. Eadem luna 2a et 8a ludi magistri una cum suis discipulis sacrificium pariter exhibent Confucio minus solemne in eorum scholis, ubi pro altari locant in medio unam quadripedem mensam, super qua nulla est Confucii tabella, nec folium aliquo nomine ejus inscriptum. Quisquis vero gradu aliquo litterario recenter donatur, templum adit Confucii in suo territorio constitutum, et omnibus praesentibus illius territorii litteratis edulia offert suo magistro Confucio, et prostrationibus eum adorat: qua functione gradum suum noviter adeptum facit omnibus innotescere. Praeterea oblationem faciunt litterati in Sinis bis singulis mensibus in novilunio et plenilunio. Verum ea res apud Tunkinenses seu Annamitas non est in usu.

Descriptio sen

Descriptio Loci pro Sacrificio Confutii.

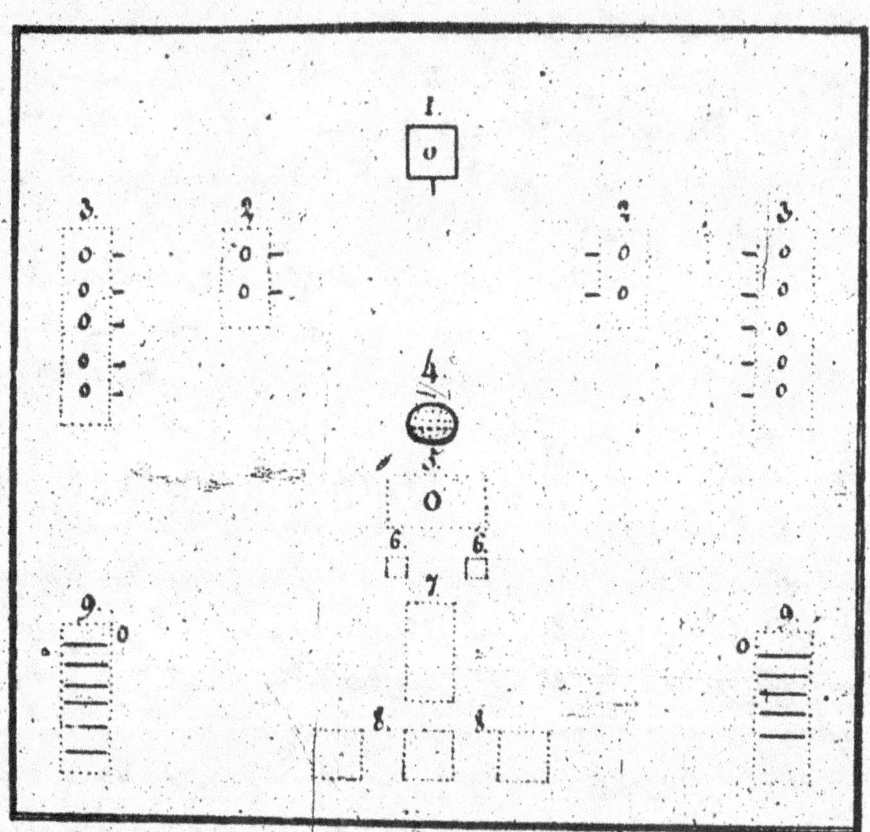

1. Altare Confutii, in quo est vasculum odorum et mensa eduliorum.
2. Altaria quatuor insignorum Confutii Discipulorum
3. Altaria decem insignium Confutii Discipulorum.
4. Locus in quo ~~apponuntur carnes~~ animalium semiustulatae et vasculum Sanguinis cum Pilis.
5. Tabula heiding'an, in qua cremantur odoramenta et antequam ritus Sacri peraguntur.
6. Caeremoniarii duo, qui praemonent ad singula, ibi adstant.
7. Minister principalis, qui sacrificat ibi se sistit et inde ascendit ad Tabulam heiding'an.
8. Assistentes tres, vel plures, qui principali Ministerio assistunt, ibi consistunt.
9. Tabulae duae in quibus parata sunt nonnulla, quae ad Sacrificium debent.

debent adhiberi. Prope illas sunt duo vascula quadrupedi imposita ad manus abluendas.

Articulus Quintus
De Solemni Confucii Sacrificio.

Paragraphus Primus
De Praeparatione ad Sacrificium

Sacrificium, quod primi litterati peragunt bis in anno in templo Confucii, his ce rebus et ritibus praeparatur. Super altari in medio locatur unum vasculum cum virgulis odorum. Ex utraque parte altaris paulo infra duae quadrupedes mensae in longum constituuntur, et super unaquaque duo vascula odoramentorum pro quatuor Confucii discipulis insignioribus Tu Phoi appellatis; duae aliae pariter mensae quadrupedes ex latere utroque inter praedictas spatio intermedio collocantur, et super unaquaque quinque odorum vascula pro aliis decem Confucii discipulis insignibus dictis Thap Triet; apponunt etiam super illis mensis seu altaribus plures papyri argentei et aurei libras, et aliquot candelas vel lucernas, nec non unam parvam in exteriorum mensarum coram singulis vasculis odoramentorum ad sacrificium. Infra omnes mensas praefatas locus est in medio ad sibi ponendas varias escas animalium occisorum, qui offeruntur. Immediate succedit ei loco una tabula seu mensa affabre elaborata, et deaurata dicta huong an, in medio directe statuta contra altare, super qua sunt odoramenta, et duae lucernae vel candelae; quae mensa adorino merito dici potest altare exterius, aut pars altaris interioris. Ab utroque latere spatio inferius ponuntur duae aliae quadrupedes mensae, super quibus variae parantur ad sacrificium adhibenda, et coram utraque mensa est unum vas aquam inhaerens quadrupedi sustentaculo ad manuum lotionem. Inter mensas laterales coram mensa huong an locus est pro sacrificii ministro principali, et pro aliis ei assistentibus.

Pridie Sacrificii primo noctis tempore omnes litterati templum ingrediuntur veste ampla et oblonga coloris violacei superinduti, et caput cooperti pyleo rotundo ejusdem coloris. Duo ex illis accedunt prope mensam hương án, et ex hinc inde stant facie ad invicem conversa, qui officium gerunt Caeremoniarii in tota functione Sacrificii, praemonendo voce elata ad singulas actiones quidquid gerendum est, et dicuntur Thày lễ, plures ministri dicti Chấp sự se sistunt in variis locis ad ministrandum, plures assistentes, saltem tres dicti Bồi tế, quam se locant in medio in conspectu mensae hương án una linea in latum; et ultimo major, seu dignior inter omnes in medium procedit coram eadem mensa, ibique stat ante praefatos assistentes, qui munus exercet Ministri Principalis Chủ tế quam nuncupatur; et merito nominari potest Sacrificulus hic vero et ejus assistentes habitum non gerunt specialem ab aliis adstantibus diversum.

Post haec principalis minister, uno caeremoniario praemonente, proxime accedit ad mensam hương án, a qua distat parumper in suo loco, et coram ea genuflectit. Aliquis vero ex ministris accendit super altare Confucii et reliquis vasculis odoramentorum, ac duo alii ministri deferunt ad altare duos [illegible], id est stillati ex oryza calices, et apponunt super praevia mensa eorum ibi locata pro Confucio. Unus deinde ex dignioribus genuflectit a sinistris Principalis ministri, atque omnium adstantium praemisso nomine, Confucium monet de sacrificio mane peragendo dicens: Kim ơi [illegible] nhật s. vọ tiên thánh Khổng tử, id est Admonemus reverenter antiquum sanctum, vel Sapientem, quod expectamus mane crastinum diei ad habendam functionem, quibus verbis Spiritus Confucii implicite invitatur, ut sacrificio faciendo intersit. Deinde dictus Minister principalis una prostratione adorat, et accedit ad locum suum, ibique facit quatuor profundas reverentias. Deinde adducitur a Janitore templi animal mactandum, et principalis Minister illud examinat, an aptum sit ad sacrificium, non tamen probatur infuso in aures ejus liquore, uti fit apud Sinenses. Illo animali electo, absolvitur functio praeparatoria quae dicitur Sơ [illegible]. Occiditur subinde animal

mal electum et approbatum, sus scrofa, vel bubalus, et si unus minime sufficiat, duo etiam occiduntur, simulque aliquot caprae. Animalia occisa excoriant, pilis abrasis; secant in partes, ac semicoquunt, ac de iis aliquid apponunt super mensis spirituum coram vasculis ornamentorum; caput vero super mensa pro Confucio; et partem reliquam in medio locant in conspectu altaris retro mensam Kiêdingân, et ibidem ponunt vasculum continens partem sanguinis et pilorum praecipui animalis occisi.

Paragraphus Secundus.
De Functione Sacrificii.

Mane sequenti, peragunt sacrificium incipientes valde diluculo. Duo Caeremoniarii, Ministri, Assistentes, et Minister Principalis se sistunt quisque suo loco, et in functione praeparatoria. Omnibus in loco suo consistentibus, Minister Principalis pergit ad inspiciendas singulas mensas, et altare, an omnibus necessariis sint instructa, atque de eo interrogat etiam Ministros illis mensis praepositos. Hac inspectione completa, unus minister, praemonente Caeremoniario, accipit vasculum sanguinis cum pilis, et pergit ad ea infodienda extra templum absque ulla praevia oblatione, quae in Sinis fieri solet, teste Episcopo a Leonissa in expositis Sacrae Congregationi; qua caeremonia ostendere intendunt, quod carnes mox offerendae munda sunt interius a sanguine, et exterius a pilis. Tum Caeremoniarius admonet obviam ire Confucio dicens: Nghenh Thánh [illegible], idest occurramus Sancto, vel Sapienti Regi, seu potius Gubernatori: atque primarius Minister, Assistentes, et omnes adstantes quatuor prostrationibus illum excipiunt adventantem.

Post haec Principalis Minister, admonitus uno Caeremoniario, qui respondet alternatim cum alio Caeremoniario, ad singula subsequentia, pergit ad mensam depositam, et manus abluit in vase quodam ibi existente, et abstergit manutergio sibi porrecto a Ministro deputato, redit ad ordinem, et genuflexus coram mensa Kiêdâng án, offert seu libat unum cyathum seu calicem vini, idest stillat utraque manu illum elevans ad oculos, oblatum quem reddit

ei...

ei, qui sibi illum tradiderat, atque is illum deponit super altare unà cum tribus aliis Ministris, qui pariter alios tres stillati caliculos ferunt ad altare, et suprà mensam adultiorem ibi collocatam imponunt. Alius verò Minister ad altare affert unum pannum, vel velum sericum album quadratum involutum, et super eo apponit. Tunc Minister Principalis prostratus semel adorat, ac surgens parumper recedit ad locum suum, ibique genuflectit. Accedit subinde quidam ex dignioribus ad mensam hương án, et coram ea genuflexus recitat offertorium ex tabellula dictâ văn tế posita super quodam parvâ tabulâ, quam sibi exhibitam manu tenet, atque recitatam locat in altari, statimque primarius Minister cum Assistentibus binâ prostratione adorat. — —

Eo autem in offertorio omnes litterati praesentes, quorum nomina, praemissis, anno, mense, die occurrentibus, exprimuntur incipiendo à nomine Principalis Ministri sacrificantis, 1° offerunt stillatum rượu appellatum, et edulia, et reliqua apposita singula exprimendo rogantes, ut ea excipiat; 2° laudant Confutium pro libris ab eo conscriptis, et pro doctrinâ posteris traditâ; 3° petunt ut eam doctrinam sibi relinquat, et proficiant in eâ, ac sapientes imitando sapientes praedecessores, sic non eamdem doctrinam conservet; et posteris tradat in perpetuum; denique concludunt iis verbis: Thượng hưởng: quibus Confutii spiritus invitatur ad comestionem modo spirituali. Confutius vero honorificis illis verbis nominatur: Đại thành chí thánh văn tuyên vương, quae suprà explicavimus. Cum quo Confutii expresso nomine faciunt etiam mentionem quatuor ejus discipulorum insigniorum communi vocabulo Tứ Phối, et decem aliorum insigniorum communi pariter vocabulo Thập Triết. Quatuor porrò insigniores discipuli sunt: 1° Nhan Tử, 2° Tăng Tử, 3° Tử Tư, 4° Mạnh Tử. Quibus nomen Thánh, idest Sancti, vel Sapientis collatum est ab Imperatore Nguyên Văn Tông anno ejus primo Christi 1307.

Factis hujusmodi offertoriis, principalis Minister offert quatuor caliculos stillati quatuor laudatis discipulis insignioribus, unum post alium pro unoquoque;

-quoque, quos quatuor ministri deferunt successivè ad binas eorum mensas, et super iis deponunt ante quatuor eorum vascula odoramentorum, ordi-ne servato, quem modò expressimus, ibique apponunt aliam pro singulis pan-num serico involutum, et cujusque panni factâ appositione, Minister Principalis unâ prostratione adorat. Decem deindè caliculi stillati apponuntur pro aliis decem discipulis inaequalibus; sed prius minimè offeruntur, nec pan-ni serici apponuntur. At ea omnia repetuntur secundò et tertiò, prius pro Confutio, posteà pro ejus Discipulis ordine praefato. Illis omnibus tertiò repe-titis, Minister Principalis genuflectit coram mensâ hiang.án, et bibit unum caliculum, aversâ facie ab altari in partem lateralem, qui cali-culus ex mensâ Confutii accipitur à Ministro deputato, et ad illum affertur; eo quia potu creditur ille accipere felicitatem à Confutio sibi impertitam, et ideo unus Caeremoniarius praemonet ad bibendum dicens: Ẩm phúc idest Ebibe Felicitatem. Et hausto caliculo, alius Caeremoniarius ministrum mo-net, ut gratias agat de tanto dono, qui statim in gratiarum actionem binâ prostratione adorat, et ad locum suum recedit. Post hoc Caeremoniarius ad-monet omnes adstantes, ut gratias agant Spiritui Confutii inquiens: Tĕ Thần; et Minister Principalis, eique assistentes, ac omnes adstantes qua-tuor prostrationibus adorant; quâ caeremoniâ intendunt cum gratiarum actione prosequi spiritum Confutii abeuntem, vel quasi abeuntem. Combu-runt denique extra templum in altis schedulam Vǎn tế, omnesque pan-nos sericos, nec non argenteas et aureas papyri libras, quae super altari-bus fuerunt apposita; in urbe autem Regiâ schedula illa et panni serici oblati non aduruntur, sed intra cystulas reposita in puteum altum projiciun-tur: quod fortè et alicubi etiam observatur. Completo sacrificio dividunt carnes et omnia edulia oblata inter Ministrum, assistentes, aliosque ad-stantes, quae magni faciunt, et partim ibi comedunt, partim domum afferunt pro suis familiaribus, et amicis./.

20. Confictii Nomina, libri et Testimonia de quibus in hoc Capite.

1.

Caput Secundum.

De Spiritibus, eorumque cultu.

Cultus Spirituum apud Sinenses ex vetustissima traditione descendit; qui Secta litteraria inhaerens cultum quidem spirituum adoravit, non tamen primo induxit. Verba jam fecimus capite praecedenti de litteratorum doctrina circa Spiritus; sermonem modo instituimus in hoc capite de Spiritibus, quos colunt tam litterati, quam omnes alii de more nationis Sinicae. Meus tamen mihi non est de omnibus, et singulis spiritibus, qui communi religione coluntur, sed de celebrioribus tantum, quibus maxime sacrificium exhibetur.

Articulus Primus.

De Spiritibus Coeli et Terrae.

Coelum imprimis, et Terram, seu coeli Spiritum, et Spiritum terrae communiter omnes tam litterati, quam illitterati, Rex et populus colunt et reverentur. Coelum appellant Regem, et Terram Reginam, Hoàng Thiên, Hậu Thổ; atque coeli Spiritum dicunt Thiên Thần, et Thượng Đế, et terrae spiritum Địa Kỳ, et Templum quidam extat dicatum Thượng Đế intra palatium Regis, quod vulgo dicitur Nhà Kính Thiên: nec alibi extat in toto regno templum aliud cultui coeli deputatum, in quo templo nulla est imago, vel tabella, sed una tantum quadrupes mensa [illegible]. Eo in templo Rex solemniter sacrificat semel in anno, prima, aut secunda, aut tertia anni ineuntis die, quod cum paucis [illegible] rex ingreditur, reliquo magnatum comitatu extra templi limen remanente; quando quidem indignos se putant in illud intrare, nec alius praeter Regem idoneus, et dignus, qui coelo ibi sacrificet existimatur; unde commune adagium est, quod solus Rex coelo sacrificare meretur, [illegible] in ejus templo. Ibi ergo Rex, manuum ablutione praemissa, ac resonantibus tympanis, aliisque musicis instrumentis, ascendit super mensam [illegible], coelum, seu Thượng Đế prostrationibus adorat, et vinum libat, atque schedula Văn tế, seu offertorium ab uno ex Primatibus reci-

tatur

-tatur, in quo Rex vinum et edulia mensae jam imposita offert, et auxilium ac pro-
-tectionem petit à Thiêng Dê pro toto regno. Terrae quoque sacrificium Rex offert
praefato triduo in ejus templo tribus victimis, quae sunt bos, capra, sus. Quando
Rex ad templum coelo dicatum se confert ibi sacrificaturus, dicitur Vua ra Giao id
est, Rex egreditur ad templum coeli, quod Giao appellatur, sicuti et templum
terrae dicatum Xã nominatur. Sacrificat insuper Rex iis diebus per suos minis-
-tros, seu magnates, montibus, et fluminibus, quatuor anni temporibus, frigori et
aestui, ventis et pluviae, seu eorum spiritibus in eorum templis distinctis, tem-
-plo prisci Imperatoris Dê Thuân, qui iis omnibus, teste Confucio in Thu Kinh
sacrificavit. In Sinis quinque sunt montes prae aliis excelsi, quibus sacrificium
offerunt Imperatores, nimirum mons Tây in parte orientali, mons Hoa in
parte occidentali, mons Hành in parte meridiali, mons Thuòng in parte
septentrionali, et mons Tung ______________ in medio quatuor illarum par-
-tium. De praefatis vide Caput 1um.

Neque vero Rex solus, sed etiam subditi Coelum colunt, eique sacrificant om-
-nibus in oppidis et pagis, semel in anno, die aliquo primi mensis, ad placitum,
sacrificant Regi superno, seu Thiêng Dê, quod sacrificium, seu functio ap-
-pellatur Kỳ yên, id est, supplicatio tranquillitatis. Illud vero sacrificium
peragunt ubicumque, sive in domo publica communitatis, sive in foro, sive
in via, sive in porticu dicto nhà quán, non tamen in aliquo templo, seu miếu,
cum nullum habeant templum dicatum Thiêng Dê, praeterquam in urbe intra
Palatium Regis, ut superius dictum est. Semel quoque in anno, mense ultimo,
omnes Praefecti, et milites, tam in civitate quam extra, solemne emittunt juramen-
-tum, quo Regi spondent fidelitatem, sibi mortem imprecantes à coelo et terrâ,
omnibusque Spiritibus, quibus omnibus faciunt solemne sacrificium, de
quâ functione agemus articulo quinto.

Praeterea communis est fama, quod Rex eo die, quo sacrificat coelo, in
agrum exeat post sacrificium, atque arrepto aratro agrum aret paulisper.
Verum perdiligenti facta inquisitione in urbe, interrogando eos qui Regem
comitari solent, quotiescumque egreditur à palatio suo ad alia loca, comper-

-tum est

-tum est Regem nusquam aratrum sumere, et agrum arare; comites quoque illi tam Christiani quam Gentiles de eâ re interrogati responderunt se nunquam vidisse Regem aratrum adhibere, et arare, nedum modò regnantem, sed et ejus prædecessores, patrem, avum et proavum. Quâ de re certiorem me reddidit Venerabilis P. Franciscus Gil de Federich, de quo in Præfatione.

Cæterum ritus ille à Rege peragendus describitur in libro Lễ Kinh iis verbis. — Thiên tử nãi dĩ nguyên nhật, kỳ cốc vu Thượng Đế, nãi trạch nguyên thần, Thiên tử thân tải lỗi trĩ, xuất tam Công, cửu Khanh, chư hầu đại phu, cung canh Đế tịch, Thiên tử tam xôi, tam Công ngũ xôi, Khanh chư hầu cửu xôi, hoc est, Cœli filius, Rex scilicet, accipit primam diem . . . disponit, vel apprehendit aratrum, jubet Aulicos Regi aperire, seu findere terram; cœli filius arat eundo et redeundo ter, Aulicus tam Công quinquies, Aulici Khanh et chư hầu novies. Obsolevit ergo ritus ille tam in aula Annamitica, quam in aula Sinensi.

Articulus Secundus.

De Regibus Thánh vocatis, et præcipuè de iis, quibus Sacrificant quatuor Anni temporibus.

Novem sunt Reges, quos Secta litteraria, et alii omnes habent et celebrant ut Sanctos, seu eximiâ virtute præditos, Thánh ab Annamitis, et Xứng à Sinis appellatos, quos distinguunt in duas classes; Antiquiores vocant Thánh Đế, et minus antiquos Thánh Vương, quæ duo nomina Đế et Vương in eo differre dignoscuntur, quod nomen Đế majorem, et nomen Vương minorem exprimat dignitatem. Reges dicti Thánh Đế sunt quinque dicti, propterea Ngũ Đế, nimirum Thái Hạo Phục Hi, Viêm Đế Thần Nông, Hoàng Đế, Đế Nghiêu, Đế Thuấn. Reges verò dicti Thánh Vương sunt quatuor, nempe Đại Vũ primus, ex familia Hạ, Thành Thang primus ex familia Thương, Văn Vương ejusque filius Vũ Vương primi ex familia Chu. Omnes illi Reges uno sub nomine Thánh Vương illustri encomio commendantur in præfatione libri

libri classici Đại học ex verbis Tích giả thánh vương kế thiên lập cực Đi đạo trị thiên hạ, tắc Phục hi, Thần Nông, hoàng Đế, Nghiêu, Thuấn, võ Thang, Văn, Võ, tiên vương truyền thừa thu học est, Ere illo Reges sancti, seu virtute eximii condentes legem, acceperunt rectam rationem ad regendum populum; illam que successive tradiderunt praefati Reges à Phục hi; Sacrificant autem prioribus quinque Imperatoribus; quia die coelo et terrae offerunt Sacrificium.

Quatuor autem anni temporibus Rex per suos aulae magnates sacrificat prisis Imperatoribus et praescribitur in Lễ Kinh, nimirum desinente hyeme sacrificat ad orientem loci Giao Imperatori Phục hi, et Spiritui Câu Mang qui egit praefectum sub illo, ad Ver introducendum lập xuân; desinente vero Sacrificat ad Austrum loci Giao Imperatori Thần Nông, et Spiritui Chúc Dung ad aestatem introducendam, lập hạ; desinente aestate Sacrificat ad occidentem loci Giao, Imperatori Thiếu hạo et Spiritui Nhục Thu ad autumnum introducendum lập thu; desinente autumno, sacrificat ad aquilonem loci giao Imperatori Chuyên húc, et Spiritui huyền Minh ad hyemem introducendam lập đông. Ad introductionem cujusque temporis astrologus triduo ante diem determinat, ac Regem praemonet de die determinato, et Rex jejunat à carnibus abstinens in praeparatione ad illam. Illis vero Imperatoribus sacrificant ob eorum merita in Rempublicam; et signanter sacrificant Phục hi, et Câu Mang, quia obedientes, seu conformes coelo legem condiderunt, seu rectam disciplinam, ut in commentariis dictis Lễ Kinh tiết Chú Đế Thánh Thần kế Thiên lập cực Sinh hữu công đức ư dân, cố báo ư xuân tắc chi.

Sacrificant quoque Thần Nông et Chúc Dung, quia subditos docuerunt agriculturam, ut in historia Sinensi refertur; Tiên mộc vi tỉ, nhu mộc vi lỗi, thủ giáo dân nghệ ngũ cốc.

Specialem autem ritum observant in Veris introductione, vel institutione lập xuân; quem describere hic juvat iisdem verbis, quibus accurate illam descripsit venerabilis P. Franciscus Gil de Federich. — Circa lập xuân (ait) milites Đội lễ Kinh, die antecedente accedunt ad domum Nha môn nghệ, et

„ et accipiunt <u>1300</u> bubalos parvos; in portâ hùng chiêu erigitur una domus
„ aperta à quatuor ventis, et ibi collocatur bubalus luteus magnus, et in unoquoque
„ bubalo est Hotua Câu Mang, in parvis parva, in magnis magna; quali tenent ip-
„ sum bubalum; acceptis 1300 bubalis, illos deferunt ad hunc carcerem orientalem;
„ et illos deponunt in atrio carceris, bubalus luteus illo die usque ad mediam noctem
„ manet in domo erecta in l'gŭ hùng chiêu, postea quo thō phiêng illum deferunt ad
„ atrium seu templum Hoa Bach Mã, ibi deponunt illum foras, sed Thân Câu Mang
„ solus erigitur in medio atrii, ibi Quan Thu Doan sacrificat Thân Câu Mang Sacrificio
„ peracto, Nha Mon storeâ involvunt Thân Câu Mang, et illam offerunt sepelire;
„ milites vero hujus carceris ad hunc carcerem deferunt bubalum, et attenuunt
„ partem capitis illius, unum pedem, et partem caudae, et deferunt offerendum Regi
„ Vua, qui expectat simul cum Proceribus hinc et inde; et ibi offerunt praedicta
„ ac simul 300 bubalos parvos, ex quibus milites ipsi attenuunt 55, et deponunt illos
„ quinos super mediam mensas vulgo mâm, et cooperiunt illos lua croceâ, et
„ ibi relinquunt, quos postea Rex mittit ad omnes Đền thờ (templa Spirituum)
„ et reliquos bubalos parvos ex 300 postea Rex partiri jubet inter omnes, qui
„ ex officio illi semper assistunt milites; deinde hujus carceris deferunt mille
„ bubalos parvos ad Thu Dang et muniant hoc Regi Chúa, accedunt omnes N ha
„ Mon sáu kiêu (sex cohortium) et sibi bubalos partiendos deferunt ad
„ omnes mandarinos, qui ad tale kiêu pertinent: quos quidem bubalos deponunt
„ in altaribus, quae habent, sive idolo, sive thân, sive progenitoribus Dicentes bu-
„ balos afferunt (ait in alio priori scripto) luteos altitudinis 5 aut 6. digitorum,
„ quos pingunt diversimodè, diverso colore caput, corpus et caudam regulariter;
„ et attentur ad hos colores pingendos quinque principiis Sinicae philosophiae,
„ quae etiam diebus et annis attribuunt, nempe hỏa, thổ, kim, thủy, mộc,
„ et quinque coloribus his principiis respondentibus: unde si primus dies Veris cor-
„ respondet igni seu hỏa, caput bubali juxtà colorem illi correspondentem ef-
„ formant; et juxtà bubalum etiam faciunt imaginem hominis quasi custo-
„ dientis, quem dicunt Thân Câu Mang, quam juxtà diversitates anni etiam
„ diversimodè pingunt."

Narratur in historiâ Sinensi, quod Xuyên Hiếu functionem Lập Xuân fecerit mense primo die primo denuo suam. nec ibi legitur quòd aliquis ejus prædecessor ante illum fecerit eam functionem. Anno Mậu Thìn, Regis Lê Cảnh Hưng nono, cæremonia illa facta fuit die 18° mensis ultimi pro anno sequenti; in Sinis verò peracta est eodem anno die 16° ejusdem mensis ultimi. Erat apud nos mensis Februarius anni 1749. Illud vel speciale habent in more pro estatis introductione, nimirum peracto Sacrificio Imperatori Thần Nông in ejus templo. Præfectus dictus Phủ Doãn in horto seu agro adjacenti accepit aratrum, et arat tantisper ter eundo et redeundo, et plantat parum oryzæ, vel rapas nomine cải khoai. Qui ritus videtur substitutus ritui qui in Lễ Kinh præscribitur peragendus à Rege mense primo, de quo egimus supra.

Præterea in singulis pagis Imperatori Thần Nông sacrificant bis in anno lunatione 6ª vel 7ª quando nimirum incipit transplantatio oryzæ, quæ dicitur hạ điền vulgò xuống đồng, seu descensus in agros, et quando completur ea transplantatio, quæ dicitur thượng điền, vulgariter lên đồng, seu ascensus ab agris. Sacrificium ad descensum in agros pluribus in locis omittitur, ac sola fit simplex oblatio eduliorum. Ad sacrificium nulla imago, aut tabella ipsius Thần Nông adhibetur. In offertorio autem quod legunt ex schedulâ 1° pluribus eum laudant, et dicunt Thánh Đế, sapientem, spiritualem; nobilissimum, et excellentissimum, atque coadjutorem Regis Superni Thượng Đế, amando, nutriendo et docendo subditos agriculturam, opportune ævo suo ac posteris relinquendo ejusmodi beneficium in perpetuum: 2° petunt ut sibi concedat plurimam felicitatem, ut terræ fertilitatem in campis, et uberem messem; nec non divitias, pacem, aerisque temperiem: quandoquidem ipse Rex sanctus auxiliatur et vires subministrat. Sic in offertorio, seu formula sacrificii. Cæterùm præfati Imperatores, quibus sacrificant quatuor anni temporibus, pro veris Sinarum Regibus haberi non possunt. Constat enim illos diluvium universale antecedere: quâ de re vide præfationem nostram de Sinensium chronologiâ, ubi et diximus Thần Nông non alium

fuisse

fuisse nisi Noe, de quo Gen. 9 legitur quod post diluvium "cæpit vir agricola exercere terram."

Articulus Tertius

De Spiritibus, quos colunt militiæ Professores.

Militiæ Professores plures numines bellica olim fortitudine celebres colunt, et præ omnibus Thái Công, qui prius familiæ nomine dictus est Lã, et proprio singulari dictus Vọng, habent in honore veluti supremum Magistrum et patronum. Floruit autem sub Imperatore Chu Vũ Vương, supra mille annos ante Christum natum, pro quo certavit contra postremum Imperatorem familiæ Thương, nomine Trụ, quem tali obsidione cinxit, ut ille nullum habens effugium in regnum sese injecerit cum suis, sic quod Vũ Vương toto imperio potitus est, quod pater ejus Văn Vương majori ex parte sibi jam devinxerat; imperioque potitus illum constituit militiæ magistrum, seu supremum Præfectum.

Honorem 2um impendunt viro valde celebri Trương Lương appellato qui imperante familia Tần primarium Præfectum egit in regno Hàn sub ejus rege [illegible], quo deinde extincto ab Imperatore Tần Thỉ Hoàng, se cum exercitu suo adjunxit Regi Hán Liêu Bang, cui postea totum imperium cessit, et dictus est Cao Tổ; postremo veritus ne ab ipso Imperatore interficeretur, ei suspectus de surripiendo sibi regno, petiit ab illo facultatem abeundi ad vitam ducendam solitariam cum spiritibus, et recessit ab aula, in qua sex annis servierat Imperatori, ac ibi latuit annis 13, usque ad annum sextum regni Huệ Đế, quo senex cessit e vita novem sæculis post Thái Công supra laudatum.

Cultum Thái Công, et Trương Lương publico decreto mandavit Imperator Đường Huyền Tông, anno regni sui 19°, Christi nati 730, iis verbis: Tề Thái Công miếu, dĩ Trương Lương phối hưởng, tuyển cổ danh tướng dĩ bị thập triết. Xuân thu hai ngày [illegible] như Khổng Tử &c. —

jussit namque templum extrui, præfecto Thái Công, accipere Trương Lương et constituere supparem Thái Công, eligere antiquos nominis duces, et collocare eorum [illegible]

mandatos,

manuscriptos, ex conoré, excepere tamen Mandarinos et eclavam, ac die illa priori Sacrificare, ... sacrificium. Ex quibus compertum est Thái Công eundem tenerem et cultum a militia professoribus obtinuisse, ac confusum apud litteratos ... illum paulo post Imperator Đàng Thủ Tông succes- immediatus ... titulo donavit Vũ Thành Vương. Superiora de Thái Công et Trương Lương ex historia Sinensi desumpta sunt.

In urbe autem Regia hujus Regni Annamitarum templum extat dictum Võ miếu in quo cultum habent duces fortes quindecim; quorum caput est praedictus Thái Công Vương. In templo sunt duae aedes; una regulariter aperta, altera semper clausa. In aede aperta sunt duodecim duces, sex ultimae sinistram, totidem dextram; in clausa vero aede manet Thái Công cum aliis Ducibus duobus, e quibus unus est Trương Lương, cum alio aliquo ejusdem gradus phẩm, ac etiam alii nomine Triệt; et, opinor, juxta decretum Imperatoris praeallegatum. Est et aliud Miếu in eadem civitate, in loco tạo constitutum, vulgo dictum Khả chài, in quo colitur celebris Dux nomine Quan Đế, dictus et Quan Vũ, erga quem majore devotione militia afficiuntur quam erga Thái Công praefatum. Ille autem floruit sub Imperatore Hậu Hán Hậu Đế, et socium habuit alterum Ducem nomine Trương Phi, cum quo simul praeliatus est pro illo Imperatore, contra Regem Ngô, et una cum eodem in praelio occisus est, anno dicti Imperatoris 2°, prope medium saeculi tertii, a Christo nato. De utroque praefato Miếu notitiam accepi a Venerabili Martyre P. Francisco Gil de Federich per Epistolam ... datam ad me die 6a Augusti 1744.

Deinde quando bellum suscipiunt, primum sacrificant militiae Inventori ante vexillum, in quo ejus imago depicta est, et equo insidens Dux qui Sacrificium offert. Deinde sic orat: — ... Vũ Thành Vương in medio, a sinistris ejus Tôn Vũ Tử, a dextris Trương Lương ... sub nomine Trương Tiên Vương.

Articulus 4us.

Articulus Quartus
De Functione Tê Ky Dao

Singulis Annis Lunatione Secunda, die à Praefecto Astrologo Quan Tu Thien appellato designato in aula, et in omnibus Provinciis fit magna functio Tê Ky Dao nuncupata. In arenaria prope urbem fit unum septum ex cannis valde amplum, intra quem 36 altaria eriguntur. 1mum in cultum coeli et terrae in sinistra illius septi, reliqua deinde altaria à dextris primi dicti altaris in plures lineas disposita subsequuntur, nimirum in prima linea sunt plura altaria in cultum praedictorum tam Regum quam Gubernatorum Regni de Republica bene meritorum; et inter Regum altaria duo sunt pro duobus Regibus antiquissimis, nempe Kinh Dương, et Lac Long Quân, qui primi sunt in chronologia Annamitarum: in secunda linea sunt quinque altaria in cultum quinque supremorum Ducum, seu militiae principum, qui sub quinque Regibus praedictis Ngũ Đế nuncupatis militarunt, ac in capite hujus lineae erectum est magnum vexillum dictum Ky Dao, quod est proprium vexillum supremi Praefecti totius exercitus, à quo desumptum est nomen hujus functionis Tê Ky Dao. Multa quoque altaria in unam et alteram lineam sunt ordinata in cultum multorum spirituum supremi gradus Thượng đẳng Thần, et super unoquoque altari ponitur tabella nomine sui spiritus inscripta; sunt quae in iis signantur altaria Tản Viên Sơn, Đổng Thiên Vương vulgò Vua Gióng et Lý Ông Trọng, vulgò Ông Trấn, de quibus specialiter agemus Articulo 8°. Regni gubernator seu Chúa cum comitatu descendit ad domum recreationis dictam Nhà Lều, quae paululum distat à loco sacrificii, et inde functionem intuetur. Regius exercitus ex ordine dispositus in arenaria cum equis et elephantibus atque militibus toto corpore armatis. Praefecti deputati in septum ingressi sacrificant spiritibus praedictis in omnibus altaribus praeparatis, gratias agentes de concessa in regno tranquillitate, ac interrogantes eorum protectionem ad continuandam et augendam eam tranquillitatem, expulsis Rebellium spiritibus, ne pacem exturbent.

Sacrificiis peractis, qui praesunt tormentis bellicis per aquilam cursoram trina explosioni excursione militum ter explodit tormentum dictum ống lệnh magno mortario simile; mox agitatur magnum vexillum positum ad januam domus praelatae, et caetera parva vexilla; subinde exploditur tormentum majus dictum bá lạng, ibidem collocatum, et reliqua tormenta subsequenter ter exploduntur, nec non milites hoquai suam catapultam explodunt, gladiosque evaginant, et lanceas attollunt. Quibus omnibus intendunt spiritus rebellium perterrefacere, et e regno procul expellere, ne sint infesti, et publicam tranquillitatem perturbent. Ultimo rursus exploditur semel ống lệnh, quo indicatur explosionem tormentorum esse completam. Tunc omnes milites conveniunt, et circa domum Chúa omnes se sistunt cum equis et elephantibus, et reliqui coram Chúa et exercitu luctantur, et ludicra alia certamina exercentur. Post haec convivatus dissolvitur, et omnes revertuntur ad propria.

Apud Praesides Provinciarum dictos quan trấn haec functio tế Kỳ đạo fit, posito solum uno altari, et una mensa hương án. Hoc anno Canh ngọ regis Cảnh Hưng undecimo, Christi 1750. Functio illa facta fuit die decima mensis secundi, concurrente die septimadecima mensis Martii.

Descriptio loci ad Juramentum.

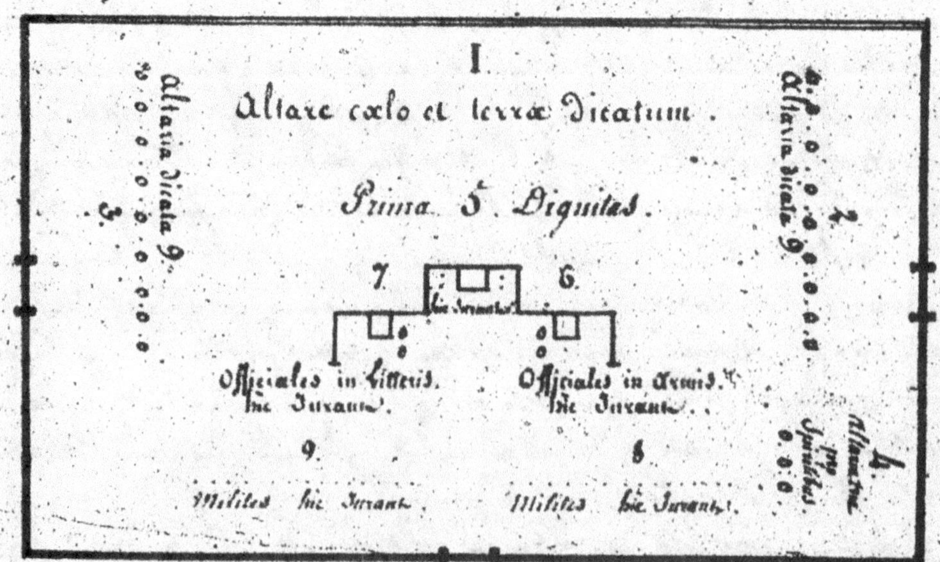

Articulus 5us

Articulus Quintus.

De Functione Hội minh, seu Juramento fidelitatis.

Functio Hội minh ea est, in quâ omnes Magistratus et Praefecti, seu aliquâ dignitate vel gradu donati, tam in litteris quam in armis, solemne juramentum emittunt de servandâ Regi fidelitate, atque appellatur Hội minh, id est, conventus ad jurandum. Ea functio peragitur tum in urbe regiâ, cum in aliis provinciis, apud eorum Praesides semel in anno mense ultimo, ac his caeremoniis in urbe celebratur. Construitur unum septum ex cannis quadratum valde amplum, in quod ingressus est ex utrâque parte laterali, et in parte anteriori. Illud intra septum erigitur in parte superiori altare coelo et terrae dedicatum, à latere sinistro illius altaris novem altaria dicata novem Regibus Lêa, ultimo defunctis, a novissimo ad praedecessores immediate; à latere dextro novem pariter altaria dicata novem Regni gubernatoribus Chúa ultimò defunctis à novissimo ad praedecessores, et ex eâdem parte sinistrâ immediate post Regum altaria subsequuntur tria altaria dicata, Primum, omnibus Spiritibus supremi gradus seu thượng đẳng thần; Secundum, Spiritibus aquarum; Tertium Spiritibus terrae. Singula vero altaria duabus umbellis cooperiuntur: et super singulis apponitur unus bubalus praevie ustulatus, oryza cocta vulgo xôi; et vinum ad sacrificium. In medio septi sunt tres quadrupedes mensae, seu tabulae, dictae hương án, super quibus virgulae odoriae cremantur, et infra illas à latere sunt vascula vino plena cum sanguine gallinae mixto, et in mensa media ensis aureus Chúa invenitur: coram hac media mensa, supremus praefectus, seu prima dignitas jurat; coram mensa laterali sinistrâ omnes officiales in armis; coram dextrâ omnes officiales in litteris jurant. In parte denique inferiori ipsius septi, ex uno et altero latere, sunt mensae 12; coram quibus milites jurant, et prope illas sunt vascula plena vino cum sanguine bubali. Pendet vero ex singulis circa mensis unum folium continens formulam Juramenti, quam recitant genuflexi qui jurant. Quae omnia ut perspicua fiant,

fiant, figuram supra exhibuimus in paginâ praecedenti 33.

Summo igitur mane ex Phủ, seu palatio gubernatoris regni Chúa, ad locum jurandi praefatum deferuntur una amphora vini grandis, una gallina, et gladius aureus ipsius Chúa. Ibi quidam Praefectus accipit gladium, et elevat ad caelum, eoque tres circulos in terrâ designat, in quos ingressi tres officiales, unus gallinam seu gallum tenet, alter forcipe apprehendit caput gallinae, alius qui medius inter utrumque, caput gallinae amputat aureo gladio, atque sanguis diffluit in amphoram vini subjectam, super quam aduritur una schedula juramenti emittendi, cineribus in eam decidentibus: et ex amphorâ illâ hauritur vinum sic mixtum in sex vascula, quorum bina locantur prope tres singulas tabulas hương án, coram quibus praefecti omnes emittunt juramentum. Plura etiam vascula vini pro militibus praeparantur, quae immixtum continent sanguinem bubali, loco gallinae cum illos sint nimis. Post haec, sacrificia peraguntur caelo et terrae, regibus novem, et novem Regni gubernatoribus, atque spiritibus, necnon sacrificuli obeuntibus vel filiis Chúa vel supremis Praefectis. Prius recitatur văn tế, seu offertorium, coram altari caelo ~~et terrae~~ dicato; cumque pronunciatur verbum duy, omnia recitantur offertoria una simul coram singulis altaribus. Sacrificiis peractis, omnes juramentum emittunt successive, unusquisque juxta gradum suum, coram tabula sibi congruente; emisso quo juramento, unusquisque uno haustu paucum bibit de vino, sanguine et cineribus simul commixtis.

Formula vero juramenti ea est: (A) Tôi lạy Hoàng Thiên Thượng Đế, Hoàng Địa Kỳ, vel Hoàng Thiên Hậu Thổ, vel Bụt Đất, cập chư linh Thần đẳng. (B) Tôi ở mỗ phủ, mỗ huyện, mỗ xã, tên tôi là mỗ, tôi niên sinh tôi là mỗ tuổi (C) Tôi làm tôi Vua Mỗ tôi; tôi làm tôi Chúa mỗ tôi cho hết lòng. (D) Vì bằng tôi ở chẳng hết ngay, thì tôi cũng chịu sau mà sây (E) nguyện kiêu Thiên Thượng Đế, Hoàng Địa Kỳ, vel Hoàng Thiên Hậu Thổ, vel Bụt Đất, cập chư linh Thần đẳng đánh chết tôi.

Cujus formulae sensus est: (A) Ego veneror magni caeli supremum Regem, et Reginam terrae spirituum; vel Regem caelum, Reginam terram; vel caelum et terram,

terram, omnes spiritus, (B) ego ex tali taparchia, ex tali territorio, ex tali oppido vocatus tali nomine, talis aetatis (C) iuro fore servum Regis N et Gubernatoris Regni N ex toto corde (D), si vero ego non maneam fidelis, bibendo de hoc vasculo vinum sanguinis (E) precor reverenter magni coeli Supremum Regem, et Reginae terrae Spirituum, vel Regem coelum, et Reginam terram, vel, coelum et terram, omnes spiritus, ut percutiendo occidant me.

Omnes qui jurant, hac una formula utuntur ad juramentum, sub diversitantum nominis coeli et terrae usurpatione; nempe Praefecti superioris ordinis seu magnates dicunt: Hoàng Thiên Thượng Đế, Hoàng Địa Kỳ; Praefecti vero ordinis inferioris dicunt: Hoàng Thiên, Hậu Thổ; milites autem dicunt Bồ Tát. Eo pariter die in palatio Vua, et in palatio Chúa juramentum fidelitatis emittunt omnes Đức Bà, seu Reginae, et quasi Reginae; omnes Quan Thị seu Thuy, id est, Eunuchi custodes regiarum, omnes qui de familia Vua et Chúa. Praeterea in unaquaque domo Bà Chúa et Đức Ông, omnes qui de familia ipsorum sunt, il re praestant juramentum: omnes quoque milites Chầu, qui pertinent ad Matrem vel Aviam Gubernatoris regni Chúa, praeter juramentum jam emissum de servanda fidelitate Vua Chúa, aliud juramentum praestant in domo suarum Dominarum de servanda illis fidelitate.

Multi insuper in pagis semel in anno, primo et plerumque mense commune juramentum faciunt de servando in pago suo, vel in territorio, concordia et unitate. Ac eodem juramento utuntur, quoties ad commune aliquod negotium, omnes pagi alicujus, aut territorii, incolae sese obstringunt, et dicuntur ăn thề. Tunc qui jurant, vel in domo publica coram Spiritu tutelari, vel in templo ejus dicto miếu, vel etiam sub dio, adhibentes potionem sanguinis gallinae vino commixti, ac juramento praemittentes oblationem adorationem. Denique ad ejusmodi juramenta quoque adiguntur litigantes a majoribus pagi in loco publico pro dirimendis eorum dissidiis.

Juvat porro illud observare circa juramentum praestitum cum potu sanguinis de fidelitate erga Regem, quod illud juramenti genus antiqua induxit consue-

tudo

-tudo, quæ fortè sumpsit exordium ab Imperatore Hán Caú Tí, qui juramentum fidelitatis exquisivit à subditis, adhibitâ potione sanguinis equi, ut refertur in historiâ Sinensi. Eam verò consuetudinem nihili facit, et rejicit Trình Tử in commentariis in librum Confucii Xuân Thu, ubi Confucius ipse improbavit vel unum exigendi à subditis simplex juramentum fidelitatis.

Omnia verò quæ dicta sunt de præfatâ functione Hội minh in civitate Regiâ celebratâ debemus erudito viro Venerabili Patri Francisco Gil. de Federich, ordinis Fratrum Prædicatorum, qui omnia suâ diligentiâ ex omnium exquisivit, invenit, et descripta ad me transmisit, designatâ etiam figurâ septi seu loci ad juramentum, prout jam suprà exhibuimus./.

Articulus Sextus.

De Spiritu tutelari nuncupato Thành hoàng

Colunt tam litterati, quam alii omnes, de more Spiritum castri, vel pagi protectorem, et rectorem, qui communi vocabulo dicitur Thành hoàng, apud Sinas Chùng hoàng. Is autem ut plurimum est homo aliquis, ob sua merita ad tantam dignitatem erectus, ut pro Spiritu loci protectore, seu tutelari habeatur atque colatur. Non rarò tamen est quidam homo celebris impietate, vel quoddam animal, vel aliqua res inanimata, ob eventum aliquem in loco Spiritum tutelarem ab incolis assumpta; quod sane valdè ridiculum est, seu potius deplorabile. Quo circa sunt aliqui pagi, qui Spiritum tigridis colunt, et plerumque, pluribus diebus ante diem sacrificii aliquem pauperem hominem capiunt, et postea occidunt statuto die, ut carnes ejus offerant Spiritui, eo quod tigrides necant homines, discerpunt, et vorent. Alii sunt, qui colunt Spiritum canis, et quia canes humano stercore vesci solent, ideo stercus quod mane aliquis juvenis ad id jejunus primò egerit, intra vasculum occludunt, et Spiritui offerunt cum aliis edulis. Plurimos alios id genus Spiritus invenimus, qui credi vix possunt ab iis, qui in his ce regionibus non commorantur.

Spiritus omnes tutelares, qui gradu aliquo sunt insigniti, ut infrà [illegible] habent speciale nomen nuncupatum. Cæteri verò qui graduati non sunt, solo

nomine

nomine Thành hoàng donati, ordinarie carent fano speciali, sed gaudent uno loco deputato in domo publicâ communitatis, qui plerumque opera caelato exornatur. Ubilibet tamen spiritus, tam graduati, quàm non graduati, tabellam habent auro delinitam, in quâ litteris argenteis scriptum est nomen ipsius cum iis duabus litteris 大王, idest Đại vương, quibus significatur Magnus Gubernator; ex utroque latere tabellae duo veluti brachia protenduntur, ac in summitate imperfecta quaedam vultûs figura, in cujus medio est parvulum quoddam speculum, exhibetur; quam alicubi etiam veste circumdant.

Originem porrò hujusmodi spirituum tutelarium ex eo aliqui deducunt, quod sub initium Imperii familiae Tấn, quae coepit imperare post Christum natum anno circiter 270; Imperator ex iis jussit in Regno templum unum in honorem spiritus caelestis custodis Regni, et ibi tabellam apponi cum eâ Inscriptione Thành hoàng thần vị — idest, sedes spiritus regentis civitatem. Quae res refertur in libro christiano Văn hằng quảng, iis verbis: Đại Minh hoàng cuộc nhất thiên vị bách niên tiền Văn Đằng Tấn tề tinh cuộc trong [illegible] nhất [illegible] cuộc Thiên Thần đi thờ thu đề ru bán [illegible] Thành hoàng Thần vị.

Verum dubia mihi ea res est; tum quia in Sinensi historia non habetur; tum quia nomine Thiên Thần à Sinensibus non intelligitur aliquis Angelus, seu Spiritus praeditus intellectu, sed sola virtus caeli intrinseca ipsi caelo, et virtutes solis, lunae, et stellarum ipsis pariter intrinseca, ut constat ex dictis Cap. 1. Artic. 2. Illud pro certo habendum, quod spiritus locorum tutelares, quales modo coluntur in Sinis et Annamitis; à Daemone inducti sint ea mente, ut opponerentur Angelis locorum custodibus, et Sanctis locorum patronis, quos Sancta veneratur Ecclesia.

His ea spiritibus locorum rectoribus, et protectoribus ter saltem in anno sacrificium offertur à communitate, nimirum tuenda primo primis diebus, et dicitur ab aliquibus kỳ yên, supplicatio tranquillitatis, quae tamen fit Regi superno, non spiritui tutelari, de quâ articulo 1°, mense decimo, et vulgaritèr et vulgariter dicitur Cơm mới, oblatio primitiarum, et mense undecimo, et dicitur Kỳ phúc, supplicatio felicitatis: quibus accedit et simplex oblatio eduliorum, quæ in fine mensis ultimi fit alicubi, in gratiarum actionem pro beneficiis eo anno acceptis. Ulterius quando pagus morbo aliquo laborat, vel malum aliquod patitur, communitas sacrificium facit spiritui tutelari, et dicitur Tống ách, deductio infortunii. Et insuper sacrificant, quando indigent pluvia ad agriculturam, et messem, et dicitur Đảo vũ, supplicatio pluviæ. Sunt et alia sacrificia, quæ in pagis ditioribus peraguntur ad libitum Majorum rectorum pagi, seu communitatis, qui quò magis epulis et jocis sunt dediti, eò plura sacrificia fieri jubent expensis communibus, ventri suo potius, quàm spiritui tutelari obsequentes.

Præterea singulis ferme annis, nisi egestas obstet, mense primo, vel tertio, vel decimo, vel undecimo instituunt cantûs solemnitatem, quæ ad plures dies, quandoque ad mensem protrahitur, fitque in domo publicâ communitatis. His autem diebus sacrificium semel in die spiritui exhibetur, mane, vel vespere, in quo una tantùm mensa eduliorum offertur, et sacrificio peracto habetur cantus, qui tota nocte, vel die continuatur. Cantores verò quasdam quidem laudes in honorem spiritus canunt, sed histrionum more cantiones obscænis, jocosis, et ridiculis satyris acutissimis refertas interponunt, quibus adstantium aures demulcent, et pecuniam multam ab illis sponte datam in remunerationem consequuntur. Tympana interim, et alia resonant instrumenta, et præsentes epulantur de mensis eduliorum, quæ nimium offeruntur in sacrificio, et ab incolis pagi contribuentibus offeruntur. Eaque solemnitas cantûs triennio luctûs pro morte Regis prohibetur.

Varios insuper ludos eo tempore agunt in honorem spiritus tutelaris; nimirum luctantur, qui ludus dicitur Đánh vật; baculis decertant, qui ludus dicitur Đánh [illegible]; duæ acies congrediuntur ad normam tabulæ lusoriæ Italis Scacco, qui ludus dicitur Đánh cờ; percutiunt utrinque quemdam globum ligneum, et excurrunt ad alterutram partem, qui ludus

ludus dicitur Đánh cầu. Qui verò victoriam obtinet, propositum praemium assequitur, et laudem.

De Sacrificio Spiritus tutelaris.

Sacrificium Spiritui tutelari his ex ritibus peragitur. In altari locata est tabella, in quâ scriptum habetur nomen illius Spiritus cum ex honoris titulo Đại Vương, id est Magnus Gubernator; quae tabella, si Spiritus templum habeat speciale, inde adducitur solemniter ad domum publicam communitatis, in proprio tabernaculo affabre elaborato. Apponunt coram illâ unum vasculum cum virgulis odoramentorum, et unam mensam orizâ coctâ xôi nuncupatâ, et unum integrum caput bovis, suis, vel bubali, nec non plures papyri libras quadratas aureas et argenteas; multas quoque aliarum mensas locant in solo propè altare in plures lineas ordinatas; atque deponunt in medio, in conspectu altaris, carnes animalis occisi in membra secti, quod animal prius mactatur absque ullâ oblatione, vel caeremoniâ; extat denique coram omnibus illis rebus una quadrupes mensa dicta hương án, super quâ cremantur odoramenta, et duo ardent candela, aut lucerna facta apparatu. Majores pagi, vesti- [illegible] induti, domum seu aulam ingrediuntur: duo caeremoniarii subsistunt propè mensam hương án ex utrâque parte; in medio coram eâdem mensa subsistit principalis Minister, et post illum aliquot assistentes, quae clarius descripta sunt capite primo, ubi agimus de Confucii sacrificio.

Omnibus in loco suo se habentibus, unus ex caeremoniariis voce clarâ pronuntiat: Nghinh Đại Vương, occurramus magno gubernatori; atque principalis Minister, et assistentes cum reliquis quater se prosternunt venerantes excipientes Spiritum advenientem, quem credunt se praesentem exhibere in suâ tabellâ. Pergit subinde Minister principalis ad lavandas manus in vase praeparato ex parte, quibus abstersis, redit ad medium propè tabulam hương án, ubi genuflexus vinum libat, calicemque elevans

usque

usque ad caelos, oblatamque reddit ministro, qui eum defert ad altare, et ponit super eduliorum mensâ ibi constitutâ. Post haec, unus à digmioribus accedit ad mensam hương án, et genuflexus à latere Ministri principalis pariter genuflexi legit offertorium, seu schedulam vǎn tế; quâ lectâ, Minister principalis unam facit inclinationem, et subinde binam prostrationem. In ea autem schedulâ omnes Majores pagi seu communitatis 1° Spiritum laudant de sua natura excellentiâ, et de suâ scientiâ, potestate, ac protectione; 2° Offerunt ei edulia, et alia ibi apposita, rogantes, ut ea dignetur acceptare; 3° Rogant, ut ipsos protegat, mala omnia arcendo, ac tribuendo tranquillitatem, ac omnia bona, ita ut dies transigant in laetitiâ. At singulare verò illud est, quod inter laudes, quibus Spiritum extollunt, eum, inquiunt, reverentiam habere, et obedientiam erga Regem illis verbis: thường hằng Khâm phụng Đế đình; omnes quippe Spiritus Regi subjectos censent, cum illos Rex attamat ad gradus, et coli faciat in regno suo, ut mox dicemus.

Offertorio hujusmodi recitato, Minister principalis iterum vinum libat secundò, et tertiò, prout primâ vice, et alius Minister defert vini caliculos ad altare, et in mensa eduliorum apponit. Postremò Caeremoniarius monet, ut gratias agant spiritui, et deducant dicens: Từ Thần; statim que Minister, et Assistentes cum caeteris adstantibus quater se prosternunt, abeuntem Spiritum grato animo prosequentes. Denique communi convivio de oblatis epulantur, quae communibus totius pagi seu oppidi expensis sunt praeparata. /.

Articulus Septimus.

De Caeremonia tạo khảo bái Thần, id est de Probatione et graduatione Spirituum.

Inter Spiritus locorum patronos plures sunt, qui gradu per Regium diploma donati sunt, et gradus eorum est triplex, minimum supremus, medius,

medius, et infimus, juxta quos illi dicuntur Thượng đẳng, Trung đẳng, hạ đẳng

thần Ad eos autem gradus publico experimento ipsi Spiritus provehuntur: quod experimentum his ce fit caeremoniis. Erigitur unum altare omnibus Thần probandis intra quoddam septum loco in urbe designato, ac in illo altari omnium dictorum Thần nomina scripta locantur. Praeterea tot adducuntur bubali prope septum, quot Thần probandi; et in unoquoque bubalo est nomen inscriptum illius Thần, ad quem bubalus pertinet. Supremus quidam Praefectus illuc missus à Rege praecipit Thần proprio nomine vocato, quod si velit ad gradum promoveri, bubalum interficiat, quamobrem bubalus inducitur intra septum; ac si illum Thần nominatus interficiat, promovetur Regio diplomate; in quo merita ejus laudantur, ejusque nomen refertur in cathalogum, in quo descripti sunt omnes Spiritus graduati. Ejusmodi vero diplomati totus postea pagus, cujus Spiritus promotus est protector, die praefixa magno apparatu obviam egreditur, pluribus prostrationibus illud veneratur, atque ad publicam domum deducit, ubi et sacrificant Spiritui promoto, epulantur post sacrificium, variisque modis collaetantur. Hanc porro functionem promotionis Spirituum nemo hac aetate fieri conspexit, abhinc enim multo tempore facta est. Spiritus omnes, qui in cathalogum regium relati sunt gradu aliquo ex tribus praefatis donati, templum habent singulare miếu nuncupatum, ibique fit illis sacrificium semel in anno à Magistratibus illius toparchiae, in qua templum existit, nimirum ab ông Chủ, ông Giáo, ông Huyện, qui tres simul peragunt sacrificium in unoquoque templo Spiritus graduati intra suam toparchiam, et intra terminos suae jurisdictionis constituto. Spiritibus vero ad supremum gradum evectis aliquis ex Regiis Magistratibus a Rege missus sacrificat, qui et facultatem habet deferendi umbellam, et attollendi vexillum ad praelium, nec non accipit singulis annis de manu Regis bubalum litaturus functionis tập xuân, de qua supra descriptio facta est. Qui transeunt ante templa Spirituum gradus supremi, tenen

Dóng Trân , tenentur galerum capiti, et calceos pedibus auferre, atque è rete in quo nobiles, et graduati deferri solent, descendere: quae honoris signa si praetermittant, poenâ mulctantur. Quae porro dicta sunt de functione Spiritus promovendi ad me scripsit iisdem fere verbis Venerabilis Martyr P. Franciscus Gil de Federich, quem super iis consului captivum in Urbe. Demum in eâ Spirituum probatione et provectione summa daemonis calliditas elucet: siquidem ritum illum spiritus probandi, et ad gradus provehendi; eorumque nomen in cathalogo describendi, ille induxit, ut facinus faceret Sanctae Ecclesiae, quae viros pietate, et virtute insignes, praevio examine, Sanctos pronuntiat, aut Beatos, et in album refert Beatorum, aut Sanctorum).

Articulus Octavus.

De Vua Dóng, et Vua Trân, et aliis nonnullis.

Inter Spiritus supremi gradus Thánh Dóng appellatos magni nominis sunt in hoc regno duo praefati, quos etiam impensè colunt Confucii docti Professores. Primus Vua Dóng vel Gióng natus est in pago Phù Đổng territorii Vũ Ninh provinciae Borealis sub Hùng Vương sexto aetatis inter Reges priscos octavo. Rex ille bello impetitus quaeri jussit, qui contra hostes dimicaret; cumque fieret inquisitio, puerulus nomine Dóng, qui annum quartum agebat, nec aliquod verbum hactenus locutus erat, extemplo dixit ad matrem suam Regium Ministrum advocare, cuique affatus est: Nguyện đắc nhất kiếm nhất mã, quân vô ưu dã ; idest, peto unum ensem, et unum equum; Rex ne sit sollicitus. Eo consecuto procedit ad praelium omnes praecedens, et hostes magnâ clade contrivit ad montem Vũ Ninh, ita ut Majori ex parte perempti sunt: reliqui vero se illi dedentes, humique prostrati adoraverunt, illum conclamantes ducem cognomine Thánh Dóng. Puerulus verò equo currenti insidens, in aerem elevatus est, et abiit,

sic disparuit

bus disparuit. Quapropter Rex imperavit ei templum construi in horto, ubi ille degebat, ac statu tempore ei sacrificari. Plurima post saecula Rex Lê Thái Tổ, qui plusquam sexties ab hinc saeculis regnabat, edicto suo illum pronuntiavit Regem seu gubernatorem spiritualem super coelis: Thượng Vị Trùng Thiên Thần Vương. Ea porro commenta narrantur in ipsius historia hujus Regni Đại Việt.

Magni etiam nominis est Spiritus Tản Viên appellatus, deque in historia Đại Việt ad Regem Hùng Vương ultimae aetatis seu Thế fabula ista narratur. Spiritus Tản Viên, et alius Spiritus Thủy Tinh venerunt ad regem Hùng Vương, et ejus filiam in sponsam petierunt. Rex vero miratus, quod Spiritus id peterent, ac duo simul peterent, dixit se unam filiam habere, nec eam dare posse ambobus, qui vero die crastino ad se munera prior detulisset, filiam suam obtenturus esset; ac postero die prior detulit plura munera Spiritus Tản Viên, et filiam Regis adeptus est, eamque ad montem suum adducens. Alter Spiritus aquae seu Thủy Tinh suscitavit tempestatem et conatus est eam pluvia et vento impedire. Hinc singulis annis importunum inter utrumque Spiritum certamina fuerunt. Spiritus autem ille montis Tản Viên favore multo patratus est. Rex autem Lý Anh Tông dictus anno ... Christi 1170 Templum ei posuit in eo monte, qui dicitur Tản Viên, et in provincia occidentali locatus est, ac ille Spiritus dicitur Tản Viên Sơn Thánh Vương Tản Viên, primus nominatus Lý Ông Trọng natus esse in territorio Từ Liêm provinciae occidentalis, et floruit tempore Regis An Dương, qui regnavit imperante Tần Thủy Hoàng, atque altus fuisse dicitur statura cubitorum 23. Adolescens verberatus a quodam Praefecto, eo quod minus aptè ageret negotium publicum, se contulit ad praefatum Imperatorem, et petiit sub eo Praefectum dictum Tư lệ hiệu úy. Missus ab illo fuit ad custodiendam regionem Lâm Thao ab hostibus Regni Hung Nô, qui eum valde timuerunt, atque expleto suo gubernio in patriam rediit senex, ibique vitam finivit. Postea

cum

cum hostes regni praefati regionem conterminam saepe irruperent, Imperator
conflavit Statuam Lí Ông Trọng mirae magnitudinis ex aere, in cujus ventre la-
-tebant triginta homines, et collocavit juxta portam urbis Imperialis: quam
Statuam videntes hostes praedicti, quia et percussa ab intra latitantibus commo-
-vebatur, putantes in ea inesse Lí Ông Trọng timore illius correpti, non sunt ausi
regionem illam amplius invadere, et diripere. Post multa saecula, praefectus
Triệu Xương, Imperante Đường Đức Tông, ineunte nimirum saeculo nono
christi nati, templum extruxit Lí Ông Trọng ad illi sacrificandum. Quod post
annos sexaginta reparavit praefectus Cao Biền dictus et Cao Vương, Imperante
Đường Tông, in eoque Statuam illi posuit ex ligno; eo quod ille auxilio sibi
fuisset in praelio contra rebellem Nam Chiếu, quem debellavit. Illud autem
templum extat in oppido Thụy Hương territorii praefati Từ Liêm. haec
habes in historia Đại Việt, cujus scriptores viderint, quam fidem merea-
-tur statura Lí Ông Trọng 23 cubitorum altitudinis, cum illa aequivaleat
altitudini sex hominum, nec non statua ejusdem, cujus venter triginta
homines capiebat. Alii autem aliter narrant historiam seu fabulam
de viro Trọng, et dicunt, quod cum Imperator Thỉ Hoàng bellum haberet
cum incolis regni Hung nô, petiit a Rege An Dương, ut ad se mitteret Lí
Ông Trọng, qui notus ipsi erat ex legatione, quam obierat tributum
exhibendo; rex vero An Dương respondit illum jam mortuum esse.
Cumque Imperator ossa defuncti ad se transmitti imperasset, Rex
An Dương veritus, ne quid mali ob mendacium sibi obveniret, sta-
-tim jussit illum occidi, ejusque ossa ad Imperatorem misit. Ita legi-
-tur in libro Thuật Thiên sinh sử; in libris tamen historiae
Đại Việt ea res minime refertur.

Magnam etiam existimationem habet vir Bạch Mã, qui fuit
militiae Praefectus proprio nomine Mã Viện appellatus, et militavit
pro Imperatore Hán Quang Vũ, a quo missus cum copiis in hoc regnum
seu provinciam dictam Giao Chỉ expugnavit mulierem Trưng
nuncupatam, quae armis praesidio Imperatoris expulso, dominationem

sibi

sibi vindicabat, dicta idcirco Trưng Vương, de quâ egimus in præfatione chronologiæ Annamitarum. In signum autem victoriæ dux ille erexit unam magnam columnam ex ære, incisis in illâ his characteribus: Đồng trụ chiết Giao Chỉ diệt; quorum sensus est; fractâ columnâ æneâ, amittetur provincia Giao Chỉ, seu Imperator eam amittet. Quæ gesta sunt anno 19° præfati Imperatoris, decennio post mortem Christi, et narrantur in historia Đại Việt; ubi est sermo de Thuộc Đông Hán. Post hoc ille reversus ad Imperatorem vitam finivit. Hinc mulier præfata, quæ ab illo victa fuerat, memor virtutis illius et meriti in rempublicam, templum ei posuit in territorio Phúc Lộc provinciæ Thanh hoa, ad ei sacrificandum, sicque cultum ex tunc ille obtinuit apud Annamitas. Nunc verò et aliud templum extat in urbe regiâ, Sadum in honorem ejus extructum, ad forum, de ejus nomine vulgo vocatum Chợ Vua Bạch Mã, quod à populo die potissimum, 1°. et 15°. cujusque mensis frequentatur.

His accedit fœmina quædam valdè celebris dicta Bà Chúa Liễu Hạnh quæ nata est in territorio Thiên Bản provinciæ Meridionalis. Cum illa cantasset, ut referunt, multa inhonesta et impudica, à quibusdam suis zelotypis occisa est, et in flumen projecta. Cujus deinde figuram et nomen diabolus assumens illius cultum pluribus in provinciis induxit, promovit, et stabilivit. Colitur autem potissimum in territorio Quỳnh Lưu in loco Bảo Tuần provinciæ Nghệ An, ubi extat templum ejus, seu miếu, in quo ei aulicant duæ puellæ, et unâ recedente, altera ei sufficitur: quæ puellæ ab ipsâ Bà Chúa Liễu Hạnh seu à dæmone ejus nomine, eliguntur, ex omnibus puellis sui territorii, et electa designatur per unam ex duabus sibi aulicantibus, seu deservientibus, quæ ad loquendum ab illâ, seu à dæmone movetur. Puella autem recedenti aliquam tribuit partem pecuniæ ad victum sibi conquirendum.

Spiritus insuper tutelaris oppidi Kẻ Sặt provinciæ Orientalis

olim

Olim, erat quaedam filia cujusdem militum Praefecti, qui antequam ad bellum pergeret, se illam idolo sacrificaturum promiserat, si victor fuisset: Victoria obtenta, dum ante idoli fanum transiret, nec filiam juxta votum vellet sacrificare, et daemonis navigium stetit, nec ultra progredi potuit, donec filiam in honorem idoli demersit. hanc igitur incolae oppidi Kẻ Sặt pro spiritu tutelari sibi adlegerunt, et coluerunt; multa quae praeter naturalia ibidem daemon operatus est: quare illam reddebant tutelam, sed ejus spiritum maximo cultu gentiles prosecuti sunt, quousque christiani fanum illius spiritus everterunt. Quae res deinceps magna materies dissidiorum inter christianos et gentiles, multarumque expensarum fuit.

Sunt et alii plurimi spiritus tutelares variis in locis, ac potissimum Vua Mẽ hả, Chúa Trì, Chúa Quê.

Primus autem ex illis Vua Bạch Mã est spiritus tutelaris urbis Regiae, seu Kẻ Chợ, ubi templum ejus habetur cum foro satis amplo, qui a populo frequentatur die potissimum primo mensis, et quinto decimo.

Articulus Nonus.

De Tiên Sư, Thổ Công, Vua bếp, et aliis qui cultum habent a Plebe.

Colunt omnes Artifices, et Mercatores primum suae artis, et Mercaturae Magistrum, seu inventorem, quem vocant Tiên Sư. Domi quamdam habent locum determinatum pro ejus altari, in quo retinent ipsius imaginem in papyro depictam sub specie senis, quam singulis annis invitant in principio, et coram illa afferunt edulia tribus primis diebus, et accendunt odoramenta. Saepe illam adorant, et invocant, potissimum quando negotium aliquod aggrediuntur, faciunt etiam, ubicumque sint, oblationem ciborum, ut bona res sibi eveniat: quam pariter oblationem frequentant, quotiescumque in convivio sunt commensales. Artifices vero, et Mercatores, qui unam constituunt societatem, semel in anno conveniunt in loco publico, et solemnem faciunt suo primo Magistro oblationem. Originem cultus Tiên Sư non ab alio esse petendam puto, quam ab eo, quod

Gens

Gens tota Sinarum colit nedum Parentes, et Progenitores defunctos, sed et Magistros maxime antiquos. Qua ratione Litterati colunt suum Confucium tanquam primum, vel principium, qui doctrinam iis tradidit, et Venefici colunt suum Lão Tử, uti primum seu principium, qui eos docuit veneficia. Pari ergo ratione omnes Artifices et Mercatores suum colunt primum Magistrum, qui adinvenit, et tradidit professionem, quam ipsi exercent.

Colunt insuper qui de plebe sunt, Spiritum Thổ Công, id est terrae, seu loci, in quo habitant, Praesidem. Qui cultum ex eo obtinuit, quod olim in Sinis tigris quaedam ferocissima viatores plurimos occidebat, nec ullus eam aggredi audebat, ne occideretur: quare Imperator publico edicto praemium ei promisit, qui eam interficeret. Quinque autem fratres ex familia Lê tigridem aggressi eam peremerunt. Deinde Imperator praeter alia praemia eos constituit Magistratus, atque protectores quinque partium regni sui proclamavit. Sicque plebs colere illos coepit et invocare sub nomine Thổ Công.

Colunt quoque Plebaei alium spiritum Thổ Chủ appellatum, hoc est dominum loci, in quo degunt. Cujus ea est, ut ferunt, origo, quod imperante familia Tấn quae regnare coepit post Christum natum anno 265; quidam dictus Hồng Chất pauper, et vilis se contulit ad ligna colligenda, ubi cum invenisset aliquos daemones ad aleam ludentes curiositatis gratia sedit ad ludum aspiciendum, interea factum est daemonis artificio, ut ferrea ejus falx a tineis fuerit corrosa, ipse quoque alter evaserit mutato vultu ob senectutem; ita ut domum reversus a suis agnitus non fuerit, nec uxor illum admittere voluerit, etiamsi se dominum illius loci ac domus esse asseveraverit, atque ab ea vix potuit obtinere, ut sibi construeret in horti angulo unam casam incompletam seu medianam, in qua habitans postea mortuus est, tunc quae agnitus fuit, quod revera loci illius dominus esset. Ac ideo cultum habere coepit a plebe, declaratus subinde Praefectus Thổ Gián.

Colunt et magnopere mulieres praesertim Vua Bếp, nempe Spiritum Regem culinae; de quo fertur ejusmodi origo. Quidam dictus Trọng Cao contentionem habuit cum uxore sua nomine Thị Nhi, propter opes, quas acquisierant, utroque conjuge industriae suae eas vindicante, quamobrem vir verberavit uxorem, quae indignata,

bonis

bonis omnibus marito relictis, ac scissis sibi crinibus, abiit ad habitandum supra-
pontem in trivio fluvii, tunc quidam dictus Phạm Lang obvius adveniens eam duxit
in uxorem, et plures exinde divitias acquisivit. Prior autem conjux ob infortunia,
et calumnias pauperrimus effectus casu venit ad illos cibum mendicans, uxorem
tamen suam minime cognovit, agnitus ab illâ, quæ cum alloquta de variis ejus
eventibus, absente marito, qui ad venandum perrexerat, ejus misertus cibum
et potum ipsi apposuit in quantitate, ita ut ille bene satur et ebrius ibi decum-
-bendo obdormierit; timens autem uxor ne deprehenderetur à marito superveniente
jussit dormientem à famulis deferri in cumulum paleæ, ea quæ cooperiri, donec
expergefactus abiret. Regressus verò Phạm Lang ex venatione cum cervo paleæ
cumulum accendit, ut cervum ustularet, in quo igne obrutus Trọng Cao vitam
amisit; cujus miseratione correpta Thị Nhi se quoque conjecit in flammas, et
periit; idque videns vir ejus ~~Phạm Lang uxoris~~ suæ misertus prosilivit in ig-
-nem, et mortuus est. hinc cæca plebs tres homines istos igne absumptos
colere cœpit sub nomine Regis culinæ, vua bếp hai ông một bà, et tres lateres,
quos supponunt lebeti ad eduliorum decoctionem tres illos dicunt significare;
quartum verò laterem, quem igni cineribus cooperto superponunt, prædictorum
conjugum ~~famulam~~ con đòi nominatam censent significare. Singulis itaque
annis primo die illorum quatuor figuram in uno papyri folio depictam nuper
emptam appendunt in culinâ, idque faciunt singulis primis tribus diebus anni
mensa eduliorum oblationem, et odoramenta incendunt, ac petiunt ab eis auxi-
-lium ad cibos bene coquendos, et parandos familiæ eo anno, et similia. Specialis
quoque est consuetudo, ut sponsa noviter domum sponsi ingressa ad adorationem
se conferat vua bếp, et postulet in culinæ officiis adjuvari.

Præter eos spiritus colunt mulieres et spiritus variis locis, ubi aliquis
terræ monticulus exurgit, vel arbor aliqua proceræ magnitudinis, qualis est
cây đa appellata consistit. Solent enim mulieres pertranseuntes invocare
ông đống, id est dominum monticuli, seu spiritum ibi dominantem, eique vovere,
quod si opem sibi ferat ad bene mercandum, in reditu aliquam terræ glebam
adjiciant, ut cumulus augeatur, vel aliquot papyraceas argenti aut auri
libras,

libras, vel torques florum, vel virgulas odoramentorum ibi apponunt, qui id praestant in reditu à foro se voto exolventes: quamobrem glebae permultae videntur coacervatae. Saepe etiam extruunt suprà eos monticulos tuguriolum quoddam, ac parvulam statuam in honorem Spiritus ibi dominantis in eo locant. Solent etiam invocare Bà Nàng in transitu alicujus arboris praefatae, cui Spiritum inesse putant, et foeminam esse, ad sua negotia, suamque salutem, ac in ejus honorem ramis arboris appendunt torques florum, et fasciculos librarum auri et argenti ex papyro, et ad ejus pedes projiciunt vascula gypsi, et virgulas odoramentorum. /.

Articulus Decimus.

De Spiritibus Defunctorum

Cultum denique Spiritibus Defunctorum caeremoniis quam pluribus impendunt: de quibus omnibus hic agere non vacat, cum tractatum exigant prolixiorem; verba tamen facere juvat de oblationibus et sacrificiis, quibus potissimum cultus ille ergà defunctos exercetur. Suis ergò defunctis quàm multas faciunt simplices oblationes, et plures oblationes cum sacrificio. Simplices oblationes peragunt singulis diebus à die obitus usquequo cadaver sepeliatur, quod ad plures plerumque menses domi detinetur in loculo inclusum, nec non singulis annis primis tribus diebus, et quatuor anni temporibus: et tunc offerunt edulia cum sola animae invitatione, absque vini seu stillati libatione, et schedulae offertorii recitatione. Oblationes autem cum sacrificio peragunt die, cineres cum biduo sequenti, die quinquagesimo, et centesimo ab obitu, ac die anniversario singulis annis, praesertim intra triennium luctus, totque lunâ septimâ prioris triennii post obitum. Ad illas vero oblationes, si cadaver domi adhuc habeatur, adhibent quamdam fasciam albam ex serico certâ formâ in ligno adaptatam, quam dicunt hồn bạch, sinis hoen pe; si verò cadaver jam fuerit tumulatum, adhibent quamdam tabellam ligneam certâ determinatâ formâ affectam, chủ nominatam, sinis chu; et in utraque credunt animam se exhibere prae-

sentem

Sentem ad oblationes. Fascia illa superextenditur duobus lignis in forma crucis altitudinis unius cubiti, ad exhibendam aliqualem imaginem defuncti; si quidem pars in summitate elevatur pro capite, duae partes in transverso pro brachiis, et duae partes sive extremitates in imum descendentes pro cruribus et pedibus. Ea quae fascia sic efformata praescribitur in Rituali Gia Lễ, ad designandam hominis figuram, et ut Anima maneat in illa: et idcirco dicitur hồn bạch, id est Anima fascia alba. Ut quae clarius exprimant eam imaginem, homines circumdant veste usuali, et pileum ipsi superimponunt. Tabella autem altitudinis unius, [illegible] palmi est, cujus pars superior prominet exterius, et in semicirculum formatur, reliquum ejus recedit interius, ejusque medium cavatum est in longum. Inscribitur vero pluribus litteris, et postremum in fine linea media illis duabus Thần vị, seu Thần chủ, quibus designatur Thronus Spiritus. Tabella ejusmodi et fasciae usus coepisse creditur auctore Chu văn Công, qui rituale Gia lễ de caeremoniis pro defunctis edidit anno sexto Imperatoris Tống Hiếu Tông, qui concurrit cum anno Christi 1168; siquidem mentio tabellae, et Animae fasciae ante tempus illius Auctoris non invenitur. At vero cultus Defunctorum per oblationes vetustissimus dignoscitur apud Sinas; quippe traditur in historia Sinensi, quod Imperator Đại Vũ sacrificaverit patri suo Cổn, et Đế Cốc, et verba textus adjecti sunt Đế Cốc. Quam Cúng tam porro oblationem cum sacrificio describere hic juvat, quam domum reversi a cadaveris sepultura faciunt ante tabellam, quae valde solemnis est, prout in Rituali exhibetur. Itaque Domum regressi tabellam deponunt supra lectum, et mensam cibis delicatioribus instructam collocant coram illa, pluresque alias vicendas adstantiorum disponunt ex utraque parte tum supra lectum, tum supra storeas in terra prope lectum tabellae. Paulo infra in medio situs est tabula odoramentorum hương án appellata in conspectu tabellae. Prope eam tabulam se sistunt duo caeremoniarii hinc inde ad praemonendum de agendis. Filii omnes, et nepotes funeris vestibus induti in medium procedunt ante tabellam praefatam, ubi humi sedent super storeis stratis, foeminae a dextris, et mares a sinistris; sed primogenitus stat solus in medio ante omnes, ibique simul

lugent

lugent omnes, et ejulant. Primogenitus deinde, seu qui primas agit partes in sacrificio principalis Minister, dictus in Rituali Chủ tế, et vulgari nomine Trưởng nam pergit ad locum determinatum ex parte, manusque abluit in tela super quadrupeda praeparata; iterum medium petit, atque incendit odoramenta super tabulam praedictam, in qua pariter ardent duae candelae, ac una prostratione tabellam adorat. Duo viri primarii, lotis similiter manibus in loco praefato, parvulam vini, id est stillati ex oriza ampullam cum uno cyatho deferunt principali Ministro, et genuflexi cum eo hinc inde ante tabellam hương án, ei ministrant: qui à dextris est, porrigit ampullam stillati, qui à sinistris cyathum manu tenet, quem principalis minister implet stillato infuso, acceptoque cyatho totum liquorem effundit, manens genuflexus, in quandam paleae manipulum colligatum in terra, qui dicitur sa mao; ac qua facta effusione, capite ad terram usque demisso adorat, inde surgens recedit inferius, et ibi simul cum fratribus, sororibus, et aliis consanguineis bina prostratione veneratur. Ea verò vini affusione intendunt de mente Ritualis attrahere deorsum spiritum defuncti vel significare ejus descensum; qua de causa, ad eam praemonent caerimoniarii dicentes: Giáng thần, sinicè Kiang xin, id est descende Spiritum, vel ut regulis latinae locutionis concordet, fac, ut spiritus descendat. Et post effusionem primogenitus, et caeteri filii cum reliquis consanguineis faciunt duas prostrationes, reverenter excipientes spiritum defuncti descendentem ad tabellam, quae ideo inscribitur sedes, seu thronus spiritûs. Effusione illa peracta, unus è ministris scutellam unam orizae coctae plenam defert, et deponit super mensâ editiorem ante tabellam constitutam. Deinde principalis minister iterum effundit vinum seu stillatum suprà paleae manipulum, sed paucas guttas ex cyatho, quem minister deputatus defert ad mensam editiorem praefatam, et ille post effusionem binâ prostratione solus adorat.

Secundâ stillati factâ effusione, unus è primariis inter adstantes accedit ad tabulam hương án, et genuflexus offertorium legit ex schedula

ab altero

ab altero genuflexo sibi exhibitâ, humili voce, et aliquantulum flebili. Recitat verò ex eâ schedulâ, praemissis anno, mense, die intercurrentibus, nomina Primogeniti, aliorumque filiorum, ac nepotum, atque eorum nomine merita parentis defuncti extollit, enumerat collata ejus beneficia, varios commiserationis, et amoris affectus exprimit, et offert edulia rogans, ut ea degustet, inquiens postremis verbis: Thượng hưởng, quorum sensus constabit Articulo sequenti. Schedulâ illâ recitatâ, filii omnes et nepotes se prosternunt ter, ejulantque simul. Tum principalis Minister accedit ad tabulam hương án, et genuflexus cum duobus aliis ministris iterum paululum stillatî effundit super paleae manipulum ibi relictum, et binâ prostratione adorat: recedit inferius rursusque superius accedit ad tabulam praefatam, et quartam stillatî effusionem facit modo praedicto. Resonant inter ea lugubri concentu varii generis instrumenta.

Post haec velamine quodam demisso tabellam et mensam eduliorum appositam coram illâ cooperiunt, ac unus ex ministris, junctis elatisque ante faciem manibus, bis rogat defunctum elatâ voce, ut eduliis oblatis vescatur: quo tempore filii omnes, et nepotes non aspiciunt ad locum tabellae, sed faciem convertunt in aliam partem, quasi non audeant aspicere ad locum, ubi comedit pater defunctus, aut progenitor. Paulò post velamen elevant, et auferunt à mensâ, et tabellâ, ac si defunctus jam comederit, seu degustaverit de eduliis, unamque scutellam potionis chè minister aliquis super eâ mensâ apponit.

Denique unus è duobus caeremoniariis, qui ad singulas actiones praefatas, quid esset agendum, praemonuerunt, enuntiat functionem esse finitam et completam dicens: Lễ thành; et alter monet, ut gratias agant Spiritui defuncti inquiens, Tạ thần. Tum primogenitus seu principalis Minister, et alii filii, nepotes, ac consanguinei binam faciunt prostrationem ejulantes; quâ caeremoniâ ad mentem Ritualis gratias agunt spiritui de sua praesentia exhibito sacrificio, et ab eodem grato animo dimittunt, atque discedunt. Comburitur subinde schedula văn tế seu offertorii; tabella colligitur, et reconditur intra ejus reductorium, relicta ante illam

illam mensa edulia cum atque omnes adstantes seu consanguinei, vel affines, qui ad funus convenerunt, quatuor prostrationibus defunctum venerantur, quorum singulis Primogenitus resalutat quaterna, vel bina, vel una prostratione, aut una tantum inclinatione juxta meritum, aut gradum personarum. Ultimo omnes communi convivio de mensis praeparatis, et una cum mensa speciali ante tabellam locata defuncto oblatis laetantur epulantur.

Articulus Undecimus.

Notatu digna circa Sacrificia

Constat ex praenarratis in hoc capite secundo et praecedenti, quod omnia Sacrificia, quae fiunt Confucio, Spiritui tutelari, aliisque Spiritibus, nec non defunctis, iisdem substantialibus caeremoniis, ac eadem credulitate peraguntur. In eorum quippe singulis altare, et quadrupes mensa dicta [illegible] habentur, Unus Minister principalis, aliquot assistentes, et alii administrantes, ac duo caeremoniarii intersunt, animalium occisorum carnes, et alia edulia offeruntur, vinum que seu stillatum orizae effunditur super paleae manipulum, et libatur, prostrationes fiunt, legitur schedula offertorii, cremantur adornamenta, et papyraceae librae argenti et auri adduntur, ac ultimo de oblatis comedunt cum laetitia. Credunt autem 1° quod Spiritus sese exhibeant praesentes ad Sacrificia in tabellis, quas plerumque adhibent cum in rem, et Spiritus sedem nempe Thần vị appellant: ideo illos certis caeremoniis excipiunt advenientes, et dimittunt abeuntes; 2° quod Spiritus suscipiant oblata, iisque perfruantur, quamobrem in fine Văn tế, seu schedulae sacrificii pro conclusione offertorii ea verba pronuntiant Thượng hưởng; 3° quod Spiritus potestatem habeant bona elargiendi suis cultoribus, idcirco gratias agunt pro beneficiis acceptis, et nova petunt ex schedula praefata.

Ex hac itaque observa 1° quod omnia illa Sacrificia aeque sint infecta Superstitione et idololatria; quare ab illis immunia censeri nequeunt Sacrificia Confucio, vel defunctis progenitoribus fieri consueta, simul ac Sacrificia, quae quæ Tien, [illegible] et aliis spiritibus de more fiunt, superstitiosa dignoscuntur et idololatrica. Quod si Confutii, et defunctorum sacrificia immunitatem haberent à cultu superstitioso et idololatrico, cæterorum quoque spirituum sacrificia eadem gauderent immunitate; quandoquidem eadem in omnibus ratio continetur. Quapropter Sedes Apostolica merito pluries pronunciavit oblationes Confutio et defunctis fieri consuetas imbutas esse superstitione.

Observa 2° quod mensa seu tabula Kiadong an, licet distincta sit, et distet ab altari, super quo posita est cæterorum mensa pro spiritu, unum tamen morale censenda est constituere cum ipso altari. Siquidem coram illa vinum seu stillatum funditur, et libatur, fiunt prostrationes, et schedula sacrificii recitatur, et ideo adhiberi videtur loco altaris, à quo necesse est Ministrum, Assistentes, et Administrantes ob mensas cæterorum interpositas procul distare. Quia vero super hujusmodi mensa Kiadong an cremantur odoramenta, nec ulla edulia et libamina apponuntur, à dæmone videtur inducta, ut exprimat altare incensi, quod in tabernaculo, et in templo Domini præter altare holocausti existebat, de quo ea Dominus præcepit Exodi C. 30. facies quoque altare ad adolendum thymiama de lignis setim .... non offeretis super eo thymiama compositionis alterius, nec oblationem, et victimam, nec libabitis libamina.

Observa 3° quod animalia, quæ occiduntur, ut carnes eorum offerantur in sacrificio, exprimunt victimas, quæ olim in sacrificiis Domini immolabantur. Attamen eorum oblatio longe diversa est ab oblatione illarum victimarum. Animalia quippe ad sacrificia Confutii, defunctorum, aliorumque spirituum non mactantur in actuali sacrificio, sed ante sacrificium occiduntur absque ulla oblatione, vel cæremonia, atque occisa, et in partes plerumque secta tantummodo offeruntur. Animalia vero in sacrificiis Domini in ipso actuali sacrificio immolabantur, necdum occisa offerebantur, ut constat ex primis libri Levitici capitulis, ubi præcipitur, quod qui obtulerit hostiam Domino, ponat manum super caput victimæ, eamque immolet, vel coram Domino, vel ad latus altaris, vel in introitu tabernaculi, vel in ejus vestibulo, et Sacerdotes fundant sanguinem

per

per altaris circuitum, vel in basim altaris, et membra caesa vel omnia, vel aliqua adoleant iidem Sacerdotes in altari juxta qualitat.. sacrificii: Ea verò in immolatione victimae ratio continet sacrificii; victima quippe Deo immolatur in protestationem supremi Dominii, quod habet in nos ipse Deus in vitam et in mortem, quae Theologi docent cum D. Thomâ 2.2ᵃ q. 85. quae ratio cum desit in mundialibus exitis ad sacrificium confutis, defunctorum aliorum quae spirituum; propriè dici non possunt sacrificia, sed solummodo solemnes oblationes cujusmodi nomine et plurimum in Sedis Apostolicae Decretis appellantur:

Animalia autem Deo offerri coeperunt a primordiis saeculi; Abel enim obtulit (Gen. c...) de primogenitis gregis sui et de adipibus eorum: et Noë post diluvium aedificavit (Gen 8) altare Domino, et tollens de cunctis pecoribus, et volucribus mundis obtulit holocausta super altare. Primus autem qui animalia obtulit in sacrificium Thượng Đế, seu Regi supremo, in historia Sinensi, occurrit Hoàng Đế, de quo ibi dicitur, quod ipse coepit ad sacrificandum Thượng Đế, et ad colendos omnes spiritus: Đế toàn lạc hộp cung tế Thượng Đế tiếp vạn linh, in quo litteralis Thiên Thai sub dit dicens: Tạo thần vị nhơn nhơn huyết thực, nhơn hưởng thần nhơn hiển sở, id est, idcirco spiritus quia habent homines se colentes, sanguine (hoc est animalibus) vescuntur, et homines quia offerunt spiritibus, habent locum (praelatum.) Solent autem Sinenses, et Annamitae in suis sacrificiis, et oblationibus offerre spiritibus carnes animalium ex his sex speciebus nempe mã equi, ngựa bubali, dương caprae, thỉ suis, kê galli, khuyển canis, quae sex species ab Annamitis dicuntur lục súc a Sinis lục chủ. Ex autem inter species tres sunt, quae conveniunt cum illis, quae olim vero Deo sacrificabantur, nimirum bubali, caprae, et galli; bubalus quippe et capra ad genus pecorum spectant, et gallus ad genus volucrum, de quo utroque genere sua Noë obtulit holocausta, et Levit. c. 1. ritus traduntur de sacrificiis utriusque generis pecorum et volucrum, ubi et explicatur pecorum nomine boves et oves comprehendi iis verbis — homo, qui obtulerit hostiam Domino de pecoribus, id est de bobus, et ovibus offerens victimas &c.

observa

Observa 4°. quod circa praesentiam Spirituum in Sacrificiis diversi-mode sentiunt litterati; alii enim dicunt illam praesentiam esse realem, alii vero esse solum imaginativam, et similitudinativam: et hi posteriores sen-tentiam suam confirmant testimonio sui magistri Confutii, qui in libro Luân ngữ ait: Tế như tại, tế thần như thần tại: hoc est, sacrificatur Spiritibus, sicuti Spiritus adessent; ubi dictio như, idest veluti, vel sicuti exprimit similitudinem praesentiae, non ipsam praesentiam. Et hanc realem praesentiam expresse negat Chu Hi in libro Thi Kinh his verbis: Nhược phụ mẫu chi kí một, dung mạo chi bất khả dĩ phục kiến, âm hưởng chi bất khả dĩ phục văn, tuy hữu cam chỉ khinh noãn, vô sở phụng chi dã. hoc est: Si pater et mater demissi sunt, (idest mortui) facies eorum am-plius non videtur, vox eorum amplius non auditur; quamvis habeantur cibi sapidi, ac vestes simplices, et duplices, sine illis (patre et matre prae-dictis) offeruntur. Verum communis est persuasio, quod Spiritus in sacri-ficiis eorum sese exhibeant praesentes. Caeterum quoad praesentiam Confutii in ejus sacrificiis, non nisi imaginariam possunt admittere litterati; siquidem uno et eodem die primo mane in omnibus ejus tem-plis ubique locorum constitutis peragitur sacrificium a litteratis luna-tione secunda, et octava: quapropter Spiritus Confutii eodem tempore pluribus in locis crederetur esse praesens ad sacrificia, si praesentia ejus crederetur esse realis, non imaginaria.

Observa 5°. quod illarum dictionum Thượng hưởng similibus Xáng hưởng, quae in fine cujusque văn tế, seu schedulae sacrificii reci-tantur, sensus est, Spiritus, quem veneramur, fruatur, seu delectatur oblatis. Dictio illa Thượng significat venerationem erga Spiritum, quem offerens alloquitur in toto offertorio, quod legit ex schedula, neque signifi-cat dubitationem de fruitione, ita ut sensus sit, fortitan fruatur oblatis, ut aliqui litterati mihi sunt interpretati, nam communiter credunt, quod revera Spiritus delectatur oblatis; si qui vero sunt, qui intelligentes dictionem Thượng pro fortitan, dubitent, an Spiritus fruantur oblatis,

ea

ea dubitatione ostendunt se certo credere, quod Spiritus frui valeant de oblatis; nisi enim illud persuasum haberent, dicere non possent, quod Spiritus forsitan sit fruiturus oblatis, Thiǔng kiǔng. Ritus autem ille pronunciandi in fine schedulae sacrificii has duas dictiones Thiǔng kiǔng, quibus Spiritus rogatur, ut oblatis perfruatur, inductus à Daemone videtur in mente, ut oblationes spiritibus factas plenius assimilaret sacrificiis olim Deo oblatis, in quibus Deus oblata suscipiebat, et signanter sacrificio, quod Deo obtulit Noë egressus ab arcâ, de quo dicitur Gen. 8. — odoratus que est Dominus odorem suavitatis. —

Denique convivio, quod habent post sacrificium, imitantur Hebraeos, qui in deserto coram vitulo aureo obtulerunt holocausta (Exodi C. 32. 6.) et hostias pacificas, et sedit populus manducare, et bibere, et surrexerunt ludere. Ambas et plenè similes se exhibent, quando nedum epulantur post oblationem, sed et varios ludos exercent, ut suo loco dictum est de Spiritu Thành Hoàng, seu Tutelari. Mos etiam fuit apud Hebraeos post sacrificium Deo vero peractum comedere de oblatis, et primò sic epulati sunt Jacob et Fratres ejus: Siquidem quando Jacob foedus iniit cum Laban, juravit (Gen. 31.) per timorem Patris sui Isaac; immolatis que victimis in monte, vocavit fratres suos, ut ederent panem, qui cum comedissent, manserunt ibi. Quando Jethro cognatus Moysi ad illum venit in desertum, (Exodi 18. 12.) obtulit holocausta, et hostias Deo: veneruntque Aaron, et omnes seniores Israel, ut comederent panem cum eo coram Deo. Et Moyses hoc praecepit (Deuteron. C. 12.) offerteis in loco illo (quem elegerit Dominus) holocausta, et victimas vestras, et primitias manuum vestrarum, et vota, atque donaria, primogenita boum, et ovium; et comedetis ibi in conspectu Domini Dei vestri.

Articulus

Articulus Duodecimus.

De Sacrificio Viventibus Vua et Chúa.

Inter Sacrificia, quae peraguntur, et illa sunt recensenda, quae viventi Vua et viventi Chúa de more exhibentur. Itaque Regi seu Vua viventi, aliquoties in anno coram ipso sacrificant cum omnibus caeremoniis, quae in aliis Sacrificiis observantur. Quod Sacrificium fieri deberet bis singulis mensibus, nimirum in novilunio, et plenilunio, quibus diebus omnes Magistratus, seu Praefecti veniunt ad salutandum. Verum Rex plerumque jubet Sacrificium praetermitti, contentus, quod quandoque solummodò fiat. potissimum autem die anniversario Nativitatis Regis celebratur.

Honor iste procul dubio excessivus est, cum aequalem faciat Regem in humanis versantem omnibus Spiritibus, quos Annamitae colunt sacrificio, atque humanam superbiam ostendit, qua Reges tantum honorem admittunt. Consultius sanè agerent, si talia Sacrificia nunquam admitterent, et fieri prohiberent, clamantes verbis Pauli et Barnabae, qui Iconii cives illos compescuerunt à Sacrificio, quod sibi facere disponebant: Viri, quid hoc facitis? (Act. c. 14.) et nos mortales sumus, similes vobis homines.

Ad nimium quoque honorem Rex coeli filius Thiên Tử anthonomastice appellatur, et videre est in libris litteratorum seu Đạo Nho, et in historiâ Sinensi; quod nomen solent etiam scribere à tergo Epistolarum, quas scribunt de More. Unde et dicunt, quod Rex Coelum habent pro Patre, et terram pro matre, sicuti et legitur in historiâ Phụ Thiên, Mẫu Địa, nhi vi Thiên Tử.

Similiter regni Gubernatori seu Chúa viventi sacrificatur bis in anno mense secundo, et mense octavo, coram ipsius Statuâ, servatis omnibus caeremoniis Sacrificii. Quod Sacrificium fit, ut mihi relatum est, in territorio Bồ chính provincia Thuận hoá, et credo etiam fieri in patriâ ipsius Chúa in territorio Thiên Thiên provincia Thanh Hoa. Eoque honore ostendunt Regni Gubernatores Chúa nominatos in omnibus praetendere cum Regibus sui Vua, quorum sibi potestatem dudum jam usurparant, æqualitatem.

Caput Tertium
De Secta Veneficorum

Articulus Primus
de Lão Tử Sectæ hujus Principe.

Secta hæc antonomastice dicitur Đạo, et illius doctrina dicitur Đạo Đạo. Princeps illius habetur quidem vulgari nomine Lão Tử, Sinis Lao zu, qui et aliis nominibus nuncupatur Lão Tiên, Lão Đam, Lão Nhuân, Lão Quân, Europæa voce à primis Missionariis dictus Lautius, natus est in Sinis in provinciâ Hồ [illegible], Annamitis Hồ Quảng, pago Tụ, sub Nguyên Định imperante Chu Linh Vương anno ejus septimo, ante christum 565; et mortuus est anno 81. Anno 35º Imperatoris Chu Kính Vương in montibus hic dictis Côn Lôn [illegible] in toparchia Bắc Lệ, quò confugerat, prævalente in Kính Vương bello civium, qui fratrem ejus natu minorem constituerant Imperatorem. Magister fuit ceremoniarum, seu disciplinæ in aula Linh Vương, ejusque filii successoris Kính Vương: libellos aliquot composuit, et singulariter eo titulo donatum Đạo Đức Kinh, qui continet varia documenta de morali disciplina. Discipulos habuit complures, et Confucius ipse aliquid instructionis ab eo accepit, ut constat ex libro Gia Ngữ in Epitome ejus vitæ, ubi refertur, quod Confucius annos natus 34 Thích Chu vấn Lễ Lão Đam; hoc est, venit ad aulam Imperatoris familiæ Chu ad interrogandum Lão Đam de ritibus.

Venefici illum habent tanquam suæ Principem, qui rei veneficæ dederit operam ad medicinam, et præcepta tradiderit de ea re, nec non docuerit esse in humano corpore quinque elementa, seu principia, nempè hỏa, thổ, kim, thủy, mộc; id est ignem, terram, metallum, aquam, lignum. Tradunt insuper de illo mira medicina [mendacia], scilicet quod fuerit in utero matris annos 81; quod natus

sit

sit non communi viâ, sed in utero stans momorderit latus matris suae sinistrum, et inde egressus sit, moriente idcirco ipsâ matre; quod quando mortuus est, apparuerit ei bubalus viridis, ipsique insidens in caelum abierit, et conscenderit.

At verò plures litterati censent Lão Đam rem veneficam non tradidisse, nec ei incubuisse, sed alios ex posteriores illam docuisse multa interferentes libro Lão Nhiễm, ut nempe tanti viri nomine auctoritatem suae doctrinae aucuparent. Quorum opinio eâ ratione persuaderi potest, quod Confutius nihil scripserit, aut dixerit contra Đạo Lão Đam, seu Lão Nhiễm; quod utique fecisset, si suo tempore doctrina illius veneficiis jam extitisset; cum Confutius mortuus sit annis sex post Lão Đam anno 41.° Chu Kính Vương. Caeterum Chu Tử in libro Lư Ngữ sentit doctrinam Dương Chu eamdem fuisse ac doctrinam Lão Tử, et contendit, quod Mạnh Tử impugnando Dương Chu simul impugnaverit et Lão Tử; siquidem ait: Lão tận thị Dương thị Mạnh Tử tịch Dương tắc thị thịch Lão. Et in praefatione libri Đại học idem Chu Tử sectam Lão Tử vocat Dị đoan hư vô chi giáo; id est, sectam nihili, contrariam et obliquam.

Docent autem in hâc secta de rerum origine, et constitutione illud principium: Đạo sinh nhất, nhất sinh nhị, nhị sinh tam, tam sinh vạn vật, hư vô tự nhiên chi Đại Đạo; id est, lex produxit unum, unum produxit duo, duo produxerunt tria, tria produxerunt innumerabiles res, seu omnia: nihilum ex semetipso est magna lex. Docent insuper esse quinque immortales, nimirum caelum, terram, aquam, spiritum, animam hominis.

Articulus Secundus.
De Sectae hujus Incremento.

Veneficorum secta magnum incrementum obtinuit sub familia Hán; tunc quippe aliqui floruerunt ex progenie Trương insignes in illâ secta; nimirum Trương Nghi, Trương Đạo Lăng, et Trương Giác.

Illis

Illis praemittunt aliqui Trương Lương virum valdè celebrem, qui primò praefectum egit sub rege Thông regni Hàn, deindè sub Imperatore Hán Cao Tổ, ac tandem ab aulâ Imperatoris secessit in montes ad vitam solitariam cum Spiritibus ducendam; quo tempore vacavit, ut illi scriptores tradunt, doctrinae Lão Tử. Dissentiunt tamen litterati dicentes, quod tantus vir recessit ab aulâ Imperatoris praetextu ducendi vitam solitariam cum Spiritibus, eâ solâ intentione ut latitaret, seque subduceret neci quam sibi minitabat ab Imperatore; non autem ut operam daret rei veneficae, quae talem virum dedecebat. Trương Nghi verò incubuit rei veneficae, seu arti medendi per veneficia, et celebris fuit in sectâ veneficorum, habuitque discipulos complures: qui natus est paulo post obitum laudati Trương Lương, et fortè nepos ejus fuit, atque adolescens in montem se recepit ad studendum doctrinae praefatae, ac anno vitae suae trigesimo mortuus est sub Imperatore Hán Văn Đế. Stupendum de eo mendacium evulgarunt de illo sectae veneficae professores, dicentes, quod mater ejus Bào Nhược Nguyệt cum liberis careret sterilis, in somnio virum celebrem dictum Nguyễn Thị, qui ei apparuit regio habitu indutus manibus gestans puerulum quemdam, quem ei tradidit; ipsa verò ex tunc concepit, et anno sequenti die nonâ lunae primae filium peperit in meridie, qui posteà Nghi appellatus est. Postquam verò migravit è vitâ, discipuli ejus frequenti acclamatione, ipsi applaudebant, quod in caelum ascendisset. Trương Đạo Lăng nepos fuit ejusdem praefati Trương Lương in octavâ generatione, et doctrinae veneficorum à suis acceptae operam dedit, quam et tradidit ~~Trương Hành~~, et iste pariter tradidit Trương Lỗ: quibus denique successit Trương Giác plurimum celebris sub Imperatore Hán Linh Đế. cum ille in montes perrexisset, ut ~~[illegible]~~, ad herbas, et radices ~~inquirendas et ad~~ medicinam inopinatè obviam habuit virum quemdam, qui proprio nomine ad se vocavit Trương Giác, et introduxit in vallem, ubi tradidit illi librum veneficiorum procuratione infirmorum, qui dicitur Thái bình yếu thuật, id est,

maxima

maximae sanitatis recondita artificia, et Tài bình yếu quiét: hoc est, maximae sanitatis doctrina. Tunc illum Trương Giác, quis esset, interrogavit, illeque respondit se esse magistrum Lão Tiên, subitòque disparuit. Cum autem primo mense sequentis anni pestis in regione esset saeva, Trương Giác juxta illius libri documenta morbo laborantibus medebatur, namque papyrum superstitiosis characteribus scriptam comburebat, et ejus cinerem aquae immixtam infirmis ad bibendum praebebat, quâ potione multi ope daemonis sanabantur. hinc illum habebant, et celebrabant magnum, mitem, ac bonum magistrum Đại hiền lương sư, prout saepe jactabat. anno sexto Imperatoris Linh Đế, christi 176, arma sumpsit contra Imperatorem cum fratre suo Trương Lương, magnamque populorum partem sublevavit, et pertraxit ad rebellandum contra Imperatorem, dumque bellum gereret, infirmatus cessit è vitâ: at victo, et perempto in certamine ejus fratre Trương Lương, Imperator jussit extrahi è loculo cadaver Trương Giác, et in partes secari, ejusque caput abscissum ad Regiam Metropolim deferri, ibique suspendi. Quam rem narratam habes in historia Sinensi ad annum 9um Hán linh Đế. Porrò praefatus Trương Lương praelio occisus diversus est, ut vides, à Trương Lương praecedenti, qui ducem egit sub Imperatore Hán Cao Tổ, ejusque nomen Lương scribitur diverso charactere à nomine senioris.

Articulus Tertius.
De Secta hujus Veneficii.

Qui sectam hanc profitentur Thầy Phù thủy appellantur, qui toti sunt in veneficiis exercendis, quae adhibent potissimum ad curationem infirmorum. Dicunt propterea spiritus, et defunctos hominibus esse maleficos, iisque infirmitates et morbos inferre, ac spiritus hujusmodi esse viginti quatuor, ex quibus constant quinque spiritus principes et capitales dicti Thần hung, atque jactant se potestatem habere

à

Süi tien, et Nji Boung, ad eos expellendos, et compellendos, ne amplius noceant ægrotantibus. Quapropter plura præstant superstitiosa, ut infirmis medeantur; edulia nimirum afferunt Spiritibus, et defunctis, auream et argenteam papyrum in eorum honorem adurunt, eos que precantur, ut desinant infirmis nocere, preces fundentes clamore magno vel in domo infirmorum, vel ad ripam fluminis, vel ubilibet; nec non eos terrent vociferatione, et strepitu, tigrides nigras hắc kồ invocantes, ut abscedant perterrefacti, inter quæ pulsant quamdam campanulam, et baculum gestant. Sæpè etiam efformari faciunt cymbulam aliquam ex papyro et cannulis cum remis et velo, quam demittunt in flumen aut piscinam, ut in eâ Spiritus nocivitos, quos in illam ascendere compellunt procul deferantur. Includunt quandoque in vitrâ ampulla noctilucam, id est insectum volucre, et lucidum, et dicunt animam, quæ vexat infirmum, esse in eâ comprehensam; ac plurimis conjurationibus, strepitu que plurimo eam conantur expellere; aperta que interim ampulla, et noctilucâ evolante, animam dicunt aufugere infirmo non amplius nociturum. Jubent quandoque infirmos in domum aliam exportari, ne animæ defunctorum, aut Spiritus domi suæ illos invenient, pejori que malo afficiant. Ossa defunctorum faciunt interdum exhumari, et alium in tumulum transferri, ut meliore loco obtento, desinant vivis esse malefica, quin imo præcipiunt aliquando ea insepulta relinqui aëris exposita intemperiei, ut nocendi virtutem perdant. Sæpius quoque fingunt animas defunctorum parentum filios, et nepotes infirmitatibus vexare, quia cruciantur in inferno, et volunt inde eorum ope liberari: quapropter faciunt functionem Phá ngục, de quâ agemus cap. 5. art. ultimo illam mutuantes à Secta cultorum Phật. faciunt quandoque aliquem sedere in medio, ac verbis, signis, et sufflatibus faciunt, ut corpus sui contendat, ut à Spiritu aliquo seu dæmone ex majoribus corripiatur, quo ille correptus apprehensâ virgâ vel percutit, et infringit quodcumque, in quo putat Spiritum infirmo nocentem latitare, ut illum expellat; vel percutit multis

ictibus

ictibus cartulam nomine inscriptam defuncti infirmo advertit, in quâ ejus Animam venefici adesse compellunt, ut desinat infirmum affligere castigata: iis que peractis ad mentem redit. Cartulas quoque variis characteribus superstitiosis inscriptas venefici illi, novo praesertim anno ineunte, distribuunt, quas plurimi emunt, et affigunt domui suae, vel collo appendunt, ut à malis liberentur: et cartulae hujusmodi vocantur bùa phép, id est veneficia praedita virtute conservativa.

Ac illas inter characteres sunt duo illi Thân Dô Sinis Xin tù, qui sunt nomen spiritus, qui malignis spiritibus praeest, eosque coercet, ne damnum inferant. Ea verò veneficia conservativa tanti faciunt, ut etiam Regni administrator Chúa omnibus rectoribus elephantum et equorum, ut singulis annis in principio, aliquibus aliter per annum cartulas illas à magistro venefico Thây Phù Thúy accipiant, et insuper liminaribus stabulorum affigant: quod si facere praetermiserint, et forte elephas vel equus aliquis aegrotet, aut moriatur, gravi poenâ puniuntur.

Faciunt insuper maleficia, et praesertim sibi faciunt spiritus seu daemones apparere, eosque jubent, ut eant ad damna aliis inferenda, atque ad haec saepè saepius utuntur quibusdam parvulis figuris, seu statuis, quasi hominis ex paleâ in formam crucis decussatae Mô Dên appellatis, quae à Diabolo motae directe, quasi viventes per domos, et super tectis discurrunt, easque admoto igne, pluribus in locis, ex toto incendunt, nec non terrae glebas in habitacula jaciunt visibiliter, stercus in ollis, seu lecticis, cibis extractis, reponunt, pecuniarum cavas effodiunt, domus supellectilia hinc inde transferunt, aliis que vexationibus habitatores ita exagitant, ut cogantur ad ipsos veneficos recurrere pro liberatione à tantis incommodis, et malis, aliis que ipsi tunc veneficiis priora destruunt maleficia. Verumtamen cùm à Rege haec ars prohibita sit sub poenâ mortis, ideò ea faciunt occulte, cumque aliunde Rex jusserit, ut illi, qui veneficia faciunt in destructionem hujusmodi maleficiorum, capiantur, et examinentur, utrùm priora maleficia ab ipsismet facta fuerint, ideò nunc rarum est, quod talia fiant, eò quia nullum afferunt lucrum, et nunquam in discrimen adducuntur; sed solùm quandoque fiunt ex odio. Similiter et veneficia amatoria faciunt, quibuscum foeminas

in familiis

in similis ceras ad se trahunt, illis abutuntur ad libitum: quibus vero rebus expetiant amentes, vestem illas dimittunt ac descendentes, antequam in se ipsas post aliquot horas virtute maleficiorum absumpta, revertantur. Illud etiam philtra vendunt, ut conjugati vel se invicem ament, vel odio habeant, et repudient: et plurima id genus damna inferunt male cautis.

Sunt et aliqui Venefici dicti Thầy [illegible], qui notitiam exquirunt, et proferunt de statu defunctorum, atque ad hoc aliquem vel aliquam statuunt in medio, ac suffitibus, et variis gestibus agunt, ut extra se actus ille rapiatur, et quasi exanimis, seu mortuus fiat, qui post aliquod tempus notabile redditus sensibus reviviscit, et refert quidquid ope daemonis sibi videre visus est, vel in sepulchro, vel in inferno, vel in caelo de statu defuncti alicujus; quae loca affirmat animam suam e corpore egressam revera adiisse, atque in via veris argenti et auri libris, in quos conversa fuerint libra papyracea, quos manu corporis tenebat, usum fuisse. Redditus vero sensibus se ille sentit defatigatum, ac viribus destitutum propter illum raptum, seu exanimationem. Videtis porro in his expressos in speciem raptus, quos famuli Dei, et famulae, gratia operante, patiuntur. Praeter ea agunt et alia plura praefati venefici, quae suae sectae non sunt, sed aliena, ut mercede quaerant sibi victum: qui circa funerationes etiam et ritus sectae cultorum [illegible] plerumque exercent, nec non operam dant artibus divinatoriis, de quibus infra.

Denique secta haec Veneficorum habet et mulieres pythonissas Bà Cốt nuncupatas, quae pariter plura faciunt veneficia. Pro infirmis curandis oblationes faciunt idolorum spiritibus, et defunctis, eosque invocant, et adorant, atque preces superstitiosas absque ullo sensu et ordine confusas clamore magno recitant. Arboris ramum quandoque statuunt supra mensam, rogantes spiritum bonum ad illum descendere, eumque bene colligatum et intra manus comprehensum deferunt ad infirmos, ut debilia ipsorum corpora vivificet. Varias aliquando imagines in spiritu faciunt apparere, quas dicunt animas esse defunctorum, cum quibus secreto colloqui simulant, ac plura ab illis sibi revelari. Rogat etiam saepe saepius pythonissa animas illas, ut cor-

-pus

-pus suum ingrediantur, et variis corporis motibus se fingit ab illis jam cor-pus suum ingressis agitari. ac jubet interea filios ac nepotes animas paren-tum in se ipsâ immanentes variis prostrationibus ergà se factis venerari; posteà fingit illas hoc vel illud velle comedere, et bibere, quod allatum ipsa comedit, et bibit, fabellas enuntiat de misero vel felici statu, in quo defunctos illos versari fingit in alio seculo. nec non praedicit futura bona vel mala, quae filii eorum, et nepotes scire desiderant. harum mulierum artem profitentur aliqui viri, qui dicuntur Ông Đồng. ac mulieribus sese vestibus induunt, barbam penitus sibi evellunt, et Bà id est Dominae vocari volunt valdè irascentes, si masculino nomine Ông, hoc est Domini appellentur. Similibus figmentis et nugis, in quibus non rarò daemon intervenit, eisque auxiliatur, alienam pecuniam sibi lucrantur hujus-modi venefici, et veneficae, quibus fidem praebet plebs incauta supersti-tionibus dedita, et quàm maximè implicata, nec ullius rationis lumine ad examinanda et discernenda ejusmodi tam aperta mendacia.

Articulus Quartus.
De Religione hujus Sectae.

Professores hujus Sectae ex pervetusta traditione spiritus colunt, pro ut Sectae litterariae professores, et prae omnibus quidem cultum exhibent Lão Tử, quem habent Principem et praeceptorem, eisque nominibus ap-pellant: Đức Thánh, Đức Tiên, Đức Tổ, id est; Regem virtute insignem, Regem priscum, Regem primaevum: ac insuper dicunt, quod ille sit in caelo Dominus omnium rerum, in terrâ Magister Regum, et in Stellis Rex maximus, iis verbis: Lão quân tại thiên vi vạn vật chi Chủ, giáng thế vi bách vương chi sư, tại tinh vi Hoàng Thái Đế. Cultum autem Lão Tử maximè promovit Imperator Tống Chân Tông, qui publico edicto gradum maximi superni Regis ei contulit anno Regni sui septimo luna prima, Christi verò nati anno 1014: Đế gia Lão Tử

gia-qui mới giết thái thượng lão quân ; quod edictum habes in historia Sinensi. Addunt alii, quod in eo edicto Imperator insuper declaravit Lão Tử esse creatorem cæli et terræ, idolorum et Spirituum: sinh thiên, sinh địa, sinh Bụt, sinh thần, at in historia ea res minime habetur. Semel autem in anno mense ac die ad libitum omnes thầy ở thầy singuli in domo propria, erecto ibi altari absque tabella, et imagine faciunt Lão Tử vel solemne sacrificium eo prorsus ritu, quo sacrificium fit Spiritui tutelari thành hoàng, de quo egimus caput 2. art. 6; vel solemnem precum recitationem tota nocte et die cum simplici oblatione iisdem ceremoniis, quibus cultores Thích, cum functionem recitationis precum Sinicarum đọc kinh, đọc kệ celebrant ad honorem suorum Idolorum. In offertorio autem seu văn tế, quod legunt ad sacrificium, 1° laudant Lão Tử, quod habeat ingenium, et prudentiam in rebus spiritualibus, quod maneat in toto mundo, et illum gubernet, quod potestatem habeat in Spiritibus iisque imperet; 2° offerunt edulia, et omnia apposita; 3° dicunt se reverenter attendere ~~ipsum~~ ministerium ut venturum, et operaturum et pluviam; 4° petunt ut ab eis avertat infortunium, et omne malum, sibique tribuat felicitatem, lucrum, et bonam famam.

Colunt potissimum ~~duodecim~~ Spiritus qui singulis annis per gyrum præsident, sibi que invicem succedunt in regimine vicissitudinum, et in potestate mundi, dicti idcirco hành khiển vương, id est, gubernatores infortunatus mundi. Eo autem ordine distribuuntur. Anno 1° Tí regit Châu vương. 2° Sửu regit Triệu vương 3° Dần regit Ngụy vương 4° Mão regit Trịnh vương 5° Thìn regit Sở vương 6° Tị regit Ngô vương 7° Ngọ regit Tần vương, 8° Vị regit Tống vương 9° Thân regit Tề vương 10° Dậu regit Lỗ vương 11° Tuất regit Việt vương 12° Hợi regit Lưu vương illis autem Spiritibus rectoribus, seu rerum unicuique suo cujusque anno bis faciunt oblationem, nempe in anni principio, et fine, in principio quidem, ut illum reverenter excipiant advenientem, in fine vero, ut illum cum gratiarum actione dimittant, et deducant ab eorum. Itaque vocetiol in ista ob, et nomen

Spiritus

Spiritus ex anno praesidentis in papyro scriptum. Simul cum illis verbis Đương niên hành khiển infirmis tradunt ad bibendum cum medicina, ut patrocinio ejus, et potestate sanentur ab infirmitate. Praefatae autem distributionis duodecim Spirituum totidem annis praesidentium auctorem faciunt quemdam Mạch Công valde celebrem Tunquinii, qui ex familia Tống imperialis dicitur fuisse. Colunt et Spiritus, seu virtutes novem constellationum, iis que faciunt [illegible] quot Spiritus, et constellationes per menses novem distribuunt successive, quibus absolutis, rursus accipiunt primam constellationem, et circulum reiterando prosequuntur. Porro de duodecim prioribus Spiritibus in totidem annos, et aliis novem posterioribus Spiritibus in totidem menses distributis librum habent specialem. Habent et alium librum in quatuordecim capita distinctum ad morbos expellendos, et alia mala avertenda, et abigenda ./.

Articulus Quintus

De Ngọc Hoàng, et aliis, quos colunt.

Magnum apud Tunquinos cultum habet Ngọc Hoàng, idest gemmeus Rex qui est Trương Nghi, de quo supra Articulo 2o., quare nunc etiam ex familiae nomine dicitur Trương Đại Đế, hoc est Trương magnus Rex. Auctor libri Vạn tấn quảng, et auctor libri Quảng [illegible] ex illo scripserunt, quod Trương Nghi ab Imperatore Tống Huy Tông fuerit praenominatus Ngọc Hoàng Thượng Đế. Sed perspicuum est ex historia Sinensi, quod ille Imperator ea nomina Caelo attribuerit, non autem alicui homini. Imo litteratus Khâu Thị, in eadem historia ad annum 6. Chính [illegible] praefato Imperatori, quod voluerit caelum, quod humanis titulis cum iisdem praedictis indignum; id circo passus sit infortunium: [illegible] tôn ... [illegible] tôn tôn giả Thượng Đế dã; vi chi hiệu Thiên Thượng Đế, Đế giả Chúa Tể [illegible] Đế, [illegible] chi Thiên chi [illegible] bất khả [illegible] Đế chi tôn [illegible] Tống Huy Tông thượng Ngọc Hoàng huy hiệu ... Chính Hòa ... [illegible] Hoàng [illegible] chi [illegible] khả [illegible] tai — cultumve Imperator Tống Tông

adeo.

adeo fuit affectus erga sectam Veneficorum, ut anno 7.o ejusdem imperii Chinh Hoa, qui occurrit anno Christi 1117. se ipsum pronunciaverit edicto publico Regem illius sectae: Tạch Đô vi giáo Chúa Đạo quân Hoàng Đê.

In cultu etiam est apud Veneficos quidam litteratus simul et Veneficus, nomine Phanlilkhan, qui eo quod congressus est cum Imperatrice, cui medebatur, jussu Imperatoris occisus est, et in tres partes discissus in amnem abjectus est. Accidit autem ut ejus cadaver ab undis illatum in flumen incideret in rete cujusdam piscatoris; quod cum piscator ejecisset, ac paulo post iterum intra rete illud reperisset, ad ripam deduxit, ac cognovit, ut in piscium captura sibi esset auxilio, si corpus esset alicujus Spiritus seu Thần, ac pisces deinde quam multos piscatus est: quamobrem domunculam ei construxit, et colere illud coepit in singulis tribus ejus partibus, quas sub nomine trium Dominorum falso veneratur; scilicet caput ejus dicitur Dominus primus, umbilicus Dominus secundus, pedes Dominus tertius.

Colunt et alii inter quidam Tư Khổng natus in Sinis sub Imperio familiae Hán, jussu Imperatoris ob scelera sua necatus fuit: et quia inquietante aliis terribilem se praestitit, ideo et ipse colitur, ne noceat. Tres quoque fratres rebelles Imperatori multo plus ..., quia non diabolus sub illorum figura quandoque apparuit, et praedixit futura, propterea cultum obtinuerunt dicti: Thiên Vua, Đa Bắc, Thủy Thần.

Sunt et alii Spiritus, quos dicunt Tướng Quân, antesignanos, seu Duces aliis praestantes; eos quippe mittunt Venefici ad expellendos alios Spiritus adversos, et maxime infernales: qui Đông Lành, Thổ Địa, Mạnh Tông, Dực Bác, Thiên Lôi, Tam Đanh, Sông Lê Tư, Chúa Quê, Chúa Liễu, qui duo Spiritus posteriores sunt Spiritus duarum feminarum. His omnibus Spiritibus, sicut et Cô Hồn, id est animabus orphanis, de quibus infra capit. 5. art. 4; offerunt edulia bis in anno, in novilunio, et plenilunio: quas illi oblationes sibi fieri volunt, et si quae omittatur, indignati damnum inferunt Veneficis, qui non praestiterint, et accidunt in eos poenas, causas habebit.

bubalos, gallinas, qui solitis edulis caruerunt. Quapropter professores hujus fanatismi, ne tantum damnum patiantur, solertes sunt ad offerendum illis adulabilis in mente, vel orationes alicujus infirmi curandi, vel alicujus defuncti tumulandi, vel propter expensas domi suae, si contra oratio habeatur.

Solent insuper ad sua sacrificia invocare cum praefatis et Spiritus subsequentes, nimirum Đức Giàng, Đức Cần, Đức Bạch Mã, Đức Bạch Hạc, Đức Đình, Đức Nhị Vị, Tam Đảo, Tam vị Tản Viên, Cửu Vĩ, Chín Sũ, Thuỷ Tề, Thuỷ Tục, qui duo ultimi sunt Spiritus magnorum piscium, et cujuslibet magnae seu extraordinariae rei, quae in aquis videatur.

Notandum vero, quod plures Spiritus cultum habent tam in Secta Đạo, quam in Secta Thích, seu ab earum sectatoribus; quod potissimum contingit de Ngọc Hoàng. Praefati vero Spiritus cum titulo Đức sunt Spiritus variorum locorum seu pagorum protectores, qui in hoc regno ab incolis coluntur.

Testimonia pro Lão Tử, ejusque Secta Đạo.

Caput quartum.
De Divinatoribus et Observatoribus.

De divinatoribus et Observatoribus sermonem hic subnectimus, cum et illi sint ex genere veneficorum, nec non ad divinationes saepe utantur documentis litteratorum.

Articulus Primus.
De Divinatoribus Thầy Bói et Thầy Khoa

Primam sedem inter Divinatores obtinent, qui dicuntur Thầy Bói hi vero ad divinandum utuntur figuris inventis ab antiquissimo Sinarum Rege Phục hi. Cum vidisset Rex ille, ut tradunt in historia Sinensi, intra aquas fluminis figuram cujusdam veluti equi simul et draconis, et super ejus dorso signa aliqua seu puncta; sumpsit inde occasionem excogitandi octo figuras linearum juxta ea signa ad distributionem et notitiam partium mundi, quae iis nominibus vocantur ab Annamitis; càn, khảm, cấn, chấn, tốn, ly, khôn, đoài, ; et generali vocabulo dicuntur quái Sinis Kua vulgariter quẻ. Ex iis octo figuris postea effecit idem Phục hi sexaginta quatuor (64) alias figuras eodem nomine dictas quái ad majorem earum distinctionem et perfectionem: quae singulae figurae constant ex senis lineis sive continuis sive interruptis, et continent duas figuras ex octo praefatis radicalibus varie copulatas: ac illae lineae omnes sunt numero 384; et dicuntur hào Sinis yáo. Porro illae 64 figurae continentur, explicantur, et illustrantur in libro Dịch Kinh nuncupato, qui liber circa eas versatur. In eo autem habes primo hos singulas figuras 64 quái dictas. Secundo interpretationem earum factam a Chu Văn Vương, tertio explicationem singularum linearum seu hào, in 64 figuris contentarum factam a Chu Công filio dicti Văn Vương, ac demum interpretationem elucidationemque Confucii in easdem figuras, quibus accedunt et aliorum litteratorum commentaria,

potissimum

peritissimum Đinh Sĩ, qui et praefationem scripsit illius libri, et Chu Sĩ magni nominis litteratorum.

Qui ergo agunt divinatores thầy bói cum praefatis figuris quae aliunde ad divinandum futura et occulta, inquirentes et explorantes, quaenam figura cadat in hominem, qui postulat divinationem, quâ inventâ et firmatâ suas enuntiant propositiones, speciosis et generalibus verbis, callide tegentes suam simulationem. quod si nesciant, quid divinando dicant, quod figura pro tali homine est figura dicta bất thuận, quae nullam in libro habet explicationem: quẻ vậy là quẻ bất thuận. Sunt ex litteratis, qui figuris illis utentes faciunt quandoque divinationes. Sed ut plurimum divinatores illi Thầy Bói appellati, sunt illiterati, qui non nisi aliqualem notitiam habent dictarum figurarum: qui ipsi caecutiunt, vel caecutientes; qui sedere solent in foris, ubi fit hominum conventus, parati ad vendendas suas divinationes, ac importune invitant praetereuntes, et trahunt ad divinationem. Eos vero consulunt praecipue circa futuros eventus vitae et mortis, sanitatis et infirmitatis, divitiarum, et paupertatis, consecutionis graduum, vel non consecutionis. Interpetunt quando quis furto aliquid amittat, quaerit a divinatore quo fur abierit, utrum Orientem versus, an Occidentem, Meridiem vel Septentrionem; et inde judicat ex illis, de quibus suspicatur, eum vere rem suam subripuisse, cujus domus existat in parte a divinatore enunciata.

Plures autem adhibent divinatores illi superstitiones. Projiciunt ante divinationem duas monetas, quae si pares deciderint, supina vel incuba, âm dicunt habere, quod nullatenus conveniat ad divinationem: si vero dispares una supina, altera incuba, dương dicunt habere, quod bonum conveniat ad divinationem, tuncque solum procedunt ad illam, ideirco toties projiciunt monetas, quousque impares cadant, et reddant dương; et ad divinationem procedant. Saepe etiam imponunt quinque corporis partibus postulantis divinationem, et eam praestant, dicentes khẩu bốc, nhĩ bốc, os divinat, aures divinant et sic de singulis. Nominibus quoque utuntur quinque elementorum, Kim metalli, mộc ligni, thủy aquae,

hỏa

hoả ignis, thổ terrae; nec non vocabulis duodecim animalium, quibus nominant, et enumerant annos, menses, dies, et horas, nimirum: tí muris, sửu bubali, dần tigridis, mão felis, thìn draconis, tị serpentis, ngọ equi, vị capra, thân simiae, dậu gallinae, tuất canis, hợi porci. Illis itaque nominibus elementorum, et animalium judicant, et pronuntiant de convenientia, vel disconvenientia rerum et personarum; quod maxime praestant ad matrimonia contrahenda, vel dissolvenda; observant enim, quo die nati sint vir et mulier conjuges facti, vel futuri, ac vito quod vir natus sit die felis, et mulier die muris, dicunt eos non esse copulandos, aut esse separandos, quia felis murem capit et manducat; vito autem quod vir natus sit die bubali et mulier die caprae, dicunt eos posse copulari, ac posse simul remanere, quia bubalus et capra simul conveniunt, et commorantur. Item est de elementis: si masculus natus sit die ignis, et foemina die aquae, eos pronuntiant nubere non debere, vel nuptos debere separari, quia aqua ignem extinguit; si vero unus die terrae natus sit, altera die ligni, eos pronunciant nubere posse, nuptosque simul remanere, quia lignum oritur ex terra, et viget in ea. Illis etiam nominibus quinque elementorum, et duodecim animalium, anni, menses, et dies notantur in communi kalendario seu lunario lịch dicto, quod editur unoquoque anno ad usum reipublicae: ut judicium fieri possit de matrimoniis contrahendis, et aliis agendis: quinimo et hujusmodi prognostica juxta ea vocabula pro singulis diebus apponuntur in eo lunario.

Praeterea frequens est divinatoribus Thầy Bói ea deprecatio ad divinandum: (A) Tiên sư, tiên thánh, tiên hiền, chiêu liêm giáng hạ, thinh vân thượng đế (B) Phục hi, Đại vũ, Văn vương, Chu công, Khổng tử, ... [illegible] giáng quyết minh bạch (C) Khổng môn khai dạ ... thập nhị ... [illegible] ... [illegible] ... Khổng ... [illegible] ... đại hiếu đồng lai ... (D) Tiểu thử ... [illegible] ... ngoạt, ... nhất, ... dư tuyệt, hoàng ... trung hạ ... hốt ngộ ... bốc vấn ... (E) Cúi cáo ... cát thần ... tâu.

trung thiên triệu, cho vị Thánh hiền đồng lai giáng hạ.
cujus orationis sensus est hujus modi = (A) Primi Magistri, primi perfecti, primi boni lumen mittite inferius: precando interrogate supernum Regem; (B) Reges Phục Hi, Đại Vũ, et Văn Vương; Chu Công, Khổng Tử, id est Confucius, omnes spiritus descendant ad resolvendum clarè et distinctè, (C) Confucii discipuli septuaginta duo boni, (alii litterati seu sapientes deinde nominantur usque ad Khang Tiết) omnes dignitate praediti, magni perfecti, magni boni una simul adjuvent lectum. (D) Anno N. Mense N. die N. hora N. instanti N. in principio, medio, vel fine lunae, sive masculus sive foemina pro divinatione interrogans quaerat aliquid, et speret aliquid. (E) omnia et singula

Caput Quintum

De Secta cultorum   seu

Articulus Primus.

de Thich Ca apud Indos secta hujus auctore.

Secta cultorum Phat primus auctor fuit famosissimus quidam Thich Ca nominatus ab annamitis; qui natus est in Indiis hic dictis Thiên Trúc in regno Ân Đô, imperante apud Sinas Chu Chiêu Vương anno vigesimo quarto, lunâ primâ, die octava, ante Christum natum millesimo vigesimo nono (1029) et mortuus est, imperante Chu Mục Vương ab annis octo, annos natus nonaginta. Pater ipsius fuit rex Tinh Phan, mater Ma Da, avus [illegible], concubina Nhu La; ipse vero Thich Ca primo vocabatur [illegible]. Cum pater ejus tributum, quod solvere quot annis debebat Regi Lê Bô, tum [illegible] praetermitteret, rex ille indignatus ipsum punire [illegible]. Quare regulus Tinh Phan ut malum impendens à se averteret, debitum vectigal ad Regem Lê Bô statuit transmittere. Omnibus vero [illegible] legationem obire detrectantibus prae timore, filius ejus [illegible] animo illud subeundum sibi exhibuit ac munera cum muneribus a patre missis tanta dexteritate rem egit cum rege Lê Bô, ut nedum illum patri suo reconciliaverit, sed et ipsius amorem sibi comparaverit adeo illi charus, ut filiam suam [illegible] Rex ei tradiderit in uxorem. Reversus ergo ad patriam effusissima omnium gratulatione ac laetitia exceptus fuit, et pater speciali cum honore prosecutus est, dato ei ad habitandum palatio orientali. At vero ipse ad nomen suum majori gloria illustrandum [illegible] discessit ab aula, vel invito patre, seque in montem recepit: ubi obvios habuit duos [illegible] A La La, et Ba La La nuncupatos, et edoctus ab illis fuit pluribus [illegible] doctrinam, quam ipse postea suis sectatoribus tradidit novo ab illis nomine appellatus Thich Ca Mâu Ni Phât, novo simul [illegible] ab illis, qui se nominarunt A Dà, A Lac. Nedum autem

debebat

sedebat inter utrumque diabolum, qui a dextris, et à sinistris, ei attentè praecepta dictabant, quae ille audiebat, ac litteris mandabat, ita ut quadraginta duos tractatus conscripserit, juxta testimonium sequenti articulo allegandum, non quatuor mille, ut aliqui scripserunt in libris Christianorum. Stupenda autem quae de Thích-ca ferunt, recensebimus articulo tertio et quarto.

Porro nomen Phât, quo Thích-ca vocatus est, significat homo caelestis. littera enim illa componitur ex duabus litteris, nempe nhân, id est homo, et thiên id est caelum. Scribi etiam aliter solet illa littera Phât, et componitur ex littera Phât id est non, et littera nhân id est homo, quasi diceretur non homo, quia nimirum evasit idolum, quod super hominem est: sed et idem nomen Phât arcanum est alio sensu in doctrina interiori hujus Sectae: siquidem in littera Phât priori habetur duplex littera nhân seu homo, et littera nhị, hoc est duo, quo significantur Vir et foemina, seu pater et Mater filium generantes.

Articulus Secundus.
De hujus Sectae apud Sinas Propagatione.

Secta Phât, Imperante familia Hán, in Sinas ex Indiis invecta est jussu Imperatoris Minh Đế anno regni ejus octavo, Christi nati circiter Septuagesimo. Quae res in libris christianis, et primum in libro Vấn Lâm Quảng Ký narratur: Vidit in somniis, inquiunt, Hán Minh Đế hominem quendam corpore aureum altitudinis sexdecim cubitorum, qui interrogatus ab Imperatore quis esset, respondit se esse hominem partis Occidentalis. Proposito regiis consiliariis hoc somnio, ut interpretationem ejus proferrent, dixerunt homines sanctos in occidente semper haberi, simul quo plurimum Imperatori gratulati sunt, quod hominem sanctum aspexisset, inde conjicientes ipsum Imperatorem esse victurum. quapropter ipsemet Imperator in occidentem ire volebat ad ibi inquirendam et addiscendam religionem et legem illius hominis Sancti. Consi-

-liariis

-liariis tamen obsistentibus Delectui Imperatoris, ne res publica ex ejus absentia perturbaretur, duos legatos Thái Âm, et Tần Cảnh appellatos misit ad ea perquirenda, et transferenda. Illi vero cum in Indias seu Thiên trúc, jam diu itinere in remotiorem occidentem necdum absoluto, pervenissent, reliquis longioris viae incommodis et difficultate absterriti, [illegible] imaginem, et libros, qui ibi habebantur, acceperunt, et ad Imperatorem detulerunt, ac simulate se imaginem et libros Sancti hominis ex occidente afferre. Quorum dictis Imperator deceptus fidem praebens cultum Phật suscepit, et subditis mandavit praecipiens fana illius idoli ubique construi, ac prohibens sub poena mortis, ne quis aliquod animal imposterum juxta doctrinam illius idoli interficeret. promulgata est ea res in libris christianis.

Verum aliter res ea refertur in libris historiae Sinensis, quibus inhaerere debemus loquentes cum litteratis. ibi ergo haec habentur: Đời Hán [illegible] Đế văn Tây vực hữu Thần, kỳ danh viết Phật, nhân khiển sứ chi Thiên Trúc cầu kỳ đạo, đắc kỳ thư, cập Sa môn dĩ lai, [illegible] thế trung quốc thủ [illegible] kỳ đạo, đồ kỳ hình tượng. —

— Idest, anno octavo Imperator (Minh Đế) fama audita in Occidentali parte esse spiritum vocatum Phật, jussit legatos pergere in Thiên Trúc, (Indias) quaerere ejus doctrinam, et obtinere ejus librum; tunc in regno habitus fuit illius mentio, et effigiata est ejus imago. Litteratus Lâm Chi Vinh in libro Tổng luận libris historicis Thông giám praemittit in eam rem aliquid addit dicens: Minh Đế khiển sứ chi Thiên Trúc, đắc Phật kinh tứ thập nhị chương, giảng chi Lan đài thạch thất; hoạ Phật tượng hội ư Thanh lương đài, cập Hiển tiết lăng. —

— Idest, Minh Đế jussit legatos ire in Thiên Trúc obtinere librum Phật quadraginta duorum tractatuum, et reponere in palatio dicto Lan in ejus aede ex lapide, et accipere imaginem Phật, et pingere in palatio dicto Thanh lương, ac in sepulchro seu terrae cumulo dicto Hiển Tiết. ex quibus compertum est, quod praefatus Imperator misit de industria in Indias ad deducendum in Sinas librum et imaginem idoli illius appellati Phật,

non autem

non autem in remotissimam occidentem seu Europam, aut Palaestinam ad dispendendam inde imaginem et doctrinam sanctorum hominum ibi permanentium. Unde autem innotuerit dicto Imperatori, quod in Indiis esset Spiritus, nomine Phật, non est difficile invenire. Siquidem enim Imperator Hán Vũ Đế ditionem Sinensem ad Indiam usque extendit, quam armis subegit annis plusquam 170. ante Minh Đế. et in historia ad annum 27.m illius Imperatoris refertur, quod Imperator nuncios misit seu ministros in regnum Đại Hạ et alia regna finitima, id est in regna Indiarum: quoque sic erat perviam iter à Sinis ad Indos, seu erat communicatio inter Sinas et Indos. Ex tunc ergo Sinenses cognoverunt Indiarum Phật ab Indis habitum in honore, ejusque notitia apud Sinas perseverante, eam accepit traditione et Imperator Minh Đế. et tunc quidem cognoverunt Phật etiam sub nomine Thiên chúa, id est Domini caeli; Siquidem ex eadem historia Sinensi narratur ad annum primum dicti Imperatoris, quod ille pluris habuit regnum Bang Trà, quod finitimum est cum regnis Indiarum, eo quod ibi afferverunt statuam auream hominis dedicati Domino caeli; Đế di Bang Trà lấy kim nhân để tế Thiên chúa. Is autem Thiên chúa seu Dominus caeli alius non est nisi Thích ca, qui ab Indis, aliis que finitimis populis Dominus caeli, imo et conditor caeli credebatur, et colebatur.

Plures deinde alii Imperatores cultum Phật promoverunt; et primo Hán Linh Đế, qui uno seculo post Minh Đế imperavit, intra suum palatium templum idoli Phật primus aedificavit, teste praefato Phan Thị Vinh: Vua Linh Đế lập tết Phật ở trong cung vua. Deinde Imperator Lương Vũ Đế qui seculo quarto à Minh Đế imperavit, magnam partem vitae exegit in uno templo idolorum, in quod postea se recepit, ibi que eorum cultui se mancipavit, ubi et captus fuit à rebelle Hầu Cảnh. Imperator Đường Hiến Tông saeculo nono à Minh Đế, accepto quoddam esse idolum magni nominis in templo dicto Pháp Môn, quod tricesimo quoque anno exponebatur, eo que anno frugum ubertatem, et reipublicae tranquillitatem tribuebat, legatum illuc misit, et ossa ejus inde ad se referunt, qui insequenti anno

18°

tii. Dicti Imperatoris adduxit ossa manus Phật ad aulam, et lucerna secunda per singula templa circumduxit: [illegible] Phật cốt chi [illegible]. Tantum vero jam crescunt cultores Phật saeculo sexto ad [illegible] sectae illius, ut centum mille viri et mulieres, qui in templis manebant cultui Phật mancipati, imperante Đường [illegible], recenserentur, ut litteratus Phó Dịch in libello supplici ad illum Imperatorem testatus est dicens; [illegible]. Haec omnia habes in historia Sinensi.

Testimonia de Phật ex libris Sinicis.

Articulus Tertius.
De Doctrina hujus Sectæ.

Duplex est Doctrina, quam Thích Ca à duobus dæmonibus magistris accepit discipulus, et discipulis suis tradidit magister, externa una, altera interna, prior circa cultum Idolorum, posterior circa atheismum versatur. Doctrina interna externæ est explicatio, qua hominis generatio, ac humani corporis tam viri, quam fœminæ membra etiam pudenda designatis sub figuris et nominibus Idolorum in doctrina externa adumbrata clarificantur, ac multa quæ fabulis, et mendaciis apparent contexta in doctrina externa, in interna tamen doctrina suam habent veritatem. Doctrinam externam Thích Ca omnibus tradidit, et vulgavit; internam verò uni soli, vel saltem paucis probatioribus et fidelioribus discipulis communicavit, quam strictè præcepit secretam retineri dictitans Bí chi. Bí chi; xiên kim bất khả khinh truyền, id est; secreta sit hæc doctrina, mille auri ponderibus [illegible] eam tradere et manifestare: quapropter nunc etiam solis familiarum Senioribus, et probatioribus communicari solet, cæteris occultata. Librum autem hujus Sectæ Bí chi appellatum tradidit Thích Ca uni ex suis discipulis auditoribus, qui rursus alteri, et alii aliis successivè tradiderunt: quorum nomina in præfatione ejusdem libri Bí chi, qui vocatur adhibetur, recensentur; eorumque ultimus appellatur Huyền Quang: mirum autem subest, quod decimus à Thích Ca inter eos sit quidam ex familiâ Tống, cum à Thích Ca ad familiam Tống decurrerint fere bis mille anni, et ad priorem familiam Tống nam bắc triều mille anni præterierint; quod utrumque annorum multo plures exigit, quam decem, qui librum illum successivè traditum acceperunt.

Dogmata autem hujus Sectæ potissimum per nomen Kinh id est libros, [illegible] in ejus libris distribuuntur, et signanter in dicto libro Bí chi et in libro Tâm đăng. Primo docetur, inquiunt, ante omnia primò fuit ex nihilo una gutta roris à se ipsa, et illa est aeterna Thai, seu idest, quæ

gutta

gutta ex seipsa evasit tres guttas, viridis una, quae caelum constituit, altera flava, quae terram; tertia alba, quae hominem constituit, mox quae habi-tum habuit nomen Nguyên thủy, idest primum principium; Tres illae deinde guttae in unum conglobatae evaserunt unum veluti ovum lapideum, quod fractum est in quatuor frusta, atque ex altero caelum, ex altero terra, ex altero pater, ex altero mater facta sunt; et ex seipso habitum est Tổ Nguyên thủy, seu originale primum principium, quod evasit quatuor partes, oriens, occidens, meridies, septentrio; quae sunt veluti quatuor fratres, ac isti quatuor fratres una cum Nguyên thủy fecerunt caelum et terram; et tunc Nguyên thủy erat in mundo, et dictum est [illegible], quae duo [illegible] idolum Thái, quod ante caelum et terram prodivit; caelo et terra primo factis, Nguyên thủy evasit Mặc Mặc; qui natura sua occultus est, et invisibilis; et tunc erat adhuc obscurum, ac caelum nondum erat compactum, et terra non-dum erat condensata. Sic ex nihilo natus vapor, seu stilla aquae effecta, idolum Thái [illegible] fecit caelum et terram, hominem, et omnes res. In doctrina istorum Nguyên thủy est primus status generationis hominis.

Secundo saeculo, ut aiunt, fuerunt duo conjuges, vir nomine [illegible], mulier [illegible], qui corpus suum adhibuerunt in adjutorium caeli et terrae, et produxerunt diem ac noctem, aquam et ignem, caelum, terram et hominem, quatuor elementa seu qualitates, solem et lunam, atque octo figuras sortium: Dựng thiên lập [illegible] Thiên Địa [illegible] Càn, Khôn, Âm dương, [illegible] [illegible] tư tượng, [illegible], bát quái [illegible].

Tertio saeculo, ut aiunt, fuere quinque fratres dicti [illegible], idest [illegible]-rum, proprio nomine singulariter appellati, primus Thái [illegible] altus 150 cubitis. Secundus Thái [illegible] altus 130 cubitis, tertius Thái [illegible] altus 120, quartus Thái [illegible] altus 110, quintus Thái [illegible] altus 100 cubitis, qui mutati sunt in quinque colores; primus nempe in colorem viridem, secundus in colorem rubrum, tertius in album, quartus in nigrum, quintus in flavum: atque pariter [illegible] condiderunt caelum et terram; [illegible] [illegible] [illegible] [illegible] [illegible] Thiên Địa [illegible] [illegible] insuper caelum [illegible] triginta sex [illegible]

seu

seu triginta sex coelos unum supra alium, ac similiter terram totidem in-aequalitatibus congeminantem extitisse.

Quarto saeculo, inquiunt, fuit Bàn Cổ, caput habens draconis, et corpus reliquum hominis, altus cubitis 50. quando omnia erant confusa, dilatavit coelum et terram, fuit que omnes res: oculos aperiendo diem faciebat, noctem vero claudendo, et postea oculus sinister conversus est in solem, dexter in lunam: quo magis coelum et dies elevabatur, et terra deprimebatur, illa statura gran-dior evadebat, vixit que mille annis. hoc in libro [illegible] et in libro Tâm Đăng quod Bàn Cổ os aperiendo aestum, et claudendo frigus, respirando ventum, loquendo tonitrua, atque spuendo pluviam producebat; quod que mor-tuus in omnes res toto corpore conversus est: nempe pili et capilli olera et ar-bores evaserunt, ossa montes, dentes aurum, sanguis aquam, excrementa pisces, pedes et omnes volatilia, bestiae et serpentes evaserunt. Hunc porro hominem Bàn Cổ ab historia Sinensi, in qua primus omnium exhibetur, [illegible], et cultores Phật acceperunt, et ibi castigatorii expressum formam [illegible] -panda superintendentem figuram.

Quinto saeculo, aiunt, fuere tam hoàng seu tres Reges communiter ap-pellati Thiên hoàng, Địa hoàng, Nhân hoàng; primus altus fuit 300 cubitis, pro cujus figura exprimunt in corona [illegible] unum caput hominis prominens majus, cum sex aliis capitibus minoribus ex una parte, et aliis quinque ex alia dependentibus: eo quia duodecim fuisse fratres dicuntur, qui omnes celebriter regnaverunt sub uno nomine Thiên hoàng, annis 18,000. Địa hoàng altus fuit 150 cubitis, pro cujus figura exprimunt unum caput hominis majus pro-minens cum decem aliis capitibus minoribus utrinque; eo quia undecim fra-tres fuisse dicuntur, qui omnes celebriter regnaverunt sub uno nomine Địa hoàng pariter annis 18,000 (corrigendum 15,000.) Nhân hoàng altus fuit 100 cubitis, pro cujus figura exprimunt unum caput hominis majus prominens cum aliis octo minoribus hinc inde; eo quia fuisse dicuntur novem fratres, qui omnes celebriter regnaverunt sub uno nomine Nhân hoàng annis 45,600 (corri-gendum 92,600) Numerus ille annorum 115,500, est [illegible] omnium annorum.

trium illorum hoàng, ut constat ex testimonio cujusdam litterati, in historiâ Sinensi allegati, qui ait tres illos hoàng regnasse 160 thế quorum quodlibet constat annis 30. Tres igitur praefati hoàng ex historiâ Sinensi desumpti sunt, in quâ primo homini Bàn Cổ immediate succedunt: quos tamen multi litterati Sinenses merito censent fabulosos. ibi tamen Thiên hoàng continet Fratres tredecim, non duodecim.

Saeculo sexto dicunt in libro Bồ chi, fuit quaedam mulier nomine Oa, quae dum coelum mundum erat omnino conjunctum, et continuum, ~~[illegible]~~ quae veluti perforatum, lapidem quinque colorum capiti suo imposuit, et coelo deficienti interuit, ac illud fecit incorruptibile. In libro autem Phàn Đăng dicunt, quod eo saeculo fuerunt quinque reges seu Ngũ Đế, nimirum 1° Nguyên Thỉ Thiên tôn, hoc est primum principium coeli altum, seu coelestis altitudo; 2° Thái hoàng Đại Đạo, hoc est, nobilis rex, magna lex; 3° Ngọc hoàng Thượng Đế, hoc est, gemmeus rex supremus imperator; 4° Thái thượng Lão quân, hoc est, maximus supremus Rex Lão tử; 5° Cửu văn Thiên sư, hoc est, expedite nubes lucida coelestis magister. Porro isti Ngũ Đế inducti sunt ad instar Ngũ Đế historiae sinensis. Illud autem observa, quod Lão quân male post ponitur Ngọc hoàng, cum is fuerit eo posterior annis circiter 300, ut patet ex dictis de utroque suo loco, utroque etiam longe recentiores sunt Thích Ca, qui posterior hic exhibetur saeculo subsequenti. Insuper tempore praefatorum Ngũ Đế fuerunt quinque [illegible], [illegible], [illegible] Chân Thể, [illegible], qui [illegible] fuderunt ex quingentis libris auri, et [illegible] totidem, ac pariter fuderunt lunam, ex libris quingentis [illegible], et totidem argenti.

Saeculo septimo, inquiunt [illegible] Thích Ca natus est, qui in libro Bồ chi male refertur natus saeculo octavo. Illius vero nativitatem ita describunt, fingunt nempe, 1° quod ille sub nomine Nhi [illegible] è coelo descendit, et obviam habens in [illegible]

Diêm Vương, qui est Rex inferorum, subito in uterum mulieris nomine Ma Da phu nhân intrusus fuit, sic que ab ea conceptus est; 2° quod genitus postea à matre statim fuit in medio novem draconum, qui aquam in ipsum ex sufflabant, atque tunc è coelo ad terram egressa est planta dicta Trầng [?], et ejus folia de more adhibentur cum aquâ ad ablutionem genitricis et geniti; 3° quod egressus ab utero matris incessit septem gressibus ad austrum, et totidem ad aquilonem, nec non totidem ad Orientem, et Occidentem, et in vestigiis ejus illicò germinarunt flores pulchri Sen appellati; 4° demum quod sic incedens habuit manum sinistram ad coelum elevatam, et dexteram ad terram demissam.

Sæculo octavo, tradunt in libro Tam Đăng, Thích Ca [illegible] præfatos, qui solem et lunam fuderunt, imitatus iterum fudit solem ex libris quingentis gemmarum, totidem auri, totidem argenti, totidem stanni, totidem que aeris; ac pari similiter lunam fudit ex gemmis, argento, stanno, et aere eodem pondere librarum quingentarum. At nihil habetur de ea re in libro Bá chi sive hoc sæculo, sive alio quocumque. Natalitas vero Thích Ca in eo libro assignata huic sæculo, debet sæculo septimo assignari, et quod ibi dicitur de fratribus supra, et oblatis Thích Ca, collocari debet sub hoc sæculo octavo, quæ res in libro Tam Đăng refertur nono, ut infra.

Sæculo nono, inquiunt, in libro Bá chi, unus vir, et una mulier, fortuiter et inaniter sibi occurrerunt, seu se convenerunt. Vir demissis oculis aspexit mulierem, et mulier elevatis oculis virum aspexit; ac illa vacuum inferius descendit inferius, et dictum est Tễ Lá, et nomen ejus Bàn Nhiễu, et factum est quoddam instrumentum musicum ad psallendum. Illud autem in libro Tam Đăng nullibi habetur. In quo narrantur sæculo nono hæc evenisse Thích Ca; ibi inquiunt, miseratus est hominum, qui nihil habebant ad se nutriendum et diu viverent, idcirco tres ejus famuli conversi sunt in tria genera piscium, in tria flumina, in quinque species frugum, et in animalia volatilia, et quadrupedia: duo prædicti Đại Nguyên Chân Đế, et Bàn Nhiễu, qui vitam agebant solitariam prope flumen nomine Bàn Cổ appellatum viderunt tres pisces vulgò ~~cá~~ chép comedere segetes, et necnon grana, et Chân Đế eos cepit,

ac

ac obtulit Thạch Lạc fortuito ibi praesenti. Thạch Lạc vero jussit Regem Thần Nông agros colere, et oryzam plantare; ac imbuere pisces praedictos, nec non colligere segetes, et excu-tere grana, ac homines nutrire, sicque posteris tradere artem colendi agros, colligendi messem, ac excutiendi grana ad eorum sustentationem. hoc in libro Sám Đăng [illegible] vide, quale absurdum sit, quod Thạch Lạc jusserit regem Thần Nông homines docere agriculturam: quandoquidem Thần Nông antiquior fuit Thạch Lạc bis mille annis, cum natus sit Thạch Lạc imperante in Sinis Chu [illegible]: quam vero falsi-lia sint, quae in praefatis novem saeculis seu cửu Kỷ enarrantur, ostendit discordantia enarrationum in libro Bách [illegible], et in libro Tân Đăng pro iis novem Kỷ, quod potissimum videre est in Kỷ 6°. 8°. et 9°. quae continent omnino diversa inter se.

Tradunt praeterea in suis libris: 1° quod in sole sit quaedam avis aurea tripes, quam vocant Chim Hạc, et in luna quaedam lepus albi coloris Con Thỏ nuncupatus, ibique palatium suum habeat Regina mater [illegible]; 2°. quod existat in coelo quidam [illegible] minister dictus Thiên Lôi, seu Thần [illegible], id est coeli fulgur, quem in hominis forma cum alis accipitris exprimunt, et quando garrit iratus, facit tonitrua, fulgura et flumina, ignemque mittit in terras, ac diffundens per mundi partes, atque homines et bestias occidit ad libitum, et alta percutit, infringit, et destruit; 3°. quod similiter in coelo sit quidam draco, qui interdum descendat ad afferendum aquam ex mari, fluminibus, et piscinis, nec non arbores evellat, homines, quadrupedia, et alia in altum abripiat, quae fieri saepe videntur a turbine, quem [illegible] illum esse putant, et vocant.

De homine demum haec docent: inesse in quolibet homine tres animas cum septem spiritibus vitalibus in viro, novem in muliere, quod vulgo illud pronunciant: Ba hồn bảy vía, ba hồn chín vía. Has autem tres animas tam masculo, quam foeminae inesse statim a nativitate seu conceptione, sed tantum ab anno aetatis quintodecimo. — Nolunt quoque vermium species humano corpori inesse, [illegible] Paradisum habere et infernum pro praemio, et poena animarum

in-

in alio saeculo, ac paradisum esse situm in caelo ad partem occidentalem in eo quo Thích Ca regem esse supremum; infernum vero infra terram locatum constare decem et octo contignationibus, seu partitionibus, ex quibus decem gubernari à Diêm Vương, alias vero octo ab octo familiis, quae sunt Tào Mã Vũ Tịch Xương Tiền Bàn &c. Animas autem ab inferno posse liberari dictos regem, et Rectores exorando, et oblationes ipsis faciendo, qui peccata eis dimittant, et à poenis absolvant. eamque liberationem sacrificuli idolorum se praestare posse gloriantur, ac solemni pompa saepius operantur, quam functionem suo loco describemus. Animarum insuper transmigrationem docent, quam appellant Luân hồi dicentes, quod animae à corporibus egressae, si bona egerint, ac praesertim si cultui Thích Ca deditae fuerint, transmigrent postea in corpora filiorum regum, magnatum, litteratorum, divitum; si vero egerint mala renascantur in filiis pauperum, idiotarum, mancipiorum, deformium, vel etiam transeant in boves, tigrides, sues, canes &c. Ex tribus autem animabus asserunt, quod una sit transmigrans, alia tumulo assistens, alia vero post annos 15. alias renascenda. alii vero dicunt, quod una descendat ad inferos, et à poenis soluta ad caelos ascendat, altera in tumulo, vel alibi se habeat, et alia transmigret in alia corpora.

Caeterum in doctrina interiori tres animae sunt pater, mater, et filius; septem vero phách seu vía non sunt septem spiritus vitales, sed septem corporis humani intestina; nec plures in foemina, quam in viro assignantur vía, sed septem tantummodo pro utroque. Similiter tam tài, de quibus sermo seu Kap. 7. id est caelum, terra, homo, in doctrina interiori, sunt tres partes corporis humani, nimirum pars superior a pectore ad caput est caelum, pars inferior ab umbilico ad pedes est terra, pars autem media est homo. pariter quinque duces, vel reges ngũ hành ngũ đế, de quibus 3o Kap., quinque sunt hominis intestina, nempe cor, jecur, pulmones, renes. Uno praecipuo, Sthomacus, quae dicuntur ngũ tạng. ea vero omnia habentur in libro Bí chỉ praecitato.

Placet hic afferre, quod eruditionem suam in praedictis adulaverit Ven. P. Franciscus Gil de Federich in ultima Epistola ad me scripta triduo ante suam passionem,

-sionem, nempe die 19 Januarii 1745. iis verbis mihi videtur quod aetates (Kiếp) quas describunt, et omnes illos reges atque conversionem idoli in illos, cum Đa uno idolo (Thích) loquuntur, et intentio est Thích Ca generationem explicare; unde ea, quae in rei veritate in generatione corporis per diversos menses contingunt, haec in illis novem Kiếp explicant; ita quod Thích Ca in primo Kiếp fuit ea, quae ibi describunt, et in 2° similiter; et cum ipsi explicant, credunt animarum transmigrationem, Kiếp Đa, Bàn Cổ &c in uno Thích Ca; hinc unde etiam haec persuadent. Sed in hoc non est delinendum, quia explicare omnes instantias illorum librorum non otiet: non vidi librum aliquem, seu materiam, quam in illo tractatur, in quo non inveniant haec ille Pater eruditus.

Articulus Quartus.

De Idolis praecipuis, quae coluntur in hac Secta.

Colunt in primis et potissimum Thích Ca, qui integro nomine dicitur Thích Ca Mâu Ni Phật, et sectam suam instituit in Indiis, ut exposuimus articulo primo. Stupenda autem mendacia de eo affirmant ejus sectatores, suis quae in libris ingerunt: praeter ea, quae diximus de ejus nativitate articulo tertio in secundo, seu Kiếp septimo, affirmant etiam sequentia: nimirum quod ex ejus capite effecti sunt viginti sex caeli, quod lingua ejus sit columna caeli ex auro et gemmis, quod duae manus ac duo pedes sint quatuor reges caeli, quod viginti costulae utriusque lateris versae sint in viginti idola, et reliqua ossa in trecenta sexaginta (360) duo... in octoginta quatuor millia (84.000) idola, quinque intestina in quinque idola, ac insuper viscera majora in flumina magna, minora in parva sunt conversa. Colunt etiam, et habent ut idola patrem, matrem, uxorem, et avunculum ejusdem Thích Ca; et alia multa idola colunt Thích Ca [illegible] genitricibus, et progenitoribus antiquiora, quorum omnium primum est Ây Âm, quem dicunt jam extitisse, antequam caelum et terra in prima rerum confusione secernerentur; Thiên Địa vị phân, Thích Ca Ây Âm Phật; ut ubi caelum et terra secedunt erant discreta, et tunc 9° fuit idolum Ây Âm. post illud quinque recensentur priscae aetates, [illegible]

Tô Lô, secundum Di Đà, tertium Di Lạc, quartum Đại Bi, quintum Nhiên Đăng; his succedunt septem idola, scilicet primum Di Nha, secundum Di Khí ber-tium Tùy Khí, quartum Câu Lưu, quintum Câu Na, sextum [illegible] Ca Diếp, septimum Thích Ca Mâu Ni Phật. ubi vides Thích Ca pluribus idolis haberi tempora posterio-rem; quibus adde etiam quae recensuimus in novem seculis seu Kiếp supradictis.

Colunt insuper Thiên Phủ, Địa Phủ, Thủy Phủ, colunt Thái Nguyên Chân quân, qui primus est inter omnes, quos vocant Tổ Đông, eumque exprimunt sub figura trium hominum in una sede. colunt plura idola quae vocant Bồ Tát, id est quae virtute pollent à malis liberandi. eaque inter est Quan Âm, cujus pater est idolum nomine Di Đà, quod et plurimi dicunt auctorem, praeditum potestate, ut homines conjugio liberentur, vel di-vortio separentur. colunt quoque plures mulieres, et praecipue Mục Liên, et Mẫu Tiên. Mục Liên, inquiunt, filia fuit Imperatoris Đàng Văn Đông quae etiam maritum reliquit, et in quodam templum Thầy se recepit, ibi quae ejus cultui sese mancipavit. Mẫu Tiên vero, aiunt filia fuit regis Mẫu Trang Vương, quae aegre ferens a patre et matre se non amari, eos dereliquit, et idolis pariter se devovit. Eam dicunt non multi eandem esse ac Quan Âm prae-dictam. Colunt specialiter subsequentia idola, quae credunt à poenis inferni eos liberare, qui statis diebus cujusvis mensis jejunium servant in eorum honorem et millies invocant nomen ipsorum. dies autem decem quae allegantur est in libro Tam Đăng hic vide dies primus Định Quang Vương Phật, dies octavus Dược Sư Lưu Ly Quang Phật, dies 14. Hiền Kiếp Thiên Phật, dies 15. A Di Đà Phật, dies 18. Địa Tạng Vương Bồ Tát, dies 23 Đại Thế Chí Bồ Tát, dies 24 Quán Thế Âm Bồ Tát, dies 28 Lô Xá Na Phật, dies 29 Dược Vương, Dược Thượng, nhị Bồ Tát, dies 30 Thích Ca Mâu Ni Phật. Sic autem invocant ea nomina, v.g. 30. Nam mô Thích Ca Mâu Ni Phật; dies 15 Nam mô A Di Đà Phật. adhibent vero multi ad eas invocationes numerandas quamdam corollam centum globulis constantem, quos percurrunt usque ad nume-rum millesimum.

Colunt denique et alia idola quam plurima, quorum hic nomina recensere catalo-gum contineret, cujus loco vide in libro Tam Đăng eorum calendarium per annos.

ab diis

et dies singulos dispositum; in quo primus mensis continet idola duodecim: secundus mensis idola quatuordecim; tertius mensis idola undecim, quartus mensis idola pariter undecim; quintus mensis idola decem; sextus mensis idola duodecim; septimus mensis idola undecim; octavus mensis idola duodecim; nonus mensis idola undecim, decimus mensis idola quatuordecim, undecimus idola tredecim; duodecimus continet idola duodecim. Illud vero notandum, quod triplicis ordinis sint idola in eo calendario, et velut illud recensita; alia primi gradus donantur nomine Phật; alia secundi gradus appellantur nomine Bồ Tát, sive Tiên ā, id est liberatoris, vel curatoris, alia tertii gradus nullo consimili nomine indigeantur, sed solo proprio singulari vocabulo nuncupantur. Omnia vero communi nomine Thánh, sive Kùng illustrantur, singulis quippe mensibus ille titulus praemittitur: Chư Thánh đản nhật vel sinh nhật; id est omnium sanctorum, seu virtute excellentium virorum natalis dies. dixerunt aliqui calendarium illud idolorum efformatum fuisse a quodam Neophyto apostata in similitudinem calendarii sanctorum, quod habet Ecclesia.

Praeter idola colunt et Cô hồn id est animas orphanas ab omnibus derelictas, quas dicunt ita debiles esse, ut ad terram descendere nequeant, et super plantis, et arbustis morentur, et ideo die prima et quintadecima cujusque mensis jusculum coquunt ex oryza, et illud projiciunt super folia plantarum, ut eo vescantur, quod jusculum coquunt valde liquidum, quia inquiunt, habent illae gutturem valde angustum ad deglutiendum. credunt vero de his Cô hồn, quod nuncia sint regis caeli, habeantque catalogum annorum vitae quos fatum pro singulis hominibus determinavit, et juxta catalogum eos necant, qui annorum numerum jam compleverunt. eamque in rem fabella haec refertur. mulier quaedam, inquiunt, nomine Nàng Bà Mẫu, pro qua decreti erant triginta anni vitae dum sederet in porta cibum et potum deferens pertranseuntibus, tres vidit Cô hồn ad se occidendum venire, quare illas humaniter excepit, et edulia et cerevisiam illis praebuit ad satietatem: illae vero satiatae, et tanti gratia beneficii vitam ei prolongarunt in annos plurimos litteram decem in mille mutantes; cum enim littera decem sinico charactere scribatur ad modum

crucis +

crucis + virgulam a super posuerunt 4, quâ additione littera decem evasit mille, et loco tria decem signata fuerunt in cathalogo annorum tria millia sicque illa mulier vixit quam diutissime.

Articulus Quintus
De Templis et Personis cultui Phât dicatis.

Templa seu fana ubique extant Phât dicata, et unusquisque pagus unum habent, et pagi grandiores plura, quae vulgo vocantur Chùa. ea vero sita sunt extra ipsos pagos, prope tamen, in loco aliquo arboribus consito, et condenso, quod idcirco lucos exprimit, quos olim Ethnici Idolis sacros habebant in Europa: aedes habent pro idolis, ac aedes pro cultoribus eorum ad habitandum, nec non atrium valdè amplum, et murum in circuitu. Templa majora plures etiam aedes habent unam post aliam ordinatas, in quibus Idola sunt collocata, usque inter aedes una est amplior caeteris, in quâ altare majus in medio est, et duo altaria minora ex utraque parte. Super his altaribus sunt Idolorum simulacra ex ligno, vel creta variis coloribus depicta, vel auro et argento oblinita, atque in altari majori sunt unum, vel duo, vel tria simulacra grandiora aspectu terribilia, et unum parvum ex aere unius quasi cubiti altitudinis, quod est Thích ca simulacrum; ejusdemque altitudinis sunt ferè omnia alia simulachra super altaribus lateralibus locata. In medio aedis est una tabula, super quam cremantur virgulae odoramentorum quam plurimae in quoddam veluti vasculum infixae ac plures accenduntur candelae ex cera. In singulis denique templis habetur una campana in altum suspensa, quae pulsatur exterius ex unâ tantum parte ictibus mallei manu hominis percutientis, ac pulsari solet in noviluniis, protoluniis et pleniluniis, et quandocumque fit solemnis aliqua oblatio.

Viri sunt, et mulieres, qui cultui Phât sunt mancipati, ac in templis Idolorum inhabitant, et caeremonias peragunt ad cultum illorum, Viri vocantur Sãi, mulieres Vãi. litterarii omnino priores dicti Tăng

presbiros

posteriores Nê nuncupata. Inter viros autem alii habent uxores, alii uxoribus carent: qui cum uxoribus vitam ducunt, Sãi Chùa dicuntur; qui absque uxoribus vitam agunt, Thầy Tu nuncupantur. Sãi Chùa ut plurimum indocti sunt, nec rigide observant praecepta suae sectae, et a majoribus pagorum templis suis deputantur; Thầy Tu docti sunt, et rigidiorem tenent suae sectae disciplinam, ac speciali regis deputatione in majoribus templis collocantur; qui plures discipulos alunt, et erudiunt, ac magna pompa sacras faciunt functiones, magnamque habent apud omnes existimationem. Mulieres vero idolis dicatae multae sunt, et caelibem vitam agunt in praecipuis templis degentes; hujus modi virorum et mulierum habitus coloris est fusci seu nigricantis, et caput gerunt abrasum, nec non comedunt solam oryzam et alios terrae fructus, semper abstinentes a carnibus, piscibus, et ovis, cum vetitum sit in eorum secta occidere viventia; quae abstinentia seu jejunium dicitur Trai vel Chay. Preces quam multas recitant singulis diebus in aedibus idolorum, et ad eas utuntur libro Hoàng Độ Viết [?], et libro Tâm Đàng [?]. Quinque sunt eis praecepta observanda. 1um Non occidere viventia quaecumque. 2um Non furari. 3um Non fornicari. 4um Non mentiri. 5um Non bibere vinum.

Denique sunt et praelati Tăng, qui aspirant ut evadant et ipsi Bụt, atque ad illam supremam dignitatem assequendam flammis etiam se tradunt exurendos, quia combustione credunt certo Phật se evasuros; et quando quis igni se tradit voluntarie, magno concursu sectatorum Phật in atrio alicujus templi functio illa celebratur. Tribus abhinc annis ea caeremonia peracta fuit in quodam templo Idolorum territorii Vĩnh Lại [?] provinciae orientalis residentiae nostrae propinquo; sed cadaver tantum igne combustum fuit; quia sacrificulus ille morte praeventus non potuerat vivus, uti proposuerat, flammis conflagrare. Functio illa dicitur Thiêu thân, id est corpus ardere. Ingens porro fuit numerus dictorum Tăng Nê imperante Đàng Cao Tổ, saeculo nimirum sexto ab inducta in Sinas secta Phật, eo tempore recensebantur centum eorum mille, teste litterato Phó Dịch, qui idcirco hortatus est illum imperatorem anno ejus nono, ut eos e templis ejiceret, et ad conjugium obligaret, ut posset postea multos milites congregare; Kim thiên hạ Tăng Ni số đương thập vạn, thú chi lệnh thất phối, tức thành thập vạn hộ, sản dục nam nữ, thập niên trưởng dưỡng, nhất kỷ giáo huấn, khả dĩ túc binh.

Vides

Vides autem in hoc Tunquino exosos nostrates religiosos et sanctimoniales, quibus sibi famulantibus vivit magna [illegible] stimulare.

De Templis insignioribus hujus Regni.

Reges familiae Lý plura idolorum templa aedificaverunt, eorum quoque cultum potissimum promoverunt. Rex Thái Tổ anno primo, ineunte saeculo Christi nati undecimo, condidit duo templa idolorum, unum intra eamdem urbem dictum Thiên ngự, alterum extra illam dictum Thắng Nghiêm, et fudit campanam ex tot librarum aeris, et anno [illegible] ubi jam incolebant plusquam mille homines Thích mancipati.

Rex Thánh Tông anno tertio condidit templum Báo Thiên nominatum, ac fudit magnam campanam duodecim mille librarum aeris, et anno quarto turrim in eo extruxit altitudinis 300 cubitorum duodecim contignationibus distinctam, nec non duo alia templa, ubique duas statuas ex auro posuit Thích ca ejusque patri Tịnh Phạn Vương.

Rex Nhân Tông Quảng Hựu anno secundo, Christi anno 1086 condidit templum Đại Lãm Sơn, et [illegible] novam turrim ibi extruxit.

Denique Rex Huệ Tông, regno filiae suae renuntiato, in templum idolorum Giáo Chùa appellatum se recepit, currente anno Christi 1225, eorumque cultui se devovit, ubi et paulo post peremptus fuit eo quod magnos clamores quereretur de regno translato in familiam Trần a filia sua Chiêu Hoàng, quae nupserat viro illius familiae nomine Trần Cảnh. Regi illi convenit, quod litterati objiciunt Imperatori Lương Vũ, nam sicut Lương Vũ liberatus non fuit a Thích cui se devoverat, quin captus ab hostibus in templo fame periret; ita nec Lý Huệ Tông liberatus fuit a Thích, cui erat mancipatus, quin ipse necaretur. De templis habes recensita in historia Annamitarum [illegible].

Porro templa Thích praecipua, quae nunc variis extant in locis, sunt; (Chùa Đàng, [illegible] templum in parte superiori provinciae meridionalis.)

lis situm; Sùng Chìn in provincia occidentali, Chùa Quỳnh Lâm in provincia orientali partes inferiores in territorio Đông Triều; denique Chùa Sùng Phúc in provincia orientali. illis verò templis plures sunt feminæ ex nobilioribus, quæ idolis dicatæ cœlibem vitam agunt; nimirum, cum et regis filiæ, vel olim concubinæ, quas inter fuit et mater Lêa gubernatoris regni vulgo Chúa, quæ se addixit templo præfato Quỳnh Lâm, et semper vitam ibi finivit. exemplo iis olim fuer-unt Mộc Liên filia Imperatoris Lang Ban Tông, et Mâu Liên filia Regis Mâu Kang de quibus supra.

Articulus Sextus
De Functionibus in honorem Phật

Oblationes faciunt idolis Phật in templis omni singulis noviluniis, et pleniluniis, offerunt nempe globos oryzæ coctæ, quos vocant Xôi, et Oản, et varios fructus, et specialiter ficus parvulos colore flavos, qui ibi vulgo dicun-tur Chuối Ngự; carnes verò non offerunt, quia mandatum est in hac secta animalia non occidere. Dum sacrificuli offerunt ad altare, prodit [illegible] cum appositio, et ad accipit reliquo, ac halitum rebus, quas offert, afflat. Accen-dunt quoque super altare ante statuas quam multas virgulas odoramentorum ignas, et aliquot candelas ex cera; atque apponunt infra invicem altaris super uno gradu multas papyraceas argenti et auri libras; quas postea comburunt in atrio ædulis super altari impositis; tympana pulsantur, et alia instrumenta, atque credunt tunc spiritus idolorum descendere, suasque statuas intrare; et functioni adesse. recitant subinde sacrificuli varias preces ex libro sedentes ante aram, in qua sunt idola; prope illius januam vario cum sonitu intermixto; quam recitationem vocant Đọc Kinh, Đọc Kệ; ac inter eam recitationem cre-dunt idola comedere, seu de oblatis degustare. Varias interim faciunt prostrationes et adorationes, sed in prostrationibus non adhibent genuflexiones; id est quibus non innituntur [illegible], et alii solent communiter in sacrificiis spirituum aut de-

-functorum

-functorum. In domibus pariter privatis cultores idolorum iisdem novilunii, et plenilunii suas faciunt oblationes, orizam nempe praedictam apponendo super tabulam, quam domi habent pro altari.

Primo cujusque anni die erigunt ante januam domus perticam unam altam in honorem Phật, ut a daemonio liberentur; cujus rei haec est origo: Fabulantur, quod olim idolum Phật litem habuerit cum daemone, eo quod daemon omnes ad partes suas pertraheret, et multam post jurgationem facta fuit inter eos conventio, ut daemon non ingrederetur, sed idolo cederet omnes domos, ad quarum januas esset pertica erecta, aliae vero domus sub daemonis essent dominio: qua conventione utrinque acceptata, idolum seu Phật illico nuncios misit fideles et fraudulentos, qui incolas monerent, ut perticam attollerent ante domos, sicque a diabolo liberarentur. hinc ritus ille inductus est, ut in exordio cujuslibet anni perticam erigant ante januas domorum, cui appendunt multas papyraceas argenti, et auri libras in fasciculos colligatas; ut nempe a daemonio immunes sint domus, quas ille ingredi non audet, sed praetergreditur tanquam pertinentes ad Phật. perticam illam vocant Nêu.

Singulis annis die octava mensis quarti in templis celebrant nativitatem Phật, id est Thích Ca Mâu Ni Phật, cujus statuam aeneam, quae super altari servatur, abluunt aqua odorifera, et calida super infusa, sicuti infantes recens nati lavantur atque emundantur.

Duas solemnes functiones ad placitum celebrant in honorem idolorum pro defunctis, quarum una dicitur Trai, altera Chay. functio Trai, peragitur in templis idolorum, et durat ad unam solam diem, aut noctem, quae fieri debet pro omnibus defunctis [illegible] aut unius familiae; altera vero functio Chay celebratur extra templa in loco aliquo spatioso, ubi amplum faciunt tabernaculum rạp appellatum, ad cujus functionem dictam vulgo Thả chay durat ad plures dies protelata; quae fieri debet pro uno vel altero defuncto intra triennium luctus. In utraque autem functione primo sacrificant tribus idolis Thích ca Phật, Di đà Phật, Thánh ông [illegible], deinde aliis idolis, precesque recitant quam multas, ac ejusmodi sacrificia et preces recitant pluries in die, ac

agitur

legitur schedula oblationis, in qua offerentium nomina exprimuntur, et deprecatio fit pro defunctis, ut ab inferni poenis liberentur; atque postremo fit insuper caeremonia destructionis inferorum dicta Phá ngục, ad liberandum animam defuncti ab inferno. Functionis Chay, seu trai auctor fuisse traditur Imperator Lương Vũ in libro Tam Giáo, ubi dicitur: Lương Vũ lập vi trai kiều. qui Imperator regnare coepit ineunte saeculo sexto Christi nati. Functionem vero tiếu prior instituit, et adhibuit Imperator Tống Huy Tông, teste Phan Thế Vinh in libro Tống Luận Thuở Tống Huy Tông chi căn, thoát tiếu chi khí khởi kiêu hồn di gia ư Đạo; id est coluit legem impensè, et instituit caeremoniam tiếu multa expendens ad illam, quia major imperatoris Huy Tông in Đạo (qui anthonomastice appellatur Đạo quân, id est doctor Đạo Rex) coepit autem Huy Tông imperare saeculo duodecimo Christi nati, et non utraque functio exprobratur contemnitur, et irridetur in rituali Gia Lễ, ubi fit sermo de hiếu hạnh, sinis không sư, ea ratione, quod qui hujusmodi habet functiones pro patre et matre, eos inhonorat, cum illos censeat peccatores, atque peccatorum remissione, ac inferni liberatione indigere. Mea autem opinio est, ne dicam persuasio, quod ritus phá ngục erat describendus daemonis calliditate sit inductus ad illum opponendum ritum, quem ex Ecclesiae instituto sacerdos celebrat circa tumulum pro defunctis, ut sibi talem cultum compararet, qualis Deo in illa actione exhibetur.

Praeter praefatas solemnes functiones in honorem idolorum pro defunctis aliam agunt non solemnem Xá anh hồi appellatam, quae ad unam vel alteram horam duntaxat durat, in qua unam tantum faciunt oblationem cum una precum recitatione absque caeremonia.

Ritus phá ngục

Inferni destructio phá ngục dicta hic peragitur caeremonia: Domunculam in medio exstruunt formae quadratae nonnullis arundinibus solo infixis, quibus super extendunt pro parietibus aliquot fascias ex tela, vel serico, vel papyro ad altitudinem unius cubiti: quinque januas designant in illa, quatuor nempe

in quatuor

in quatuor lateribus, et unam in medio, quae correspondent quatuor mundi partibus, earumque medio, et unaquaeque suum idolum habet custodem, janua orientalis habet Thanh Đế viridem regem, occidentalis Bạch Đế album regem, meridionalis Xích Đế rubeum regem, septentrionalis Hắc Đế nigrum regem, media Hoàng Đế flavum regem. ad hujusmodi domunculam sacrificulus accedit cum suis ministris cappa indutus ad modum nostri pluvialis; pileo varii coloris valde pulchro coopertus caput, et baculum manu tenens; quandoque tres sacrificuli, sed unus eo modo induuntur. sacrificant edulia offerendo, et virgulas odoramentorum accendendo primo idolis decem simul, quae una simul regnant in inferno, et dicuntur Thập Điện Minh Vương; sacrificant secundo idolo Địa Tạng quod deducit ad inferos, et ostendit quo in loco anima, quae petitur liberari, detineatur; sacrificant tertio ad singulas januas singulis earum custodibus, ut januas recludant, et animam exire permittant. ante quodcumque vero sacrificium circumeunt domunculam tribus vicibus, et sacrificio peracto, faciunt duos nummulos, qui si dispares cadunt, unus supinus, incubus alter, conjectantur idola preces exaudire; si vero pares supini, vel incubi cadant, colligunt idola preces minime exaudire: quare toties reiterant sacrificium, et precationes, quousque nummuli projecti decidant, et jaceant differentes. habito autem eo signo exauditionis, sacrificulus baculo percutit, et frangit, vel abjicit scutellas aliquas in janua locatas, quo inferni januam censent recludi. finitisque omnibus oblationibus et precibus, ac ita januis omnibus reseratis, domuncula igne destruitur, pluribus telis, vel sericis, vel papyros circumpositis cartaceis abripientibus; sicque animam credunt ab inferno liberari. porro hic juvat claritatis gratia figuram exhibere praefatae domunculae igneae, qualis exprimitur in libro, cui Titulus Hoàng Đế vịnh, quo ad suas preces, et functiones utuntur Doctorum sacrificuli.

Figura

Figura [illegible]

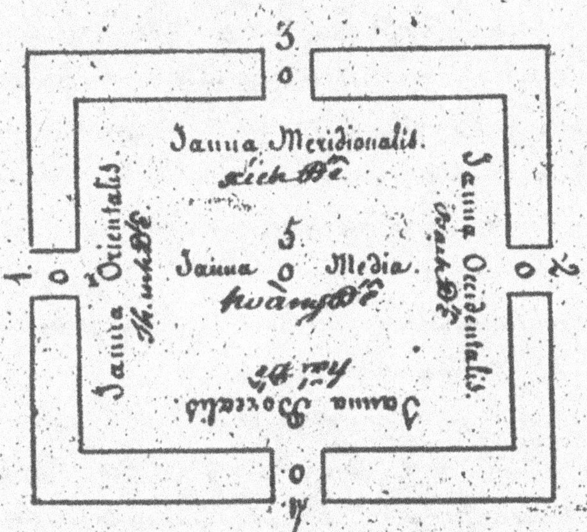

Solemnem præterea faciunt quandoque processionem ad honorem idolorum, quæ antonomasticè dicitur [illegible], seu [illegible], et maximo concursu ad plures dies celebratur; conveniunt quippe ex omnibus pagis territorii [illegible], vel [illegible], prævia invitatione pagi celebrantis festivitatem. Pridie processionis habendæ à pagis advenientibus, sacrificulus se confert cum aliis è templo, ad quod processionaliter convenire debent invitati, ad aliud templum alterius pagi, ut indè idolum [illegible] ad templum suum deducat. Ea tamen idoli deductio non fit accipiendo et deferendo ejus statuam, sed tanquam illius spiritum veluti conducendo; undè tabernaculum quoddam vacuum gestatur absque ulla statua, aut imagine, quod non nulla similiores idolis dicata subsequuntur gerentes super capita [illegible] fasciam unam albam protensam, quam dicunt pontem [illegible], super quo spiritus idoli progreditur, et templum advenit. hæc verò idoli deductio, quæ vulgò dicitur [illegible] aliis quoque occasionibus peragitur. Diebus consequentibus fiunt processiones pagorum advenientium, quorum quilibet suam facit processionem solus, et unus post alium tempore diverso. Progrediuntur verò in ejusmodi processionibus speciales vestes induti vario cum sonitu instrumentorum, ad templum [illegible]

-tant, et circumeunt illud, atrium ejus ingrediuntur, et ante ædem idolorum transeun-
-tes prostrationibus illa venerantur. Præcedunt verò nonnullæ puellæ cô đồng appellatæ
quæ vestibus ornatæ ac facie fucatæ procedunt oculis defixis in folium scriptum, vel
in forcipem, vel in cultrum, quem tenent utraque manu, nec audent in hanc, vel
illam partem aspicere; quod si minime servent, contemnuntur et privantur remuneratione:
In atrium templi ingressæ ~~folium scriptum~~ seu schedulam tradunt majoribus pagi
ibi assistentibus et sedentibus, in quo signatur nomen pagi, qui venit ad processionem,
et numerus pecuniarum, quæ ab eo tunc offeruntur. Finita processione tradunt co-
-mœdias agunt, et lautè epulantur, conviviis à majoribus pagi habentis hội præ-
-paratis. Hæc de Functionibus Idolorum ——

Ad complementum hujus rei juvat adjicere, quod sectam et cultum Phật plu-
-rimis impugnant in suis libris litterati; quos inter præcipui sunt litteratus Phó
Dịch, qui imperatori Đường Cao Tổ anno ejus nono, Christi nati 626: sup-
-plicem libellum exhibuit ad ejiciendam legem et cultum Phật; litteratus Hàn
Dũ, qui pariter contra sectam Phật libellum præbuit Imperatori Đường Hiến
Tông anno regni ejus quarto decimo, Christi nati 819; nec non litteratus Phan
Thế Vinh, qui floruit sub primo Imperatore familiæ Minh, et in
libro Thông giám de historia Sinensi, cui præmittitur, plura intermiscet
contra imperatores cultores Phật.

Triplici verò de causa litterati sectam Phật contemnunt, aversantur,
et impugnant. Prima est, quia Phật est homo exterus et barbarus, siquidem
Thích Ca in montibus Indiarum versatus est ibique à Dæmonibus suæ sectæ
rationem accepit. Secunda est, quia Phật tollit debitum obsequium subdi-
-torum ergà Regem, et filiorum ergà parentes; quandoquidem qui sunt sectæ
Phật specialiter addicti, Reges, ac patrem, et matrem prostrationibus juxta
Regni consuetudinem non venerantur, sed tantum inclinationibus. Tertia
est, quia Phật à malis minime liberat; quin imò cultus illius est causa
malorum, Reges quippe cultores Phật plura perpessi sunt, et res publica multis
afflicta est, ex quo Phật coli cœpit. Hæc illi in libris suis pronunciant et decantant.

Caput Se[illegible]um

Caput Sextum
De
Christianâ Religione
apud
Sinas et Annamitas.

Postquàm egimus de Sectis Sinarum et Annamitarum, aequum
planè est ut etiam de Religione Christianâ apud Utrosque dudum praedi-
-catâ, et latè propagatâ verba faciamus.

Articulus Primus.
De Christianâ Religione in Sinis.

Christi Fides bis olim Sinensibus annunciata fuit.

1°. Saeculo Christi nati sexto desinente, et septimo ineunte. Nam cum Ma-
-hometes armis praevaluisset, et Graecorum Imperium subjugasset, dirum perse-
-cutionem contra Christi Fideles in Asia auspicatus est in fine Saeculi sexti. Qua-
-propter multi christiani declinandae persecutionis causâ in alienas terras abierunt.
Eo tempore quidam Presbyter Parthicus nomine Isbozaddes primus in Indias pene-
-trâvit, deinde paulatim ad Sinas usque profectus est, ubi provinciam [illegible] im-
-bus praedicatione suâ multos ad christi fidem perduxit, regnante familia
Suy, Annamitis Tuy, quae familiam Tang seu Đàng immediate prae-
-cessit. Illum proximè subsecuti sunt nonnulli Sacerdotes Syri, qui exemplo
ejus excitati ad Sinas ex Syriâ se contulerunt, Imperatore Tang Tai Tsong
seu Đàng Thái Tông, qui regnavit annis 23. ab anno Christi 627.
Quos inter praecipuus fuit Sacerdos Olopuen, qui meritò dictus est Sina-
-rum Apostolus, cum fidem christianam invexerit in provinciam [illegible]
Khang Si, et [illegible] hujusce rei celebre monumentum inventum
fuit anno Christi 1625. in Urbe Si Gan metropoli provinciae [illegible]
-rum una tabula lapidea figura pyramidalis effossa, quae crucem habebat [illegible]

[illegible]

summitate, et plures Syriacos et Sinicos characteres in parte inferiori inscriptos, quibus significabatur Christianae fidei praedicationem magnum in Sinis incrementum habuisse per Sacerdotem Olopuen praefatum ab anno Christi 636. quae tabula collocata est in templo idolorum frequentissimo dictae civitatis, ubi omnibus est conspicua in ejus atrio aut horto. Figuram illius tabulae exhibet P. Athanasius Kirkerius Societatis Jesu in sua China illustrata, apud quem et ego illam vidi Mediolani in nostra bibliotheca conventus SS. Cosmae et Damiani. De his vide Mappamundum historicum P. Antonii Foresti tom. 7 in vita secundi Imperatoris Familiae Taingae, id est, Tâng, et in vita Imperatoris XV familiae Mingae, id est Ming.

2° Christiana fides Sinensibus praedicata est post sex saecula, Imperante Scing Sy Zung, cognomento Tong Sy Tong, qui coepit imperare ab anno Christi 1280. Illius enim tempore dum Tartari occidentales Sinicum imperium suo dominio subjiciebant, primi omnium ex Europaeis in Sinas venerunt duo illustres viri veneti Nicolaus, et Marcus Polo, pater et filius, qui in Sinis strenue pugnaverunt pro Tartaris contra praefatum Imperatorem, pluresque urbes expugnaverunt. Quo tempore et venerunt in Sinas duo Praecones Evangelii ex ordine fratrum minorum, nempe P. Nicolaus Vicentinus, et P. Guillelmus Tripolitanus, qui paulo ante missi fuerant in Tartariam a Gregorio Papa X: et illuc adducti a Nicolao Veneto praefato, qui illos a Summo Pontifice postulaverant; eorumque opera fides Christi 2° in Sinis invaluit, et latius propagata est, quae et diu viguit, plurimosque habuit sectatores et professores, quamdiu Tartari occidentales Imperium Sinicum tenuerunt. Laudatus vero Marcus Polo in Italiam reversus notitiam gentis Sinicae primus omnium detulit, et vulgavit. Porro hoc habes in Mappamundo historico praefato tom. 7°

Postremo fides christiana post tria saecula ab incepta praedicatione praecedenti iterum in Sinis praedicata est a Praeconibus Europaeis. Et Primus omnium tantum opus tentavit P. Martinus de Herrada hispanus ordinis nostri fratrum Eremitarum S. P. Augustini, qui anno Christi 1575, et anno tertio Imperatoris Ming Xin Zung, cognomento Mien Shin Tong imperium Sinicum ingressus est, ad annunciandam christianam fidem, appulsus navi Sinico in provinciam Chê Kiang ex insulis Philippinis cum sodali suo Hieronymo Marino Mexicano, sed immorari in Sinis diu non potuit,

juxta

jussu Proregis illius provinciae ad Manillam redire compulsus. Duo illi ministri Evangelii à paucis annis fidem invexerant in insulas Luzon appellatas, ad quas tunc primum inventas pervenerunt cum celebri navi victoria anno christi 1565; quae distant leucis 160 a continente Sinensi, et dictae sunt ab hispanis Philippinae in honorem sui regis Philippi Secundi, in quarum principali Manilla nuncupata suam primariam civitatem iidem hispani aedificarunt anno christi 1571. Post fratres Eremitas S. P. Augustini, fratres minores Sancti Francisci pariter hispani christianam fidem in Sinis praedicare tentaverunt. Primum anno 1578. P. Petrus de Alfaro et alii quatuor socii ex Philippinis ad civitatem metropolim provinciae Kuang Tung pervenerunt die 12. Junii; sed apud praefectos accusati tanquam exploratores Regis hispaniarum redire ad Philippinas coacti sunt. Rursus anno 1582. P. Martinus Ignatius à S. Francisco, et sex alii sodales pariter hispani ad eandem provinciam Kuang Tung venerunt ex Philippinis mense Junio desinente. Ubi prius capti ut exploratores, postea dimissi christianam fidem praedicare coeperunt: sed invidia Sacerdotum idolorum rursus capti, et in carcerem conjecti sunt, unde educti et dimissi operâ cujusdam ducis lusitani macaum cum eo reversi sunt, et inde in Europam. Caeterum fratres minores lusitani ante fratres suos hispanos Evangelium jam annunciaverant in confiniis Sinarum, nempè in insula macao, ubi suam civitatem lusitani aedificaverunt, impetrata facultate ab Imperatore Sinensi praefato anno ejus quinto, christi 1577. Demum anno 27 ejusdem Imperatoris desinente; et christi 1600. ineunte P. Matthaeus Riccius Italus maceratensis ex Societate Jesu fidem primus advexit in aula Pe King media mathesi, qua pollebat. Et exinde christiana Religio mirificè in Sinis propagata est. Ille verò prius venerat ad civitatem principuam provinciae Kuang Tung anno 1583. sed ibi permanere à Gubernatore prohibitus fuit, et Goam reversus est. Quod et contigerat biennio ante P. Michaeli Ruggerio Neapolitano ex eadem Societate. Haec omnia ex mappamundo praecitato, nec non quae sequuntur desumpta sunt.

Eadem aetate, qua agebatur in Sinis, primam persecutionem in christianos movit in Japonia ille Imperator nomine Faxiba anno christi 1596. Annis nimi-

-rum

-rum 48 à Fide illuc primùm invecta à Sancto Francisco Xaverio. Quin in Persecutione in Cruce alligati lanceâ confossi sunt tres Sancti Martyres Societatis Jesu, nec non sex alii martyres Ordinis FF. minorum, eodem martyrio omnes affecti una die quintâ Februarii 1597. Eo mortuo Imperatore, christiana fides ibi invaluit, et latiùs propagata est sub duobus ejus filiis successoribus Sanimo et Cugozio. At succedente filio Imperatoris Sancamadich Congigendayemon, nova persecutio, et acerbissima excitata est anno Christi 1621 in qua plurimi tum Christiani cujusque conditionis, cum Missionarii crudele martyrium multiplici poenarum genere passi sunt. Ac inter Missionarios mira constantia claruerunt igne combusti P. Ludovicus Flores ex ordine FF. Praedicatorum, P. Carolus Spinola ex Societate Jesu, et P. Petrus Zuniga ex ordine FF. Eremitarum.

Articulus Secundus
De Persecutionibus Fidei christianae in Sinis:

Fides ergò christiana ab uno jam saeculo cum dimidio in florentissimo Sinarum Imperio viget per omnes ejus Provincias disseminata et exculta industriâ et labore cujusvis Ordinis et Status operariorum. Suas verò passa est variis temporibus persecutiones. Duae priores excitatae sunt in provinciâ Nankim. Prima minimum anno Christi 1616. Imperatoris Ming xin zung, anno 39°. altera verò anno Christi 1622. ejusdem Imperatoris 46°. Utraque persecutio nec diu duravit, nec magna fuit. Majoris autem fuit momenti tertia persecutio, quae excitata est à quatuor Aulae Magnatibus initio Imperii Zùng Khanghi, dum Imperator esset in minoritate, lato edicto anno quarto illius Imperatoris, Christi 1665. quo prohibebatur promulgatio Fidei christianae, et ingressus Praeconum ejus in ditionem Sinicam, ac libri christiani flammis dati sunt in pleno concilio. Verùm quadriennio post Missionariis permissum fuit ad Ecclesias suas redire, suasque functiones exercere, salvo interdicto praedicationis fidei. Novam

persecutionem

Persecutionem movit in Provincia Tche Kiang illius prorex, lato etiam Edicto anno 30° praefati Imperatoris et Christi 1691 qui christianos undique exagitavit, omnesque eorum Ecclesias diruit in ea provincia constitutas. Cessavit vero in posterum expresso Decreto Tribunalis Rituum in favorem fidei jussu Imperatoris emanato eodem anno die 20° Martii, quo statutum fuit liberum esse Europaeis suam exercere Religionem ut pote conformem rectae rationi, ac eorum Ecclesias ipsis debere restitui, et cuicumque pro libito in illas ingredi, et reverentiam ibi exhibere. Quod Decretum ab ipso Imperatore confirmatum fuit, et in omnibus provinciis promulgatum. hactenus continuantur Mappamundi historici praecitati.

Quousque Imperator Kang hi in vivis fuit, pacem exinde habuit, et processum Christiana Religio; controversiae tamen diudum exortae inter Missionarios circa ritus Sinenses sub eo Imperatore diu exarserunt. Ad quas dirimendas plura emanarunt Apostolica Decreta, et pro eorum executione missi sunt a Clemente Papa XI, duo Dni Patriarchae Visitatores Apostolici Generales, nimirum D. Carolus Thomas Maillard de Tournon Taurinensis, Patriarcha Antiochenus postea Cardinalis qui in Sinas pervenit anno 1705, et D. Carolus Ambrosius mediobarbus Ticinensis, Patriarcha Alexandrinus, qui Sinas advenit anno 1720.

Mortuo Imperatore Kang hi, qui imperavit annis 61. filius ejus successit dictus Yung Tching, annominatis Uong Chiuh. Tunc supremus praefectus Provinciae Fo Kien edictum edidit contra Religionem Christianam, ejusque confirmationem obtinuit ab Imperatore, qui illud a Tribunali Rituum prius examinatum et approbatum confirmavit anno Regni sui 1° [illegible] Sinice nomine Kuei Mao et Christi 1724 ineunte die 10 Januarii. Eo edicto et Decreto mandatum fuit ut Ministri Evangelici per provincias dispersi vel ad Aulam Pe King se conferrent, vel Macaum abirent, atque Ecclesiae eorum in templa progenitorum vel in aulas litteratorum converterentur: quod et factum est. Imperante autem Imperatore Kien Lung, annominatis Tien [illegible] [illegible] aliud Decretum emanavit a Tribunali Rituum contra sanctam Religionem; deinde aliud statutum est ab ipso Imperatore anno ejus 11° mense 6° [illegible], anno Christi 1746

die

die 12. Augusti. Et hinc persecutio, quam exercere jam ceperat in Provincia Fö Kien, in aliis etiam provinciis statim efferbuit. hac in novissima perse-cutione plures Missionarii capti sunt, et poenis affecti cum multis christianis. Ac inter missionarios praecipuus fuit Venerabilis Petrus Sans Ordinis fratrum praedicatorum hispanus, Episcopus Mauricastrensis, et Vicarius Apostolicus in provincia Fö Kien, qui captus cum sociis anno 1746 die 30 Junii, et subinde coram judicibus, immò et Prorege de fide interrogatus, atque diris colaphis, aliisque verberibus pluries caesus demum die 26 maii 1747 hilaris excepit capitis obtruncationem coram populo in magna civitate Fö Cheu totius provinciae metropoli. Quatuor verò illius sodales pariter hispani in carcere strangulati sunt die 28 octobris anni sequentis 1748: quo pariter anno die 17 Septembris eodem mortis genere necati sunt duo Patres Galli ex Socie-tate Jesus in provincia Nân King. 1.us autem omnium in Sinis martyrium sudam fuit Venerabilis P. Franciscus de Capilla ejusdem Ordinis Fratrum Praedicatorum qui capite plexus fuit pro christo sub Imperatore Xún Chý familiae modò imperantis primo, qui imperare cepit anno christi 1645. Cujus rei testis est Venerabilis P. Franciscus Serranus in sua relatione de martyrio praelaudati Episcopi, ei concaptivus, et postea consors ejusdem gloriae.

Ultio porrò divina in persecutores exarsit. Namque Prorex Provinciae Fö Kien sua dignitate privatus fuit, bonisque ejus fisco assignatis, ob malam ejus gu-bernationem. Prorex verò provinciae Nân King suspectus de rebellione captus fuit

Index
Capitum et Articulorum totius Opusculi.

Articulus 3us.

Ad Majorem Dei Gloriam Virginisq. Dei Paræ .

SOUTHEAST ASIA PROGRAM PUBLICATIONS

Cornell University

Studies on Southeast Asia

Number 33 *Opusculum de Sectis apud Sinenses et Tunkinenses (A Small Treatise on the Sects among the Chinese and Tonkinese): A Study of Religion in China and North Vietnam in the Eighteenth Century,* Father Adriano de St. Thecla, trans. Olga Dror, with Mariya Berezovska. 2002. 363 pp. ISBN 0-87727-732-X.

Number 32 *Fear and Sanctuary: Burmese Refugees in Thailand,* Hazel J. Lang. 2002. 204 pp. ISBN 0-87727-731-1.

Number 31 *Modern Dreams: An Inquiry into Power, Cultural Production, and the Cityscape in Contemporary Urban Penang, Malaysia,* Beng-Lan Goh. 2002. 225 pp. ISBN 0-87727-730-3.

Number 30 *Violence and the State in Suharto's Indonesia,* ed. Benedict R. O'G. Anderson. 2001. Second printing, 2002. 247 pp. ISBN 0-87727-729-X.

Number 29 *Studies in Southeast Asian Art: Essays in Honor of Stanley J. O'Connor,* ed. Nora A. Taylor. 2000. 243 pp. Illustrations. ISBN 0-87727-728-1.

Number 28 *The Hadrami Awakening: Community and Identity in the Netherlands East Indies, 1900-1942,* Natalie Mobini-Kesheh. 1999. 174 pp. ISBN 0-87727-727-3.

Number 27 *Tales from Djakarta: Caricatures of Circumstances and their Human Beings,* Pramoedya Ananta Toer. 1999. 145 pp. ISBN 0-87727-726-5.

Number 26 *History, Culture, and Region in Southeast Asian Perspectives,* rev. ed., O. W. Wolters. 1999. 275 pp. ISBN 0-87727-725-7.

Number 25 *Figures of Criminality in Indonesia, the Philippines, and Colonial Vietnam,* ed. Vicente L. Rafael. 1999. 259 pp. ISBN 0-87727-724-9.

Number 24 *Paths to Conflagration: Fifty Years of Diplomacy and Warfare in Laos, Thailand, and Vietnam, 1778-1828,* Mayoury Ngaosyvathn and Pheuiphanh Ngaosyvathn. 1998. 268 pp. ISBN 0-87727-723-0.

Number 23 *Nguyễn Cochinchina: Southern Vietnam in the Seventeenth and Eighteenth Centuries,* Li Tana. 1998. Second printing, 2002. 194 pp. ISBN 0-87727-722-2.

Number 22 *Young Heroes: The Indonesian Family in Politics,* Saya S. Shiraishi. 1997. 183 pp. ISBN 0-87727-721-4.

Number 21 *Interpreting Development: Capitalism, Democracy, and the Middle Class in Thailand,* John Girling. 1996. 95 pp. ISBN 0-87727-720-6.

Number 20 *Making Indonesia,* ed. Daniel S. Lev, Ruth McVey. 1996. 201 pp. ISBN 0-87727-719-2.

Number 19 *Essays into Vietnamese Pasts,* ed. K. W. Taylor, John K. Whitmore. 1995. 288 pp. ISBN 0-87727-718-4.

Number 18 *In the Land of Lady White Blood: Southern Thailand and the Meaning of History,* Lorraine M. Gesick. 1995. 106 pp. ISBN 0-87727-717-6.

Number 17 *The Vernacular Press and the Emergence of Modern Indonesian Consciousness,* Ahmat Adam. 1995. 220 pp. ISBN 0-87727-716-8.

Number 16 *The Nan Chronicle,* trans., ed. David K. Wyatt. 1994. 158 pp. ISBN 0-87727-715-X.

Number 15 *Selective Judicial Competence: The Cirebon-Priangan Legal Administration, 1680–1792,* Mason C. Hoadley. 1994. 185 pp. ISBN 0-87727-714-1.

Number 14 *Sjahrir: Politics and Exile in Indonesia,* Rudolf Mrázek. 1994. 536 pp. ISBN 0-87727-713-3.

Number 13 *Fair Land Sarawak: Some Recollections of an Expatriate Officer,* Alastair Morrison. 1993. 196 pp. ISBN 0-87727-712-5.

Number 12 *Fields from the Sea: Chinese Junk Trade with Siam during the Late Eighteenth and Early Nineteenth Centuries,* Jennifer Cushman. 1993. 206 pp. ISBN 0-87727-711-7.

Number 11 *Money, Markets, and Trade in Early Southeast Asia: The Development of Indigenous Monetary Systems to AD 1400,* Robert S. Wicks. 1992. 2nd printing 1996. 354 pp., 78 tables, illus., maps. ISBN 0-87727-710-9.

Number 10 *Tai Ahoms and the Stars: Three Ritual Texts to Ward Off Danger,* trans., ed. B. J. Terwiel, Ranoo Wichasin. 1992. 170 pp. ISBN 0-87727-709-5.

Number 9 *Southeast Asian Capitalists,* ed. Ruth McVey. 1992. 2nd printing 1993. 220 pp. ISBN 0-87727-708-7.

Number 8 *The Politics of Colonial Exploitation: Java, the Dutch, and the Cultivation System,* Cornelis Fasseur, ed. R. E. Elson, trans. R. E. Elson, Ary Kraal. 1992. 2nd printing 1994. 266 pp. ISBN 0-87727-707-9.

Number 7 *A Malay Frontier: Unity and Duality in a Sumatran Kingdom,* Jane Drakard. 1990. 215 pp. ISBN 0-87727-706-0.

Number 6 *Trends in Khmer Art,* Jean Boisselier, ed. Natasha Eilenberg, trans. Natasha Eilenberg, Melvin Elliott. 1989. 124 pp., 24 plates. ISBN 0-87727-705-2.

Number 5 *Southeast Asian Ephemeris: Solar and Planetary Positions, A.D. 638–2000,* J. C. Eade. 1989. 175 pp. ISBN 0-87727-704-4.

Number 3 *Thai Radical Discourse: The Real Face of Thai Feudalism Today,* Craig J. Reynolds. 1987. 2nd printing 1994. 186 pp. ISBN 0-87727-702-8.

Number 1 *The Symbolism of the Stupa,* Adrian Snodgrass. 1985. Revised with index, 1988. 3rd printing 1998. 469 pp. ISBN 0-87727-700-1.

SEAP Series

Number 19 *Gender, Household, State: Đổi Mới in Việt Nam,* ed. Jayne Werner and Danièle Bélanger. 2002. 151 pp. ISBN 0-87727-137-2.

Number 18 *Culture and Power in Traditional Siamese Government,* Neil A. Englehart. 2001. 130 pp. ISBN 0-87727-135-6.

Number 17 *Gangsters, Democracy, and the State,* ed. Carl A. Trocki. 1998. Second printing, 2002. 94 pp. ISBN 0-87727-134-8.

Number 16 *Cutting across the Lands: An Annotated Bibliography on Natural Resource Management and Community Development in Indonesia, the Philippines, and Malaysia,* ed. Eveline Ferretti. 1997. 329 pp. ISBN 0-87727-133-X.

Number 15 *The Revolution Falters: The Left in Philippine Politics after 1986,* ed. Patricio N. Abinales. 1996. Second printing, 2002. 182 pp. ISBN 0-87727-132-1.

Number 14 *Being Kammu: My Village, My Life,* Damrong Tayanin. 1994. 138 pp., 22 tables, illus., maps. ISBN 0-87727-130-5.

Number 13 *The American War in Vietnam*, ed. Jayne Werner, David Hunt. 1993. 132 pp. ISBN 0-87727-131-3.

Number 12 *The Political Legacy of Aung San*, ed. Josef Silverstein. Revised edition 1993. 169 pp. ISBN 0-87727-128-3.

Number 10 *Studies on Vietnamese Language and Literature: A Preliminary Bibliography*, Nguyen Dinh Tham. 1992. 227 pp. ISBN 0-87727-127-5.

Number 9 *A Secret Past*, Dokmaisot, trans. Ted Strehlow. 1992. 2nd printing 1997. 72 pp. ISBN 0-87727-126-7.

Number 8 *From PKI to the Comintern, 1924–1941: The Apprenticeship of the Malayan Communist Party*, Cheah Boon Kheng. 1992. 147 pp. ISBN 0-87727-125-9.

Number 7 *Intellectual Property and US Relations with Indonesia, Malaysia, Singapore, and Thailand*, Elisabeth Uphoff. 1991. 67 pp. ISBN 0-87727-124-0.

Number 6 *The Rise and Fall of the Communist Party of Burma (CPB)*, Bertil Lintner. 1990. 124 pp. 26 illus., 14 maps. ISBN 0-87727-123-2.

Number 5 *Japanese Relations with Vietnam: 1951–1987*, Masaya Shiraishi. 1990. 174 pp. ISBN 0-87727-122-4.

Number 3 *Postwar Vietnam: Dilemmas in Socialist Development*, ed. Christine White, David Marr. 1988. 2nd printing 1993. 260 pp. ISBN 0-87727-120-8.

Number 2 *The Dobama Movement in Burma (1930–1938)*, Khin Yi. 1988. 160 pp. ISBN 0-87727-118-6.

Translation Series

Volume 4 *Approaching Suharto's Indonesia from the Margins*, ed. Takashi Shiraishi. 1994. 153 pp. ISBN 0-87727-403-7.

Volume 3 *The Japanese in Colonial Southeast Asia*, ed. Saya Shiraishi, Takashi Shiraishi. 1993. 172 pp. ISBN 0-87727-402-9.

Volume 2 *Indochina in the 1940s and 1950s*, ed. Takashi Shiraishi, Motoo Furuta. 1992. 196 pp. ISBN 0-87727-401-0.

Volume 1 *Reading Southeast Asia*, ed. Takashi Shiraishi. 1990. 188 pp. ISBN 0-87727-400-2.

CORNELL MODERN INDONESIA PROJECT PUBLICATIONS

Cornell University

Number 75 *A Tour of Duty: Changing Patterns of Military Politics in Indonesia in the 1990s*. Douglas Kammen and Siddharth Chandra. 1999. 99 pp. ISBN 0-87763-049-6.

Number 74 *The Roots of Acehnese Rebellion 1989–1992*, Tim Kell. 1995. 103 pp. ISBN 0-87763-040-2.

Number 73 *"White Book" on the 1992 General Election in Indonesia*, trans. Dwight King. 1994. 72 pp. ISBN 0-87763-039-9.

Number 72 *Popular Indonesian Literature of the Qur'an*, Howard M. Federspiel. 1994. 170 pp. ISBN 0-87763-038-0.

Number 71 *A Javanese Memoir of Sumatra, 1945–1946: Love and Hatred in the Liberation War,* Takao Fusayama. 1993. 150 pp. ISBN 0-87763-037-2.

Number 70 *East Kalimantan: The Decline of a Commercial Aristocracy,* Burhan Magenda. 1991. 120 pp. ISBN 0-87763-036-4.

Number 69 *The Road to Madiun: The Indonesian Communist Uprising of 1948,* Elizabeth Ann Swift. 1989. 120 pp. ISBN 0-87763-035-6.

Number 68 *Intellectuals and Nationalism in Indonesia: A Study of the Following Recruited by Sutan Sjahrir in Occupation Jakarta,* J. D. Legge. 1988. 159 pp. ISBN 0-87763-034-8.

Number 67 *Indonesia Free: A Biography of Mohammad Hatta,* Mavis Rose. 1987. 252 pp. ISBN 0-87763-033-X.

Number 66 *Prisoners at Kota Cane,* Leon Salim, trans. Audrey Kahin. 1986. 112 pp. ISBN 0-87763-032-1.

Number 65 *The Kenpeitai in Java and Sumatra,* trans. Barbara G. Shimer, Guy Hobbs, intro. Theodore Friend. 1986. 80 pp. ISBN 0-87763-031-3.

Number 64 *Suharto and His Generals: Indonesia's Military Politics, 1975–1983,* David Jenkins. 1984. 4th printing 1997. 300 pp. ISBN 0-87763-030-5.

Number 62 *Interpreting Indonesian Politics: Thirteen Contributions to the Debate, 1964–1981,* ed. Benedict Anderson, Audrey Kahin, intro. Daniel S. Lev. 1982. 3rd printing 1991. 172 pp. ISBN 0-87763-028-3.

Number 60 *The Minangkabau Response to Dutch Colonial Rule in the Nineteenth Century,* Elizabeth E. Graves. 1981. 157 pp. ISBN 0-87763-000-3.

Number 59 *Breaking the Chains of Oppression of the Indonesian People: Defense Statement at His Trial on Charges of Insulting the Head of State, Bandung, June 7–10, 1979,* Heri Akhmadi. 1981. 201 pp. ISBN 0-87763-001-1.

Number 57 *Permesta: Half a Rebellion,* Barbara S. Harvey. 1977. 174 pp. ISBN 0-87763-003-8.

Number 55 *Report from Banaran: The Story of the Experiences of a Soldier during the War of Independence,* Maj. Gen. T. B. Simatupang. 1972. 186 pp. ISBN 0-87763-005-4.

Number 52 *A Preliminary Analysis of the October 1 1965, Coup in Indonesia (Prepared in January 1966),* Benedict R. Anderson, Ruth T. McVey, assist. Frederick P. Bunnell. 1971. 3rd printing 1990. 174 pp. ISBN 0-87763-008-9.

Number 51 *The Putera Reports: Problems in Indonesian-Japanese War-Time Cooperation,* Mohammad Hatta, trans., intro. William H. Frederick. 1971. 114 pp. ISBN 0-87763-009-7.

Number 50 *Schools and Politics: The Kaum Muda Movement in West Sumatra (1927–1933),* Taufik Abdullah. 1971. 257 pp. ISBN 0-87763-010-0.

Number 49 *The Foundation of the Partai Muslimin Indonesia,* K. E. Ward. 1970. 75 pp. ISBN 0-87763-011-9.

Number 48 *Nationalism, Islam and Marxism,* Soekarno, intro. Ruth T. McVey. 1970. 2nd printing 1984. 62 pp. ISBN 0-87763-012-7.

Number 43 *State and Statecraft in Old Java: A Study of the Later Mataram Period, 16th to 19th Century,* Soemarsaid Moertono. Revised edition 1981. 180 pp. ISBN 0-87763-017-8.

Number 39 Preliminary Checklist of Indonesian Imprints (1945-1949), John M. Echols. 186 pp. ISBN 0-87763-025-9.

Number 37 *Mythology and the Tolerance of the Javanese,* Benedict R. O'G. Anderson. 2nd edition 1997. 104 pp., 65 illus. ISBN 0-87763-041-0.

Number 25 *The Communist Uprisings of 1926–1927 in Indonesia: Key Documents,* ed., intro. Harry J. Benda, Ruth T. McVey. 1960. 2nd printing 1969. 177 pp. ISBN 0-87763-024-0.

Number 7 *The Soviet View of the Indonesian Revolution,* Ruth T. McVey. 1957. 3rd printing 1969. 90 pp. ISBN 0-87763-018-6.

Number 6 *The Indonesian Elections of 1955,* Herbert Feith. 1957. 2nd printing 1971. 91 pp. ISBN 0-87763-020-8.

LANGUAGE TEXTS

INDONESIAN

Beginning Indonesian through Self-Instruction, John U. Wolff, Dédé Oetomo, Daniel Fietkiewicz. 3rd revised edition 1992. Vol. 1. 115 pp. ISBN 0-87727-529-7. Vol. 2. 434 pp. ISBN 0-87727-530-0. Vol. 3. 473 pp. ISBN 0-87727-531-9.

Indonesian Readings, John U. Wolff. 1978. 4th printing 1992. 480 pp. ISBN 0-87727-517-3

Indonesian Conversations, John U. Wolff. 1978. 3rd printing 1991. 297 pp. ISBN 0-87727-516-5

Formal Indonesian, John U. Wolff. 2nd revised edition 1986. 446 pp. ISBN 0-87727-515-7

TAGALOG

Pilipino through Self-Instruction, John U. Wolff, Maria Theresa C. Centeno, Der-Hwa V. Rau. 1991. Vol. 1. 342 pp. ISBN 0-87727—525-4. Vol. 2. 378 pp. ISBN 0-87727-526-2. Vol 3. 431 pp. ISBN 0-87727-527-0. Vol. 4. 306 pp. ISBN 0-87727-528-9.

THAI

A. U. A. Language Center Thai Course, J. Marvin Brown. Originally published by the American University Alumni Association Language Center, 1974. Reissued by Cornell Southeast Asia Program, 1991, 1992. Book 1. 267 pp. ISBN 0-87727-506-8. Book 2. 288 pp. ISBN 0-87727-507-6. Book 3. 247 pp. ISBN 0-87727-508-4.

A. U. A. Language Center Thai Course, Reading and Writing Text (mostly reading), 1979. Reissued 1997. 164 pp. ISBN 0-87727-511-4.

A. U. A. Language Center Thai Course, Reading and Writing Workbook (mostly writing), 1979. Reissued 1997. 99 pp. ISBN 0-87727-512-2.

KHMER

Cambodian System of Writing and Beginning Reader, Franklin E. Huffman. Originally published by Yale University Press, 1970. Reissued by Cornell Southeast Asia Program, 4th printing 2002. 365 pp. ISBN 0-300-01314-0.

Modern Spoken Cambodian, Franklin E. Huffman, assist. Charan Promchan, Chhom-Rak Thong Lambert. Originally published by Yale University Press, 1970. Reissued by Cornell Southeast Asia Program, 3rd printing 1991. 451 pp. ISBN 0-300-01316-7.

Intermediate Cambodian Reader, ed. Franklin E. Huffman, assist. Im Proum. Originally published by Yale University Press, 1972. Reissued by Cornell Southeast Asia Program, 1988. 499 pp. ISBN 0-300-01552-6.

Cambodian Literary Reader and Glossary, Franklin E. Huffman, Im Proum. Originally published by Yale University Press, 1977. Reissued by Cornell Southeast Asia Program, 1988. 494 pp. ISBN 0-300-02069-4.

HMONG

White Hmong-English Dictionary, Ernest E. Heimbach. 1969. 8th printing, 2002. 523 pp. ISBN 0-87727-075-9.

VIETNAMESE

Intermediate Spoken Vietnamese, Franklin E. Huffman, Tran Trong Hai. 1980. 3rd printing 1994. ISBN 0-87727-500-9.

* * *

Southeast Asian Studies: Reorientations. Craig J. Reynolds and Ruth McVey. Frank H. Golay Lectures 2 & 3. 70 pp. ISBN 0-87727-301-4.

Javanese Literature in Surakarta Manuscripts, Nancy K. Florida. Vol. 1, *Introduction and Manuscripts of the Karaton Surakarta*. 1993. 410 pp. Frontispiece, illustrations. Hard cover, ISBN 0-87727-602-1, Paperback, ISBN 0-87727-603-X. Vol. 2, *Manuscripts of the Mangkunagaran Palace*. 2000. 576 pp. Frontispiece, illustrations. Paperback, ISBN 0-87727-604-8.

Sbek Thom: Khmer Shadow Theater. Pech Tum Kravel, trans. Sos Kem, ed. Thavro Phim, Sos Kem, Martin Hatch. 1996. 363 pp., 153 photographs. ISBN 0-87727-620-X.

In the Mirror: Literature and Politics in Siam in the American Era, ed. Benedict R. O'G. Anderson, trans. Benedict R. O'G. Anderson, Ruchira Mendiones. 1985. 2nd printing 1991. 303 pp. Paperback. ISBN 974-210-380-1.

www.ingramcontent.com/pod-product-compliance
Lightning Source LLC
Chambersburg PA
CBHW080117020526
44112CB00037B/2767